GENES IN ECO

THE 33RD SYMPOSIU

OF THE BRITISH ECOLOGICAL

UNIVERSITY OF EAST ANGLIA

1991

EDITED BY

R. J. BERRY
Department of Biology,
University College London

T. J. CRAWFORD
Department of Biology,
University of York

G. M. HEWITT
School of Biological Sciences,
University of East Anglia

b

Blackwell
Science

Editorial Offices:
Osney Mead, Oxford OX2 0EL
25 John Street, London WC1N 2BL
23 Ainslie Place, Edinburgh EH3 6AJ
238 Main Street, Cambridge
Massachusetts 02142, USA
54 University Street, Carlton
Victoria 3053, Australia

Other Editorial Offices:
Arnette Blackwell SA
1, rue de Lille
75007 Paris
France

Blackwell Wissenschafts-Verlag GmbH
Kurfürstendamm 57
10707 Berlin
Germany

Feldgasse 13
A-1238 Wien
Austria

First published 1992
Reprinted 1994, 1995

Set by Setrite Typesetters, Hong Kong
Printed and bound in Great Britain
at the University Press, Cambridge

DISTRIBUTORS

Marston Book Services Ltd
PO Box 87
Oxford OX2 0DT
(*Orders*: Tel: 01865 791155
Fax: 01865 791927
Telex: 837515)

USA
Blackwell Science, Inc.
238 Main Street
Cambridge, MA 02142
(*Orders*: Tel: 800 215-1000
617 876-7000
Fax: 617 492-5263)

Canada
Oxford University Press
70 Wynford Drive
Don Mills
Ontario M3C 1J9
(*Orders*: Tel: 416 441-2941)

Australia
Blackwell Science Pty Ltd
54 University Street
Carlton, Victoria 3053
(*Orders*: Tel: 03 347-0300)
Fax: 03 349-3016)

A catalogue record for this title
is available from the British Library

ISBN 0-632-03468-8 hbk
ISBN 0-632-03504-8 pbk

CONTENTS

PART 3: ECOLOGY IN GENETICS

PREFACE

Genetics and ecology are complementary disciplines, at least at the population level. Textbooks and courses are increasingly labelled 'population biology' instead of 'population ecology' and 'population genetics'. But this is logic, not reality. In practice geneticists and ecologists are frequently in different departments in universities; genetics tends to be relegated in ecology courses to a few simple notions in a subsidiary part of the subject called 'evolutionary ecology', instead of being fully integrated; geneticists graduate with little understanding of the life-style of different organisms, and hence how natural selection and population processes work. Indeed genetical and ecological emphases are often so different that the disciplines in which they are taught seem to be dealing with different concepts.

The BES 1991 Symposium faced up to this split in the heart of ecology and sought to bring geneticists and ecologists together to confront the implications of the others' discipline for their own work. Most papers were coauthored by a geneticist and an ecologist. The results were mixed; commensalism did not always lead to symbiosis. But there were some excellent examples of the importance of one discipline for the other, and the meeting (and this volume) was valuable in exposing the divisions within population biology, and hence providing a framework for dealing with the weaknesses. Two sessions at the meeting were devoted to practical demonstrations of molecular and genetical techniques that may be useful to ecologists; a selection of protocols is printed at the end of this book.

We offer this volume as an indication of the state of affairs in population biology, and hope that the concepts discussed and techniques described will lead to major advances for the understanding of 'genes in ecology'.

R. J. Berry
T. J. Crawford
G. M. Hewitt
April 1992

PART 1
GENES IN ECOLOGY

1. GENES AND ECOLOGY IN HISTORY

ARTHUR J. CAIN* AND WILLIAM B. PROVINE†
* *Department of Environmental and Evolutionary Biology, University of Liverpool, P.O. Box 147, Liverpool L69 3BX, UK and* † *Division of Biological Sciences, Corson Hall, Cornell University, Ithaca, NY 14853, USA*

VIEWS IN OXFORD IN THE 1930s AND 1940s (A.J.C.)

Some time soon after 1945 I was rash enough to use the word *ecology* when speaking to E.B. Ford, who was not in a good mood. He glared, and remarked in his thinnest manner:

> It seems to be...
> what animals do...
> when they are doing *nothing interesting*.

The explanation of this apparent hostility goes back to the 1930s. There is some indication that it was partly reciprocated. Charles Elton (1938) wrote, in an article entitled 'Animal numbers and adaptation':

> At a time when ecology and genetics are each racing swiftly towards one new concept after another, yet with little contact of thought between the two subjects, there may be some advantage in surveying, if only synoptically and in a preliminary fashion, the largely uncharted territory between them.

He points out that Darwin had had a clear insight into the struggle for existence, but no reliable theory of variation. Geneticists, in contrast, are good on variation:

> But their training and experience prevent them from knowing much about the struggle for existence in nature, that is to say, the section of ecology which deals with animal populations, competition, and similar subjects.

This, while perhaps true in general, was hard upon Ford, who had already linked type of variation and absolute numbers in his joint paper with his father on the Marsh Fritillary, *Melitaea aurinia*, in 1930, and who had collaborated, in the perhaps slightly unexpected role of protozoologist, with Elton and J.R. Baker from 1925 to 1928 in a study of the fluctuations in numbers of voles in Bagley Wood near Oxford (Elton *et al.* 1931). Elton, eminently fair-minded, goes on:

> Ecologists, correspondingly, although they are being drawn into a deep study of numbers, have inclined to believe that evolution was

> long and ecology was short, that variation and the formation of new races and species take place too seldom to be of much significance in ordinary ecological studies. Generally speaking, one of the assumptions made in most ecological work is that the species will remain constant. The best field studies of the species problem have usually been done by systematists, but their results have naturally lacked the experimental analysis of variation, or the background of population research which is needed in order to discover how these interesting systematic distributions may have arisen.

Plenty of workers could echo these words today. Ecology is a more than full-time study, and enough for anyone without complicating it. So is genetics; and the complexities of applying genetics to ecology could discourage the hardiest. I suspect that it is really evolutionists, however disguised, that want to bring the two together.

In fact it was Elton, surely an ecologist if ever there was one, who, as far back as 1924 had linked fluctuations in animal numbers, or rather the smallness of populations in the troughs of cycles, with the spread of non-adaptive characters. But why did he do so? As an ecological systematist, ranging widely over many groups and species and knowing them in the field, he was deeply impressed with the impossibility of seeing any adaptive significance in so many of the characters in which related species differ. This was a very usual attitude in the 1920s, partly because of the strong emotional reaction against natural selection and 'Nature red in tooth and claw' which turned many minds to vitalism and Lamarckism and was memorably expressed by George Bernard Shaw in the preface to *Back to Methuselah*.

In his book *Animal Ecology* (1927), Elton spelt out in detail his views on non-adaptive characters, and the light that could be thrown on evolution by studies of changes in animal numbers (ch. 12, pp. 179–187):

> Every biologist accepts the fact that evolution has taken place. The problem which has not yet been really solved is the exact manner in which it has happened. The existence of vast numbers of undoubted and complicated adaptations in physiological, psychological, and structural characters makes it reasonably certain that Darwin's theory of natural selection must be essentially true, however we may disagree about parts of it.

But after describing the apparent camouflage of arctic animals in their summer brown and grey coats or plumages and their winter white, he points out some 'awkward facts' which hardly fit the hypothesis of adaptive camouflage:

> All over the arctic regions the arctic fox possesses two colour phases, one of which is brown in summer and white in winter, while the other is grey or black in summer and 'blue' — often quite black — in winter. The writer has seen a 'blue' fox in summer which was the colour of a black cat, and startlingly visible against rocks and vegetation at a distance of a quarter of a mile. The blue and white phases occur equally in males and females, and interbreed freely, and in different parts of the arctic regions are found in various proportions in the population. ... If the whiteness in winter is an adaptation, the blackness of the other phase cannot also be advantageous. If the black colour is not adaptive, *how did it evolve*? If the white colour is not adaptive, *how does the black survive*? We have in addition to reckon with the fact that in many parts of the arctic, the fox can have no possible use for its colour in winter, because it subsists at that season upon carrion left by bears, out on the frozen sea-ice, or if it is on land, it depends almost entirely on caches of animals collected and stored up in the autumn. [His italics.]

Characters, in pure Darwinian theory, can be spread only by natural selection, but if so, 'all the characters possessed by animals — at any rate those which separate closely allied species — must be of some direct use to the species' or to one sex, or be 'intimately bound up in development with some other character which is useful...'. This cannot be the case with the arctic (as against the red) fox, and naturalists with field experience, Elton points out, have indeed nearly all rejected the idea of colour adaptation in mammals (though not in all other groups):

> It can always be argued...that even if the colours are not directly adaptive they may be correlated in development with some character (perhaps physiological) which *is* adaptive. But such arguments cannot apply to species which are dimorphic, like the arctic fox or the white-eared cob.

He goes on to give three other mammalian examples, to refer to Stresemann for numerous examples in birds, and to instance 'exactly comparable colour dimorphism' in some American dragonflies. That very phenomenon, therefore, which was to be used with such effect by Fisher and Ford in studies on natural selection is here shown by cogent argument and the facts of field natural history to be inexplicable by selection. But Elton knew that a far greater range of other characters have the same implications, namely all, or nearly all, the differences (non-polymorphic) between closely related species:

> There is another important line of evidence on the subject of adaptation which has recently been investigated very carefully by Richards and Robson and reviewed in a paper[29]. The gist of their conclusions is that very closely allied species practically never differ in characters which can by any stretch of the imagination be called adaptive. If natural selection exercises any important influence upon the divergence of species, we should expect to find that the characters separating species would in many cases be of obvious survival value. But the odd thing is that although the characters which distinguish genera or distantly allied species from one another are often obviously adaptive, those separating closely applied species are nearly always quite trivial and apparently meaningless.

The reference 29 is to Richards and Robson's paper, 'The species problem and evolution', in *Nature* (1926). The argument in it was repeated in Robson's *The Species Problem* (1928), and developed with a wealth of detailed observations in Robson and Richards's *The Variation of Animals in Nature* (1936). (The species problem was not then what it is now.) Charles Elton gave especial thanks to O.W. Richards in his 1927 book for extensive help both with insect examples and in the discussion of ideas. Robson and Richards's book was highly influential, being quoted (for example) by Sewall Wright (see Provine 1986, for discussion). It deserves rather more respectful attention than it has received recently. They were as critical of Elton's and their own ideas as of other authors' — not too common a trait; they had an excellent classification of isolating mechanisms antedating Dobzhansky's; and they were rightly critical of most of the little work done on *Cepaea* to that time. Their detailed list of characters in psammocharid (pompilid)) wasps showing non-adaptive differences is so similar in format and intent to that of Dobzhansky's for *Drosophila* species in his 1956 paper, 'What is an adaptive trait?', that one suspects an undocumented connection.

Nevertheless, it must be allowed that Robson and Richards showed a surprising reluctance to allow any example of natural selection; their cautious qualification that characters were non-adaptive as far as they could see became too often a certainty that they were non-adaptive; and their arguments were sometimes one-sided. Thus they allowed that some pompilid wasps were stoutly built anteriorly for digging out spiders but did *not* draw the inference that the more lightly built were adapted for ranging widely. It is as if one should say that Geoff Capes is adapted for putting the shot, but Steve Cram and Carl Lewis are not adapted for running. Their requirement that selection should be shown not merely to act but to have changed a character was over-rigorous when discussing the scope of selection; and at the very end of the book, they let the cat out of the bag:

> In arguing that an element of self-regulation and self-organisation has had an influence [as against both natural selection and chance] in evolution we are aware that we are touching certain profound and speculative issues. If this organising activity is indeed an agent in producing the main adaptive tendencies in evolution, it might be argued that the gradual upbuilding and perfection of adaptations, because they involve so large an element of design, must also involve some reference to a purpose independent of survival value and chance, and existing as an end in itself. . . . For those who believe that all organisation is produced by the material processes envisaged by the traditional theories, the scheme of evolution must seem to be clear, at least in outline. For those with whom the difficulties we have outlined in this work have any weight, it must remain to attempt a clearer definition of the purposeful activity with which we seem confronted.

In this vitalistic or perhaps theistic attitude, Robson and Richards were far from alone. Alister Hardy, an undergraduate with Elton and J.R. Baker and later the Linacre Professor of Zoology at Oxford, was an earnest Unitarian and certainly a vitalist. Others, perhaps less extreme, limited the action of selection severely. There was in Oxford a fine tradition of work on crypsis and polymorphic mimicry in the Hope Department of Entomology, beginning with E.B. Poulton, a friend of Alfred Russel Wallace, and continued by his successor, G.D. Hale Carpenter. Yet Hale Carpenter, an ardent believer in natural selection producing crypsis and polymorphic mimicry in insects, with extensive field experience and experiment in Africa to his credit, took considerable pains to find in the collection a lepidopteran with a non-selectable character (a violet-purple sheen only to be seen by viewing the wing very obliquely) to show me, and challenged me to explain it by natural selection.

Even my supervisor John Baker, an amazing polymath and firm believer in evolution, returned our first paper on *Cepaea* to me with the remark that there were fashions in science, and sometimes it was fashionable to believe in natural selection, and sometimes it was not. When I expostulated that we had the prey, its genetically mediated variation, the predator, and a significant difference in the polymorphism in woodlands and in green habitats, he indicated that he distrusted statistics. He said he would look at the paper again (and I'm sure he did — he was a most truthful man) but it reappeared on my desk without comment.

In Cambridge matters were even worse. The excellent naturalist W.H. Thorpe came to Oxford one year to give the Balliol lectures. A party from the Department of Zoology went to hear the first one and did not attend the rest. The lectures were on evolution, and he produced the example of the cuckoo which needs five simultaneous adaptations to function as a parasite, none of which would work unless fully developed — with the obvious conclusion that the cuckoo's adaptations could not be evolved by natural selection. He appeared totally ignorant of the Great Spotted Cuckoo which, parasitizing host-species of its own size, does not have all these adaptations. This seems to have been a popular argument in Cambridge: Charles Raven, naturalist and Regius Professor of Divinity to 1950, used it in detail in his Gifford lectures 1951–52 (pp. 137–139 in the Second Series) with the comment:

> It will be seen that each one of this sequence of conditions is essential to the success of the whole. Yet each by itself is useless. The whole *opus perfectum* must have been achieved simultaneously. The odds against the random occurrence of such a series of coincidence are, as we have already stated, astronomical. Nor could a single accidental performance if it should happen establish any guarantee of its fixation and repetition. The last consideration is one to which the advocates of randomness have paid insufficient attention.

He urged the same argument also in relation to the larval symbiosis, as he called it, of the Large Blue caterpillar in the nest of the red ant, and to the perfection of the orb-web of the spider *Epeira diademata* (First Series, pp. 211–212 and footnote; Second Series, pp. 13–17), with the comment on Darwin:

> This was of course repeatedly urged by critics like Asa Gray in Darwin's own lifetime. He never succeeded in answering it or even appreciating its character. His successors have not been much more successful.

Sir James Gray referred in a letter to *Nature* to the 'cheating' that would have to go on if evolution were to proceed by natural selection; and J.W.S. Pringle treated me with great hauteur for believing in natural selection; he had consulted his father-in-law (the Cambridge botanist H. Gilbert-Carter) who had assured him that no-one could explain leaf-shapes by selection — you could see all sorts growing happily together on any roadside.

Raven was answered by David Lack who pointed out the very various adaptations of different species of cuckoo, but never accepted Lack's arguments (Dillistone 1975, appendix 1). Lack, who migrated from Cambridge to Oxford, had convinced himself from his own studies of Darwin's finches, that their specific characters were truly adaptive, after starting with the opposite belief (see Provine 1986). He was the only religious man whom I knew at the period who did not allow his religion to dictate his view of natural selection. He took a great interest in our work on *Cepaea*. Elton was a very private man; I never knew what his religious or philosophical beliefs were.

Elton had a well-founded distrust of mathematical theorizers. Haldane (1932) had rejected his idea of the spread of neutral genes during population cycles, having calculated that random extinction could play only a 'very subordinate part in evolution, even in favourable cases'. Elton (1938), not inclined to give up a good idea for what might well be dubious reasons, replied:

> The calculation may require revision in the light of the undoubted fact that reduction of numbers takes place patchily...[and there might be a local isolated refuge from which the mutant could spread]. This sort of process might not happen very often, but when it did, the result would perhaps be crucial.... There is no way in which we can calculate the probability of this process taking place for a particular species or a particular mutation. The only way in which the matter can be carried further is to undertake marking experiments on various mixed populations on a large scale in the field, and follow their fate through several cycles of increase and decrease. Until this has been done, the matter cannot be considered as closed. The fact that mathematical calculations about field populations are at present limited very closely by their framework of assumptions, e.g. about random distribution, and that there are many irregular field phenomena that cannot be treated theoretically, is often forgotten.

Neither Robson (1928) nor Robson and Richards (1936, pp. 320–322) appear to have had any idea that, given a sufficient number of small fluctuating populations, a spread of neutral mutations would occur simply by chance in some of them. Elton himself (1930, pp. 79–82, duly noted by Robson and Richards 1936) recognized as a serious difficulty to his theory that only selection, apparently, could spread a gene, but did think it possible by chance, and worked out a numerical example. He even said explicitly that adaptations had two sources, by selection and by chance (p. 76). Professor W. B. Provine points out to me that the first exposition of a stochastic function in evolution was by Fisher in 1922; he dismissed it as merely generating unimportant noise in evolution. It must have been infuriating when Sewall Wright expanded the treatment in the 1930s and made it a major process in producing new gene combinations. Elton and Wright, so far as I know, do not mention each other before 1948, nor does Elton mention Fisher in 1927, 1930, 1933 or 1938.

When we turn to Ford in the 1930s his resemblance to Robson and Richards is at first startling. In the first edition of his *Mendelism and Evolution* (1931) we read:

> The strong probability that the effects of the genes are multiple has already been discussed. This consideration may throw some light on the nature of the characters which separate local races and closely allied species. That these are sometimes entirely non-adaptive has been demonstrated, we believe successfully, by Richards and Robson (1926).
>
> It is evident that certain genes which either initially or ultimately have beneficial effects may at the same time produce characters of a non-adaptive type which will therefore be established with them. Such characters may sometimes serve most easily to distinguish different races or species; indeed, they may be the only ones ordinarily available, when the advantages with which they are associated are of a physiological nature. Further, it may happen that the chain of reactions which a gene sets going is of advantage, while the end-product to which this gives rise, say a character in a juvenile or the adult stage, is of no adaptive significance. For this latter suggestion I am indebted to Mr. C.S. Elton.
>
> J.S. Huxley (1924, 1927a and b) has pointed out another way in which non-adaptive specific differences may arise. For he has shown that changes in absolute body-size, in themselves probably adaptive, may automatically lead to disproportionate growth in a variety of structures, such as horns and antlers in Mammalia and the appendages in Arthropoda. The effects so produced may be very striking, but, as they are the inevitable result of alteration in size, they can rarely have an adaptive significance.
>
> It is not perhaps always recognised how complete has been the demonstration provided by the above authors that the characters available to systematists for the separation of allied species may be of a wholly non-adaptive kind.

So far, then, Ford was as ready to recognize non-adaptive characters as Elton, no doubt partly from his own taxonomic experience, and quoted Richards and Robson in support. But he was well aware, and documents the phenomenon in his book, that mutants have effects on viability, as apparently did the unidentified genes responsible for the non-adaptive change in the wing pattern in the Marsh Fritillary. He continues, therefore:

> We are not justified, however, in assuming that they [the specific characters] have been established by a process of non-adaptive evolutionary change. Many of them are very invariable. An example is provided by the chitinous processes within the claspers of some male moths. These may show most constant differences in allied species; yet the female parts are often identical with each other and quite unmodified to fit those of the male, which therefore appear almost certainly to be non-adaptive. Yet it is gravely to be doubted if the uniformity of each male type could be preserved in the absence of at least associated stabilizing selection. Even if a non-adaptive character were to be established by chance survival, it appears to the author in the highest degree improbable that it could be maintained in a constant condition purely fortuitously.

Most of this quotation, except for the last few sentences, was preserved nearly intact in the 1939 and even 1954 editions of the book. Ford was right to notice the constancy of the genital armature, rather less critical in accepting the inevitability of allometric growth (it is itself a relationship selected for). What surprised me was that he never asked himself, nor did Elton, nor Robson and Richards, nor anyone else that I knew of, whether what they could see by simple looking was all that there was to a character. Fisher was no exception, being dependent on Ford for observation both in the field and in the collection. In 1931, quoting Ford, he remarked of the pleiotropic effect of a colour-pattern gene in a ladybird on the shape of the spermatheca, described by Dobzhansky, that:

> ...in the case of a small change in the proportions of an internal organ we have exceptionally good grounds for presuming the absence of selective action.

What was it, then, that led Ford, in contrast to Elton or Robson and Richards, to the belief that many characters might be in themselves non-adaptive, but the genes determining them and other, adaptive, characters were always under some selective influence? He was much impressed by, and often referred to, Fisher's mathematical demonstration (a field demonstration was out of the question) in *The Genetical Theory of Natural Selection* (1930, p. 80) that a neutral gene derived from a single mutation could only be in about the same number of individuals as there had been generations since its inception (Ford 1931, p. 81) and by Fisher's showing (1927) that for a polymorphism to be stable, there must be a balance of advantages and disadvantages. The disadvantage preventing fixation could be frequency-dependent, as was obvious in polymorphic mimicry when the mimetics became too common and attracted the predator; but it could also be constant in the case of linked deleterious recessives. Even in an *apparently* neutral polymorphism such as Elton's arctic foxes, there must be selection. There was plenty of evidence, direct or presumptive, for such associated disadvantages in the breeding data on the grouse locusts in America, obtained by Nabours and looked at by Fisher. Ford of course knew of and referred to much American work on *Drosophila* in which trivial variants were associated with differences in viability, which could be improved by selection.

What Ford thought of the paper by Dobzhansky and Queal (1938) proclaiming that third chromosome inversions in *Drosophila pseudoobscura* in the Rockies were varying by genetic drift, I do not know, but can guess. He certainly welcomed the later work in population cages showing them to be heavily selected in relation to temperature, producing balanced polymorphisms. He was on excellent terms with Dobzhansky, and they exchanged visits.

Ford was already in 1931 referring to melanism, but it was protective melanism in Sumner's deer mice (*Peromyscus*) on dark soil. Somewhat in contrast to the remarks quoted above on non-adaptive characters in species, he used Sumner's work as a model of geographical isolation producing divergent *adaptive* differences which could be improved into specific differences on crossing in the manner suggested by Haldane (1922), namely by disadvantage of the heterogametic sex. He also quoted (1931, p. 93) the two 'races' of '*Drosophila obscura*' in Washington and Oregon as evidence 'that isolation of a genetic as well as a geographical kind is possible...'. He offered these and other examples in a chapter entitled 'Special problems of evolution', in the first section of it, 1. *The Origin of Species*, giving the explicitly unsupported suggestion that the genetical split might occur between differently adapted types in a polymorphism. These were his contributions to a solution of the species problem.

The comparative abundance, then, of evidence for associated physiological disadvantages agreed with Fisher's theoretical calculations, which Ford admired. I do not know whether he understood them; Elton did not understand Haldane's, and Robson and Richards were refreshingly frank about their own inability. All of them, however, could check the inferences in the field or collections with better skill than any mathematician. In later years, Ford could add, in his re-review of polymorphism (1945) an extensive survey of melanism, especially in Lepidoptera, showing that rare recessive melanics were poorly viable, but the spreading industrial melanics were actually hardier than the wild-type in polluted conditions. By that time he believed that, although the black colour abolished the normal protective pattern, it:

> ...will not be such a handicap, perhaps even an asset, in industrial districts, and this for two reasons. (1) It will tend to match the smoke-grimed tree-trunks and fences. (2) There may well be fewer predators in such places, so that the selection pressure in favour of the correct colouring will be less intense. Here then the species may at last be able to avail itself of those genes which confer greater viability, even though they may involve an excessive formation of melanin.

It is remarkable that even Ford had hardly as yet achieved the idea of strong visual selection *for* the melanic form in polluted areas. Kettlewell and Tinbergen's demonstration of strong selective predation must have come as a surprise to both Ford and Fisher. Kettlewell himself told me that he was assured, by lepidopterists and ornithologists alike, that birds did not take moths resting on tree trunks, certainly not in polluted districts. (Equally, David Lack told me that when he first lectured on adaptation in Darwin's finches, he was flatly contradicted by distinguished ornithologists, who told him that beak shape was of no significance — you could walk beside a hawthorn hedge and see birds with all sorts of beaks eating the same berries. It was this that sent him to Lapland to see what happened in the winter when reserves were low.)

If Charles Elton, to Ford, was the enemy within the gates, there was another Englishman nearby who must have been an even greater irritant. Cyril Diver, a clerk to the House of Commons, was celebrated in scientific circles for his efficient committee work. He was even more celebrated for his excellent scientific work. With A.E. Boycott and others he had worked out (1930) the peculiar inheritance of sinistrality in the water snail *Limnaea peregra*; he had disentangled phenotypic and genotypic variation in tarn populations of the same species; he had published on the genetics of polymorphism in the land snail *Cepaea*, which he had also studied in subfossil populations. He and Fisher collaborated on studies of linkage in *Cepaea* (Fisher & Diver 1934). This work was later disputed on the grounds that they had used adults still storing sperm from previous matings, and Ford agreed, but their correspondence shows that Diver was fully aware of the danger and used juveniles (Cook 1969).

Diver became aware from his field studies of the importance of detailed mapping of the plant carpet, of highly clumped distributions of both plants and animals, of the virtual non-existence of large-scale randomly mating populations such as Fisher discussed, partly to simplify the mathematics but largely because he and Ford believed that small populations could only head for eventual extinction — they could contribute nothing to evolution.

Diver had convinced himself that there was no sign of differential predation on the colour and banding forms of *Cepaea*; most unfortunately, being a perfectionist, he never published his data, which were never available for scrutiny. His expressed opinion was enough to convince everyone (Haldane 1932, pp. 83, 174, was an outstanding example) that the polymorphism in *Cepaea* was neutral; he was a man of obvious experience and integrity, and there was no reason why anyone should doubt him. Fisher and Ford, however, would argue (Ford 1931, p. 85; 1945, p. 80) from Diver's subfossil finds that the polymorphism must be balanced, and therefore physiological selection at least must be acting on linked or pleiotropic characters.

Diver (1939, p. 97) was uneasy — it was a criticism also produced by Robson and Richards — that selection could lead only to closer and closer specialization, and that the species involved could only become senescent and, with changing conditions, eventually extinct. (I don't know who first said that strong selection could promote genetic diversity; probably it was already said of adaptive polymorphisms, but at this period, they would be thought of as a special case.) He was sure that most specific characters were non-adaptive, and that species existed in small or tiny isolated or semi-isolated populations. In 1940, in the same volume in which Ford was confidently quoting *Cepaea* (pp. 494, 498) as an example of balanced polymorphism, Diver used a range of animal and plant species, including *Cepaea*, as examples of non-adaptation. He did not quote Robson and Richards, but that was simply because he was speaking directly from his own experience. But he quoted Sewall Wright in the same volume — he had been shown the proof-sheets — and after giving most impressive figures for the number of colonies of *Cepaea* he had sampled and the shells he had scored, he concluded:

> If the few facts that are known about the unselected cases given above are considered dispassionately, it seems that selective forces and adaptive values have played little direct part in these specific differentiations; nor is there any evidence to suggest that geographical isolation, which obviously plays a large part in different circumstances, has been operative here, though the possibility is by no means excluded. The most probably general cause is random differentiation in small partially isolated populations which Wright (1939) [i.e. 1940] shows in chap. 5 to be statistically possible.

And he rounds off with a reassertion that selection in other circumstances does transform or multiply species, but:

> The truth seems to be that speciation and evolution are brought about in different ways in different cases, that a number of

different factors may be brought into play, and that the importance of the role of each will vary with the particular circumstances.

I can only suppose that our work on *Cepaea nemoralis* (Cain & Sheppard 1950, 1954) came as a much greater surprise, for rather different reasons, to Haldane, to Diver, and to Fisher and Ford, than I realized at the time. My own approach was a quite different one, and seemed obvious enough to me. As a small boy I had read the illustrated edition of H.G. Wells's *Outline of History* with its convincing exposition in the first few chapters of Darwinian evolution theory and palaeontology (including dinosaurs). I had also read Charles Kingsley's *The Water-Babies*, with its splendid remark that:

> no one has a right to say that no water-babies exist, till they have seen no water-babies existing; which is quite a different thing, mind, from not seeing water-babies; and a thing which nobody did, or perhaps ever will do.

All I wanted to know from all these great people was, how exactly did they *know* that any character was non-adaptive or neutral, totally devoid of any significance either way for the life of the animal or plant bearing it? They didn't know and they couldn't know. Philip Sheppard took the point at once when I first showed him *Cepaea* shells.

Their attitude, as I know now but had no inkling of then, was that of Plato and Aristotle (and most philosophers to the present day). Ford took a degree in classics before turning to zoology. Elton studied Greek at school, and apparently enjoyed the discipline. Some of them might have got the attitude from the philosophy, politics and economics course at Oxford, supposed to be a preparation for public life. But this may be false historicism; for most of the actors in this comedy, it was probably a matter of absorbing unconsciously an all-pervading atmosphere, which was indeed generated, but only very remotely, from ancient Greek thought. This *intellectualism* still reigns triumphant; some of the most widely known names in evolutionism have built their theories on it. It may well turn out to be as distorting an influence as was the Aristotelian essentialism in the last thousand years.

RISE OF THE NULL SELECTION HYPOTHESIS (W.B.P.)

Arthur Cain has shown that non-adaptive interpretations of differences between closely related species was a common view among geneticists, systematists and even ecologists in Britain in the period between 1920 and the early 1940s. Indeed, our conclusion is that during the 1920s and

1930s there existed a concerted, conscious campaign to advocate the null hypothesis (to use a modern expression) that if no use could be seen for physical characters in a species, then one could conclude that the characters had no adaptive value and had spread by some chance process, random genetic drift in particular. Advocacy of this null hypothesis long pre-dated the widespread understanding of random genetic drift and was as prevalent in the United States and continental Europe as in Britain. Consider, for example, these comments from Frank E. Lutz's prize-winning monograph entitled 'Apparently non-selective characters and combinations of characters, including a study of ultraviolet in relation to the flower-visiting habits of insects' (A. Cressy Morrison Prize for 1923 of the New York Academy of Sciences). Lutz had studied venation patterns in bee wings and also analysed and extended the early work of von Frisch on ultraviolet colours of flowers and attractiveness of flowers to bees. Following T.H. Morgan's view that mutations were produced at random with respect to adaptation, Lutz (1924, p. 228) concluded:

> If characters have arisen without such ulterior motive and are inherited, it is to be expected that creatures possess many totally useless characters — quite a different notion from the not-very-old teleological idea of the origin of all characters. These useless but not detrimental characters totally escape any action, for or against, of natural selection simply because they are neither useful or detrimental.

And the final paragraphs of the monograph argued that the null hypothesis of usefulness of characters should be changed.

> All this is not to say that natural selection is purely imaginary. There is no doubt that natural selection does set bounds beyond which variation can not go and succeed. It is also quite conceivable and altogether probable that certain variations are of so great a benefit to a creature that natural selection favors that variation. It is even conceivable and probable that many non-selective variations are so linked up, so correlated with a variation of selective value, that they will be carried along by the favoring of the valuable variation. But it is just as conceivable and probable that multitudinous variations have arisen, been perpetuated, and become distinguishing characteristics of species, genera, or larger taxonomic groups without having in themselves any selective value. They may even be used by the creature without their having selective value, the creature being perfectly able to get along just as well or perhaps even better without them. Grasshoppers use their long hind legs for jumping (or else they jump because they

> have long hind legs), but their more ancient relatives, the roaches, are still doing very well with ordinary legs.
>
> It is certainly not going too far to change the old expression, 'Whatever is is good,' to a more moderate one, 'whatever is is not bad.' If we can succeed in bringing ourselves to do this we may expect 'that creatures may possess many totally useless characters,' and we can think of even the colors of flowers in terms of plant physiology instead of solely in the more attractive and exciting terms of advertising and the struggle for existence. (Lutz 1924, pp. 282–283.)

When Sewall Wright conceived his shifting balance theory of evolution in nature in 1925–1932, he believed, following his reading of systematists, that differences between closely related species were almost always non-adaptive. Wright's concept of random genetic drift indicated that genes determining characters that were subject to small selection rates could become effectively selectively neutral if the population were sufficiently small. Thus, Wright argued that genes subject to selection coefficients of the order of mutation rates, such as Fisher hypothesized to account for the gradual evolution of dominance, were effectively neutral in the sizes of actual natural populations.

From the modern perspective of ecological genetics it may be difficult to accept the historical reality that in the period 1900–1940, views like those of Lutz were widespread and (in our opinion) dominant in the biological community. Yet it is only in the perspective of this non-adaptive view of evolution that the origins and early aims of ecological genetics can be understood.

From the perspective of the active non-adaptive null hypothesis (look quickly for adaptive use — find none, assume non-adaptive evolution), the programme of Fisher and Ford to change the null hypothesis to a selective interpretation (look quickly for adaptive use — find none, assume the adaptive use is there but hard to find) must be viewed as both audacious and extremely ambitious. The only reason why their programme appeared so natural and obvious by the time of the Darwin Centennial in 1959 was because of the great and almost unexpected success of the programme in achieving its aims.

The start of the experimental adaptationist programme was somewhat rocky. The late 1930s and early 1940s were a particularly encouraging time for the drifters and discouraging for Fisher and Ford, as demonstrated earlier in this paper.

Fisher and Ford began their serious field work on *Panaxia dominula* during the early 1940s for the express purpose of taking a relatively small population and finding in it incontrovertible evidence that changes in gene frequency from year-to-year could not be explained by random genetic drift. They certainly did find fluctuations of gene frequency in a conspicuous polymorphism that were greater than could be explained by sampling drift from the finite population size. But this was not 'ecological' genetics. Nothing whatever was known or demonstrated about the selective forces that caused the observed changes in gene frequency. But this did not prevent them from making the clear conclusion that their analysis of the data indicated that random genetic drift could not be of 'any significance' in evolution (Fisher & Ford 1947, p. 173).

The first Cain and Sheppard paper on selection in *Cepaea* (1950) forcefully raised the issue of how realistic was the prevailing non-selectionist interpretation of definite characters in natural populations. This general implication of their work was palpable in their paper because they had chosen the most celebrated example of supposed non-selective conspicuous characters, banding patterns in snails. They concluded that *all* supposed cases of random drift in polymorphisms should be reinvestigated. This paper was far more convincing than the 1947 paper of Fisher and Ford on *Panaxia dominula* because the ecological factors producing selective changes (ecological backgrounds and predation by thrushes) were specified and correlated with the colour and banding patterns.

In case any doubts remained about the general implications of this research on *Cepaea*, Cain's two *Nature* papers (1951a, 1951b) issued an unmistakable challenge to the thesis that if no selective interpretation of a character were obvious, then a non-selective interpretation was warranted (for that view, see the replies of G.S. Carter 1951). Not only that, he stated that *all* cases so far investigated of apparently non-adaptive characters turned out to have significant selection coefficients. Further, he argued that:

> The more the interactions between genes and their environments are studied, the less likely does it become that genes controlling definite characters can possess, except perhaps for very short periods, the very low selective coefficients necessary for extensive drift. . . what is wanted is more investigation; but it is doubtful whether any example of variation in Nature can be so completely analysed that, after selective effects have been estimated, the residual variation can be ascribed with confidence to genetic drift. There is always the possibility, indeed the likelihood, that the analysis of selective effects was not complete. (Cain 1951b, p. 1049.)

Sewall Wright's reactions to the *Cepaea* work were very different from his earlier reactions to the *Panaxia dominula* research (Wright 1948).

When Wright replied to Fisher and Ford, among his arguments were these three:

1 Even if Fisher and Ford were completely correct that yearly changes in frequency of the *medionigra* gene were caused by large fluctuations in selection rates, their further conclusion that all genes were subject to similar selection rates was wholly unwarranted.

2 The deduction by Fisher and Ford that, if the changes in gene frequency were not caused by sampling drift due to finite population size, then they had to be caused by natural selection, was not substantiated. Wright argued instead that random fluctuations in rates of selection and immigration could have caused the observed fluctuations in gene frequency.

3 Finally, Wright held out the possibility that the fluctuations in frequency of the *medionigra* gene were still possibly due to random drift because Fisher and Ford had not sufficiently determined population numbers in the years they were claiming selection had to be acting, and he gave theoretical reasons for suspecting that effective population sizes were smaller than calculated.

In 1948, Wright had by no means given up the possibility that conspicuous polymorphisms were subject to significant random drift (see also his article on organic evolution in the *Encyclopaedia Britannica* for 1948). But when Cain wrote to Wright in March of 1950 telling him about the *Cepaea* work, Wright replied:

> If we classify pairs of alleles in two categories — pairs that determine conspicuous differences and ones which do not but which act as modifiers or which contribute to quantitative variability — I suspect that variation in selection would in most cases dominate the gene frequencies of the former practically to the exclusion of drift while selection and sampling would either be more or less equal or there would be predominantly more drift in most of the latter. (Wright to Cain, November 14, 1950.)

The *medionigra* gene certainly determined a conspicuous character, as did the genes controlling banding patterns in *Cepaea*. Wright had changed from his views only two years earlier, in direct response to a convincing refutation of his earlier assertion that banding patterns in snails probably represented the effects of random drift. Soon Wright wrote:

> It is probable that conspicuous polymorphism is usually a device for adaptation to diverse conditions encountered by the species. It may relate to adaptation to different seasonal conditions as shown by Dobzhansky in the case of chromosome patterns in *Drosophila pseudoobscura*. In other instances it may give a basis for adaptation to diverse microenvironments. The observations of

> Cain and Sheppard on the frequencies of different color patterns in the land snail *Cepaea nemoralis* under different ecological conditions suggest this interpretation. (Wright 1951b, p. 455.)

Wright's change of view on the selective significance of conspicuous polymorphisms was directly related to Cain's challenge and the results of the Cain and Sheppard research. Further work by Sheppard indicated that Wright was probably wrong in his surmise that changes in frequencies of the *medionigra* gene in *Panaxia dominula* could have been caused by random genetic drift (Sheppard 1951). Indeed, Wright for the next few years took great pains to disassociate himself from the view that conspicuous polymorphisms were strongly affected by random genetic drift, and emphasized that his view of evolution in nature was deeply selectionist (see especially his address to the 1955 Cold Spring Harbor Symposium, Wright 1956).

Ecological genetics was on the way up in strength and influence. There is good evidence that this work was taken very seriously at international meetings, especially the Cold Spring Harbor Symposia in 1955 (devoted to population genetics) and 1959 (genetics and twentieth century Darwinism). Julian Huxley, Ernst Mayr, Ledyard Stebbins, G.G. Simpson, Theodosius Dobzhansky and many others became demonstrably more selectionist in their outlook and writings in the period 1950–1959. The Darwin centennial year (of *On the Origin of Species*) contained more celebrations of the power and ubiquity of natural selection than at any time since Darwin invented the idea. The change since the earlier Darwin centennial (of his birth; it was also the fiftieth anniversary of the *Origin of Species*) in 1909 is striking. Then, most of the speakers gathered in Cambridge to celebrate Darwin actually believed that natural selection was less important than Darwin believed (Seward 1909); by 1959, most evolutionists believed that natural selection was more pervasive than Darwin believed (Tax 1960). The evidence is good that the work of ecological geneticists was crucial in this change to a more selectionist view.

When A.D. Bradshaw made the following statements in 1962, most evolutionists from all over the world could agree. What determines local variation in plant species?

> The primary factor involved is natural selection. Apart from the possibility in very small populations of some genetic drift, and the remote possibility of continuous mutation in one direction, natural selection is the only factor that can cause changes in gene frequency and therefore changes in the genetic constitution of populations. The pattern of differentiation within species, therefore, depends primarily upon the pattern of natural selection itself....

> Evolutionary differentiation within species is therefore predominantly, if not entirely, due to the selective effects of the environment, and its pattern must resemble that of the environment. (Bradshaw 1962, pp. 9–10.)

Following this view, Bradshaw became a leader in showing the influence of natural selection upon quantitative variation in natural populations of plants, an extremely difficult undertaking compared with studying a conspicuous polymorphism (see Briggs & Walters 1984 for a comprehensive presentation, in historical perspective, of quantitative ecological genetics in plants).

Between 1950 and 1964 Ford and his associates had indeed multiplied the cases of conspicuous polymorphism under the influence of natural selection. Almost no one continued to argue that conspicuous polymorphism were subject to significant random genetic drift. Ford's *Ecological Genetics* (1964) was directed in part against Wright, but, ironically, Wright had stated his agreement with the thesis of the book in 1950 and never later changed his mind. During this time Ford could have directed greater attention to natural selection in relation to quantitative variation in both animals and plants, an aspect of ecological genetics he considered very important and to which Wright had made many theoretical contributions, including the lecture he gave at Oxford in 1950 (Wright 1951a).

Ford's 1964 book glories in the triumph of natural selection over random genetic drift, of 'scientific natural history' over the greatly exaggerated and distorted 'drift' of Sewall Wright. There is an excellent reason for this triumphal tone. Ford had little reason to believe, when he and Fisher began on the *Panaxia dominula* work in 1941, that it and the other field-work inspired by the same viewpoint would in only a decade and a half rout the widespread reliance on random drift, so visible in 1940, to explain variations in natural populations. Yet selectionism was enormously successful during this time. Most of the credit belongs to ecological genetics.

The proof for this assertion can be found in Mayr's influential book, *Animal Species and Evolution* (1963), which was published in the year before Ford's book. Similar shifts to a greater emphasis upon the all-pervasive influence of natural selection can be found in Stebbins, Julian Huxley, Dobzhansky and many others.

The changes in Dobzhansky's views can be seen by comparing the third edition of *Genetics and the Origin of Species* (1951) with his later revision under a new title, *Genetics of the Evolutionary Process* (1970). In the first two editions of *Genetics and the Origin of Species*, Dobzhansky had argued that random drift was the explanation for local variation in many species of land snails, including those studied by Gulick in Hawaii,

Crampton in Tahiti and Moorea, Welch in Oahu and Diver in England. But in 1951 Dobzhansky was well aware of the new research by Cain and Sheppard. After retaining his older discussion of land snails complete with the random drift explanation, Dobzhansky (1951, pp. 170–171) addressed the work of Cain and Sheppard:

> Cain and Sheppard (1950) find, however, that at least some of these microgeographic variations are correlated with certain features of the local environment.... Cain and Sheppard rightly argue that such correlations indicate that the variations observed by them fall into the class of adaptive polymorphism, possibly balanced polymorphism. The local differentiation in the traits which they observed is, then, due to natural selection and not to genetic drift. It should, however, be noted that not all variable characteristics in the snail show such correlations, and, hence, the participation of the genetic drift in the microgeographic differentiation is by no means excluded in the species which Cain and Sheppard have studied. The differentiation of human populations with respect to the skin color is almost certainly caused by selection, but it does not follow from this fact that the racial differentiation of, for example, the blood-group frequencies is also conditioned by selection. Indeed, Birdsell (1951) has published detailed data on variation of blood-group frequencies in some tribes of Australian aborigines which are strongly indicative of genetic drift in these populations.

Here Dobzhansky not only minimizes the implications of the Cain and Sheppard research, he also cites Birdsell's 1951 paper from the Cold Spring Harbor Symposium of 1950 as evidence of random drift in action, never mentioning that Cain had provided at the meeting (with Dobzhansky present) a stinging critique of Birdsell's assertions about random drift in human populations, nor or that Cain's critique had been published in the discussion section following Birdsell's paper.

By 1970, Dobzhansky's report on variation in land snails was a little different. After summarizing the older work of Gulick and others he said that 'random genetic drift seemed a more plausible explanation.' He continued: 'The works of Cain and Sheppard (1951, 1954) and of their numerous disciples in Britain...changed the situation' (Dobzhansky 1970, p. 279). Then he added the by now almost predictable caveat: 'Although the evidence adduced by Cain and Sheppard and their school has established beyond a doubt that natural selection is involved in the formation of local races of *Cepaea*, it does not rule out the possibility that some of the differences may also be due to random drift and to the operation of the founder principle' (Dobzhansky 1970, p. 279). This passage is followed by discussion of the work of Lamotte, and of the 'area effects' that Cain and Currey had discovered and published beginning in 1963 – Dobzhansky's interpretation was that 'area effects' were probably nothing other than random genetic drift.

The programme that Ford had set for himself and his 'ecological genetics' was intensely successful, more so than he had any good reason to believe possible when he was writing his essay on polymorphism for Julian Huxley's book *The New Systematics* (1940). By 1962, Fisher could die knowing that his selectionist enterprise had been terribly successful. The null hypothesis had been changed at least in some minds from the assumption of selective neutrality to the assumption of selective determination of every observable physical character of organisms in the wild.

THE NEUTRAL THEORY OF MOLECULAR EVOLUTION, RANDOM DRIFT AND NATURAL SELECTION (W.B.P.)

The deep extent of the change to a selectionist interpretation of all genetically based variability in natural populations can be measured by the reaction to the neutral theory of molecular evolution, first published in detail by Kimura (1968).

Kimura's lifelong interest in population genetics was sparked by the papers of Fisher, Ford and Wright on selection and random drift in *Panaxia dominula*. There was no population geneticist in Japan, and Kimura learned the field by reading the original papers of Fisher, Haldane, Wright and many others. In the late 1940s and early 1950s, Kimura's reading suggested to him that the controversy between Wright and Fisher was primarily one of random drift versus selection. This was precisely the dichotomy that Wright was trying his best to play down in the early 1950s, especially after seeing the results of Cain and Sheppard.

Kimura's greatest early success was deriving exact mathematical formulations of random genetic drift from both random sampling and random fluctuation of selection rates (see especially Kimura 1956). He did this in the hope and expectation that his results would buttress Wright's views on random drift in evolution, and would help to settle the controversy between Wright and Fisher.

As Kimura came to know Wright better during the years 1954–1960, however, he discovered to his great surprise that Wright was almost as much a selectionist as Fisher or Ford or Mayr. By the early 1950s, Wright's only role for random drift in the evolutionary process was to produce shifts of gene frequencies in the small subdivisions of a large population, occasionally producing a more adaptive local population, which then spread its gene structure by selective diffusion to others (his shifting balance theory). As Wright saw it in the 1950s, this process would rarely if ever produce non-adaptive differences between closely related species.

As the world's leader in the theoretical understanding of random drift, Kimura accurately perceived that he was the master of a process that evolutionists considered minor in the evolutionary process. He thus turned his attention to the deeper understanding of natural selection. His first major project was a revision of Fisher's Fundamental Theorem of Natural Selection, published by Fisher in *Heredity* (Kimura 1958).

Not until the summer of 1967 did Kimura begin to suspect that random genetic drift might have greater importance than he thought in the early 1950s. At this time a number of evolutionists and geneticists pointed out that two DNA triplets differing in third-position codons might still code for exactly the same protein. They concluded that the differences between the two genes was therefore probably selectively neutral and that some part of evolution at the molecular level must be neutral.

Kimura was the first to quantify the amount of neutral evolution by examining the existing molecular data for rates of evolutionary substitution. Using his own version of Haldane's famous 'cost of selection' paper (which Haldane had sent to Kimura for pre-publication comments: Haldane 1957), Kimura calculated that nucleotide substitutions were about 150 times more frequent than Haldane's highest possible rate. Kimura deduced that the vast majority of these substitutions must be selectively neutral, thus escaping the cost of selection.

Kimura was basically arguing that molecular evolution was dominated by selectively neutral evolution. Thus, at the molecular level, the proper null hypothesis about evolutionary changes was that they were selectively neutral until proved selective. At the phenotypic level, Kimura declared that changes in characters were probably dominated by natural selection rather than sampling drift.

When King and Jukes published their blast at the neo-Darwinians in their famous paper on 'Non-Darwinian evolution', they used physiological and biochemical arguments as well as population genetics to argue that molecular evolution was dominated by random drift. Their primary target was the null hypothesis of selection for explaining molecular differences between populations or species (King & Jukes 1969).

The initial reaction to the neutral theory of Kimura, King and Jukes was generally very negative, particularly from ecological geneticists. (See

Kimura 1983 for a substantial bibliography of negative reactions to the neutral theory.) The bone of contention was specifically what null hypothesis to use with molecular variability.

As long as the database was drawn from protein variation, the controversy between the neutralists and the selectionists was pretty much a draw, and reasons to change the selectionist null hypothesis were not compelling (for example, see Lewontin 1974). But when DNA sequence data began to pour in after the early 1980s, the situation changed dramatically for molecular evolutionists. The vast amount of non-coding DNA (junk DNA, pseudogenes) in addition to the synonymous changes indicated strongly that at the DNA level, neutral evolution might be really important. Evidence indicating more rapid molecular evolution at selectively unconstrained loci and codons accumulated. By 1990, molecular evolutionists had largely abandoned the null hypothesis of selection to explain observed molecular differences and accepted the neutral theory. If a DNA sequence change were observed, the starting point was the assumption of non-selective difference unless selective constraints were indicated. Even the molecular evolutionists who argue for the importance of selection at the DNA level construct and use models for which the neutral theory is the assumption (see Kreitman, Shorrocks & Dytham, Ch. 11, this volume).

Some neo-Darwinian selectionists have accepted the neutral theory. Dawkins, for example, says that he hopes the neutral theory is true because it is irrelevant to ecological genetics and yet has great possibilities for systematics (Dawkins 1986). Others such as Bryan Clarke and Cain reject the neutral null hypothesis on the supposition that in time most of the molecular genome will be proved to have selective importance.

This is the one significant issue in this paper on which Cain and Provine (amicably) part company. Cain's wager is that in 50 years intellectualism will be discarded, and the neutral theory forgotten as a once plausible but wrong view of molecular evolution. Provine's wager is that in 50 years the neutral theory of molecular evolution will be considered banally true, in the same sense that the heliocentric solar system in which we live is now considered true. But we agree that whatever the outcome of the neutral theory of molecular evolution, its importance for ecological genetics is small.

FINAL COMMENT (A.J.C., W.B.P.)

We are both concerned about the future of ecological genetics. Funding of science and university reward structures lack support for extended research projects. Even lifetimes of research are required for a robust ecological genetics. Scientific natural history is exceedingly complex and requires intensive field research. No molecular technique can ever provide a quick fix to the basic problems of ecological genetics. There will be no deep understanding of mechanisms of speciation unless the field of ecological genetics flourishes. A constant effort will be required to maintain funding for research and to provide the setting in which ecologists and geneticists can co-operate and collaborate in producing the ecological genetics of the future.

ACKNOWLEDGEMENTS

A.J.C. wishes to thank M.H. Williamson and D.J. Thompson for comments.

REFERENCES

Birdsell, J. B. (1951). Some implications of the genetical concept of race in terms of spacial analysis. *Cold Spring Harbor Symposia on Quantitative Biology (1950)*, **15**, 259–314.

Boycott, A. E., Diver, C., Garstang, S. & Turner, F. M. (1930). The inheritance of sinistrality in *Limnaea peregra* (Mollusca, Pulmonata). *Philosophical Transactions of the Royal Society of London*, B, **219**, 51–131.

Bradshaw, A. D. (1962). The taxonomic problems of local geographic variation in plant species. *Taxonomy and Geography* (Ed. by D. Nichols). Systematics Association Publication Number 4. The Systematics Association, London, UK.

Briggs, D. & Walters, S. M. (1984). *Plant Variation and Evolution* (2nd edn). Cambridge University Press, Cambridge, UK.

Cain, A. J. (1951a). So-called non-adaptive or neutral characters in evolution. *Nature*, **168**, 424.

Cain, A. J. (1951b). Non-adaptive or neutral characters in evolution. *Nature*, **168**, 1049.

Cain, A. J. & Sheppard, P. M. (1950). Selection in the polymorphic land snail *Cepaea nemoralis*. *Heredity*, **4**, 275–294.

Cain, A. J. & Sheppard, P. M. (1954). Natural selection in *Cepaea*. *Genetics*, **39**, 89–116.

Carter, G. S. (1951). Non-adaptive characters in evolution. *Nature*, **168**, 700, 1049.

Cook, L. M. (1969). Results of breeding experiments of Diver and Stelfox on *Helix aspersa*. *Proceedings of the Malacological Society of London*, **38**, 351–358.

Dawkins, R. (1986). *The Blind Watchmaker*, pp. 303–304. Norton, New York, NY, USA.

Dillistone, F. W. (1975). *Charles Raven. Naturalist, Historian, Theologian*. Hodder & Stoughton, London, UK.

Diver, C. (1939). Aspects of the study of variation of snails. *Journal of Conchology London*, **21**, 91–141.

Diver, C. (1940). The problem of closely related species living in the same area. *The New Systematics* (Ed. by J. S. Huxley), pp. 303–328. Oxford University Press, Oxford, UK.

Dobzhansky, T. (1951). *Genetics and the Origin of Species* (3rd edn). Columbia University Press, New York, NY, USA.

Dobzhansky, T. (1956). What is an adaptive trait? *American Naturalist*, **90**, 337–347.

Dobzhansky, T. (1970). *Genetics of the Evolutionary Process*. Columbia University Press, New York, NY, USA.

Dobzhansky, T. & Queal, M. L. (1938). Genetics of natural populations. I. Chromosome variation in populations of *Drosophila pseudoobscura* inhabiting isolated mountain ranges. *Genetics*, **23**, 239–251.

Elton, C. S. (1924). Periodic fluctuations in the numbers of animals: their causes and effects. *British Journal of Experimental Biology*, **2**, 119–163.

Elton, C. S. (1927). *Animal Ecology*. Macmillan, New York, NY, USA.

Elton, C. S. (1930). *Animal Ecology and Evolution*. Clarendon Press, Oxford, UK.

Elton, C. S. (1933). *The Ecology of Animals*. Methuen, London, UK.

Elton, C. S. (1938). Animal numbers and adaptation. *Evolution: Essays on Aspects of Evolutionary Biology Presented to Professor E. S. Goodrich on his Seventieth Birthday* (Ed. by G. R. De Beer), pp. 127–137. Clarendon Press, Oxford, UK.

Elton, C., Ford, E. B., Baker, J. R. & Gardner, A. D. (1931). The health and parasites of a wild mouse population. *Proceedings of the Zoological Society of London (1931)*, 657–721.

Fisher, R. A. (1922). On the dominance ratio. *Proceedings of the Royal Society of Edinburgh*, **42**, 321–341.

Fisher, R. A. (1927). On some objections to mimicry theory, statistical and genetic. *Transactions of the Entomological Society of London*, **75**, 269–278.

Fisher, R. A. (1930). *The Genetical Theory of Natural Selection*. Clarendon Press, Oxford, UK.

Fisher, R. A. (1931). The evolution of dominance. *Biological Reviews*, **6**, 345–368.

Fisher, R. A. & Diver, C. (1934). Crossing-over in the land snail *Cepaea nemoralis* L. *Nature*, **133**, 834.

Fisher, R. A. & Ford, E. B. (1947). The spread of a gene in natural conditions in a colony of the moth *Panaxia dominula*. *Heredity*, **1**, 143–174.

Ford, E. B. (1931). *Mendelism and Evolution*. Methuen, London, UK.

Ford, E. B. (1940). Polymorphism and taxonomy. *The New Systematics* (Ed. by J. S. Huxley), pp. 493–513. Oxford University Press, Oxford, UK.

Ford, E. B. (1945). Polymorphism. *Biological Reviews*, **20**, 73–88.

Ford, E. B. (1964). *Ecological Genetics*. Methuen, London, UK.

Ford, H. D. & Ford, E. B. (1930). Fluctuation in numbers, and its influence on variation, in *Melitaea aurinia*. *Transactions of the Entomological Society of London*, **78**, 345–351.

Haldane, J. B. S. (1922). Sex ratio and unisexual sterility of hybrid animals. *Journal of Genetics*, **12**, 101–109.

Haldane, J. B. S. (1932). *The Causes of Evolution*. Longman, Green, London, UK.

Haldane, J. B. S. (1957). The cost of natural selection. *Journal of Genetics*, **55**, 511–524.

Huxley, J. S. (1924). Constant differential growth-ratios and their significance. *Nature*, **114**, 895–896.

Huxley, J. S. (1927a). Further work on heterogonic growth. *Biologische Zentralblatt*, **47**, 151–163.

Huxley, J. S. (1927b). Studies on heterogonic growth. *Journal of Genetics*, **18**, 45–53.

Kimura, M. (1956). Stochastic processes and distribution of gene frequencies under natural selection. *Cold Spring Harbor Symposia on Quantitative Biology (1955)*, **20**, 33–53.

Kimura, M. (1958). On the change of population fitness by natural selection. *Heredity*, **12**, 145–167.

Kimura, M. (1968). Evolutionary rate at the molecular level. *Nature*, **217**, 624–626.

Kimura, M. (1983). *The Neutral Theory of Molecular Evolution*. Cambridge University Press, Cambridge, UK.

King, J. L. & Jukes, T. H. (1969). Non-Darwinian evolution. *Science*, **164**, 788–798.

Lewontin, R. C. (1974). *The Genetic Basis of Evolutionary Change*. Columbia University Press, New York, NY, USA.

Lutz, F. E. (1924). Apparently non-selective characters and combinations of characters, including a study of ultraviolet in relation to the flower-visiting habits of insects. *Annals* *of the New York Academy of Sciences*, **29**, 181–283.

Mayr, E. (1963). *Animal Species and Evolution*. Harvard University Press, Cambridge, USA.

Provine, W. B. (1986). *Sewall Wright and Evolutionary Biology*. University of Chicago Press, Chicago, IL, USA.

Raven, C. E. (1953a). *Natural Religion and Christian Theology. The Gifford Lectures 1951. First Series: Science and Religion*. Cambridge University Press, Cambridge, UK.

Raven, C. E. (1953b). *Natural Religion and Christian Theology. The Gifford Lectures 1952. Second Series: Experience and Interpretation*. Cambridge University Press, Cambridge, UK.

Richards, O. W. & Robson, G. C. (1926). The species problem and evolution. *Nature*, **117**, 345–347 and 382–384.

Robson, G. C. (1928). *The Species Problem*. Oliver & Boyd, London, UK.

Robson, G. C. & Richards, O. W. (1936). *The Variation of Animals in Nature*. Longmans, London, UK.

Seward, A. C. (Ed.) (1909). *Darwin and Modern Science*. Cambridge University Press, Cambridge, UK.

Sheppard, P. M. (1951). A quantitative study of two populations of the moth, *Panaxia dominula*. *Heredity*, **5**, 349–378.

Tax, S. (Ed.) (1960). *Evolution after Darwin* 3 vols. University of Chicago Press, Chicago, IL, USA.

Wright, S. (1940). The statistical consequences of Mendelian heredity in relation to speciation. *The New Systematics* (Ed. by J. S. Huxley), pp. 161–183. Oxford University Press, Oxford.

Wright, S. (1948). On the role of directed and random changes in gene frequency in the genetics of populations. *Evolution*, **2**, 279–294.

Wright, S. (1951a). The genetical structure of populations. *Annals of Eugenics*, **15**, 323–354.

Wright, S. (1951b). Fisher and Ford on 'the Sewall Wright effect'. *American Scientist*, **39**, 452–458, 479.

Wright, S. (1956). Classification of the factors of evolution. *Cold Spring Harbor Symposia on Quantitative Biology (1955)*, **20**, 16–24.

2. STOCHASTIC PROCESSES IN POPULATIONS: THE HORSE BEHIND THE CART?

JOHN R.G. TURNER
Department of Genetics, University of Leeds, Leeds LS2 9JT, UK

CHANCE AND NECESSITY, OR GOD AND MEPHISTOPHELES

History is full of ironies; the history of science is not excepted.

I shall present the thesis that Britain's foremost statistician was instrumental in turning Britain's evolutionists and ecologists away from the stochastic modelling of population processes. More seriously, he turned them away from thinking stochastically about populations.

In the course of this, I shall discuss the neutralist–selectionist controversy in evolution, and a similar problem over adaptationism versus population modelling which has now surfaced in ecology. It is not my aim to discuss which theory is right in either case, but rather to examine the basis on which other scientists have formed their opinions. I shall not therefore examine evidence in detail, and I shall not deal with anything on neutral evolution subsequent to Kimura's book (Kimura 1983). My own view is that there is (to that date at least) no good evidence in favour of the neutral theory but *only one* good argument against it.

Just what is a stochastic as distinct from a deterministic process? We do not understand what causation is: all that we know of it comes from our observation of correlation. But it seems unlikely that there are two kinds of causation, the one stochastic and the other deterministic. Whether causation is predominantly determinate or indeterminate depends on what one wants to believe, among other things, about free will, predestination and John Calvin. However, depending on the consistency of the correlations, in particular whether the effect we are interested in has a high and consistent correlation with only one or two causes, it may be convenient to model the causal network deterministically. If not, it may be more helpful to use a probabilistic approach.

Thus we have the relatively uninteresting question, not what processes are stochastic and what deterministic, as all are at bottom equally determinate (or stochastic), but which processes can be more profitably modelled in which way? But we do know that there is an interesting question involved in the conflict between theories that attribute evolution to natural selection, and theories that attribute it to other factors which change gene frequencies. Predominant in our thinking about these have of course been the aleatory effects produced by finite population size.

'Random' genetic drift is *not* truly a random process. The gene for pyruvate kinase (PK) deficiency has an abnormally high frequency among the Old Order Amish of Mifflin County, Pennsylvania (McKusick *et al.* 1964). It is known from pedigrees that it was introduced by one 'Strong Jacob' Yoder, one of a small number of Mennonites who founded this population in 1742. As the gene is deleterious, this adds up to almost the best evidence one can imagine that we are seeing not the effects of local natural selection in enhancing the frequency of the gene, but a classical founder effect due to the population bottleneck. Yet we could construct a believable causal, or if we like, determinate history of how that gene came to be there. The history of Calvinism, and of the religious upheavals of central Europe, would tell us why a number of Mennonites chose to escape to the New World. If we had sufficient information we could give an account of why Jacob Yoder was among them, and why he went to Mifflin County. A combination of family history and the physics of sperm mobility might tell us how he came to be carrying the PK deficiency allele.

Clearly what we mean when we say that founder effects of this kind are best looked at stochastically is that we can see no direct functional connection between the presence of the allele in Strong Jacob and his arrival in Mifflin County. It could just as well have been any other allele, as indeed it was among the founders of other Amish communities, and detailed descriptions of the causation of the presence of a particular allele in a particular county are not so much tedious as uninteresting from an evolutionary point of view. Only more generalized descriptions of the behaviour of any allele in any small population are of interest.

Natural selection, likewise, cannot be regarded as any more determinate than random drift. The distinction between them is not so easy as many imagine, and is impossible for complete diploid genomes in a sexual population. Consider the outcome of Jacob Yoder dying on the voyage to America. None of his genes would now be in Mifflin County. Was this natural selection or a random event? If we regard Jacob's diploid genome as a unique configuration of genes, then we cannot say. All his genes contributed to his destiny, and their mass extinction permits no distinction between selection and random drift. Only when we consider a few loci at a time, and are able therefore to replicate the experiment by asking whether more Mennonites made it to America when they carried say blood group O than blood group A, are we able to make a start on distinguishing changes of gene frequency that are selective from those that are random.

The long-standing debate over the importance of random processes and natural selection in evolution does not result merely from the practical difficulty of determining what is causing gene frequency to change: there is a fundamental problem of distinguishing these two factors in principle (Hodge 1987).

The interesting question then is not whether a process is best understood through stochastic or deterministic modelling, but whether a particular biological process is aleatory, that is to say merely an aspect of the second law of thermodynamics, which causes everything to degenerate into chaos, or whether it is a selective system which works in the opposite direction, as the 'infinite improbability drive', generating objects of very low probability (Fisher 1954). The two chief aleatory processes for an evolutionist are mutation — the disordering of the molecular genetic structures of organisms — and random drift — the disordering of the genetic structure of populations. To these the ecologist should add local extinction, which randomly disorders the structure of ecological communities by removing some of their members. A macroevolutionist would add the global creation and extinction of species and of life forms (such as all the flying vertebrate taxa), which have the same outcome on a much longer time scale.

We now come to a paradox. A 'creative' process like natural selection operates only by selecting from the products of the same degenerative processes that, by themselves, would cause organisms to vanish into a mess of randomized atoms. We can have selection only if mutation causes potentially degenerative decay in the genetic material. Other randomizing/aleatory processes may similarly produce a base for selection, as is proposed by the 'species selection' part of the theory of punctuated equilibrium, or they may produce randomized patterns on top of any tendency of natural selection to hold the organism together (see for instance the discussion of species selection and species drift in Turner 1986 and in Levinton *et al.* 1986).

It is possible that all 'creation' is like this: that even art is aleatory, selecting from the products of the very thermodynamic chaos which it apparently counters. Landscape painting consists of selecting pleasing angles from the undoubtedly aleatory phenomenon of landscape; creative writing consists of making a selection from a large randomized set of possibilities drawn from the writer's lexical store.

This is a Manichaean doctrine: we need both God the Creator and Mephistopheles the Denier: 'the spirit that says "No!"' (Goethe, *Faust* pt 1). It is a delicate mental balancing act to perceive how much weight should be given to each process. Thus the historical record (e.g. Olby 1981) shows considerable difficulty from 1890 to 1930 in figuring out the balance between selection and mutation (a matter that population geneticists now regard as largely solved), and deciding how big are the mutational steps that selection is working with, a question that is still unresolved.

THE ORIGIN OF THE NEUTRAL THEORY

It has been said many times (originally apocryphally by Agassiz commenting on the reception of Darwin) that the response of scientists to a new theory comes in three stages: (1) it's ridiculous, (2) it's obvious, (3) we thought of it first. The neutral theory of evolution has in Britain had a fair share of the first two treatments: I shall now give it the third treatment by pointing out that it was derived by R. A. Fisher in 1930 (Fisher 1930a).

Fisher's evolutionary theory is a theory of evolutionary flux (I shall not give detailed citations: extensively documented discussions of Fisher's thought are Hodge 1992, Leigh 1986, 1987, and Turner 1985, 1987; his collected papers are published by Bennett 1971–1974, and his letters on which I have drawn extensively by Bennett 1983). Very different from the views of evolutionary stasis, encouraged alike by E.B. Ford's later concept of balanced polymorphism and the Eldredge–Gould theory of equilibrium with jerks, it sees evolution as a continuous, but slow, substitution of new mutant genes at the expense of their ancestral alleles. As befitted Darwin's intellectual heir (and the psychologically adopted 'son' of Darwin's youngest son Leonard), Fisher conceived the driving force of this genetic flux as natural selection, the superiority in survival or reproduction of the new allele over the old, and viewed the adaptation and highly improbable level of organization built up by this process as a kind of optimistic reverse coin of the depressing second law of thermodynamics (Fisher 1930b): it was this philosophical view that he crystallized mathematically in the difficult and controversial fundamental theorem of natural selection. His demonstration that 'fitness' (roughly, adaptation) would perpetually increase formed a Darwinian ladder to counter the thermodynamic snake, which will eventually swallow the universe by the maximization of entropy.

Fisher believed fundamentally in indeterminism; and 'fundamentally' is to be read as meaning 'from the bottom of his heart', not 'when you finally strip off the excess baggage'. It was this that allowed him to reconcile his religious beliefs about freedom of will and the absence of predestination (he was no Calvinist) with his Darwinian view that the human psyche was subject to natural law and to full scientific investigation (Hodge 1992). He therefore accepted the importance of aleatory changes in gene frequency and regarded natural selection itself as being a non-determinate process. Initially, the theoretical discovery of genetic drift as the 'Hagedoorn effect' (Hagedoorn & Hagedoorn 1921) had posed a problem for Mendelian evolutionary theory, by suggesting that the genetic variance needed for evolution would be lost through random fixation. Fisher successfully wrestled with this problem when devising his flux theory: the drip-feed of continual mutation would sufficiently counter the loss through drift, to maintain a reservoir of variation on which selection would act. While the fate of most new mutants was loss by genetic drift within a few generations of their occurrence, a small proportion but large number would remain drifting at low frequency for a substantial time. It was from this reservoir that natural selection would pull the alleles that eventually became fixed. Fisher believed that *the majority of new mutations were approximately neutral in their effects on survival*. Over time, they would cease to be so, as either the environment or the rest of the genome altered. Those that had survived through the risky period of potential loss would then either tend to be removed by selection (an uninteresting process not obviously distinguishable from their loss due to drift) or would rise in frequency to become part of the positive evolutionary flux (Fisher 1930a).

In the course of this derivation, Fisher calculated the probability that a newly arisen neutral mutation would become fixed by random walk alone: his solution is the now well-known $1/2N$, where N is the population size. He also produced a close approximation to the minimum time it would take for a newly arisen neutral allele to become fixed (see Kimura & Ohta 1971, p. 9). Fisher was thus in a position to propose the neutral theory of evolution in 1930. He did not do so, not because he failed to notice its significance but because he believed that the neutral theory was empirically (*not* mathematically) invalid. His argument was the one I mentioned as the one good argument against the theory.

Thus, having derived the theory Fisher concluded that it was wrong. He therefore published only his own disproof and left the theory itself to be read between the lines (Fisher 1930a).

THE NECESSITY OF CHANCE

Fisher had a valuable analogy: a balanced roulette wheel is as near to a perfect random number generator as one can get. Yet the casino steadily makes money out of it at the expense of the gamblers by an appropriate loading of the odds. Natural selection can be seen as a loading of the odds in the random process of evolution, which ensures that alleles which confer adaptive properties upon organisms become fixed in species' gene pools just as surely as the proprietor of a casino dines well every night (Fisher 1930b).

Evolutionary biologists have been correct in their perception of natural selection as the important force in evolution. Without it, organisms would be prey to unbiased randomization and would no longer be recognizable as adapted organisms. Provided we reject the other potentially adequate explanations for adaptations (vitalism, divinely directed evolution, the Lamarckian process and special creation), we have to assign a very important place to natural selection in any evolutionary theory. Dawkins (1982, 1986) has expressed this point of view eloquently in books that are not less worthy of attention by serious workers for being addressed to a wider audience.

It is not, however, inevitable that we should go on to assume that natural selection is the only process in evolution, or that every feature of an organism is an 'adaptation'.

ECOLOGICAL GENETICS AND SEWALL WRIGHT

Fisher's conflict with Sewall Wright over the role of random genetic drift in evolution fuelled a great deal of research in evolutionary genetics up to the 1970s at least, and became increasingly personal and acrimonious over the years. (The whole story has been magnificently documented by Provine 1985, 1986.)

The reasons for this dispute are obscure. Clearly, Fisher did not accept Wright's view that random drift had a creative role to play in evolution by making new, adaptive configurations of genes in isolated populations. Fisher's reasons were equally clearly theoretical, or of the nature of a hunch, as empirical evidence was not at hand. Wright's theory involved a further stage, in which the new combinations of genes spread through the species either by some kind of migrational swamping (the population with the successful combination producing excess emigrants) or by some kind of population selection (the population with the better combination out-surviving the poorer adapted populations). Fisher was always extremely cautious about evoking group selection.

Fisher had also a strong emotional attachment to natural selection as the sole creative process of evolution and even saw it as the still present activity of the Creator. It was at this point that Creator and Creature between them selected the future from its range of statistical possibilities. The human duty would eventually be to take control of our own evolution and create a better future, using our free will, through the practice of eugenics. Fisher had of course allowed the aleatory process of mutation to play a crucial role but he had minimized the creative nature of that role with his theorem that, statistically, only mutations with vanishingly small effects on fitness and phenotype would be successful in evolution. (This solution was as extreme as you can get; its correctness is still in dispute.)

Thus mutation fed its variation to the selective machinery in the most finely divided form possible. The importance of this in Fisher's intellectual development was that it was a decisive counter to the mutationist view that prevailed among Mendelian evolutionists during Fisher's formative years, in which very large mutational changes were held to produce whole adaptive systems, even the phenotype of a whole new species, at one step. The problem, as has been eloquently pointed out by Dawkins (1986), is that it pulls the central rug out from under Darwinism: if a whole jumbo jet can be assembled by a tornado in a junk yard, then on the one hand natural selection becomes a redundant hypothesis and we are back to divine intervention, or on the other the whole theory of evolution becomes ridiculous.

Fisher's demolition of mutationism had been an intellectual *tour de force*; just as he completed it, Wright produced another theory proposing that an aleatory process played a crucial creative role in evolution. It is easy to imagine that Fisher was not emotionally disposed to accept such a theory. As Cain (Ch. 1, this volume) suggests, it must have been infuriating.

But Fisher did not reject Wright's theory on its fundamental mathematical premises. Fisher believed in stochasticity as firmly as did Wright, and in one of his letters to Leonard Darwin even toyed with the idea that new interacting combinations of genes could come into being which would be important new adaptive types. He seems to have rejected the thought because he could see no way in which they could be held together against the destructive force of recombination. Wright's solution, that such new combinations could be fixed in small isolated subpopulations, was perhaps even more infuriating (there is nothing more annoying than the elegant solution one has just missed). At the time Fisher's disagreement with Wright seemed to boil down to a set of empirical questions about the degree to which the populations of real species are actually isolated from one another; if there is too much genetically effective migration between them, Wright's theory will not work, and it was this point that Fisher stuck to, maintaining that the effective genetic number of a natural species was the enumerated number of the whole species, not of its component populations.

In the ensuing decades Fisher found an experimental ally in E.B. Ford, who set about investigating the phenomena of microevolution in the field. The work of Ford and the Oxford school of ecological genetics, among whom must be numbered in various kinds of association, Sheppard, Cain, Clarke and Kettlewell, was a major scientific advance. There can hardly be a biology textbook now which does not mention Kettlewell's demonstration of strong natural selection; other demonstrations of selection also became widely known, for example through the beautiful diorama illustrating the Cain–Sheppard collaboration on selection in *Cepaea* which used to grace the main hall of the Natural History Museum. Sheppard's conviction that he could demonstrate natural selection on the human blood groups led directly to a major advance in paediatrics (see Turner 1990a, 1990b). It is only in recognition of these achievements that I present a critique.

It is a matter still for historical investigation how much influence Fisher had on the thinking of the Oxford group, collectively or severally, and how much their appearance as men of Fisher's (Turner 1988) derives from convergence from independent beginnings; Cain (1988) has been at pains to point out that his own apparent agreement with Fisher resulted from independent thinking. It is undoubtedly the case that Ford's early book *Mendelism and Evolution* (1931) is in part a magnificently lucid and readable exposition of Fisher's theory of evolution, without the mathematics and therefore accessible in a way that Fisher's was not. The alliance did conceal some rather large differences of opinion, which developed as the experimental results from Ford and his friends came in: whereas Fisher's disagreement with Wright hinged on questions of population structure, the Oxford group tended to see the question as one of the strength of natural selection.

Cain (Ch. 1, this volume) shows how a crucial question in the formation of the Oxford view was the old taxonomists' problem of which differences between taxa were adaptive: it was seen as central to the creation of any evolutionary taxonomy that the 'non-adaptive' and therefore slowly evolving (or perhaps non-evolving) differences should be used to define the natural groups, and the literature was full of *a priori* assertions that certain types of character fell into this category. As Cain argues, it was equally rational to assume that *no* characters were non-adaptive. The problems that this created for taxonomy were overcome first of all by the invention of phenetic, non-evolutionary taxonomy by Cain and Harrison (1958), and then, following on the development of this into numerical phenetic taxonomy, by its re-invented evolutionary version, cladistics. Thus was born the Oxford version of adaptationism, in which the hypothesis that all taxonomic character differences were adaptive became allied with a Fisherian view that random genetic drift was evolutionarily insignificant. The anti-Wright stance that resulted had something of a paradox at its core because Wright himself accepted the adaptationist view of character differences (Provine, Ch. 1, this volume). (Note that the statement 'character difference *x* is/is not adaptive' remained largely unanalysed: as it has many possible meanings (Turner 1987) it is not surprising that there was confusion and controversy.)

In the end at least, the Oxford view of evolution differed considerably from Fisher's in emphasizing stasis and balanced polymorphism, which Ford believed was almost exclusively maintained by heterozygous advantage. Concomitantly, the Oxford group emphasized the importance of genes with large effects on phenotype and fitness, and therefore effectively reversed the central tenet of Fisher's theory that the majority of alleles which became fixed during evolution had very small effects on survival. On the other hand they were very much with him on the difficult and obscure question of the evolution of dominance (although again their approach was completely different: Fisher had been concerned with the dominance of rare recurrent mutations, whereas Ford and Sheppard were predominantly concerned with the dominance of alleles in polymorphic systems).

There is no doubt that the Oxford group saw their work as providing excellent evidence against Wright's view and against an evolutionarily significant role for the effects of finite population size. It was indeed the case that with selection coefficients as strong as they had discovered, random drift would be ineffective in influencing gene frequencies in any permanently interesting way except in populations that were so small as to be on the verge of extinction. Or as Ford modestly put it:

> Up to about 1940, it was assumed that the advantage possessed by genes spreading in natural populations rarely exceeded 1 per cent. As it is now known that it quite commonly exceeds 25 per cent and is frequently [*sic*] far more..., it will be realized how restricted is the field in which random drift is of importance. (Ford 1964, p. 32.)

Random drift, according to this view, verged on the non-existent: there are even passages which suggest (perhaps not intentionally) that this might be literally true, that there really were circumstances in real populations in which the effects of finite population size on gene frequency actually ceased:

> Just what evolutionary importance should be ascribed to genetic drift is a matter of considerable controversy. On the one hand,

> the process is mathematically certain to occur, *given the right conditions*, and may even, as claimed, produce by a non-selective process particular combinations of genes which happen to be highly advantageous and can spread, once they have originated, by natural selection. On the other hand, selection coefficients actually determined are all (or almost all) much too high to allow drift to occur, even although they refer to apparently very trivial characters. And it may very well be doubted whether under the changing conditions normal in nature any gene can possess, except for a very short time, a selection coefficient near enough to neutrality for drift to become important in determining its distribution. (Cain 1954, p. 146.) (My italics.)

A population which is on the verge of extinction can of course recover, and some admittance was granted in this theoretical structure for founder effects, which had been to some extent given clearance by Ernst Mayr's (1954) adaptationist version of them. Ford was, however, determined that no hint of compromise with Wright should emerge even when considering population bottlenecks. His work (for the original citations, see Ford 1964) on the Marsh Fritillary butterfly in its day was an elegant piece of field observation. Ford's findings, of the modal phenotype of the population changing radically after a bottleneck produced by a population crash, can be most obviously interpreted as an example of the phenomena that Wright had conjectured (Turner 1987). Ford, however, was at pains to interpret the observations as refuting Wright's ideas.

The Ford–Cain–Sheppard position was not irrational. We must make inferences from what we know; natural selection had been shown to be not nearly as feeble as had been universally supposed. If I insist that there are fairies at the bottom of the garden, you can challenge me to let you see them. A few nights' watching fails to produce the little people; I can then insist that my garden is ecologically unsuitable but that no end of assorted hobgoblins will be found in Bryan Clarke's garden. When further watches in Hamilton's, Maynard Smith's and Parker's gardens have failed to produce so much as a whisker of a leprechaun, you would all be entitled to the view, in the absence of further strong evidence, that the whole idea was ridiculous. This was largely the view taken on random genetic drift within English ecogenetic circles: natural selection was strong, and random drift was effectively non-existent.

Implicit in this is a theoretical approach which assumes that the baseline theory of population genetics is exemplified by the Hardy–Weinberg theorem of constant gene frequency in an infinite population. Evolution is conceived as a series of deviations from this norm, selection and random drift being two of these. This is the way most of us have been taught, and in turn have taught theoretical population genetics to undergraduates. This is misleading: the baseline is of course the events in a finite population, which immediately generate evolution of a sort (Gale 1990). One can then think of adaptive evolution as a set of deviations from that norm.

The final curious intellectual balancing act that resulted from this anti-Wright, anti-drift position can be seen in the last edition of Philip Sheppard's classic *Natural Selection and Heredity*:

> Recent work on polymorphism, for example in ladybirds, snails, flies, moths, mammals and primroses, to mention only a few, suggest [*sic*] that *genes having easily recognisable effects are usually subject to very strong selection.* Moreover, characters affected by polygenes, such as birth weight in man, egg size in ducks, or spot number in the Meadow Brown have been shown to be equally influenced by selection. The evidence at the moment suggests, therefore, that changes large enough to be detected easily are unlikely to be controlled by genetic drift, except in populations of very small size, which are unlikely to persist for long periods of time.... That selection is controlling the expression of characters does not mean, however, that the polygenes controlling such characters cannot drift in frequency, for several different combinations can produce the same effect, and it is the effect that is being controlled by selection. However, if these genes interact with one another in producing a particular character, a change in their frequency is much less likely to be neutral with respect to its effect on selection. These arguments, of course, do not mean that genetic drift never causes a change in wild populations, but only that it is probably of rather minor importance in evolution. *A possible exception would be mutants which have no effect on the development or physiology of an individual (if such exist...), and, therefore, would have no effect on the phenotype in evolution.* (Sheppard 1975, p. 134.) (My italics.)

Sheppard therefore admits the possibility of alleles which are completely neutral. He then omits to mention that between these alleles with zero selection coefficients and the strongly selected ones which are his main subject matter, there are likely to be alleles which are weakly selected. In this way the theory that selection comes only in the form of strong coefficients is precariously maintained.

Looked at this way, the Oxford, or English, position does not seem so reasonable. What it is asserting is that selection coefficients are *always* large. But this, to adapt Cain's rhetorical question (p. 15) is to assert that because one has found only big water babies, one can safely conclude that there are no little ones.

The Oxford position then is rather different from Fisher's. He had argued for very small selection coefficients, for evolutionary minimalism, and for population structure as eliminating a creative role for genetic drift. The Oxford group believed that genetic drift was effectively impossible because natural selection was normally too strong. It was a view largely influenced by, if not originating from, the group's own empirical findings: a series of stunning and elegant studies showing that natural selection could be very strong indeed.

The outcome was clear. In England, or at least within the widespread influence of the Oxford school of ecological genetics, a belief in strong selection coefficients and the total inefficacy of random drift became *de rigueur*. Deviation within the group was not permitted. Outsiders who came up with interpretations of field phenomena involving significant amounts of genetic drift (e.g. Crosby 1959) got some pretty rough handling.

I date the collapse of the Oxford position from the demonstrations, which became increasingly frequent, of marked founder effects in human populations. While such effects had been postulated by Sam Berry, among others, for non-human mammalian populations (Berry 1964), it was only when the human populations could be examined by pedigree, so that the introduction of the gene by a named individual could be clearly demonstrated (as with 'Strong Jacob', p. 30), that the evidence became totally convincing. Although they had always admitted certain aspects of founder effects, the Oxford school remained silent on these findings.

ECOLOGICAL GENETICS AND KIMURA

Thus it was that finite population size effects came to have the status of a 'lunar green cheese theory'. This is an important concept in the philosophy and practice of science: it is not true that science consists of the impartial investigation of all possible hypotheses. Most possible hypotheses are so improbable as to be not worth investigating: suggestions that the moon is made of green cheese are simply not worth refuting. The English view of random drift as lunar green cheese came into head-on collision with the revivals by Kimura (1968) and by King and Jukes (1969) of the neutral theory that had been thought up and rejected by Fisher.

Much of the debate (e.g. Clarke 1970) centred on empirical evidence, which I shall not deal with. The implicit bottom line was that no alterations, even at the most intimate molecular level, could produce changes in organisms which were so small that natural selection would not override random drift in determining their fate. (This it will be noted is totally different from Fisher's viewpoint, which was that a substantial proportion of new mutations were indeed neutral.) If one was brought up in Oxford it was quite difficult to see just how unreasonable (although not irrational) this position was. This is a problem in the development of science which has been identified by Travis and Collins (1991) with the name 'cognitive particularism': briefly the inability on the part of a group of scientists to conceive that what the opposition is saying makes any sense whatever!

But consider the distribution derived from a paper by Crow (1972) (Fig. 2.1a): there are known to be advantageous mutations, perhaps sometimes with selection coefficients up to 50%. There are known to be deleterious mutations, right down to lethality (coefficients of −100%).

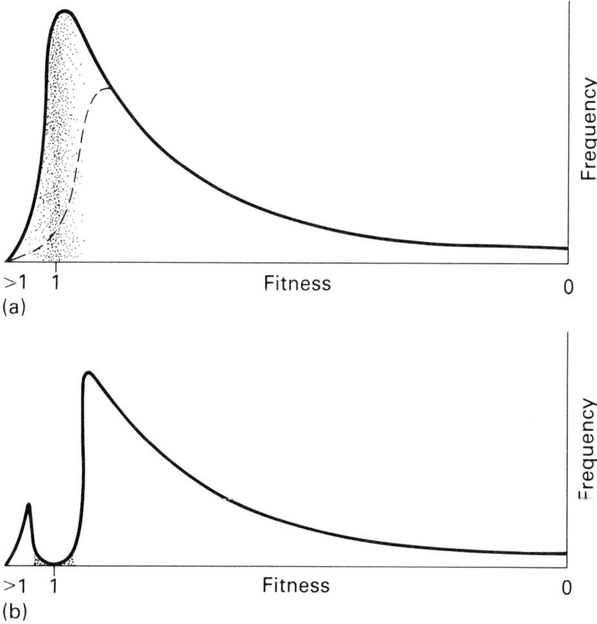

FIG. 2.1. Some possible frequency distributions of new mutations against their effect on individual survival, from lethal (fitness zero), through neutrality (fitness 1) to somewhat advantageous. (a) A reasonable distribution, based on Crow (1972); the proportion of effectively neutral mutations (the stippled zone) exceeds the advantageous mutations. The overall frequency of the effectively neutral alleles can be reduced by assuming that the distribution follows the dashed line, but it still exceeds the proportion of advantageous mutations in most reasonable ways of drawing the graph. (b) An 'Oxford' distribution, drawn to show what the graph would look like if there truly were virtually no neutral alleles.

Somehow this distribution has to cross the point where the mutations are neutral (fitness = 1) or, if one wants a more sophisticated view, it has to pass through the zone where the mutations are effectively neutral (selection coefficients roughly less than the reciprocal of population size), represented by the stippled band. How does the distribution cross this line? It is known that mildly deleterious mutations are more common than semilethals, so the distribution rises in this area. Crow considered that it might peak at neutrality, or slightly to the deleterious side of it. But what it is extremely unlikely to do (Fig. 2.1b), is to dip to zero in this region! Not that anybody ever explicitly suggested that the distribution did that; this would have exposed the unreasonableness of the view that there are no weak selection coefficients. Sheppard's compromise (p. 39) suggests the even more bizarre possibility that the distribution dips to zero in the effectively neutral zone, and has an infinitely thin mode precisely on neutrality!

The adaptationist reaction was in part a reaction to a view which seemed to emerge in the early neutralist literature that proteins and other macromolecules were merely random strings of residues. If organisms are no more than the epiphenomena of the interaction, dynamic and structural, of their macromolecules — i.e. if there is no vital principle — and if organisms are adapted, then this random string view of molecules is plainly ridiculous. Organisms would then be totally in the realm of thermodynamic chaos. Further, the more we get to know about microstructure, the more unlikely it seems that the molecules are merely random packing, with very small evolutionarily undetectable selected active sites (the view that there is a large random process riding piggyback on a small selective one).

It is not therefore similarly unreasonable to assert that it is impossible to make an alteration in the integrated and intricate structure that is an organism, which can *never* have any effect on its survival, in any circumstances of the external environment or of the internal functioning of the organism. As the external environment is perpetually changing, and as the internal and genetic constitution of organisms is just as perpetually changing in response, the effect on survival of any particular mutation or allele must be constantly changing. Although we do not know how rapid or slow such changes are, we do know that the time required for a neutral gene substitution is on average $4N_e$ generations (Kimura & Ohta 1971), and at the minimum about N_e generations. For most successful evolutionary lines, most of the time, this is likely to be a very long time indeed. It is thus plausible, if unproved, that very few mutations remain in the realm of effective neutrality for long enough to allow them to be substituted purely by random drift. It may be the case that the nearest an allele ever gets to neutral evolution is to drift upwards in frequency for part of the distance between loss and fixation, during which time the change in its circumstances will render it, while still well short of fixation, an advantageous gene which then completes its journey to fixation under the influence of natural selection. (Or of course, circumstances may render it deleterious, in which case it will be lost under natural selection — some mysteriously high-frequency deleterious genes, such as the *bimacula* allele of the moth *Panaxia dominula* (again, for original citations, see Ford 1964) may have reached their anomalously high frequency in this way — this being roughly Wright's (1978) interpretation of this case.) Alternatively, some alleles will commence their journey of substitution under selection as advantageous alleles, and complete fixation neutral and drifting. Either way, although random drift and neutrality are playing a role in evolution, the role is substantially trivial: every allele that becomes fixed has done so because it is adaptively advantageous. (In terms of the distribution (Fig. 2.1a) what this theory proposes is that the positions of alleles are perpetually changing along the *x*-axis, and that the time for which they remain in the stippled zone is too short to permit fixation.)

This is Fisher's theory: it was his reason for rejecting the neutral theory in 1930(a); it is the argument which I mentioned as being the only good one against the neutral theory. The argument has been rather seldom revived, although it can be found in Ford (1976) and Lewontin (1974); indeed, Fisher's whole evolutionary theory is long overdue for re-examination and perhaps revival.

Thus, the question for neutral evolution is not what proportion of alleles is effectively neutral at any one time but what proportion can remain neutral for the very long periods required to effect their total substitution in the species. It follows from this, that tests which investigate the proportion of currently neutral alleles present in populations are irrelevant to the question whether neutral evolution occurs: there may be a substantial proportion of neutral alleles at any one time (as Fisher predicted) but *no* neutral evolution. As it is impossible to observe the history of alleles over the vast periods of time required, only retrospective studies of evolution as it has already happened have any hope of resolving the issue.

Perhaps then the English or Oxford school of ecological genetics were indeed right: most observable evolutionary changes in the phenotypes of organisms are probably due to selection. But if they were right about neutral evolution, it was apparently for the wrong reasons. Where I think they will eventually be seen to have gone seriously wrong is in promulgating the belief that deterministic, adaptationist views of evolution were all-sufficient, and that stochastic phenomena could be totally discounted.

CAN THE DEVIL HAVE THE FIRST SUBJECT?

Is it helpful to ignore aleatory elements when setting up a theory of populations? Should we, when possible, set up the stochastic theory, and then find the deterministic approximation, having satisfied ourselves that the stochastic elements in the process are insignificant (Gale 1990)? Clearly as a matter of practicality this is not always possible, since the deterministic equations may be readily soluble when the stochastic process is intractable — a problem which can now surely be almost always overcome at some cost by the use of high-speed computation. Do we need to convince ourselves of some deep philosophical point, that the world is essentially stochastic or chaotic, before we are willing to abandon the approach of starting with determinism, or do we merely need to say to ourselves that there has been a 'stochastic revolution' in which deterministic thinking has been steadily replaced by stochastic thinking since 1890 (Krüger *et al.* 1987) and that, if we want to be part of the trend, population biology had better join in?

In population genetics at least we need subscribe to neither of these views. We should commence with the stochastic viewpoint for a very simple reason indeed: random drift is the one thing we can be certain will happen to all alleles in all populations, *a priori* and with very little empirical observation. This conclusion arises merely from the observation that no population is infinite in size. Perhaps next to that in certainty comes mutation, which *is* a matter of empirical observation. Only after that comes natural selection. All but the most eccentric biologists are as convinced of the reality of natural selection as they are of the fact that populations are finite; the difference is that we can be certain that all alleles undergo random drift but we cannot be certain, however much we huff and puff, that all alleles are subject to natural selection.

The problem with relegating Wright's and Kimura's theories to the 'lunar green cheese' category is not that a possibly correct theory is being ignored — for all we still know both these theories may be wrong — but in training population geneticists that they can ignore stochastic, or finite population size effects. There are many circumstances in which such effects are particularly important, an outstanding one being the theory of the evolution of recombination and sexual reproduction (Maynard Smith 1978). Models that lack a stochastic base are likely always to suffer from dynamic insufficiency and to concentrate excessively on 'biological' phenomena such as adaptation.

But worse than that, has been the view that adaptation itself was unproblematical: that everything about organisms could be seen as adaptive. Leaving aside the philosophical problem of deciding just what that actually means, we do not know that natural selection is *always* the overriding determinant of everything about organisms, although this was a belief held by Wallace, and even more strongly by August Weissman, and hence by many later workers. We do not know that aleatory processes are always unimportant in determining the course of events: in fact we know that they frequently are important. Yet the view that it is adaptation that matters supremely has permeated not simply ecological genetics but ecology and sociobiology. The chief attack on adaptationism has in fact come from a group of radical Harvard biologists who for quite other reasons did not like sociobiology, and who saw that if they could demolish adaptationism they could get sociobiology's rug right out from under it. I believe that this particular attack was misguided: in saying that adaptation may not be universal and primary I do not mean to propose that it is non-existent. The problem comes when a whole school of thought becomes so thoroughgoingly adaptationist that the other factors take on the status of lunar green cheese.

AN ALEATORY PROBLEM IN POPULATION ECOLOGY?

The deterministic, adaptationist approach is less obviously an error in population ecology. The aleatory effects of population turnover (extinction and recolonization) are less obvious *a priori* than random genetic drift, and might be seen as of no greater empirical certainty than such 'deterministic' effects as adaptation. Nonetheless, considerable advances have been made by adopting a stochastic viewpoint: the coexistence of species for example can be modelled without reference to competition if we take into account the stochastic colonization of spatially patchy resources (Shorrocks & Rosewell 1987).

Consider the two models of community structure shown in Fig. 2.2. The one, which I have named the *structural* model is unashamedly deterministic and adaptationist: it assumes that what structures communities is the width of realized ecological niches, and that this is determined by the evolutionary history of the species, the course that natural selection has taken in moulding them to their environment (specifically in most versions that a stable environment permits niche specialization through slow adaptation, thereby reducing competition and allowing more species to co-exist — see for example Connell and Orias 1964, expanded into a sophisticated mathematical theory by May 1973).

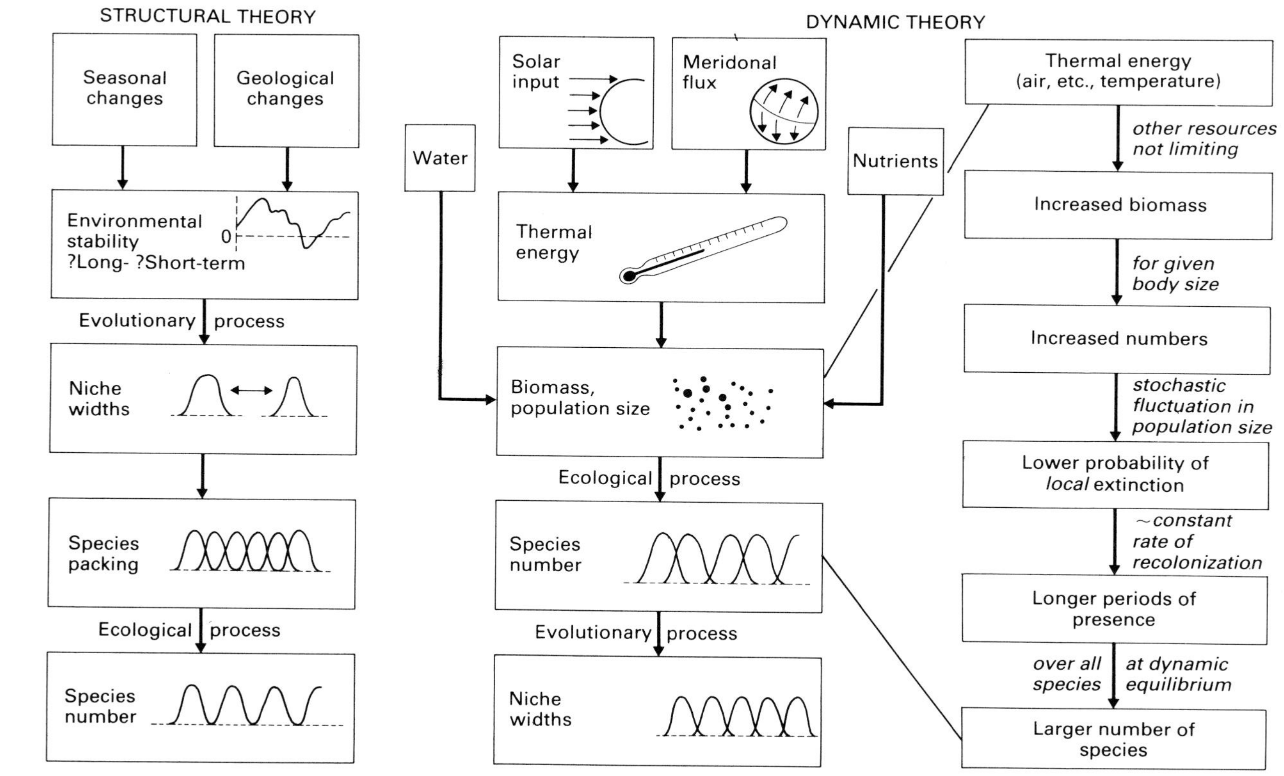

FIG. 2.2. Flow diagrams illustrating two possible ways in which the global diversity gradient is related to models of community ecology.

The other, which I have named *dynamic*, assumes that the heart of the process is the repeated local extinction and recolonization of populations. As a result when resources, particularly energy but also water and nutrients, are plentiful, larger populations (for a given body size) will result in lower rates of extinction and hence higher numbers of species in the community at dynamic equilibrium. Only after that number has been set, will the slow process of coadaptation between the species adjust their mutual ecological requirements.

The different implications of these two models are not trivial. The structural model maintains that species richness is related to the stability of the environment; the dynamic model that species richness is related to the overall energy and resource supply. Both theories can therefore 'explain' the global latitudinal gradient in species richness — the 'bulging biosphere' (Arthur 1991) — but the two models predict different outcomes for biotic diversity at mid-latitudes as a result of the 'changing greenhouse effect'. In the one, the increase in species richness from climatic amelioration will be rapid, being in the time-scale of recolonization; in the other, it will require evolutionary time.

We do not know which of these models is valid; indeed both might be. A sophisticated approach, favoured by a number of population biologists, is that both the colonization/extinction process and the adaptation of niche width process are occurring simultaneously. This view, unfortunately, begs the question which process occurs at the faster rate, and which process is therefore in major control of the system. It is again the problem of the primacy of ecological versus evolutionary processes that taxed Elton and his contemporaries (see Cain, Ch. 1, this volume).

What I want to consider is the attitude of population biologists to the two theories. The one we must remember is purely adaptationist; the other acknowledges natural selection but puts aleatory population processes first. There are no prizes for guessing which theory is universally regarded. The structural, adaptationist theory is dealt with in all textbooks. It is also, for example, the received orthodoxy almost everywhere that there are huge numbers of species in a tropical rainforest because there is such narrow niche specialization. The dynamic theory, which usually raises its head as the so-called *species–energy theory* (because of the predicted relation between species richness and average thermal energy input), is mentioned in barely any front-line textbook, and if mentioned, gets a one-line dismissal. It hardly ever occurs to anyone to suggest that tropical species have extremely narrow niches because so many of them are crammed into the forest!

The difference in the treatment of the theories could of course be because nobody of any standing has proposed the dynamic theory. But this explanation will not work: *both* theories, as was first noticed by Cousins (1989), derive from the classic *Homage to Santa Rosalia* paper of Hutchinson (1959). Only the structural theory has been developed: the passage in which Hutchinson proposed the dynamic theory has, with the honorable and recent exception of Lawton (1990), been invisible to generations of ecologists.

Worse is to come. The reaction that we encountered when we started to work on the dynamic/energy theory was quite startling in its vehemence, and was accompanied by the sound of substantial ecologists fainting in coils. We were told that our results were obviously silly, as it was clear to anyone that gradients in species richness were produced by gradients in the variety of habitats available, and that our climatic correlations (Turner *et al.* 1987, 1988) were a local aberration within the British Isles: a different result would certainly be obtained if we took the whole of temperate Eurasia (to paraphrase Cain again, how did our interlocutor know *that*?). The dynamic/energy hypothesis itself was described variously as 'grandiose and pretentious' or 'weak and feeble'. It was not so much that our fellow ecologists thought that the theory was wrong (which it may well be), or that alternate theories were *also* correct (a result which would not surprise me) but that in our colleagues' view the dynamic theory was so obviously ludicrous that it was a total waste of time to investigate it. This theory like the neutral evolution theory before it, had been relegated to the realm of lunar green cheese.

Why should such a simple and obvious theory, one that is moreover immediately testable and therefore open to annihilation if wrong, by data which already exist, arouse such violent opposition? The salient explanation is that we are encountering yet another episode of mutual incomprehension and 'cognitive particularism' (Travis & Collins 1991) arising from the old problem of adaptationism and the reluctance of population biologists, particularly in Britain, to think stochastically.

The clear difference between the dynamic theory and the structural theory is that the former has a stochastic model at its core, whereas the structural theory is purely adaptationist. The dynamic theory starts by considering the stochastic extinction and recolonization of local populations; the structural theory by considering how the adaptation of species to their fluctuating or constant environments regulates the size of their realized ecological niches.

Not that anybody consciously examines the dynamic theory, sees a stochastic model in the middle, and thinks 'I don't believe in stochastic models'. What appears to be happening is that the traditional adaptationist model sits comfortably within the traditional framework of British thinking in population biology: natural selection and adaptation placed foremost, and in the end providing the ultimate explanation for everything. The dynamic theory in this context looks bizarre, ridiculous and not worth even considering.

If you are unconvinced, try explaining to an imaginary TV interviewer why there are so many invertebrate species in your square metre of Amazonian stream: the adaptationist structural explanation trips lightly off the tongue — the species have narrow ecological requirements and do not compete. It is an almost insuperable challenge to explain the dynamic stochastic theory in three simple sentences.

If historians ever examine this bizarre episode they will naturally have to consider other explanations for this resistance to the dynamic theory. Honesty compels me to summarize those I have identified. The theory seems to have met much more opposition in Britain than in America. Partly this results from our deep attachment to Darwinism but no doubt from other aspects also of our scientific culture: a commitment to historicism, seen for instance in the *New Naturalist* books, several of which including Ford's *Butterflies* (Ford 1945) explained faunal distributions by highly speculative, not to say fictional, reconstructions of the post-glacial recolonization. This gives British naturalists a strong attachment to an historical explanation for diversity gradients. This has been allied with a British empiricist mistrust of intellectuals and theorizing, the national knee-jerk rejection of innovation, and a strong hegemony of reductionist thinking by physiological ecologists, who see little value in investigating climatic relationships at the community level until the physiological processes are entirely known.

Second, there is a not unreasonable belief that the energy theory has indeed been empirically disproved. This stems from the argument 'Energy will not be related to species richness; *a priori* the relationship will be between *productivity* and species richness. But we know of many individual examples of species-poor productive habitats such as papyrus swamps, and of species-rich deserts; besides Rosenzweig's (1971) discovery of the "paradox of enrichment" finally disproved that relationship.' This argument relies to a considerable extent on individual observations which may merely be the exceptions lying on the minor axis of an overall correlation which goes the other way, and the perceptive will see that it contains a major logical *non sequitur* or undistributed middle, but otherwise it is a respectable argument; Currie (1991) discusses it further.

ENVOY

Prince of statisticians, Fisher was influential in turning English population biologists away from stochastic thinking. He did this in part through his commitment to synthesizing Darwinism and Mendelism in such a way that no creativity could be assigned to aleatory processes, and hence through his opposition to Wright's belief in the creativity of random drift. In part, he exerted his influence through an alliance with the Oxford school of ecological genetics, who had the very different concern of disputing the view that there were some taxonomic differences, particularly those between closely related species, that were non-adaptive. As Cain shows in Ch. 1, this volume, the view that most of the taxonomic differences that were believed to be neutral were in fact adaptive was not an empirical deduction but an *a priori* hypothesis to be pursued and tested with all vigour, and preferably confirmed. This is indeed the normal and proper way to perform scientific research: when the programme seeks to correct the views of those who want, as perhaps did Robson and Richards (1936), to introduce vitalism or divine intervention into evolution, thus placing it outside the realm of natural law, it will be viewed positively by most modern biologists (Fisher saw the process as both divine and *within* the bounds of natural law).

But aleatory processes are themselves within the bounds of natural law, and while the *a priori* hypothesis that they have a minimal part to play in evolution and ecology is not in the realm of lunar green cheese, and deserves respect and empirical testing, the opposite view is not in the realm of lunar green cheese either: it is not safe to assume that everything about organisms is equally adaptive, or that adaptation is the ruling process about which the aleatory processes merely create a certain degree of noise.

There seems to have been an aleatory association in the history of evolutionary theory in which the desire to remove non-natural processes became identified with a desire to remove aleatory processes as well. Yet selection operates solely on the products of the aleatory processes. If we do not understand the role they play our interpretations will fail. 'Cognitive particularism' is a failing common to all of us as scientists; the cultivation of a greater self-awareness than has been customary among scientists would help us to avoid its more disastrous consequences.

ACKNOWLEDGEMENTS

I am most grateful to Dr M.J.S. (Jon) Hodge of the unit for the History and Philosophy of Science at the University of Leeds for his comments on a draft, and for our continuing collaboration on the work of R.A. Fisher, to Dr Jerry Ravetz for introducing me to Travis and Collins, and to the editors of this volume for their help in shortening this chapter.

REFERENCES

Arthur, W. (1991). The bulging biosphere. *New Scientist*, 29 June, 42–45.

Bennett, J. H. (Ed.) (1971–74). *Collected Papers of R. A. Fisher* 5 vols. University of Adelaide Press, Adelaide, Australia.

Bennett, J. H. (Ed.) (1983). *Natural Selection, Heredity, and Eugenics. Including selected correspondence of R. A. Fisher with Leonard Darwin and others.* Clarendon Press, Oxford, UK.

Berry, R. J. (1964). The evolution of an island population of the house mouse. *Evolution*, **18**, 468–483.

Cain, A. J. (1954). *Animal Species and their Evolution.* Hutchinson, London, UK.

Cain, A. J. (1988). A criticism of J. R. G. Turner's article 'Fisher's evolutionary faith and the challenge of mimicry'. *Oxford Surveys in Evolutionary Biology*, **5**, 246–248.

Cain, A. J. & Harrison, G. A. (1958). An analysis of the taxonomist's judgement of affinity. *Proceedings of the Zoological Society of London*, **131**, 85–98.

Clarke, B. C. (1970). Darwinian evolution of proteins. *Science*, **168**, 1009–1011.

Connell, J. H. & Orias, E. (1964). The ecological regulation of species diversity. *American Naturalist*, **98**, 399–414.

Cousins, S. H. (1989). Species richness and the energy theory. *Nature*, **340**, 350.

Crosby, J. L. (1959). The effect of random fluctuations on groups of rapidly evolving populations. *Heredity*, **13**, 412.

Crow, J. F. (1972). Darwinian and non-Darwinian evolution. *Proceedings of the Sixth Berkeley Symposium on Mathematical Statistics and Probability*, Vol. V, pp. 1–22. University of California Press, Berkeley, CA, USA.

Currie, D. J. (1991). Energy and large-scale patterns of animal- and plant-species richness. *American Naturalist*, **137**, 27–49.

Dawkins, R. (1982). *The Extended Phenotype.* Freeman, Oxford, UK.

Dawkins, R. (1986). *The Blind Watchmaker.* Longman Scientific and Technical, Harlow, UK.

Fisher, R. A. (1930a). The distribution of gene ratios for rare mutations. *Proceedings of the Royal Society of Edinburgh*, **50**, 205–230.

Fisher, R. A. (1930b). *The Genetical Theory of Natural Selection* (1st edn). Clarendon Press, Oxford, UK.

Fisher, R. A. (1954). Retrospect of the criticisms of the theory of natural selection. *Evolution as a Process* (Ed. by J. Huxley, A. C. Hardy & E. B. Ford), pp. 84–98. George Allen & Unwin, London, UK.

Ford, E. B. (1931). *Mendelism and Evolution* (1st edn). Methuen, London, UK.

Ford, E. B. (1945). *Butterflies* (1st edn). Collins, London, UK.

Ford, E. B. (1964). *Ecological Genetics* (1st edn). Methuen, London, UK.

Ford, E. B. (1976). *Genetics and Adaptation.* Edward Arnold, London, UK.

Gale, J. S. (1990). *Theoretical Population Genetics.* Unwin Hyman, London, UK.

Hagedoorn, A. L. & Hagedoorn, A. C. (1921). *The Relative Value of the Processes Causing Evolution.* Martinus Nijhoff, Den Haag, The Netherlands.

Hodge, M. J. S. (1987). Natural selection as a causal, empirical, and probabilistic theory. *The Probabilistic Revolution*, Vol. 2, *Ideas in the Sciences* (Ed. by G. Gigerenzer, L. Krüger & M. Morgan), pp. 233–270. MIT Press, Cambridge, MA, USA.

Hodge, M. J. S. (1992). Biology and philosophy (including ideology): a study of Fisher and Wright. *The Founders of Modern Population Genetics* (Ed. by S. Sarkar), pp. 231–293. Kluwer, Boston, MA, USA.

Hutchinson, G. E. (1959). Homage to Santa Rosalia or why are there so many kinds of animals? *American Naturalist*, **93**, 145–159.

Kimura, M. (1968). Evolutionary rate at the molecular level. *Nature*, **217**, 624–626.

Kimura, M. (1983). *The Neutral Theory of Molecular Evolution*. Cambridge University Press, Cambridge, UK.

Kimura, M. & Ohta, T. (1971). *Theoretical Aspects of Population Genetics*. Princeton University Press, Princeton, NJ, USA.

King, J. L. & Jukes, T. H. (1969). Non-Darwinian evolution. *Science*, **164**, 788–798.

Krüger, L., Gigerenzer, G. & Morgan, M. S. (1987). *The Probabilistic Revolution* 2 vols. MIT Press, Cambridge, MA, USA.

Lawton, J. H. (1990). Species richness and population dynamics of animal assemblages. Patterns in body size: abundance space. *Philosophical Transactions of the Royal Society of London*, B, **330**, 283–291.

Leigh, E. G. (1986). Ronald Fisher and the development of evolutionary theory. I. The role of selection. *Oxford Surveys in Evolutionary Biology*, **4**, 187–223.

Leigh, E. G. (1987). Ronald Fisher and the development of evolutionary theory. II. Influences of new variation on evolutionary process. *Oxford Surveys in Evolutionary Biology*, **4**, 212–263.

Levinton, J. S., Bandel, K., Charlesworth, B., Müller, G., Nagl, W., Runnegar, B., Selander, R. K., Stearns, S. C., Turner, J. R. G., Urbanek, A. J. & Valentine, J. W. (1986). Organismic evolution: the interaction of microevolutionary and macroevolutionary processes. *Patterns and Processes in the History of Life* (Ed. by D. M. Raup & D. Jablonski), Dahlem Konferenzen, pp. 167–182. Springer Verlag, Berlin, Federal Republic of Germany.

Lewontin, R. C. (1974). *The Genetic Basis of Evolutionary Change*. Columbia University Press, New York, NY, USA.

May, R. M. (1973). *Stability and Complexity in Model Ecosystems*. Princeton University Press, Princeton, NJ, USA.

Mayr, E. (1954). Change of genetic environment and evolution. *Evolution as a Process* (Ed. by J. S. Huxley, A. C. Hardy & E. B. Ford), pp. 157–180. George Allen & Unwin, London, UK.

McKusick, V., Hostetler, J. A., Egeland, J. A. & Eldridge, R. (1964). The distribution of certain genes in the Old Order Amish. *Cold Spring Harbor Symposia on Quantitative Biology*, **29**, 99–114.

Maynard Smith, J. (1978). *The Evolution of Sex*. Cambridge University Press, Cambridge, UK.

Olby, R. C. (1981). La théorie génétique de la sélection naturelle vue par un historien. *Revue de Synthèse*, IIIe serie **103–104**, 251–289.

Provine, W. B. (1985). The R. A. Fisher–Sewall Wright controversy. *Oxford Surveys in Evolutionary Biology*, **2**, 159–196.

Provine, W. B. (1986). *Sewall Wright and Evolutionary Biology*. University of Chicago Press, Chicago, IL, USA.

Robson, G. C. & Richards, O. W. (1936). *The Variation of Animals in Nature*. Longmans, Green, London, UK.

Rosenzweig, M. (1971). Paradox of enrichment: destabilization of exploitation ecosystems in ecological time. *Science*, **171**, 385–387.

Sheppard, P. M. (1975). *Natural Selection and Heredity* (5th edn). Hutchinson, London, UK.

Shorrocks, B. & Rosewell, J. (1987). Spatial patchiness and community structure: coexistence and guild size of drosophilids on ephemeral resources. *Organisation of Communities Past and Present* (27th Symposium of the British Ecological Society) (Ed. by J. H. R. Gee & P. S. Giller), pp. 29–51. Blackwell Scientific Publications, Oxford, UK.

Travis, G. D. L. & Collins, H. M. (1991). New light on old boys: cognitive and institutional particularism in the peer review system. *Science, Technology and Human Values*, **16**, 322–341.

Turner, J. R. G. (1985). Fisher's evolutionary faith and the challenge of mimicry. *Oxford Surveys in Evolutionary Biology*, **2**, 159–196.

Turner, J. R. G. (1986). The genetics of adaptive radiation: a neo-Darwinian theory of punctuational evolution. *Patterns and Processes in the History of Life* (Ed. by D. M. Raup & D. Jablonski). Dahlem Konferenzen, pp. 183–207. Springer Verlag, Berlin, Federal Republic of Germany.

Turner, J. R. G. (1987). Random genetic drift, R. A. Fisher, and the Oxford School of Ecological Genetics. *The Probabilistic Revolution*, Vol. 2, *Ideas in the Sciences* (Ed. by G. Gigerenzer, L. Krüger & M. Morgan). pp. 313–354. MIT Press, Cambridge, MA, USA.

Turner, J. R. G. (1988). Reply: men of Fisher's? *Oxford Surveys in Evolutionary Biology*, **5**, 249–252.

Turner, J. R. G. (1990b). Kettlewell, Henry Bernard Davis. *Dictionary of Scientific Biography*, Vol. 17 (suppl. II), pp. 469–471. Charles Scribner's Sons, New York, NY, USA.

Turner, J. R. G. (1990a). Sheppard, Philip MacDonald. *Dictionary of Scientific Biography*, Vol. 18 (suppl. II), pp. 814–816. Charles Scribner's Sons, New York, NY, USA.

Turner, J. R. G., Gatehouse, C. M. & Corey, C. A. (1987). Does solar energy control organic diversity? Butterflies, moths and the British climate. *Oikos*, **48**, 195–205.

Turner, J. R. G., Lennon, J. J. & Lawrenson, J. A. (1988). British bird species distributions and the energy theory. *Nature*, **335**, 539–541.

Wright, S. (1978). *Evolution and the Genetics of Populations*, Vol. IV. University of Chicago Press, Chicago, IL, USA.

3. POPULATION DYNAMICS, NATURAL SELECTION AND CHAOS

H.C.J. GODFRAY*, L.M. COOK† AND M.P. HASSELL*

**Department of Biology and NERC Centre for Population Biology, Imperial College at Silwood Park, Ascot, Berkshire SL5 7PY, UK and* †*Department of Environmental Biology, Williamson Building, Oxford Road, Manchester M13 9PL, UK*

INTRODUCTION

The fields of genetics, ecology and evolutionary biology have been inextricably linked throughout their historical development. For example, there is an active controversy among historians of science about the major influence that crystallized in Darwin's mind the concept of evolution by natural selection (Sober 1984). Was it his knowledge and exploration of animal breeding and artificial selection, the precursors of modern genetics, or was it his reading of Thomas Malthus's *An Essay on the Principle of Population* (1798)? Despite his rather frightening politics (both to modern and contemporary eyes), Malthus must rank as one of the fathers of population ecology. The conclusion Malthus drew from considering the parameter that bears his name was of the wisdom of sexual abstinence by the poor. It is perhaps a mark of progress that one of the main recommendations of modern population dynamicists is both more moderate and more egalitarian: sexual restraint — by all classes of society (Anderson & May 1991)!

In its most basic form, population dynamics is the study of changes in population density brought about by birth, death, emigration and immigration. Given a knowledge of how these four processes combine, and of the demographic parameters that determine their rates, ecologists predict levels and changes of population densities. Population genetics and evolutionary biology have major roles in a number of areas of population ecology. Here, we concentrate on one particular contribution. Can a consideration of the evolutionary process help explain the values and distributions of demographic parameters across species? In other words can we predict, *a priori*, the dynamic behaviour of populations in different environments by a knowledge of how natural selection operates in these environments?

In this chapter we shall be particularly concerned with the question of whether natural selection reduces the likelihood of chaos being observed in natural populations. In the first section, we review the search for chaos in natural populations and distinguish the three main techniques that have been employed in this quest. In the second section we trace the study of the evolution of demographic parameters from the pioneering contribution of MacArthur and Wilson (1967) to very recent studies of evolution in structured populations in stochastic environments, and of life history evolution in populations with chaotic dynamics. Much of the work on the evolution of demographic parameters has concentrated on single-species populations. In the final section we outline some of the problems that arise in considering the evolution of demographic parameters in complex assemblies of species.

CHAOS IN ECOLOGY

One of the most startling discoveries in population ecology during the 1970s was that many of the simple models used as abstract descriptions of animal population dynamics were capable of displaying chaotic fluctuations (May 1974, 1976, May & Oster 1976). Chaotic fluctuations are purely deterministic, yet are seemingly indistinguishable from random fluctuations. Moreover, and the defining property of chaos, two population trajectories initiated with arbitrarily close starting conditions will inevitably diverge. Though it is possible to predict the statistical properties of ensembles of chaotic populations, the long-term prediction of specific population trajectories is impossible. To display chaos, population models must contain time lags and strong density dependence: the time lags may be explicit as in discrete generation models, or implicit as in systems of species interacting with overlapping generations. Strong, overcompensating density dependence is necessary to prevent the system from achieving a stable equilibrium.

The discovery of the potential for chaos in population models initiated a search for chaos in real populations. This search has been conducted on three fronts, two initiated in the 1970s while the third is more recent.

Model fitting to field data

The first technique involves fitting flexible population models to field data. A model is used that is capable of predicting stable, cyclic or chaotic dynamics, depending on the value of one or several parameters that are estimated from the field data. The fit to the field data is achieved using standard statistical techniques (e.g. non-linear, least-squares regression).

The first application of this technique was by Hassell *et al.* (1976). They used a model that had been earlier developed by Hassell (1975) as a robust descriptor of single-species density dependence. The model contains three parameters — fecundity (λ), a measure of density dependence (b) and a third parameter (a) that characterizes the population levels at which the density-dependent effects become important:

$$N_{t+1} = N_t \left\{ \frac{\lambda}{(1 + aN_t)^b} \right\} \tag{1}$$

where N_t is population density at time t. Perfect contest competition ($b \rightarrow 1$) and perfect scramble competition ($b \rightarrow \infty$) can both be described by this model. Stability depends only on the two parameters b and λ. Hassell *et al.* (1976) fitted Eqn (1) to 28 data sets, the majority of them from the field. The estimated parameter values for each population, together with the model's stability boundaries, are illustrated in Fig. 3.1. With the exception of two populations, all the estimated parameter values were in

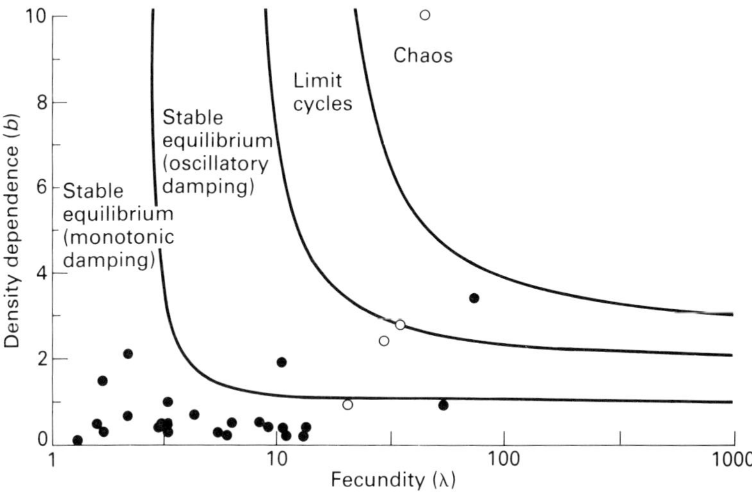

FIG. 3.1. The stability properties of the Hassell (1975) model of density dependence in a single-species population as a function of the two parameters fecundity (λ) and the form of the density dependence b. The lines demarcate regions of parameter space with different stability properties. The points represent estimates of $\{\lambda, b\}$ from different insect populations (Hassell *et al.* 1976). Solid points are from field populations, hollow points from laboratory populations.

the stable region of parameter space. The two exceptions were the Colorado Beetle (*Leptinotarsus quadrilineata*), a well-known outbreak pest of potatoes, for which cyclic population dynamics were predicted, and a laboratory population of blowflies studied by Nicholson (1957) which were predicted to be chaotic. We shall discuss Nicholson's experiments further later (p. 78).

There are a number of problems in inferring dynamic behaviour through fitting simple, and general, population models (Perry 1990, Morris 1990). Perhaps the worst problem is that the conclusions of such analyses are strongly influenced by the choice of model. This point was stressed by Hassell *et al.* (1976) who noted that one species for which they predicted stable dynamics, the Grey Larch Tortrix (*Zeiraphera diniana*), in fact showed very pronounced cycles. The cycles are probably caused by an interaction of the moth with its food plant or a pathogen; a phenomenon that the single-species model was unable to capture. Nevertheless, this study has been much cited as evidence for the rareness of chaos in natural populations.

In recent years there has been much interest in using techniques from non-linear mathematics to detect the signature of chaos in long time series. These techniques, which we describe later (p. 60), are model independent. However, they have the major difficulty of requiring extremely long time series of data. This obstacle has prompted renewed interest in the detection of chaos by model fitting. For example, Turchin and Taylor (1992) have fitted rather general models using the statistical technique of response surfaces. They analysed a similar data set to that used by Hassell *et al.* (1976) and came to broadly similar conclusions, though there was some evidence of an increased likelihood of more complicated dynamics.

Similar criticisms to those levelled at Hassell *et al.* (1976) can be levelled at Turchin and Taylor: that they assume a particular type of underlying population model, and a particular way that environmental variation interacts with the population dynamics (i.e. they assume a particular form of error term when fitting the model). Their model and fitting techniques, however, are considerably more general than those used in the earlier study. The similar conclusions of the two approaches do suggest the real rarity of chaos, at least in field populations of insects. The next few years are likely to see further development and sophistication of this type of analysis.

Study of laboratory populations

The world's best-studied insects live in bottles. Although the majority of research on *Drosophila* has concerned its genetics, a number of workers have also studied fruitfly dynamics in serial laboratory culture. The significance of such studies for the dynamics of field populations must be treated with caution. However, the enormous advantages of ease of study, and availability of background information, amply compensate for the artificiality of the laboratory culture.

Thomas *et al.* (1980) and Mueller and Ayala (1981) analysed the dynamics of a variety of species and strains of *Drosophila* maintained in serial culture. As in the studies described in the previous section, simple population models, capable of displaying a variety of dynamics, were fitted to data. Thomas *et al.* (1980) directly fitted models using non-linear, least-squares regression to predict the stability of the system, while Mueller and Ayala (1981) assessed stability by estimating the linear dynamics about the carrying capacity (the equilibrium) directly from the data. Both studies concluded that the population dynamics of the flies were best described by models with parameters predicting stable equilibria. Both groups of workers suggested that part of the reason they found no evidence of chaos was that natural selection tended to produce stable population dynamics. We shall return to their arguments in the second part of the chapter.

More recent studies of the dynamics of *Drosophila* in serial culture have revealed complexities that may strongly influence the dynamics. Prout and McChesney (1985) have shown that density dependence not only affects egg-to-adult survival, the mechanism modelled by previous authors, but also adult fertility. Females that developed in crowded cultures are smaller and lay fewer eggs. Prout and McChesney fitted several models to their laboratory data and, while they found stable dynamics to be the most common prediction, for some experiments and models they predicted cyclic and even chaotic dynamics. Mueller (1988) has developed yet more sophisticated models of *Drosophila* dynamics incorporating an explicit description of the probability of larval survival as a function of food intake, as well as a more detailed description of the effect of larval density and interactions between adults on fecundity. The dynamics of the resulting models can only be studied numerically but show both point stability and more complicated dynamics for biologically reasonable parameter values. More worryingly, the dynamic results depend quite critically on assumptions about the biology of the flies. Mueller (1988) also studied parameter evolution in his models.

Chaos has been sought in a few other laboratory systems in addition to *Drosophila*. Perhaps the most famous system is that of blowflies studied by Nicholson (1957). The evolution of demographic parameters during Nicholson's experiments has received considerable attention and is discussed later (p. 78). Here we note only that blowfly populations in laboratory cages supplied with limited food initially cycled with a period of approximately 40 days. There is some variability in the form of the cycle and limited evidence that some of the variation can be explained as deterministic chaos (Blythe & Stokes 1988, Godfray & Blythe 1990). Another laboratory insect whose dynamics have been closely studied is the bean weevil, *Callosobruchus maculatus*, and its hymenopterous parasitoids. The parameters of a detail-rich age-structured simulation model were estimated from laboratory experiments by Bellows and Hassell (1988). Time series of population densities produced by the simulation model showed apparently random fluctuations that appear, at least superficially, chaotic.

The overall picture that emerges from laboratory studies is somewhat contradictory. It is clear that cyclic or chaotic dynamic behaviour is seldom predicted when simple population models are used to describe laboratory experiments. However, when more complicated models are used, the range of possible dynamic behaviour increases markedly, in parallel with an increase in the difficulty of accurate parameterization. The techniques described in the next section offer a potential way of avoiding the need to make *a priori* assumptions about underlying population mechanisms.

New techniques from non-linear mathematics

The branch of mathematics concerned with non-linear dynamics has flowered in the last 20 years, fertilized by the enormous interest in chaos in fields as diverse as fluid mechanics and economics. There has been much research on techniques to identify deterministic chaos in time series of experimental data. These techniques are beginning to be applied in population biology, in large part through the advocacy and enthusiasm of W.M. Schaffer and colleagues. We describe these new techniques and their applications only briefly as there are a number of recent reviews (Schaffer 1985, Schaffer *et al.* 1988, Godfray & Blythe 1990, Sugihara *et al.* 1990).

An important concept in non-linear dynamics is that of an attractor. Consider an interaction between a predator and a prey and plot the trajectory of the system in a two-dimensional phase space with axes representing the densities of the two interacting species. Suppose the system has a stable (global) equilibrium: system trajectories initiated at any point in the phase space will be 'attracted' to the point at which the system is at equilibrium. In this case there is a point attractor of zero dimensions. Now suppose that after initial transients have decayed away, the predator–prey system shows persistent cycles. When plotted in phase space, trajectories will appear to be 'attracted' on to a closed loop. In this case there is a linear attractor of one dimension. In more complicated interactions, the persistent behaviour of the system may have to be represented in a phase space of many dimensions and the attractor may be of high dimension. The persistent trajectories of chaotic systems are also governed by attractors. However, chaotic trajectories have fractal structure with non-integer dimension. Whereas the structure of a two-dimensional attractor remains the same at whatever scale it is viewed, the structure of a nearly two-dimensional, chaotic attractor is influenced by scale. In particular, as a portion of the attractor is magnified, greater and greater detail is revealed, though this detail is approximately self-repeating.

Thus, attractor structure and dimensionality allow a taxonomy of dynamic behaviour. Two potentially orthogonal questions can be asked of natural systems: (1) are the dynamics of natural systems governed by attractors of relatively low dimension; and (2) are attractors integer or non-integer; that is, are natural systems chaotic? Together, these questions can be rephrased as asking what is the complexity of nature. It should be noted, however, that the answer will depend on how closely the system is observed. What may appear as a stable equilibrium when studied using coarse data may reveal evidence of more complicated dynamics when exposed to closer scrutiny. We now briefly describe four techniques that provide evidence on the structure of attractors.

Attractor reconstruction

Attractors exist in phase space and one way to reveal their structure would be directly to plot the system trajectory in a space with appropriate dimensions. However, biologists very seldom have long time series from all the species involved (or potentially involved) in an interaction. Packard *et al.* (1980) and Takens (1981) proved that attractor structure can be estimated from a time series of a single component of a mutually interacting complex of species by using a phase space constructed from lagged co-ordinates. Thus, a point in a three-dimensional phase space has co-ordinates representing population density now, one time-unit ago and two time-units ago. Once an attractor has been constructed in this way, further evidence about its possibly fractal structure can be obtained. Suppose the attractor is essentially a twisted sheet in a three-dimensional phase space. A plane intersecting the sheet is called a Poincaré section and the sequence in which the system trajectory intersects the Poincaré section can be used to determine whether or not the attractor is fractal.

This technique has been applied by Schaffer and his colleagues to a number of long-term data sets: for example, lynx population densities as estimated by the returns of fur trappers, measles epidemics in North American cities and the famous *Thrips imaginis* data set (Davidson & Andrewartha 1948). All three data sets show pronounced cycles. Schaffer (1984) suggested there was some evidence for chaos in the lynx data, possible arising as an interaction between a strong periodic cyclic and environmental stochasticity. The measles data also showed evidence of a chaotic modulation of an underlying cycle (Schaffer & Kot 1985a). Similarly, Schaffer & Kot (1985b, 1986) concluded that the reconstructed attractor for the thrips data appeared to have the characteristics of chaos.

One problem with attractor reconstruction is that much of the final analysis depends on recognizing pattern by eye, a difficult and subjective exercise, especially with the relatively poor data sets available to ecologists. There is also the risk of artefacts associated with the choice of time lag when analysing strongly cyclic populations (Ellner 1992). Ellner (1992) has constructed a model that closely mimics the thrips data and incorporates random variation around seasonal trends but has non-chaotic dynamics. If the techniques of attractor reconstruction are applied to data generated by the model, one would incorrectly conclude there was evidence of underlying deterministic chaos.

Estimating dimensions

Instead of the complete reconstruction of the attractor, there is a series of techniques available for the direct estimation of the dimension of an attractor. Probably the most useful technique for ecologists is the Grassberger–Procaccia algorithm that allows the estimation of a quantity called the correlation dimension (Grassberger & Procaccia 1983a, b). The correlation dimension can be shown to be a good estimate of attractor dimension. The Grassberger–Procaccia algorithm can be applied to time series of a single component of a complex system and also involves the construction of a phase space using lagged co-ordinates. The technique is 'data hungry' and probably would not work on time series with less than about 400 data points covering about 20 orbits of the attractor.

There have been as yet relatively few applications of this technique in ecology. Schaffer and Kot (1985a) found evidence for a non-integer attractor in measles data confirming their analysis of the reconstructed attractor. No evidence of a low-dimensional attractor was found when this technique was applied to the data from Nicholson's blowfly experiments or to data from long-term plankton surveys in the North Sea (Godfray & Blythe 1990).

Non-linear forecasting

As the trajectory of a system moves around an attractor in a deterministic orbit, a knowledge of the system's position allows a prediction to be made of the course of the trajectory, at least in the short term. A variety of different methods of prediction is possible, their utility depending in large part on the quality of data available. A method developed by Sugihara and May (1990) is particularly suited to the relatively poor-quality data available to ecologists.

Sugihara and May (1990) reconstruct the attractor in a phase space of appropriate dimensions using lagged co-ordinates. The data set is then divided into two parts, and one half used to construct predictions of the second half. Consider a single point in the second half of the time series: it is hoped to predict the system's trajectory some way into the future from this point. Each point in the time series is represented by a point in phase space and nearby points in phase space may be some distance apart in the time series. The first stage is to construct a simplex around the test point using the nearest neighbours from the first half of the time series. The next stage is to identify the points that succeed each neighbour in the time series: these points form a new simplex and its centre of mass is the predicted state of the system one time-unit hence. Predictions further into the future are obtained in similar manner. Finally, the predicted and observed points can be compared.

One of the main functions of this technique is the prediction of the future state of a complicated system. In addition, the manner in which the success of the prediction decays with time can be used as evidence of the underlying dynamics (see also Wales 1991). In particular, if the underlying attractor is chaotic, the success of the prediction decays exponentially with time. Sugihara and May (1990) and Sugihara *et al.* (1990) have applied this technique to both plankton data collected on the pacific coast of California and to the measles data discussed earlier (p. 62), and find evidence for the presence of an underlying chaotic attractor. Care has to be taken in interpreting the fall in prediction ability with time because some forms of correlated noise can give similar signatures to those of chaos (Sugihara and May 1990, Ellner 1992).

Statistical techniques

Chaos is normally thought of as a purely deterministic phenomenon that results in extreme sensitivity to initial conditions. However, sensitivity to initial conditions may also arise in systems that are deterministically non-chaotic but are constantly perturbed by stochastic noise. To see how this may happen, consider a system with a non-chaotic attractor in a region of parameter space close to where a chaotic attractor may be found. The set of points that will form the chaotic attractor may still influence the dynamics, not by attracting trajectories but by repelling them: a chaotic repellor (Rand & Wilson 1992). Stochastic noise may perturb the system away from its attractor to a position where it falls under the influence of the chaotic repellor and where, using an apt metaphor of Rand and Wilson (1992), the system trajectory bounces around the repellor like a ball in a pinball machine. In consequence, it is not possible to predict the trajectory of the system, no matter how much information one has about the initial conditions, and the nature of the stochastic perturbations. Some mathematicians define chaos purely in terms of sensitivity to initial conditions (Ruelle 1989).

Sensitivity to initial conditions can be measured by the magnitude of the Lyapunov exponents of a system. Lyapunov exponents describe the average expansion or shrinkage of small volumes of phase space containing system trajectories; one exponent is defined for each orthogonal axis of the small volume of phase space. In a non-chaotic system, the small volume shrinks to nothing from all sides as the system is attracted on to the attractor: all exponents are negative. In chaotic systems, the small volume also shrinks to zero (the sum of the Lyapunov exponents is negative), but in some directions the volume expands (at least one Lyapunov exponent positive). The presence of a positive Lyapunov exponent shows the presence of extreme sensitivity to initial conditions and hence chaos.

Ellner and colleagues (Ellner *et al.* 1991, McCaffrey *et al.* 1992, Nychka *et al.* 1992) have developed techniques for the statistical estimation of Lyapunov exponents from time series of biological data. Their method involves the non-parametric fitting (using either spline or neural-network techniques) of a generalized, non-linear time series model. Experiments with artificial data suggest that the method performs well, even for relatively short and noisy data sets. When applied to Lynx cycle data, the Lyapunov estimates are negative indicating the absence of chaos (Ellner 1992).

All the techniques described in this section are relatively new and not fully explored. Formidable problems oppose their routine use in ecology. All techniques require relatively long runs of data, of a quality rare in population biology. Many of the techniques were developed in the physical sciences where the signal-to-noise ratio is much higher than that commonly encountered by biologists. Noise, especially when it is temporally correlated, will frequently obscure the underlying deterministic dynamics. The application of these techniques also assumes the absence of initial transients and that the system has approached the underlying attractor. If transients are in fact present, attractor dimensions can be seriously over- or under-estimated (Blythe & Stokes 1988, Godfray & Blythe 1990). Finally, and of particular relevance here, Darwinian evolution can change the shape of the underlying attractor. This is a particular worry as very long time series are needed to characterize an attractor. Nicholson's blowflies (see p. 78) provide an example of a case where attractor structure may have changed during the course of data collection. Despite all the caveats listed here, the application of these new techniques to ecological data is an enormously exciting advance in the analysis of the dynamics of real systems.

EVOLUTION OF DEMOGRAPHIC PARAMETERS

We conclude from the last section that it remains ambiguous from the empirical evidence whether or not chaos is common or rare in nature. Nevertheless, a number of workers have argued *a priori* that chaos is likely to be rare because of the action of natural selection. This problem is part of the larger question of how natural selection and population dynamics interact. We begin this section with a brief review of density-dependent natural selection and its application to the evolution of demographic parameters. We then discuss r- and K-selection which spurred much of the early work on the interaction of population dynamics and evolution. After a brief digression to consider age-structured models, we review recent work on life history evolution in chaotic and cyclic populations.

Density-dependent natural selection

The classic analysis of evolution acting on two alleles segregating at a single locus is simply extended to the case where fitnesses are density dependent (e.g. Roughgarden 1979). Suppose that p_t is the frequency of the A allele and q_t the frequency of the alternative a allele. Let the fitness of each genotype be a function of total population size, $w_{AA}(N_t)$ etc., where N_t is population size. Assuming that the Hardy–Weinberg rule can be used to calculate genotype frequencies, mean fitness is $\overline{w}(N_t) = p_t^2 w_{AA}(N_t) + 2p_t q_t w_{Aa}(N_t) + q_t^2 w_{aa}(N_t)$ and the frequency of the A allele in the next generation is:

$$p_{t+1} = \frac{p_t^2 w_{AA}(N_t) + p_t q_t w_{Aa}(N_t)}{\overline{w}(N_t)} \qquad (2)$$

To pursue this genetic recursion, it is also necessary to know the population size in the next generation. In density-independent gene recursions, genotype fitnesses may take arbitrary absolute values as long as their relative values are preserved. It is thus possible to define fitness as the expected number of progeny produced by an individual of a particular genotype and to use fitness in a recursion for population size:

$$N_{t+1} = N_t \overline{w}(N_t) \tag{3}$$

The dynamics of Eqns (2, 3) may be very complex. Considerable simplification is achieved if the analysis is restricted to the invasion of a rare allele (A) into a stable population. When rare, an allele will almost exclusively be represented as a heterozygote at frequency $2p_t(1 - p_t) \approx 2p_t$. However, the size of the stable population (K_{aa}) will be determined almost exclusively by the properties of the resident genotype aa while mean fitness $\approx w_{aa}(K_{aa}) = 1$ (every female exactly replaces itself). Thus:

$$p_{t+1} = p_t w_{Aa}(K_{aa}) \tag{4}$$

The rare allele thus invades if $w_{Aa}(K_{aa}) > 1$. Suppose this condition is met and the A allele spreads. When common, can it be invaded by the a allele? A completely symmetrical argument shows that invasion is possible only if $w_{Aa}(K_{AA}) > 1$. If just one of these conditions holds, then the direction of evolution is clear. However, if both conditions are true then (at least deterministically) neither allele will be excluded. There is thus a protected polymorphism and it is necessary to study the full recursion to discover the end points of the genetic and population processes.

r- and *K*-selection

The terms *r*- and *K*-selection were introduced by MacArthur and Wilson (1967) to describe selection acting on populations far from or close to their equilibrium carrying capacity respectively. Their work has led to two rather separate areas of investigation (Mueller 1988). First, there has been extensive investigation of genetic models incorporating density-dependent selection. Second, a very large verbal theory has grown up around the concepts of *r*- and *K*-selection. Attempts have been made to relate many aspects of the life history of plants and animals to their position on an $r-K$ continuum (Pianka 1970, Boyce 1984). In addition, it has been suggested that evolutionary feedback loops will tend to turn the $r-K$ continuum into a dichotomy (Horn & Rubenstein 1984). While achieving limited success in synthesizing disparate aspects of life history theory, the diversity of life histories has largely frustrated such a procrustian approach and many biologists have become rather suspicious of the whole concept of *r*- and *K*-selection.

MacArthur and Wilson's (1967) verbal arguments on density-dependent selection were quickly formalized by a number of authors working with the techniques described in the last section (Anderson 1971, Charlesworth 1971, King & Anderson 1971, Roughgarden 1971, Clarke 1972). In simple additive models, where the phenotype of the heterozygote is intermediate between the two homozygotes, selection in stable populations acts to maximize equilibrium population size while selection in populations away from carrying capacity maximizes the intrinsic rate of increase. Stable polymorphisms are possible in the case of overdominance.

The reason why competitive ability and hence equilibrium population size in stable populations is maximized can be seen by examination of Eqn (4). An invading allele only spreads if $w_{Aa}(K_{aa}) > 1$; clearly this will only be true if the invading genotype is more resistant to competition than the resident genotype, and greater resistance to competition implies larger equilibrium population size. Now consider a population that increases exponentially until reduced to a fixed sized by a catastrophic mortality. Assume also that the probability of survival is independent of genotype. As the frequency distribution of genotypes is the same before and after the catastrophe, the (ecological) population dynamics themselves have no effect on the genetic dynamics. The genotypes can thus be viewed as competing clones and in an additive model natural selection will favour the allele with the greatest capacity for increase.

Will natural selection acting on stable populations at equilibrium tend to maintain stability or to lead to demographic parameters that give rise to other forms of population behaviour? The answer to this question depends on whether the parameters that determine maximum population size also influence stability. Consider first the Ricker–Moran model for single-species density dependence:

$$N_{t+1} = N_t \exp\left\{r\left(1 - \frac{N_t}{K}\right)\right\} \quad (5)$$

where $\exp(r)$ is the maximum growth rate in a low-density population and K is the equilibrium population size. The stability properties of this equation have been fully analysed by May and Oster (1976) and depend only on the parameter r (Fig. 3.2). In this case, unrestrained natural selection has no effect whatsoever on stability (but see later for the addition of environmental noise).

Now consider the equation used by Hassell *et al.* (1976) in their analysis of insect time series (Eqn 1). We shall assume that evolution acts only on λ and b and that a is constant (though the analysis could be extended to include a). Equilibrium population size (N^*) is given by:

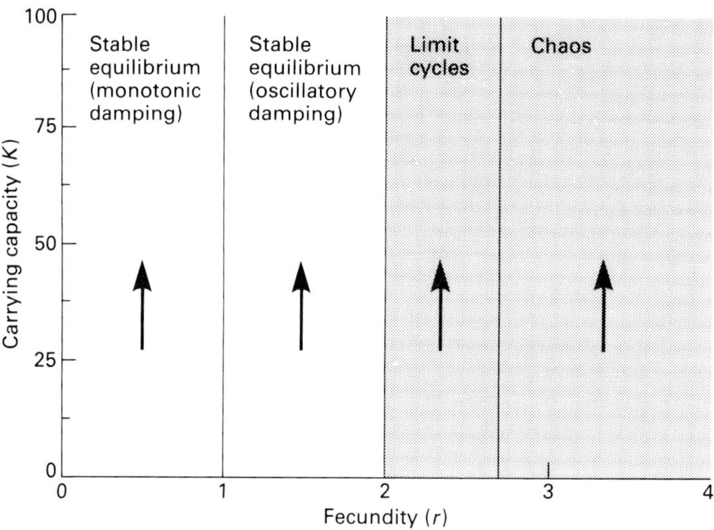

Fig. 3.2. The stability properties of the Ricker–Moran model of density dependence in a single-species population as a function of the two parameters fecundity (r) and carrying capacity (K). Evolution acts to maximize K as shown by the arrows. Different arguments are required to show the direction of evolution when the population is point stable (unshaded region) or cyclic or chaotic (shaded region): see the text.

$$N^* = \frac{1}{a}\left(\lambda^{\frac{1}{b}} - 1\right) \tag{6}$$

and hence maximizing population size is equivalent to maximizing $\ln(\lambda)/b$. In Fig. 3.3 we plot lines of equal population size and indicate the direction in which natural selection will act. If selection is unhindered by other factors, it is capable of changing the stability properties of the population and may even lead a population into a cyclic region of parameter space. However, it is important to realize that selection is not acting directly on stability. Changes in stability occur as a population level side-effect of selection acting on competitive ability. In general, the presence of this type of side-effect is likely to be model specific and generalizations on the effect of natural selection on stability will be difficult.

So far we have assumed the absence of trade-offs between the different components of an organism's life history. Trade-offs form the basis of life history theory and, although notoriously hard to demonstrate experimentally, are assumed to be both widespread and important (Stearns 1976). Consider again the Ricker–Moran model (Eqn 5) which caricatures the

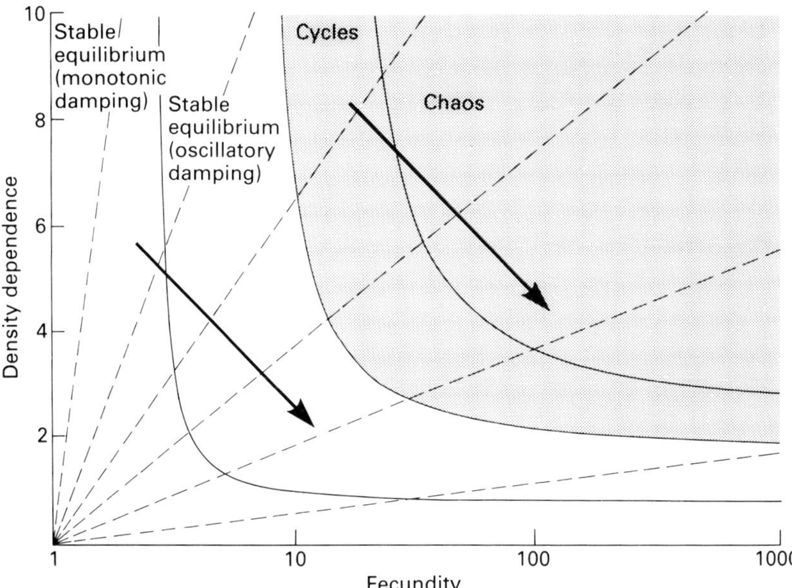

FIG. 3.3. Evolution acts to maximize population size in systems described by the Hassell (1975) model. The dashed lines show points in parameter space connected by equal equilibrium population sizes. Lines with lower slope represent high population densities. Evolution acts in the direction shown by the arrows. Different arguments are required to show the direction of evolution when the population is point stable (unshaded region) or cyclic or chaotic (shaded region): see the text.

animal's life history in terms of two parameters, r and K. As MacArthur and Wilson (1967) first suggested, there is likely to be a trade-off between fecundity and competitive ability: individuals that invest limiting resources in trophic functions will have less resources available for reproductive functions. In Fig. 3.4 we superimpose on the stability diagram of the Ricker–Moran equation a possible strategy set for a species. We assume that very small fecundities and very low competitive abilities are unable to evolve and that the maximum values of r and K are limited by trade-offs. The set of possible phenotypes is thus triangular. As discussed earlier, unhindered natural selection will operate purely on K. However, as shown in the figure, selection purely on K will lead to a reduction in fecundity when the trade-off line is reached. Thus it seems likely that in the case of a population described by the Ricker–Moran equation, natural selection will lead to a reduction in fecundity. It is harder to predict the shape of the strategy set for an animal whose dynamics are governed by Eqn (1), and we do not attempt that here.

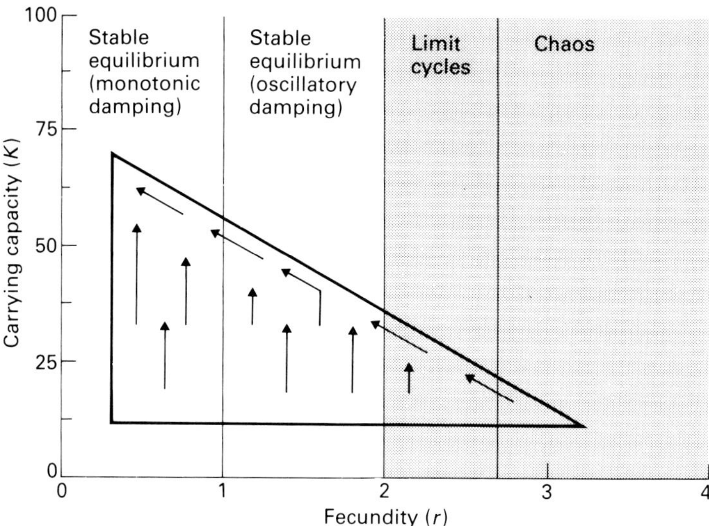

FIG. 3.4. Hypothetical set of possible life history strategies in a population described by the Ricker–Moran model shown with the stability criteria. A trade-off between fecundity and the ability to compete in crowded populations is assumed. The lines roughly represent evolutionary trajectories.

Thus, deterministic models of single-species populations at equilibrium population size predict that population density should be maximized and that the effect on stability depends on the presence of either population level side-effects of selection for competitive ability or of trade-offs. An important question is whether these conclusions are robust to the incorporation of stochastic variability; all individuals will experience some environmental variability in both their fecundity and their competitive ability. This problem has been examined in the context of the discrete logistic equation by Heckel and Roughgarden (1980) and more generally by Turelli and Petry (1980).

To study the spread of a rare gene in a stochastic environment a stochastic version of the invasion criteria (Eqn 4) is required. Haldane and Jayakar (1963) showed that when selective values varied in a set sequence over time, the relevant measure of long-term fitness was the geometric mean of the fitness in each generation. Gillespie (1973) and Karlin and Liberman (1974, 1975) have extended this work to show that in a truly stochastic environment, an allele will invade if the geometric mean fitness of the heterozygote is greater than that of the resident homozygote. In the context of density-dependent selection, the logarithm of the geometric mean fitness of the resident allele is zero; the population is fluctuating around the equilibrium population size and in the long run neither increases nor declines. Thus the condition for the spread of the rare heterozygote is:

$$E[\ln w_{\mathrm{Aa}}(N_t)] > 0 \tag{7}$$

Turelli and Petry (1980) analysed a series of discrete-time models of the form:

$$N_{t+1} = N_t G\left[r, \left(\frac{N_t}{K}\right)^{\theta}\right] \tag{8}$$

where r and K have their usual meaning. In a deterministic environment, selection acts solely on K, the only parameter to influence population size. Stability is determined jointly by r and also by the parameter θ which measures the severity of the density dependence: in general, larger values of r and θ lead to instability. Turelli and Petry explored three forms of the arbitrary function G (linear, exponential and hyperbolic) and assumed environmental stochasticity either to act on equilibrium population size ($K = K + \varepsilon_t$) or, multiplicatively, on per capita growth rate ($G = G(1 + \varepsilon_t)$). Finally, they assumed that environmental variation was relatively small and that it could be approximated purely by its variance.

How selection acts on r is highly model dependent — selection for higher r, lower r, or the absence of selection were all found. Turelli and Petry conclude that the most likely result of selection is for r to increase which is in accord with the general principle that environmental uncertainty favours increased intrinsic growth rates. Although the analysis is restricted to the invasion of resident populations with stable dynamics, Turelli and Petry were able to show that under some conditions life histories that would result in chaotic dynamics were able to invade. Clearer predictions emerge if θ is allowed to evolve. Environmental noise acting on the equilibrium population size tends to push θ towards zero, irrespective of the model. When $\theta = 0$ the eigenvalue of the system is one and thus neutral oscillations about the equilibrium are predicted. However, noise acting on the per capita growth rate leads to selection on θ towards a positive constant associated with an eigenvalue of less than one. Thus the net effect of evolution acting on θ is to promote stability.

Structured populations

So far, we have discussed the evolution of demographic parameters in the context of population models without age or size structures. For most real populations, age and/or size structures are likely to be of crucial importance but, as yet, there has been rather little analysis of how evolution in structured populations influences population dynamics. In contrast, the more general problem of life history evolution in structured populations has received considerable attention, especially in the last 10 years. In this section, we briefly discuss this work and how it lays the foundation to study the relationship between population and evolutionary dynamics. In the following section we will revert to unstructured populations to study evolution in chaotic resident populations, before, in the final section, returning to structured populations to discuss an example of evolution in the laboratory.

Consider first deterministic models without density (or frequency) dependence. In the non-structured case, natural selection maximizes r, the intrinsic rate of increase when rare, which is thus a measure of the fitness of a strategy. In models with age structure (for extensions to populations with other forms of structure see Caswell (1989) and Metz and Diekmann (1986)) the correct measure of fitness is also the intrinsic rate of increase when rare (Charlesworth 1980). Unfortunately, r can now only be defined implicitly as the solution of the Euler–Lotka equation:

$$1 = \int_0^{\infty} l_t m_t e^{-rt}\, \mathrm{d}t \tag{9}$$

where l_t is the probability of surviving until age t and m_t is fecundity at age t. The term e^{-rt} acts to discount young born later in life; young born early in life are more efficient propagators of a parent's genes as they themselves will go on to produce offspring — a form of compound interest. There is now a large literature on optimizing life cycles in density-independent environments based on Eqn (9). For example, in a series of papers, Sibly and Calow (1983, 1984, 1987) have systematically examined all possible life history trade-offs in a discrete-time version of Eqn (9) with the assumption that survival and fecundity is constant after maturity is reached.

The assumption of density independence limits the use of this approach for the study of parameters that affect population dynamics. In the limit, where a population is perfectly regulated, natural selection will select the genotype with the greatest life-time reproductive success. As the population is neither growing nor declining, there is no special benefit from the production of offspring either early or late in life. Thus in some ways, the strict density-dependent case is simpler than density independence. In these circumstances, natural selection will tend to maximize population size, as in the case of non-structured populations (Charlesworth 1980, Sibly & Calow 1983).

Cases other than perfect regulation and strict density independence have been little studied. Problems arise in particular when the assumption of a stable age distribution is violated. A second problem, whose resolution is relevant to evolution in deterministically varying environments, is evolution in stochastic environments. Great progress has been made in recent years in the study of randomly varying environments (Tuljapurkar 1989, 1990, reviewed in Metz *et al.* 1992). In particular, the criterion for the invasion of a rare allele into a stochastically varying population has been generalized to structured populations.

Consider an age-structured population in discrete time whose density can be described by the vector $\boldsymbol{N}_t$ whose elements are the density of individuals of age 0, 1 . . . *max* (for extensions to populations structured in other ways see Tuljapurkar 1990). The population dynamics are now described by:

$$\boldsymbol{N}_{t+1} = \boldsymbol{B}_t \boldsymbol{N}_t \tag{10}$$

where $\boldsymbol{B}_t$ is a square matrix of order *max*. This equation includes no density dependence and is thus linear in $\boldsymbol{N}$. In the deterministic case, $\boldsymbol{B}$ (independent of time) would be the Leslie Matrix and the fate of the population would be determined by its dominant eigenvalue. In the case of a stochastically varying environment, the place of the dominant eigenvalue is taken by the dominant Lyapunov exponent, a, defined as:

$$a = \lim_{T \to \infty} \left\{ \frac{1}{T} \ln \left\| \prod_{t=1}^{T} \boldsymbol{B}_t \right\| \right\} \tag{11}$$

where $\|\cdot\|$ is any matrix norm. In the same way as evolution maximizes r in a deterministic environment, evolution will maximize a in a stochastic environment. Recall that in the non-structured stochastic case, the fate of an invading allele was determined by the long-term geometric mean fitness. The dominant Lyapunov exponent can also be interpreted as a geometric mean, although in the structured case, the complete transition matrix has to be considered. Except in the most simple case, analytical calculation of the Lyapunov exponents will be impossible (Tuljapurkar 1990). Nevertheless, the result is still very valuable as the exponent can be estimated from simulation data and provides a criterion for assessing the invasibility of an allele.

How important are stochastic effects in the evolution of life histories? It is still too soon to give a definite answer but initial work suggests that at least sometimes they are very important (see for example, Orzack & Tuljapurkar 1989).

Chaotic populations: simple, discrete-time models

Soon after chaos came to the attention of population biologists, it was suggested that it might be rare in natural populations because natural selection favoured stable population dynamics. Two arguments were advanced in support of this proposition. The first (deliberately) invoked group selection: Thomas *et al.* (1980) suggested that chaotic dynamics would lead to high frequencies of population extinction in comparison with stable dynamics. Alleles that caused chaos would thus be at a comparative disadvantage through selection at the group or population level. In contrast, Mueller and Ayala (1981) argued that individual selection may result in populations evolving out of chaotic regions of parameter space. They illustrated their argument using a single-species population model.

The role of group selection in populations with chaotic dynamics has been little explored since Thomas *et al.* (1980), though a similar argument has recently been repeated by Berryman and Millstein (1989). One misconception sometimes made is that chaotic dynamics are *always* associated with sufficiently severe population fluctuations to increase markedly the probability of stochastic population extinction. This is certainly not necessarily true and group selection is unlikely to be a general force preventing chaotic dynamics in nature. Having said that, it may be important in preventing some kinds of chaos from being found in natural populations.

Turning to the evolution of demographic parameters, with one exception (Felsenstein 1979), studies of evolution in chaotic populations have involved numerical simulations of the invasion of rare alleles. Very recently, J.A.J. Metz and colleagues (Metz 1990, Metz *et al.* 1992, J.A.J. Metz and R.M. Nisbit personal communication) have suggested that the dominant Lyapunov exponent provides a measure of the fitness of an allele invading a resident chaotic population. As with the stochastic, density-independent case, it will not normally be possible to calculate the Lyapunov exponent analytically for anything but very simple cases (see later). However, estimation of the exponent from numerical data provides a useful criterion to judge invasibility.

In the case of single-species models, the dominant Lyapunov exponent is simply the long-term geometric mean of the per capita rate of increase. Consider the Ricker–Moran equation (Eqn 5); this can be rewritten as:

$$N_{t+1} = B_t N_t \qquad (12)$$

where $B_t = \exp(r(1 - N_t/K))$. As the population is persistent and shows no long-term trends over time, the dominant Lyapunov exponent of the resident population is zero. This is true, whether the resident population is stable, cyclic or chaotic. (The use of the Lyapunov exponent in this context should not be confused with its use to describe the geometry of attractors where positive exponents are associated with chaos; see p. 64). Thus:

$$a = \lim_{T\to\infty}\left\{\frac{1}{T}\sum_{t=1}^{T}\ln \boldsymbol{B}_t\right\} = \lim_{T\to\infty}\left\{\frac{1}{T}\sum_{t=1}^{T} r\left(1-\frac{N_t}{K}\right)\right\} = 0 \qquad (13)$$

The Lyapunov exponent is particularly simple in this case as the logarithm of the geometric mean disappears with the exponent of the Ricker–Moran equation. Rearranging the last equality and noting that r and K are time invariant we find, as expected, that the long-term average value of N_t is K, the carrying capacity.

Now consider a mutant whose life history can be summarized by the pair of parameters r' and K'. The mutant will invade the population if it has a higher fitness than the resident life history. If the dominant Lyapunov exponent is used as a measure of fitness then the mutant must have an exponent (a') greater than zero. Thus, using primes to distinguish the density and dynamics of the mutant:

$$a' = \lim_{T\to\infty}\left\{\frac{1}{T}\sum_{t=1}^{T}\ln \boldsymbol{B}'_t\right\} = \lim_{T\to\infty}\left\{\frac{1}{T}\sum_{t=1}^{T} r'\left(1-\frac{N_t}{K'}\right)\right\} > 0$$

$$\Rightarrow K' > \lim_{T\to\infty}\left\{\frac{1}{T}\sum_{t=1}^{T} N_t\right\} \qquad (14)$$

Note that the density dependence experienced by the rare mutant is solely a property of the density of the resident strain. In addition, we know that the long-term mean population density of the resident strain is K. Thus, the last inequality implies that the rare mutant will spread if $K' > K$ or, in words, if the rare mutant has a higher carrying capacity.

Thus, at least when the population is described by the Ricker–Moran equation, natural selection in a population with chaotic (or cyclic) dynamics maximizes carrying capacity. As stability depends on r and not on K, selection will have no effect on dynamics (though note we are at this stage ignoring possible trade-offs between the two parameters). This is exactly the same result as was obtained in the analysis of the identical equation in regions of parameter space where it displays stable dynamics. (See Holt (1983) for a similar argument used in a different context.) Consider now the single-species model of Hassell *et al.* (1976) (Eqn 1). Analysis of the invasion of a population with stable dynamics concluded that evolution maximized the quantity $\ln(r)/c$ which again was equivalent to maximizing population density. Applying the above techniques to the problem of evolution in areas of parameter space with cyclic and chaotic dynamics shows that exactly the same quantity is maximized (Metz *et al.* 1992). Thus evolution may affect the nature of the population dynamics (Fig. 3.3), though essentially this is a population level side-effect of selection on competitive ability.

Further confirmation of the usefulness of Lyapunov exponents is obtained by comparing the results of using this technique with simulation studies. As discussed earlier (p. 54), Mueller and Ayala (1981) fitted single-species population models to data obtained from laboratory populations of *Drosophila melanogaster*. They fitted two models:

$$N_{t+1} = (S - sFN_t)FN_t \tag{15a}$$

$$N_{t+1} = S\exp(-sFN_t)FN_t \tag{15b}$$

where F is fecundity, S is maximum juvenile survival and s is a measure of density dependence. Stability depends only on the quantity FS and not on the extent of density dependence. Mueller and Ayala then asked whether natural selection will tend to move the population from regions of chaotic or cyclic dynamics into regions of stability. They chose a test point in parameter space that gave rise to a resident population with cyclic or chaotic dynamics and examined by simulation whether alternative life histories could invade. Their models were fully genetic and they distinguished between recessive and dominant alleles. We have repeated their analysis using the techniques described above (although an analytical solution is only possible for one model). Our criteria for the spread of a mutant life history are almost identical to Mueller and Ayala's criteria for the spread of a mutant life history determined by a dominant gene (we believe the one discrepancy is due to a numerical error in Mueller and Ayala's paper).

Until recently, the only analytical treatment of evolution in a population with chaotic dynamics was that of Felsenstein (1979). Felsenstein analysed a very simple discrete-time model that had previously been discussed by Williamson (1974):

$$N_{t+1} = \begin{cases} R_1 N_t, & N_t \leq K \\ R_2 N_t, & N_t > K \end{cases} \tag{16}$$

The population growth rates are piecewise linear, declining above the carrying capacity (K) and growing below (Fig. 3.5). Population density thus oscillates in a chaotic manner (for all non-integer R_1/R_2) around the carrying capacity. Now consider a potential invader, differing in R_1, R_2 and K. The mutant will grow in numbers when $N_t > K'$ (the prime denotes the mutant values) and decline when the inequality is untrue.

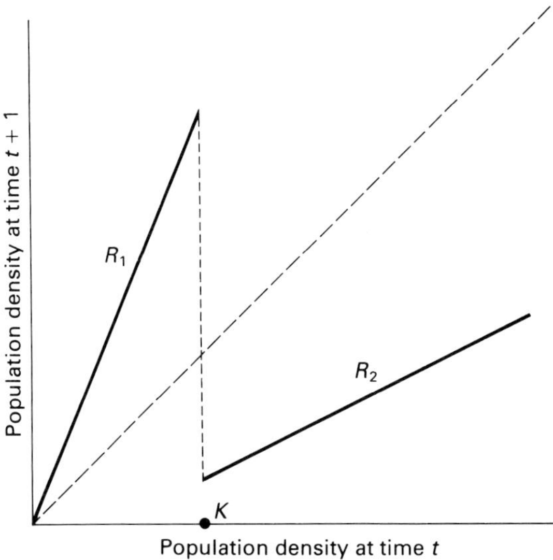

FIG. 3.5. The map assumed by Felsenstein (1979) in his analytical study of parameter evolution in a chaotic population. Below population sizes of K, the population increases each generation by a factor $R_1 > 1$; above K, population size decreases (i.e. the rate of increase $R_2 < 1$).

Using a geometrical argument, it is straightforward to calculate the fraction of time $N_t > K'$ as a function of R_1, R_2 and K (Felsenstein 1979). From this one can calculate the long-term geometric mean of the mutant growth rate: the mutant spreads if the mean growth rate is greater than one. In effect, Felsenstein calculates the Lyapunov exponent from first principles; the criterion he derives for the spread of a mutant is:

$$(k' - k) > \frac{r_1' r_2 - r_2' r_1}{r_1' - r_2'} \tag{17}$$

where the lower-case symbols refer to the natural logarithms of the corresponding upper-case symbols. This example displays one property that was not found in any of the single-species models discussed above. Here, no simple quantity is maximized and the fact that one life history can invade a second does not imply that the reverse is impossible (Eqn (17) is not symmetric in switching symbols with and without primes). As Felsenstein demonstrates more rigorously, protected polymorphisms are possible with more than one life history persisting in a population.

To conclude, the use of the long-term, geometric average growth rate (the one-dimensional Lyapunov exponent) is a valuable tool with which to study the evolution of demographic parameters in populations with chaotic dynamics. In the case of simple, discrete-time models, analytical solutions are often possible. It appears that the ability to compete in crowded populations is maximized *irrespective of the nature of the underlying population dynamics*. Whether natural selection influences population behaviour purely depends on whether selection for increased competitive ability, subject to physiological trade-offs, also leads to a change in stability properties. We conjecture that the answer to the question, 'Does individual selection (*ceteris paribus*) tend to stabilize population dynamics?' will normally be 'yes' for two reasons: (1) an increased ability to cope with crowded conditions will tend to reduce non-linearities in density dependence and thus reduce the likelihood of chaos; and (2) trade-offs between fecundity and competitive ability will lead to reduced fecundity which again will normally be associated with a reduction in the likelihood of chaotic dynamics. There are (at least) two important caveats. First, this conclusion is based on the analysis of a restricted class of models. Second, we have not examined environmental stochasticity in populations with chaotic or cyclic dynamics. The lesson of Turrelli and Petry's (1980) work on stable resident populations is an important warning about the complications of environmental stochasticity. It will be interesting to discover whether their conclusions about the invasion of alleles in stochastic environments are influenced by the nature of the dynamics of the resident population.

Nicholson's blowflies

In this section we briefly describe one study of the evolution of demographic parameters in a more complicated system with non-stable population dynamics. For a second example, see Mueller (1988).

One of the classic laboratory data sets in population ecology shows evidence of the evolution of demographic parameters. Nicholson (1954, 1957) kept blowflies (*Lucilia cuprina*) in laboratory cages where they were fed on a limited supply of liver renewed every 20 days. In the longest experiments (722 days), the numbers of flies initially oscillated with a pronounced cycle of approximately 40 days. However, towards the end of the time series, distinct changes in the dynamics are clearly visible: the mean population density increases, and the period of the dominant cycle falls from 40 days to 20 days (Fig. 3.6).

Gurney *et al.* (1980) have shown that the dynamics are largely captured by a differential equation with a time lag:

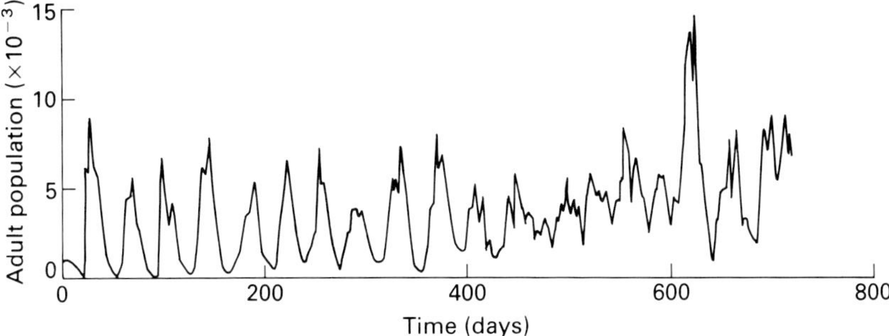

FIG. 3.6. Fluctuations in adult blowfly numbers in Nicholson's (1957) 'long' experiments. (After Nisbet *et al.* 1989.)

$$\frac{dN}{dt} = R(N_{t-\tau}) - \delta N_t \qquad (18)$$

Here $R(N_t)$ describes density dependent recruitment to the adult stage (N_t), δ is the *per capita* death rate of the adult and τ is a time delay representing the development time of the fly. Recruitment is density dependent since the egg production of the adult fly depends on food supply and thus on population crowding. Stokes *et al.* (1988) estimated the parameters of Eqn (18) from Nicholson's data at different stages of the time series. They found that two parameters changed significantly over the course of the experiment: (1) the fecundity of the flies, which decreased; and (2) the resistance of the fly to the effects of crowding, which increased. The overall effect of these changes was to increase equilibrium population size and to change the deterministic dynamics from cycles to a stable point. If realistic levels of environmental noise are included in the model, quasicycles are observed instead of the stable equilibrium and simulations of the model show a remarkable resemblance to the real data.

Fitting the model with time-varying parameters to the data does not demonstrate that the changes in the values of the parameters are consistent with the operation of natural selection. To show this Stokes *et al.* (1988) and Nisbet *et al.* (1989) asked whether a mutant with a life history characteristic of flies at the end of the experiment could invade a resident population with a life history characteristic of flies at the beginning of the experiment. They used simulation techniques since the study of evolution in continuous-time, single-species models with time delays is substantially less tractable than single-species discrete-time models, and found that the rare life history was able to invade the resident life history.

Thus natural selection increases carrying capacity, as expected from the analysis of the models in the last section. A rise in carrying capacity can be achieved either by an increase in fecundity, or an increase in tolerance of crowding. The observed increase in the blowfly experiments was exclusively due to a raised tolerance of crowding — the decrease in fecundity acted to limit the rise in carrying capacity. However, the change in the stability properties of the system is almost exclusively due to the decrease in fecundity. A consistent explanation of these results is that there is a trade-off between crowding tolerance and fecundity: carrying capacity is maximized by increasing crowding tolerance although the increase is modulated by the concomitant decrease in fecundity. Furthermore, the change in the stability properties occurs simply as a by-product of selection for increased carrying capacity. We predict that, unencumbered by trade-offs, natural selection would act simultaneously to raise both fecundity and tolerance (though this has yet to be shown). The demonstration that this has not occurred is a novel demonstration of the presence of a life history trade-off.

COMPLEX COMMUNITIES

We now turn from a consideration of simple single-species systems to problems posed by complex assemblages of species. Animals invading new habitats face many novel challenges, both biotic and abiotic. One of us has studied the terrestrial snail fauna of the Madeiran islands (Cook *et al.* 1990) and the questions of speciation, persistence and colonization that they raise. This work is discussed in this section.

The small, isolated Madeiran archipelago has over 250 species of snails (a large terrestrial fauna). Over 70% of species are endemic and most occupy only parts of the territory. At a higher taxonomic level diversity is low; 90% of the species are in five families compared with 15 families for the European fauna from which most of them are derived. This appears to be a classic case in which allopatric speciation and repeated colonizations over long or short distances have built up the groups of coexisting species in each part of an island. Numbers of species living sympatrically are not high; an average of 9.2 species was found in 56 samples collected in a survey of one particular region (Cook *et al.* 1990). The evidence for competitive interaction and niche occupancy, derived from comparison of the island with continental faunas, was also examined (Cameron & Cook 1989). The range of size and shape in the endemic families extends into the dimension space usually occupied by some of the families that are missing, suggesting the existence of niches that would otherwise be unfilled, but other tests fail to indicate competitive interactions.

Many analytical studies have been made of competition between species (e.g. MacArthur & Levins 1967, May 1973, Levins 1979, Abrams 1983, 1987). These give us a picture of the general outcome or the result of particular types of interaction. Simple simulations provide a feel for the kind of patterns which would be expected if species repeatedly made contact with each other as a result of accidental introduction. Exploratory studies have been carried out (Cook & Mani, unpublished) and some results are summarized here as a means to examine the evolutionary consequences.

At its most basic the dynamic representation of the relation of a species to its environment has to start with some expression like the Ricker–Moran equation (Eqn 5). There is potential for increase and environmental restraint such that individuals compete for resources, and also a time lag in the response to the restraining effects. If several species occupy the same area they may interact, in which case there may be interference, as well as exploitative competition. This could also be true of interacting genotypes within a species but has not been assumed above in the discussion of single species. For a species i the pattern of competition can then be represented by:

$$N_i(t + 1) = N_i(t) \exp\left[r\left\{1 - \sum_{j=1}^{n} \frac{a_{ij}N_j(t)}{K_j}\right\}\right] \qquad (19)$$

If all species have similar effects on each other (the a_{ij} values are about unity) then few species could survive. The preceding discussion indicates that these would be the ones with highest K values, ones which are most efficient at using resources. On the other hand, if we imagine a series of similar species introduced to an area, then the r and K values will be similar, and the outcome depends to a great extent on the a_{ij} matrix. We assume $a_{ij} = 1$ for $i = j$ (i.e. for intraspecific interference) and the other values to be greater than zero if there is any interaction.

A series of simulations was carried out with a range of parameters. In some cases, groups of up to 40 species were assumed to reach a given location at once, while in others there was serial introduction. The most relevant conclusions (Cook & Mani, unpublished) may be summarized as follows.

1 When there was a rectangular random distribution of a_{ij} from zero to some limit k, then whatever the initial number of species, the value k prescribed a mean number of surviving species. When the starting number of individuals was small the number of surviving species plateaued at

about 8 when $k = 1.1$ and about 4 when $k = 2.0$. The frequency distribution of a_{ij} among surviving species changed from its initial rectangular shape to one where there was a predominance of small values.

2 Serial introduction of species, rather than group introduction, tended to reduce the chance of survival. For example, in one pair of runs started with initial numbers of 10 the mean number of surviving species was 5.6 ± 0.64 for serial introductions and 7.6 ± 0.40 when all commenced at once.

3 There is a strongly limiting effect of interference under the very artificial conditions assumed. Two modifications were made which raise the number of coexisting species. One of these was rarification by random mortality, which reduces the interspecific competition. The other was to cause the a_{ij} values to decline progressively as they diverge from the major diagonal of the a matrix. This is equivalent to saying that species are less likely to interfere with each other as they become taxonomically more distinct.

4 The random a_{ij} matrix is unrealistic in that it assumes the effect of one species on another to be uncorrelated with its effect on a third. If correlation is introduced between the elements in columns of the a_{ij} matrix the result is sensitive to the degree of association used. In general, the effect on the mean number of surviving species is small but the variance is increased. The ability to predict the number of surviving species for a given set of conditions therefore goes down.

5 When r was raised to ln(4.0) species became extinct after a short time if introduced on their own. Introduction in groups had a powerful damping effect so long as the a_{ij} values were small but not negligible, so that, unlike the preceding conditions, interspecific interference at a low level increased the chance of survival and coexistence. The implication is that weed species may do better if they are introduced to new territory in groups than if they arrive on their own.

The above computer experiments have only examined the ecological factors affecting coexistence. Evolutionary factors will also be extremely important. There is a large literature on the evolution of the avoidance of competition by character displacement (e.g. Grant 1975, Slatkin 1980, Milligan 1985, Taper & Case 1985, Abrams 1986) which often explicitly includes both evolutionary and population dynamics. Evolution may modify the response to competition in ways other than avoidance. For example, Krietman *et al.* (Ch. 11, this volume) discuss the influence of within-species distribution among resource patches on the probability of coexistence. It would be interesting to know how the balance of inter- and intraspecific competition affects distribution patterns over evolutionary time. Another aspect of the within-species response to resource competition is phenotypic flexibility which is discussed by Jones *et al.* (Ch. 16, this volume). We believe that the best way to understand complex communities such as Madeiran snails is through an approach integrating both population dynamic and evolutionary considerations.

REFERENCES

Abrams, P. (1983). The theory of limiting similarity. *Annual Review of Ecology and Systematics*, **14**, 359–376.

Abrams, P. (1986). Character displacement and niche shift analysed using consumer–resource models of competition. *Theoretical Population Biology*, **29**, 107–160.

Abrams, P. (1987). The functional responses of adaptive consumers of two resources. *Theoretical Population Biology*, **32**, 262–288.

Anderson, R. M. & May, R. M. (1991). *The Population Biology of Infectious Diseases.* Oxford University Press, Oxford, UK.

Anderson, W. W. (1971). Genetic equilibrium and population growth under density-regulated selection. *American Naturalist*, **105**, 489–498.

Bellows, T. S. & Hassell, M. P. (1988). The dynamics of age-structured host–parasitoid interactions. *Journal of Animal Ecology*, **57**, 259–268.

Berryman, A. A. & Millstein, J. A. (1989). Are ecological systems chaotic — and if not, why not? *Trends in Ecology and Evolution*, **4**, 26–28.

Blythe, S. P. & Stokes, T. K. (1988). Biological attractors, transients and evolution. *Ecodynamics* (Ed. by W. Wolff, C.-J. Soeder, & F. R. Drepper), pp. 309–318. Springer Verlag, Berlin, Federal Republic of Germany.

Boyce, M. S. (1984). Restitution of *r*- and *K*-selection as a model of density-dependent natural selection. *Annual Review of Ecology and Systematics*, **15**, 427–447.

Cameron, R. A. D. & Cook, L. M. (1989). Shell size and shape in Madeiran land snails: do niches remain unfilled? *Biological Journal of the Linnean Society*, **36**, 79–96.

Caswell, H. (1989). *Matrix Population Models.* Sinauer, Sunderland, MA, USA.

Charlesworth, B. (1971). Selection in density regulated populations. *Ecology*, **52**, 469–474.

Charlesworth, B. (1980). *Evolution in Age-structured Populations.* Cambridge University Press, Cambridge, UK.

Clarke, B. (1972). Density-dependent selection. *American Naturalist*, **106**, 1–13.

Cook, L. M., Cameron, R. A. D. & Lace, L. A. (1990). Land snails of eastern Madeira: speciation, persistence and colonization. *Proceedings of the Royal Society of London*, B, **239**, 35–79.

Davidson, J. & Andrewartha, H. G. (1948). Annual trends in a natural population of *Thrips imaginis* (Thysanoptera). *Journal of Animal Ecology*, **17**, 193–199.

Ellner, S. (1992). Detecting low-dimensional chaos in population dynamics data: a critical review. *Chaos* (Ed. by J. Logan). University of Ohio Press, Ohio, OH, USA.

Ellner, S., Gallant, A. R., McCaffrey, D. & Nychka, D. (1991). Convergence rates and data requirements for Jacobian-based estimates of Lyapunov exponents from data. *Physics Letters* A, **153**, 357–363.

Felsenstein, J. (1979). *r*- and *K*-selection in a completely chaotic population model. *American Naturalist*, **113**, 499–510.

Gillespie, J. H. (1973). Polymorphism in random environments. *Theoretical Population Biology*, **4**, 193–195.

Godfray, H. C. J. & Blythe, S. P. (1990). Complex dynamics in multispecies communities. *Philosophical Transactions of the Royal Society of London*, B, **330**, 221–233.

Grant, P. R. (1975). The classical case of character displacement. *Evolutionary Biology*, **8**, 237–337.

Grassberger, P. & Procaccia, I. (1983a). Characterization of strange attractors. *Physics Review Letters*, **50**, 346–349.

Grassberger, P. & Procaccia, I. (1983b). Measuring the strangeness of strange attractors. *Physica*, **9D**, 189–208.

Gurney, W. S. C., Blythe, S. P. & Nisbet, R. M. (1980). Nicholson's blowflies revisited. *Nature*, **287**, 17–21.

Haldane, J. B. S. & Jayakar, S. D. (1963). Polymorphism due to selection of varying direction. *Journal of Genetics*, **58**, 237–242.

Hassell, M. P. (1975). Density-dependence in single-species populations. *Journal of Animal Ecology*, **44**, 283–296.

Hassell, M. P., Lawton, J. H. & May, R. M. (1976). Patterns of dynamical behaviour in single species populations. *Journal of Animal Ecology*, **45**, 471–486.

Heckel, D. & Roughgarden, J. (1980). A species near its equilibrium size in a fluctuating environment can evolve a lower intrinsic rate of increase. *Proceedings of the National Academy of Sciences, USA*, **77**, 7497–7500.

Holt, R. D. (1983). Models for peripheral populations: the role of immigration. *Population Biology* (Ed. by H. I. Freedman & C. Strobeck), pp. 25–32. Springer Verlag, Berlin, Federal Republic of Germany.

Horn, H. S. & Rubenstein, D. I. (1984). Behavioural adaptations and life history. *Behavioural Ecology, An Evolutionary Approach* (2nd edn) (Ed. by J. R. Krebs & N. B. Davies), pp. 411–429. Blackwell Scientific Publications, Oxford, UK.

Karlin, S. & Liberman, U. (1974). Random temporal variation in selection intensities: case of large population size. *Theoretical Population Biology*, **6**, 355–382.

Karlin, S. & Liberman, U. (1975). Random temporal variation in selection intensities: one locus two allele model. *Journal of Mathematical Biology*, **2**, 1–17.

King, C. E. & Anderson, W. W. (1971). Age-specific selection. II. The interaction between *r* and *K* during population growth. *American Naturalist*, **105**, 137–156.

Levins, R. (1979). Coexistence in a variable environment. *American Naturalist*, **114**, 765–783.

MacArthur, R. H. & Levins, R. (1967). The limiting similarity, convergence, and divergence of coexisting species. *American Naturalist*, **101**, 377–385.

MacArthur, R. H. & Wilson, E. O. (1967). *The Theory of Island Biogeography*. Princeton University Press, Princeton, NJ, USA.

May, R. M. (1973). *Stability and Complexity in Model Ecosystems*. Princeton University Press, Princeton, NJ, USA.

May, R. M. (1974). Biological populations with non-overlapping generations: stable points, stable cycles and chaos. *Science*, **186**, 645–647.

May, R. M. (1976). Simple mathematical models with very complicated dynamics. *Nature*, **261**, 459–467.

May, R. M. & Oster, G. F. (1976). Bifurcations and dynamic complexity in simple ecological models. *American Naturalist*, **110**, 573–599.

McCaffrey, D. F., Ellner, S. P., Gallant, A. R. & Nychka, D. W. (1992). Estimating the Lyapunov exponent of a chaotic system with nonparametric regression. *Journal of the American Statistical Association* (in press).

Metz, J. A. J. (1990). Chaos en Populatie-Biologie. *Dynamische systemen en chaos* (Ed. by H. W. Broer & F. Verhulst), pp. 320–343. Epsilon Uitgaven, Utrecht, The Netherlands (in Dutch).

Metz, J. A. J. & Diekmann, O. (1986). *The Dynamics of Physiologically Structured Populations* (Lecture Notes in Biomathematics **68**). Springer Verlag, Berlin, Germany.

Metz, J. A. J., Nisbet, R. M. & Geritz, S. A. H. (1992). How should we define 'fitness' for general ecological scenarios? *Trends in Ecology & Evolution*, **7**, 198–202.

Milligan, B. G. (1985). Evolutionary divergence and character displacement in two phenotypically variable competing species. *Evolution*, **39**, 1207–1222.

Morris, W. F. (1990). Problems detecting chaotic behaviour in natural populations by fitting simple discrete models. *Ecology*, **71**, 1849–1860.

Mueller, L. D. (1988). Density-dependent population growth and natural selection in food-limited environments: the *Drosophila* model. *American Naturalist*, **132**, 786–809.

Mueller, L. D. & Ayala, F. J. (1981). Dynamics of single-species population growth: stability or chaos. *Ecology*, **62**, 1148–1154.

Nicholson, A. J. (1954). An outline of the dynamics of natural populations. *Australian Journal of Zoology*, **2**, 9–65.

Nicholson, A. J. (1957). The self adjustment of populations to change. *Cold Spring Harbor Symposia on Quantitative Biology*, **22**, 153–173.

Nisbet, R. M., Gurney, W. S. C. & Metz, J. A. J. (1989). Stage structure models in applied evolutionary ecology. *Applied Mathematical Ecology. Lecture Notes in Biomathematics*, **18**, pp. 428–449. Springer Verlag, Berlin, Germany.

Nychka, D., Ellner, S., McCaffrey, D. & Gallant, A. R. (1992). Finding chaos in noisy systems. *Journal of the Royal Statistical Society*, B, **54**, 451–474.

Orzack, S. H. & Tuljapurkar, S. (1989). Population dynamics in variable environments. VII. The demography and evolution of iteroparity. *American Naturalist*, **133**, 901–923.

Packard, N. H., Crutchfield, J. P., Farmer, J. D. & Shaw, R. S. (1980). Geometry from a time series. *Physics Review Letters*, **45**, 712–716.

Perry, J. N. (1990). See published discussion following Godfray & Blythe (1990) *loc. cit.*.

Pianka, E. R. (1970). On *r*- and *K*-selection. *American Naturalist*, **104**, 592–596.

Prout, T. & McChesney, F. (1985). Competition among immatures affects their adult fertility: population dynamics. *American Naturalist*, **126**, 521–558.

Rand, D. A. & Wilson, H. (1992). Chaotic stochasticity: a ubiquitous source of unpredictability in epidemics. *Philosophical Transactions of the Royal Society of London*, B (in press).

Roughgarden, J. (1971). Density-dependent natural selection. *Ecology*, **52**, 453–468.

Roughgarden, J. (1979). *Theory of Population Genetics and Evolutionary Ecology*. Macmillan, New York, NY, USA.

Ruelle, D. (1989). *Chaotic Evolution and Strange Attractors*. Cambridge University Press, Cambridge, UK.

Schaffer, W. M. (1984). Stretching and folding in lynx fur returns: evidence for a strange attractor in nature? *American Naturalist*, **124**, 798–820.

Schaffer, W. M. (1985). Order and chaos in ecological systems. *Ecology*, **66**, 93–106.

Schaffer, W. M. & Kot, M. (1985a). Nearly one dimensional dynamics in an epidemic. *Journal of Theoretical Biology*, **112**, 403–427.

Schaffer, W. M. & Kot, M. (1985b). Do strange attractors govern ecological systems? *BioScience*, **35**, 342–350.

Schaffer, W. M. & Kot, M. (1986). Chaos in ecological systems: the coals that Newcastle forgot. *Trends in Ecology and Evolution*, **1**, 58–63.

Schaffer, W. M., Truty, G. L. & Fulmer, S. L. (1988). *DYNAMICAL SOFTWARE, Users Guide and Introduction to Chaotic Systems*. Vols I & II. Dynamical Systems, Tucson, Arizona, USA.

Sibly, R. M. & Calow, P. (1983). An integrated approach to life-cycle evolution using selective landscapes. *Journal of Theoretical Biology*, **102**, 527–547.

Sibly, R. M. & Calow, P. (1984). Direct and absorption costing in the evolution of life cycles. *Journal of Theoretical Biology*, **111**, 463–473.

Sibly, R. M. & Calow, P. (1987). Ecological compensation — a complication for testing life-history theory. *Journal of Theoretical Biology*, **125**, 177–186.

Slatkin, M. (1980). Ecological character displacement. *Ecology*, **61**, 163–177.

Sober, E. (1984). *The Nature of Selection*. MIT Press, Cambridge, MA, USA.

Stearns, S. C. (1976). Life history tactics: a review of the ideas. *Quarterly Review of Biology*, **51**, 3–47.

Stokes, T. K., Gurney, W. S. C., Nisbet, R. M. & Blythe, S. P. (1988). Parameter evolution in a laboratory insect population. *Theoretical Population Biology*, **33**, 248–265.

Sugihara, G. & May, R. M. (1990). Nonlinear forecasting as a way of distinguishing chaos from measurement error in time series. *Nature*, **344**, 734–741.

Sugihara, G., Grenfell, B. & May, R. M. (1990). Distinguishing error from chaos in ecological time series. *Philosophical Transactions of the Royal Society of London*, B, **330**, 235–251.

Takens, F. (1981). Detecting strange attractors in turbulence *Dynamical Systems and Turbulence* (Ed. by D. A. Rand & L. S. Young) pp. 366–381. Springer Verlag, Berlin, Federal Republic of Germany.

Taper, M. & Case, T. J. (1985). Quantitative genetic models for the evolution of character displacement. *Ecology*, **66**, 355–371.

Thomas, W. R., Pomerantz, M. J. & Gilpin, M. E. (1980). Chaos, asymmetric growth and group selection foı dynamical stability. *Ecology*, **61**, 1312–1320.

Tuljapurkar, S. (1989). An uncertain life: demography in random environments. *Theoretical Population Biology*, **35**, 227–294.

Tuljapurkar, S. (1990). *Population Dynamics in Variable Environments*. Springer Verlag, Berlin, Germany.

Turchin, P. & Taylor, A. (1992). Complex dynamics in ecological time series. *Ecology*, **73**, 289–305.

Turelli, M. & Petry, D. (1980). Density-dependent selection in a random environment: an evolutionary process that can maintain stable population dynamics. *Proceedings of the National Academy of Sciences, USA*, **77**, 7501–7505.

Wales, D. J. (1991). Calculating the rate of loss of information from chaotic time series by forecasting. *Nature*, **350**, 485–488.

Williamson, M. (1974). The analysis of discrete time cycles. *Ecological Stability* (Ed. by M. B. Usher & M. H. Williamson), pp. 17–33. Chapman & Hall, London, UK.

4. LIFE-HISTORY EVOLUTION

RICHARD SIBLY* AND JANIS ANTONOVICS[†]
**Department of Pure and Applied Zoology, University of Reading, Reading RG6 2AJ, UK and [†]Department of Botany, Duke University, Durham, North Carolina 27706, USA*

SUMMARY

The life history is a focal point for the intersection of population genetics and population ecology. Nevertheless historically life-history variation has been studied either from a 'genetic' or from an 'ecological' point of view. The genetic approach has involved a detailed analysis of selection acting on multivariate age-specific life-history components. The ecological approach has used optimality analysis to determine the life-history features that will produce the highest population growth rate in a particular environment. We make explicit the relationship between these two approaches and show them to be complementary. Optimality analysis is illustrated by considering how big offspring should be, how fast they should grow, whether they should continue to grow after first reproduction, and what size and how fecund adults should be. We discuss various approaches to testing life-history theory and the special challenges that life-history traits present to the empiricist.

INTRODUCTION

The life history, defined as the schedule of age-specific birth and death rates of a population or class of individuals, has been the focal point for the merger of the disciplines of population genetics and population ecology. This merger, a belated evolutionary synthesis (Anderson & King 1970, Charlesworth & Giesel 1972a, b), converted the subject of ecological genetics from a discipline that simply studied genetic variation in an ecological (and by implication natural) context (Ford 1964), to a discipline that promised truly to integrate ecological and evolutionary thinking. The life history was an expression of fitness of a phenotype in the context of natural selection as well as an expression of the contribution of that class of phenotypes to population growth. Theoretical studies (e.g. Charlesworth & Giesel 1972a, b) showed clearly that the relative fitness of genotypes could depend critically on population growth rates, and that population growth rates could be influenced by genotypic composition (King & Anderson 1971).

In an ideal world, all individuals should have an infinite number of offspring which have an infinite life span and which reproduce as soon as they are born! The biological reality is that different species have widely divergent life histories, and once this obvious fact was pointed out by Deevey (1947), the life history and the forces that mould its evolution became an object of fascination and study. This generated a research agenda that has lasted to the present day. Much of this fascination was fuelled by Cole's (1954) paper, which presented the now famous but by no means irresolvable dilemma that the fitness of an annual (semelparous) species will be equal to the fitness of a perennial (iteroparous) species if it produced one extra offspring. This made it hard to see why perennials would ever evolve.

In spite of these seminal papers, very little theoretical progress in understanding life-history evolution was made until the development of the ideas of r- and K-selection by MacArthur (1962). His theory integrated genetic and ecological ideas in that it was based on genetic variation in the parameters of the logistic population growth equation. He showed in populations obeying logistic growth dynamics, that under low density, genotypes with high r would be favoured, but that at high density, i.e. at carrying capacity, r was now irrelevant and that genotypes with high K would be favoured. Given a trade-off between high fecundity at low density and high performance in resource-limited conditions of high density, it was easy to see that organisms may indeed evolve quite different life histories.

The prospect of being able to explain life-history evolution by the $r-K$ continuum was a seductive one but the idea rapidly gained as many opponents as converts. At one level the theory fits what we know about the world (weeds versus trees, aphids versus elephants) but at the same time it was clearly over-simplified. A number of other classificatory schemes for life histories were therefore developed. However, because of the multitude of selective forces acting on life histories and the diversity of responses by different organisms to similar forces, none of these schemes has gained general acceptance (see Southwood 1988, for a review of 'ecological periodic tables').

Since the 1970s numerous approaches have been used to model life history evolution. The raw genetic approach is to use explicit single-locus or two-locus genetic models, where genotypes are assigned life-history schedules of births and deaths; this permits exploration of the dynamics of gene frequency change and equilibrium outcomes (e.g. Anderson &

King 1970). This approach can be extended to a quantitative genetics scenario, where now the life-history traits are described by a genetic variance–covariance matrix, and evolutionary trajectories are explored under different types and intensities of selection (e.g. Lande 1982). A very common method has been to compare the intrinsic rates of increase of contrasting life-history phenotypes, and to ask under what circumstances a particular phenotype will have the highest increase (e.g. Bell 1980). A similar approach is to use some form of options set or trade-off surface (see later) to predict which combination of life-history parameters will have the highest fitness under particular circumstances (e.g. Pianka & Parker 1975). Such ecological models are seemingly gene free but they can be conceptually grounded in genetic models given some not unreasonable assumptions. An explicit mathematical reconciliation of the optimality and quantitative genetics approaches has recently been described by Charlesworth (1990); such a reconciliation is dependent on weak selection and trade-off curves that can as a first approximation be treated as linear functions.

Not only has it come to be appreciated that the processes of life history evolution are diverse but the theoretical approaches taken by ecologists and geneticists in trying to understand life-history evolution have also been wide ranging (e.g. Schaffer 1974a, b, Lande 1982). The ecologists have focused on asking which specific life histories might produce higher population growth rates in which environments, and they have considered trade-offs among life-history processes as the inevitable outcome of individual limits to resource acquisition and allocation of these limited resources to competing physiological functions. The geneticists on the other hand have viewed life-history evolution as the result of selection of alleles with age-specific effects; they have considered trade-offs to be due to pleiotropic gene effects within populations that produced genetic covariances among traits that constrained the joint evolution of multiple (life history) character states. It is almost as if ecologists viewed the life history as a property of a population and trade-offs as a property of an individual, whereas the geneticists saw the life history as a property of individual alleles and trade-offs as a property of the population in which those alleles resided. These two approaches, for want of better terms we shall call the 'ecological approach' and the 'genetic approach'.

To understand the relationship between ecological and genetic approaches to life-history evolution, we begin by describing in the next section how the rate of increase of an allele depends on its effects on life-history components. We then describe how such a population genetic approach relates to optimality theories based on trade-off curves and fitness functions. We illustrate the optimality approach by considering some general predictions of life-history theory. In the last section we discuss explicitly how life-history theory is testable but also emphasize why life-history evolution presents unique challenges for the empiricist.

EVOLUTION: PROCESS AND OUTCOME

We start our analysis by considering what happens in asexual populations because in this case there is a direct link with population dynamics in the concept of the rate of increase of a population. Later we proceed to the sexual case, which we introduce with a simple graphical approach (Figs 4.1 and 4.2).

Ecologists have traditionally translated the overall age-specific survivorship and fecundity schedules of individuals into estimates of intrinsic rates of increase of the population, r, using the Euler–Lotka equation:

$$1 = \sum_{x=1}^{\infty} n(x)l(x)e^{-rx}$$

where $n(x)$, $l(x)$ are the female age (x) specific fecundity and survival respectively.

If we consider any population as a collection of genotypes, each with its own age-specific life-history characteristics, and *for the moment assume that these genotypes are asexual*, then the intrinsic rate of increase of the ij^{th} genotype would be given by:

$$1 = \sum_{x=1}^{\infty} n_{ij}(x)l_{ij}(x)e^{-r_{ij}x} \qquad (1)$$

The absolute fitness of the ij^{th} genotype would be $\lambda_{ij} = e^{r_{ij}}$, which can easily be relativized to the most fit genotype to give the more traditional relative fitnesses of population genetics. However, this parallel between the ecological and genetic approaches is based on a large number of assumptions, the most important being that the genotypes are asexual. If the genotypes are interbreeding, then there will be Mendelian assortment of genes every generation.

Before proceeding to the algebraic treatment of what happens in sexual populations, consider Fig. 4.1, which provides a simple graphical account of the main ideas. The evolutionary process is envisaged, put very simply, as consisting of the creation (by mutation) of new alleles, which either displace or are displaced by their counterparts. In Fig. 4.1, alleles A–E affect two life-history traits of carriers. Note that most individuals carry the A allele in Fig. 4.1a and so have small values of both

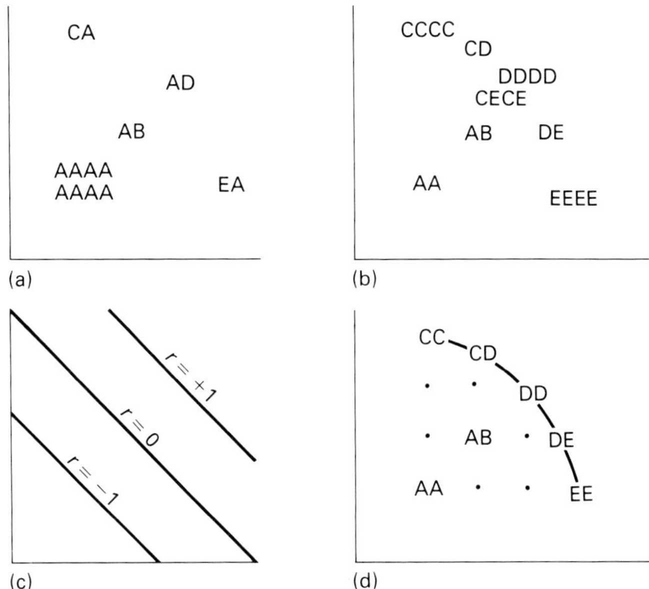

FIG. 4.1. Simple example of an evolutionary process. Axes represent two life-history traits. Note that the alleles far from the origin (C–E) have increased in numbers between (a) and (b) whereas those near the origin (A) have decreased. Per copy rates of increase (i.e. fitnesses) are shown in (c). The extant genetic options set with genotypes obtainable by recombination represented as dots is shown in (d). The boundary of the options set is the trade-off curve (thick line). See text for further details.

traits, but a few individuals have larger values so that overall there is a small positive correlation between individuals. If there is not much environmental variation, this reflects a positive genetic correlation (e.g. the two traits are correlated because they are determined by alleles that have an effect on the magnitude of both traits).

Figure 4.1b represents a hypothetical situation at some later time in the selection process. Now most of the small-trait A alleles have disappeared but the numbers of the large-trait alleles (C–E) have increased. Furthermore, the genetic correlation between individuals is now negative, whereas earlier it was positive. Empirical evidence for such a scenario has been given by Holloway *et al.* (1990).

Clearly all depends on whether or not an allele spreads in the population — i.e. on the rates of increase of the alleles (called *fitness* hereafter). Since these depend on their effects on life histories, they can be plotted out in the space of Fig. 4.1, as shown in Fig. 4.1c. In our example the small-trait alleles have negative rates of increase, corresponding to their decline in the population, whereas the large-trait alleles have positive rates of increase, since they are spreading. Evolutionary change can also occur, however, if both small- and large-trait alleles increase but at different rates.

In general, as selection proceeds, the cloud of points in Fig. 4.1 changes shape. In the absence of environmental variation, the shape of the cloud is measured by genetic correlations and variances (i.e. the G matrix) and as the cloud changes shape, the genetic correlations and variances change accordingly. In the absence of further mutation, where would this process end up?

In considering the eventual outcome of this selection process it is natural to restrict attention to a constant environment, or one in which the environmental variation is specified by constant parameters (e.g. randomly changing or cycling annually). It is important to realize that the environment of an individual depends not only on physical features (e.g. temperature, rainfall) and biotic features determined by other species (e.g. food availability, predation) but also has characteristics determined by conspecifics, such as territory size, availability of mates, competition for food and so on.

In this environment many alleles will affect life-history components. Plotting out all these genetically-codable options (including all possible recombinants) in a space like that of Fig. 4.1a gives us a set of points we shall call the *extant genetic options set* (Fig. 4.1d). However, the evolutionary process is a dynamic one, and we consider that there also exists for any population (or set of populations) within any time scale a *potential genetic options set* which represents what is possible given mutation and recombination. When considering different genetic possibilities, care is needed in saying what we mean by the 'study organism' — how far are we allowed to change it before it is no longer the same organism (Maynard Smith 1991)? Technically this is the same problem as specifying the set of alleles defining a species. The potential genetic options set has also been variously referred to as a 'strategy set' (Parker & Maynard Smith 1990) or as a 'fitness set' when the traits contribute linearly and equally to fitness (e.g. Charnov 1982).

A three-dimensional example of an options set is shown in Fig. 4.2a. We will not here distinguish between a genotype options set (as in Fig. 4.1d) and an allele options set, representing the average characteristics of each allele, but note that the type of options set should match the fitness accounting system, so either both should use alleles, or both should use genotypes.

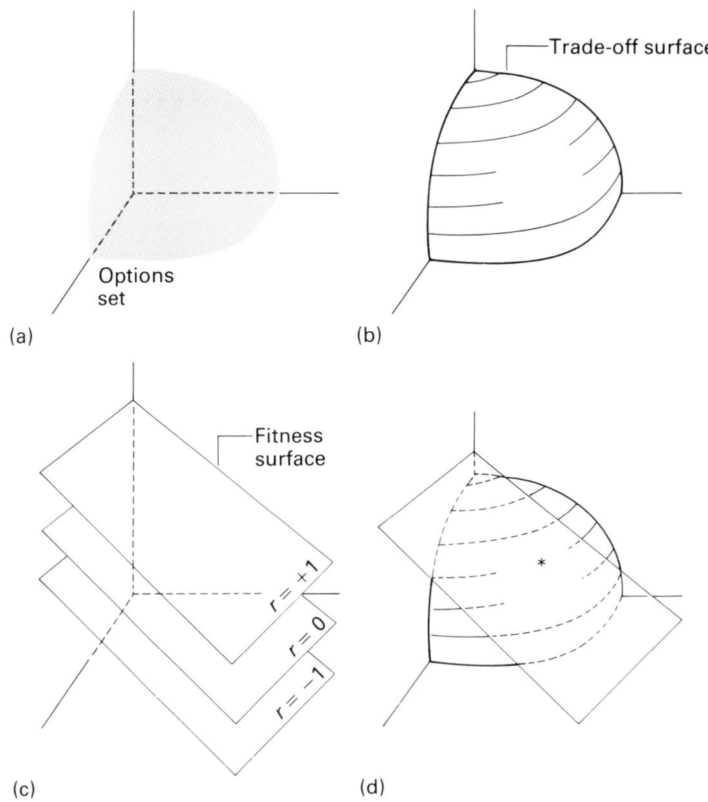

FIG. 4.2. The options set in three dimensions. (a) The options set comprises a volume. (b) The boundary of the options set is a trade-off surface. (c) Points giving equal fitness r now form surfaces (cf. Fig. 4.1c). (d) The outcome of selection — i.e. the optimal strategy — is the point (*) in the options set giving the highest fitness in the study environment.

Of particular interest, because it limits selection, is the boundary of the options set. We shall call this the *trade-off curve* (two dimensions) or *trade-off surface* (three dimensions) or, in general, the *trade-off hypersurface* (n dimensions) (Fig. 4.2b). This trade-off (hyper)surface represents the best that this type of organism can achieve genetically in the study environment.

Putting together the information about fitness (Figs 4.1c and 4.2c) with the information on options sets (Figs 4.2a and b) the optimal strategy is readily identified (Fig. 4.2d) as that having the highest fitness in the study environment. This point, then, represents the eventual outcome of selection in this environment.

For short-term evolutionary predictions within local populations, the fitness surfaces together with the extant genetic options set as defined by the genetic variance–covariance matrix will determine the evolutionary trajectories. On the other hand if we wish to make predictions over a longer term, and/or for example, within a taxonomic group, there may be no direct method of estimating the potential options set (indeed, it may be in a strict sense 'unknowable', given the stochasticity of mutational events). However, within a particular taxonomic group, a number of aspects of the physiology and ecology of the group may be relatively invariant, thus allowing us to infer the likely shape of the trade-off surface. We can now caricature more precisely the views of the 'geneticist' and the 'ecologist' as to what a trade-off represents. For the geneticist, it is a population property because the trade-off is measured on an extant options set. The ecologist, on the other hand, views the trade-off in terms of the potential options set, best estimated by understanding the 'underlying physiology' of the individual. Such within-individual trade-offs must, however, have implications for the shape of the genetic options set (Smith *et al.* 1987, Partridge & Sibly 1991, Smith 1991).

In this section we have made a distinction between the process and the outcome of selection. This makes explicit the relationship between quantitative genetics, which models the process, and optimality theory (ecology) which locates the outcome of the selection process.

In the next section we give algebraic form to some of these ideas.

How fitness (rate of increase) depends on life-history components

As we have seen, whether or not an allele is able to spread in a population depends on its rate of increase. Suppose that at some locus there are only two alleles, A_1 and A_2, in proportions p and q, with $p + q = 1$. Then the rate of increase of the proportion of A_1 is $\mathrm{d}p/\mathrm{d}t$. How is gene frequency change related to the life-history characteristics of the two genotypes in which the A_1 allele occurs, namely A_1A_1 and A_1A_2? The solution was given by Charlesworth (1980). The first step is to define the age-specific life-history characteristics of each genotype (Fig. 4.3a); thus let $l_{ij}(x)$ be the chance of survival from birth to age x of individuals of the ij genotype (i.e. here A_1A_1, A_1A_2 or A_2A_2), and let $n_{ij}(x)$ be the expected number of daughters at age x. Intrinsic rate of increase of the ij genotype is then defined as the number, r_{ij}, which solves the Euler–Lotka (Eqn 1). We assume that the sexes have identical life histories and that the life-history characteristics do not change with allele frequencies (otherwise the formulations are more complex: Charlesworth 1980, Abugov 1988).

Charlesworth (1980, p. 206) showed that under weak selection the proportionate rate of increase of A_1 is given approximately by:

$$dp/dt = pq(pr_{11} + (q - p)r_{12} - qr_{22}) \qquad (2)$$

Examining Eqn (2), we now ask, what causes dp/dt to increase, or in other words what causes A_1 to spread faster? Clearly anything increasing r_{11} will. When r_{12} is increased but r_{11} and r_{22} are unaffected dp/dt is increased when A_1 is rare ($p \simeq 0$), so A_1 will spread. However, if A_1 were ever to approach fixation, it would be selected against, since then $q \simeq 0$, and dp/dt is decreased. Thus A_2, not A_1, then spreads because of 'heterozygous advantage'.

Therefore, a new mutant will spread in the population (at least initially) if it results in a greater intrinsic rate of increase of the genotypes which now carry it. Intrinsic rate of increase, defined as in Eqn (1), therefore provides a measure of genotypic fitness.

A similar approach, but one which simplifies some of the calculations by restricting attention to dominant alleles, was suggested by Sibly and Calow (1986, see Sibly & Curnow, in press). In this case the life history of the heterozygote is the same as that of the homozygote, and it turns out that an allele's per copy rate of increase (hereafter called allelic fitness) is given by r in an equation looking like Eqn (1), viz.

$$1 = \tfrac{1}{2} \sum_{x=1}^{\infty} n(x)\ l(x)\ e^{-rx} \qquad (3)$$

where $l(x)$ and $n(x)$ are characteristics of individuals carrying the allele: $l(x)$ is the chance of carriers surviving from birth to age t, and $n(x)$ is the number of offspring at age x (Sibly 1989). In Eqn (3) the $\frac{1}{2}$ represents the chance of a given allele being transferred from parent to offspring: a given allele is transferred to half the offspring on average by Mendel's laws. However, if segregration is distorted, for example by meiotic drive, or if there is selfing, the $\frac{1}{2}$ should be adjusted appropriately. Although A_2 is contained in the heterozygote and it might seem that the per copy rate of increase of A_1 would depend on the genotypes carrying it, with dominance one can show it is not necessary to take into account the frequency of A_2.

An attraction of this approach is that general life histories can be handled directly — examples are given in Fig. 4.3. Note that although genotypic and allelic fitnesses are interchangeable for some purposes, they may not be interchangeable when timing of the life history is affected as in some of the models in Fig. 4.3, since genotypic equivalents have not been derived for all the allelic treatments. In Fig. 4.3b, the timing of the

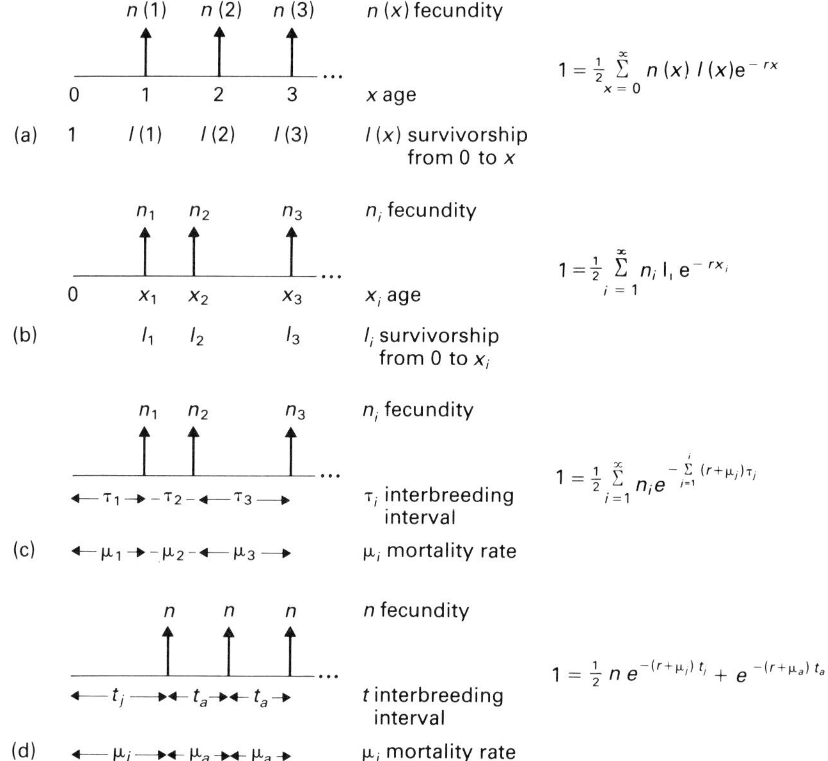

FIG. 4.3. The life histories and associated equations discussed in the text. (a) Life history with regular breeding. (b) Life history with irregular breeding. (c) Reparameterization of (b) to obtain independent variables τ and μ. (d) Simple regular life history in which parameters vary between juvenile, j, and adult, a, phases.

different breeding episodes is now one of the key life-history variables, allowing consideration of irregular breeding, which cannot be handled within the framework of Fig. 4.3a. The modified form of the Euler–Lotka equation is shown on the right of Fig. 4.3b.

The parameterization of the life history shown in Fig. 4.3b suffers from the disadvantage that the parameters are not independent of each other. Thus the timing of the ith breeding event (x_i) is likely to depend on the timing of the $(i-1)^{\text{th}}$ event — if that is delayed, there are likely to be effects for subsequent reproduction. Similarly l_i, the probability of survival from birth until the ith breeding attempt, obviously depends on when the ith breeding attempt occurs — if it is delayed, the chances of survival are reduced because of extrinsic mortality. Furthermore, survivorship to the

i^{th} breeding attempt depends on survivorship to the $(i-1)^{th}$ breeding attempt, and so on. Thus the l_i variables are not independent of each other either. Both these problems can be circumvented by replacing the x and l variables by a set of independent variables τ and μ defined as in Fig. 4.3c. The mortality rates μ are independent of each other, and in the absence of trade-offs they are independent of the timing of breeding events.

We shall later consider in some detail the case in which adult characteristics do not change after the age of first reproduction. The resultant life history and associated equation are shown in Fig. 4.3d.

In principle the fitness of alleles in organisms such as plants which use both sexual and vegetative reproduction can be handled by methods similar to those shown in Fig. 4.3 (Sibly 1989).

The above life-history components can be divided into two categories: those that depend on rate of production of new biomass and those that affect the survival of that biomass. We can call these 'production rate' (Sibly & Calow 1986) and 'mortality rate' variables. For example, production rate affects age to first reproduction, offspring size, fecundity and interval between breeding. In this way the timing and extent of reproduction are determined by production rate. The remaining life-history components represent mortality rates, μ_i defined as in Fig. 4.3c. It is interesting to note that mortality rate always appears in the equations added to r.

Using the above formulation it is easy to show that in the absence of trade-offs there is always selection to increase fecundity, decrease mortality rate and breed early (Sibly 1989). In the next section we outline what happens when trade-offs occur, using the concepts of genetic options sets and fitness surfaces to illustrate the richness of life-history theory and the diversity of possible evolutionary outcomes, following the general approach of Sibly and Calow (1986). We go through an organism's life history, and consider the types of forces that might mould offspring size, juvenile growth rate, post-reproductive growth, adult size and adult fecundity. We then illustrate how this approach can be extended to considerations of sex allocation involving extension of the models to frequency-dependent processes.

TRADE-OFFS BETWEEN LIFE-HISTORY COMPONENTS

Limits to life history evolution are obviously set by the fact that organisms cannot, to any large degree, simultaneously increase their fecundity, decrease their mortality and decrease the age at reproduction. There are trade-offs between these (and other) aspects of the life history. Trade-offs are often viewed by ecologists as the inevitable consequence of the physiological and behavioural allocations of an individual. Thus, resources can be allocated to growth or reproduction, or resources devoted to reproduction can be partitioned among a few large offspring or many small offspring; time spent handling prey items will be at a cost to time spent foraging; and so on. Functional relationships between life-history traits will almost certainly be evident whenever these traits vary. For present purposes we assume that each such trade-off has a genetic basis and we present an optimality analysis for the life history in Fig. 4.3d.

How big should offspring be?

The product of offspring size and offspring numbers is here taken to be fixed (equal to 'reproductive effort'). Offspring size can affect a number of life-history characters, for example juvenile mortality rate (Taylor & Williams 1984) but here we consider only development period (i.e. time to first reproduction). If we assume that size at first reproduction is fixed, then there will be a trade-off between offspring size and juvenile development period, since smaller offspring have further to grow (Fig. 4.4). Fitness contours can be calculated from the equation in Fig. 4.3c or d and have slope $-1/(r + \mu_j)$ (Sibly & Calow 1985). Optimal offspring size is the point where one such line touches the trade-off curve (starred in

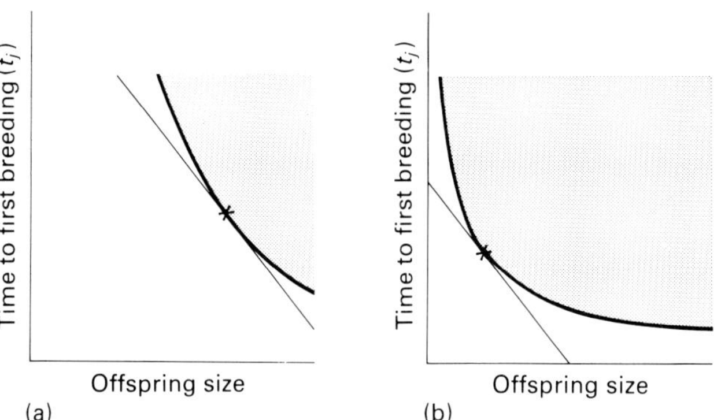

FIG. 4.4. The trade-off curve (thick line) relating offspring size to development period t_j in an environment with (a) low and (b) high production rate. In this and subsequent figures shaded areas represent genetic option sets, thick lines represent trade-off curves, thin lines represent contours and * represents the selection outcome (optimal strategy). See text for further details.

Fig. 4.4). One of the most interesting applications of this result is to use it to compare optimal strategies in habitats differing in production rate. Suppose the trade-off in Fig. 4.4a represented the situation when production rate was low and consider the likely changes if production rate was increased (Fig. 4.4b). Note that the trade-off in the good habitat is everywhere below and steeper than that in the poor one (Sibly & Calow 1985). Assuming for simplicity that μ_j is the same in the two habitats and that ecological compensation (by other components of the life history, Sibly & Calow 1987) has resulted in r also being the same (e.g. zero), then it is easy to see that optimal offspring size in the good habitat is smaller than that in the poor (Fig. 4.4, Sibly & Calow 1985). In this way, if trade-offs with mortality are not involved, the effect of the habitat on production rate will determine offspring size, with smaller offspring being produced where production rate is higher.

How fast to grow?

After birth a variety of growth strategies may be possible but this may also affect the risks that the individual takes and hence the mortality rate. Thus it may be possible for animals to increase production rate by feeding more at increased cost in terms of personal safety, or for better quality food in more dangerous places or at more dangerous times of day. Alternatively, resources may be allocated to personal defence which could otherwise have gone to production. Thus energy, nutrient or water reserves may help avoid starvation or desiccation. Other examples would include thorns, toxins, protective coloration, or immune and detoxification systems. The relationships between mortality and allocation to defence can be plotted as an options set in a space with axes mortality rate and growth rate, and a trade-off curve defined as the boundary of such a set (Fig. 4.5). The resultant curve has the features that: (1) even when growth rate is maximal (zero allocation to defence) growth rate is finite — equal to the limiting production rate in the study environment; (2) even if all resources are allocated to defence, mortality rate is still greater than zero, equivalent to the 'extrinsic' mortality rate in that environment. The simplest shape the trade-off curve can take is therefore that shown in Fig. 4.5, i.e. convex seen from below. The $r = 0$ fitness contour is a straight line through the origin (Sibly & Calow 1989).

What happens to the optimal strategy if the production or mortality regimes change? In general, such changes will change the shape as well as the position of the trade-off curve, but since we lack insight into how shape might change, we shall hold shape constant for the purposes of

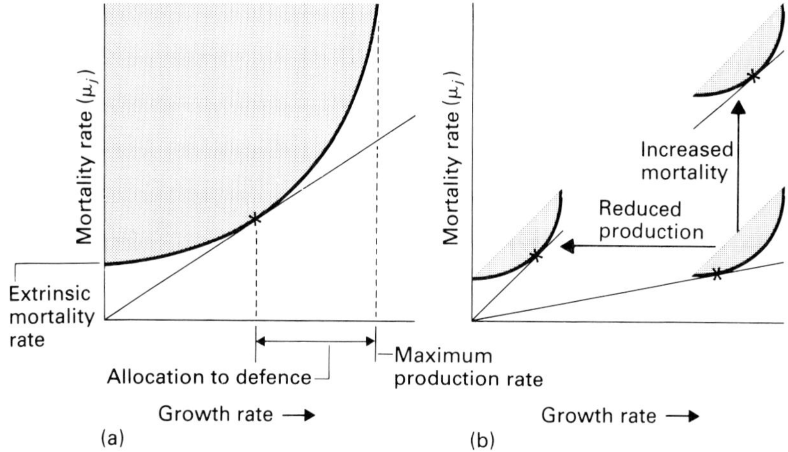

FIG. 4.5. (a) Allocation of resources to defence reduces mortality rate but simultaneously cuts growth, here defined as $1/t_j$, i.e. growth rate is inverse time to first reproduction. The $r = 0$ fitness contour is a straight line through the origin. (b) If only the position of the trade-off curve is changed, by reducing maximum production or increasing mortality rate, the effect on optimal strategy is a reduced allocation to defence. See text for further details.

discussion. Allowing only the position of the trade-off curve to change, it is clear that increasing (extrinsic) mortality rate moves the curve vertically upwards, whereas decreasing production rate moves the curve horizontally to the left (Fig. 4.5b). Assuming ecological compensation acts elsewhere in the life history to keep r zero in all three situations, the optimal strategy lies in each case on a straight line through the origin (Fig. 4.5b). Thus, either sort of worsening of the environment (increasing mortality or decreasing production) results in a reduced optimal allocation to defence.

Should organisms continue to grow after first reproduction?

This is one of the classical problems of life-history theory: if production and mortality rates depend solely on body size, and if maximum life span is given, then what is the optimal size at first reproduction, and how (if at all) should the organism grow thereafter? It is usually assumed that production is split between growth and reproduction, and that birth rate and specific growth rate are linearly proportional to their allocations from production. Analyses so far include infinite life span models with general production and mortality regimes (e.g. Taylor *et al.* 1974 and Sibly *et al.* 1985), and models with limited life span but no size-dependent mortality (Ziolko & Kozlowski 1983). These analyses concluded that generally fixed adult size is optimal, i.e. growth followed by reproduction, with no intermediate phase of simultaneous reproduction and growth. These conclusions are surprising given the ubiquity of growth after first reproduction in nature (but see also Gabriel (1982), who used numerical methods to show that intermediate strategies could be optimal if life span was finite and both production and mortality rates increased with size, and see also Kozlowski (1991), Pugliese and Kozlowski (1990) and Taylor and Gabriel (1992)).

From now on we assume for simplicity that there is no growth after first reproduction.

What size adults?

Now suppose that egg size is fixed so that, since it necessarily takes longer to grow to be bigger, larger adult size can only be achieved at the cost of a longer development period. As noted above, in the absence of trade-offs there is always selection to minimize development period, and hence adult size. Thus in the absence of trade-offs, adults should be as small as possible.

What usually prevents this happening in practice is a trade-off that arises because larger adults are more fecund. This produces a trade-off between development period and fecundity, as shown in Fig. 4.6a. If the options set is known, optimal body size can be readily identified.

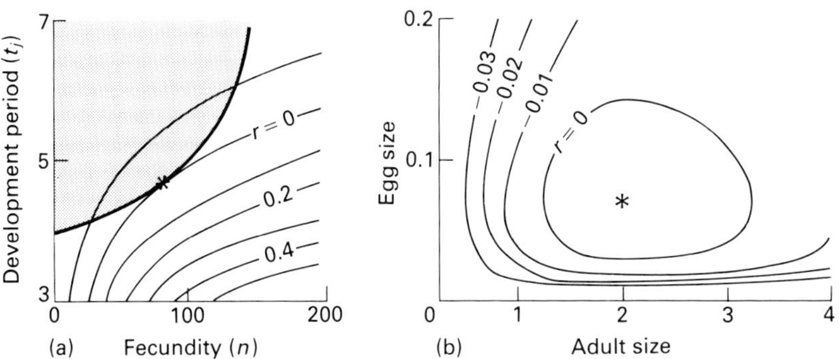

FIG. 4.6. Calculation of adult body size with offspring size fixed (a) or allowed to vary (b). Larger adults are more fecund but take longer to develop, so fecundity trades off against development period (a) (from Sibly *et al.* 1985). To construct the example in (b) it was supposed that $n\times$(egg size) = $(1-\exp(-0.3\times$(adult size)) and that t_j = (adult size) + $0.5(\log_e$(egg size)$)^2$ + 2.

What happens if both egg size and adult size are allowed to vary? Both have consequences for development period. A simple example to illustrate what might happen is shown in Fig. 4.6b.

How fecund?

A classic problem in life-history theory concerns the number of offspring to produce in the case that increased fecundity results in an increase in post-reproductive adult mortality. Other costs of reproduction, perhaps more serious in practice, but not considered here, include delays and decreases in subsequent reproduction (see for example, Lessells 1991). Also important, and also not treated here, is the Lack case in which number of offspring trade off against their individual survivorship, in species with parental care (Lack 1954, Nur 1984).

Certain features of the curve specifying the trade-off between fecundity and mortality can be deduced *a priori*. Even when fecundity is nil, mortality must be greater than zero (extrinsic mortality), but maximum fecundity is finite, and then, since all resources are devoted to reproduction, no resources are left for maintenance, so the organism dies (i.e. infinite mortality rate). Hence the options set is likely to be convex (Fig. 4.7). In this case there is no very easy way to find the optimal strategy. However, the optimal strategy can be characterized by a differential equation:

$$\frac{\delta\mu_a}{\delta n} = \frac{S_j}{t_a S_a} e^{-rt_j + rt_a} \tag{4}$$

where μ_a, S_a and t_a represent adult mortality rate, survivorship between breedings and interval between breedings respectively; t_j represents age

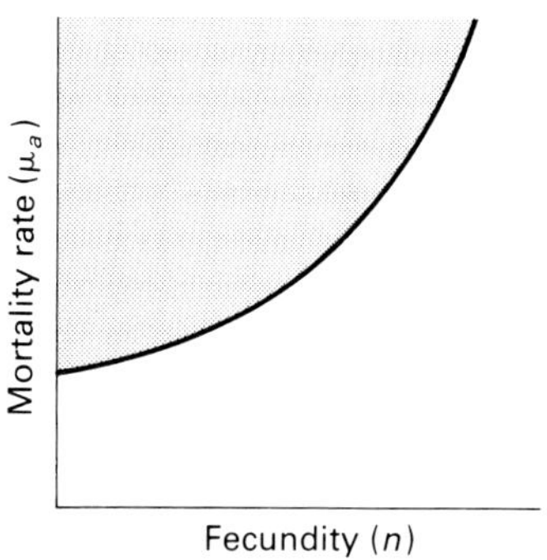

FIG. 4.7. The classic cost of reproduction trade-off.

at first reproduction, and S_j is survivorship to first reproduction (model of Fig. 4.3d).

What happens if the production or mortality regime changes? Keep, as ever, the shape of the trade-off curve constant (for simplicity) and consider comparisons made with $r = 0$. Ecological compensation is unusually difficult to take into account because so many life-history components have an effect on the optimal strategy (Eqn (4), Sibly & Calow 1987). For example if S_j is better in one environment, then to keep $r = 0$, if n were unchanged, S_a must decrease. These complications can, however, be handled mathematically, and the conclusion is that however ecological compensation acts (through extrinsic adult mortality or t_a) the result is the same: selection acts to increase n if S_j/t_aS_a is increased (Sibly & Calow 1987). Thus, environments that offer higher S_j/t_aS_a, through an improvement in either production or mortality, select for increased fecundity, i.e. towards semelparity.

Male and female, or hermaphrodite?

The approach developed so far is quite general and can be applied directly to sex-allocation theory, as developed principally by Charnov (1982). We illustrate this in the next two sections.

Given two types of gamete (sperm and eggs), it is easy to imagine that their production requires specialist structures, which may be carried by all individuals (hermaphrodites, monoecious) or may alternatively be more efficiently carried by specialized individuals (males/females, dioecious). This may be examined formally by considering whether a given individual should be male or female or both (hermaphrodite), and whether gender should be constant or change through life, and if so when? The modern approach to these questions was pioneered by E.O. Charnov in the 1970s and is synthesized in his 1982 book. Suppose the options set is concave (Fig. 4.8a) so that more offspring are obtained by single-sex individuals than by hermaphrodites. It is easy to imagine this coming about as a result of advantages of specialization. For example, since only one type of reproductive organ needs to be built, the costs of building the other type are saved by specialists. Hermaphrodites, by contrast, have to pay the costs of building and maintaining both male and female organs. Since fitness depends on the total number of offspring produced, fitness contours are straight lines with slope -1, and so the optimal strategies are to be either male or female. On the other hand, if the options set was convex (Fig. 4.8b) the optimal strategy would be hermaphrodite.

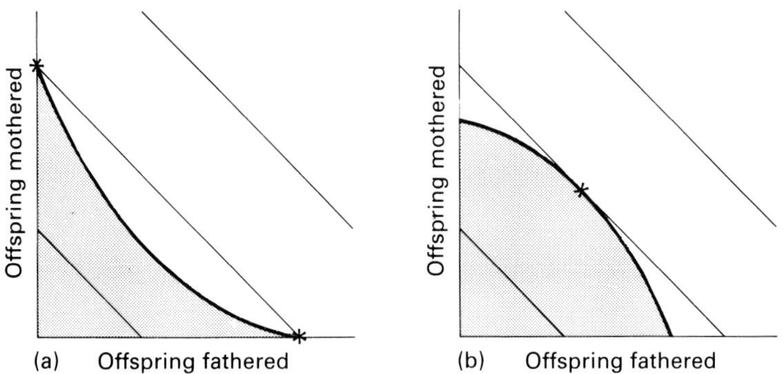

Fig. 4.8. Options sets for hermaphrodites. Offspring fathered is the number of offspring to which sperm have been contributed via male organs. Offspring mothered is defined analogously. A concave options set (a) has twin optima corresponding to dioecy whereas a convex options set (b) has a single optimum corresponding to hermaphroditism. (After Charnov 1982 and Maynard Smith 1989).

The analysis can be extended to consider when to change sex by changing the axes in Fig. 4.8 so that the x-axis now represents the number of offspring fathered in the male part of the life history, and the y-axis the number mothered in the female part. The options set now shows the consequences of spending different amounts of time as a male — the longer spent, the more offspring fathered, and so on. The optimality analysis proceeds as before. Sex change is advantageous if the options set is convex as in Fig. 4.8b, but not if the options set is concave, as in Fig. 4.8a.

Accepting the form of reproductive system is now chosen, we continue the analysis of life history by considering the allocation of resources between sons and daughters in the two-sex system.

Sons or daughters?

This is one of the classic trade-offs first considered by Fisher (1930). If sons and daughters cost the same to produce, in terms of resources, then the trade-off between them is linear (Fig. 4.9a). What then is the optimal ratio of sons to daughters? The answer depends on whether sons or daughters can be expected to pass on more alleles to future generations. Suppose an allele causing mothers to produce only sons spreads initially — this could not continue for long, since a very fundamental feedback operates against such alleles. If initially successful, they thereby tip the balance of advantage against themselves. This comes about because

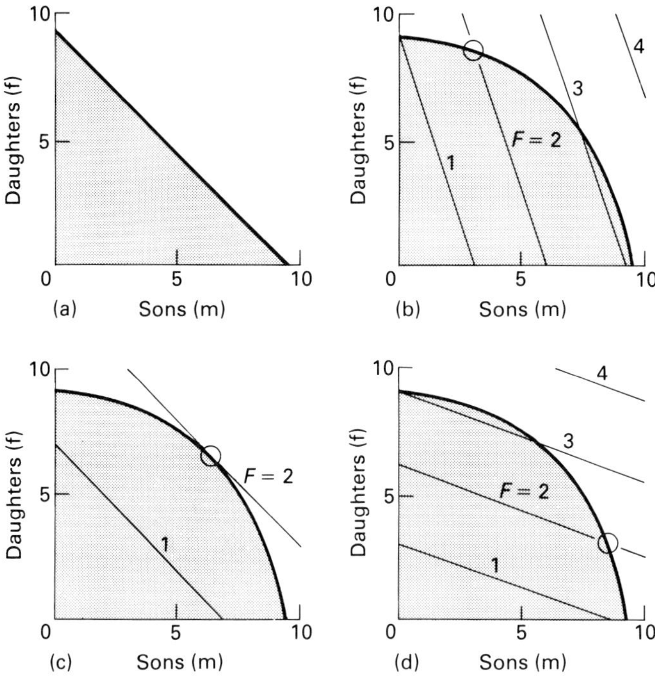

FIG. 4.9. Trade-off constraining offspring production. Sons can theoretically be traded for daughters on a one-to-one basis if they cost the same (a). (b)–(d) show a convex options set with fitness contours from Eqn (5) giving the fitness of a rare mutant. ○ represents the population strategy (m', f'). See text for discussion.

after their initial success there are more breeding males than females in the population, so the success of males becomes lower than that of females. Resources invested in sons would then be more profitably invested in daughters and alleles that do not make sons are favoured over those that do.

The argument can be formalized using fitness contours calculated using the Shaw–Mohler equation (Charnov 1982, p. 14) for the fitness of a rare mutant producing m sons and f daughters:

$$\text{fitness} = \frac{m}{m'} + \frac{f}{f'} \tag{5}$$

where m' and f' are the numbers of sons and daughters, respectively, produced by individuals not carrying the mutant allele. Fitness contours are shown in Fig. 4.9b–d for a non-linear trade-off curve (application to the linear case is discussed by Charnov 1982, p. 14). In the case shown in

Fig. 4.9b, where there are more females than males in the population, mutants producing more sons have higher fitness. The converse holds in Fig. 4.9d. Only in Fig. 4.9c, where the fitness contours are parallel to the options set, do mutants have lower fitness than non-mutants. Note that both the fitness contours and the direction of selection are frequency dependent. Only the situation in Fig. 4.9c is evolutionarily stable (*sensu* Maynard Smith 1982). For a recent review of the topics covered in the last two subsections see Frank (1990).

General patterns of productivity and mortality

In this section we have distinguished two types of life-history variable — production variables and mortality variables. We have analysed what happens when they are traded off against each other, and we have considered the impact of production stress and mortality stress. Throughout we have taken some account of the basic requirement of existence, that, put simply, production has to balance mortality. Do any general life-history patterns emerge?

In the search for general patterns, consider first the case that extrinsic mortality is low throughout life. This might be true of some top carnivores, for example. If mortality rate is low, then production rate must be low too, to balance the low mortality rate. What offspring size is favoured by selection if both production and mortality rates are low? Low production implies low growth rate, and with juvenile mortality rate also low, selection favours offspring about as large as possible, and offspring produced one at a time (Fig. 4.4). This is a feature of many top carnivores, from freshwater flatworms to albatrosses. The prediction does, however, need formal testing.

Next, what growth rate of juveniles is favoured? Should resources be allocated to defence or should juveniles grow as fast as possible? Since production rate is low, relatively low allocation to defence is favoured (Fig. 4.5b), and juveniles are therefore expected to grow nearly as fast as possible — though limited, of course, by low production rate.

Will the organism be semelparous or iteroparous? Semelparity can here be ruled out on other grounds — if only one offspring is produced at a time a semelparous population could not sustain itself. Fixed-size populations with unit fecundity are necessarily iteroparous. Furthermore, since fecundity is already fixed, at one, no further analysis of the cost of reproduction trade-off is needed.

The above has dealt with the case in which extrinsic mortality is low. If extrinsic mortality is higher, for example as a result of transplanting the population to a new environment, production rate must also be higher if the population persists, and now selection favours smaller offspring. Allocation to defence is again expected to be relatively low (Fig. 4.5b) though the rationale this time is the existence of mortality stress (as opposed to production stress, before). The reproductive strategy is not this time constrained, and could be either semelparous or iteroparous, but in predicting which, ecological compensation has to be taken into account. All the above assumes the shapes, though not the positions, of the trade-off curves are invariant.

TESTING LIFE-HISTORY THEORY

Over the past 20 years, empirical and theoretical studies of life histories and their evolution have generated a body of broad and generally accepted knowledge that may be termed 'life-history theory'. The main achievement of this theory has been to answer the question posed by Deevey in the 1940s, namely, how do diverse life histories arise and what is their selective significance. However, while some answers have been given to the 'how possibly' questions of life-history evolution, a much more difficult task is to answer the 'how actually' question, i.e. whether the process posited by a model has actually occurred, or is occurring, in a group of organisms. As we will see, this problem is particularly challenging given the difficulty of measuring life histories, their sensitivity to environmental conditions, and the closeness of life-history traits to fitness itself.

A model of a biological process can be 'tested' in two ways. One way is to demonstrate that the assumptions of the model are met for many (or several) biological situations, i.e. that the phenomena and processes posited in the model actually occur. The other way is to test the model's predictions, i.e. that given a range of starting conditions the outcomes of the hypothesized process are actually as expected. Clearly, both types of test are desirable. Assumptions may be met but other unknown forces may impinge on the process; or outcomes may be correct but for the wrong reasons. When we are dealing with evolutionary predictions about outcomes, we can study these outcomes either at a 'microevolutionary' level (i.e. by looking at evolution as an ongoing phenomenon in present-day populations) or at a 'macroevolutionary' level (i.e. by using the comparative method in a phylogenetic context). In the present paper we mainly consider microevolutionary approaches.

There are two major requirements for testing evolutionary predictions about life-history outcomes. One is to measure the shapes and positions of the trade-off surfaces that bound the options set. The other is to measure the associated fitness surface.

ESTIMATION OF TRADE-OFFS: PHENOTYPIC METHODS

Observation of phenotypes

Observational studies of phenotypes, either within species, or comparative studies between species, often stimulate hypotheses about the trade-offs that influence the evolution of a particular type of organism. Sometimes, indeed, it is hard to think of explanations other than trade-offs to account for observed character correlations (see for example, Tuttle & Ryan 1981, Clutton-Brock *et al.* 1982, Gustaffson & Part 1990).

In general, however, because phenotypic correlations confound genetic and environmental influences, and these may act on character combinations in quite different ways, extreme caution has to be exercised in their interpretation. Environmentally induced correlations can come about for many reasons. There may be ecological compensation such that under density-dependent limitation, an environmentally induced increase in local mortality may result in a corresponding increase in individual size and fecundity. Or accidents and chance events early in life (e.g. an individual's location) may affect an individual's overall 'quality' (e.g. size) which then affects more than one life-history variable.

Experimental manipulation

Changing the phenotype of an individual with regard to one trait experimentally, and examining the response in a second trait, has the advantage that it ensures that the covariance of the life-history characteristics is not due to some common environmental factor affecting each trait independently. It also has the advantage that phenotypes can be produced that are more extreme than the extant types in a given population; the potential options set may therefore be better explored by this method. However, there is still no guarantee that a genetic change, and the ensuing correlated genetic change in the other trait, will be in the same direction as in the experimentally manipulated system. To translate the experimental effect into a genetic effect, one has to assume that the experimental manipulation provides an exact 'phenocopy' of the genetic effect. It is well-known that actual alleles can have seemingly quite bizarre pleiotropic effects (Gromko *et al.* 1991), and an actual genetic change in a trait may have repercussions on other traits that are different from the effects of a manipulation.

We illustrate this method using Møller's (1988, 1989) study of swallows. The basis of the study was that Moller was able: (1) to catch 83 males shortly after arrival at their breeding colonies; (2) to manipulate male tail length, with scissors and superglue; and (3) to observe males thereafter and to record various features of their behaviours and life histories. Males caught at the start of the breeding season were assigned to one of four groups: short tails, long tails, and two control groups with tails of normal length, one unmanipulated, and the other cut and stuck. The males with experimentally lengthened tails were more successful in attracting mates, and fledged more young in the year their tails were lengthened (Fig. 4.10a). Conversely, the group with shortened tails fledged fewer

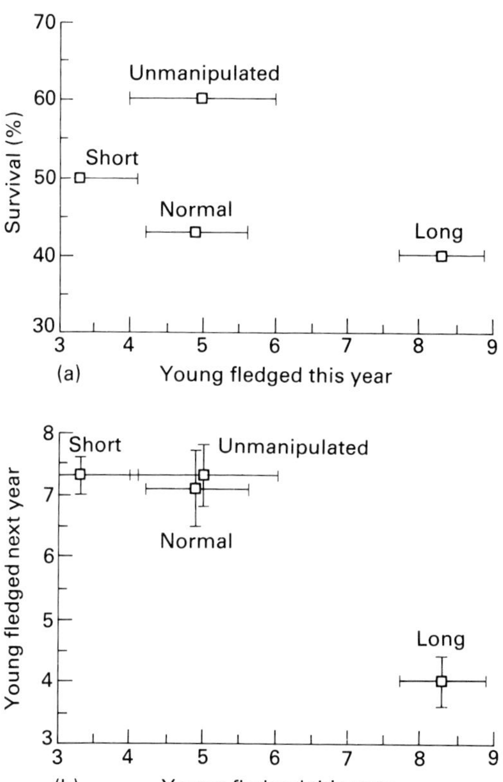

FIG. 4.10. Experimental manipulation of swallow tail length to identify costs of reproduction (data of Møller 1988, 1989). The lengths of male tails were manipulated into four groups, 'short', 'long', 'normal' and 'unmanipulated' (bars indicate standard errors). (a) shows the effects on number of offspring fledged in the year the manipulation was performed, and on the survival of the male until the following year (standard error was not calculated for survivorship). (b) shows the effects on the number of offspring fledged in the following year. See text for further details.

young. The two control groups did not differ in terms of young fledged, indicating that the manipulation procedure did not itself affect the results. There was, however, no detectable cost of reproduction in terms of male survival to the following year (Fig. 4.10a). However, sample size was small for the detection of survivorship differences, being about 20 per group. Figure 4.10b shows there were costs in terms of the number fledged the following year. Note that these data suggest a curvilinear trade-off (but see also Smith *et al.* 1991).

In an experiment of this type, it is obviously not possible to obtain evidence about the initial cost of growing a tail, nor of the effects sacrifices earlier in the life history might have on tail length. This illustrates a general point about experimental manipulations — they can only inform us about trade-offs with events later in the life history, never about trade-offs with events before the manipulation occurred (Partridge & Sibly 1991).

Experiments of this sort are much more easily performed with plants. The pink Lady's Slipper orchid *Cypripedium acaule* is well suited to such designs because naturally occurring flowering plants only rarely fruit, whereas virtually all hand-pollinated flowers develop into fruits. Plants manipulated to fruit more grew and flowered less later, thereby demonstrating a cost of reproduction (Primack & Hall 1990). In *Plantago lanceolata* it is possible to induce flowering by exposing plants to 30 minutes of very dim light during the night. Plants manipulated to flower more grew fewer leaves (Antonovics 1980). Experimental manipulation has also been used to measure the cost of nectar production in Christmas Bells (*Blandfordia nobilis*) (Pyke 1991).

ESTIMATION OF TRADE-OFFS: GENETIC METHODS

As explained earlier, direct short-term predictions of life-history evolution are possible from a knowledge of the extant genetic options set; this genetic options set is normally described by a genetic variance–covariance matrix, under the assumption its shape is multivariate normal. The interpretation of genetic covariances in terms of trade-offs has to be done cautiously if there are more than two interacting traits (i.e. the options set is multidimensional). For example, two traits may be negatively correlated given a uniform genetic background for all other traits but this may be obscured if there is a strong correlation of these two traits with another third trait that varies. In this way, the genetic covariances among some pairs of traits may be positive (Charlesworth 1990, Smith 1991) even though their trade-off functions are negative.

A large number of difficulties are associated with the estimation of genetic correlations. Sample sizes have to be large, there are problems in estimating confidence intervals, and estimates (though not the true values) can and do exceed the range (−1, +1). However, the statistical problems are being addressed by a number of recent studies (for example, Shaw 1991). Another weakness of the genetic correlation *per se* is that it gives no information about the curvilinearity of the trade-off relationship. However, this can perhaps be assessed by appropriate data transformations, or by non-linear regressions of breeding values of the two traits.

If the population is 'at equilibrium' (i.e. has been in the same environment for a long time, it has not undergone a radical change in its breeding system, and there is a low mutation rate), it is often assumed that the extant genetic options set will be at or close to the boundary (see Fig. 4.1) and will therefore reflect the trade-off curve. There is some evidence for this assumption (Holloway *et al.* 1990), and the converse can certainly be expected to be true. Thus, a novel environment, inbreeding in a normally outbred population (Rose 1984), or a high mutation rate (Houle 1991), can be expected to produce genes that have very different fitnesses, resulting in correlations among life-history traits which in principle could be positive. The trade-off surface of the extant options set is therefore ideally estimated from the genetic correlations measured using progeny from crosses among parents derived from a long-standing population, where those progeny are transplanted back into the same natural environment.

We present, as an example, a study by Moller *et al.* (1989) of the cowpea weevil, *Callosobruchus maculatus*, a stored product pest. An advantage of working on stored product pests is that their ancestral environment is readily re-created in the laboratory. As mentioned above, this is an important point, because the values of genetic parameters are in general environment dependent, so studies that have moved populations to the laboratory to make measurements have generally also changed their environments, making the measurements of doubtful value.

A specially designed breeding study was used to allow efficient calculation of genetic parameters such as breeding value (Fig. 4.11), which provides an estimate of the effects of the alleles carried by each individual (here, each male). Figure 4.11a shows that genetically larger individuals produced more eggs, but Fig. 4.11b shows that this was at a cost in terms of juvenile growth rate — because it takes longer to grow to be bigger. The methods of quantitative genetics allowed accurate estimation of genetic correlations from these data, and these are shown in Table 4.1.

The requirement that the genetic correlation be measured in the

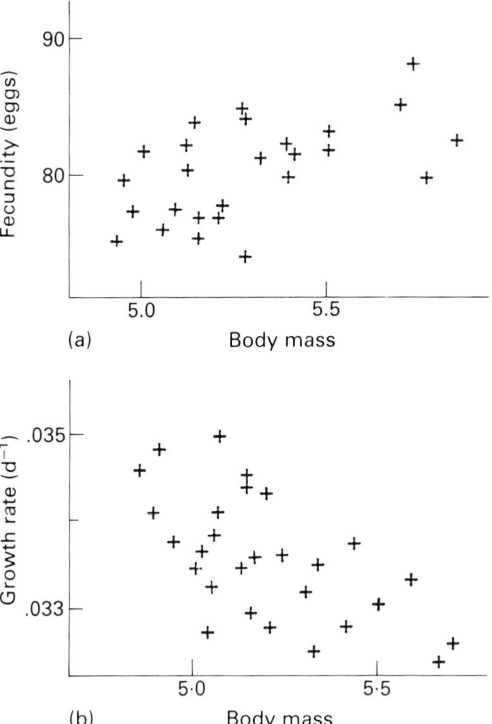

FIG. 4.11. Plots of breeding values (family means) of three life-history characters of seed weevils (data of Moller *et al.* 1989, cf. Sibly *et al.* 1991). Growth rate is here the reciprocal of juvenile development period. Data were obtained from a full sib/half sib design in which measurements were taken of 17 to 33 offspring from the 4 or 5 females that were mated to each of 30 males. Each point represents one male, and is an average of the measurements of his offspring. See text for discussion.

TABLE 4.1. Genetic correlations for the data in Fig. 4.11 (from Moller *et al.* 1989)

	Growth rate	Fecundity
Body mass	−1.01 ± 0.22	.68 ± 0.26
Growth rate		−1.26 ± 0.58

population's natural environment places large restrictions on the usefulness of the method in practice, since the designs are intricate and require large samples (761 in the above example) if precise estimation is to be achieved. Prerequisites for application of the technique are the abilities to control parentage and to track individuals for long enough to be able to measure life-history components. These prerequisites are far more easily satisfied in plants than in animals. As an example see Roach's (1986) demonstration of a negative genetic correlation between juvenile and adult traits in *Geranium carolinianum*.

If we wish to consider evolutionary outcomes over an evolutionary time scale, which we wish to test by a comparative study of several populations or taxa, then genetic approaches to measuring the trade-off surface become tenuous. Clearly the extant options set, measured even on an 'equilibrium' population, may not reflect the longer term evolutionary boundaries of the lineage under consideration. In such situations, a comparative study of character relationships within a taxon may be the best guide to the nature of the boundary of the options set for those characters. Of course among species (or among populations, etc.) comparisons must be genetic and not simply the result of differences in the environments of the different species. However, to determine whether such differences are genetic may require growing the different species in a standard environment: this in itself may be artefactual as the specific environment that is chosen could alter the life-history traits themselves in a very unnatural way (e.g. remove natural sources of mortality or induce mortality if the environment is unusual). The lability of life-history traits can again create difficulty for the empiricist.

An example is the study of Primack (1979) on different species in the genus *Plantago*. Annuals had a far higher reproductive effort than perennials, not an unexpected finding, but consistent with the genus wide trade-off curve and life history expectation.

Transplant experiments

Transplant experiments represent an underused technique for examining the process and outcomes of life-history evolution. In the past, reciprocal transplant experiments have largely been used to demonstrate genetic differentiation among populations and to analyse the selection components responsible for such differentiation (for life-history examples, see Berven 1982, Antonovics & Primack 1983). However, transplant experiments can also be used to examine evolutionary outcomes. The method consists in transplanting individuals from a number of habitats to a common habitat in which their life-history components are then measured. Care must be taken that there are no maternal or other residual non-genetic effects carried over from the previous habitat. Since all individuals are assessed in a common environment, population differences must then reflect genetic differences. Since these can be estimated with relatively small sample sizes, the technique would seem to be well suited to the job of mapping the options set. The principal difficulty from the point of view of identifying the trade-off surface is that one cannot be certain that the genetic options so identified lie on the boundary rather than in the interior of the extant genetic options set. However, this can be overcome by maintaining the populations in the study environment for several generations; lack of change would indicate they were on the boundary.

Transplant experiments can also be used to study microevolutionary processes within populations directly. If transplants into a novel environment are the result of a formal crossing design, then it should be possible from measurements in this new habitat to identify both the genetic options set and, using the methods suggested above, the fitness surface for that environment. If the population is allowed to persist in that environment, actual changes in life-history characteristics can then be examined.

In one such study (Jordan 1989, also Jordan 1991), but involving morphological and growth characteristics rather than life history traits, families of a non-weed ecotype of *Diodia teres* were transplanted into a dense stand of soybeans. This permitted calculation of genetic variances and covariances, as well as forces of selection on a number of covarying traits. Comparing the weed and non-weed ecotypes, the direction of selection was as predicted in four out of five characters studied.

In a reciprocal transplant experiment a further prediction can be made. If the transplanted populations are genetically distinct, it is unlikely that the alleles evolved in other habitats will be superior in the study environment to the alleles that evolved there. Hence, in each habitat the population that evolved there should outperform the others. This prediction has often been confirmed by reciprocal transplant experiments (especially in plants) showing that resident populations outperform aliens (Briggs & Walters 1984, Levin 1984). The life history components that result in such overall fitness differences have, however, rarely been studied explicitly (for exceptions see McGraw & Antonovics 1983, Jordan 1991) or put in the context of expectations from life history theory (Antonovics & Primack 1982). More explicit use of transplant experiments to test life-history theory, rather than overall fitness differences, could be rewarding.

DIRECT STUDY OF THE EVOLUTIONARY PROCESS

A particular challenge is to test life-history theory in prospective, microevolutionary studies, where there can be direct observation of evolutionary changes in life history. Such studies may involve laboratory selection experiments or may be field based.

An interesting example of the latter approach is the work of Reznick *et al.* (1990). Earlier work had shown that guppies (*Poecilia reticulata*) occurred in streams differing with respect to whether juveniles or adults were more affected by predation. Where predation was mainly on adults, guppies matured at an earlier age, had higher reproductive effort, and had more and smaller offspring per brood (Reznick & Endler 1982, Reznick *et al.* 1990). These differences were heritable and could be explained on the following basis. First, where predation is mainly on juveniles, production rate is thought to be lower (on the basis of temperature and food supply, Reznick 1982). This selects for larger eggs. In addition, larger eggs would give juveniles a 'head start' and so allow them to hurry through the juvenile stages (Reznick 1982, Taylor & Williams 1984). Second, where predation is mainly on juveniles, juvenile survivorship is lower but adult survivorship is higher, and this combination selects for lower reproductive effort assuming the costs of reproduction are paid after reproduction has occurred. Lastly, although we have not treated it formally here, it would seem adaptive to mature earlier and therefore at lower size where adult predation is more intense, since the increased mortality on larger fish can thereby be to some extent avoided (Reznick *et al.* 1990). To show that predation was the cause of the observed life-history differences, Reznick *et al.* (1990) introduced 200 guppies from a site with predominantly adult predation to one with mainly juvenile predation. By the end of the study 11 years (30–60 generations) later, field phenotypes had lower reproductive effort, and fewer and larger offspring, as predicted. To see if these differences were heritable, Reznick *et al.* first reared fish from both localities in a common environment for two generations, to eliminate environmental influences on the life histories. When they then measured the life histories they found they had changed in the predicted directions (Table 4.2).

Other examples of selection experiments include Rose and Charlesworth (1981), Luckinbill *et al.* (1983) and Moller *et al.* (1990) (for a review see Lessells 1991).

ESTIMATION OF FITNESS SURFACES

In theoretical studies such as those described earlier, fitness surfaces are estimated by solving the Euler–Lotka equation to calculate r for the relevant trait variables. In any particular real-world situation, the actual observed relationship between the trait combination and fitness may be different from this theoretical expectation for many reasons. For example, the trait 'seed number at age x' might seem easily equatable with $n(x)$ in a

TABLE 4.2. Life-history traits of two lines of guppies (*Poecilia reticulata*) exposed to either adult or juvenile predation in the field for 11 years (SE in brackets, data from Reznick *et al.* 1990). *, $p < 0.05$; NS, $p > 0.05$. Although the overall difference in reproductive effort was not significant, as shown, the difference at 8 weeks was

Life-history trait	Adults predated	Juveniles predated	
Male age at maturity (days)	48.5 (1.2)	58.2 (1.4)	*
Female age at first parturition (days)	85.7 (2.2)	92.3 (2.6)	*
Brood size, litter 1	4.5 (0.4)	3.3 (0.4)	*
Brood size, litter 2	8.1 (0.6)	7.5 (0.7)	NS
Offspring size (mg-dry), litter 1	0.87 (0.02)	0.95 (0.02)	NS
Offspring size, litter 2	0.90 (0.03)	1.02 (0.04)	*
Interbrood interval (days)	24.5 (0.3)	25.2 (0.3)	NS
Reproductive effort (%)	22.0 (1.8)	18.5 (2.1)	NS

fitness function but such a measure may fail to take into account seed quality (inbred versus outbred, large versus small), may fail to take into account dispersal differences (due to, for example, variation of plant height with age), may fail to consider the level of interaction among the seedlings from the same sibship in the next generation, etc. Ideally we would like to know the actual relationship between the traits in question and fitness. However, an important empirical problem arises if we attempt to measure the traits and fitness on the same individuals because of confounding by environmental variables that affect both (Rausher 1992). There is also the problem that the life-history character should not be part of the fitness measure of those self-same individuals.

There are ways out of these difficulties but none of them is easy. One could measure the trait in question on one set of individuals and measure fitness on another related (e.g. same family or clone) set of individuals. Alternatively, one can look at the correlations among breeding values (Rausher 1992). Another approach is to use two (or multiple) generation experiments, where life histories of individuals from a crossing design are measured in one generation, and the contribution of these individuals to the next generation are estimated using genetic markers (see Lacey *et al.* 1983, for a discussion of this issue). An example of such a study is that of Meagher (in press) which although it did not explicitly investigate life-history traits, showed using paternity analysis based on genetic markers, that large males of the dioecious plant *Chamaelirium luteum* actually tended to sire fewer offspring (perhaps because of reduced pollinator movement from those males).

Another possible source of error arises if the options set is multidimensional but some relevant characters are omitted ('the missing characters' problem). One method to test for whether all the relevant traits have been identified is to ask how completely variation (and covariation) in the observed traits predict the observed variation in fitness. If there is little residual unexplained variation in fitness, then one can assume that the relevant traits (or their correlates) have been identified. If, however, the residual variation is high, then clearly important traits are missing. In a study of selection for herbivore resistance, 91% of the variance in breeding value of individuals for fitness (as measured by seed production) could be accounted for by variation in their breeding values for leaf area and damage by four different herbivores (Rausher & Simms 1989, calculated from their Table 3).

Of particular interest are cases where there is a large amount of unexplained genetic variance in a component life-history trait but little genetic variance in fitness (Mousseau & Roff 1987). Such a discrepancy could have two interpretations; either the trait is neutral, or it indicates that there is a negatively covarying fitness component that has not been measured. If the negative correlation is close to -1 then these two possibilities are hard to distinguish empirically.

In conclusion, the estimation of the fitness surface presents non-trivial issues for the evolutionary biologist interested in life-history evolution. These issues are common to any rigorous quantitative analysis of natural selection acting on multivariate traits but are exacerbated in life-history work by the closeness of the traits to fitness and by their phenotypic flexibility. The resolution of this issue may well be dependent on the growing use of genetic markers to trace parentage. Such methods are therefore likely to play a large role in empirical studies of life-history evolution.

CONCLUSIONS

Detailed consideration of the fate of individual alleles affecting life-history traits to a large extent reconciles the 'ecological' and the 'genetic' approaches that were juxtaposed in the introduction to this chapter. The genetic approach gives a predictive framework within which to study the microevolutionary process, and the ecological approach identifies expected outcomes in particular environments using optimality analysis. Both assume trade-offs among life-history traits and knowledge of the form of these trade-offs is critical to predicting evolutionary outcomes.

The present status of life-history theory can best be described as being in the 'work-horse' phase. We now have a wealth of theories and more useful ideas continue to be forthcoming. We also have a large number of empirical investigations which are important in having shown life-history variation within and among species, in showing these are correlated with habitat/community features, and in illustrating at least the potential occurrence of trade-offs. However, few if any studies have rigorously delineated the forces responsible for the evolution of a particular life history.

We can liken the present status of life-history theory to that of the theory of natural selection after the publication of Darwin's book *Origin of Species*. It is clear that the general mechanisms and the environmental conditions that can lead to the evolution of diverse life histories are well established; similarly, the theory of natural selection was first posed as a logical inference from well-supported biological phenomena. But just as the theory of natural selection remained in need of 'testing' for a long period, so there is now a need to instantiate life-history theory, so as to establish which mechanisms are general or important in which groups, and under what ecological circumstances.

ACKNOWLEDGEMENTS

R.S. has benefitted greatly in the development of some of these ideas from discussions with Robert Smith and Nicolas Perrin.

REFERENCES

Abugov, R. (1988). A sex-specific quantitative genetic theory for life history and development. *Journal of Theoretical Biology*, **132**, 437–447.

Anderson, W. W. & King, C. E. (1970). Age-specific selection. *Proceedings of the National Academy of Sciences, USA*, **66**, 780–786.

Antonovics, J. (1980). Concepts of resource allocation and partitioning in plants. *Limits to Action* (Ed. by J. R. Staddon), pp. 1–35. Academic Press, London, UK.

Antonovics, J. & Primack, R. B. (1983). Experimental ecological genetics in *Plantago*. VI. The demography of seedling transplants of *P. lanceolata*. *Journal of Ecology*, **70**, 55–75.

Bell, G. (1980). The costs of reproduction and their consequences. *American Naturalist*, **116**, 45–76.

Berven, K. A. (1982). The genetic basis of altitudinal variation in the Wood frog *Rana sylvatica*. I. An experimental analysis of life history traits. *Evolution*, **36**, 962–983.

Briggs, D. & Walters, S. M. (1984). *Plant Variation and Evolution* (2nd edn). Cambridge University Press, Cambridge, UK.

Charlesworth, B. (1980). *Evolution in age-structured populations*. Cambridge University Press, Cambridge, UK.

Charlesworth, B. (1990). Optimization models, quantitative genetics and mutation. *Evolution*, **44**, 520–538.

Charlesworth, B. & Giesel, J. T. (1972a). Selection in populations with overlapping generations. II. Relations between gene frequency and overlapping generations. *American Naturalist*, **106**, 388–401.

Charlesworth, B. & Giesel, J. T. (1972b). Selection in populations with overlapping generations. IV. Fluctuations in gene frequency with density-dependent selection. *American Naturalist*, **106**, 402–411.

Charnov, E. L. (1982). *The Theory of Sex Allocation*. Princeton University Press, Princeton, NJ, USA.

Clutton-Brock, T. H., Guiness, F. E. & Albon, S. D. (1982). *Red Deer*. University of Chicago Press, Chicago IL, USA.

Cole, L. C. (1954). The population consequences of life history phenomena. *Quarterly Review of Biology*, **29**, 103–137.

Deevey, E. S. (1947). Life tables for natural populations. *Quarterly Review of Biology*, **22**, 283–314.

Fisher, R. A. (1930). *The Genetical Theory of Natural Selection*. Oxford University Press, Oxford, UK.

Ford, E. (1964). *Ecological Genetics*. Methuen, London, UK.

Frank, S. A. (1990). Sex allocation theory for birds and mammals. *Annual Review of Ecology and Systematics*, **21**, 13–55.

Gabriel, W. (1982). Modelling reproductive strategies of *Daphnia*. *Archiv fur Hydrobiologie*, **95**, 69–80.

Gromko, M. H., Briot, A., Jensen, S. C. & Fukui, H. (1991). Selection on copulation duration in *Drosophila melanogaster*: predictability of direct response versus unpredictability of correlated response. *Evolution*, **45**, 69–81.

Gustaffson, L. & Part, T. (1990). Acceleration of senescence in the collared flycatcher *Ficedula albicollis* by reproductive costs. *Nature*, **347**, 279–281.

Holloway, G. J., Povey, S. R. & Sibly, R. M. (1990). The effect of new environment on adapted genetic architecture. *Heredity*, **64**, 323–330.

Houle, D. (1991). Genetic covariance of fitness correlates; what genetic correlations are made of and why it matters. *Evolution*, **45**, 630–648.

Jordan, N. (1989). Predicted evolutionary response to selection for tolerance of soybean (*Glycine max*) and intraspecific competition in a non-weed population of poorjoe (*Diodia teres*). *Weed Science*, **37**, 451–457.

Jordan, N. R. (1991). Multivariate analysis of selection in experimental populations derived from hybridization of two ecotypes of the annual plant *Diodia teres* W. (Rubiaceae). *Evolution*, **45**, 1760–1772.

King, C. E. & Anderson, W. W. (1971). Age-specific selection. II. The interaction between *r* and *K* during population growth. *American Naturalist*, **105**, 137–156.

Kozlowski, J. (1992). Optimal allocation of resources of growth and reproduction: implications for age and size at maturity. *Trends in Ecology and Evolution*, **7**, 15–19.

Lacey, E. P., Real, L., Antonovics, J. & Heckel, D. (1983). Variance models in the study of life histories. *American Naturalist*, **122**, 114–131.

Lack, D. (1954). *The Natural Regulation of Animal Numbers*. Clarendon Press, Oxford, UK.

Lande, R. (1982). A quantitative genetic theory of life history evolution. *Ecology*, **63**, 607–615.

Lessells, C. M. (1991). The evolution of life histories. *Behavioural Ecology* (3rd edn) (Ed. by J. R. Krebs & N. B. Davies), pp. 32–68. Blackwell Scientific Publications, Oxford, UK.

Levin, D. A. (1984). Immigration in plants: an exercise in the subjunctive. *Perspectives on Plant Population Biology* (Ed. R. Dirzo & J. Sarukhan), pp. 242–260. Sinauer, Sunderland, MA, USA.

Luckinbill, L. S., Arking, R., Clare, M. J., Cirocco, W. C. & Buck, S. A. (1983). Selection for delayed senescence in *Drosophila melanogaster*. *Evolution*, **38**, 996–1003.

MacArthur, R. H. (1962). Some generalized theorems of natural selection. *Proceedings of the Natural Academy of Sciences, USA*, **38**, 1893–1897.

Maynard Smith, J. (1982). *Evolution and the Theory of Games*. Cambridge University Press, Cambridge, UK.

Maynard Smith, J. (1989). *Evolutionary Genetics*. Oxford University Press, Oxford, UK.

Maynard Smith, J. (1991). The evolution of reproductive strategies: a commentary. *Philosophical Transactions of the Royal Society of London*, B, **332**, 103–104.

McGraw, J. B. & Antonovics, J. (1983). Experimental ecology of *Dryas ocopetala* ecotypes I. Ecotypic differentiation and life-cycle stages of selection. *Journal of Ecology*, **71**, 879–897.

Meagher, T. R. Analysis of paternity within a natural population of *Chamaelirium luteum*. II. Male reproductive success. *American Naturalist* (in press).

Mòller, A. P. (1988). Female choice selects for male sexual tail ornaments in the monogamous swallow. *Nature*, **332**, 640–642.

Møller, A. P. (1989). Viability costs of male tail ornaments in a swallow. *Nature*, **339**, 132–135.

Moller, H., Smith, R. H. & Sibly, R. M. (1989). Evolutionary demography of a bruchid beetle. I. Quantitative genetical analysis of the female life history. *Functional Ecology*, **3**, 673–681.

Moller, H., Smith, R. H. & Sibly, R. M. (1990). Evolutionary demography of a bruchid beetle. III. Correlated responses to selection and phenotypic plasticity. *Functional Ecology*, **4**, 489–493.

Mousseau, T. A. & Roff, D. A. (1987). Natural selection and the heritability of fitness components. *Heredity*, **59**, 181–197.

Nur, N. (1984). The consequences of brood size for breeding blue tits. II. Nestling, weight, offspring survival and optimal brood size. *Journal of Animal Ecology*, **53**, 497–517.

Parker, G. A. & Maynard Smith, J. (1990). Optimality in evolutionary biology. *Nature*, **348**, 27–33.

Partridge, L. & Sibly, R. (1991). Constraints in the evolution of life histories. *Philosophical Transactions of the Royal Society of London*, B, **332**, 3–13.

Pianka, E. R. and Parker, W. S. (1975). Age-specific reproductive tactics. *American Naturalist*, **109**, 453–464.

Primack, R. B. (1979). Reproductive effort in annual and perennial species of *Plantago* (Plantaginaceae). *American Naturalist*, **114**, 51–62.

Primack, R. B. & Hall, P. (1990). Costs of reproduction in the pink lady's slipper orchid: a four-year experimental study. *American Naturalist*, **136**, 638–656.

Pugliese, A. & Kozlowski, J. (1990). Optimal patterns of growth and reproduction for perennial plants with persisting or not persisting vegetative parts. *Evolutionary Ecology*, **4**, 75–89.

Pyke, G. H. (1991). What does it cost a plant to produce floral nectar? *Nature*, **350**, 58–59.

Rausher, M. D. (1992). The measurement of selection on quantitative traits: biases due to environmental covariances between traits and fitness. *Evolution*, **46**, 616–626.

Rausher, M. D. & Simms, E. L. (1989). The evolution of resistance to herbivory in *Ipomoea purpurea*. I. Attempts to detect selection. *Evolution*, **43**, 563–572.

Reznick, D. A. (1982). Genetic determination of offspring size in the guppy (*Poecilia reticulata*). *American Naturalist*, **120**, 181–188.

Reznick, D. A. & Endler, J. A. (1982). The impact of predation on life history evolution in Trinidadian guppies (*Poecilia reticulata*). *Evolution*, **36**, 160–177.

Reznick, D. A., Bryga, H. & Endler, J. A. (1990). Experimentally induced life-history evolution in a natural population. *Nature*, **346**, 357–359.

Roach, D. A. (1986). Life history variation in *Geranium carolinianum*. 1. Covariation between characters at different stages of the life cycle. *American Naturalist*, **128**, 47–57.

Rose, M. R. (1984). Genetic covariation in *Drosophila* life history: untangling the data. *American Naturalist*, **123**, 565–569.

Rose, M. R. & Charlesworth, B. (1981). Genetics of life-history in *Drosophila maelanogaster*. II. Exploratory selection experiments. *Genetics*, **97**, 187–196.

Schaffer, W. M. (1974a). Optimal reproductive effort in fluctuating environments. *American Naturalist*, **108**, 783–790.

Schaffer, W. M. (1974b). Selection for optimal life histories: the effects of age structure. *Ecology*, **55**, 291–303.

Shaw, R. G. (1991). The comparison of quantitative genetic parameters between populations. *Evolution*, **45**, 143–151.

Sibly, R. M. (1989). What evolution maximizes. *Functional Ecology*, **3**, 129–135.

Sibly, R. M. & Calow, P. (1985). Classification of habitats by selection pressures: a synthesis of life-cycle and *r*/*K* theory. *Behavioural Ecology: Ecological Consequences of Adaptive Behaviour* (Ed. by R. M. Sibly & R. H. Smith), pp. 75–90. (The 25th Symposium of The British Ecological Society). Blackwell Scientific Publications, Oxford, UK.

Sibly, R. M. & Calow, P. (1986). *Physiological Ecology of Animals*. Blackwell Scientific Publications, Oxford, UK.

Sibly, R. M. & Calow, P. (1987). Ecological compensation — a complication for testing life-history theory. *Journal of Theoretical Biology*, **125**, 177–186.

Sibly, R. M. & Calow, P. (1989). A life-cycle theory of responses to stress. *Biological Journal of the Linnean Society*, **37**, 101–116.

Sibly, R. M., Calow, P. & Nichols, N. (1985). Are patterns of growth adaptive? *Journal of Theoretical Biology*, **112**, 553–574.

Sibly, R. M. & Curnow, R. N. An allelocentric view of life-history evolution. *Journal of Theoretical Biology* (in press).

Sibly, R. M., Smith, R. H. & Moller, H. (1991). Evolutionary demography of a bruchid beetle. IV. Genetic trade-off, stabilizing selection and a model of optimal body size. *Functional Ecology*, **5**, 594–601.

Smith, H. G., Montgomerie, R., Poldmaa, T., White, B. N. & Boag, P. T. (1991). DNA fingerprinting reveals relation between tail ornaments and cuckoldry in barn swallows, *Hirundo rustica*. *Behavioural Ecology*, **2**, 90–98.

Smith, R. H. (1991). Genetic and phenotypic aspects of life-history evolution in animals. *Advances in Ecological Research*, **21**, 63–120.

Smith, R. H., Sibly, R. M. & Moller, H. (1987). Control of size and fecundity in *Pieris rapae*: towards a theory of butterfly life cycles. *Journal of Animal Ecology*, **56**, 341–350.

Southwood, T. R. E. (1988). Tactics, strategies and templets. *Oikos*, **52**, 3–18.

Taylor, B. & Gabriel, W. (1992). Models for optimal growth and reproduction of *Daphnia*. *American Naturalist*, **139**, 248–266.

Taylor, P. D. & Williams, G. C. (1984). Demographic parameters at evolutionary equilibrium. *Canadian Journal of Zoology*, **62**, 2264–2271.

Taylor, H. M., Gourley, R. S., Lawrence, C. E. & Kaplan, R. S. (1974). Natural selection of life history attributes: an analytical approach. *Theoretical Population Biology*, **5**, 104–122.

Tuttle, M. D. & Ryan, M. J. (1981). Bat predation and the evolution of frog vocalizations in the neotropics. *Science*, **214**, 677–678.

Ziolko, M. & Kozlowski, J. (1983). Evolution of body size: an optimization model. *Mathematical Biosciences*, **64**, 127–143.

5. THESE HIERARCHICAL VIEWS OF LIFE: PHYLOGENIES AND METAPOPULATIONS

PAUL H. HARVEY*, SEAN NEE*, ARNE Ø. MOOERS* AND LINDA PARTRIDGE[†]

**Department of Zoology, University of Oxford, South Parks Road, Oxford OX1 3PS, UK and* [†]*Department of Zoology, University of Edinburgh, West Mains Road, Edinburgh EH9 3JT, UK*

INTRODUCTION

Recently, much has been written about the advantages and the disadvantages of a hierarchical perspective applied to evolution (e.g. Harvey 1985, Brooks & Wiley 1986, Vrba & Gould 1986, Vrba 1989) and to ecology (e.g. Allen & Starr 1982, Gilpin & Hanski 1991). The two hierarchies considered in this paper represent natural hierarchies in the analysis of evolutionary and ecological questions. They are, respectively, temporal phylogenies and spatial metapopulations. The impetus for the work we describe arises from new developments in phylogeny reconstruction and our interest in the conservation consequences of metapopulation dynamics. Using established empirical and theoretical foundations, we ascribe fecundities, mortality rates and measures of fitness to clades and to populations. In so doing, we produce results that are reciprocally illuminating to ecology and evolution. We consider the phylogenetic hierachy first, reaching down to the ecological scale as we proceed. The metapopulation work that follows will, as we shall see, have distinct bearing on and relation to evolution theory.

A KEY ADVANCE IN PHYLOGENY RECONSTRUCTION AND A KEY PHYLOGENY

The revolution in molecular systematics is resulting in the production of much more accurate phylogenetic trees than has previously been possible. Different parts of the genome diverge at different rates so that, given the assumptions of the molecular clock (Kimura 1968, Thorpe 1982), appropriate choice of nucleotide sequence comparison allows phylogenetic reconstruction among any taxa, however closely or distantly related they may be (Hillis & Moritz 1990, Harvey & Pagel 1991). Ribosomal RNA is useful for discriminating very distant levels of relationship because of its relatively conservative structure; for example, Ghiselin (1988) has used it to throw new light on the origin of the molluscs. Solution hybridization of total single-copy nuclear DNA (DNA hybridization) provides data that distinguish relationships among closer relatives; for example, Sibley and Ahlquist (1990) have used it to produce a near complete phylogenetic classification of the birds, from the level of the tribe and above. At lower taxonomic levels, some regions of the mitochondrial genome can be used to determine even closer phylogenetic relatives, such as among species or populations (Wilson *et al.* 1985). Finally, following the pioneering work of Jeffreys *et al.* (1985), hypervariable DNA sequences are now routinely used to decide familial relationships within local single-species populations (see Burke 1989).

Perhaps the most ambitious project in molecular systematics to date has been Sibley and Ahlquist's (1990) attempt to produce a phylogeny of the birds based on DNA hybridization data. Sibley and Ahlquist used 1700 of the 9700 species of birds, drawn from 171 of the recognized 174 families, to produce 26554 DNA hybrids. Genetic divergence between species is measured in units of delta $T_{50}H$. $T_{50}H$ is the temperature in degrees Celsius at which 50% of all potentially hybridizable single-copy DNA sequences are in the hybrid form and 50% have dissociated (more dissociation occurs at higher temperatures). Delta $T_{50}H$ is the difference in degrees Celsius between the $T_{50}H$ for a homoduplex DNA hybrid (the two strands are from the same species) and that for the heteroduplex (i.e. strands from different species) under consideration. According to Sibley and Ahlquist, to a rough approximation each delta $T_{50}H$ unit in a comparison between two species represents 4.5 million years since they last shared a common ancestor. Therefore, a delta $T_{50}H$ value of 10 means that the most recent common ancestor of two species lived about 45 million years ago. Two clustering algorithms were used to produce phylogenetic trees, the nodes on which were given approximate dates. In what follows, we have used Sibley and Ahlquist's (1990) tree (the earlier divisions of which are shown in Fig. 5.1) produced from Sokal and Michener's (1958) clustering unweighted pair group method using arithmetic averages (UPGMA). Some of our analyses make use of dates of nodes, although any conclusions concerning dates rest only on the assumption that dates of splitting are a constant multiple of those given. Other analyses simply use the tree structure, ignoring dates of splitting, though sometimes using relative timings to define taxonomic groupings.

The motivation for our analyses is to seek answers to questions that could not be tackled without a reliable phylogeny. The reliability of our

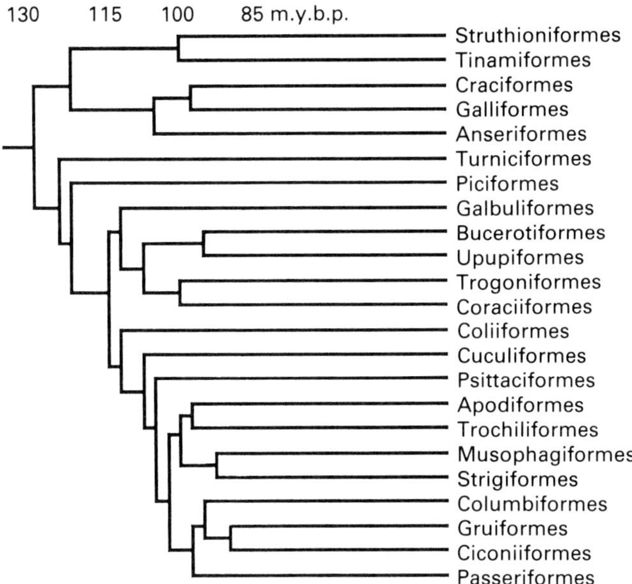

FIG. 5.1. Sibley and Ahlquist's (1990) DNA hybridization tree showing the major divisions of the class Aves determined by the UPGMA method. Most divisions are further subdivided many times in their complete tree. We have multiplied Sibley and Ahlquist's delta $T_{50}H$ values by 4.5 to give approximate dates of splitting. Subsequent figures and tables refer directly to delta $T_{50}H$ values.

results is constrained by the reliability of Sibley and Ahlquist's tree. If their timings are wrong, then so will some of our results be wrong. And if their branching patterns are wrong, then so will others of our results be wrong. Sibley and Ahlquist have their critics (e.g. Sarich *et al.* 1989). It might be argued reasonably that Sibley and Ahlquist took too broad-brush an approach, that their delta $T_{50}H$ measure was not the most appropriate, and that many of their analyses should have been performed differently. They reply, 'Our data are not perfect and we did not subject them to every available statistical analysis; that we should have done many things better is undeniable, but hindsight is always crystal-clear.... We are satisfied with the results, but we know that many questions remain unanswered and that we have raised new ones. That is progress; perfection is for the future.' (Sibley & Ahlquist 1990, p. xvii.) Our analyses are performed in the spirit of that quotation.

The questions that we pose using Sibley and Ahlquist's tree fall under two main headings. The first is: does Sibley and Ahlquist's tree display anything unusual in the pattern of cladogenesis which might implicate ecology? The second question is: can viewing an ecological relationship — that between population density and body weight — from a phylogenetic perspective reveal anything new? The answer to both questions is yes.

Does Sibley and Ahlquist's tree demonstrate unexpected structure?

Our expectations are based on statistical null hypotheses.

Are all lineages equally prone to effective cladogenesis?

Sibley and Ahlquist's tree is, for the most part, bifurcating. It is constructed using data collected from extant taxa. One consequence of the data source is that lineages which became extinct do not appear in the tree. If we observe high rates of splitting in particular parts of the tree, we cannot tell whether they result from high rates of lineage division (high lineage birth rates), low rates of lineage extinction (low lineage death rates), or some combination of the two. Branching on the tree is referred to as 'effective cladogenesis'. A radiation that was more prone to branching had a lineage-splitting rate per lineage-extinction rate (one measure of lineage fitness) that was higher than a radiation that was less prone to branching.

A simple test of whether particular radiations are prone to higher rates of effective cladogenesis (that is, whether rates of cladogenesis are, in a sense, heritable) is given in Fig. 5.2. Does the shorter of two branches descended from a single common ancestor itself give rise to shorter branches? In order to maximize our sample size, we have compared only the shorter of the two branches emanating from each daughter node. The reason for this is that longer branches sometimes extend to tribal status or below and, because not all species in each tribe are represented in the data, it is therefore not possible to determine when the longer branch split (if indeed it did at all). We were also careful to eliminate nodes from our analysis for which the shorter branch may not have been correctly identified. In order that the shorter daughter branches be correctly identified, the longer branches must each have split into separate monophyletic groups (at the limit, two genera) or include all the members of the lowest discernible monophyletic group, the genus (in fact, the longer branches often end in the only member of their genus).

Sixty-eight ancestral nodes were used. These were grouped into those found high in the tree between the root and 20 delta $T_{50}H$ units (17 nodes), those falling between 20 and 10 units (26 nodes), and those found

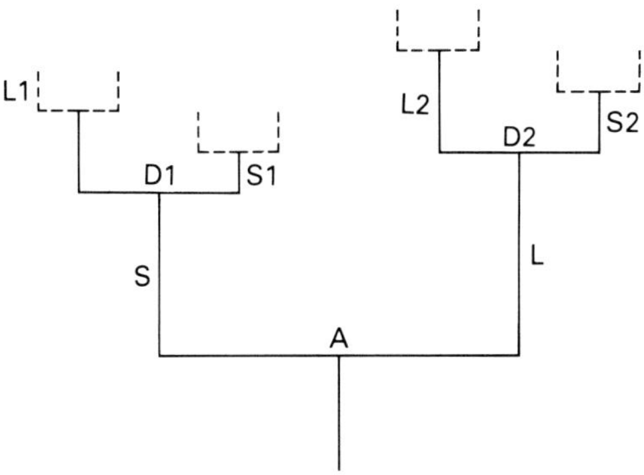

FIG. 5.2. Do short branches generate short branches? Or is cladogenesis heritable? Data were provided whenever an ancestral node (A) in Sibley and Ahlquist's (1990) UPGMA tree gave rise to two daughter nodes (D1, D2), from each of which we could calculate the length of the shorter branch (S1, S2). The null hypothesis is that S1 is equally likely to be shorter or longer than S2, whether it arose from the shorter (S) or the longer branch (L) emanating from the ancestral node. If short branches generate short branches, S1 (being descended from S) should be shorter than S2 (being descended from L).

below 10 units (25 nodes). These are artificial categorizations but correspond very well with the taxonomic categories of order and above, between order and family, and below family. Shorter branches emanating from nodes above 20 units tend themselves to give rise to shorter branches (Table 5.1; S1 tends to be less than S2 in Fig. 5.1), although this result is not found for ancestral nodes belonging to the more recent node categories (Table 5.1).

Measurement error resulting from node displacement is likely to lead to a pattern of shorter branches emanating from longer branches. For

TABLE 5.1. Short branches generate short branches high in Sibley and Ahlquist's phylogenetic tree but not lower down. Data from 68 ancestral nodes were used. S1 < S2 when shorter branches gave rise to shorter branches, and *vice versa* (see Fig. 5.2). Overall heterogeneity $\chi_2^2 = 6.11$, $p < 0.05$. Pooling the two higher levels (10 and above) which are not heterogeneous, produces 30 nodes with S1 < S2 versus 13 with S1 > S2, a highly significant departure from the null expectation ($\chi_1^2 = 6.72$, $p < 0.01$)

Age of node	S1 < S2	S1 > S2	χ_1^2	p
>20	13	4	4.76	<0.05
10–20	17	9	1.88	NS
<10	10	15	1.00	NS

NS, non-significant.

example, imagine that D1 in Fig. 5.2 is misplaced in the tree to occur further back in time than was actually the case. The result would be to shorten S but lengthen S1: shorter branches would appear to produce longer daughter branches. Therefore, the significant pattern found early in the tree would be countered by measurement error.

The above suggests that nodes arising from short branches themselves are more likely to give rise to short branches, but only high in the tree. A simple two-sample t test comparing ages of those of the 68 ancestral nodes in which the short branches give rise to the shorter branches with those in which short branches give rise to longer branches tends to support the suggestion that the pattern is more typical of higher parts of the tree ($t_{66} = 1.92$, $p < 0.06$).

These analyses show that, high in the tree, short branches tend to give rise to nodes which themselves yield short branches, but that this pattern dissipates as we move towards the tips of the tree.

Does the rate of effective cladogenesis change with time?

The previous analyses demonstrate patterns that occur earlier in the tree but not later. We now ask if rates of effective cladogenesis change with time. Our null hypothesis is based on a simple birth process. If the rate of effective cladogenesis was constant through the tree (i.e. the probability of any lineage splitting was the same at any time in the past) then, if nodes were ranked from earliest to latest, a plot of time of splitting since the first node against rank of node should yield a straight line if the rank-of-node axis is logarithmically transformed. The plot is evidently non-linear (Fig. 5.3), with rates of effective cladogenesis declining from the root of the tree towards the present. A good fit to the data is provided by density-dependent cladogenesis of the following form:

$$\text{per lineage rate of cladogenesis} = b\left(\frac{1}{n}\right)^r \qquad (1)$$

where b and r are constant and n is the number of lineages. The forms of density dependence commonly used in population biology (May 1976) do not provide good fits to the data.

The distribution of subtaxa per taxon

There is a considerable literature examining the number of subtaxa per taxon, such as the number of species per genus, or genera per family (e.g. Williams 1964, Burlando 1990). However, previous studies of which we

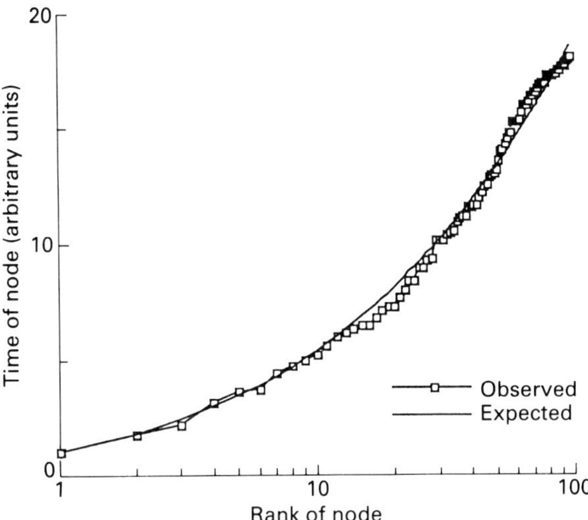

FIG. 5.3. Plot of time of node (since first node, measured in delta $T_{50}H$ units) against rank of node, with the latter drawn on a logarithmic scale. The plot would be a straight line if effective cladogenesis rates had remained constant through time. In fact, rates seem to have declined with time, resulting in a upward curved line. A density-dependent model in which the rate of cladogenesis declines as a multiple of $(1/n)^r$, where n is the number of clades and r is a constant provides a good fit to the data as seen by the 'expected' line in the figure.

are aware have not been purely phylogenetic but are based on evolutionary or phenetic classifications, neither of which attempts to describe phylogenetic relationships (see Ridley 1986, Harvey & Pagel 1991). Insofar as such classifications do reflect phylogeny, time units are inevitably amalgamated so that the age of any given taxon relates to divergence from a common ancestor between x and y time units ago. For example, we might say that each single lineage which existed more than 25 million years should be granted family status, whereas those existing less than 10 million years ago be called genera. If a split occurred 25 million years ago to produce two extant species, and another occurred 10 million years ago each pair of species would be placed within the same family but in different genera. However, a split occurring 9 million years ago would place the species within the same genus.

Over DNA divergence units between, say, 20 and 15 time units and between 15 and 10 time units, rates of effective cladogenesis remained roughly constant (that is, the curve in Fig. 5.3 approximates to a straight line during each of those periods). Under the assumption of constant rates of effective cladogenesis for the different lineages within each of

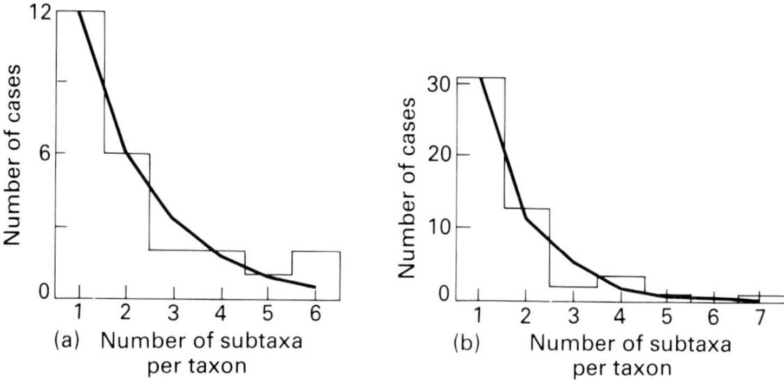

FIG. 5.4. Observed (histogram) and expected (heavy lines) numbers of subtaxa per taxon. Expected values are derived from a model in which rates of effective cladogenesis remain constant in each lineage through the time period considered. Each taxon and subtaxon respectively is defined as a lineage (a) 20 and 15, and (b) 15 and 10 time units ago by delta $T_{50}H$ divergence values. In (b) two radiations are excluded from both observed and expected values: the Ciconiiformes with 19 subtaxa, and the Passeri with 15 subtaxa defined as lineages 10 time units ago.

those two time frames, we can estimate the frequency distribution of subtaxa per taxon. This is equivalent to fitting the data to Eqn (1) above with $r = 0$, so that only b is estimated. As is evident from Fig. 5.4a, the frequency distribution of taxa recognized at 15 delta $T_{50}H$ units from the present descended from each lineage occurring 20 units ago fits the null expectation very well indeed. Similarly, the distribution of taxa 10 units ago descended from those 15 units ago also fits the null model so long as two major radiations, the Ciconiiformes (containing the Charadrii and the Ciconii which, together, include the sandpipers, plovers, gulls, auks, diurnal birds of prey and grebes) and the Passeri (songbirds), are not included (Fig. 5.4b). The number of taxa containing eight or more subtaxa is expected to be about 0.085, yet the Ciconiiformes and Passeri contain 15 and 19 subtaxa respectively, both highly unlikely events under our model.

Assessment

On the face of it, Fig. 5.3 demonstrates that avian effective cladogenesis has been slowing down over time, as a consequence of lower clade production rates, higher clade extinction rates, or both. However, such an interpretation is particularly dependent on Sibley and Ahlquist's delta $T_{50}H$ units representing a molecular clock that ticks at a constant rate. If each successive delta $T_{50}H$ unit measures less evolutionary change, then it is still perfectly possible that rates of effective cladogenesis have remained constant through time. Sibley and Ahlquist claim that the clock is not constant among avian lineages and argue that taxa with longer generation times evolve at a slower rate in real time (Sibley & Ahlquist 1990, ch. 13). However, it is not clear how such differences among lineages would result in the temporal trend shown in Fig. 5.3. The possibility that the real degree of molecular divergence among taxa is not linearly related to time since divergence is best tested by matching molecular data against a timed palaeontological record. Wayne *et al.* (1991) have done exactly that with the relatively sparse data available for carnivores and primates. The carnivores show rates of molecular divergence which appear to decrease the longer that lineages have been separated, while the primate data show no clear pattern (Nee *et al.*, in press). If the bird data in Fig. 5.3 were corrected in line with the results from carnivores, the decreased rate of effective cladogenesis with time would become even stronger.

It would, of course, be far more interesting to ecologists if cladogenesis decreased as a consequence of niche saturation. We might imagine that, shortly after the origin of birds, there were many new niches to occupy but these have slowly become filled to provide increasing resistance to further cladogenesis. Eqn (1) provides a functional description of such density-dependent cladogenesis. It will be interesting to construct models of niche filling and creation which lead to Eqn (1).

Further back in time, but not more recently, we have also provided evidence for lineage-dependent rates of cladogenesis: some lineages were more prone to cladogenesis than others (Table 5.1). However, part of this pattern also accords with Fig. 5.3 because branches emanating from shorter branches start further back in time than those emanating from longer branches, and therefore might be expected to have higher rates of effective cladogenesis. However, that could not account for the temporal heterogeneity shown in Table 5.1: the pattern is found only high in the tree. Why do we lose the pattern as we move down the tree? One possibility is that the signal-to-noise ratio increases as we move from the root towards the tips. Nodes high in the tree are calculated from data of many DNA-hybridization experiments, while nodes near the tips are reconstructed from few replicates, often only one. The error variance is therefore likely to be much higher near the tips (see Sibley & Ahlquist 1990) and we might expect the observed pattern of dissipation.

Finally, although a constant probability of cladogenesis within time windows can account for most of the frequency distribution of subtaxa per taxon, there are startling exceptions. We have pointed to two such exceptions: the Passeri and the Ciconiiformes. The factors responsible for those radiations remain unknown.

Is population density associated with phylogenetic affinity?

It has long been known that bigger birds and those living on more widely dispersed food supplies have larger territories (Schoener 1968). If territories were contiguous, then those same species would have lower population densities. Following Brown and Maurer's (1987) work on the birds of North America, we have examined the data for British birds, collected by British Trust for Ornithology (BTO) volunteers (Nee *et al.*, 1991). The BTO data are of unusually high quality because the number of individuals of the rarest species tends to be known quite precisely. Population density decreases with increased body size raised to the −0.75 power, in accord with Damuth's (1981, 1987) energetic equivalence hypothesis. However, we were surprised to find that this correlation vanished when the passerine birds, which are generally small-bodied, were removed from the data set. Furthermore, there was no equivalent correlation within the passerines themselves. This suggested to us that the relationship between population density and body size might differ according to phylogenetic affinity.

Using the data from all the birds, about 65% of the 45 correlations among species within genera and generic means within tribes were actually positive (binomial $p = 0.072$), compared with only 25% of the 16 comparisons at the parvorder level and above (binomial $p = 0.077$). The pattern within higher taxa is significantly different from that among lower taxa ($\chi_1^2 = 7.40$, $p < 0.007$). Why should this be? The negative correlations found within the higher taxa are as expected (Schoener 1968, Harvey & Mace 1983). It is the positive correlations within the lower taxa that require explanation. One possibility is distinctly ecological: closely related species within a community are likely to constitute an ecological guild (Root 1967) and, if food resources are limiting, larger bodied competitors may displace their smaller bodied relatives in direct competition. As a consequence, larger bodied species within guilds would be found at higher population densities.

Nee *et al.* (1991) were able to make a test of the guild structure hypothesis. They argued that those tribes most likely to comprise a complete guild would be the ones without close relatives within the community being studied. Species belonging to tribes with close phylogenetic relatives represented in the data set would be likely to share a similar life-style with their relatives, and to compete with them for resources. Therefore, the positive correlation between body size and population density should be found most commonly in those tribes without close phylogenetic relatives because the confounding effects of the presence of other direct competitors would be absent. In accord with their expectation, Nee and co-workers found that those tribes among whose species there is a positive correlation between population density and body size are the ones that root into the phylogenetic tree more deeply: they have fewer close phylogenetic relatives within the community than the tribes for which the correlation is negative. Similar results have been found across 91 bird communities sampled from around the world (P. Cotgreave, personal communication). So, if the guild structure and competition hypotheses turn out to be unfounded, the rootedness phenomena remain in need of explanation.

PATCH REMOVAL AND METAPOPULATION DYNAMICS

The world is becoming increasingly fragmented, at least as far as populations are concerned. Metapopulation theory describes the dynamics of populations among which there is limited migration. Populations die out from time to time, to be re-established by successful invasion from other populations. Probably all species persist as metapopulations at an appropriate spatial scale. Such a world consists of habitable patches but in the real world the number of such patches is likely to be changed, typically decreased, as a result of human activity. We describe here a model developed by Nee and May (1992) which shows how reduction in the number of patches can have unforeseen consequences on community structure.

Nee and May examine what will happen to coexisting competitors in a fragmented world in which habitable patches become less common. In their model, one competitor is superior to the other, and three types of habitable patches are defined: unoccupied patches, patches occupied by superior competitors and patches occupied by inferior competitors. Unoccupied patches can be invaded by superior competitors or by inferior competitors. Patches occupied by superior competitors can become unoccupied through population extinction. And patches occupied by inferior competitors can either become unoccupied or be invaded by superior competitors. The model system is illustrated in Fig. 5.5.

A necessary condition for inferior competitors to persist in such a system is that:

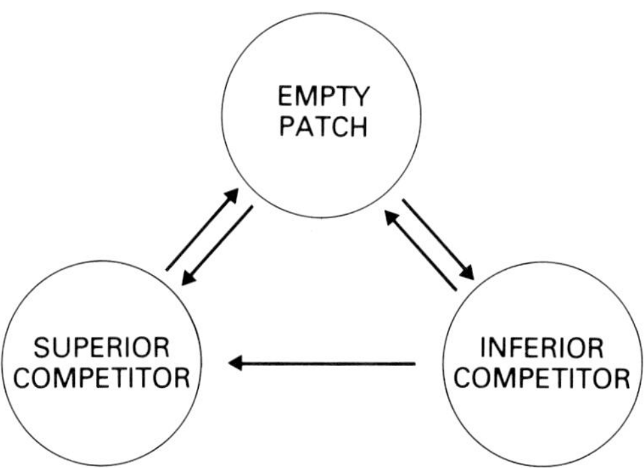

FIG. 5.5. The structure of the model analysed by Nee and May (1992), showing the three types of patches and the permitted routes of transition from one patch type to another. (For example, the arrow pointing from inferior competitor patches to superior competitor patches denotes that patches occupied by inferior competitors may turn into patches occupied by superior competitors.) Under necessary conditions for inferior competitors to persist in the system, a reduction in the number of patches can lead to an increase in the regional abundance of inferior competitors. The reason is that the number of both superior and inferior competitor patches is reduced, but the reduction in the number of superior competitor patches means less infection of inferior competitor patches by superior competitors.

$$\frac{c_B}{e_B} > \frac{c_A}{e_A} \quad (2)$$

where B is the inferior competitor, A is the superior competitor, c is patch colonization rate and e is patch extinction rate. Each side of the equation is a measure of the life-time reproductive success of the patches containing one type of competitor and can be viewed as a product of the fertility and survival of particular patch types. In fact, Eqn (2) says that a necessary condition for the inferior competitor to persist is that it has a higher R_0 (Anderson & May 1979) than the superior or, less rigorously, a higher 'metapopulation level fitness'. Even though the superior competitor wins in competition within patches, the inferior competitor may persist if it is a superior patch colonizer or if patches containing it are less likely to go extinct. As Nee and May point out, providing several references to papers published between 1951 and 1987, it has long been known that there are circumstances under which inferior competitors can persist within metapopulations. What we have just pointed out is the connection between these ecological theories and the evolutionary theories of group selection.

Now, what happens when patches are removed? Since inferior competitors persist by virtue of colonizing empty patches, the naive expectation is that patch removal will be to their detriment. If patch removal is indiscriminate, patches containing both superior and inferior competitors will be reduced in number. However, because patches with superior competitors can 'infect' patches with inferior competitors, the removal of the former reduces that infection rate so that the proportion and, in fact, the number of patches with inferior competitors may actually increase because of the decreased transition rate of patches from state B to state A. As Nee and May (1992) write 'Thus, patch removal can actually increase the regional abundance of inferior competitors. We discuss the implications of these results for understanding biodiversity changes in a changing world'.

CONCLUDING DISCUSSION

We live in a hierarchical world and the analysis of biological data is usually performed at one level of each particular hierarchy. For example, evolutionary biologists usually analyse selection at the level of the gene or of the individual, while ecologists may range in their discussions from the individual through the population, the trophic level to the community, or even the ecosystem. The links between evolution and ecology have, for the most part, been forged at the level of the individual genotype. However, as we hope to have illustrated in this chapter, selection among clades or among populations can provide interesting biological insights. Indeed, we should go further and say that understanding the interaction between ecology and evolution requires a hierarchical approach.

When history is written, the fading of ecological genetics from the scientific firmament, after a promising flurry in the 1950s and 1960s, may become generally interpreted in terms of the failure of its practitioners to broaden their hierarchical perspectives to take into account selection among populations and, indeed, clades. The group selection debate in the 1960s, which quite rightly drew attention to loose thinking and incorrect conclusions, seems to have stultified the general acceptance of a hierarchical approach being important to evolutionary processes. This may be partly because the debate was concerned primarily with how to understand the evolution of altruism, a social behaviour, rather than competitive ability, which, in retrospect, would have been more natural. As we have seen in this paper, and as has been long evident, clades and populations have fecundity and survival rates that allow us to define appropriate fitness measures for our analyses. Rather than analysing the strength of selection at the level of the gene against selection at other levels, it may be useful to define the properties of populations and clades which allow them to persist and to multiply. We do not yet know, for example, why the Passeri radiated but they certainly did, presumably because some property possessed by individuals or by the group as a whole resulted in much higher rates of cladogenesis than was true for sister taxa. To argue whether this may or may not have been due to species selection is, perhaps, tantamount to placing semantic issues above biological investigation. We must define our terms but in so doing it can be useful to have examples to cite that illustrate the different processes among which we are attempting to distinguish.

REFERENCES

Allen, T. F. H. & Starr, T. B. (1982). *Hierarchy: Perspectives for Ecological Complexity*. Chicago University Press, Chicago, IL, USA.

Anderson, R. M. & May, R. M. (1979). Population biology of infectious diseases: Part I. *Nature, London*, **280**, 361–367.

Brooks, D. B. & Wiley, E. O. (1986). *Evolution as Entropy: Toward a Unified Theory of Biology*. Chicago University Press, Chicago, IL, USA.

Brown, J. H. & Maurer, B. A. (1987). Evolution of species assemblages: effects of energetic constraints and species dynamics on the diversification of the North American avifauna. *American Naturalist*, **130**, 1–17.

Burke, T. (1989). DNA fingerprinting and other methods for the study of mating success. *Trends in Ecology and Evolution*, **4**, 139–144.

Burlando, B. (1990). The fractal dimension of taxonomic systems. *Journal of Theoretical Biology*, **146**, 99–114.

Damuth, J. (1981). Population density and body size in mammals. *Nature, London*, **290**, 699–700.

Damuth, J. (1987). Interspecific allometry of population density in mammals and other animals: the independence of body mass and population energy-use. *Biological Journal of the Linnean Society*, **31**, 193–246.

Ghiselin, M. T. (1988). The origin of molluscs in the light of molecular evolution. *Oxford Surveys in Evolutionary Biology*, **5**, 66–95.

Gilpin, M. & Hanski, I. (Eds) **(1991).** Metapopulation dynamics. *Biological Journal of the Linnean Society*, **42**, 1–323.

Harvey, P. H. (1985). Intrademic group selection and the sex ratio. *Behavioural Ecology: Ecological Consequences of Adaptive Behaviour* (Ed. by R. M. Sibly & R. H. Smith), pp. 59–73. Blackwell Scientific Publications, Oxford, UK.

Harvey, P. H. & Mace, G. M. (1983). Foraging models and territory size. *Nature, London*, **305**, 14–15.

Harvey, P. H. & Pagel, M. D. (1991). *The Comparative Method in Evolutionary Biology*. Oxford University Press, Oxford, UK.

Hillis, D. M. & Moritz, C. (1990). *Molecular Systematics*. Sinauer, Sunderland, MA, USA.

Jeffreys, A. J., Wilson, V. & Thein, S. L. (1985). Hypervariable 'minisatellite' regions in human DNA. *Nature, London*, **314**, 67–73.

Kimura, M. (1968). Evolutionary rate at the molecular level. *Nature, London*, **217**, 624–626.

May, R. M. (1976). Models for single populations. *Theoretical Ecology: Principles and Applications* (Ed. by R. M. May), pp. 4–25, Blackwell Scientific Publications, Oxford, UK.

Nee, S. & May, R. M. (1992). Dynamics of metapopulations: habitat destruction and competitive coexistence. *Journal of Animal Ecology*, **61**, 37–40.

Nee, S., Mooers, A. Ø. & Harvey, P. H. The tempo and mode of evolution revealed from molecular phylogenies. *Proceedings of the National Academy of Sciences, USA* (in press).

Nee, S., Read, A. F., Greenwood, J. J. D. & Harvey, P. H. (1991). Taxonomic relationships between abundance and body size in British birds. *Nature*, **351**, 312–313.

Ridley, M. (1986). *Evolution and Classification: The Reformation of Cladism*. Longman, London, UK.

Root, R. B. (1967). The niche exploitation pattern of the blue-gray gnatcatcher. *Ecological Monographs*, **37**, 317–350.

Sarich, V. M., Schmid, C. W. & Marks, J. (1989). DNA hybridization as a guide to phylogeny: a critical analysis. *Cladistics*, **5**, 3–32.

Schoener, T. W. (1968). Sizes of feeding territories among birds. *Ecology*, **49**, 704–726.

Sibley, C. J. & Ahlquist, J. E. (1990). *Phylogeny and Classification of Birds: A Case Study in Molecular Evolution*. Yale University Press, New Haven, CT, USA.

Sokal, R. R. & Michener, C. D. (1958). A statistical method for evaluating systematic relationships. *University of Kansas Science Bulletin*, **38**, 1409–1438.

Thorpe, J. P. (1982). The molecular clock hypothesis. *Annual Review of Ecology and Systematics*, **13**, 139–168.

Vrba, E. S. (1989). Levels of selection and sorting with special reference to the species level. *Oxford Surveys in Evolutionary Biology*, **6**, 111–168.

Vrba, E. S. & Gould, S. J. (1986). The hierarchical expansion of sorting and selection: sorting and selection cannot be equated. *Paleobiology*, **12**, 217–228.

Wayne, R. K., Van Valkenburgh, B. & O'Brien, S. J. (1991). Molecular distance and divergence time in carnivores and primates. *Molecular Biology and Evolution*, **8**, 297–319.

Williams, C. B. (1964). *Patterns in the Balance of Nature*. Academic Press, London, UK.

Wilson, A. C., Cann, R. L., Carr, S. M., George, M., Gyllensten, U. B., Helm-Bychowski, K. M., Higuchi, R. G., Palumbi, S. R., Prager, E. M., Sage, R. D. & Stoneking, M. (1985). Mitochondrial DNA and two perspectives on evolutionary genetics. *Biological Journal of the Linnean Society*, **26**, 375–400.

6. THE COEVOLUTION OF PLANT–INSECT AND HOST–PARASITE RELATIONSHIPS

DOUGLAS J. FUTUYMA* AND ROBERT M. MAY†
*Department of Ecology and Evolution, State University of New York, Stony Brook, NY 11794, USA and †Department of Zoology, University of Oxford, South Parks Road, Oxford OX1 3PS and Imperial College, London SW7 2BB, UK

INTRODUCTION

The chapters in this volume are written by unlike pairings, and this chapter is no exception. There are, however, good reasons for thinking it might be a sensible idea to treat coevolution between plant hosts and phytophagous insects and between animal hosts and microparasites (*sensu* Anderson & May 1979; broadly viruses, bacteria and protozoans), within a common framework.

To begin with, both kinds of associations involve an exploiting and an exploited population, with consequent pressures upon each population to evolve to foil the other. This immediately leads to the general question of whether we expect such evolutionary pressures to produce some static or cyclic (even chaotically shifting) balance, or whether we may expect indefinite escalation in an 'arms race' of, as it were, escape and pursuit. More particularly, host–microparasite and plant–insect systems have some common features that distinguish them from prey–predator systems in general, making it sensible to compare them. These common features typically include a marked disparity in generation times (with the exploiter — insect or microparasite — commonly having a life expectancy that is several orders of magnitude shorter than that of the exploited plant or animal host), and a tendency for many insects and microparasites to be specific to a single kind of host (as distinct from many generalist vertebrate predators).

These commonalities being acknowledged, there remain several significant differences between plant–insect and host–microparasite systems. Among these are differences in the way the exploiters get from host to host: phytophagous insects by dispersal (often flying), and microparasites sometimes by direct (or effectively direct, such as coughing or sneezing infectious droplets) contact between hosts and sometimes indirectly via intermediate vectors. It follows that, other things being equal, microparasites will often optimize transmissibility by not harming their host too much, whereas such considerations are likely to be less significant for phytophagous insects. Hence, movement from host to host may often act to limit the evolution of virulence for microparasites but seldom for phytophagous insects.

In what follows, we will consider first animal hosts and microparasites and second plants and phytophagous insects. It will quickly become clear that the two kinds of system, although apparently similar, have been explored in different ways both from a theoretical perspective and in relating theory to data. To a large extent this is a consequence of emphasis on different questions.

One set of questions, exemplified by some studies of coevolution of microparasites with their hosts, is posed within the framework of population biology *sensu stricto*. One asks how a system will behave, with respect to genetic and demographic dynamics, over relatively short time scales, when the theoretical parameters are fairly well defined. In a few instances, some parameters can be estimated well enough from data to explore the relation of data to theory; in the best of cases, time series data are available.

Another set of questions asks why systems have evolved their present characters. Such questions are more historical and macroevolutionary in nature, although population-level processes are often invoked to explain historical patterns. This is the approach taken by most research on plant–insect interactions. The attempt is largely to explain species-typical characters, even though intraspecific variation may be used to probe these questions. For the ecologist, this approach to coevolution has implications mostly for community ecology, including issues such as species diversity and the structure of food webs.

The development of theory, and its relation to empirical investigation, differs between the two approaches. The theoretical formulations of population biology (as used for infectious diseases) are based on: (1) relatively simple ecological interactions, such as one parasite and one host; (2) explicit parameters, such as dispersal and fitnesses, which one might hope to estimate; and (3) a specified and constant set of genotypes (or quantitative genetic parameters such as genetic variances), the behaviour of which is followed (perhaps to equilibrium) within 'ecological time'. For example, Mode's (1958) model was a direct extension from standard population genetics, and like most later theory takes a set of genotypes as given. The advantage of this approach is its concreteness and relation to measurable parameters. The concomitant limitation of the approach is that it says little about long-term dynamics, such as whether or not further evolutionary change, not included within the model, might cause extinction.

In contrast, much of the theory on plant–insect coevolution addresses longer-term outcomes of coevolution, such as whether there is a prolonged, indefinite 'arms race', or what determines the number of species associated with a plant species, or what accounts for the host specificity of insects. Some of these questions can be framed in terms of population genetic models, such as those of Gould (1986), Castillo-Chávez *et al.* (1988) and Rausher (in press a, b) on the evolution of host specificity. But other questions (e.g. whether or not there is an indefinite 'arms race') require one to consider not only a specific set of genotypes but also those that might be imagined to arise over evolutionary time. Such models are highly generalized, to the point of being almost metaphorical. These include: Rosenzweig *et al.*'s (1987) models that embrace, among other things, mutation rates for defensive and counterdefensive characters; Abram's (1990) phenotypic models of cost and benefits (coupled with population dynamics); and the highly abstract models of Stenseth and Maynard Smith (1984), which predict stasis or change for systems of many interacting species, based on conflicting selection imposed on each species by large aggregates of other species.

For the empirical worker, general models of this kind do not offer precise, context-specific predictions. Rather, their results differ little from verbal models, providing broad statements rather than specific conditions under which different outcomes are to be expected. For example, these models tend toward the conclusion that a character (e.g. a plant defence) will evolve to a condition of evolutionary stasis when selection for increase is balanced by counterselection based on investment costs or conflicting species interactions. But there needs no ghost come from the grave to tell us this. This leaves the empirical worker with the tasks of: (1) trying to determine, from historical and functional information, whether coevolutionary histories fit a pattern of continuous escalation, stasis, or punctuational change; and (2) trying to determine if costs or other constraints exist.

The next two sections contrast the relation between theory and data, by considering research on microparasites and their animal hosts, undertaken in a population biological framework, and on 'parasitic' insects and their plant hosts, in which, although the methods of analysis include those of population biology, the questions are more macroevolutionary in nature.

ANIMAL HOSTS AND MICROPARASITES

The various infectious agents that afflict humans and other animals are conventionally classified along taxonomic lines. In discussing the ecology or evolution of host–parasite associations, however, it is more sensible to make distinctions on the basis of the population biology of the interaction.

Microparasites (*sensu* Anderson & May 1979) are those that have direct reproduction — usually at very high rates — within the host. They characteristically have small sizes and short generation times; the duration of infection is typically very short relative to the expected life span of the host, and hosts that recover from infection usually acquire immunity against re-infection for some time, often for life. The result is that most microparasitic infections are transient in individual hosts. Most viral and bacterial parasites, and (more equivocally) many protozoan and fungal parasites, fall broadly into the microparasite category. To analyse the interaction between populations of such microparasites and their hosts, we may divide the host population into relatively few classes of individuals: susceptible, infectious, recovered-and-immune. Our operational definition of a microparasite is, indeed, an infectious agent whose population biology can, to a sensible first approximation, be described by some such compartmental model.

A variety of other kinds of parasites, whose life cycles and evolution are intimately entwined with those of one or more host species, can be distinguished. *Macroparasites* (*sensu* Anderson & May 1979) — broadly, parasitic helminths and arthropods — may be thought of as those having no direct reproduction within the host. They are typically larger and longer lived than microparasites, with generation times that often are an appreciable fraction of the host life span. Lasting immune responses are rarely elicited, so that macroparasitic infections are characteristically persistent, with hosts being continually re-infected. The various factors that characterize host–macroparasite associations — egg output per female parasite, pathogenic effects on the host, parasite death rates, and so on — can all depend on the number of parasites in a given host, and mathematical models must take account of the details of the way the population of macroparasites is distributed among the hosts. *Parasitoids* are arthropods (usually dipteran or hymenopteran species) that lay their eggs in or on the larvae or pupae of other insects; the parasitoid offspring kill their host. This life-style accounts for as much as 10% or more of all metazoan species. Dobson (1982) has given a useful summary of some of the relations among life-history characteristics of microparasites, macroparasites, parasitoids and conventionally defined predators. This summary would serve as a point of departure for a wider discussion of similarities and differences among various categories of host–parasite associations, if space permitted. Interspecific and intraspecific brood parasitism is yet another category of animal host–parasite association, with themes running parallel to those below. We shall offer a brief guide to the literature on coevolution in the systems mentioned in this paragraph later (p. 148).

Dynamics of host–microparasite associations

Suppose we have a population of hosts where generations overlap completely, so that population change is a continuous process. The basic model for the interaction between such a host population and a microparasitic agent takes the familiar form of differential equations, describing the rate of change in the number or density of susceptible, infected-and-infectious, and recovered-and-immune hosts, $X(t)$, $Y(t)$, $Z(t)$, respectively:

$$\mathrm{d}X/\mathrm{d}t = B(X, Y, Z) - \mu X - \beta XY + \gamma Z \tag{1}$$

$$\mathrm{d}Y/\mathrm{d}t = \beta XY - (\mu + v + \alpha)Y \tag{2}$$

$$\mathrm{d}Z/\mathrm{d}t = vY - (\mu + \gamma)Z \tag{3}$$

Here $B(X, Y, Z)$ represents the rate at which new hosts are born; μ is the per capita death rate; v and α are the rates at which hosts move out of the infectious category by recovering or by dying from the infection, respectively; and γ is the rate at which immunity is lost ($\gamma = 0$ if immunity is lifelong). A key feature is the non-linear term βXY, which in this simplest model describes the rate at which new infections appear (proportional both to the number susceptible, X, and the number infectious, Y; β is a rate parameter characterizing transmission efficiency). The total host population is $N = X + Y + Z$.

The population dynamics of these and related equations have been thoroughly studied (for a review, see Anderson & May 1991). The details depend on the assumptions made about density dependence in the birth rate, B, but broadly the microparasite can regulate an otherwise exponentially-growing population to a stable equilibrium value (either monotonically or via damped oscillations), provided the disease-induced death rate or virulence, α, is large enough. The equations also describe the epidemics that arise when infection is introduced into a susceptible population. Analogous equations describe the regulatory effects of microparasites in host populations with discrete, non-overlapping generations (as found in many temperate zone insects); here the 'regulated' state may be chaotic fluctuations in host abundance (May 1985).

Genetics of host–microparasite associations

The previous subsection dealt with epidemiology, with no reference to genetics. We now sketch work on the coevolutionary genetics of host–microparasite associations that makes essentially no reference to the epidemiology. The next subsection will draw these two strands together.

Following the early work of Mode (1958), Day (1974) and Van der Plank (1975), there has been much work on the population genetics of 'gene-for-gene' interactions between hosts and pathogens. These studies assume specific associations between individual genotypes of hosts and corresponding genotypes of pathogens. The work is mainly directed toward pathogens of plants, where there are documented instances of such gene-for-gene associations (for a detailed and critical review see Ennos, Ch. 10, this volume). Constant values are assigned to the fitnesses of each host genotype when attacked by a specific parasite genotype, and the ensuing net fitnesses of the various host genotypes are weighted sums over the appropriate fitnesses (weighted according to the relative abundances of the parasite genotypes). Similar calculations give the fitnesses of the various parasite genotypes. The result is a system in which the host fitnesses depend on the relative gene frequencies within the parasite population and parasite fitnesses depend on host gene frequencies. The simplicity of these assumptions is, however, such that threshold and other important density-dependent effects associated with epidemiological processes are neglected.

These studies of gene-for-gene associations between hosts and microparasites suggest that polymorphisms in the gene frequencies of both hosts and pathogens can easily arise and be maintained. The polymorphisms may be stable, or cyclic, or even chaotic. Levin (1983), however, emphasizes that many of the simpler models can be seen to be neutrally stable, although this fact is often obscured by round-off errors and by the proliferation of parameters in numerical studies.

The essential mechanisms responsible for maintaining polymorphisms in these models, whatever the dynamical details, are the interplay between parasite virulence and the costs of host resistance.

Coevolution of host–microparasite associations

What we need are studies that take the earlier gene-for-gene framework and combine it with fitness functions computed from epidemiological analyses that pay full respect to the non-linear nature of the transmission process. The pioneering study here is by Gillespie (1975) who, however, only considered the statics and not the dynamics of his model. Studies of the full dynamics of such combined genetic and epidemiological models reveal interesting biological and mathematical features (Hamilton 1980, Levin *et al.* 1982, May & Anderson 1983, 1990, Beck 1984, Seger 1988, Seger & Hamilton 1988); for a recent review, see Anderson & May (1991).

Most of these studies are for the conventional metaphor of one locus with two alleles. The studies typically show that gene-for-gene associations between hosts and microparasites promote genetic diversity, with polymorphisms that may be stable or varying from generation to generation in cyclic or even chaotic fashion. The reason is straightforward: once the epidemiological dynamics are recognized, rarer alleles of hosts or parasites are seen often to be favoured (essentially because rare host genotypes are typically less susceptible to currently prevailing parasite genotypes, and rare parasite genotypes typically find few hosts resistant to them), which leads to polymorphisms that may be static or shifting, depending on the details.

Going beyond single-locus studies, Seger (1988; see also Seger & Hamilton 1988) has used computer simulations to explore the coevolutionary properties of a model in which two loci in the host determine a strain-specific defence against parasites. He finds that intermediate rates of recombination tend to produce cyclically varying polymorphisms (while extreme recombination rates do not). Seger's model suggests that parasites can, in effect, act as a fluctuating environment which favours the evolution of intermediate rates of recombination in the host population.

In short, it has long been recognized that the frequency-dependent and density-dependent selective effects that act reciprocally between animal host populations and microparasites are likely to create and maintain genetic polymorphisms (Haldane 1949). But essentially all earlier work, both theoretical and empirical, has implicitly assumed that such polymorphisms will be at some steady level. It now appears that host–microparasite interactions will often produce polymorphisms that vary cyclically or chaotically. These may even have wider implications for the evolution of sex (Hamilton 1980; Seger & Hamilton 1988). All this has obvious and important implications for empirical studies of such polymorphisms, both in the laboratory and in the field.

Evolution of virulence

It is commonly asserted that 'well adapted' or 'successful' parasites will be relatively harmless to their hosts. While it is possible to assemble data that seem to support this view (Allison 1982, Holmes 1982; for a more equivocal look at the data, see May & Anderson 1983), the theoretical arguments advanced to support it are blatantly group selectionist: it is supposedly in the interest of the parasite population not to harm its host population too much. More careful appraisal makes it clear that the coevolutionary trajectories of hosts and microparasites depend on the detailed interplay among the transmission and virulence of the parasite and the costs of host resistance. If virulence were entirely unconnected with other factors, then indeed the evolutionary interests of both hosts and parasites would, independently, be best served by avirulence. But transmissibility, virulence and resistance costs are rarely unconnected, which makes things more complex.

Some feeling for what is involved can be gained by returning to Eqns (1–3), and focusing only on the parasite. The intrinsic fitness (Fisher's 'net reproductive value') of a microparasite is measured by the number of new infections produced, on average, by each infected host in a population that is almost entirely susceptible. Looking at Eqn (2) in this limit (when $X \simeq N$), we see that this net reproductive value, R_0, is given by:

$$R_0 = \beta N/(\alpha + \mu + v) \qquad (4)$$

This result can be understood intuitively. Each infected individual produces new infections at a rate βN per unit time, and does so, on average, for a time that is the reciprocal of the sum of the rates of moving out of the infected class (by dying from disease, α, or other causes, μ, or by recovering, v), namely $1/(\alpha + \mu + v)$. As Eqn (2) makes clear, the microparasite can invade and maintain itself only if $R_0 > 1$, and the larger R_0, the higher the parasite's reproductive capacity or fitness.

If recovery rates (v) and transmission (βN) were uncoupled from virulence (α), then clearly the microparasite maximizes R_0 by being avirulent ($\alpha \rightarrow 0$). But most of the nasty effects that parasites have on hosts are connected with producing transmission stages, so that both transmission efficiency (β) and recovery rates (v) will in general be explicitly connected with α. Once this is recognized, it is obvious that the value of α that maximizes R_0 — the optimal degree of virulence — depends on the details of the functional relations among βN, v and α. Evolution could favour decreasing virulence, increasing virulence, or convergence to some intermediate level. There is no *a priori* way of knowing. The details matter.

It must be emphasized that the argument in the preceding two paragraphs focuses exclusively (and in a frankly oversimplified way) on the evolutionary pressures experienced by parasite individuals. It is not a coevolutionary argument. Even so, the argument in general, and Eqn (4) in particular, make it clear that the extent to which parasites will tend to evolve toward avirulence depends on the degree to which transmissibility and recovery rates are linked with harmful effects on host physiology or behaviour. Unfortunately, virtually no information is available about these kinds of linkages. Yet, without such information, studies of the evolution of virulence are doomed to sterile abstraction.

There is one example where sufficient data are available to make a very rough assessment of the interrelationships in Eqn (4), and thence to say something about the likely evolution of avirulence in a specific instance. This example is the Australian rabbit–myxoma virus system, following the introduction of the virus into Australia in 1950. This case study has been fully discussed elsewhere (Anderson & May 1982; for a summary see Anderson & May 1991, pp. 649–652). Suffice it to say that a theoretical analysis based on Eqn (4) (with relations among α, v and βN roughly estimated from data) suggests myxoma evolves from the highly virulent strain that was originally introduced, to a strain of intermediate virulence. Too high a virulence kills rabbits too fast, whereas too low a virulence allows them to recover too fast; R_0 is maximized at intermediate values of α. This theoretical conclusion is not the story commonly told in introductory texts (which usually tell of ever-diminishing virulence) but it matches the facts.

To our knowledge, no other studies provide enough information to infer the shape of functional relationships among virulence, transmissibility and recovery rates. But there are certainly instances where empirical evidence indicates that transmissibility and damage to the host are so entangled that it is difficult, and probably impossible, for the parasite to evolve toward harmlessness. Moore (1984), for example, has reviewed many instances where parasites with indirect life cycles modify the behaviour of their vertebrate or invertebrate hosts in such a way as to facilitate transmission to the next stage in the parasite's life cycle, even though this behaviour increases host mortality. Many invertebrate hosts have relatively short lives anyway, and such pressures toward avirulence as do exist are correspondingly weak; thus many baculoviruses kill their insect hosts and, in doing so, effectively turn them into masses of viral transmission stages.

To summarize, both theory and some empirical evidence suggest that the coevolution between hosts and microparasites can follow many evolutionary paths, depending on the relations among parasite transmissibility and virulence, and host cost of resistance.

Other 'host–parasite' systems

At the start of this section, we mentioned other associations that could be gathered under the umbrella of 'animal hosts and parasites'. Lacking space to pursue these in detail, we provide here a guide to the literature on coevolutionary aspects of such associations (with the warning that much of the work really deals with evolution of one partner, or non-interactively with both, rather than with genuine coevolution).

For macroparasites, as defined earlier, the trade-offs among transmissibility, virulence and cost of host resistance are as for microparasites, but further complicated by the facts that most hosts harbour many worms or ectoparasitic arthropods and that macroparasite life-times are usually significantly longer (relative to the hosts) than are microparasites. There has not been much theoretical work in this area (May & Anderson 1978). Among the many complexities that need to be dealt with, notice that parasites (such as trypanosomes) that keep 'changing their coat' in a programmed sequence not only evade immune responses but also reduce intraspecific competition within the host (because later invasions by fellow parasite individuals find it harder to establish themselves in a host whose immune system is already mobilized against the early stages of this particular invader).

Hosts and parasitoids typically have life cycles that are roughly synchronized, which moves them yet further than macroparasites away from the very disparate generation times characteristic of host–microparasite and most plant–insect systems. For theoretical and empirical work on the coevolutionary dynamics of host–parasitoid systems see Price (1980) and Godfray and Hassell (1991).

The population dynamics of the interaction between species-specific avian brood parasites and their hosts has formal similarities to host–parasitoid systems (May & Robinson 1985). This is a variety of host–parasite association where there has been a good deal of work combining field observations with verbal models (for recent reviews, see Rothstein & Mason 1986 and Davies & Brooke 1988), and a limited amount of analysis of the population dynamics, but little connection either between the two approaches or with other host–parasite systems (and very little on population genetics).

Finally, intraspecific brood parasitism, among birds and other animals, poses some of the basic host–parasite coevolutionary questions in sharp form (Andersson 1984, Møller & Petrie 1991). Theoretical work that blends game theory with population dynamics suggests that once the habit of brood parasitism arises in a population, it is likely to spread, in turn eliciting some kind of vigilant response. The result is likely to be a population where different genotypes within the population play, as it were, different strategies or where individual birds play mixed strategies. In either event, this kind of behavioural polymorphism can, in principle, drive cycles in the overall abundance of the population (May *et al.* 1991). If this theoretical possibility turns out to be manifested by real animals, it will be a surprising example where the coevolution of host and parasite behaviour within a single population leads to cyclic changes in population density.

PHYTOPHAGOUS ARTHROPODS AND THEIR HOST PLANTS

Speculations about coevolution among plants and herbivores have historically been stimulated by observations on the host specificity of many phytophages, on taxonomic patterns (e.g. associations of related insects with related plants), and on differences among plant taxa in the diversity of their associated faunas and in characteristics thought to affect their susceptibility to herbivores. The major thrust of work in this field has consequently been to explain how and why these patterns have arisen — an understanding that bears on evolutionary questions about the genesis of diversity and on ecological questions about the structure of communities (Southwood 1961, Ehrlich & Raven 1964, Strong *et al.* 1984). These questions are largely historical. Although population biological studies have been used to explore processes responsible for the patterns, the chief focus has been on the historical genesis of pattern, rather more than on the genetic and demographic dynamics of interacting species in 'ecological' time.

Coevolution of plants and herbivores: meaning and models

As mentioned earlier, the term 'coevolution' has sometimes been used so broadly as to mean little more than evolution (as by some authors who attribute adaptations of an insect to a plant to coevolution, without reference to evolutionary responses of the plant). Janzen (1980), Futuyma and Slatkin (1983) and others have urged that the term be restricted to instances in which both parties to an interaction (where a 'party' may be a single species or an aggregate of ecologically similar species) evolve in response to mutually imposed selection. Even if restricted, the term embraces several phenomena (Thompson 1989, Brooks & McLennan 1991, Futuyma & Keese 1992). These include the following.

1 Coadaptation, or adaptation and counteradaptation. This may be pairwise, as when single plant and insect species impose much stronger selection on each other than do other species; or 'diffuse', when at least one species (e.g. a plant) is strongly affected by many species of antagonists (e.g. many arthropod species, but perhaps pathogens and mammalian herbivores as well).

2 'Escape-and-radiate' coevolution, Thompson's (1989) term for the frequently misunderstood scenario of Ehrlich and Raven (1964). These authors postulated that a plant species, under selection from herbivores, evolves a new defence that largely frees it from herbivory. As a consequence (although the mechanism is obscure), the lineage diversifies, with the descendant species of the clade sharing the novel defence. At some later time, one or more of these species is 'colonized' by an insect lineage that undergoes its own adaptive radiation, with descendant species shifting to related plants that provide underused resources. Hence, related insect species will be associated with related plants. However, because the diversification of plants has preceded that of the insect clade, there need not be strong congruence between the phylogenetic structure of the insect clade and that of the host clade.

3 Congruent cladogenesis. It is at least conceivable that, as for some associations of 'traditional' parasites and hosts (Brooks & McLennan 1991), the diverging species in an insect lineage have retained an uninterrupted association with their diverging hosts and have at least sometimes speciated in concert with them. Thus the cladograms of plants and insects would be congruent except for asynchronous extinction and speciation. An uninterrupted history of association would imply extensive opportunity for coadaptation and would also imply strong constraints on the ability of insects to adapt to other plants. To the extent that contemporary plant–insect associations stem from recent colonizations (as in the escape-and-radiate model) rather than congruent cladogenesis, the defensive features of plants are likely to have evolved in response to former, perhaps phylogenetically distant, enemies, rather than to currently associated insect species or their immediate ancestors.

Very little formal theory treats these issues in other than the most general terms. The gene-for-gene models discussed earlier were developed to describe pathogen–host systems but they may provide a general basis for thinking about pairwise coevolution. They are to a limited extent applicable to the interaction between wheat and Hessian fly (*Phytophaga destructor*), in which allelic series at complementary 'resistance' and 'virulence' loci have been identified (Gallun 1978, Gould 1986). Such models will not necessarily apply to diffuse coevolution, nor to polygenic traits that affect the interactions. Although (to our knowledge) explicit genetic models have not been developed for these cases, there is a prevailing expectation that selection will tend toward an 'escalation' (Vermeij 1987) of defences and of insect virulence (ability to attack and survive), limited only by exhaustion of genetic variation or by counterselection (which will establish optimal levels of defence or virulence). Some very general models of predator–prey coevolution (Schaffer & Rosenzweig 1978, Rosenzweig *et al.* 1987) assume that genetic variation can be exhausted, so that the mutation rate for traits affecting the interaction can determine the course of coevolution. No empirical information exists on mutation rates for relevant traits, and it would be very difficult to obtain, because we have little idea of how many such traits might exist. Any of a number of chemical, morphological and phenological plant features can affect susceptibility to at least some insects, and an insect's ability to respond to and grow on a plant is likewise affected by many sensory, biochemical and other features. In phenotypic models of predator–prey coevolution (e.g. Abrams 1990), the outcome is largely determined by benefits versus costs (e.g. of investment in defences). Abrams argues that predator or prey species may evolve in a direction opposite to the popular expectation because population densities may be altered by evolution of one antagonist so as to reduce selection on the other. This conclusion has not been examined experimentally.

Although explicit models of coevolution *per se* are few and highly general, models do exist for components of coevolution, taken separately. These include models of investment in defence by plants (e.g. Fagerström 1989) and of optimal host range (monophagy versus polyphagy) in insects (Futuyma 1983, Castillo-Chávez *et al.* 1988, Rausher in press a). These too are cast largely in terms of costs versus benefits, although the models of insect host range include also the effects of gene frequencies. In particular, whether an insect evolves adaptation to or avoidance of a toxic plant depends on the relative levels of genetic variation for physiological tolerance and for host preference.

The thrust of these considerations is that one might expect indefinitely prolonged investment in, and elaboration of, defence and counterdefence (unless Abrams is right), and selection for polyphagy in insects, except insofar as constraints counter these trends. This is not a deep insight. It means that the chief tasks of the empirical researcher are to determine if plant–herbivore associations are very old and if they have undergone escalation, and to elucidate the constraints on coevolution and on insect host range. Because these topics are reviewed elsewhere (e.g. Jaenike 1990, Rausher in press b, Mitter & Farrell 1991, Futuyma & Keese 1992), we touch on only a few of these issues, and that only superficially.

Historical evidence

Much of the burden of Ehrlich and Raven's (1964) stimulating paper was the evidence that related species of butterflies frequently, although by no means always, feed as larvae on related plants. For example, all the species of Heliconiini feed on Passifloraceae. From this we may infer that plant–insect associations are frequently quite old. This conclusion is reinforced by fossil evidence of the great age (Oligocene or earlier) of many extant insect genera, and by the conservative host associations of some insect genera that have persisted since biogeographic disjunctions dated at almost 50 Ma (Zwölfer & Herbst 1988, Moran 1989, Mitter *et al.* 1991, Mitter & Farrell 1991). Such evidence implies that these insects may be strongly constrained from adapting to unrelated plants, and that there has been extensive opportunity for them to have influenced the evolution of their host lineages. However, conservative associations of large clades of insects and plants do not necessarily imply that each of the included insect lineages has had a continuous association with one of the included plant lineages. For example, all the species of *Ophraella*, a North American genus of chrysomelid beetles, feed on certain Asteraceae, but the best current estimate of the phylogeny of *Ophraella* does not correspond to the phylogeny of the tribes of Asteraceae (Futuyma & McCafferty 1990; Fig. 6.1). Moreover, palynological data indicate that the tribes, and even some genera, of the host plants evolved before the diversification of *Ophraella*, estimated from genetic distances. Thus the distinctive secondary compounds of asteraceous tribes, many of which are toxic or repellent and which may well have evolved to serve a defensive function, cannot be ascribed to these particular insects. Although *Ophraella* species have adapted to these compounds (Futuyma 1991), the origin of the compounds may be ascribed to diffuse coevolution, inasmuch as the plants are attacked by numerous species of insects. Most of the rather few other contrasts of the phylogeny of insect taxa and their host plants have similarly provided little evidence of phylogenetic congruence (Mitter & Farrell 1991), although one genus of chrysomelids provides a striking exception (Farrell & Mitter 1990).

As several authors (e.g. Futuyma 1983, Jermy 1984, Strong *et al.* 1984) have noted, cospeciation appears less common than shifts of insect species from one pre-existing host species to another, although often, as

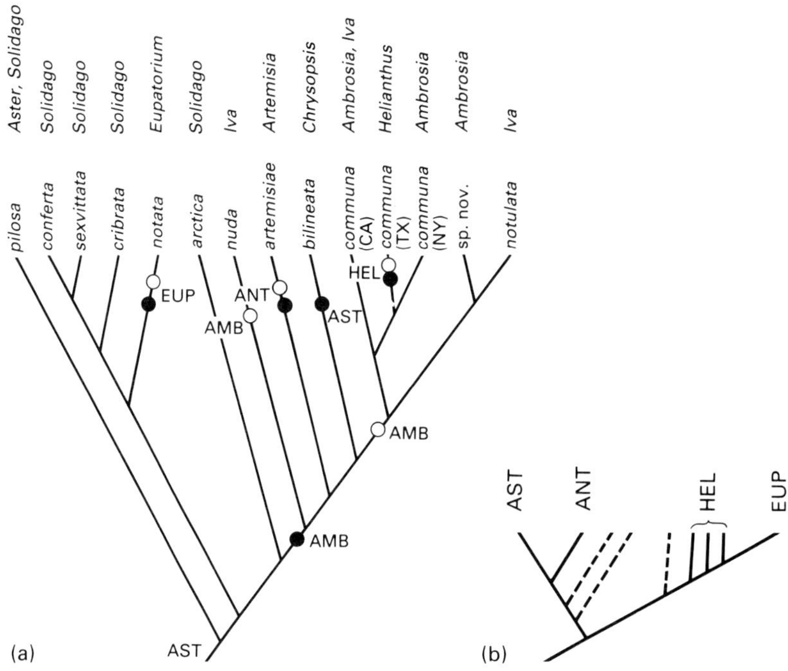

FIG. 6.1. (a) Best current estimate of phylogenetic relationships among species of *Ophraella*. Host plants of species and populations are listed by genus across the top. Filled and open symbols on the phylogenetic tree indicate two equally parsimonious reconstructions of transitions in host affiliation among tribes or subtribes of Asteraceae (AMB, Ambrosiinae; ANT, Anthemideae; AST, Astereae; EUP, Eupatorieae; HEL, Helianthinae). (b) Phylogenetic relationships among tribes of Asteraceae that include hosts of *Ophraella*, based on chloroplast DNA restriction fragment length polymorphism data (Jansen *et al.* 1991). Broken lines indicate position of tribes that do not include *Ophraella* hosts. (After Futuyma and McCafferty 1990.)

in *Ophraella*, within rather narrow taxonomic limits. In the case of *Ophraella*, phylogenetic inference of the history of host shifts suggests that species are more likely to shift to chemically similar than to dissimilar Asteraceae, in accord with Ehrlich and Raven's (1964) proposition.

To assess the extent to which plant features have been escalated during evolution, it would be necessary to show from phylogenetic analysis an historical progression toward more complex or effective defences (e.g. chemicals). The necessary combination of phylogenetic data and experimental data on physiological effects hardly exists but there are instances in which some species in a plant taxon have 'atypical' compounds that appear to liberate them from certain herbivores that feed on related plants (Mitter *et al.* 1991, Futuyma & Keese 1992). In *Asclepias* (milkweeds), there may be a phylogenetic progression from simple to complex, more toxic cardenolides, a progression to which the phylogeny of *Tetraopes* beetles may correspond (Farrell & Mitter in press).

Many insect clades are rather conservative in host affiliation, but the apparently low frequency of cospeciation suggests that associations of individual species of insects and plants often are not very old. Moreover, many individual species of insects, largely because of their rarity, appear to have little impact on plant growth and reproduction, although the impact of herbivores in the aggregate may be considerable (Strong *et al.* 1984). Prevalent opinion therefore holds that coevolution is more likely to be diffuse than pairwise (Strong *et al.* 1984).

Constraints

Constraints on evolutionary change may, for our present purposes, be divided into those arising from selection and those arising from the genetic developmental system. The latter include, for example, lack of genetic variation and pleiotropy, which will often be manifested by genetic correlations among traits. Selective constraints, often referred to as trade-offs, arise from conflicting selection pressures. These may be intimately related to pleiotropy; for example, an optimal combination of egg size and egg number follows from a negative genetic correlation between the traits, owing to allocation of fixed resources. Trade-offs might be inferred from comparisons among species or populations: for instance, one might find that each of several insect species performs better on its own host plant than on the others. However, this is weak support for trade-offs because each species is likely to have evolved adaptations to its peculiar environment (host), and has simply not been faced with the others. Thus the search for trade-offs in insect and plant adaptations has increasingly become a search for negative genetic correlations within populations.

Constraints on plant defences

We say little on this topic because it has been addressed extensively by other authors (e.g. Fritz & Simms 1992, Rausher in press b). Two obvious candidates for constraints on the level of a plant's defence (e.g. amounts of secondary compounds) present themselves: optimal allocation of energy and materials, and conflicting selection by different enemies on the level of any given defence.

Genetic variation in the profile and amounts of plant compounds has been found in most (if not all) the cases in which it has been sought. There is abundant opportunity for selection by herbivores for plant defence, and actual selection has been demonstrated in some cases (Berenbaum *et al.* 1986, Rausher in press b). In a few instances, including comparisons of genotypes, evidence has been presented that high levels of chemical investment (or high levels of resistance, where the resistance factors have not been identified) are negatively correlated with growth or seed set in the absence of herbivores but much of this evidence has been questioned (Rausher in press b, Fritz & Simms 1992). In other experiments, no evidence has been found for an allocation trade-off (Simms & Rausher 1989; see Vrieling 1990, Fritz & Simms 1992).

Certain plant defences surely experience opposing selection pressures by different enemies; for example, glucosinolates in crucifers and hypericin in *Hypericum* are toxic to 'non-adapted' insects but are attractants and/or feeding stimulants to some insects that specialize on these plants (Rees 1969, Chew 1988). However, there is little quantitative information at the population level. In one of the earlier tests for antagonistic selection in natural plant populations, Hare & Futuyma (1978) sought to explain the negative correlation, both within and among local populations, between attack by two seed predators (the tortricid moth *Phaneta imbridana* and the tephritid fly *Euaresta inaequalis*) on the cocklebur *Xanthium strumarium*. Within natural populations and in a greenhouse, largely different sets of morphological and chemical features were correlated with moth versus fly attack individually, and still other features were correlated with apparent resistance to both species. One morphological feature and one chemical compound were positively correlated with attack by one species but negatively correlated with the other: a possible instance of antagonistic selection. On the whole, the insects appeared to respond to different attractant or deterrent characters, and this appears to be the prevailing pattern in field studies of genetic variation in attack by multi-species assemblages of insects (Simms & Rausher 1989, Marquis 1990, Maddox & Root 1990). For example (Maddox & Root 1990), censuses of 17 species of insects on 18 half-sib families of *Solidago altissima* provide evidence of positive genetic correlations in attack by certain suites of insects (clusters of insects with positively correlated distributions over plant families) but few instances of negative genetic correlations in attack by insects in different suites. There is rather little genetic evidence, then, for antagonistic selection by different insects.

The idiosyncratic responses of different insects to plant genotypes or characters may appear surprising, in view of laboratory tests of repellent or toxic compounds that generally yield consistent results across a wide variety of insect taxa, including in some instances those that specialize on the plant. This may imply that major defensive barriers evolve in response to a diverse assemblage of insects that collectively impose strong selection. Those insects that have become adapted to the major barriers may discriminate among plants in a species-specific idiosyncratic way, on the basis of numerous other plant characters. Whether or not these characters evolve in response to the affected insect species is not known. Many of the insect species may be individually too rare to impose substantial selection on the particular traits to which these insects respond. This line of reasoning would predict higher levels of genetic variation for such features than for broadly effective defences, on which selection may be more intense. This hypothesis, which if supported would provide evidence on the function of supposedly defensive secondary compounds, has not (to our knowledge) been advanced before, and has not been tested.

Constraints on insect adaptation

Much of the genetic study of phytophagous insects has been directed more toward understanding reasons for the limited range of host species used, than toward limits on adaptation to variable characters of the host plant (but see Denno & McClure 1983). It should be noted that monophagous or oligophagous species often prefer or perform better on individual plants with relatively low titres of certain defence compounds, and so may be subjected to selection for improved adaptation (references in Futuyma & Keese 1992). Genetic evidence on constraints on adaptation to different plant species should be relevant also to constraints on coevolution with single plant species.

Host specificity is proximally mediated by behaviour, in the form of evolved host preferences. The traditional explanation for the selective advantage of a specialized preference is that some plant species are superior as hosts, owing to the physiology of the plant–insect interaction or to ecological factors such as competition, host-associated predation, or host abundance. The need for an explanation of specialization is particularly acute when two sister species occupy different host species, since this implies that at least one of them abandoned an ancestral host in favour of a new one.

For more than 35 years (see Dethier 1954), the common supposition has been that chemical differences among plants impose constraints on insects' physiological adaptations, so that specialization is favoured because of trade-offs. Genetic studies at Stony Brook and elsewhere have yielded equivocal evidence on this point. Under strong selection, a laboratory population of the spider mite *Tetranychus urticae* became adapted to cucumber (perhaps to its toxic cucurbitacins), but displayed some loss of the capacity to survive on cucumber after several generations of relaxed selection, i.e. maintenance on a superior host (Gould 1979). Fry (1990) obtained a similar result in a fairly similar experiment on this species. Whether or not these results provide evidence for trade-offs may be questioned. Strong artificial selection (or strong natural selection, as in these experiments) is likely to generate linkage disequilibrium between deleterious alleles and loci governing the selected trait. This is a common explanation for the loss of selection gains after relaxation of artificial selection (e.g. Yoo 1980). If so, the selected trait *per se* may not have a fitness cost. A striking outcome of Gould's experiment, directly contrary to expectations from the trade-off hypothesis, was that the cucumber-adapted population displayed positive cross-adaptation to solanaceous plants, as well as to several insecticides (Gould *et al.* 1982).

Several studies of genetic correlation in performance on two different hosts have failed to provide evidence of trade-offs (reviewed by Jaenike 1990, Via 1990, Futuyma & Keese 1992). These include studies of variation among aphid clones, in which rates of growth in numbers provide especially satisfying measures of fitness. An exception is Mackenzie's (1991) elegant analysis of a negative correlation between fitness on *Vicia* and *Tropaeolum* in *Aphis fabae*. Many searches for negative genetic correlations may be criticized, however (Rausher 1988). When genotypes are tested only on natural hosts, it is possible that adaptive genetic change has eliminated trade-offs that existed at one time, and which might have impelled the switch from ancestral to derived hosts. Another problem is that genetic variation in overall 'vigour' may obscure or override a negative genetic correlation, and actually generate a positive genetic correlation.

The latter problem may be addressed by rearing each genotype on more than two plant types, so that overall 'vigour' may be 'factored out', much as a morphometrician studies shape by correcting for differences in 'size'. Futuyma and Philippi (1987) reared asexually propagated genotypes of *Alsophila pometaria*, a geometrid moth, on four species of natural hosts (*Acer rubrum* [Aceraceae] and three species of Fagaceae: *Castanea dentata*, *Quercus coccinea*, *Q. alba*). In both the laboratory and in the field, all the pairwise genotypic correlations in growth rate were positive and many were significant. In an attempt to control for differences in vigour, the authors calculated 'residual' growth rates on three hosts as deviations from each genotype's mean growth on the 'best' host (*Q.*

coccinea). Of the pairwise correlations among the 'residuals', two were statistically significant: one positive and one negative. Futuyma and Philippi were sceptical that this provided evidence for a trade-off. Jaenike (1990) reanalysed their data by principal components analysis, and reported a negative correlation between growth rate on *Acer* versus the Fagaceae. Jaenike concluded that 'the only study to consider more than two hosts simultaneously does support the genetic trade-off hypothesis'. However, the mechanics of principal component analysis ensure loadings of opposite sign in the several principal components.

Constraints on the evolution of host utilization might well arise from a lack of selectable genetic variation. A model is provided by metal tolerance in plants. Only a few species have evolved tolerance to metal-contaminated soils, and in samples of plants from normal soils, genetic variation for metal tolerance was found in all species that have metal-tolerant populations but not in any of those which have not (Bradshaw 1991). The question arises, then, whether the host shifts realized in the history of an insect clade have been guided by differences in levels of genetic variation in features required to use one versus another plant. If constraints on genetic variation have been important, one might expect that although two sister species might display genetic variation in ability to use each other's host, such variation might be less evident with respect to the host of a distant relative, a plant that has not figured in the species' evolutionary history.

The phylogenetic analysis of *Ophraella* (Futuyma & McCafferty 1990), referred to above, was undertaken with such genetic investigations in mind. As described elsewhere (Futuyma 1991), tests of *Ophraella* species on their congeners' hosts show that barriers to host utilization include larval mortality and retarded development (probably due in part to plant toxicity), as well as partial or complete blocks to oviposition and to adult and larval feeding. Our work to date (Futuyma *et al.* in preparation) has focused on feeding behaviour. Each of several *Ophraella* species has been screened for genetic variation in feeding response to several of their congeners' hosts, using in some instances a half-sib design (each male mated to two females) and in other cases families from wild-collected inseminated females (each family may include both full- and half-sibs). Among species examined to date, *Ophraella communa* and *O. notulata* are near relatives; phylogenetic analysis (Fig. 6.1) implies that the host association (*Iva frutescens*) of *O. notulata* has been derived from that of *O. communa* (viz. *Ambrosia*). This lineage has never (based on available data) been associated with *Eupatorium*, the host of the distantly related *O. notata*, and if the lineage's ancestors ever fed on *Solidago*, they did so well before the *communa–notulata* divergence. *Ophraella conferta* feeds on *Solidago altissima* and several related species; its close relative *O. notata* feeds on *Eupatorium*, but the *O. conferta* lineage has had no evolutionary experience of the ambrosiine genera *Ambrosia* and *Iva*.

The details of the experiments will be published elsewhere. Briefly, each individual is presented with discs of fresh leaf material in a petri dish with moist filter paper, and the leaf area grazed or consumed is measured after 24 hours (or at two successive 24-hour intervals). At present, it appears that *O. communa* and *O. notulata* are genetically variable (as expected) in their feeding responses to each other's host (Tables 6.1 and 6.2) and in their responses to *Eupatorium*. No individuals of these species have displayed any feeding response to *Solidago altissima*; thus there is no indication of either phenotypic or expressed genetic variation. Likewise, *O. conferta* displays almost no feeding response to either *Eupatorium* (the host of its fairly close relative) or to *Ambrosia* or *Iva*; the very limited feeding on these plants, by a few individuals, provided no hint of a genetic pattern.

A study of the sister (and sibling) species *Ophraella notulata* and *O. slobodkini*, presently undertaken by Mark Keese for his dissertation at Stony Brook, includes a search for trade-offs that might explain a host shift (cf. remarks above). The phylogenetic study (Fig. 6.1, in which *O. slobodkini* is denoted sp. nov.) implies that *O slobodkini.* retains the common ancestor's association with *Ambrosia* and that *O. notulata* has shifted to *Iva*. Keese has divided full-sib families of each species between

TABLE 6.1. *Ophraella communa* first-instar larval feeding response to *Iva frutescens* and *Eupatorium perfoliatum*. An example of half-sib analysis of variance of consumption data. Each male was mated to two females, and several progeny of each female were scored. A significant sire effect implies an (additive) genetic component to the phenotypic variation

Source	df	SS	*F*	*P*
Iva frutescens				
Model	87	1751.27	2.83	0.0001
Sire	43	1336.52	4.38	0.0001
Dam (Sire)	44	414.74	1.33	0.1029
Error	176	1249.89		
Eupatorium				
Model	87	4393.60	3.06	0.0001
Sire	43	2858.55	4.03	0.0001
Dam (Sire)	44	1535.05	2.12	0.0003
Error	176	2901.40		

TABLE 6.2. Summary of beetle–plant combinations in which evidence for genetic variation in feeding response was either found or not

Test plant	Host of within-clade congener		Host of other-clade congener	
	+	−	+	−
Ophraella communa	Iva		Eup	Sol. alt.
O. slobodkini	Iva			
O. notulata	Amb		Eup	Sol. alt.
O. conferta		Eup		Amb Iva

+, −: Evidence for genetic variation found/not found.
Amb, *Ambrosia artemisiifolia*; Iva, *Iva frutescens*; Eup, *Eupatorium perfoliatum*; Sol. alt., *Solidago altissima*.

the two plants. A negative genetic correlation in performance on the two hosts might imply that a physiological cost imposed selection for the complete switch from one plant to the other. Family means of larval development time appeared positively correlated in *O. slobodkini* (Spearman rank correlation $r_s = 0.17$, $n = 10$) and negatively correlated in *O. notulata* ($r_s = -0.29$, $n = 32$), but neither correlation is statistically significant. Both species displayed a significant family × host interaction, indicating genetic variation in developmental response to the plants. Keese plans to repeat the experiment on a larger scale.

More assays of beetle–plant combinations will be necessary before it will be possible to say if patterns of genetic variation and constraint match the history of host shifts to any extent. The tests so far provide no overwhelming evidence of such a match but they do suggest strongly that differences exist in levels of genetic variation in behavioral responses to different plants. There is good reason to believe that the evolution of host associations can be guided not only by selection but by the availability of genetic variation.

Implications for ecology of studies of plant–insect interactions

Genetic variation exists in insects' adaptations to their host plants (Futuyma & Peterson 1985, Via 1990) and in plant resistance to insects (Denno & McClure 1983, Fritz & Simms 1992), so it is to be expected that coevolutionary effects at the population level will be uncovered, as they have been for certain plant–pathogen interactions (e.g. Parker 1991). These may well affect the distribution and abundance of the interacting species. For example (although there is no evidence of coevolution in this case), poplars (*Populus*) in hybrid zones support far higher populations of *Pemphigus* aphids than do pure species populations of these plants (Whitham 1990). Thus genetic variation within and among populations has important consequences for the ecology of insect–plant systems, as for most other ecological phenomena. At the same time, evidence from both systematics and from the genetic studies described above implies that there are often strong 'historical' constraints on insect feeding habits (and on many organismal features generally). Although phylogenetic conservatism and historical constraints are not news to systematists and historical biogeographers, community ecology appears to be reawakening to this message (Wanntorp *et al.* 1990, Ricklefs & Schluter in press).

The insect associates of a given plant species include, in varying proportions, polyphagous species, stenophagous species related to others that feed on unrelated plants, and stenophagous species that represent a long evolutionary history of association between the insect clade and the plant clade (Southwood 1961, Holloway & Hebert 1979, Strong *et al.* 1984). The course of colonization of an introduced plant, the diversity of a plant's fauna, and the structure of local communities depend both on contemporary ecological processes and on evolutionary events extending deep into the past.

DISCUSSION

It would be nice to conclude with a crisp catalogue of similarities and differences between evolutionary patterns in host–parasite and plant–insect systems. But, as we foreshadowed in our introduction, we do not see our way clear to doing this.

The quite different emphases in our discussion of hosts and microparasites compared to plants and phytophagous insects reflect our personal interests, as well as the differences between the bulk of the literature on these interactions. They may also reflect, in some degree, differences between the kinds of ecological interactions. The great specificity of most microparasites, their documented capacity for rapid genetic change, and their clearly evident demographic and genetic impacts on host populations make it natural to study the dynamics of these systems in 'ecological time'. Furthermore, the medical or economic importance of many pathogens focuses attention on particular species. Conversely, there exists rather little information on the community structure of pathogens and hosts, or on the phylogeny and evolutionary history of the interactions.

In the study of plant–insect interactions, in contrast, we are still trying to determine the extent to which species have any demographic or genetic impact on each other. The wealth of taxonomic and ecological data on patterns of association has focused attention on the historical processes responsible for the patterns revealed by systematics and community ecology. The complexity of linkages between primary producers and consumers has also, undoubtedly, made population models less prominent in this field.

Despite the different traditions of research on these interactions, we suggest that one overriding similarity be recognized. Coevolutionary trajectories in both kinds of systems are constrained by the contingencies of past history, expressed in the life histories of associated organisms. There are no grand generalizations such as 'successful parasites evolve to commensal associations with their hosts', or 'plants and insects are locked in an endless arms race'. Whether or not parasitism evolves toward commensalism depends, *inter alia*, on mechanisms of movement and transmission; whether or not resistance and virulence evolve indefinitely depends on costs. But the exact character of the trade-offs, mechanisms of transmission, and other features that determine the course of coevolution depends on historically contingent details of life histories. We think it likely that the contingencies of life histories would make for as much variety in the coevolutionary patterns found among host–parasite associations or among plant–insect associations, as there are differences between them.

REFERENCES

Abrams, P. (1990). The evolution of anti-predator traits in prey in response to evolutionary change in predators. *Oikos*, **59**, 147–156.

Allison, A. C. (1982). Coevolution between hosts and infectious disease agents, and its effects on virulence. *Population Biology of Infectious Diseases* (Ed. by R. M. Anderson & R. M. May), pp. 245–268. Springer Verlag, New York, NY, USA.

Anderson, R. M. & May, R. M. (1979). Population biology of infectious diseases: Part I. *Nature*, **280**, 361–367.

Anderson, R. M. & May, R. M. (1982). Coevolution of hosts and parasites. *Parasitology*, **85**, 411–426.

Anderson, R. M. & May, R. M. (1991). *Infectious Diseases and Control*. Oxford University Press, Oxford, UK.

Andersson, M. (1984). Brood parasitism within species. *Producers and Scroungers* (Ed. by C. J. Barnard), pp. 195–228. Chapman & Hall, London, UK.

Beck, K. (1984). Coevolution: mathematical analysis of host–parasitism interactions. *Journal of Mathematical Biology*, **19**, 63–78.

Berenbaum, M. R., Zangerl, A. R. & Nitao, J. K. (1986). Constraints on chemical coevolution: wild parsnips and the parsnip webworm. *Evolution*, **40**, 1215–1228.

Bradshaw, A. D. (1991). The Croonian Lecture, 1991. Genostasis and the limits to evolution. *Philosophical Transactions of the Royal Society of London*, B, **333**, 289–305.

Brooks, D. R. & McLennan, D. A. (1991). *Phylogeny, Ecology, and Behavior*. University of Chicago Press, Chicago, IL, USA.

Castillo-Chávez, C., Levin, S. A. & Gould, F. (1988). Physiological and behavioral adaptation to varying environments: a mathematical model. *Evolution*, **42**, 986–994.

Chew, F. C. (1988). Searching for defensive chemistry in the Cruciferae, or, do glucosinolates always control interactions of Cruciferae with their potential herbivores and symbionts? No! *Chemical Mediation of Coevolution* (Ed. by K. C. Spencer), pp. 81–112. Academic Press, New York, NY, USA.

Davies, N. B. & Brooke, M. L. (1988). Cuckoos versus reed warblers: adaptations and counteradaptations. *Animal Behaviour*, **36**, 262–284.

Day, P. R. (1974). *Genetics of Host Parasite Interactions*. W. H. Freeman, San Francisco, CA, USA.

Denno, R. & McClure, M. (Eds) (1983). *Variable Plants and Herbivores in Natural and Managed Systems*. Academic Press, New York, NY, USA.

Dethier, V. G. (1954). Evolution of feeding preferences in phytophagous insects. *Evolution*, **8**, 33–54.

Dobson, A. P. (1982). Comparisons of some characteristics of the life histories of microparasites, macroparasites, parasitoids, and predators. *Population Biology of Infectious Diseases* (Ed. by R. M. Anderson & R. M. May), p. 5. Springer Verlag, New York, NY, USA.

Ehrlich, P. R. & Raven, P. H. (1964). Butterflies and plants: a study of coevolution. *Evolution*, **18**, 586–608.

Fagerström, T. (1989). Anti-herbivore chemical defense in plants: a comment on the concept of cost. *American Naturalist*, **133**, 281–287.

Farrell, B. & Mitter, C. (1990). Phylogeny of host affiliation: have *Phyllobrotica* (Coleoptera: Chrysomelidae) and the Lamiales diversified in parallel? *Evolution*, **44**, 1389–1403.

Farrell, B. D. & Mitter, C. Phylogenetic determinants of insect/plant community diversity. *Historical and Geographic Determinants of Community Diversity* (Ed. by R. Ricklefs & D. Schluter). University of Chicago Press, Chicago, IL, USA (in press).

Fritz, R. S. & Simms, E. L. (Eds) (1992). *Plant Resistance to Herbivores and Pathogens: Ecology, Evolution, and Genetics*. University of Chicago Press, Chicago, IL, USA.

Fry, J. (1990). Trade-offs in fitness on different hosts: evidence from a selection experiment with the phytophagous mite *Tetranychus urticae*. *American Naturalist*, **136**, 569–580.

Futuyma, D. J. (1983). Selective factors in the evolution of host choice by phytophagous insects. *Herbivorous Insects: Host-seeking Behavior and Mechanisms* (Ed. by S. Ahmad), pp. 227–244. Academic Press, New York, NY, USA.

Futuyma, D. J. (1991). Evolution of host specificity in herbivorous insects: genetic, ecological, and phylogenetic aspects. *Plant–Animal Interactions: Evolutionary Ecology in Tropical and Temperate Regions* (Ed. by P. W. Price, T. M. Lewinsohn, G. W. Fernandes & W. W. Benson), pp. 431–454. Wiley, New York, NY, USA.

Futuyma, D. J. & Keese, M. C. (1992). Evolution and coevolution of plants and phytophagous arthropods. *Herbivores: Their Interaction with Secondary Metabolites* (Ed. by G. A. Rosenthal & M. R. Berenbaum), pp. 439–475. Academic Press, New York, NY, USA.

Futuyma, D. J. & McCafferty, S. S. (1990). Phylogeny and the evolution of host plant associations in the leaf beetle genus *Ophraella* (Coleoptera: Chrysomelidae). *Evolution*, **44**, 1885–1913.

Futuyma, D. J. & Peterson, S. C. (1985). Genetic variation in the use of resources by insects. *Annual Review of Entomology*, **30**, 217–238.

Futuyma, D. J. & Philippi, T. E. (1987). Genetic variation and covariation in responses to host plants by *Alsophila pometaria* (Lepidoptera: Geometridae). *Evolution*, **41**, 269–279.

Futuyma, D. J. & Slatkin, M. (1983). Introduction. *Coevolution* (Ed. by D. J. Futuyma & M. Slatkin), pp. 1–13. Sinauer, Sunderland, MA, USA.

Gallun, R. L. (1978). Genetics of biotypes B and C of the Hessian fly. *Annals of the Entomological Society of America*, **71**, 481–486.

Gillespie, J. H. (1975). Natural selection for resistance to epidemics. *Ecology*, **56**, 493–495.

Godfray, H. C. J. & Hassell, M. P. (1991). Encapsulation and host–parasitoid population biology. *Parasite–Host Associations: Coexistence or Conflict?* (Ed. by C. A. Toft, A. Aeschlimann & L. Bolis), pp. 131–147. Oxford University Press, Oxford, UK.

Gould, F. (1979). Rapid host range evolution in a population of the phytophagous mite *Tetranychus urticae* Koch. *Evolution*, **33**, 791–802.

Gould, F. (1986). Simulation models for predicting durability of insect-resistant germ plasm: Hessian fly (Diptera: Cecidomyiidae)-resistant winter wheat. *Environmental Entomology*, **15**, 11–23.

Gould, F., Carroll, C. R. & Futuyma, D. J. (1982). Cross-resistance to pesticides and plant defenses: a study of the two-spotted spider mite. *Entomologia Experimentalis et Applicata*, **31**, 175–180.

Haldane, J. B. S. (1949). Disease and evolution. *La Ricerca Sciences Supplemento*, **19**, 68–76.

Hamilton, W. D. (1980). Sex versus non-sex versus parasite. *Oikos*, **35**, 282–290.

Hare, J. D. & Futuyma, D. J. (1978). Different effects of variation in *Xanthium strumarium* L. (Compositae) on two insect seed predators. *Oecologia*, **37**, 109–120.

Holloway, J. D. & Hebert, P. D. N. (1979). Ecological and taxonomic trends in macrolepidopteran host plant selection. *Biological Journal of the Linnean Society*, **11**, 229–251.

Holmes, J. C. (1982). Impact of infectious disease agents on the population growth and geographical distribution of animals. *Population Biology of Infectious Diseases* (Ed. by R. M. Anderson & R. M. May), pp. 37–51. Springer Verlag, New York, NY, USA.

Jaenike, J. (1990). Host specialization in phytophagous insects. *Annual Review of Ecology and Systematics*, **21**, 243–273.

Jansen, R. K., Michaels, H. J. & Palmer, J. D. (1991). Phylogeny and character evolution in the Asteraceae based on chloroplast DNA restriction site mapping. *Systematic Botany*, **16**, 98–115.

Janzen, D. H. (1980). When is it coevolution? *Evolution*, **34**, 611–612.

Jermy, T. (1984). Evolution of insect/host plant relationships. *American Naturalist*, **124**, 609–630.

Levin, B. R. *et al.* (1982). Evolution of parasites and hosts (group report). *Population Biology of Infectious Diseases* (Ed. by R. M. Anderson & R. M. May), pp. 212–243. Springer Verlag, New York, NY, USA.

Levin, S. A. (1983). Some approaches to the modelling of coevolutionary interactions. *Coevolution* (Ed. by M. Nitecki), pp. 21–65. University of Chicago Press, Chicago, IL, USA.

Mackenzie, A. (1991). Host utilization in aphids. PhD Thesis, University of East Anglia, UK.

Maddox, G. D. & Root, R. B. (1990). Structure of the encounter between goldenrod (*Solidago altissima*) and its diverse insect fauna. *Ecology*, **71**, 2115–2124.

Marquis, R. J. (1990). Genotypic variation in leaf damage in *Piper arieianum* (Piperaceae) by a multispecies assemblage of herbivores. *Evolution*, **44**, 104–120.

May, R. M. (1985). Regulation of populations with non-overlapping generations by microparasites: a purely chaotic system. *American Naturalist*, **125**, 573–584.

May, R. M. & Anderson, R. M. (1978). Regulation and stability of host–parasite population interactions. II. Destabilizing processes. *Journal of Animal Ecology*, **47**, 249–267.

May, R. M. & Anderson, R. M. (1983). Epidemiology and genetics in the coevolution of parasites and hosts. *Proceedings of the Royal Society of London*, B, **219**, 281–313.

May, R. M. & Anderson, R. M. (1990). Parasite–host coevolution. *Parasitology*, **100**, S89–S101.

May, R. M. & Robinson, S. K. (1985). Population dynamics of avian brood parasitism. *American Naturalist*, **126**, 475–494.

May, R. M., Nee, S. & Watts, C. (1991). Could intraspecific brood parasitism cause population cycles? *Acta xx Congressus Internationalis Ornithologici*, Vol. II (Ed. by B. D. Bell), pp. 1012–1022. NZ Ornithological Congress Trust Board, Wellington, NZ.

Mitter, C. & Farrell, B. (1991). Macroevolutionary aspects of insect/plant relationships. *Insect–Plant Interactions*, Vol. 3 (Ed. by E. Bernays). CRC Press, Boca Raton, FL, USA.

Mitter, C., Farrell, B. & Futuyma, D. J. (1991). Phylogenetic studies of insect–plant interactions: insights into the genesis of diversity. *Trends in Ecology and Evolution*, **6**, 290–293.

Mode, C. J. (1958). A mathematical model for the co-evolution of obligate parasites and their hosts. *Evolution*, **12**, 158–165.

Møller, A. P. & Petrie, M. (1991). Evolution of intraspecific variability in birds' eggs: is intraspecific nest parasitism the selective agent? *Acta xx Congressus Internationalis Ornithologici*, Vol. II (Ed. by B. D. Bell), pp. 1041–1048. NZ Ornithological Congress Trust Board, Wellington, NZ.

Moore, J. (1984). Altered behavioural responses in intermediate hosts — an acanthocephalan parasite strategy. *American Naturalist*, **123**, 572–577.

Moran, N. A. (1989). A 48-million-year-old aphid–host plant association and complex life cycle: biogeographic evidence. *Science*, **245**, 173–175.

Parker, M. A. (1991). Local genetic differentiation for disease resistance in a selfing annual. *Biological Journal of the Linnean Society*, **42**, 337–349.

Price, P. W. (1980). *Evolutionary Biology of Parasites*. Princeton University Press, Princeton, NJ, USA.

Rausher, M. D. (1988). Is coevolution dead? *Ecology*, **69**, 898–901.

Rausher, M. D. (a). The evolution of habitat preference. III. The evolution of avoidance and adaptation. *Evolution of Insect Pests: The Pattern of Variations* (Ed. by K. C. Kim). Wiley, New York, NY, USA (in press).

Rausher, M. D. (b). Natural selection and the evolution of plant–animal interactions. *Evolutionary Perspectives in Insect Chemical Ecology* (Ed. by B. D. Roitberg & M. B. Isman). Routledge, Chapman & Hall, New York, NY, USA (in press).

Rees, C. J. C. (1969). Chemoreceptor specificity associated with choice of feeding site by the beetle *Chrysolina brunsvicensis* on its food plant *Hypericum hirsutum*. *Entomologia Experimentalis et Applicata*, **12**, 565–583.

Ricklefs, R. & Schluter, D. (Eds) *Historical and Geographical Determinants of Community Diversity*. University of Chicago Press, Chicago, IL, USA (in press).

Rosenzweig, M. L., Brown, S. J. & Vincent, T. L. (1987). Red Queens and ESS: the coevolution of evolutionary rates. *Evolutionary Ecology*, **1**, 59–94.

Rothstein, S. I. & Mason, P. (1986). Coevolution and avian brood parasitism: cowbird eggs show evolutionary response to host discrimination. *Evolution*, **40**, 1207–1214.

Schaffer, W. M. & Rosenzweig, M. L. (1978). Homage to the Red Queen. I. coevolution of predators and their victims. *Theoretical Population Biology*, **14**, 135–157.

Seger, J. (1988). Dynamics of some simple host–parasite models with more than two genotypes in each species. *Philosophical Transactions of the Royal Society of London*, B, **319**, 541–555.

Seger, J. & Hamilton, W. D. (1988). Parasites and sex. *The Evolution of Sex* (Ed. by R. E. Michod & B. R. Levin), pp. 176–193. Sinnauer, Sunderland, MA, USA.

Simms, E. L. & Rausher, M. D. (1989). The evolution of resistance to herbivory in *Ipomoea purpurea*. II. Natural selection by insects and the costs of resistance. *Evolution*, **43**, 573–585.

Southwood, T. R. E. (1961). The number of species of insects associated with various trees. *Journal of Animal Ecology*, **30**, 1–8.

Stenseth, N. & Maynard Smith, J. (1984). Coevolution in ecosystems: Red Queen evolution or stasis? *Evolution*, **38**, 870–880.

Strong, D. R., Lawton, J. H. & Southwood, R. (1984). *Insects on Plants: Community Patterns and Mechanisms*. Harvard University Press, Cambridge, MA, USA.

Thompson, J. N. (1989). Concepts of coevolution. *Trends in Ecology and Evolution*, **4**, 179–183.

Van der Plank, J. E. (1975). *Principles of Plant Infection*. Academic Press, New York, NY, USA.

Vermeij, G. J. (1987). *Evolution and Escalation: An Ecological History of Life*. Princeton University Press, Princeton, NJ, USA.

Via, S. (1990). Ecological genetics and host adaptation in herbivorous insects: the experimental study of evolution in natural and agricultural systems. *Annual Review of Entomology*, **35**, 421–446.

Vrieling, K. (1990). Costs and benefits of alkaloids of *Senecio jacobaea* L. Thesis, University of Leiden.

Wanntorp, H.-E., Brooks, D. R., Nilsson, T., Nylin, S., Ronquist, F., Stearns, S. C. & Wedell, N. (1990). Phylogenetic approaches in ecology. *Oikos*, **57**, 119–132.

Whitham, T. G. (1990). Plant hybrid zones as sinks for pests. *Science*, **244**, 1490–1493.

Yoo, B. H. (1980). Long-term selection for a quantitative character in large replicate populations of *Drosophila melanogaster*. I. Response to selection. *Genetical Research*, **35**, 1–17.

Zwölfer, H. & Herbst, J. (1988). Präadaptation, Wirtskreiserweiterung, und Parallel-Cladogenese in der Evolution von phytophagen Insekten. *Zeitschrift für Zoologische Systematik und Evolutionsforschung*, **26**, 320–340.

PART 2
MOLECULES IN ECOLOGY

7. ADAPTATION IN BACTERIA: UNANSWERED ECOLOGICAL AND EVOLUTIONARY QUESTIONS ABOUT WELL-STUDIED MOLECULES

J. P. W. YOUNG* AND B. R. LEVIN†
*Department of Biology, University of York, York YO1 5DD, UK and
†Department of Biology, Emory University, Atlanta, GA 30322, USA

...I have to be molecular. Who is not? [A. Lwoff, 1965]

INTRODUCTION

Ultimately, the adaptation of organisms to their environment comes down to selection favouring specific forms of molecules: proteins and RNAs and, in turn, the nucleotide sequences of the DNA (or RNA) that codes for and regulates the synthesis of these molecules. With higher organisms one can, with some justification, study much of what is biologically interesting about adaptation and evolution without considering its molecular basis or even the genetics of the characters involved. In the case of bacteria, the phenotypes responsible for particular adaptations are often single molecules, and the molecular biology, genetics and ecology of these phenotypes are intimately connected. One cannot fully understand the ecology and evolution of these characters without considering their mode of inheritance (chromosomal, plasmid, prophage or transposon-borne genes) and occasionally transgressing into the technology, at least, of molecular biology.

In this presentation we consider six classes of 'molecular adaptations' of bacteria: restriction–modification, allelopathy (antibiotics and bacteriocins), proteins and other molecules associated with pathogen virulence, resistance to antibiotics, signal molecules involved in interactions with plants and natural genetic engineering by *Agrobacterium*. A great deal is known about the molecular biology and genetics of one or more example of each of these classes of adaptations. However, relatively less and, in some cases, very little is known about the ecological role of these characters in natural habitats and thus the selective pressures responsible for their evolution and maintenance.

RESTRICTION–MODIFICATION

Restriction and modification are two components of systems that, on the surface, appear to have the function of defending bacteria against foreign DNA. Restriction, in the contemporary use of the word, is the cutting of DNA at specific sequences by enzymes, restriction endonucleases. Modification is the alteration of DNA to preclude its being cut by the restriction endonucleases produced by that same cell. This is usually accomplished by the addition of methyl groups to the adenines or cytosines at specific sequences of base by DNA-modification methyltransferases (Bickle 1986). Restriction–modification systems are diverse and ubiquitous. More than 1200 restriction endonucleases and 130 DNA-modification methyltransferases have already been isolated from more than 1000 different species of eubacteria and archaebacteria (Kessler & Manta 1990) and found to be coded for by both chromosomal and plasmid-borne genes.

The phenomenon of restriction–modification was first discovered because of the effects of these enzymes on bacteriophages (Luria & Human 1952; and review by Arber 1965). When injected into a bacterium with a restriction–modification system, unmodified DNA or DNA of the wrong modification state from a restriction-sensitive phage is, with a high probability, destroyed and the infection aborted. With a low probability (10^{-3} and often less), however, the infecting phage DNA will be modified by the host's modification enzymes. Under these conditions, the lytic cycle continues and the 'progeny' phages released carry DNA modified to attack bacteria of the host's restriction–modification state with impunity.

In theory, as long as restriction-sensitive phages are present, restriction–modification will result in stabilizing frequency-dependent selection (Levin 1986, 1988). Phage-sensitive bacteria of each restriction–modification state will have an advantage when rare. The magnitude of this selective advantage can be considerable and make up for a substantial disadvantage of the rare restriction–modification cell type. Besides restriction–modification, bacteria can also acquire resistance to phages by means of alterations of the cell envelope that render it refractory to adsorption by a whole class of related phages. In the absence of this 'envelope resistance', cells of rare restriction–modification states will ascend very rapidly. If phage-resistant bacteria and phages are present, however, they will dominate the community and retard the rate of ascent of higher-fitness sensitive cells of rare restriction–modification states.

Experimental results with *Escherichia coli* K-12, *E. coli* B and the phage λ-vir are qualitatively consistent with these predictions but, at the same time, can be interpreted as equivocal with respect to the broader hypothesis that restriction–modification systems are maintained by phage-mediated selection. In the presence of λ-vir, bacteria of the rare restriction–modification type have an initial advantage, relative to that in phage-free controls (Levin 1988). However, in these experiments, envelope resistance developed rapidly and the outcome of interclone competition was almost entirely determined by the relative fitnesses of the phage-resistant mutants of the different cell lines, rather than their restriction–modification states.

It remains to be seen if this limited effect of restriction would also obtain if resistance to phages is more difficult for the bacteria to acquire, for example if resistance engendered a considerable disadvantage or multiple phages with different adsorption sites were present. Currently, Ryszard Korona (in B.R. Levin's laboratory) is doing experiments to explore the latter situation. Under these conditions, multiple mutations would be required for a bacterium to become resistant to all the phages in its environment, while restriction–modification would provide that cell with general protection against these viruses. The preliminary results of these experiments with *E. coli* B, a plasmid-borne type II restriction system, *Sbo*13, and the phages λ-vir and T5 and an uncharacterized wild phage, W1, indicate that with two and three phages present, the initial advantage of the rare restriction–modification type is greater than that with any single phage alone. However, cells resistant to the two and even three phages evolved rapidly, and once again, the final outcome of competition was determined by the relative fitness of the resistant cell lines, rather than restriction–modification.

At this juncture all of the results of the modest number of experimental studies of the population dynamics of restriction–modification of which we are aware suggest that the greatest individual fitness advantage for this character obtains when bacteria colonize new habitats in which marauding phages are present, rather than in sustained populations (Levin 1988, Korona & Levin unpublished). In the absence of restriction–modification, a single phage particle would be sufficient to prevent the establishment of a bacterial population (or a colony on a surface). With this immune system, it would take from 10^2 to 10^5 (the reciprocal of the modification probability) or even more phages of the wrong modification state to prevent the establishment of a bacterial population. Not so clear, is whether the colonization of phage-infested habitats is a frequent event in the natural population ecology of *E. coli* or other bacteria, sufficiently frequent to select for and maintain restriction–modification.

Three additional observations also question whether protection against phages is the unique selective agent responsible for maintaining restriction–modification systems in contemporary populations of *E. coli* and, by induction, other bacteria.

First, the majority of coliphages that have been studied in the laboratory have mechanisms to avoid the effects of at least some host restriction–modification systems (Kruger & Bickle 1983). To be sure, the existence of these restriction-avoiding mechanisms suggests that phages had to deal with host restriction–modification, but this would be the case whatever the selected-for function of restriction–modification may be. Thus, if the majority of naturally occurring bacteriophages are unaffected by host restriction, these viruses would play little role as the selective agent for bacteria with these 'defences'.

Second, it's not at all clear whether the densities of phages in natural habitats are sufficient for these viruses to be an important selective agent, even if they were sensitive to restriction–modification. To illustrate this, consider a mass action (liquid habitat) situation where the adsorption rate constant for a lytic phage is of the order of 10^{-8} ml/hour, a relatively high value (Levin *et al.* 1976), and a phage density of 10^4 particles per ml. Under these conditions, the hourly probability that a sensitive bacterium would be killed by a phage is 10^{-4}. If, because of periodic selection and low rates of recombination, the genetically effective sizes of bacterial populations are as small as suggested by Levin (1981), this small a selection pressure would have little if any effect on the fate of the genes coding for restriction–modification. Our estimates of the densities of coliphages in sewage (Laursen & Levin, unpublished) is not much greater than 10^4. Coliphages are not commonly found in the guts of mammals like mice, voles and people, and when present are usually at densities lower than 10^4 (D. Gordon, personal communication). Furthermore, in these habitats, the majority of coliform bacteria are resistant to infection by the coexisting phages.

Finally, restriction–modification systems occur in organisms that live in habitats that appear to be inhospitable to bacterial viruses as we know them. One of these is *Thermoplasma acidophilum* (McConnell *et al.* 1978). There has yet to be a demonstration of bacteriophages that attack this archaebacterium. Also, the hot (60°C), acidic (pH 2) environment in which this cell wall-less archaebacterium lives does not seem an amenable habitat to an organism composed of little more than a protein coat and some DNA. This, of course, does not rule out the possibility that there are *Thermoplasma* phages, as there are phages that attack other thermophiles.

While we can raise the possibility that there are other selective pressures ('functions') for restriction endonucleases and modifying methyltransferases responsible for the evolution and maintenance of restriction–modification, we have no really good idea what those pressures and functions may be. It seems unlikely that restriction endonucleases are maintained because they protect bacteria against other sources of foreign DNA such as plasmids (Levin 1988) or free DNA picked up by bacteria with transforming mechanisms. These DNAs are usually not lethal or very deleterious. Although the carriage of plasmids could confer a selective disadvantage on their host bacterium they can also be beneficial because of the genes they carry, e.g. resistance to antibiotics. Furthermore, plasmids enter bacteria as single-stranded DNA while most restriction endonucleases cut only double-stranded DNA. Naturally transforming bacteria have mechanisms that protect the transforming DNA from the cell's restriction endonucleases.

Be all this as it may, there are few quantitative data on the ecology and population dynamics of bacteria and phages in natural communities (see the review by Lenski 1988). Until we have those data, we cannot properly evaluate the phage-protection hypothesis for both the evolution and maintenance of restriction–modification.

ANTIBIOTICS AND BACTERIOCINS

Bacteria produce a variety of molecules that kill or inhibit the growth of other bacteria or fungi. The best known of these allelopathic agents are antibiotics — small molecules that attack a wide range of bacteria and some fungal species — and bacteriocins — proteins that kill closely related bacteria. Antibiotics are coded for by both chromosomal and plasmid-borne genes, while the genes coding for bacteriocins and immunity to bacteriocins are exclusively borne on plasmids.

On first consideration, it would seem that the ecological role of these molecules, and the selective pressure responsible for their maintenance and possibly their evolution, is to inhibit the growth of competing microorganisms. And, in theory, the production of compounds that kill or inhibit the growth of competing bacteria of different species or genotypes can confer an advantage on clones that carry genes coding for these allelopathic compounds, as long as the producing cells are at least somewhat immune to their action. Selection can favour allelopathy, even when the synthesis of the allelopathic compounds is somewhat deleterious or, as in the case of bacteriocins, lethal to the minority of cells that are induced to produce these allelopathic agents (Reeves 1972). In mass (liquid) culture, the intensity and direction of selection for allelopathy depends on the frequency of the producing genotype relative to that of the sensitive (Chao 1980, Chao & Levin 1981, Levin 1988). If the producing genotypes are intrinsically less fit than the sensitive, they will only increase in frequency when they are sufficiently common to produce enough of the allelopathic substance to inhibit the growth of the sensitive cells adequately to overcome their intrinsic disadvantage. However, when the producing and sensitive bacteria are growing as colonies in fixed habitats, the allelopath-producing bacteria can increase in frequency when they are initially rare as well as when they are common. In this fixed habitat, the diffusing allelopathic substance kills sensitive bacteria in the vicinity of the colony producing it. This, in turn, enables that colony to sequester resources and thus grow larger (produce more cells) than colonies of surviving sensitive bacteria.

Both of these anticipated results have been observed in experimental populations of *E. coli* K-12 and the colicin plasmid, Col E3 (Chao & Levin 1981). (Colicins are bacteriocins produced by *E. coli* and other coliform bacteria.) In competition with cells sensitive to colicin E3 in liquid serial transfer culture, the frequency of bacteria carrying the Col E3 plasmid increased only when their frequency exceeded $\sim 10^{-2}$. Below this unstable equilibrium point, the frequency of the bacteria carrying the Col E3 plasmid declined because of the lethal synthesis of colicin and their intrinsically lower fitness. In fixed, soft agar, serial transfer culture, however, cells carrying the Col E3 plasmid increased over the entire range of frequencies studied, 10^{-6} to 10^{-1}. And, as anticipated, there were zones of inhibition, no bacterial growth, around rare colicinogenic colonies, and the number of bacteria in the colicin-producing colonies exceeded that in surviving colonies of sensitive cells.

Antibiotics, when used in purified form and in relatively high concentrations are extremely effective in killing or preventing the growth of bacteria in (and on) animal and plant hosts. In laboratory culture, antibiotic-producing colonies are able to inhibit the growth of sensitive microorganisms in the same way as observed for colicins. In fact, zones of inhibition on lawns of bacteria or fungi is the classical assay to identify colonies of antibiotic-producing microorganisms (Waxman 1967).

Thus, it would seem that there should be conditions where, by inhibiting the growth of competitors, the production of bacteriocins and antibiotics would confer a selective advantage on the bacteria producing them. Not so clear, however, is whether these conditions obtain for bacteriocinogenic and antibiotic-producing bacteria in their natural communities. From a perusal of the modest literature that addresses this question for bacteriocins and clinically used antibiotics — commonly no more than remarks added to articles and chapters written for other, more serious, purposes — the evidence that in natural populations the inhibition of competitors is the evolutionary *raison d'être* for these compounds is, at best, underwhelming.

In their review of colicins and col plasmids, Luria and Suit (1987) conclude that 'Colicinogy appears to be an unnecessary complication in the life of coliform bacteria.... One would guess that bacteria as organisms could do very well without these nuances;...'. In the case of antibiotic-producing *Actinomyces*, there was actually some question about whether these allelopathic compounds are as toxic to the cells producing them as they are to competitors. This question was answered in the negative by Gause *et al.* (1981) (yes, the same G.F. Gause). Still, it is not at all clear that in natural communities the antibiotics produced by the actinomycetes are at sufficiently high concentrations to be effective in inhibiting the growth of sensitive competitors (Hopwood & Merrick 1977).

At the same time, there is compelling evidence for allelopathy, or 'amensalism' (term used by Bull & Slater 1982), playing a role in bacterial competition in more-or-less natural habitats. This role appears to be more for defence against invading competitors than a mechanism to facilitate invasion of established communities. Bacteria are mixed with seeds and seedlings to protect them from infections by fungi and other bacteria (Bull & Slater 1982). One example of this is the control of crown gall tumour by inoculating the seeds or seedlings of crop plants with *Agrobacterium radiobacter* which prevents the pathogenic *A. tumefaciens* from transferring its Ti (Tumour-inducing) plasmid to the host plant (Moore & Warren 1979).

There is also a long-standing, if not trendy, tradition of using bacterial interference for medical intervention. Non-pathogenic strains of bacteria are inoculated to control or prevent infections by pathogenic bacteria responsible for skin, nasal, throat, genital, gastrointestinal and other symptomatic infections; see the various chapters in Aly and Shinefield (1982). Also included in this intriguing collection of articles is a number of lines of evidence in support of the hypothesis that the normal microbial flora of the gastrointestinal tract plays an important role in preventing symptomatic infections by pathogenic microorganisms. Not so clear, however, is the role of bacteriocins and antibiotics in bacterial interference.

One of the best characterized examples of specific allelopathic substances being used by bacteria is the suppression of 'take-all' disease of wheat (caused by a fungus, *Gaeumannomyces graminis*) by strains of *Pseudomonas fluorescens* that produce an antibiotic, phenazine-1-carboxylate (Tomashow & Weller 1988). *In vitro*, this compound suppresses the growth of fungus, as do strains of pseudomonads that produce it, but non-producing strains do not. In sterilized soil, the non-producing mutants colonize plant roots just as well as wild-type, but suppress disease less effectively. In raw soil, however, which presumably contains many other microbial species, the wild-type strains persist in significantly larger populations than the mutant strains, both in the soil itself and on the surfaces of wheat roots (Thomashow & Pierson 1991). Furthermore, significant quantities of phenazine-1-carboxylate can be recovered from root systems but only if they are colonized by producing strains (Thomashow *et al.* 1990). Since 'take-all' causes severe stunting of plant growth, it seems reasonable to suppose that the antibiotic allows producing strains to colonize a larger niche (that is, a healthier root system) than non-producers. It will not be possible to assess the real significance of antibiotic production, however, until there are quantitative estimates of the fitness differentials between producers and non-producers at each stage of the life cycle.

MOLECULES ASSOCIATED WITH THE VIRULENCE OF PATHOGENIC BACTERIA

Virulence, the ability of a bacterium to cause disease (symptomatic infections) in multicelled eukaryotic hosts with uncompromised defences, is the end-product of a complex interaction between the host and the bacterium. Despite this complexity, a good deal of recent research on the mechanisms, genetics and molecular biology of bacterial pathogenesis has focused on a few, well-defined characters known as virulence determinants or virulence factors. These phenotypes may be encoded by genes borne on chromosomes, plasmids or prophages and are sometimes associated with transposons. By definition, the loss of these genes or their function would make a bacterium less pathogenic without affecting its viability (Davis *et al.* 1980). Many virulence determinants are single molecules which endow a bacterium with one of four capacities: (1) to adhere specifically to particular somatic cells, (2) to produce toxins, (3) to avoid host defences, or (4) to enter, survive and replicate in somatic cells (for reviews see Brubaker 1985, Finlay & Falkow 1989).

Is the capacity to cause disease in a host the selective pressure responsible for the evolution and maintenance of virulence determinants? In theory, the answer can be affirmative. It is possible that the expression of these characters augments the fitness of a bacterium by (1) facilitating its colonization of a host, (2) increasing its rate of proliferation, survival or range of habitats (the tissues it infects or the resources it uses) within (or on) a host, or (3) increasing its rate of infectious transmission between hosts. In accord with the 'enlightened view' of parasite–host coevolution (Levin & Pimentel 1981, Anderson & May 1982, Levin *et al.* 1982, May & Anderson 1983, Ewald 1983, 1988, Levin & Svanborg Edén 1990), not only can the virulence of a parasite be favoured in the short term, but natural selection could maintain the virulence of parasites for extended periods. Because of the much shorter generation times of parasites, relative to those of their hosts, and the generalized, somatic cell evolution mechanism of the immune systems of higher organisms (Svanborg Edén & Levin 1990), it is possible that the virulence of a parasite will not be countered by the evolution of resistance in the host.

While the *a priori* arguments that virulence determinants can be favoured by natural selection may be appealing to evolutionary theorists and their groupies, the empirical evidence in support of this interpretation (hypothesis) is, at best, modest. This evidence is also almost exclusively retrospective (story telling). It is conceivable that some 'virulence determinants' and the pathogenicity caused by them are coincidental to other features of the parasite's biology, a 'spandrel' after Gould and Lewontin (1979), or a perverse response of the host's defences.

The best evidence for a bacterial virulence determinant being favoured by natural selection is that for the capsule of the pneumonia-causing bacterium, *Streptococcus pneumoniae*. This sheath protects the bacterium from being destroyed by macrophages. Mutant *S. pneumoniae* that lack the capsule are unable to cause disease. As demonstrated in the classical transformation experiments of Griffith (1928) — the experiments that ultimately led to the evidence that DNA is the genetic material — when heat-killed, capsulated pneumococci are mixed with uncapsulated mutants in a mouse, capsulated pneumococci are produced by transformation. These virulent transformants increase in frequency, cause pneumonia and replace the uncapsulated mutants as the dominant cell type.

Is this so for other virulence determinants? Is the production of toxins by *Vibrio cholerae*, *Corynebacterium diphtheriae* and *Clostridium difficile* favoured by within or between host (infectious transfer or colonization) selection? Are the proteins and other molecules required for invasion, survival and proliferation in somatic cells produced by *Shigella dysenteriae*, *Mycobacterium tuberculosis* and *Salmonella typhimurium* adaptations for colonization? Are the adhesins produced by *Neisseria gonorrhoeae*, *Treponema pallidum*, and *Streptococcus pyogenes* adaptations for colonization and maintenance within hosts? Or are these toxins, invasiveness molecules and adhesins spandrels? Levin and Svanborg Edén (1990) argue that some of the adhesins responsible for the virulence of uropathogenic *E. coli* are actually adaptations for colonization and maintenance in the gut. In their interpretation, the symptoms that these adhesins cause in urinary tract infections are the result of coincidental evolution, and these adhesins may well confer a selective disadvantage in that environment. Levin and Svanborg Edén cite evidence in support of this idea, including the observations that the receptors for these adhesins are present in the gut as well as the bladder, and that adhesion to cells in the bladder causes an inflammatory response that ultimately leads to the clearing of that bacterium.

Currently we do not have answers to these questions about selection and the evolution of virulence determining molecules in bacteria. However, as suggested by Levin and Svanborg Edén (1990), whether a virulence determinant confers an advantage on the bacteria that encode for it is a question that can be addressed and even answered with straightforward experiments.

RESISTANCE TO ANTIBIOTICS

The dramatic increase in the frequency of bacteria resistant to antibiotics over the past 40 years is an impressive and frightening illustration of the potential and power of 'natural' selection. This resistance has been achieved in several ways. In some cases, small changes in existing molecules have frustrated the antibiotics: the uptake system is modified so that they are excluded, or their target is altered and their action prevented. This kind of change, often achieved by a single mutation, is the basis of the spontaneous mutations to resistance that occur in most bacteria and can be selected on media containing antibiotics. Resistance to streptomycin, for example, is conferred by a small change in one of the ribosomal proteins (Bohman *et al.* 1984), and such mutations have been widely used as genetic markers. In the absence of antibiotic, resistant mutants sometimes have an obviously lowered fitness, manifested by slower growth rates. However, this is not always the case, and streptomycin-resistant mutants of *Rhizobium* have been used as marked strains in ecological experiments. They form normal nitrogen-fixing nodules on legume roots, though there is some indication that resistant mutants may suffer a competitive disadvantage (Bromfield & Jones 1979). Since wild-type rhizobia are nevertheless sensitive to streptomycin, we must conclude either that all mutations to resistance carry some fitness penalty in the field, or that rhizobia are not often exposed to this antibiotic, despite the fact that the producing organism, *Streptomyces*, is also a soil-dweller.

Resistance mediated by modified versions of normal cell components may sometimes involve more than a simple spontaneous mutation. In the case of pathogenic *Neisseria* species, penicillin resistance has apparently been achieved by replacing part of a so-called 'penicillin binding protein' (whose actual function is to produce the cell wall and not to bind penicillin) (Spratt 1988, Spratt *et al.* 1989, reviewed by Maynard Smith *et al.* 1991).

The new, resistant part of the molecule has apparently been acquired by genetic transformation events that have replaced part of the gene with the corresponding part from a related species that is naturally resistant but non-pathogenic. Not enough is known about the ecology of the donor species to speculate fruitfully on the natural importance, if any, of its penicillin resistance.

Much of the clinically important antibiotic resistance, however, is not mediated through changes in the targets of antibiotic action, but by molecules that appear to function specifically against antibiotics. These may be enzymes that degrade them, for example, or transport systems that pump them out of the cell. In many cases, these resistance genes are associated with transposable elements and reside on plasmids that are likely to carry resistance for a number of other antibiotics (Falkow 1975). These plasmids can often be transferred by conjugation between widely different genera of proteobacteria (Gram-negatives), so that essentially the same set of genes may be found in enteric bacteria and in pseudomonads, for example. It is clear that the recent ascent of these resistance genes, transposons and plasmids can be attributed to human use of antibiotics, but their ready transmissibility makes it hard to trace where they came from and how widespread they were in the past. One possible source is the antibiotic-producing organisms themselves, and the 3′-aminoglycoside phosphotransferase (kanamycin resistance) genes found on Gram-negative transposons are certainly homologous to the corresponding genes in *Bacillus* and *Streptomyces* species that produce this class of antibiotics (reviewed by Trieu-Cuot *et al.* 1987), but the sequences are highly diverged, and could even date back to the common ancestor of these bacteria. There are some clear examples of recent lateral transfer of resistance genes to Gram-negatives from Gram-positives. Kanamycin resistance that has recently appeared in *Campylobacter* is due to a phosphotransferase gene that is identical to that commonly found in *Enterococcus*, while *E. coli* resistant to erythromycin have a gene for rRNA methylase that is identical to that of *Streptococcus* (Trieu-Cuot *et al.* 1987). Furthermore, this methylase gene has a G + C content of 33%, typical of *Streptococcus* but very different from the 50% that is average in *E. coli*. The fosfomycin resistance gene found on a TN*10*-related transposon on a plasmid in *Serratia marcescens* is more than 99% identical to the corresponding gene of *Streptomyces fradiae*, which is a producer of the antibiotic (Suárez *et al.* 1989). It is possible that these transfers from Gram-positive to Gram-negative bacteria were mediated by a conjugative transposon like Tn*916*, which can readily cross this supposed barrier (Bertram *et al.* 1991).

As for the plasmids and transposons that have spread the resistance genes, these are normal components of the bacterial genome; perhaps they should be considered as selfish accessory elements that just took advantage of the antibiotic era to expand their niche. Both plasmids and transposable elements are ubiquitous in natural strains of *Rhizobium* (Simon *et al.* 1991), for example, even though these are soil bacteria and have not been significantly exposed to clinical antibiotics and do not as a rule have the resistance genes. The plasmids and transposons associated with antibiotic resistance are unusual only in their wide host range, and it is not hard to see why those with the widest host range should have been the most successful in the circumstances. A survey of *E. coli* isolates that had been stored since before the era of clinical antibiotics revealed the presence of conjugative plasmids, but they did not carry the resistance genes that were later associated with them (Hughes & Datta 1983). Although the recent spread of resistance genes among clinical bacteria has an obvious explanation in terms of human activities, their wider ecological significance and evolutionary history are still obscure.

THE SPECIFICITY OF PLANT–MICROBE INTERACTIONS

Although many plant–microbe interactions are deleterious to the plant, we will take the symbiosis between rhizobia and legumes as our primary example, as this is still the best-characterized plant–microbe interaction. This symbiosis is commonly assumed to be mutual, although the evidence for mutual benefit in nature is certainly far from watertight. Mutualism has always held a special fascination for evolutionary biologists (perhaps because antagonistic interactions seem so much more common and, to some at least, more natural). The rhizobia (*Rhizobium*, *Bradyrhizobium* and *Azorhizobium*) are bacteria that invade the roots of legumes, inducing nodules (galls) in which they multiply and fix nitrogen — that is, they convert atmospheric dinitrogen into ammonia — which is taken up by the plant in exchange for energy and nutrients. How the plant can prevent 'cheating' by bacteria that take the food handouts but fail to pay the ammonia tax is a question that should interest ecologists and game theorists; the answer must be based on evidence from physiological and molecular studies (Kahn *et al.* 1985).

Rhizobia are entirely restricted to legumes (plus one oddball plant in the Ulmaceae) but no one rhizobium strain is able to nodulate all possible host plants. Every strain has a definite host range, which is sometimes so broad that it includes hosts from many genera and more than one subfamily of the legumes, but can in other cases be confined to a few species or even distinguish between genotypes within a species (Young & Johnston 1989). This implies that there is no strongly selected optimum breadth of host range, and perhaps suggests that specificity may have a number of different causes.

This suspicion is confirmed by the detailed analysis of the bacterial genes involved in nodule initiation (Young & Johnston 1989, Martinez *et al.* 1990). Briefly, the molecular story is that flavonoids and related compounds present in legume root exudates interact with the product of the bacterial *nodD* gene, which then activates a whole suite of other *nod* genes, whose function is to elaborate another signal molecule, a substituted oligosaccharide (Lerouge *et al.* 1990), that is secreted by the bacterium and causes the plant to initiate the nodule. The NodD proteins of different rhizobium species respond to different ranges of flavonoids — indeed, some are activated by compounds that act as inhibitors in other species — and this is an important component of specificity. However, there are also differences in the signal molecule elaborated by the bacterium, due to small differences in the *nod* genes or to the presence of extra genes that have no counterpart in other species. There are also additional signals in some species, and other bacterial features such as extracellular polysaccharide, which are necessary for successful symbiosis with some legumes but not with others.

What does all this molecular complexity mean for the ecologist? It provides some rationale for the wide variation in niche (host range) breadth — there are constraints imposed by the available molecules, in addition to any ecological considerations. It suggests that a simplistic model based on a single class of 'host-range determinants' will be a poor approximation to reality. More positively, the molecular knowledge and the techniques that led to it provide the opportunity to construct strains with specific host-range characteristics; these could be used in experimental systems of general ecological interest, such as competition between specialists and generalists.

Clearly, there has been great progress in understanding the mechanisms of host specificity in the rhizobium–legume symbiosis. But a more general question remains: why should this system evolve specificity in the first place? In a pathogenic interaction it is easy to see that the host's attempts to escape, and the pathogen's counterattacks, will lead to increasing specialization if the molecular mechanisms involved do not permit unlimited pathogenicity, or unlimited resistance; however, there seems to be no comparable driving force that is intrinsic to a mutual interaction. Indeed, there is a good argument for both plant and bacterium to have catholic tastes, and hence increase the probability of finding a partner even where partners are scarce.

It is a cliché to liken any example of specific recognition to a 'lock and key', but in this case the analogy may be unusually apt. If we keep watch on an average home, we will see the family lock and unlock the doors as they depart and return. Why? The answer, of course, is external to the house–family mutualism, and cannot be deduced by studying this in isolation. The existence of pathogens may force mutualisms to become specific, just as the existence of burglars forces us all to have different locks on our doors. Plants have evolved a variety of complex chemical defences against pathogens, and rhizobia have had to refine their keys in order to track these changes, and have at the same time had to specialize.

Can we test this hypothesis by reference to the molecular details of legume–pathogen interactions? Not yet, unfortunately, because our molecular knowledge of pathogenic interactions is much less detailed, though it is improving rapidly. There is a great deal of genetic and physiological information, of course, and this had led to the 'gene-for-gene' concept of avirulence: a particular 'avirulence' gene product from the pathogen triggers a 'hypersensitive response' (HR) in the plant. The HR is a kind of scorched-earth strategy in which a small number of plant cells around the pathogen are stimulated to produce antimicrobial compounds and then to die, isolating the pathogen in a hostile non-living environment. In this instance, therefore, positive recognition leads to abortion of the interaction; the microbial 'toxin' is not a pathogenicity factor but quite the reverse.

Quite a few avirulence genes have now been cloned, and we can soon expect to learn about the molecular phenotypes to which they lead. For example, the *avrD* gene of *Pseudomonas syringae* pathovar *tomato* encodes a function (presumably an enzyme) that leads to the production of a molecule ($C_{13}H_{20}O_6$) that elicits a hypersensitive response in the leaves of soybeans that carry the *Rpg4* resistance allele (Keen *et al.* 1990). The elicitor has not been completely identified but has a heterocyclic ring and a saturated alkyl side-chain (Keen *et al.* 1991) — in this it resembles the *Rhizobium* elicitor, though that is much larger. As in *Rhizobium*, too, the production of the elicitor is stimulated by some (unknown) signal from the plant. Since the production of an elicitor leads to the failure of infection and the death of the pathogen, the obvious evolutionary question is 'why not stop making it?'. The obvious answer is 'because it performs some vital function'. Unfortunately, this is not true, since mutants deficient in *avrD* are not only viable but are still pathogenic on tomato (Keen *et al.* 1990). A quantitative reduction in fitness is our remaining hope — that has yet to be tested.

If we are going to make genetic models of the evolution of gene-for-gene systems, we need to have some idea about the nature of the alternative alleles at the avirulence and resistance loci. The molecular genetics of avirulence genes gives us little ground for generalization, though — there are examples in which the virulent strains have no homologous gene at all, and others in which the virulent allele is a non-functional mutant, or an apparently functional allelic variant of the allele that causes avirulence (Staskawicz *et al.* 1987, Kearney & Staskawicz 1990, Keen *et al.* 1990, 1991, van Kan *et al.* 1991).

Even the biochemical nature of the elicitor may vary widely. It is generally assumed that the proteins encoded by bacterial avirulence genes are not themselves the elicitors, since they appear not to be secreted. This may not be universally true, though, since the product of the *avr9* gene of the fungus *Fulvia fulva* is a peptide that itself triggers the HR response in tomato plants with the corresponding *Cf9* resistance gene (Keen *et al.* 1991). Clearly the room for evolutionary manoeuvre possessed by both pathogen and host will depend very much on the genetic nature and complexity of the relevant genes and the constraints imposed on them by other functions. It is not surprising that plants have latched on to a variety of different signals in order to detect pathogens, and pathogens have adopted a range of strategies to avoid detection. We have just scratched the surface of this diversity: the challenge in future will be to extract, from the welter of data, enough plausible generalizations to construct evolutionary models.

THE *AGROBACTERIUM*–PLANT INTERACTION

Agrobacterium is a close relative of *Rhizobium* but its interaction with plants is very different. Like *Rhizobium*, it is spurred into action by molecules from the plant, but in this case they are acetosyringone and other phenolic compounds that are normally released from damaged plant tissue (Stachel *et al.* 1985). *Agrobacterium* is only able to invade tissue that is damaged, but although strains do show differences in host range they are generally much more catholic in their choice of host species than are rhizobia. The gene products of the *virA* and *virG* genes detect acetosyringone and activate a whole suite of other *vir* genes, setting in motion an extraordinary process (Hohn *et al.* 1991, Nester & Gordon 1991). A copy of part of the *Agrobacterium* genome, called the T-DNA, is injected into the plant cytoplasm; it enters the nucleus and is integrated into the plant chromosomes. The T-DNA carries genes for the synthesis of plant growth regulators, and the expression of these leads to the development of a tumour. This tumour is not, however, full of

Agrobacterium cells: indeed, it may contain no bacteria at all because once the plant cells are transformed the tumour is self-sustaining and does not require the continuing presence of the bacteria.

Why, then, does *Agrobacterium* do it? The answer usually given is 'opines' (Tempé & Petit 1983). The term 'opine' covers a range of small carbon compounds, derivatives of sugars and amino acids. The T-DNA carries, in addition to the genes that produce the tumour, genes for the synthesis of an opine. The tumour therefore becomes an opine factory, but opines are rather unusual nutrients and most microbes are unable to digest them. *Agrobacterium* strains, however, carry the necessary genes for opine catabolism. There are a number of different opines, and each strain has the ability to use the opine that is specified by its own T-DNA: thus, by engineering the plant, it provides itself with a private larder, and the assumption is (though the data are lacking) that this gives it a large fitness advantage over other bacteria. This physiological linkage between production and consumption is ensured by genetic linkage between the corresponding genes: the T-DNA and the opine catabolic genes are located, along with the *vir* genes, on a single plasmid. There are more than a dozen different *Agrobacterium* opines known, each handled by a corresponding plasmid. It seems that essentially all transforming plasmids carry opine genes but usually only one opine is associated with each plasmid. The relevant theory and experiments remain to be done but one can imagine that the diversity might be maintained by frequency-dependent selection: the producer/user of a rare opine runs less risk of its larder being raided by other strains. The strains that catabolize a particular opine are not necessarily closely related; indeed, one interesting (but perhaps inevitable) adjunct is that all kinds of molecular freeloaders have invited themselves to lunch. A range of quite unrelated plant-colonizing bacteria, such as pseudomonads, can be isolated from the vicinity of *Agrobacterium*-induced galls and be shown to have catabolic pathways for the relevant opine (Nautiyal & Dion 1990). Clearly, there is scope for some interesting studies to unravel the significance of all this for the ecology of *Agrobacterium*. One would think that a smart *Agrobacterium* might have the plant make an antibiotic to keep these marauders from its food supply but this is an extra level of sophistication that has not (yet) been reported.

Generally, the genetic colonization of the plant genome by T-DNA would not be expected to have long-term genetic consequences for the plant, since it is usually cells of the lower stem or roots that are transformed, and the transformed tissue does not normally give rise to flowers and seed. However, it is a major goal of today's plant genetic engineers to regenerate whole, fertile plants from transformed tissue, and they are having success with an increasing number of species, so occasional natural transformation cannot be ruled out. In fact, a potential case of this has been reported: sequences homologous to a characteristic part of the T-DNA have been identified in the chromosomal DNA of some species of *Nicotiana* (Furner *et al.* 1986).

NATURE'S JUMBLE SALE: THE ORIGIN OF NOVEL ADAPTATIONS

We have outlined a number of quite different systems through which bacteria interact with other organisms, each furnished by a special set of genes. Where did the genes for all these adaptations come from? Now that we have a wealth of comparative DNA sequence information, we can see clearly that Nature has cobbled together each specialized genetic system by borrowing and adapting genes that were already around. Most of the genes we have discussed are recognizably related to other bacterial genes, and some belong to extensive families. In some cases this family resemblance probably dates back to the common ancestors of the bacteria themselves, but bacterial gene transfer mechanisms can potentially operate across very wide taxonomic ranges, so that new genes need not be separately invented by all lineages that find the need for these genes. This is clearly illustrated by the examples of antibiotic resistance discussed above. The horizontal transfer of genes among genetically distinct lineages can accelerate evolution, and may have been crucial in allowing the evolution of the present astonishing complexity and diversity of bacteria in a mere 3.5×10^9 years. The balance and apparent conflict between clonality and hybridization, between species identity and horizontal transfer, is currently an area of considerable interest in bacterial population genetics (Young 1989).

Many of the interactions we have discussed are mediated by genes that are members of extensive families that are spread across many genera and many different functions. Thus, for example, the NodD protein (product of the *nodD* gene), which activates the synthesis of the *Rhizobium* nodulation signal in response to flavones, is clearly related to both NocD of *Agrobacterium*, which activates opine uptake in response to opine (White *et al.* 1990), and AmpR of enteric bacteria, which activates an antibiotic resistance mechanism in response to β-lactams (Honoré *et al.* 1989). These are just three members of the large LysR family of response regulators, which all bind to promoters and activate genes in response to molecular signals from the environment (Henikoff *et al.* 1988). Similarly,

VirA and VirG, which activate T-DNA transfer in response to acetosyringone, belong to a different family of response regulators, all of which have a membrane-bound sensor component (VirA) which, in response to the appropriate signal, triggers (by phosphorylation) a regulator (VirG) that activates genes (Ronson *et al.* 1987, Miller *et al.* 1989). To interact with their environment, bacteria also need to import and export molecules across the cell surface, and it is no surprise to find that these transport systems, too, come in kit form (Ferro-Luzzi Ames 1986). One of the standard types of transport system has a pore in the membrane made of two protein types, and an associated protein that provides the motive energy by hydrolysing ATP. This ATP-binding 'power unit' is specific to each type of pump, but is very conserved so that the homology of different systems is readily apparent. Pumps in this family are involved in both the uptake of iron (Staudenmaier *et al.* 1989) and the export of haemolysin (Bhakdi *et al.* 1988) by *E. coli* (these are important components of pathogenicity), in opine uptake by *Agrobacterium* (White *et al.* 1990), and in the secretion of cyclic β-1,2-glucans (needed for successful interaction with their plant hosts) by both *Agrobacterium* and *Rhizobium* (Stanfield *et al.* 1988, Cangelosi *et al.* 1989).

Even the origins of the bizarre genetic engineering practised by *Agrobacterium* can be traced, at least in outline (Stachel & Zambryski 1989). The mobilization of the T-DNA from the bacterium has strong similarities with the transfer of plasmids during conjugation between two bacterial cells, and in fact the *vir* genes can also mobilize plasmids into plants (Buchanan-Wollaston *et al.* 1987), while it has been suggested that the subsequent behaviour of the T-DNA in the plant cell has much in common with that of plant viruses (Hohn *et al.* 1991). Thanks to molecular genetics, we can explain in considerable detail the mechanisms by which bacteria interact with their environment, and we can often guess at the evolutionary ancestry of a particular mechanism. On the other hand, the selective pressures that led to these mechanisms, and that maintain them today, have not received much critical thought yet.

IN CONCLUSION: BACTERIA MAY BE GOOD FOR YOU

In this essay on molecules and niche we have, for good reasons, dealt exclusively with bacterial examples. One good reason is that we both work on bacteria, so we have saved ourselves some effort and had an opportunity to advertise what we do. There are real advantages in looking at evolutionary questions in bacteria, though. One is that there has been relatively little effort in this area, so it is easy to come up with something new. A more important reason is that bacteria are the ideal organisms for many evolutionary and ecological studies. Their adaptations can be understood at the molecular level and can be manipulated experimentally because their genetic systems are amenable and well-studied. Furthermore, they are cheap to house and feed, and large populations can be put through thousands of generations within the duration and budget of a single research grant, so experimental studies of evolution and ecological interactions are feasible on a scale that no macroorganism can match.

We have tried to convince you that bacterial biology is swarming with interesting evolutionary questions that are tractable but so far unsolved. These include examples of some of the universal preoccupations of biologists, as well as uniquely bacterial phenomena. By our choice of illustrations we have attempted to show that even biotic interactions can be reduced to comparatively simple molecular mechanisms. Of course, we believe that this is often true of eukaryotes as well as prokaryotes: after all, the partners/victims in some of our examples were eukaryotes. If anything, the interaction of organisms with their inanimate environment ought to be more straightforward than that with other organisms, and indeed there has already been considerable progress in exploring the adaptation of bacteria to nutrient sources (Dykhuizen & Dean 1990).

Our message, then, is that for those who are serious about solving ecological/evolutionary problems, rather than merely describing them, bacteria can provide a rich and largely untapped resource.

REFERENCES

Aly, R. & Shinefield, H. R. (1982). *Bacterial Interference.* CRC Press, Boca Raton, FL, USA.

Anderson, R. M. & May, R. M. (1982). Coevolution of hosts and parasites. *Parasitology*, **85**, 411–426.

Arber, W. (1965). Host controlled modification of bacteriophage. *Annual Review of Microbiology*, **19**, 365–368.

Bertram, J., Strätz, M. & Dürre, P. (1991). Natural transfer of conjugative transposon Tn*916* between gram-positive and gram-negative bacteria. *Journal of Bacteriology*, **173**, 443–448.

Bhakdi, S., Mackman, N., Menestrina, G., Gray, L., Hugo, F., Seeger, W. & Holland, I. B. (1988). The hemolysin of *Escherichia coli*. *European Journal of Epidemiology*, **4**, 135–143.

Bickle, T. (1986). DNA restriction and modification systems. *Escherichia coli* and *Salmonella typhimurium. Cellular and Molecular Biology* (Ed. by F. C. Neidhart, J. L. Ingram, K. Brooks Low, B. Magasanik, M. Schaechter & E. Umbargar), pp. 692–696. American Society for Microbiology, Washington, DC, USA.

Bohman, K., Ruusala, T., Jelenc, P. C. & Kurland, C. G. (1984). Kinetic impairment of restrictive streptomycin-resistant ribosomes. *Molecular and General Genetics*, **198**, 90–99.

Bromfield, E. S. P. & Jones, D. G. (1979). The competitive ability and symbiotic effectiveness of doubly labelled antibiotic resistant mutants of *Rhizobium trifolii*. *Annals of Applied Biology*, **91**, 211–219.

Brubaker, R. R. (1985). Mechanisms of bacterial virulence. *Annual Review of Microbiology*, **39**, 21–50.

Buchanan-Wollaston, V., Passiatore, J. E. & Cannon, F. (1987). The *mob* and *oriT* mobilization functions of a bacterial plasmid promote its transfer to plants. *Nature*, **328**, 172–175.

Bull, A. T. & Slater, J. H. (Eds) (1982). *Microbial Interactions and Communities*, Vol. 1. Academic Press, New York, NY, USA.

Cangelosi, G. A., Martinetti, G., Leigh, J. A., Lee, C. C., Theines, C. & Nester, E. W. (1989). Role of *Agrobacterium tumefaciens* ChvA protein in export of beta-1,2-glucan. *Journal of Bacteriology*, **171**, 1609–1615.

Chao, L. (1980). *The Population Biology of Colicinogenic Bacteria: A Model for the Evolution of Allelopathy*. PhD Thesis, University of Massachusetts, Amherst, MA, USA.

Chao, L. & Levin, B. R. (1981). Structured habitats and the evolution of anticompetitor toxins in bacteria. *Proceedings of the National Academy of Sciences, USA*, **78**, 6324–6328.

Davis, B. D., Dulbecco, R., Eisen, H. N. & Ginsberg, H. S. (1980). *Microbiology* (3rd edn). Harper & Row, New York, NY, USA.

Dykhuizen, D. E. & Dean, A. M. (1990). Enzyme activity and fitness: evolution in solution. *Trends in Ecology and Evolution*, **5**, 257–262.

Ewald, P. W. (1983). Host–parasite relations, vectors, and the evolution of disease severity. *Annual Review of Ecology and Systematics*, **14**, 465–485.

Ewald, P. W. (1988). Cultural vectors, virulence, and the emergence of evolutionary epidemiology. *Oxford Surveys in Evolutionary Biology*. Vol. **5** pp. 215–245. Oxford University Press, Oxford.

Falkow, S. (1975). *Infectious Multiple Drug Resistance*. Pion Press, London, UK.

Ferro-Luzzi Ames, G. (1986). Bacterial periplasmic transport systems: structure, mechanism, and evolution. *Annual Review of Biochemistry*, **55**, 397–425.

Finlay, B. B. & Falkow, S. (1989). Common themes in microbial pathogenicity. *Microbiological Reviews*, **53**, 210–230.

Furner, I. J., Huffman, G. A., Amasino, R. M., Garfinkel, D. J., Gordon, M. P. & Nester, E. W. (1986). An *Agrobacterium* transformation in the evolution of the genus *Nicotiana*. *Nature*, **319**, 422–427.

Gause, G. F., Maksimova, T. S. & Olkhovatova, O. L. (1981). Resistance of Actinomycetes to their own antibiotics and its possible significance to ecology. *Actinomycetes* (Ed. by K. P. Schaal & G. P. Pulverer), pp. 181–184. Fischer Verlag, Stuttgart, Germany.

Gould, S. J. & Lewontin, R. C. (1979). The spandrels of San Marco and the Panglossian paradigm: a critique of the adaptationist programme. *Proceedings of the Royal Society of London*, B, **205**, 581–598.

Griffith, F. (1928). Significance of pneumococcal types. *Journal of Hygiene, Cambridge*, **27**, 113.

Henikoff, S., Haughn, G. W., Calvo, J. M. & Wallace, J. C. (1988). A large family of bacterial activator proteins. *Proceedings of the National Academy of Sciences, USA*, **85**, 6602–6606.

Hohn, B., Koukolíková-Nicola, Z., Dürrenberger, F., Bakkeren, G. & Koncz, C. (1991). The T-DNA on its way from *Agrobacterium tumefaciens* to the plant. *Advances in Molecular*

Genetics of Plant–Microbe Interactions (Ed. by H. Hennecke & D. P. S. Verma), pp. 19–27. Kluwer, Dordrecht, Germany.

Honoré, N., Nicolas, M.-H. & Cole, S. T. (1989). Regulation of enterobacterial cephalosporinase production: the role of a membrane-bound sensory transducer. *Molecular Microbiology*, **3**, 1121–1130.

Hopwood, D. A. & Merrick, M. J. (1977). The genetics of antibiotic production. *Bacterial Reviews*, **41**, 595–635.

Hughes, V. M. & Datta, N. (1983). Conjugative plasmids in bacteria of the 'pre-antibiotic' era. *Nature*, **302**, 725–726.

Kahn, M. L., Kraus, J. & Somerville, J. E. (1985). A model of nutrient exchange in the *Rhizobium*–legume symbiosis. *Nitrogen Fixation Research Progress* (Ed. by H. J. Evans, P. J. Bottomley & W. E. Newton), pp. 193–199. Martinus-Nijhoff, Dordrecht, Germany.

Kearney, B. & Staskawicz, B. (1990). Widespread distribution and fitness contribution of *Xanthomonas campestris* avirulence gene *avrBs2*. *Nature*, **346**, 385–386.

Keen, N. T., Kobayashi, D., Tamaki, S., Shen, H., Stayton, M., Lawrence, D., Sharma, A., Midland, S., Smith, M. & Sims, J. (1991). Avirulence gene *D* from *Pseudomonas syringae* pv. *tomato* and its interaction with resistance gene *Rpg4* in soybean. *Advances in Molecular Genetics of Plant–Microbe Interactions* (Ed. by H. Hennecke & D. P. S. Verma), pp. 37–44. Kluwer, Dordrecht, Germany.

Keen, N. T., Tamaki, S., Kobayashi, D., Gerhold, D., Stayton, M., Shen, H., Gold, S., Lorang, J., Thordal-Christensen, H., Dahlbeck, D. & Staskawicz, B. (1990). Bacteria expressing avirulence gene D produce a specific elicitor of the soybean hypersensitive reaction. *Molecular Plant–Microbe Interactions*, **3**, 112–121.

Kessler, C. & Manta, V. (1990). Specificity of restriction endonucleases and DNA modification methyltransferases — a review (Edition 3). *Gene*, **92**, 1–248.

Krüger, D. H. & Bickle, T. A. (1983). Bacteriophage survival: multiple mechanisms for avoiding deoxyribonucleic acid restriction systems of their hosts. *Microbiological Reviews*, **47**, 345–360.

Lenski, R. E. (1988). Dynamics of interactions between bacteria and virulent bacteriophage. *Advances in Microbial Ecology*, **10**, 1–44.

Lerouge, P., Roche, P., Faucher, C., Maillet, F., Truchet, G., Promé, J. C. & Dénarié, J. (1990). Symbiotic host specificity of *Rhizobium meliloti* is determined by a sulphated and acylated glucosamine oligosaccharide signal. *Nature*, **344**, 781–784.

Levin, B. R. (1981). Periodic selection, infectious gene exchange and the genetic structure of *E. coli* populations. *Genetics*, **99**, 1–23.

Levin, B. R. (1986). Restriction–modification and the maintenance of genetic diversity in bacterial populations. *Proceedings of Conference on Evolutionary Processes and Theory* (Ed. by E. Nevo & S. Karlin), pp. 669–688. Academic Press, New York, NY, USA.

Levin, B. R. (1988). Frequency dependent selection in bacteria. *Philosophical Transactions of the Royal Society of London*, B, **319**, 459–472.

Levin, B. R. & Svanborg Edén, C. (1990). Selection and the evolution of virulence in bacteria: an ecumenical excursion and modest suggestion. *Parasitology*, **100**, S103–S115.

Levin, B. R., Allison, A. C., Bremermann, H. J., Cavalli-Sforza, L. L., Clarke, B. C., Fentzel-Beyme, R., Hamilton, W. D., Levin, S. A., May, R. M. & Thieme, H. R. (1982). Evolution of parasites and hosts. *Population Biology of Infectious Disease* (Ed. by R. M. Anderson & R. M. May), pp. 213–243. Springer Verlag, Berlin, Germany.

Levin, B. R., Stewart, F. M. & Chao, L. (1976). Resource limited growth, competition and predation: a model and experimental studies with bacteria and bacteriophage. *American Naturalist*, **111**, 3–24.

Levin, S. A. & Pimentel D. (1981). Selection of intermediate rates of virulence in parasite–host systems. *American Naturalist*, **117**, 308–315.

Luria, S. E. & Human, M. L. (1952). A non-hereditary, host-induced variation of bacterial viruses. *Journal of Bacteriology*, **64**, 557–563.

Luria, S. E. & Suit, J. L. (1987). Colicins and Col. plasmids. *Escherichia coli* and *Salmonella typhimurium* (Ed. by F. C. Neidhart, J. L. Ingram, K. Brooks Low, B. Magasanik, M. Schaechter and M. Umbarger), pp. 1615–1624. American Society for Microbiology, Washington, DC, USA.

Martinez, E., Romero, D. & Palacios, R. (1990). The *Rhizobium* genome. *Critical Reviews in Plant Sciences*, **9**, 59–93.

May, R. M. & Anderson, R. M. (1983). Parasite–host coevolution. *Coevolution* (Ed. by D. J. Futuyma & M. Slatkin), pp. 186–206. Sinauer, Sunderland, MA, USA.

McConnell, D. J., Searcy, D. G. & Sutcliff, J. G. (1978). A restriction enzyme, Tha I, from the thermophilic mycoplasmid, *Thermoplasma acidophilum*. *Nucleic Acids Research*, **5**, 1729–1739.

Maynard Smith, J., Dowson, C. G. & Spratt, B. G. (1991). Localized sex in bacteria. *Nature*, **349**, 29–31.

Miller, J. F., Mekalanos, J. J. & Falkow, S. (1989). Coordinate regulation and sensory transduction in the control of bacterial virulence. *Science*, **243**, 916–922.

Moore, L. W. & Warren, G. (1979). *Agrobacterium radiobacter* strain 84 and biological control of crown gall. *Annual Review of Phytopathology*, **17**, 163–169.

Nautiyal, C. S. & Dion, P. (1990). Characterization of the opine-utilizing microflora associated with samples of soil and plants. *Applied and Environmental Microbiology*, **56**, 2576–2579.

Nester, E. W. & Gordon, M. P. (1991). Molecular strategies in the interaction between *Agrobacterium* and its hosts. *Advances in Molecular Genetics of Plant–Microbe Interactions* (Ed. by H. Hennecke & D. P. S. Verma), pp. 3–9. Kluwer, Dordrecht, Germany.

Reeves, P. (1972). *The Bacteriocins*. Springer Verlag, New York, NY, USA.

Ronson, C. W., Nixon, B. T. & Ausubel, F. M. (1987). Conserved domains in bacterial regulatory proteins that respond to environmental stimuli. *Cell*, **49**, 579–581.

Simon, R., Hötte, B., Klauke, B. & Kosier, B. (1991). Isolation and characterization of insertion sequence elements from gram-negative bacteria by using new broad-host-range, positive selection vectors. *Journal of Bacteriology*, **173**, 1502–1508.

Spratt, B. G. (1988). Hybrid penicillin-binding proteins in penicillin-resistant strains of *Neisseria gonorrhoeae*. *Nature*, **332**, 173–176.

Spratt, B. G., Zhang, Q.-Y., Jones, D. M., Hutchison, A., Brannigan, J. A. & Dowson, C. G. (1989). Recruitment of a penicillin-binding protein gene from *Neisseria flavescens* during the emergence of penicillin resistance in *Neisseria meningitidis*. *Proceedings of the National Academy of Sciences, USA*, **86**, 8988–8992.

Stachel, S. E. & Zambryski, P. (1989). Generic trans-kingdom sex? *Nature*, **340**, 199–200.

Stachel, S. E., Messens, E., Van Montagu, M. & Zambryski, P. (1985). Identification of the signal molecules produced by wounded plant cells that activate T-DNA transfer in *Agrobacterium tumefaciens*. *Nature*, **318**, 624–629.

Stanfield, S. W., Ielpi, L., O'Brochta, D., Helinski, D. R. & Ditta, G. S. (1988). The *ndvA* gene product of *Rhizobium meliloti* is required for beta-1,2-glucan production and has homology to the ATP-binding export protein HlyB. *Journal of Bacteriology*, **170**, 3523–3530.

Staskawicz, B., Dahlbeck, D., Keen, N. T. & Napoli, C. (1987). Molecular characterization of cloned avirulence genes from race 0 to race 1 of *Pseudomonas syringae* pv. *glycinea*. *Journal of Bacteriology*, **169**, 5789–5794.

Staudenmaier, H., van Hove, B., Yaraghi, Z. & Braun, V. (1989). Nucleotide sequences of the *fecBCDE* genes and locations of the proteins suggest a periplasmic-binding-protein-dependent transport mechanism for iron(III) dicitrate in *Escherichia coli*. *Journal of Bacteriology*, **171**, 2626–2633.

Suárez, J. E., Arca, P., Villar, C. J. & Hardisson, C. (1989). Evolutionary origin, genetics and biochemistry of clinical fosfomycin resistance. *Genetics and Microbiology of Industrial Microorganisms* (Ed. by C. L. Hershberger, S. W. Queener & G. Hegeman), pp. 93–98. American Society for Microbiology, Washington, DC, USA.

Svanborg Edén, C. & Levin, B. R. (1990). Infectious disease and evolution in human populations: a critical reexamination. *Disease and Populations in Transition: Anthropological and Epidemiological Perspectives* (Ed. by A. Swedlund & G. Armelagos), pp. 31–46. Bergan and Garby Press, South Hadley, MA, USA.

Tempé, J. & Petit, A. (1983). La piste des opines. *Molecular Genetics of the Bacteria–Plant Interaction* (Ed. by A. Pühler), pp. 14–32. Springer Verlag, New York, NY, USA.

Tomashow, L. S. & Pierson, L. S. (1991). Genetic aspects of phenazine antibiotic production by fluorescent pseudomonads that suppress take-all disease. *Advances in Molecular Genetics of Plant–Microbe Interactions* (Ed. by H. Hennecke & D. P. S. Verma), pp. 443–449. Kluwer, Dordrecht, Germany.

Tomashow, L. S. & Weller, D. M. (1988). Role of a phenazine antibiotic from *Pseudomonas fluorescens* in biological control of *Gaeumannomyces graminis* var. *tritici*. *Journal of Bacteriology*, **170**, 3499–3508.

Tomashow, L. S., Weller, D. M., Bonsall, R. F. & Pierson, L. S. (1990). Production of the antibiotic phenazine-1-carboxylic acid by fluorescent *Pseudomonas* species in the rhizosphere of wheat. *Applied and Environmental Microbiology*, **56**, 908–912.

Trieu-Cuot, P., Arthur, M. & Courvalin, P. (1987). Origin, evolution and dissemination of antibiotic resistance genes. *Microbiological Sciences*, **4**, 263–266.

van Kan, J. A. L., van den Ackerveden, G. F. J. M. & de Wit, P. J. G. M. (1991). Cloning and characterization of cDNA of avirulence gene *avr9* of the fungal pathogen *Cladosporium fulvum*, causal agent of tomato leaf mold. *Molecular Plant–Microbe Interactions*, **4**, 52–59.

Waxman, S. A. (1967). *The Actinomycetes: A Summary of Current Knowledge*. Ronald Press, New York, NY, USA.

White, D. R. W., Pritchard, M. & Marincs, F. (1990). Genetic and sequence analysis of *Agrobacterium* opine catabolism genes. *5th International Symposium on the Molecular Genetics of Plant–Microbe Interactions*, 53 (abstract).

Young, J. P. W. (1989). The population genetics of bacteria. *Genetics of Bacterial Diversity* (Ed. by D. A. Hopwood & K. F. Chater), pp. 417–438. Academic Press, London, UK.

Young, J. P. W. & Johnston, A. W. B. (1989). The evolution of specificity in the legume–rhizobium symbiosis. *Trends in Ecology and Evolution*, **4**, 341–349.

8. ENZYMES AND ADAPTATION

ANDREW G. CLARK* AND RICHARD K. KOEHN[†]
*Genetics Program and Department of Biology, Pennsylvania State University, University Park, PA 16802, USA and [†]210 Park Building, University of Utah, Salt Lake City, UT 84112, USA

INTRODUCTION

Evolutionary geneticists working at the molecular and the whole organism levels can be engaged in such different problems that they may appear to have little in common. DNA sequence data provide tremendous power in reconstructing the evolutionary relationships among species, and in combination with population genetic models, the forces of natural selection and drift can to some extent be quantified. Such studies, however, rarely examine the effects of the DNA sequence variation on a target phenotype. Indeed, in many studies of DNA sequence variation (e.g. restriction site polymorphism), the probable phenotype of a stretch of sequence may not be at issue and may never be known. In such cases, DNA polymorphism is strictly a marker of genetic variation, much the way enzyme variation was treated in early studies of protein polymorphism. In regard to proteins, we now know that such an approach ignores the real biological significance of the genetic and metabolic systems we seek to understand.

Physiological geneticists focus their attention on the phenotype and try to understand the genetic and environmental causes for physiological variation. Although breeding studies have shown a multitude of physiological phenotypes to have a genetic basis, these have rarely been precisely identified in terms of DNA sequence variation. Indeed, it is uncommon that specific genes have been correlated with specific physiological effects and only rarely has any causal relationship been established.

The thesis of this chapter is that metabolic control theory, including both experimental and theoretical extensions, provides a 'glue' to hold physiology and genetics together. As such, it is a mechanism within which to describe how natural selection can act on a phenotype to effect evolutionary changes in genotype. It is also our contention that we cannot understand the evolution of enzyme-encoding genes outside the context of cellular metabolism, whether we are concerned with factors that influence the behaviour of specific metabolic pathways or the physiological energetics of whole organisms, or both.

To develop these points in the following sections, we will describe the theoretical foundation of metabolic control theory. We will demonstrate that the behaviour of metabolism is predictable from the characteristics of some individual enzyme components and that metabolic flux can be correlated with, if not directly a determinant of, fitness. We will use both theory and empirical observations to draw a connection between the properties of individual enzymes and global properties of metabolic pathways, including whole-organism energy balance.

BRIEF OVERVIEW OF METABOLIC CONTROL THEORY

A large body of theory has been developed that relates the properties of individual enzymes in a metabolic pathway to global properties of the pathway (Kacser & Burns 1973, 1979, 1981, Heinrich & Rapoport 1983). For any phenotype that might be determined by a global property (such as rate of flux through the pathway or concentration of an intermediate metabolite), metabolic control theory provides the mechanistic model to relate a series of traits (such as enzyme activities) that may have a simpler genetic basis to the global phenotype. In order to see how natural selection acting on a metabolic character can influence properties of individual enzymes, we first review the basic principles of metabolic control theory, and then consider how genetic transmission of metabolic traits can constrain the evolutionary change.

The simplest metabolic pathway is linear, with each substrate converted by first-order kinetics to the subsequent product:

$$S_1 \xrightarrow[E_1]{} S_2 \xrightarrow[E_2]{} S_3 \xrightarrow[E_3]{} S_4 \longrightarrow \ldots \longrightarrow S_n \xrightarrow[E_n]{} S_{n+1}$$

We will assume that the concentrations of the first substrate (S_1) and the last substrate (S_{n+1}) are held constant by some homoeotic mechanism external to the pathway. Each of the enzymes in the pathway satisfies the kinetics of the Briggs and Haldane (1925) formulation, which means the substrate concentration is not saturating, and the enzyme–substrate complex formation occurs essentially instantaneously. Under these conditions, the rate of conversion of substrate S_i to S_{i+1} is:

$$v_i = \frac{(V_i/K_i)(S_i - S_{i+1}/k_{i,i+1})}{1 + S_i/K_i + S_{i+1}/K_i'}$$

In this equation, V_i is the maximum velocity of the reaction under substrate-saturating conditions (often called $V_{\max}$), K_i is the Michaelis constant (also called K_m) for the reaction from S_i to S_{i+1}, and K_i' is the Michaelis constant for the reverse reaction. $k_{i,i+1}$ is the equilibrium constant across the step. When $[S_i]$ is sufficiently low for all substrates such that none of the enzymes is saturated, it is possible to solve a steady-state condition, at which the velocity across all steps is the same and is equal to the pathway flux, J. Kacser and Burns (1973) solved an expression for the steady-state flux by solving the system of simultaneous equations $v_i = J$. The solution is:

$$J = \frac{S_1 - S_{n+1}/k_{1,n+1}}{\sum_i K_i/(V_i k_{1,i})}$$

where $k_{1,n+1}$ is the equilibrium constant across all the steps from 1 to $n + 1$, and is $k_{1,2} \times k_{2,3} \times k_{3,4} \ldots \times k_{n,n+1}$. If we define the activity of an enzyme as $E_i = V_i k_{1,i}/K_i$, and note that the numerator is a constant for fixed initial and terminal substrate concentrations ($C = S_1 - S_{n+1}/k_{1,n+1}$), then the steady-state flux can be re-written:

$$J = \frac{C}{(1/E_1) + (1/E_2) + \ldots + (1/E_n)}$$

The relationship between flux and activity of any one enzyme shows saturation kinetics (Fig. 8.1), and Kacser, Burns and others have shown that many physiological systems are on the plateau of this curve. Kacser and Burns (1981) argued that this can explain the molecular basis of dominance, since halving the activity of an enzyme will result in a much smaller effect on flux. The numerator of the above expression is the concentration gradient, so doubling the initial substrate concentration will double the flux (provided no enzyme approaches saturation). Similarly, if all enzymes in the pathway were halved in activity, the steady-state flux would halve. The steady-state of this system can also be solved to get an expression of the concentration of any of the substrates. We are particularly interested in the influence of varying the activity of one enzyme on the steady-state concentration of one substrate. If E_u is the activity of an upstream enzyme, the steady-state solution has the form:

$$[S] = \frac{aE_u + b}{cE_u + d}$$

where a, b, c and d are functions of S_1, S_{n+1}, V_i and k_{ij} (Clark, unpublished). If the activity of the downstream enzyme (E_d) varies, the solution is of the form:

$$[S] = \frac{a' + b'E_d}{c' + E_d}$$

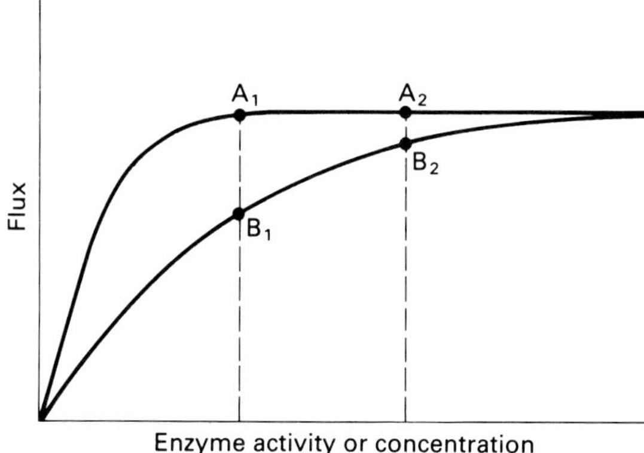

FIG. 8.1. The relationship between flux and enzyme activity (or concentration) for two enzymes (A and B). Curve A illustrates the form of the function for flux derived in the text. Curve B represents another enzyme with a lower control coefficient, also defined in the text. From Koehn (1991) with permission.

Figure 8.2 shows that substrate concentration shows a plateau effect with respect to either upstream or downstream enzymes but, as expected, increasing upstream enzyme activity increases the steady-state concentration of its product, while increasing the activity of a downstream enzyme decreases the steady-state concentration of its substrate. Both of these saturation effects show that Kacser and Burns' idea for molecular dominance holds whether the phenotype is a property of flux or of substrate concentration.

Metabolic control theory may be relevant to evolutionary adaptation because it provides a link between discrete characters like enzyme activities, whose molecular basis is accessible to genetic and molecular methods, and a physiological phenotype like growth rate or fat storage.

Before we pursue this application it is useful to comment on some of the caveats that have been levelled at metabolic control theory. The theory employs biochemical assumptions that have caused some concern, including the assumption that the reactions occur in homogeneous solution (which cells are not), that the system is in steady state, that none of the reactions is saturated, and that branched pathways do not introduce serious complications (Burton & Place 1986). We think the most serious of these criticisms is that living organisms are metabolically dynamic; steady-state conditions usually prevail for only a small proportion of the time. The induction of enzyme synthesis in response to various forms of stress (reviewed by Hoffmann & Parsons 1991) bears evidence that the

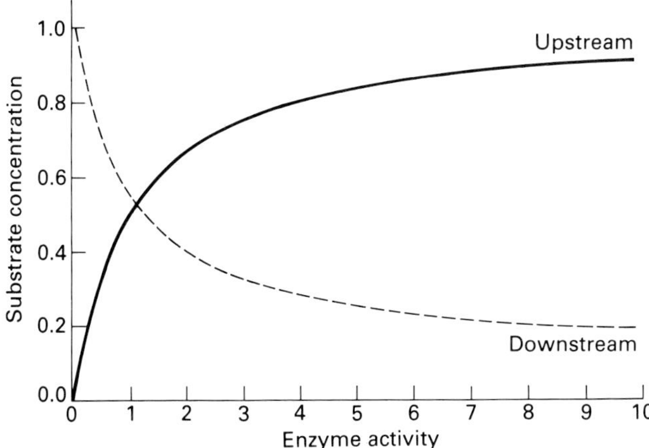

FIG. 8.2. Relationship between upstream (E_u) and downstream (E_d) enzyme activity and steady-state concentration of flanking substrate.

rate of flux can be drastically altered in response to particular environmental conditions. When the system is not at steady state the relationships between the activity of a particular enzyme and metabolic flux may be very different from the steady-state situation.

The issue that has aroused the most controversy is the equating of metabolic flux with fitness (Hartl *et al.* 1985). In nutrient-limited chemostats, Dykhuizen, Hartl, Dean and co-workers have repeatedly demonstrated the utility of this simple model, and have empirically demonstrated the equivalence of fitness and flux through nutrient-uptake pathways (Dykhuizen & Hartl 1983, Dean *et al.* 1986, Dykhuizen *et al.* 1987). It is important to realize in other cases that there need not be an equivalence but only a correlation between fitness and flux for most of the conclusions of evolutionary models of metabolic control to be applicable. Even if fitness has nothing to do with flux, metabolic control theory makes quantitative predictions about other global properties of metabolic pathways that may be associated with fitness (such as substrate concentration). Having said this, it is also true that the relationship between fitness and flux in eukaryotes may be more complicated than suggested by the results from chemostat studies with *Escherichia coli*. Enzyme activity differences can result from differences in catalysis and/or concentration. Only the former has been considered in any depth by other authors, since the theory describes the control of the *rate* of flux. The maintenance of enzyme pools is a substantial metabolic cost that must be 'deducted' from the benefits of flux. Both the rate of flux and the efficiency of flux can act to determine fitness, a point that is elaborated later.

Metabolic control theory also makes predictions about control coefficients, defined as the effect on flux of a change in the activity of an enzyme, or $\delta J/\delta E_i$. Control coefficients are useful for understanding steady states, but they too may vary with nutritional and environmental conditions (e.g. Heinstra *et al.* 1990, Heinstra & Geer 1991). These criticisms have motivated additional extensions of the original formulation of metabolic control theory (e.g. Easterby 1973, LaPorte *et al.* 1984).

QUANTIFICATION OF GENETIC VARIATION IN ENZYME ACTIVITIES

Variation in activity among products of distinct structural alleles

During the burst of work surveying natural populations for electrophoretic variants of enzymes, a number of workers investigated the potential adaptive significance of electrophoretic variation. They pursued the effects of the genetic variation by measuring biochemical and/or physiological differences among genotypes. Some physiological examples include endurance of ethanol in the environment by alcohol dehydrogenase (ADH) variants of *Drosophila* (Oakeshott 1976, Cavener & Clegg 1981), adaptation to osmotic conditions by leucine aminopeptidase (LAP) variants of the mussel *Mytilus edulis* (Koehn & Hilbish 1987), ability to use starch in the diet by amylase variants of *Drosophila* (DeJong & Scharloo 1976, Hickey 1979, Powell & Amato 1984), the effect of lactic dehydrogenase (LDH) allozymes on blood chemistry and various measures of performance in the teleost fish *Fundulus heteroclitus* (Powers *et al.* 1983), the series of papers on phosphoglucose isomerase (PGI) and other enzymes of energy metabolism in *Colias* by Watt and colleagues (Watt 1983, Watt *et al.* 1983, 1985, Carter & Watt 1988), and endurance of osmotic shock by glutamic–pyruric transaminase (GPT) variants of the copepod *Tigriopus californicus* (Burton & Feldman 1983). For these few successful cases, where enzyme variants were demonstrated to have an effect on whole animal physiology, there were dozens of studies where the effect was inferential only.

Even in the clearest associations between enzyme variants and physiology, the adaptive mechanism of the polymorphism is not very clear. This does not mean that the range of activities of most of the enzymes is irrelevant to normal metabolism. It may mean that there was insufficient kinetic variation at the structural locus, and/or an excess of confounding variation in the remainder of the genome influencing the expression of the structural gene.

Quantitative genetic variation in enzyme activities

The work of Laurie-Ahlberg *et al.* (1980, 1982, 1985) began a new level of rigour in the quantitative genetic analysis of enzyme activities. Here the product of a structural locus, specifically the variation in function of the product, was treated as a quantitative trait with a genetic contribution from both the structural enzyme variants of the locus and the 'regulatory' effects of other genes. Variation in enzyme activity can be caused by variation in rates of transcription, transcript processing, translation, post-translational modification, or in the stability of the transcript or protein product. Most of these processes result in variation in amounts of enzyme product produced, so the enzyme's affinity and catalytic activity (activity per molecule) are not altered. Enzyme activity, measured as the rate at which the catalysed reaction proceeds per unit live weight or per unit total protein of the animal and the quantitative genetic basis of this trait have been examined in several ways that we describe next.

Activity variation among chromosome replacement lines

Chromosome replacement lines have a common homozygous genetic background and differ in only one targeted chromosome (e.g. the second chromosome represents about 30% of the genome of *D. melanogaster*). A distinct advantage of such genetically defined lines is that genotypes can be replicated at different developmental stages and environments. In cases where the structural gene for an enzyme is not on the second chromosome, the variation can definitively be identified as non-structural.

Analysis of variation among the second chromosome replacement lines of *Drosophila melanogaster* has demonstrated that there is significant genetic variation in metabolic traits (Laurie-Ahlberg *et al.* 1980, 1982, Clark & Keith 1988). Significant among-line variation was found in triacylglycerol and glycogen storage, and the activities of fatty acid synthase (FAS), glucose-6-phosphate dehydrogenase (G6PD), glycogen phosphorylase (GP), α-GPDH, glycogen synthase (GS), hexokinase (HEX), malic enzyme (ME), 6-phosphogluconate dehydrogenase (6PGD), phosphoglucoisomerase (PGI), phosphoglucomutase (PGM) and trehalase (TRE) (Clark 1989). Supplementation of the medium with 10% sucrose resulted in a number of coordinated changes in enzyme activities and identified several gene-by-environment interactions (Fig. 8.3).

Genetic correlations in the broad sense (including non-additive terms) were estimated from covariances of line effects divided by the product of the standard deviations of respective line effects. Of all the possible correlations, the most strikingly consistent is the strong positive correlation

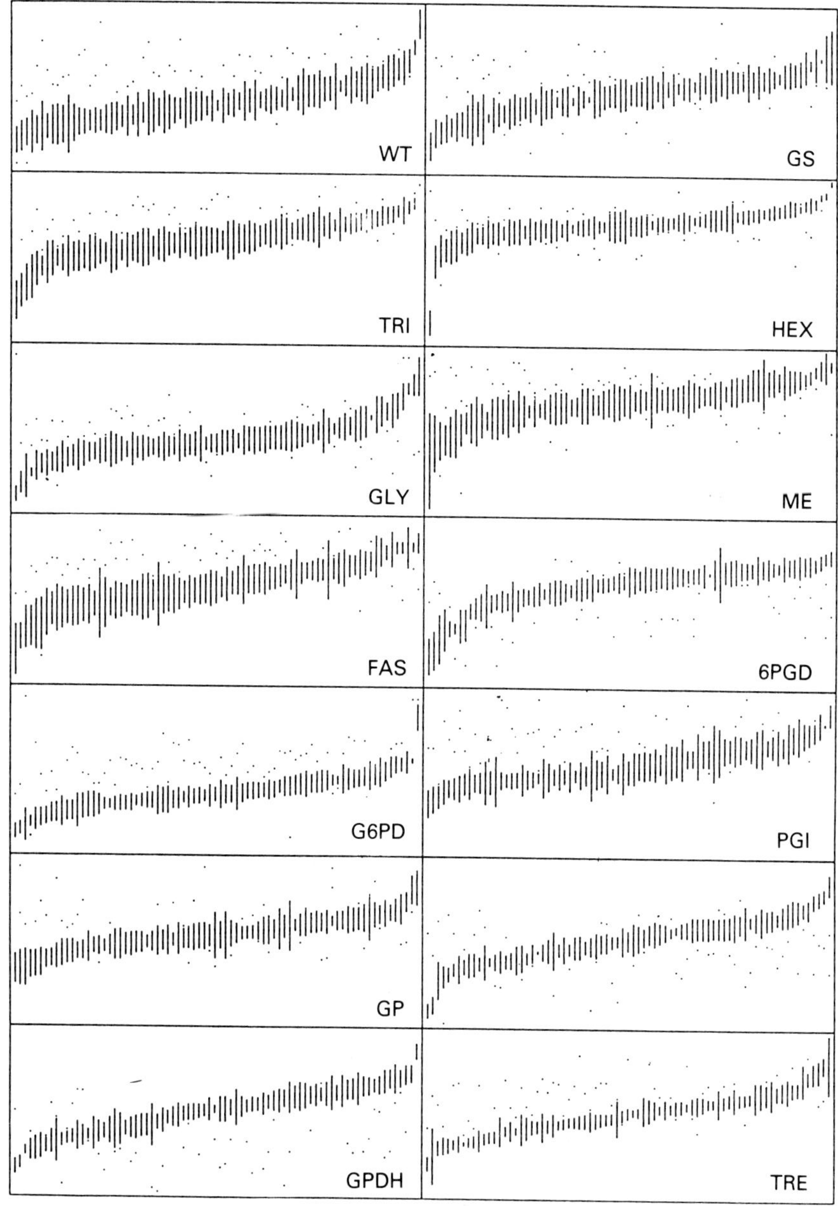

FIG. 8.3. Results of the second chromosome replacement line experiment of Clark (1989). Twelve different characters were measured in 83 different lines. They are presented in rank order by line mean for each character. Error bars are ±1 SE. The dots represent line means for flies reared on sucrose medium. Abbreviations are defined in the text. From Clark (1989) with permission.

between the activities of G6PD and 6PGD, the first two enzymes in the pentose phosphate shunt (Fig. 8.4). Significant positive phenotypic and genetic correlations were seen between G6PD and 6PGD in the studies of Hori and Tanda (1981), Hori *et al.* (1982) and Wilton *et al.* (1982), as well as studies of second chromosome lines, X chromosome lines, half-sib families, artificial selection lines and wild fly surveys of Clark and co-workers. Aspects of natural selection acting on these enzymes have been investigated by Bijlsma and van Delden (1977), Bijlsma (1980) and Eanes *et al.* (1985).

The two storage compounds, triacylglycerol and glycogen, were positively correlated, suggesting that there is not a trade-off between the two pools. Rather some genotypes store large quantities of both, while other genotypes store little of either. Several other consistently positive correlations were observed, including those among stored lipid, fatty acid synthase and the two leading enzymes in the pentose phosphate shunt, which supplies nicotinamide-adenine-dinucleotide phosphate (NADPH) for lipogenesis. The quantity of stored glycogen frequently exhibits a

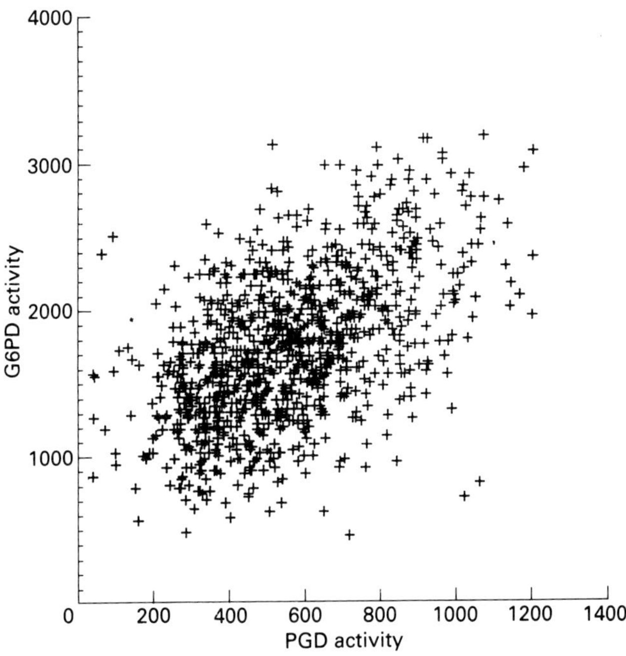

Fig. 8.4. Scattergram of line means of glucose-6-phosphate dehydrogenase (G6PD) and 6-phosphogluconate dehydrogenase (6PGD) activities, showing that they are highly correlated (data from Clark 1989).

strong positive correlation with the activity of glycogen synthase. The enzymes that share glucose-6-phosphate as a substrate, including G6PD, HEX, PGI and PGM, generally showed positive intercorrelations in activity, in both Wilton *et al.* (1982) and Clark (1989).

Regression techniques showed surprising success in predicting the amount of stored lipids and carbohydrates from the enzyme kinetic assays. On normal medium, 20% of the variance among lines in adult lipid storage could be explained by the activity of fatty acid synthase (Clark & Keith 1988). Over 50% of the variance in stored glycogen could be explained by the activities of PGM, PGI and TRE in adults on normal medium. These patterns varied somewhat across developmental stage and media but in all cases a substantial portion of the variance in storage compounds could be explained by enzyme activities. Flight power, which can be considered a property of metabolic flux, was also related to enzyme kinetic properties but only weakly (Barnes & Lauric-Ahlberg 1986).

Sib analysis and artificial selection quantifies additive effects

Chromosome replacement lines allow replicated genotypes but this method does not allow estimation of additive genetic variance, which is crucial for prediction of response to selection. Classical quantitative genetic approaches, such as sib analysis, permit quantification of additive variance. Clark (1990) reports the results of a large half-sib study in which 1157 half-sib families were scored for the same set of metabolic characters as in the chromosome replacement line studies. Each male was mated to 10 females and two offspring were scored from each female. The purpose was to partition the total variance into its 'causal' components. The flies were from a population cage that had been started with offspring from 92 isofemale lines collected in the summer of 1985. Components of variance were estimated in three different ways, including analysis of variance on offspring only, parent–offspring regression and maximum likelihood methods. Estimates of heritability are presented in Fig. 8.5. Additive genetic variances and correlations estimated by these three methods are expected to be different due to the positive sampling correlation between the parent–offspring regression and the full-sib correlation (Hill & Nicholas 1974). Despite the large sampling effort, the genetic correlations had large sampling variances (Robertson 1959a, b). Previous studies of chromosome replacement lines had indicated several significant genetic correlations among the metabolic characters, and the sib analysis showed that much of the correlation was due to additive effects (a number of

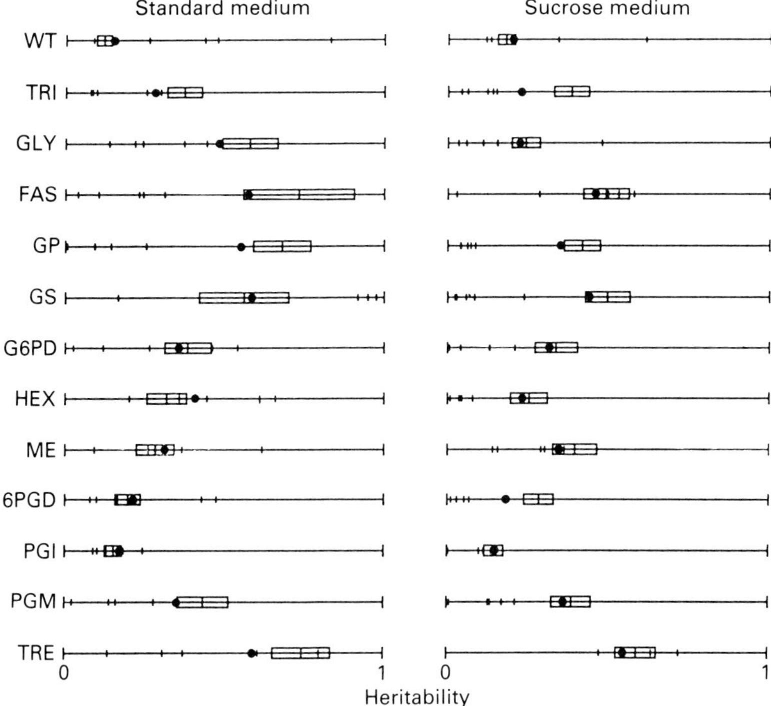

FIG. 8.5. Narrow-sense heritabilities of metabolic characters. These characters all exhibit significant additive genetic variation. From Clark (1990) with permission.

additive genetic correlations were significantly different from zero). The results show that there is substantial opportunity for natural and artificial selection to act on quantities of stored lipid and glycogen, and that the response to selection is likely to be mediated in part by changes in the kinetics of enzymes targeted in these studies (Clark 1990) (Fig. 8.6).

The prospect for response to artificial selection on triacylglycerol and glycogen storage, and the associated correlated responses were tested in the studies reported in Clark *et al.* (1989). In the first triacylglycerol selection experiment, the raw measures of fat content (μg per fly) were used as the selection criterion. The result was surprising in that there was no direct response in fat content but the lines selected for low fat content decreased in total body weight. We then learned that the allometric relation between body weight and fat content (expressed as percentage of weight) has a slope less than one (so that, generally, larger flies have a

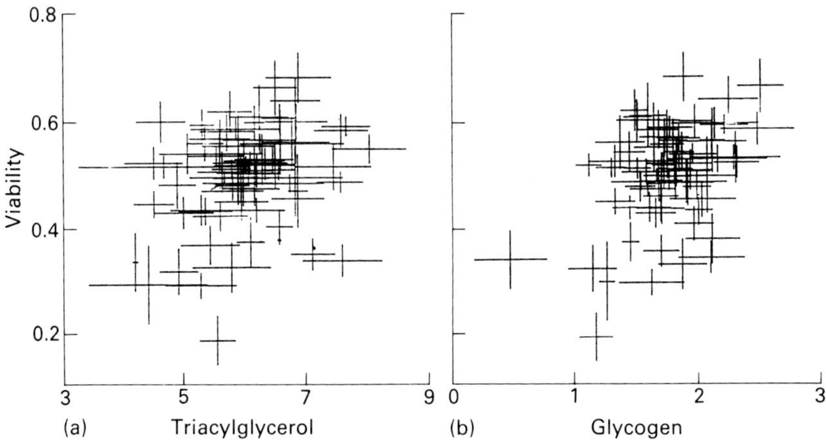

FIG. 8.6. (a) Relationship between triacylglycerol storage (in percentage live weight) and viability based on line means from the second chromosome replacement line tests (Clark 1989). (b) Relationship between glycogen storage (in percentage live weight) and viability. Both traits are significantly correlated with viability.

lower fat percentage than smaller flies). Subsequent selections used weight-adjusted measures for the selection criterion, and significant response was obtained for both fat and glycogen content. The realized heritabilities for fat content were 0.43 and 0.40 for the two replicates. These were somewhat higher than the estimates from the sib analysis, in part because of the correlated responses that enter due to the allometry of fat and total body weight. Realized heritabilities of glycogen content were 0.25 and 0.31 for the two replicates. Several correlated responses were detected and the directions were generally consistent with results of the chromosome replacement studies and the sib analysis.

Combining the theory of metabolic control with quantitative genetics

By combining the tools of metabolic control theory and the theory of evolutionary quantitative genetics, it will be possible to make a number of testable predictions about the evolution of metabolic pathways and their component enzymes. Rather than being just a special case of the general theory of evolutionary quantitative genetics, the specific consideration of metabolic control theory will provide an excellent opportunity to examine suites of mechanistically interrelated phenotypes, and to obtain predictions for which a large experimental base has been established. Metabolic control theory provides a coherent mapping from properties of individual gene products (enzymes), to global properties of metabolic pathways. Two very general properties of this mapping are that it is non-linear, and that it exhibits saturation (higher activity results in diminishing change in flux or metabolite concentration). What is needed is a formulation that expresses the partitioning of genetic variance into its causal components, when the underlying genes affect activity in a specified way, and when the phenotype of interest is a global property of a metabolic pathway. Kacser and Burns (1981) were the first to bring together the results of metabolic control theory with the consequences of genetic transmission of enzyme kinetic properties. They showed that under a wide range of conditions, a halving of the activity of one enzyme is expected to have a much smaller effect on the flux through the pathway. This is consistent with the empirical observation that heterozygotes for null alleles are often phenotypically normal, and is a plausible mechanism for molecular dominance. Keightley and Kacser (1987) extended these results by showing that pleiotropic effects are also expected to be shared among enzymes in a pathway.

Keightley (1989) has made a good start on part of this problem by partitioning variance in flux into an additive and non-additive component. He considered a haploid population with the activities of each enzyme in a pathway determined by one locus with two alleles. After specifying allele frequencies, he obtained expressions for the total genetic variance in flux and for the additive variance. The additive variance in flux is calculated by first determinating α, the average effect of an allelic substitution and is expressed as $\delta F/\delta q$, where F is the population mean flux and q is the allele frequency. For one locus the additive variance is $\alpha^2 q(1 - q)$, and a like quantity for each locus is summed over loci to give the multiple locus formula. Keightley (1989) showed that the interaction component of variance ($V_i = V_g - V_a$) is generally a small proportion of the total variance unless there are many loci with large differences in activity between the alleles. The theory supports the notion that pleiotropic effects should be prevalent, since any change in the pathway will change its global properties. The degree of dominance of various pleiotropic effects is expected to be the same in all but extreme cases of branched pathways (Keightley & Kacser 1987). Ward (1990) has considered the within-sibship genetic mean and genetic variance for metabolic flux, with the purpose of understanding how to obtain statistical power in tests of associations between allozyme variation and inter-individual variation.

TARGETS OF SELECTION

Once we accept that many adaptive changes are mediated by enzymatic processes, we are faced with the question of the mechanism by which metabolic differences are manifested as differences in fitness. The emphasis of attempts to exploit evolutionary predictions from the use of metabolic control theory has been on the relationship between metabolic flux and fitness. For example, Fig. 8.1 compares two enzymes, one with a small control coefficient (A), the other large (B). Clearly, an activity change from B_1 to B_2 will produce a larger change in flux than an equivalent change in the activity of enzyme A (e.g. A_1 to A_2). Moreover, if A_1 and A_2 represent allele- or genotype-specific activity differences, and fitness is taken to be proportional to flux, Hartl *et al.* (1985) have shown that for the case of enzyme A, A_1 and A_2 would be functionally and adaptively equivalent, since the phenotype of selective relevance, namely flux, does not differ between A_1 and A_2. This conclusion follows inescapably from equating fitness with flux. A_1 and A_2 would differ in reaction rate but this difference would not be expressed in flux. The two hypothetical alleles, or genotypes, would be metabolically and evolutionarily equivalent, if we only consider a kinetic basis for the activity difference between A_1 and A_2.

On the other hand, since $V_{max} = k_{cat}[E]$, enzyme activity differences, including those between genetic variants, can also result from differences in steady-state enzyme concentrations (i.e. $[E]$), where $[E] = K_s/K_d$. K_s is the zero-order rate constant of enzyme synthesis and K_d is the first-order rate constant of enzyme degradation (Schimke & Doyle 1970). Mutations that alter transcription efficiency, promoter action, protein stability and so forth, can result in steady-state activity differences between enzymes, irrespective of their catalytic properties. In the case of A_1 and A_2 (Fig. 8.1), differences in concentration, reflecting differences in the cost of synthesis and degradation, could be potentially non-neutral with respect to one another if selection detects differences in cost and not simply rate. If genetic differences in enzyme activity were exclusively catalytic, then we need only consider a potential relationship between the rate of flux and fitness. On the other hand, since genetic differences in enzyme activity can also result from non-catalytic regulatory factors, we need to examine the possible differences in fitness that could result from variation in metabolic efficiency.

Efficiency can be related to productivity and cost. At the level of a metabolic pathway, we can measure efficiency as productivity of the pathway in energy equivalents relative to the energy costs of maintaining the constituent enzymes of the pathway. In the case of A_1 and A_2 (Fig. 8.1), the productivity of this hypothetical pathway would be equivalent in each case but the efficiency of the pathway with A_1 would be higher than with A_2 because of the lower cost of maintaining the A enzyme step.

Thus, the concept of efficiency in this context has to do with maintenance costs, the energy required to maintain an enzyme, or group of enzymes at some steady-state concentration.

The concept of a maintenance cost, or more precisely the energy demands of maintenance metabolism, is well established at the whole organism level as the total cost of metabolism in the absence of growth, reproduction, behaviour, etc. In short, the basal metabolic costs of maintaining normal cell function in the absence of all other sources of energy demand. This cost, at least that part reflected by the dominant metabolic costs of protein turnover, is merely a summation of the costs of synthesis and degradation of individual enzymes, or groups of such enzymes in a specific metabolic pathway.

Although the rate of flux and the efficiency of flux should not be interpreted as two mutually exclusive properties of metabolism, it is important to consider how each might be the phenotypic target of natural selection. Does evolution merely favour enzyme variants that tend to increase the rate of flux or is the efficiency of flux also a property of a pathway that can be subject to natural selection?

In proposing that evolution maximizes metabolic flux, Hartl *et al.* (1985) reviewed a considerable body of evidence to support this point (but see Burton & Place 1986). Indeed, the many chemostat experiments of Dykhuizen and Hartl and collaborators (Dykhuizen & Hartl 1983, Hartl *et al.* 1985, Dyhuizen *et al.* 1987, Dean *et al.* 1988, Dean 1989, Hartl 1989) with *E. coli* have demonstrated a very strong positive relationship between fitness (as the rate of cell division) and the rate of flux. As these authors correctly claim, there is much evidence from these studies that natural selection favours alleles that enhance the rate of flux.

It is likely, however, that these data cannot be extrapolated directly to more complex organisms. This is because the cost of maintenance is a major portion of the energy demand in higher organisms, whereas prokaryotes have essentially no maintenance costs (Battley 1987, p. 410), especially during unrestricted growth (Marr *et al.* 1963). More precisely, because of the rapid rate of cell division, the total heat of metabolism (a measure of total energy expenditure) is associated with growth and cell division, not maintenance. The rate of metabolism and the rate of cell division (i.e. fitness) are one and the same process. It is for this reason that the *rate* of flux is closely equivalent to fitness in prokaryotes. Since there is essentially no cost for the maintenance of a pathway, the performance of a pathway can be measured in rate but not efficiency.

The situation is strikingly different for adult eukaryotes. In mammals, for example, maintenance constitutes more than 50% of the heat production at body mass equilibrium; more than 99% of the total life-time energy expenditure in humans (assuming a life span of 70 years) is devoted to meeting maintenance requirements (Reeds *et al.* 1985). In eukaryotes, the cost of maintenance is a significant source of energy expenditure; the biological significance of any change in energy demand will derive from its potential impact upon the cost of maintenance. In the next section, we determine the cost of enzyme synthesis and metabolic efficiency as a potential target of natural selection.

NATURAL SELECTION ON METABOLIC EFFICIENCY

The cost of enzyme synthesis

The energy required for protein turnover is dependent upon high-energy phosphate (ATP). The formation of each peptide bond requires 4 ATP-equivalents (Millward *et al.* 1976). An additional ATP is probably required for the active transport of the amino acid across the cell membrane, giving a cost of 5 ATPs per peptide bond (cf. Reeds *et al.* 1985, Milligan & Summers 1986). Milligan and Summers (*op. cit.*) note that this value for the cost of protein synthesis is likely to be conservative; it excludes other known sources of energy expenditure such as RNA synthesis, protein degradation and other cellular processing events.

The cost of enzyme synthesis (Z) will be proportional to K_s and linear with $[E]$ at a constant K_d. This cost is the ATP-equivalents required to maintain steady-state $[E]$ per unit time and will increase proportionally with increasing $[E]$ (Fig. 8.7). $A_1 - Z_1$ and A_1/Z_1 (Fig. 8.7) represent the metabolic profit and the efficiency of flux, respectively, both with respect to enzyme A_1.

The slope of the cost function will be determined by several properties of an enzyme. For example, the energetic cost (assuming all else to be equal) to synthesize a molecule of molecular weight (MW) 200 000 will be ten times that of a molecule of MW 20 000. Similarly, if the steady-state $[E]$ is 80 μM, the cost of maintaining steady state will be greater than if $[E]$ is 40 μM, with the same K_d in each case, since a higher rate of synthesis will be required. At steady state, the rate of enzyme turnover is $t_{1/2} = \ln 2/K_d$ where $t_{1/2}$ is the time required to replace half of $[E]$. All else being equal, the cost of maintaining a particular enzyme concentration is greater for an enzyme with a faster turnover rate. Lastly, the total cost of whole-organism protein turnover will be a function of the biomass containing the enzyme. The cost of a particular turnover rate for an enzyme

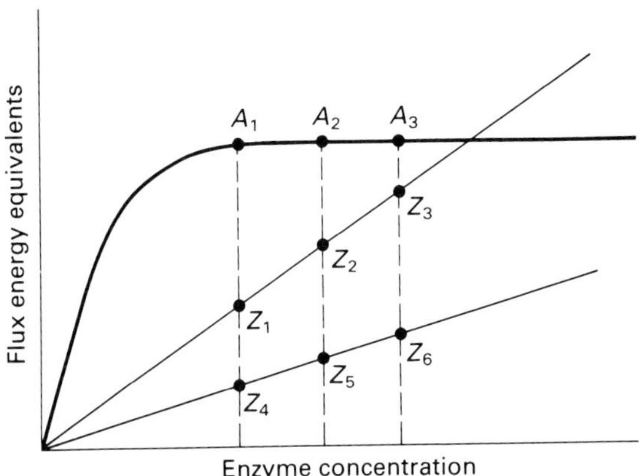

FIG. 8.7. As in Fig. 8.1 for enzyme A but assuming that differences in activity (e.g. A_1–A_3) are due to differences in enzyme concentration. Linear functions represent the change in the cost of enzyme synthesis with increasing $[E]$. The upper line (Z_1-Z_3) illustrates a higher cost of steady-state concentrations of enzyme A, relative to the lower line. Since increases in enzyme activity beyond A_1 do not increase the rate of flux, both the profit of flux ($A-Z$) and the efficiency of flux (A/Z) decline to the right of A_1. The slope of the cost function is affected by several factors discussed in the text. From Koehn (1991) with permission.

at 40 μM in human liver would be less than at 40 μM in muscle, as muscle constitutes a much greater proportion of total biomass.

The cost of protein synthesis is 3.53 kJ/g (Koehn 1991). At the level of the whole organism, the actual energy required to synthesize a specific enzyme can be given as:

$$Z = 3.53 \text{ kJ/g}\left[\frac{(F)(W)(T)K_s}{W^{0.75}}\right]$$

where F is the soluble fraction of biomass within which the enzyme occurs (see later) in litres/kg, W is the mass of the organism in kg, T is the ratio of the tissue mass in which the enzyme occurs to the total mass, K_s is the rate constant of synthesis, and $W^{0.75}$ is the metabolic mass in kg. At steady state, measures of the rate of synthesis are normally made as the rate of degradation. Since at steady state $-K_d[E] + K_s = 0$,

$$Z = 3.53 \text{ kJ/g}\left[\frac{(F)(W)(T)(K_d[E])}{W^{0.75}}\right]$$

Finally, at steady state, the rate of enzyme turnover is $t_{1/2} = \ln 2/K_d$. Therefore, the cost of maintenance for a given enzyme pool is:

$$Z = 3.53 \text{ kJ/g}\left[\frac{(F)(W)(T)(\ln 2[E])}{(W^{0.75})\ (t_{1/2})}\right]$$

Z is in units of kJ per $W^{0.75}$ per day, for reasons that will be apparent below.

The various parameters of this expression are present for reasons noted earlier but a detailed rationale and description of each are given by Koehn (1991). Briefly, F is the amount of fluid volume per tissue mass containing the enzyme of interest and is needed to calculate the *total* amount of enzyme in the organism at some particular concentration; F permits micromoles of enzyme to be related to tissue mass. W is the total body mass of the organism but T reflects the proportion of total body mass in which $[E]$ is measured. For example, in adult humans, muscle and liver constitute 43% and 2.3%, respectively, of total body mass (Diem 1962). Thus, in computations of Z, T will be 0.027 and 0.470 for liver and muscle enzymes, respectively. Finally, Z is expressed with respect to $W^{0.75}$, or 'metabolic mass' to scale the metabolic processes to linearity with total biomass.

There are apparently no data where the concentration and $t_{1/2}$ of an enzyme have been measured simultaneously under the same conditions. It is not possible, therefore, to calculate Z for a list of specific enzymes. Hence, some values of Z are given (Table 8.1) for a variety of representative parameter values where the cost of maintaining individual enzyme pools can be seen to vary over several orders of magnitude. This cost will determine the overall slope of the cost function (Fig. 8.7) and the rate of decline in pathway efficiency with increasing $[E]$.

TABLE 8.1. Representative values of Z in kJ/$W^{0.75}$ per day for various parameter values of molecular weight (MW) in kilodaltons, turnover ($t_{1/2}$) in days and $[E]$ in μM. F is taken as 0.4 and W as 70 kg, but T is either 0.027 (liver) or 0.430 (muscle). (After Koehn 1991.)

MW	$t_{1/2}$	$[E]$	Z^a	Z^b
30	0.25	5	0.046	0.730
30	0.25	60	0.550	8.763
30	2	60	0.069	1.095
200	0.25	5	0.305	4.868
200	2	60	0.458	7.302
150(E_1)[d]	2	200	1.146	1.825[c]
150(E_2)	2	220	1.261	2.008[c]
150(E_3)	2	240	1.376	2.191[c]

[a] liver; [b] muscle; [c] $t_{1/2}$ = 20 days in muscle; [d] see Fig. 8.9 and text.

For example, consider A_1, A_2 and A_3 (Fig. 8.7) as alternate genotypes that differ from one another in $[E]$ by about 10% (see Table 8.1). If A has a very small Z, then differences in cost among A_1-A_3 (Z_4-Z_6) will reflect only small changes in Z and genotypic differences in efficiency of flux will be small. On the other hand, if A has a larger Z, then the increase in cost with increasing $[E]$ will be greater, the change in efficiency will decrease at a faster rate, and the range of maximum flux efficiency will be smaller. The slope of the Z function will determine the potential strength of natural selection against lower efficiency (see later).

Whether the cost of $[E]$ is large or small, selection or metabolic efficiency differs from selection for the rate of flux proposed by Hartl *et al.* (1985) in several respects. One important difference is the evolutionary consequence of changes in $[E]$. When fitness is equivalent to the rate of flux, selection is directional, maximizing flux. When flux is equivalent to both rate and efficiency, there exists an optimum range for $[E]$ over which maximum flux at minimum cost can occur. Enzyme concentrations below this range would be selected against because of decreased flux (Hartl *et al.* 1985), whereas enzyme concentrations above this range could be selected against because of lower efficiency. There will be a balance between mutational changes and the selective elimination of such mutants that decrease or increase $[E]$ away from the range of maximum flux at maximum efficiency.

Secondly, whether or not a change in flux efficiency has any selective consequences depends on several other factors that determine whole-organism energy balance. These factors can be genetic and/or environmental. The strength of selection will vary as an inverse function of the energy available for protein synthesis, for reasons that have been elaborated elsewhere (Koehn 1991). Any increase in energy demand, however small, can have potential selective consequences if there is no energy available to meet that demand.

The cellular protein pool must consist of several thousand proteins. Many enzymes, perhaps the majority, will contribute very little to the overall energy expenditure of maintenance metabolism, especially if they are present in cells for only a limited time (e.g. during a specific stage of development) or are at very low cellular concentrations (e.g. regulatory molecules). Some enzymes, on the other hand, represent a significant proportion of the costs of total maintenance metabolism. Muscle may be nearly 50% of total biomass (e.g. mammals). In adult skeletal muscle three glycolytic enzymes, triose phosphate isomerase, aldolase and glyceraldehyde phosphate dehydrogenase, can constitute nearly 20% of the total soluble cellular protein (Penhoet *et al.* 1967, Harris & Waters 1976).

The fasting metabolic energy demand (i.e. maintenance net energy) of most mammals is about 300 kJ/$W^{0.75}$ per day and there is very little variation in this value from rats to humans (McDonald *et al.* 1988, p. 289). Of total maintenance, minimally 25% can be attributed to the costs of protein turnover (Millward *et al.* 1976, Meier *et al.* 1981, Waterlow & Jackson 1981, Lundholm *et al.* 1982, Houlihan *et al.* 1986, Muramatsu *et al.* 1987). If we assume that total maintenance is about 300 kJ per day, of which 75 kJ per day are required solely for the turnover of the total protein pool, then individual enzymes can, with appropriate characteristics, constitute a fairly large proportion of total maintenance. For the examples in Table 8.1, a single enzyme can constitute from 6.1×10^{-2} to 1.8% of total protein pool costs in liver and about 1 to nearly 12% in muscle. These estimates do not include factors that would make the turnover cost even higher; the ATP-equivalent costs of tRNA and mRNA syntheses are unknown but clearly exist. The cost of degradation is poorly understood; so is the precise nature of the degradation processes, though there is evidence that these require energy (Goldberg & St. John 1976, Houlihan *et al.* 1986).

In summary of this point, the cost of maintaining a single gene product can constitute a fairly large fraction of the total costs of metabolism. Clearly, metabolic efficiency is a potential target for natural selection, though as we will see later, the strength of selection will vary in response to other environmental and genetic factors that affect the energy balance of an organism.

THE STRENGTH OF NATURAL SELECTION FOR METABOLIC EFFICIENCY

The strength of natural selection against a genotype of higher Z and lower flux efficiency will be a function of individual energy balance. A simple example can illustrate this point. Assume the three regressions in Fig. 8.8 correspond to three individuals that are completely isogenic, except for differences in steady-state turnover costs at the locus under consideration (Table 8.1 for E_1-E_3). Each would differ in maintenance by the amount Z from Table 8.1 (i.e. about 0.2 kJ per day, assuming a muscle enzyme). Clearly, at the same level of available energy, each would differ in net energy balance. More important, the *relative* differences in energy balance are a function of available energy, or more precisely, metabolizable energy (ME), defined as the energy available

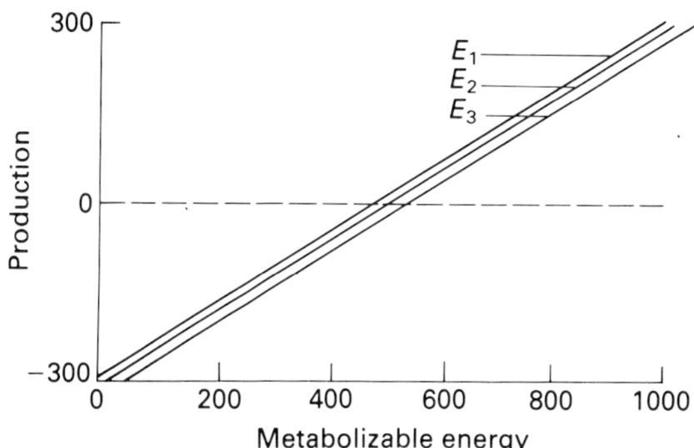

FIG. 8.8. The change in net energy balance (production) with a change in metabolizable energy. Units of both axes are kJ/$W^{0.75}$/day. $E_1 - E_3$ represent genotypes differing from one another in the costs of maintaining [E]. See Table 8.1 and text. From Koehn (1991) with permission.

from the digestion and assimilation of ingested food. At high ME, say 1000 kJ per day, a relative measure of production (e.g. growth) would be trivially different, reflecting a net energy balance difference of E_1 = 578.01 kJ/day, E_2 = 577.81 kJ/day and E_3 = 577.61 kJ/day (i.e. 1000 − 420 − Z from Table 8.1). In contrast, if ME was barely above maintenance at 424 kJ/day, then the relative differences would be greater (E_1 = 2.01 kJ/day; E_2 = 1.81 kJ/day and E_3 = 1.61 kJ/day). If available energy were used exclusively for growth (unrealistic but illustrative), the latter case would suggest very significant genotype-dependent growth rates; in the former case the differences would not be measurable. A computation of relative fitnesses (W) for the two sets of values would further illustrate this point.

Any factor that reduces ME per unit consumption will reduce energy balance and the intensity of selection against decreased efficiency would increase accordingly, including decreased food availability, disease, psychological stress, physiological (Wilton *et al.* 1982) and metabolic responses to changing conditions of the environment (Webster & Murphy 1988, Hoffmann & Parsons 1991), or genetic background (Geer & Laurie-Ahlberg 1984). Hence, the phenotypic consequences of genetic differences in the cost of turnover are environmentally dependent; there is a genotype-by-environmental interaction that enhances genetic effects under conditions of stress.

NATURAL SELECTION ACTING ON A METABOLITE CONCENTRATION

Human inborn errors of metabolism

Perhaps the strongest motivation for examining the potential for natural selection to act on metabolite concentration is the observation that most human inborn errors of metabolism are associated with abnormal metabolite accumulation. Although the proximal cause for the phenotype is the loss of enzyme function and consequent loss of flux through the respective pathway, the deleterious phenotypic effects generally seem to be caused by the abnormally high serum concentrations of relevant metabolites. This is shown to be true in those cases where dietary or other intervention can be made to control serum levels of the metabolite, and this often results in prevention or amelioration of the diseased phenotype.

Errors of amino acid metabolism are particularly likely to result in high serum levels of the respective amino acid, and these metabolic defects generally result in mental retardation (Table 8.2). Most of the examples, including the particularly well-studied case of phenylketonuria (PKU), result from a lesion in an enzyme involved in the degradation of an amino acid absorbed from the diet. In the case of PKU, defects in phenylalanine hydroxylase, result in excess phenylalanine which enters other metabolic pathways and results in accumulation of phenylpyruvic acid and several other metabolites. All of the defects in amino acid metabolism listed in Table 8.2 are recessive (heterozygous carriers are asymptomatic), providing another (Kacser and Burns 1981) example of the molecular basis of dominance.

TABLE 8.2. Inborn errors of amino acid metabolism. (After Feuer & de la Iglesia, 1985.)

Disease	Enzyme defect
Hyperglycaemia	Glycine metabolism
Hypervalinaemia	Valine transaminase
Hyperprolinaemia	Proline oxidase
Histidinaemia	Histidase
Maple syrup disease	Branched-chain ketoacid decarboxylase
Phenylketonuria	Phenylalanine hydroxylase
Alkaptonuria	Homogentisic acid oxidase
Albinism	Tyrosinase
Homocystinuria	Cystathionine synthetase
Cystathionuria	Cystathionase

The inborn errors of carbohydrate metabolism provide additional lessons about the metabolic consequences of a single lesion (Table 8.3). Galactosaemia, caused by a defect in galactose-1-phosphate uridyl transferase, results in high serum levels of galactose, one of the moieties of lactose. Feeding milk to infants triggers vomiting and diarrhoea, and ensuing dehydration and poor nutrition result in mental retardation, jaundice and cataracts. Dietary intervention can largely avoid these grim consequences, and unlike PKU, a change in the diet can result in a rapid regression of the diseased phenotype. This case is to be contrasted with fructosuria and pentosuria, both of which lead to elevated serum and urinary levels of the respective carbohydrates but neither condition is deleterious.

Glucose-6-phosphate dehydrogenase is an enzyme that is widely studied by population geneticists, and has been shown to exhibit extensive activity variation in *Drosophila* (Laurie-Ahlberg *et al.* 1980, 1982, Eanes 1984, Eanes & Hey 1986). In humans, the defect is manifested as a lowered capacity to produce NADPH. Drugs such as primaquine, and certain foods such as fava beans, place a demand on erythrocyte production of NADPH. The more oxidized state of the cells results in oxidation of glutathione, and ultimately haemolysis, producing painful and potentially fatal episodes.

Eight different steps in the pathway for glycogen synthesis and catabolism have associated defects in the human population (Table 8.4). Glycogen is present in all tissues and serves as an important energy storage compound. The regulation of glycogen storage requires the coordinate regulation of a series of enzymes, accounting for the multiplicity of defects found. A defect in the debranching enzyme (amylo-1,6-glucosidase) results in glycogen with very short branched chains, and a defect in the branching synthetic enzyme (amylo-(1,4–1,6)-transglucosidase) results in

TABLE 8.3. Inborn errors of carbohydrate metabolism. (After Feuer & de la Iglesia, 1985.)

Disease	Enzyme defect
Diabetes mellitus	Several
Galactosaemia	Galactose-1-phosphate uridyl transferase
Fructosuria	Fructokinase
Pentosuria	l-Xylitol dehydrogenase
Lactose intolerance	Lactase
G6PD deficiency	Glucose-6-phosphate dehydrogenase
Glycogen storage	Several
Oxalosis	Glyoxylic dehydrogenase

TABLE 8.4. Glycogen storage diseases. (After Feuer & de la Iglesia, 1985.)

Disease	Enzyme defect
von Gierke	Glucose-6-phosphatase
Pompe	α-1,4-Glucosidase (maltase)
Forbes	Amylo-1,6-glucosidase (debrancher)
Andersen	Amylo-(1,4–1,6)transglucosidase (brancher)
McArdle–Schmid–Pearson	Phosphorylase (muscle)
Hers	Phosphorylase (liver)
Type VII	Phosphofructokinase
Type VIII	Phosphorylase β kinase

glycogen with very long unbranched chains. In all other glycogen storage diseases, the glycogen has normal structure. Glycogen can be completely hydrolysed by phosphorylase and the debranching enzyme, and defects in phosphorylase result in severe hypertrophy of the liver caused by the excess glycogen deposition. Consideration of glycogen metabolism in an evolutionary context brings the realization that regulation can be far more important than maximization of flux.

Defects in other metabolic pathways also frequently result in an abnormal phenotype because of excess metabolite concentrations. Loss of hypoxanthine guanine phosphoribosyl transferase (HGPRT), an enzyme in purine metabolism, results in an inability to interconvert the purines guanine and hypoxanthine. These purines are consequently excreted as uric acid, which is present in the urine of patients at unusually high concentration. Infants are born normal but the defect in purine metabolism leads within a few months to spasticity and mental retardation in a suite of defects known as the Lesch–Nyhan syndrome. A defect in hexosaminidase A, an enzyme in a sphingolipid synthetic pathway, results in accumulation of defective lipids in the central nervous system and causes Tay–Sachs disease. Again, both of these disorders are recessive, so a single copy of the functional gene produces enough enzyme for a normal phenotype.

While an asymptotic relation between enzyme activity and phenotype seems to be quite general, allosteric modification of enzymes and disruption of feedback inhibition can result in unusual dominant inborn errors of metabolism. For example, mutations of uroporphyrinogen I synthetase result in dominant acute intermittent porphyria, with resulting high levels of δ-aminolevulinic acid (ALA). ALA synthetase is highly elevated in activity in this disease due to loss of feedback inhibition.

Lipid and glycogen storage are associated with fitness in Drosophila

Earlier we noted that there is significant genetic variation among *D. melanogaster* in storage of both triacylglycerol and glycogen. The relationship between these storage phenotypes and fitness were tested by the classical viability test of Mukai (1964). Each of the 83 second chromosome replacement lines had triacylglycerol and glycogen contents measured, and the viability test allowed quantification of the relative viability of homozygotes for each second chromosome to heterozygotes (Clark 1989). Both triacylglycerol storage and glycogen storage were positively correlated with viability (Fig. 8.6). The partial correlations of line means were $r = 0.335$ and 0.318, respectively (both $p < 0.01$). The figures suggest that there is directional selection favouring higher storage of both compounds, rather than balancing selection as we have modelled the system. Some of the variability present among these lines may have been generated in the process of replacing the genetic background, a process that took 10+ generations. Most such mutations would be deleterious, and if they resulted in a loss in storage pools, the positive correlation we observed could be in part a result of these pleiotropic mutations. Some of the effect may be more general — recessive alleles present on the second chromosome make homozygous flies sick, and we measure this as reduced viability. A consequence of the lowered vitality might be that they feed less vigorously, which could also account for the lowered energy storage. A definitive distinction between specific lesions in the relevant metabolic pathway and a generalized vitality effect has yet to be made. That the effects may be specific is suggested by the observation that the correlation between viability and storage disappears when the flies are reared on a 10% sucrose medium.

ARE ENZYME ACTIVITIES TRAITS IN A STATE OF MUTATION–SELECTION BALANCE?

Beginning with the papers of Kimura (1965), Bulmer (1972), Latter (1970) and Lande (1975), an extensive literature on the theory of the evolution of a quantitative character in the face of mutation and selection has accumulated. Controversies have arisen over the assumptions involved in invoking Gaussian optimizing selection (Barton 1986, Barton & Turelli 1987, Turelli 1988, Nagylaki 1989, Lynch & Gabriel 1990), which, while mathematically convenient, are not always justified biologically. These models have been extended to include pleiotropic mutations, which add an important genetic constraint to joint evolution of multiple characters

(Lande 1980, Turelli 1985, Bürger 1986, 1989, Wagner 1989). There remain a number of significant controversies centring around the issue of whether these models can explain observed levels of variation (reviewed by Turelli 1984, 1986). It appears that even though it is clear that mutation provides an important source of genetic variation in natural populations, the resolution of these controversies will require empirical tests.

One of the critical parameters for models of mutation–selection balance is the rate of polygenic mutation (Lynch 1988). Two classes of experiments that have been done include those that quantify the rate of divergence among initially identical lines and artificial selection studies. The three parameters of importance in quantifying polygenic mutation are the mutation rate, the variance of mutational effects and the degree of dominance. When effects are assumed to be additive and there is no epistasis, these are collapsed to one parameter, V_m, defined as twice the sum over loci of the products of per locus mutation rates and variances in mutational effects. Lynch (1988) calculated the ratio of variance of mutational effect to the environmental variance (V_m/V_e) to scale the results among disparate experiments, and in studies of *Daphnia, Drosophila* and crop plants, this ratio fell to between 10^{-2} and 10^{-4}.

A model of mutation–selection balance

Consider a simple linear metabolic pathway, with genetic variation influencing the activity of one of the enzymes in the pathway. Let the genetic transmission be haploid, with one locus and a continuum of alleles (Crow & Kimura 1964). Under the assumption that none of the enzymes is saturated, and that the initial and final pool concentrations are constant, the flux and metabolite concentrations can be expressed as shown earlier, p. 195. These functions allow a conversion from the phenotypic distribution of enzyme activities to phenotypic distributions of flux and of substrate pool concentration. We can equally use these as expressions of the distributions of genetic effects on activity, flux and substrate concentration.

Natural selection will be assumed to operate on the distribution of either fluxes or substrate pool sizes, since these are global properties of the metabolic pathway. The fitness may be an arbitrary function of flux or pool concentration, and if we assume Gaussian optimizing selection, the fitness can be written:

$$w(x) = \exp[-(J(x)-J_{opt})^2]/\sigma_s^2$$

where J_{opt} is the optimum flux (or pool concentration), and σ_s represents the strength of selection (smaller σ_s implies that fitness falls off rapidly as

J deviates from J_{opt}). Fitnesses are scaled so that the fitness of J_{opt} is 1.0. Figure 8.9 presents the Gaussian fitness functions that map substrate concentration into fitness (here there is optimizing selection on substrate concentration), and the resulting relation between enzyme activity and fitness, which is obtained as the compound function of activity → flux and

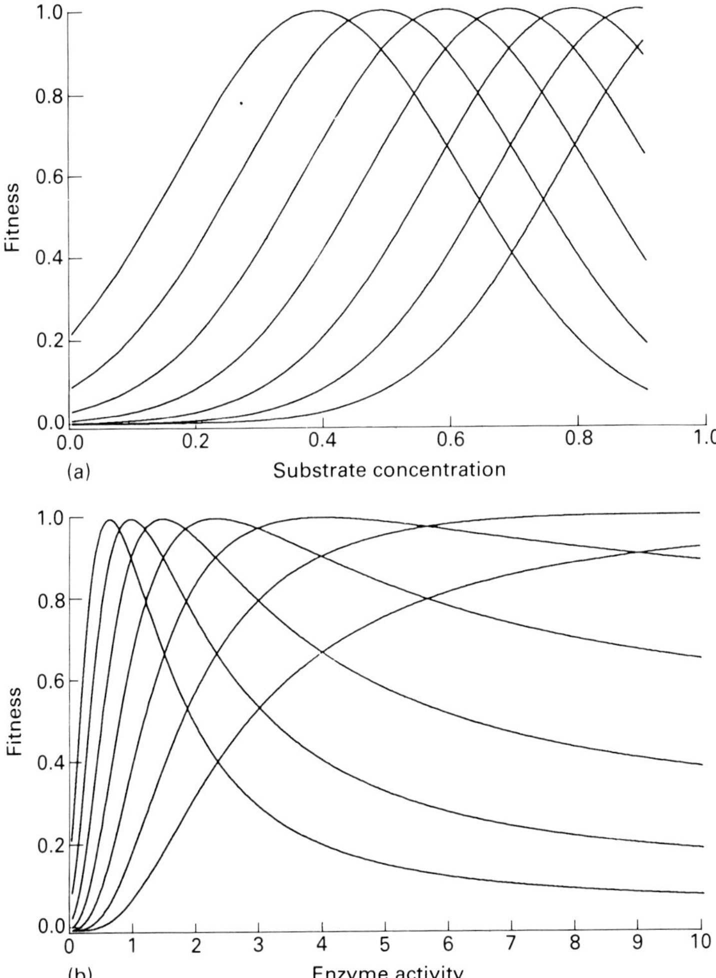

FIG. 8.9. Distributions of fitness as functions of enzyme activity when selection optimizes substrate concentration. As the optimum of the selection function moves right, the distributions become more skewed. For a sufficiently high optimum $[S]$, the selection becomes directional for higher upstream enzyme activity.

flux → fitness. The fitness functions appear to be distinctly skewed, and as the fitness optimum gets closer to saturation, the selection becomes more directional. The relation between activity and fitness when flux is optimized shows patterns similar to those of Fig. 8.9.

Mutations enter the haploid continuum-of-alleles model at a rate μ per generation, and the allelic effect of a mutation is assumed to follow a Gaussian distribution. If the allelic effect after mutation depends on the allelic effect before mutation, then the change in the distribution of allelic effects, $p(x)$ can be expressed by the 'Kimura–Lande–Fleming' model (Turelli 1984):

$$p_{t+1}(x) = (1-\mu)p_t'(x) + \mu \int p_t'(y)g(x-y)\mathrm{d}y$$

where $p'(x)$ is the density function after selection (selection occurs before mutation). If the allelic effect after mutation is independent of its effect before mutation, then the 'house of cards' model is appropriate, and analysis of that case can be found in Clark (1991). $p'(x)$ follows classical haploid selection:

$$p_t'(x) = \frac{w(x)p_t(x)}{\overline{w}}$$

where:

$$\overline{w} = \int w(x)p_t(x)\mathrm{d}x$$

is the mean fitness at time t. $g(x)$ is the density function of mutational effects and is assumed to be Gaussian with variance σ_m^2. Turelli (1984) reviewed the literature on solving the equilibrium distribution and the solutions depend on the Gaussian approximation of $p_t(x)$, which is accurate for sufficiently weak selection and small mutational effects.

Numerical simulations were performed for a range of all parameters in order to explore the behaviour of the model (Clark 1991). The distribution of allelic effects was first discretized into 200 segments. The above recurrence system was then approximated by its discrete form and iterated numerically. The parameters that were varied in the simulations included the mean of the selection function, σ_s^2, μ, the mean of the mutation function $\overline{g}(x)$, and σ_m^2. The criterion for equilibrium was a change over 100 successive generations of less than 10^5 in the mean of $p(x)$, and at that time the mean, variance and skew $(E(x^3)/E(x^2)^{3/2})$ were tallied.

Table 8.5 reports the results of the one-enzyme mutation–selection simulations when metabolite concentration is subjected to optimizing selection. As predicted the equilibrium distribution of allelic effects is globally stable. This was verified numerically by starting the simulations

TABLE 8.5. Simulations of mutation–selection balance model

$\bar{s}$	σ_s^2	μ	$\bar{g}(x)$	s_m^2	$\bar{p}(x)$	V_p	Skew
Altering selection optimum ($\bar{s}$)							
0.40	0.20	0.00010	1.50	1.00	2.971	0.0443	−0.0104
0.50	0.20	0.00010	1.50	1.00	1.674	0.0141	0.0194
0.60	0.20	0.00010	1.50	1.00	1.006	0.0051	0.1121
0.70	0.20	0.00010	1.50	1.00	0.603	0.0018	0.4205
0.80	0.20	0.00010	1.50	1.00	0.302	0.0005	2.5687
Altering strength of selection (σ_s^2)							
0.60	0.20	0.00010	1.50	1.00	1.006	0.0051	0.1121
0.60	0.30	0.00010	1.50	1.00	1.009	0.0051	0.1669
0.60	0.40	0.00010	1.50	1.00	1.012	0.0052	0.2188
0.60	0.50	0.00010	1.50	1.00	1.016	0.0053	0.2680
0.60	0.60	0.00010	1.50	1.00	1.019	0.0053	0.3147
Altering mutation rate (μ)							
0.60	0.20	0.00001	1.50	1.00	1.000	0.0050	0.0117
0.60	0.20	0.00010	1.50	1.00	1.006	0.0051	0.1121
0.60	0.20	0.00100	1.50	1.00	1.058	0.0059	0.3808
0.60	0.20	0.01000	1.50	1.00	1.350	0.0109	0.5399
0.60	0.20	0.10000	1.50	1.00	1.603	0.0162	0.6716
Altering the mean of the distribution of mutational effects $\bar{g}(x)$							
0.60	0.20	0.00010	1.00	1.00	1.003	0.0051	0.0540
0.60	0.20	0.00010	1.50	1.00	1.006	0.0051	0.1121
0.60	0.20	0.00010	2.00	1.00	1.007	0.0051	0.2040
0.60	0.20	0.00010	2.50	1.00	1.008	0.0051	0.3383
0.60	0.20	0.00010	3.00	1.00	1.008	0.0052	0.5228
Altering the variance of mutational effects (σ_m^2)							
0.60	0.20	0.00010	1.50	0.50	1.008	0.0051	0.0760
0.60	0.20	0.00010	1.50	1.00	1.006	0.0051	0.1120
10.60	0.20	0.00010	1.50	1.50	1.006	0.0051	0.1475
0.60	0.20	0.00010	1.50	2.00	1.005	0.0051	0.1828
0.60	0.20	0.00010	1.50	2.50	1.005	0.0051	0.2183

from several different initial distributions. The first set of parameters in Table 8.5 examines the effect of increasing the mean of the selected optimum. As the optimum metabolite concentration moves closer to the saturation level, the fitness function shifts to the right and becomes less peaked. This results in increasing equilibrium mean activity and variance. The degree of skewness of $p(x)$ decreases as the mean increases, in part because the population is shifted away from the truncation at 0. The second parameter set in Table 8.5 examines the effect of increasing σ_s^2. As prediced, the mean and variance increase only slightly as the strength of selection increases, in part because of the relatively low mutation rate.

The third parameter set in Table 8.5 varies the mutation rate. Because of the asymmetry built into the model, as the mutation rate increases, the mean and variance of the distribution of allelic effects increases. In the fourth set of parameters in Table 8.5 the mean of the distribution of mutational effects increases. Because of the high variance in mutational effects, and the relatively low mutation rate, the equilibrium mean is largely determined by selection, and is only slightly affected by varying the mutational mean. The last set of parameters varied σ_m^2, the variance in the distribution of mutational effects. The effects on the mean and the variance of the distribution of allelic effects at equilibrium were negligible but the skewness increased with increasing mutational variance.

There are two significant consequences of the fact that the deleterious effects of most metabolic errors are due to a departure from metabolic homoeostasis. The first is that concentration control coefficients are generally more local than are flux control coefficients, so that changes in activity of an enzyme will affect the immediately flanking metabolite pools more than pools more distant in the pathway. This means that natural selection on a pool concentration can have a greater effect on flanking enzymes. In addition, the simulations show that selection on pool concentration results in a striking tendency for positive correlations in activity, and experimental observations indicate that positive correlations are far more frequent than negative correlations (Wilton *et al.* 1982, Clark & Keith 1988, Clark 1989, 1990).

While the initial development of metabolic control theory required many restrictive assumptions (a linear pathway of unsaturated enzymes all in homogeneous solution), most of the results described here do not depend on these assumptions. All that is really needed to derive the results obtained here is that there be an asymptotic relation between enzyme activity and whatever is the global property undergoing selection (flux, metabolite concentration, or whatever). The argument of Kacser and Burns (1981) for molecular dominance can be turned around to support the idea that natural populations are near this asymptote. Regardless of the biochemical details, the fact that heterozygotes for nulls are generally closer to wild phenotype than the null homozygote argues that the mean phenotype is up on the plateau of the relation between activity and fitness (or phenotype). In the absence of natural selection, mutations that decrease activity predominate, and the population would inexorably move towards fixation for zero activity as pseudogenes occur and are fixed. Rather than the population evolving toward neutrality, it might be more precise to view it as evolving toward a balance between natural selection retaining activity, and mutational loss of activity.

SUMMARY AND CONCLUSIONS

1 There is abundant genetic variation in enzyme activities in natural populations. In some cases only a small fraction of the variation is mediated by the structural gene encoding the enzyme.

2 Lack of steady state due to ecological complications weakens the ability of metabolic control theory to make predictions about evolution of metabolism.

3 Natural selection may act on flux, efficiency or metabolite concentrations.

4 Natural selection may maximize, minimize, or optimize the trait.

5 If flux is maximized by natural selection, this tendency may be opposed by the directional effect of mutations, most of which result in a decrease of enzyme activity. These two forces can balance each other (see 8).

6 Natural selection may favour higher flux but response may be limited by the metabolic cost of synthesis of the needed enzyme.

7 Human inborn errors of metabolism provide abundant examples of the manner in which deviation from homoeostasis in control of metabolite concentrations can be deleterious or fatal.

8 Models of mutation–selection balance derive equilibrium distributions of genetic effects. Experimental parameterization of models of mutation–selection balance remains a difficult challenge, but the context of metabolism is one of the best for doing so because constituent parts of genetically complex phenotypes can be identified and manipulated.

REFERENCES

Barnes, P. T. & Laurie-Ahlberg, C. C. (1986). Genetic variability of flight metabolism in *Drosophila melanogaster*. III. Effects of GPDH allozymes and environmental temperature on power output. *Genetics*, **112**, 267–294.

Barton, N. H. (1986). The maintenance of polygenic variation through a balance between mutation and stabilizing selection. *Genetical Research*, **47**, 209–216.

Barton, N. H. & Turelli, M. (1987). Adaptive landscapes, genetic distance and the evolution of quantitative characters. *Genetical Research*, **49**, 157–173.

Battley, E. H. (1987). *Energetics of Microbial Growth*. Wiley Interscience, New York, NY, USA.

Bijlsma, R. (1980). Polymorphism at the G6PD and 6PGD loci in *Drosophila melanogaster*. IV. Genetic factors modifying enzyme activity. *Biochemical Genetics*, **18**, 699–715.

Bijlsma, R. & van Delden, W. (1977). Polymorphism at the G6PD and 6PGD loci in *Drosophila melanogaster*. I. Evidence for selection in experimental populations. *Genetical Research*, **30**, 221–236.

Briggs, G. E. & Haldane, J. B. S. (1925). A note on the kinetics of enzyme action. *Biochemical Journal*, **19**, 338–339.

Bulmer, M. G. (1972). The genetic variability of polygenic characters under optimizing selection, mutation and drift. *Genetical Research*, **19**, 17–25.

Bürger, R. (1986). On the maintenance of genetic variation: global analysis of Kimura's continuum-of-alleles model. *Journal of Mathematical Biology*, **24**, 341–351.

Bürger, R. (1989). Linkage and the maintenance of heritable variation by mutation–selection balance. *Genetics*, **121**, 175–184.

Burton, R. S. & Feldman, M. W. (1983). Physiological effects of an allozyme polymorphism: glutamate–pyruvate transaminase and response to hyperosmotic stress in the copepod *Tigriopus californicus*. *Biochemical Genetics*, **21**, 239–251.

Burton, R. S. & Place, A. R. (1986). Evolution of selective neutrality: further considerations. *Genetics*, **114**, 1033–1036.

Carter, P. A. & Watt, W. B. (1988). Adaptation at specific loci. V. Metabolically adjacent enzyme loci may have very distinct experiences of selective pressures. *Genetics*, **119**, 913–924.

Cavener, D. R. & Clegg, M. T. (1981). Evidence for biochemical and physiological differences between enzyme genotypes of *Drosophila melanogaster*. *Proceedings of the National Academy of Sciences, USA*, **78**, 4444–4447.

Clark, A. G. (1989). Causes and consequences of variation in lipid and carbohydrate storage in Drosophila. *Genetics*, **123**, 131–144.

Clark, A. G. (1990). Genetic components of variation in energy storage in *Drosophila melanogaster*. *Evolution*, **44**, 637–650.

Clark, A. G. (1991). Mutation–selection balance and metabolic control theory. *Genetics*, **129**, 909–923.

Clark, A. G. & Keith, L. E. (1988). Variation among extracted lines of *Drosophila melanogaster* in triacylglycerol and carbohydrate storage. *Genetics*, **119**, 595–607.

Clark, A. G., Szumski, F. M., Bell, K. A., Keith, L. E., Houtz, S. & Merriwether, D. A. (1989). Direct and correlated responses to artificial selection on lipid and glycogen contents in *Drosophila melanogaster*. *Genetical Research*, **56**, 49–56.

Crow, J. F. & Kimura, M. (1964). The theory of genetic loads. *Proceedings of the XIth International Congress of Genetics*, **2**, 495–505.

Dean, A. M. (1989). Selection and neutrality in the lactose operon of *Escherichia coli*. *Genetics*, **123**, 441–454.

Dean, A. M., Dykhuizen, D. E. & Hartl, D. L. (1986). Fitness as a function of β-galactosidase activity in *Escherichia coli*. *Genetical Research*, **48**, 1–8.

Dean, A. M., Dykhuizen, D. E. & Hartl, D. L. (1988). Theories of metabolic control in quantitative genetics. *Proceedings of the Second International Conference on Quantitative Genetics* (Ed. by B. S. Weir, E. J. Eisen, M. M. Goodman & G. Namkoong), pp. 536–548. Sinauer Sunderland, MA, USA.

DeJong, G. & Scharloo, W. (1976). Environmental determination of selective significance or neutrality of amylase variants in *Drosophila melanogaster*. *Genetics*, **84**, 77–94.

Diem, K. (ed.) (1962). *Scientific Tables*. Geigy (U.K.) Ltd, Macclesfield.

Dykhuizen, D. E. & Hartl, D. L. (1983). Functional effects of PGI allozymes in *Escherichia coli*. *Genetics*, **105**, 1–18.

Dykhuizen, D. E., Dean, A. M. & Hartl, D. L. (1987). Metabolic flux and fitness. *Genetics*, **115**, 25–31.

Eanes, W. F. (1984). Viability interactions, in vivo activity and the G6PD polymorphism in *Drosophila melanogaster*. *Genetics*, **106**, 95–107.

Eanes, W. F. & Hey, J. (1986). In vivo function of rare G6PD variants from natural populations of *Drosophila melanogaster*. *Genetics*, **113**, 679–693.

Eanes, W. F., Bingham, B., Hey, J. & Houle, D. (1985). Targeted selection experiments and enzyme polymorphism: negative evidence for octanoate selection at the G6PD locus in *Drosophila melanogaster. Genetics*, **109**, 379–391.

Easterby, J. (1973). Coupled enzyme assays: a general expression for the transient. *Biochimica et Biophysica Acta*, **293**, 552–558.

Feuer, G. & de la Iglesia, F. A. (1985). *Molecular Biochemistry of Human Disease*. CRC Press, Boca Raton, FL, USA.

Geer, B. W. & Laurie-Ahlberg, C. C. (1984). Genetic variation in the dietary sucrose modulation of enzyme activities in *Drosophila melanogaster. Genetical Research*, **43**, 307–321.

Goldberg, A. L. & St. John, A. C. (1976). Intracellular protein degradation in mammalian and bacterial cells: Part 2. *Annual Review of Biochemistry*, **45**, 747–803.

Harris, J. I. & Waters, M. (1976). Glyceraldehyde-3-phosphate dehydrogenase. *The Enzymes*, Vol. 13 (Ed. by P. D. Boyer). Academic Press, New York, NY, USA.

Hartl, D. L. (1989). Evolving theories of enzyme evolution. *Genetics*, **122**, 1–6.

Hartl, D. L., Dykhuizen, D. E. & Dean, A. M. (1985). Limits of adaptation: the evolution of selective neutrality. *Genetics*, **111**, 655–674.

Heinrich, R. & Rapoport, S. M. (1983). The utility of mathematical models for the understanding of metabolic systems. *Biochemical Society Transactions*, **11**, 31–35.

Heinstra, P. H. W. & Geer, B. W. (1991). Metabolic control analysis and enzyme variation: nutritional manipulation of the flux from ethanol to lipids in *Drosophila. Molecular Biology and Evolution*, **8**, 703–708.

Heinstra, P. W. H., Seykens, D., Freriksen, A. & Geer, B. W. (1990). Metabolic physiology of alcohol degradation and adaptation in *Drosophila* larvae as studied by means of carbon-13 nuclear magnetic resonance spectroscopy. *Insect Biochemistry*, **20**, 343–348.

Hickey, D. A. (1979). Selection on amylase in *Drosophila melanogaster*: selection experiments using several independently derived pairs of chromosomes. *Evolution*, **33**, 1128–1137.

Hill, W. G. & Nicholas, F. W. (1974). Estimation of heritability by both regression of offspring on parent and intraclass correlation of sibs in one experiment. *Biometrics*, **30**, 447–468.

Hoffmann, A. A. & Parsons, P. A. (1991). *Evolutionary Genetics and Environmental Stress*. Oxford University Press, Oxford, UK.

Hori, S. H. & Tanda, S. (1981). Genetic variation in the activities of glucose 6-phosphate dehydrogenase and 6-phosphogluconate dehydrogenase in *Drosophila melanogaster. Japanese Journal of Genetics*, **56**, 257–277.

Hori, S. H., Tanda, S., Fuzukawa, K. & Hanaoka, T. (1982). Further studies on the modifier gene system regulating activities of X-linked enzymes in *Drosophila melanogaster. Japanese Journal of Genetics*, **57**, 535–550.

Houlihan, D. F., McMillan, D. N. & Laurent, P. (1986). Growth rates, protein synthesis, and protein degradation rates in rainbow trout: effects of body size. *Physiological Zoology*, **59**, 482–493.

Kacser, H. & Burns, J. A. (1973). The control of flux. *Symposium of the Society of Experimental Biology*, **27**, 65–104.

Kacser, H. & Burns, J. A. (1979). Molecular democracy: who shares the controls. *Biochemical Society Transactions*, **7**, 1149–1160.

Kacser, H. & Burns, J. A. (1981). The molecular basis of dominance. *Genetics*, **97**, 639–666.

Keightley, P. D. (1989). Models of quantitative variation of flux in metabolic pathways. *Genetics*, **121**, 869–876.

Keightley, P. D. & Kacser, H. (1987). Dominance, pleiotropy and metabolic structure. *Genetics*, **117**, 319–329.

Kimura, M. (1965). A stochastic model concerning the maintenance of genetic variability in quantitative characters. *Proceedings of the National Academy of Sciences, USA*, **54**, 731–736.

Koehn, R. K. (1991). The cost of enzyme synthesis in the genetics of energy balance and physiological performance. *Biological Journal of the Linnean Society*, **44**, 231–247.

Koehn, R. K. & Hilbish, T. J. (1987). The adaptive importance of genetic variation. *American Scientist*, **75**, 134–141.

Lande, R. (1975). The maintenance of genetic variability by mutation in a polygenic character with linked loci. *Genetical Research*, **26**, 221–234.

Lande, R. (1980). The genetic covariance between characters maintained by pleiotropic mutations. *Genetics*, **94**, 203–215.

LaPorte, D. C., Walsh, K. & Koshland, D. E. (1984). The branchpoint effect: ultrasensitivity and subsensitivity to metabolic control. *Journal of Biological Chemistry*, **259**, 14068–14075.

Latter, B. D. H. (1970). Selection in finite populations with multiple alleles. II. Centripetal selection, mutation, and isoallelic variation. *Genetics*, **66**, 165–186.

Laurie-Ahlberg, C. C., Barnes, P. T., Curtsinger, J. W., Emigh, T. H., Karlin, B., Morris, R., Norman, R. A. & Wilton, A. N. (1985). Genetic variability of flight metabolism in *Drosophila melanogaster*. II. Relationship between power output and enzyme activity levels. *Genetics*, **111**, 845–868.

Laurie-Ahlberg, C. C., Maroni, G., Bewley, G. C., Lucchesi, J. C. & Weir, B. S. (1980). Quantitative genetic variation of enzyme activities in natural populations of *Drosophila melanogaster*. *Proceedings of the National Academy of Sciences, USA*, **77**, 1073–1077.

Laurie-Ahlberg, C. C., Wilton, A. N., Curtsinger, J. W. & Emigh, T. H. (1982). Naturally occurring enzyme activity variation in *Drosophila melanogaster*. I. Sources of variation for 23 enzymes. *Genetics*, **102**, 191–206.

Lundholm, K., Edstrom, S., Karlberg, I., Ekman, L. & Schersten, T. (1982). Glucose turnover, gluconeogenesis from glycerol, and estimation of net glucose cycling in cancer patients. *Cancer*, **50**, 1142–1150.

Lynch, M. (1988). The rate of polygenic mutation. *Genetical Research*, **51**, 137–148.

Lynch, M. & Gabriel, W. (1990). Mutation load and the survival of small populations. *Evolution*, **44**, 1725–1737.

Marr, A. G., Nilson, E. H. & Clark, D. J. (1963). The maintenance requirement of *Escherichia coli*. *Annals of the New York Academy of Science*, **102**, 536–548.

McDonald, P. R., Edwards, A. & Greenhalgh, J. F. D. (1988). *Animal Nutrition*. Longman Scientific & Technical, Essex, UK.

Meier, P. R., Peterson, R. G., Bonds, D. R., Meschia, G. & Battaglia, F. C. (1981). Rates of protein synthesis and turnover in fetal life. *American Journal of Physiology*, **240**, E320–E324.

Milligan, L. P. & Summers, M. (1986). The biological basis of maintenance and its relevance to assessing responses to nutrients. *Proceedings of the Nutrition Society*, **45**, 185–193.

Millward, D. J., Garlick, P. J. & Reeds, P. J. (1976). The energy cost of growth. *Proceedings of the Nutrition Society*, **35**, 339–349.

Mukai, T. (1964). The genetic structure of natural populations of *Drosophila melanogaster*, I. Spontaneous mutation rate of polygenes controlling viability. *Genetics*, **50**, 1–19.

Mukai, T., Chigusa, S. I., Mettler, L. E. & Crow, J. F. (1972). Mutation rate and the dominance of genes affecting viability in *Drosophila melanogaster*. *Genetics*, **72**, 335–355.

Muramatsu, T., Aoyagi, Y., Okumura, J. & Tasaki, I. (1987). Contribution of whole-body protein synthesis to basal metabolism in layer and broiler chickens. *British Journal of Nutrition*, **57**, 269–277.

Nagylaki, T. (1989). The maintenance of genetic variability in two-locus models of stabilizing selection. *Genetics*, **122**, 235–248.

Oakeshott, J. G. (1976). Selection at the Adh locus in *Drosophila melanogaster* imposed by environmental ethanol. *Genetical Research*, **26**, 265–274.

Penhoet, E. E., Kochman, M., Valentine, R. & Rutter, W. J. (1967). The subunit structure of mammalian fructose diphosphate aldolase. *Biochemistry*, **6**, 2940–2949.

Powell, J. R. & Amato, G. D. (1984). Population genetics of Drosophila amylase. V. Genetic background and selection on different carbohydrates. *Genetics*, **106**, 625–629.

Powers, D. A., DiMichelle, L. & Place, A. R. (1983). The use of enzyme kinetics to predict differences in cellular metabolism, developmental rate and swimming performance between LDH-B genotypes of the fish, *Fundulus heteroclitus. Isozymes: Current Topics in Biological and Medical Research*, Vol. 10, (Ed. by M. C. Rattazzi, J. G. Scandalios & G. S. Whitt), pp. 147–170. Alan R. Liss, New York, NY, USA.

Reeds, P. J., Fuller, M. F. & Nicholson, B. F. (1985). Metabolic basis of energy expenditure with particular reference to protein. *Substrate and Energy Metabolism in Man* (Ed. by J. S. Garrow & D. Halliday), pp. 46–57. John Libbey, London, UK.

Robertson, A. (1959a). Experimental design in the evaluation of genetic parameters. *Biometrics*, **15**, 219–226.

Robertson, A. (1959b). The sampling variance of the genetic correlation coefficient. *Biometrics*, **15**, 469–485.

Schimke, R. T. & Doyle, D. (1970). Control of enzyme levels in animal tissues. *Annual Review of Biochemistry*, **39**, 929–976.

Turelli, M. (1984). Heritable genetic variation via mutation–selection balance: Lerch's zeta meets the abdominal bristle. *Theoretical Population Biology*, **25**, 138–193.

Turelli, M. (1985). Effects of pleiotropy on predictions concerning mutation–selection balance for polygenic traits. *Genetics*, **111**, 165–195.

Turelli, M. (1986). Gaussian versus non-Gaussian genetic analyses of polygenic mutation–selection balance. *Evolutionary Processes and Theory* (Ed. by S. Karlin & E. Nevo), pp. 607–628. Academic Press, New York, NY, USA.

Turelli, M. (1988). Population genetic models for polygenic variation and evolution. *Proceedings of the Second International Conference on Quantitative Genetics* (Ed. by B. S. Weir, E. J. Eisen, M. M. Goodman & G. Namkoong), pp. 601–618. Sinauer, Sunderland, MA, USA.

Wagner, G. P. (1989). Multivariate mutation–selection balance with constrained pleiotropic effects. *Genetics*, **122**, 223–234.

Ward, P. J. (1990). The inheritance of metabolic flux: expressions for the within sibship mean and variance given the parental genotypes. *Genetics*, **125**, 655–667.

Waterlow, J. C. & Jackson, A. A. (1981). Nutrition and protein turnover in man. *British Medical Bulletin*, **37**, 5–10.

Watt, W. B. (1983). Adaptation at specific loci. II. Demographic and biochemical elements in the maintenance of Colias PGI polymorphism. *Genetics*, **103**, 691–724.

Watt, W. B., Carter, P. A. & Blower, S. M. (1985). Adaptation at specific loci. IV. Differential mating success among glycolytic allozyme genotypes of Colias butteflies. *Genetics*, **109**, 157–175.

Watt, W. B., Cassin, R. C. & Swan, M. S. (1983). Adaptation at specific loci. III. Field behavior and survivorship differences among Colias PGI genotypes are predictable from in vitro biochemistry. *Genetics*, **103**, 725–739.

Webster, K. A. & Murphy, B. J. (1988). Regulation of tissue-specific isozyme genes: coordinate response to oxygen availability in myogenic cells. *Canadian Journal of Zoology*, **66**, 1046–1058.

Westerhoff, H. V. & Chen, Y. (1984). How do enzyme activities control metabolite concentrations? An additional theorem in the theory of metabolite control. *Journal of Biochemistry*, **142**, 425–430.

Wilton, A. N., Laurie-Ahlberg, C. C., Emigh, T. H. & Curtsinger, J. W. (1982). Naturally occurring enzyme activity variation in *Drosophila melanogaster*. II. Relationships among enzymes. *Genetics*, **102**, 207–221.

9. MOLECULAR VARIATION AND ECOLOGICAL PROBLEMS

T. BURKE*, W.E. RAINEY[†] AND T.J. WHITE[‡]
*Department of Zoology, University of Leicester, Leicester LE1 7RH, UK; [†]Museum of Vertebrate Zoology, University of California, Berkeley, CA 94720, USA and [‡]Roche Molecular Systems Inc., 1145 Atlantic Avenue, Suite 100, Alameda, CA 94501, USA

INTRODUCTION

Recent developments in molecular genetics have led to many new and powerful techniques of value to the ecologist. While these techniques are likely to be fundamental to solving problems in ecological genetics and evolutionary ecology, they are also starting to provide tools of value to many other ecological disciplines. There is a tendency to criticize the enthusiasm with which many ecologists have greeted and started to apply the new techniques as a bandwagon, or perhaps as the latest 'fad' in ecology (Abrahamson *et al.* 1989) but we regard this to be a very positive response by ecologists for many of whom the new possibilities really will provide a critical technological leap.

The techniques of immediate importance are those that now allow the efficient detection of differences between the DNAs of individual organisms. The apparently simple linear arrangement of just four nucleotides of which all DNA molecules are comprised belies a tremendous and complex heterogeneity in evolutionary rates, a consequence of widely differing sequence organization, mutation rates, fixation rates and selective pressures (Fig. 9.1). Many organisms have several genomes with differing patterns of inheritance and rates of sequence evolution (see Fig. 9.2) and comparison among these can yield valuable insights. Additionally, the available molecular techniques themselves offer various levels of sensitivity. It has therefore recently become possible to select a combination of target DNA class and molecular method appropriate for quantifying genetic difference (or similarity) at every level from closely related individuals to anciently diverged species.

In the longer term, ecologists interested in phenotypic variation and its maintenance will be able to isolate and study the genetic component directly by isolating the genes that have allelic variation which contributes to the phenotype. This will be a natural progression from similar molecular

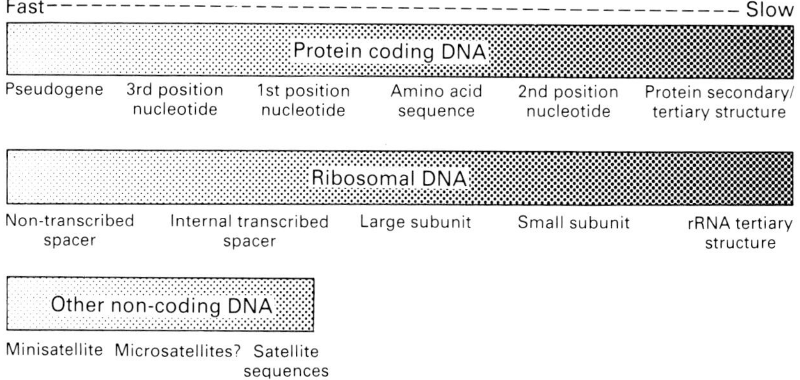

FIG. 9.1. Relative rates of DNA sequence evolution.

genetic studies which are already underway in commercially important plant and animal species.

In this review we concentrate mainly on the analysis of DNA variation, rather than on the study of the function of specific sequences or selective processes at particular loci. We illustrate the range of applications with reference to examples of relevance to ecological problems. The ecological problems that have so far been tackled using various molecular approaches are summarized in Table 9.1. The areas of application are dealt with in turn, where in each case we endeavour to emphasize those approaches that now seem likely to be most profitable. As most of the techniques are used in tackling a variety of problems, to minimize repetition, a brief description of the main techniques will be given first.

Nuclear/ Chromosomal
Mitochondrial
Plastid
Bacteria
Non-photosynthetic protists
Algal protists
Plants
Fungi
Animals

FIG. 9.2. Genomes available for analysis in different taxa.

TECHNIQUES AND TERMINOLOGY

The aim in this section is to give an overview of the different techniques that are used. Two manuals which are particularly relevant to the needs of the ecologist are those edited by Hoelzel (1992) and Hillis and Moritz (1990). These contain detailed descriptions and protocols for the main established methods described throughout this section; other references are given where necessary.

Source material

Virtually any cellular tissue is potentially a suitable source of DNA. In studies of vertebrates, blood is the most commonly used tissue as it can be obtained non-destructively. The quantity of DNA required will vary according to the technique that is to be used. For example, for methods based on DNA–DNA hybridization, such as multilocus DNA fingerprinting, as much as 5 μg of DNA may be required per sample run (and it is usually desirable to have sufficient material for several runs). This might be obtained from as little as 1–2 μl of avian blood, in which the red cells are nucleated, but require up to 1 ml blood from mammals, in which only the white cells are nucleated. For methods which allow the use of amplification techniques, such as the polymerase chain reaction (PCR), it is possible under ideal conditions to run an analysis starting from a single haploid genome (see p. 236), though it is normally desirable to avoid such a small sample because of the potential problem of contamination.

Though the predominant laboratory approach to preserving tissues for extraction of DNA has been freezing, a variety of chemical cocktails (involving chaotropes, chelating agents, alcohols and concentrated salt solutions) have been tested and shown to preserve relatively long DNA molecules suitable for most analytical approaches for periods of at least weeks or months at ambient temperatures (see Bruford *et al.* 1992). For example, animal tissues preserved in ethanol for 6 years have been found to provide high yields of DNA which can be cut with restriction enzymes (Smith *et al.* 1987). However, another study reported low yields and rapid degradation (Seutin *et al.* 1990). The difference may be attributable to contaminants present in commercial ethanol (Ito 1992).

DNA–DNA hybridization

Hybridization methods are used either (i) to assess overall similarity between the genomes of two species or (ii) to detect a specific, previously

Table 9.1. Examples of the application of various molecular genetic methods to ecological problems

Type of DNA / Molecular method	Ecological application								
						Species identification			
	Sex identification	Mating systems	Population structure	Migration & gene flow	Hybrid zones/ introgression	General	Host/parasite & host/symbiont interactions	Systematics	Community diversity
Total genome									
Hybridization	–	–	–	–	–	Bacteria[1]	–	Birds[2]	–
RAPD	*	Dragonfly[39]	*	*	Iris[3]	***Borellia***[40]	–	–	–
Highly repetitive									
Dot blot	Gull[4]	–	–	–	–	–	Trypanosome[5]	–	–
VNTR									
Multilocus minisatellite	Stripe-backed Wren[6]	**Dunnock**[7]	**Clonal species**[8] Channel Island Fox[9]	–	–	–	–	–	–
Single locus minisatellite	–	**Red-winged Black bird**[10]	**Human**[41]	*	*	–	–	–	–
Single locus microsatellite (PCR)	–	*	**Plants**[42]	*	*	–	–	–	–
Ribosomal									
RFLP	–	*Drosophila*[11]	*Clematis*[12]	–	Gopher[13]	*Aeromonas*[43]	–	–	–
Diagnostic PCR product	–	–	–	–	–	–	**Zooxanthellae**[14]	–	–
Oligonucleotide probes (PCR)	–	–	–	–	–	–	**Mycorrhizae**[15]	–	–
Sequencing	–	–	–	–	–	–	**Mycorrhizae**[15]	**Bacteria**[1] **Fungi**[16]	**Bacterio-plankton**[17] **Cyano-bacteria**[18]

Individual nuclear loci									
RFLP	Snow Goose[19]	Snow Goose[20]	Phytopathic Fungi[21]	Mosquito[22]	–	–	–	Galliformes[23]	–
Diagnostic PCR product	–	–	–	–	–	–	***Borrelia*[24]**	–	–
Oligonucleotide probes (PCR)	**Mammals[25]**	–	–	–	–	–	***Onchocerca*[26]**	–	–
DGGE/SSCP (PCR)	–	–	*	*	**Gopher[27]**	–	–	–	–
Sequencing	–	–	–	–	–	–	–	***Drosophila*[28]**	–
Mitochondrial									
Mapping (RFLP)	–	–	**Various[29]**	**Newt[30]**	**Various[31]**	–	–	**Various[32]**	–
DGGE/SSCP (PCR)	–	–	*	*	*	*	–	–	–
Sequencing	–	–	**Kangaroo Rat[33]**	**Human[34]**	–	Sea Cucumber[44]	–	**Warblers[35]**	–
Plastid									
Mapping (RFLP)	–	–	**Red Algae[36]**	–	**Iris[37]**	–	–	**Various[38]**	–
DGGE/SSCP (PCR)	–	–	*	*	*	–	–	–	–
Sequencing	–	–	*	–	–	–	–	**Various[45]**	–

For each area of application examples which used the most popular technique, or the most promising new approach, are shown in **bold** typeface. Some of the examples given under Mapping and Sequencing predate the availability of PCR-based methods which would now usually be preferred.

* Indicates new methods which may prove to be very valuable for particular applications. 1 Woese 1987, 2 Sibley & Ahlquist 1990, 3 Arnold *et al.* 1991, 4 Griffiths & Holland 1990, 5 Kukla *et al.* 1987, 6 Rabenold *et al.* 1991, 7 Burke *et al.* 1989, 8 e.g. Nybom & Schaal 1990; Turner *et al.* 1990, 9 Gilbert *et al.* 1990, 10 Gibbs *et al.* 1990, 11 Williams & Strobeck 1986, 12 Learn & Schaal 1987, 13 Baker *et al.* 1989, 14 Rowan & Powers 1991, 15 Gardes *et al.* 1990, 16 Bruns *et al.* 1991, 17 Giovanonni *et al.* 1990, 18 Ward *et al*, 1990, 19 Quinn *et al.* 1990, 20 Quinn *et al.* 1987, 21 McDonald & Martinez 1990, 22 Raymond *et al.* 1991, 23 Helm-Bychowski & Wilson 1986, 24 Persing *et al.* 1990, 25 Sinclair *et al.* 1990; Gubbay *et al.* 1990, 26 Harnett *et al.* 1989, 27 Lessa 1992, 28 Thomas & Hunt 1991, 29 reviewed in Avise *et al.* 1987, 30 Arntzen & Wallis 1991, 31 reviewed in Harrison 1989, 32 reviewed in Moritz *et al.* 1987, 33 Thomas *et al.* 1990, 34 Vigilant *et al.* 1991, 35 Richman & Price 1992, 36 Goff & Coleman 1988, 37 Arnold *et al.* 1991, 38 reviewed in Palmer 1987, 39 Hadrys *et al.* 1992, 40 Welsh *et al.* 1992, 41 Balazs *et al.* 1992, 42 Rogstad in press, 43 Lucchini & Altwegg 1992, 44 Olson *et al.* 1991, 45 reviewed in Soltis *et al.* 1992.

cloned, sequence. In its simplest form a dot blot is performed in which a small aliquot of DNA (or even blood) is spotted and fixed on to a filter membrane before hybridizing against a labelled probe. The probe is most frequently labelled radioactively but non-radioactive labelling methods are being developed and becoming increasingly popular. The presence of probe sequences in the target sample is assessed by comparing the strength of hybridization with appropriate controls. The hybridization is detected autoradiographically on X-ray film or by chemically staining the probe on the membrane directly. When investigating a specific sequence the probe may consist of a cloned segment of DNA or else a very short, artificially synthesized, oligonucleotide sequence of typically 20–30 base pairs (bp). Oligonucleotide probes can be designed once a clone has been sequenced, and in principle allow the relatively rapid and convenient collection of data on sequence variation (e.g. Gardes *et al.* 1991).

Restriction fragment analysis

Often the simple detection of similar sequences in a dot blot is insufficient and more detailed sequence information is required about the hybridizing target DNA. Until recently, the simplest way to assay DNA sequence variation has been through the use of restriction fragment (or restriction fragment length polymorphism, RFLP) analysis. The sample DNA is first cut into defined fragments using one of the many available restriction enzymes and the fragments are then separated electrophoretically according to their length. Restriction fragments may be observed directly by staining in the electrophoretic gel or else detected by hybridization, as above, following permanent transfer on to a filter membrane by the Southern blotting procedure. (Some procedures now avoid the blotting step by drying the fragments into the gel and hybridizing the gel directly, e.g. Schäfer *et al.* 1988). The presence or absence of a DNA fragment implies variation in the specific target sequence recognized by the particular restriction endonuclease used.

DNA fingerprinting

There are now two separate classes of DNA fingerprint analysis — multi-locus and single locus fingerprinting. In the latter, allelic DNA restriction fragments of variable size are detected at a single locus by hybridizing a Southern blot with a cloned minisatellite probe (Wong *et al.* 1987). A minisatellite DNA sequence is typically up to 20 000 bp in length, comprising repeated copies of a short, 10–60 bp non-coding sequence. The number of repeats may vary markedly, producing restriction fragments having easily detectable length differences, and resulting in very high levels of polymorphism (with heterozygosity approaching 100%) at some minisatellite loci. Minisatellite loci are examples of 'variable number tandem repeat' (VNTR) loci.

In multilocus DNA fingerprinting a 'poly-core' probe is used which will hybridize simultaneously to part of the repeat unit (known as the 'core') common to the minisatellites at many separate loci (Jeffreys *et al.* 1985a, b). Different core probes may be used to detect largely independent minisatellite profiles. A major advantage of multilocus fingerprinting is that the available core probes produce results in a very wide range of organisms (e.g. Burke & Bruford 1987, Dallas 1988, Taggart & Ferguson 1990, Carvalho *et al.* 1991; see reviews in Burke *et al.* 1991a). Detailed laboratory protocols concerning multilocus and single locus minisatellite DNA fingerprinting are provided in Bruford *et al.* (1992).

A disadvantage of multilocus fingerprinting is that the fingerprint profiles are complex and difficult to compare, especially when obtained in separate gels. Also, the constituent DNA fragments cannot be ascribed to specific loci. Single-locus fingerprinting circumvents these problems, by allowing genotypes to be ascribed at often highly variable loci, but has the disadvantage that a marker system has to be developed in each species of interest, or at least in a closely related species (Hanotte *et al.* 1991a, b, 1992). A relatively efficient method for the isolation of such loci is, however, now available (Armour *et al.* 1990, Hanotte *et al.* 1991a, b; protocols in Bruford *et al.* 1992).

The other class of VNTR loci comprises simple sequence, or *micro*-satellite polymorphisms (Tautz 1989). Microsatellites consist of variable numbers of a simple short tandem repeat, such as (GT)*n* or (CAC)*n*. The difference between a minisatellite and microsatellite is arbitrary but the practical distinction is that the overall length of a microsatellite is small enough to allow analysis by means of PCR (see p. 236). The analysis of microsatellite variation is therefore potentially much less labour-intensive than for minisatellites (for methods see Rassmann *et al.* 1991, Schlötterer *et al.* 1991). Locus-specific microsatellite systems are often applicable across a wide range of related species (Schlötterer *et al.* 1991), perhaps to a greater extent than minisatellite probes. There are as yet too few data to allow a detailed comparison of the typical variability at each of the two classes of loci. The highest levels of polymorphism seem likely to be attained at minisatellite loci but the variability of microsatellites is likely to be adequate for most applications.

DNA amplification

A relatively new approach applicable to most DNA samples — including rather crude extracts of total DNA — is the polymerase chain reaction (PCR) (Mullis & Faloona 1987, Saiki *et al.* 1988). This technique produces a highly enriched preparation of DNA of defined length which is suitable for further analysis by a variety of methods, e.g. RFLP, sequencing and hybridization to specific probes. In the polymerase chain reaction a thermostable DNA polymerase is used to copy cyclically the sequence between two priming sites on opposite DNA strands; the reaction requires the presence of two synthetic oligonucleotide primers complementary to these sites and the amount of product doubles with every cycle. The sensitivity of the procedure makes it useful for the analysis of remarkably small amounts of DNA which may be derived, for example, from single sperm cells (Arnheim *et al.* 1990), single hairs (Higuchi *et al.* 1988), single feathers (Taberlet & Bouvet 1991), ancient bone (Hagelberg *et al.* 1989) or museum specimens (Thomas *et al.* 1989, Thomas *et al.* 1990). Since few intact copies of the sequence of interest are required, and even fixed or embedded tissues can be suitable for DNA extraction for PCR (Greer *et al.* 1991), highly simplified field sample preservation and laboratory extraction protocols are usually satisfactory.

PCR now often provides an alternative to the hybridization methods as enough amplified PCR product can be produced to allow it to be examined directly on an electrophoretic gel. This allows, for example, detection of length variation between the primer sites, or detection of variation in a priming site itself. Alternatively, the PCR product can be used as the target material in DNA–DNA hybridization using dot blots, or for restriction analysis. These and other techniques (see p. 237) may allow the relatively easy collection of useful sequence-based marker data without the need for extensive sequencing.

DNA sequencing

Until recently it was necessary to clone a sequence from the study organism of interest before a sequence could be obtained. A study of DNA polymorphism across an entire gene, for example, required that the gene be cloned separately from each individual (e.g. Kreitman 1983). The advent of PCR will now usually allow the cloning step to be bypassed once a particular locus has been cloned and sequenced in at least one related organism from which oligonucleotide primers can be designed. For some loci it is possible to identify stretches of flanking sequence which are highly conserved across a wide range of taxa, allowing the design of 'universal' primers (Kocher *et al.* 1989, Hillis & Dixon 1991, Taberlet *et al.* 1991). There are now excellent protocols for the direct sequencing of PCR products (e.g. Winship 1989, Innis *et al.* 1990, Lee 1991). Some workers have preferred to subclone PCR products before sequencing, but this can create considerable extra work, especially as multiple sequences are then required to exclude the possibility of artefactual nucleotide substitutions.

Denaturing gradient gel electrophoresis

Even with the relative ease of acquiring sequence data via PCR and direct sequencing, amassing data suitable for comparing population frequencies of nuclear gene alleles or mitochondrial haplotypes is a daunting task. Though not yet widely applied outside medical genetics, denaturing gradient gel electrophoresis (DGGE) and related methods (e.g. thermal gradient gel electrophoresis (TGGE) (Riesner *et al.* 1989) and PCR-single-strand conformation polymorphism (SSCP) analysis (Hayashi 1991)) offer a less labour-intensive alternative to sequencing tens of samples. Lessa (1992) and Myers *et al.* (1989) offer detailed guidance on DGGE methods but, in brief, the approach entails preparing a primer to the region of interest which has a long G–C tail. Amplified products with this denaturation-resistant G–C clamp are run in a gel containing a gradient of urea concentration. Products differing in sequence partially denature at different urea concentrations. For products under 500 bp in length, alterations as small as single base-pair substitutions can be seen as mobility differences. Frequency data (including detection of heterozygotes) can be obtained directly from the gel. If desired, samples from bands representing the mobility classes identified can be reamplified and sequenced. In this application, DGGE is most useful for a DNA fragment which is moderately variable within the populations or other study units (i.e. not all individuals are likely to be unique). However, it may have equal value for preliminary surveys (with either a population genetic or phylogenetic focus) assessing whether the DNA fragment initially amplified has appropriate levels of variation within or among populations or taxa, before beginning to sequence fragments from selected individuals.

Random amplified polymorphic DNA

The random amplified polymorphic DNA (RAPD, pronounced 'rapid') approach is now being explored widely, in part because of its apparent simplicity. It relies on screening DNA (sometimes from isolated organelles) from organisms of interest for variability using panels of single short primers of arbitrary sequence (Williams *et al.* 1990; see Hadrys *et al.* 1992). When the amplification products are compared by agarose gel electrophoresis and ethidium bromide staining, some primers will yield a few discrete bands and a subset of those may be polymorphic within or among populations. Where tested, the markers have usually shown dominant Mendelian inheritance (Williams *et al.* 1990, Arnold *et al.* 1991). The markers can be used to create genetic linkage maps in both plants and animals (Williams *et al.* 1990).

Given that the regions amplified are unknown and that relatively few published studies are yet available, replicability of product patterns from individuals over several independent extractions and amplifications (and heritability, where possible) should be tested in each new organism. In successful applications, this approach can provide a substantial number of polymorphic markers by a procedure requiring only DNA isolation, amplification and agarose electrophoresis. The cost and greater complexity of using restriction enzymes and radioactive labelling are avoided.

ECOLOGICAL APPLICATIONS

In this section we discuss a range of areas of interest to the ecologist. Examples of studies in which the different categories of problem have been tackled, and the methodological approach used, are provided in Table 9.1. We have attempted where possible to select examples having particular relevance to the ecologist and to include a representative range of taxa. In many cases a new and promising technique has been identified but there is as yet no published example of its application, reflecting the pace of technical development in this area. Attention is drawn to these possibilities in Table 9.1. The reader should also be aware that in other cases the selected example, as cited in Table 9.1, no longer necessarily represents the most efficient methodological approach.

Sex identification

Fisher (1930) predicted that in sexual species a parent should make an equal total investment in its offspring of each sex. Trivers and Willard (1973) argued that when parental investment affects an offspring's eventual reproductive success and the variance in reproductive success is greater in one of the sexes, then a parent should make a greater investment in that sex. Extensive tests of these and related hypotheses, and life history studies in general, have been impeded by the difficulty of sexing juveniles in many popular study organisms. As an example where sexing was possible morphologically, in the eastern bluebird (*Sialia sialis*) it was found that males invested more in their female offspring (Gowaty & Droge 1991). It was suggested that this reflected the very low natal-to-breeding dispersal in this species as philopatric males might potentially compete with their own father for females, so that female offspring would represent a greater proportion of a male's fitness.

Where sex is determined genetically there must per se be some DNA specific to at least one sex. While in principle this only needs to be an allelic difference at a single locus, the differences are usually much more extensive, often involving sex-specific chromosomes. In such cases, cytological sexing is possible but usually impractical for the large sample sizes required (but see Parker *et al.* 1991). There are now several examples of the use of molecular techniques to detect sequences characteristic of particular sex chromosomes. For example, Griffiths and Holland (1990) used a subtraction cloning technique to isolate a probe specific for the W (female-specific) chromosome in the herring gull (*Larus argentatus*). Unfortunately, as with other examples of similar probes, this probe is only of value in a few closely related species. Sex-linked probes for other species have on occasion been found fortuitously (e.g. Quinn *et al.* 1990, Rabenold *et al.* 1991).

In the longer term, this problem is likely to be avoided by identifying and analysing the sex-determining gene itself. The sex-determining region on the Y-chromosome (SRY) gene was recently isolated and is believed to be the sex-determining locus in humans (Sinclair *et al.* 1990, Gubbay *et al.* 1990). It can be used as a probe in blot analyses to determine the sex of a range of mammals (Sinclair *et al.* 1990). While it seems possible that it will have a homologue with equivalent function in other vertebrate taxa, a first search for an homologous gene in birds was not successful (Griffiths 1991). (It is intriguing to speculate about the possible functional organization of such a locus where the female is the heterogametic sex.) Once appropriate sequence data are available it should be possible to design and synthesize oligonucleotide probes that work in a wide range of mammalian species, at least, or to design oligonucleotide primers that allow the use of PCR.

Mating systems

Mating systems are of particular interest to evolutionary ecologists who wish to measure the reproductive success of individuals under natural conditions. Alternatively, there may be a requirement to measure relatedness among cooperating individuals. In practice, testing maternity or paternity is a particular case of measuring relatedness (e.g. Birkhead *et al.* 1990). The use of molecular methods — especially multilocus DNA fingerprinting and random RFLP analysis — for this purpose has been reviewed elsewhere (Burke 1989). More recently, the application of single locus fingerprinting has, somewhat unexpectedly, developed rapidly and may often now be the method of choice (Burke *et al.* 1991b).

Multilocus analysis has been applied in several completed field studies of breeding systems and is now an almost routine component of many more. Most studies have so far focused on birds, reflecting the popularity of birds as study organisms for behavioural ecology, and have concerned either the confirmation of maternity or paternity in essentially monogamous systems (see Burke *et al.* 1991b, Birkhead & Møller 1992) or else the distribution of parentage and degree of relatedness among members of cooperatively breeding groups (Burke *et al.* 1989, Rabenold *et al.* 1990, Jones *et al.* 1991, Packer *et al.* 1991, Davies *et al.* 1992).

The first category of studies has been concerned with the occurrence of alternative mating strategies, such as extra-pair copulation or intraspecific brood parasitism, detected through exclusion analyses where offspring genotypes are found to be incompatible with those of their putative parents. For example, studies of the copulation behaviour of zebra finches (*Taeniopygia guttata*) in aviaries led to the expectation that extra-pair paternity might occur in natural populations. A fingerprinting study of the putative, behaviourally-assigned parents in a wild population was therefore completed and while extra-pair paternity was confirmed by exclusion analysis to occur at a low frequency, in 2 out of 82 offspring, intraspecific brood parasitism was unexpectedly found to be rather more significant, accounting for 9 out of 80 offspring (Birkhead *et al.* 1990).

As an example of a species in which the aim has been to assign parentage, the dunnock (*Prunella modularis*) most commonly breeds in a polyandrous group in which two or more males associate with a single breeding female; the males, which are normally unrelated, have a dominance relationship and either or both may assist the female to feed the brood. By the use of multilocus fingerprinting, it was shown that males were significantly more likely to feed the brood if they had some paternity, though they showed no preference towards their own offspring (Burke *et al.* 1989). A male was much more likely to assist if he had been observed to have some exclusive access to the female during the fertile pre-laying period, and his proportion of the male-supplied feeds was significantly correlated with his proportion of exclusive access. The fingerprinting data showed that observed access was a good predictor of paternity, and it was therefore suggested that male dunnocks use some measure of their access to determine whether to feed the brood. This was subsequently verified experimentally by artificially manipulating the mating success (confirmed by DNA fingerprinting) of individual males in a series of removal experiments (Davies *et al.* 1992).

Assignment of parentage can be achieved efficiently by multilocus fingerprinting only when there are a small number of candidates, as was generally the case in the dunnock study, but it is often desirable to test many potential parents. In such instances, it is more efficient to use a single locus fingerprinting system in which individuals can be assigned genotypes at a series of highly polymorphic loci. Gibbs *et al.* (1990) used a combination of multilocus and single locus fingerprinting to identify almost all the fathers of the 28% of 111 red-winged blackbird chicks which were not sired by the male owning the territory in which they were born. This revealed that there was no significant correlation between the number of offspring produced on a male's territory and his actual reproductive success, and that those males which sired a higher proportion of the offspring in their own territory also achieved more extra-pair fertilizations. The one single locus probe available to Gibbs and co-workers was a mouse histocompatibility locus cDNA, the usefulness of which seems to have resulted from its fortuitous hybridization to a single minisatellite-containing restriction fragment; it has not been found to be generally useful in other species of bird (H. L. Gibbs, personal communication). Generalized methods for obtaining probes or primers specific to highly polymorphic minisatellite or microsatellite loci, respectively, are now available (see earlier) and the use of several such loci in combination can make multilocus fingerprinting obsolete (Wong *et al.* 1987, Hanotte *et al.* 1991a).

Other molecular methods have occasionally been used. Quinn and co-workers showed that a series of randomly cloned RFLPs from snow geese detected considerable variability and could be used for parentage analysis in this species (Quinn & White 1987, Quinn *et al.* 1987). Williams and Strobeck (1986) identified RFLPs specific to the ribosomal genes of *Drosophila* Y chromosomes, and so were able to show the occurrence of multiple mating by female *D. melanogaster* in wild populations.

A more detailed review of this area is beyond the scope of this article and the reader is referred to the published reviews (Burke 1989, Burke *et al.* 1991b and other papers in Burke *et al.* 1991a).

Population structure

Population structure is a broad topic, including the study of genetic relationships and genetic differentiation at many levels from within social groups to among populations. The analysis of close familial relationships has been discussed separately in the previous section.

Apart from allozymes, which are outside the scope of this review, mitochondrial DNA (mtDNA) has been the macromolecule of choice for many studies of population differentiation (reviewed in Avise *et al.* 1987). As an example, RFLP analysis of mtDNA from skin biopsies of 84 humpback whales demonstrated a marked segregation of haplotypes among subpopulations as well as between populations from the North Atlantic and North Pacific oceans (Baker *et al.* 1990). There was excellent agreement between the geographic distribution of haplotypes and previously reported patterns of migration between summer feeding grounds and winter breeding areas. The authors suggested that the genetic segregation reflected 'maternal traditions in migratory destination', illustrating the importance of considering behaviour patterns in analyses of population structure.

In plants, plastid DNA offers many of the same advantages as mtDNA and has been used in a small number of studies of population structure (e.g. Goff & Coleman 1988).

Random clones isolated from total genomic libraries have been used for RFLP studies at the population level. For example, McDonald and Martinez (1990) examined the population structure of the fungal pathogen *Mycosphaerella graminicola* from a single wheat field. They found a high level of genetic variation, including differences among lesions on a single leaf. Their study emphasizes the importance of assessing the spatial scale of variation before assuming that a few samples from different geographic locations adequately represent population level variation.

Other types of DNA markers, such as ribosomal DNA (e.g. Learn & Schaal 1987), have occasionally been used. While minisatellites were generally perceived as too rapidly evolving for analysis at the population level, Gilbert *et al.* (1990) showed fingerprint patterns were informative regarding the phylogeny of, and relative levels of genetic variability among, the small, isolated populations of dwarf foxes on the Channel islands of southern California. For the most isolated island, they observed no fingerprint variation among the foxes sampled, a pattern not even encountered in inbred laboratory mice. Multilocus fingerprinting may also be of particular value for identifying members of clones in natural populations (Nybom & Schaal 1990, Turner *et al.* 1990, Carvalho *et al.* 1991, Brookfield 1992).

PCR now makes it feasible to collect actual DNA sequences in population studies. It also allows the use of material held in museum collections. Thomas *et al.* (1990) took advantage of this to show that there had been no significant change in the population structure of three kangaroo rat populations during a 78-year period.

Migration and gene flow

Migration is, of course, an important component of population structure, and the same methodological approaches are therefore applicable. We mention some examples under this heading to highlight that migration patterns can in themselves sometimes be inferred using molecular methods.

For example, on the controversial question of the geographical origin of modern humans, sequence comparison of the mtDNA displacement loop region from a diverse sample of humans and the chimpanzee appears to confirm an African root for the human mtDNA tree (Vigilant *et al.* 1991; but see Templeton 1992). Hagelberg *et al.* (1989) extended the usefulness of PCR for studies of human population migrations and, implicitly, the identification of morphologically non-diagnostic bone fragments for a range of studies, by demonstrating the feasibility of amplifying mtDNA from human bone up to 5450 years old.

MtDNA was similarly used, in an RFLP analysis in combination with allozymes, to investigate and confirm genetically the movement of an historically charted hybrid zone between two species of newt (Arntzen & Wallis 1991). It was found that populations of the crested newt, *Triturus cristatus*, which had replaced the marbled newt, *T. marmoratus*, were characterized by the presence of a low but detectable frequency of introgressed *marmoratus* alleles.

The mosquito *Culex pipiens* is commonly resistant to organophosphate insecticides through the overproduction of non-specific esterases. Among the latter is an electrophoretically detectable, amplified B2 allele at the B locus. Restriction analysis of the sequences flanking the B2 esterase structural gene in samples from Africa, Asia and North America revealed a very high degree of homology, indicating that the B2 allele arose from a single mutation event and has, through its insecticide-induced selective advantage, spread rapidly among the world's populations (Raymond *et al.* 1991).

Introgression and hybrid zones

The techniques appropriate to population structure analysis are again appropriate to the special case of hybrid zones. MtDNA has been particularly valuable in the analysis of genetic introgression across hybrid zones (reviewed in Harrison 1989). Ribosomal DNA has also been used to some extent (e.g. Baker *et al.* 1989).

Arnold *et al.* (1991) used PCR of a selected chloroplast gene and RAPD to investigate hybrid speciation in the Louisiana Iris. The geo-raphical distribution of species-specific RAPD markers supports the hypothesis that *Iris fulva* and *I. hexagona* have undergone gene flow resulting in localized and dispersed introgression. RFLP analysis of an amplified chloroplast gene fragment (carried in the female cytoplasm) indicated that the gene flow resulted from pollen transfer rather than seed dispersal.

This area provides some of the first examples of the successful application of DGGE. Lessa (1992) used DGGE to study a hybrid zone in a gopher species.

To examine levels of gene exchange among potentially hybridizing white oak species in regions where morphologically recognizable hybrids are absent, Whittemore and Schaal (1991) surveyed blots of genomic DNA restriction fragment digests with cloned probes from both *Petunia* chloroplasts and a soybean nuclear ribosomal repeat. They found that, though there was some large-scale geographic variation in chloroplast genotypes, co-occurring species at a single site (including evergreen and deciduous species) frequently had the same chloroplast genotype. While single species had different chloroplast genotypes at different localities, a nuclear ribosomal marker showed a distribution pattern congruent with expected species boundaries. The strongly contrasting patterns of geographic variation and apparent gene flow that they observed in chloroplast and nuclear DNA underline the need for caution in the interpretation of population or taxon boundaries on the basis of limited data sets from organellar DNA (Pamilo & Nei 1988).

Species identification

The degree of cross-hybridization between total DNA extracts has been widely used as a method for estimating relatedness among species. Among prokaryotes in particular, this approach has been associated with a rough approximation defining species as organisms which have cross-hybridization values of 90% or above (Woese 1987). However, the resolution and taxonomic range of this approach are often low and the need for pairwise comparisons requires large amounts of DNA.

Probes specific to species are especially useful in the investigation of host-vector-parasite systems. Kukla *et al.* (1987) identified species and subspecies of trypanosomes in the tissues of tsetse flies using radioactively-labelled cloned restriction fragments containing repetitive sequences. They developed a procedure adaptable to field use in which gut trypanosomes were detected and identified by simply pressing the severed abdomens of whole flies on to nylon filters which were then hybridized to the labelled probe. By screening a genomic library, Harnett *et al.* (1989) detected and subsequently sequenced an oligonucleotide probe that discriminates between *Onchocerca volvulus*, the nematode causing human river blindness, and other morphologically similar *Onchocerca* species which are not human pathogens, but may occur in the same blackfly vector.

Persing *et al.* (1990) used *Borrelia*-specific primers and PCR to detect diagnostic DNA fragments in museum specimens of deer ticks, showing that Lyme disease must have occurred in the United States at least 30 years before its clinical recognition. Sequence analysis of another random clone from the Lyme disease pathogen *Borrelia burgdorferi* permitted the design of PCR primers that could distinguish North American from European and Asian isolates (Rosa *et al.* 1991).

Goff *et al.* (1988) used a probe for a surface protein gene from *Anaplasma marginale* to monitor tick and cattle infection frequencies. Host carrier status, modes of disease transmission, and prevalence of infected ticks within enzootic areas could be monitored. Rowan and Powers (1991) sequenced segments of the small subunit rDNA from 131 individual isolates of unicellular algal symbionts in 22 marine animal host taxa. Closely related algae were found in phylogenetically distant hosts. The eclectic and apparently broad ranges for the algal symbionts is a pattern of association quite distinct from that of some animal parasites whose cladistic histories are sometimes largely congruent with that of their host (Page 1990).

DNA analysis can potentially allow the identification of the prey of haematophagous arthropods. As an illustration of the potential power of this approach, Coulson *et al.* (1990) obtained the genotype of a human bitten by a mosquito by single locus minisatellite fingerprint analysis of the mosquito's gut contents.

Systematics

Ecologists are interested in systematics from the points of view both of recognizing distinct species and understanding the evolutionary relationships among species. Molecular techniques are being widely applied in systematics and the field has been extensively reviewed elsewhere (Hillis & Moritz 1990, Hewitt *et al.* 1991; examples in Table 9.1). Virtually any objective, genetically based character has the potential to be taxonomically informative, and the value of different approaches will vary according to the degree of genetic divergence within the group under study. While the phenetic approach offered by DNA–DNA hybridization has been successfully used (especially in birds; Sibley & Ahlquist 1990), the phylogenetic analysis of DNA sequences is to be preferred and has now become more generally feasible since the advent of PCR. Previously only ribosomal RNA genes had been sequenced to any significant extent (Woese 1987, Hillis & Dixon 1991).

The first studies using PCR have exploited mtDNA sequences for which universal primers have been characterized (Kocher *et al.* 1989). For example, Richman and Price (1992) used such primers to obtain 910 base pairs of mitochondrial cytochrome *b* gene sequence from eight sympatric species of *Phylloscopus* warblers in order to construct a phylogeny for the group. This phylogeny was then used to control for the effects of common ancestry in a comparative analysis which in turn supported adaptive explanations for the association between morphology, feeding behaviour and ecology in these species.

The classification of species is of particular relevance to conservation, and this has been emphasized by a number of studies of variation in mtDNA which have shown a lack of significant differentiation between supposedly separate species or subspecies of pocket gophers (Laerm *et al.* 1982) and seaside sparrows (Avise & Nelson 1989), the probable hybrid origins of the red wolf (Wayne & Jenks 1991), and introgression of foreign genes into endangered populations of panther and grey wolf (see O'Brien & Mayr 1991). In the red wolf study it was possible to rule out the possibility that hybridization was a very recent phenomenon through the analysis of museum specimens using PCR. Molecular systematics is also likely to reveal instances where separate taxa have been lumped into a single species, especially in lineages which are morphologically conservative (Daugherty *et al.* 1990).

Community diversity

The simultaneous amplification of multiple small subunit rDNA sequences provides a useful approach for examining the natural diversity of microorganisms. Giovannoni *et al.* (1990) sequenced clones of amplified portions of the 16S rRNA genes from natural populations of bacterioplankton. The observed diversity was increased over that detected by culturing, and some of the previously unknown taxa were both phylogenetically distinct and quantitatively important members of the microbial community.

Ward *et al.* (1990) similarly examined the species composition of microbes in the cyanobacterial mat of a terrestrial hot spring. Using a conserved oligonucleotide primer they synthesized DNA from environmental samples of 16S rRNA. Cloning, sequencing and comparison with 16S rRNA sequences of organisms cultured from similar habitats revealed that *none* of the eight sequence types detected was identical with the 14 previously known organisms from the site. It is clear that molecular tools can reveal previously undetected diversity in microbial communities and that the new organisms detected are not necessarily limited to rare taxa.

CONCLUDING REMARKS

The extent and types of variation at the DNA level, especially within species, have only become known relatively recently. Even newer technical developments, especially PCR, are making the problem of assaying this variability much more tractable. In general, PCR-based approaches either already are, or seem likely to soon become, the methods of choice (Table 9.1).

MtDNA has been the most popular source of information at the DNA (restriction fragment) level for various kinds of population study for a variety of good reasons (see Hillis & Moritz 1990). This continues to be the case for sequence data obtained by PCR, probably because of the mtDNA molecule's frequent (but not universal – see Kreitman 1991) higher overall nucleotide substitution rate than for nuclear sequences, the presence within it of regions having known and highly different evolutionary rates, the availability of 'universal' primers (Kocher *et al.* 1989) and the haploid nature of the mitochondrial genome. The latter allows avoidance of the potential problem, in diploid nuclear genomes, of identifying sequence haplotypes (discussed in Kreitman 1991). Often nuclear markers are also desirable (Pamilo & Nei 1988) and while allozymes are often used, DNA markers potentially provide more flexibility in identifying a level of variability appropriate to the resolution required by the problem being tackled. As typical levels of nucleotide polymorphism within species are of the order of 1% or less (Kreitman 1991), the mass sequencing of samples will not generally be the most profitable approach for the ecologist to take. We have therefore drawn attention to the short-cuts that are possible by the use of, for example, DGGE, oligonucleotide probing, restriction fragment digestion, or simple sizing of PCR products from polymorphic regions that have been characterized at the sequence level.

Though the techniques are becoming more tractable, their successful implementation remains an intellectually demanding activity, and ecologists should be careful not to fall into the trap of regarding the laboratory work, condescendingly, as a simply technical activity. Ultimately, the most successful application of molecular approaches in the study of ecological processes will result from a genuine collaboration between field and laboratory based scientists who take the trouble to understand each others' interests and problems.

ACKNOWLEDGEMENTS

T.B. is supported by a Royal Society University Research Fellowship. We thank J.W. Arntzen, B. Best, B. Bowman, O. Hanotte, S.A. Harris, E. Lessa, C. Orrego, T. Quinn, W.K. Thomas and A.C. Wilson for discussions.

REFERENCES

Abrahamson, W. G., Whitham, T. G. & Price, P. W. (1989). Fads in ecology. *BioScience*, **39**, 321–325.

Armour, J. A. L., Povey, S., Jeremiah, S. & Jeffreys, A. J. (1990). Systematic cloning of human minisatellites from ordered array charomid libraries. *Genomics*, **8**, 501–502.

Arnheim, N., Li, H. & Cui, X. (1990). PCR analysis of DNA sequences in single cells: single sperm gene mapping and genetic disease diagnosis. *Genomics*, **8**, 415–419.

Arnold, M. L., Buckner, C. M. & Robinson, J. J. (1991). Pollen mediated introgression and hybrid speciation in Louisiana irises. *Proceedings of the National Academy of Sciences, USA*, **88**, 1398–1402.

Arntzen, J. W. & Wallis, G. P. (1991). Restricted gene flow in a moving hybrid zone of the newts *Triturus cristatus* and *T. marmoratus* in western France. *Evolution*, **45**, 805–826.

Avise, J. C. & Nelson, W. S. (1989). Molecular relationships of the extinct dusky seaside sparrow. *Science*, **243**, 646–648.

Avise, J. C., Arnold, R. M., Ball, E., Bermingham, T., Lamb, G. E., Neigel, C. A., Reeb, C. A. & Saunders, N. C. (1987). Intraspecific phylogeography: the mitochondrial bridge between population genetics and systematics. *Annual Review of Ecology and Systematics*, **18**, 489–522.

Baker, C. S., Palumbi, S. R., Lambertsen, R. H., Weinrich, M. T., Calambokidis, J. & O'Brien, S. J. (1990). Influence of seasonal migration on geographical distribution of mitochondrial DNA haplotypes in humpback whales. *Nature*, **344**, 238–240.

Baker, R. J., Davis, S. K., Bradley, R. D., Hamilton, M. J. & Van Den Bussche, R. A. (1989). Ribosomal-DNA, mitochondrial-DNA, chromosomal, and allozymic studies on a contact zone in the pocket gopher, *Geomys*. *Evolution*, **43**, 63–75.

Balazs, I., Neuweiler, J., Gunn, P., Kidd, J., Kidd, K. K., Kuhl, J. & Mingjun, L. (1992). Human population genetic studies using hypervariable loci. *Genetics*, **131**, 191–198.

Birkhead, T. R. & Møller, A. P. (1992). *Sperm Competition in Birds*. Academic Press, London, UK.

Birkhead, T. R., Burke, T., Zann, R., Hunter, F. M. & Krupa, A. P. (1990). Extra-pair paternity and intraspecific brood parasitism in wild zebra finches, *Taeniopygia guttata*, revealed by DNA fingerprinting. *Behavioural Ecology and Sociobiology*, **27**, 315–324.

Brookfield, J. F. Y. (1992). DNA fingerprinting in clonal organisms. *Molecular Ecology*, **1**, 21–26.

Bruford, M. W., Hanotte, O., Brookfield, J. F. Y. & Burke, T. (1992). Single locus and multilocus DNA fingerprinting. *Molecular Genetic Analysis of Populations: A Practical Approach* (Ed. by A. R. Hoelzel), pp. 225–269. IRL Press, Oxford, UK.

Bruns, T. D., White, T. J. & Taylor, J. W. (1991). Fungal molecular systematics. *Annual Review of Ecology and Systematics*, **22**, 525–564.

Burke, T. (1989). DNA fingerprinting and other methods for the study of mating success. *Trends in Ecology and Evolution*, **4**, 139–144.

Burke, T. & Bruford, M. W. (1987). DNA fingerprinting in birds. *Nature*, **327**, 149–152.

Burke, T., Davies, N. B., Bruford, M. W. & Hatchwell, B. J. (1989). Parental care and mating behaviour of polyandrous dunnocks *Prunella modularis* related to paternity by DNA fingerprinting. *Nature*, **338**, 249–251.

Burke, T., Dolf, G., Jeffreys, A. J. & Wolff, R. (Eds) (1991a). *DNA Fingerprinting: Approaches and Applications*. Birkhäuser, Basel, Switzerland.

Burke, T., Hanotte, O., Bruford, M. W. & Cairns, E. (1991b). Multilocus and single locus minisatellite analysis in population biological studies. *DNA Fingerprinting: Approaches and Applications* (Ed. by T. Burke, G. Dolf, A. J. Jeffreys & R. Wolff), pp. 154–168. Birkhäuser, Basel, Switzerland.

Carvalho, G. R., Maclean, N., Wratton, S. D., Carter, R. E. & Thurston, J. P. (1991). Differentiation of aphid clones using DNA fingerprinting from individual aphids. *Proceedings of the Royal Society of London*, B, **243**, 109–114.

Coulson, R. M. R., Curtis, C. F., Ready, P. D., Hill, N. & Smith, D. (1990). Amplification and analysis of human DNA present in mosquito bloodmeals. *Medical and Veterinary Entomology*, **4**, 357–366.

Dallas, J. F. (1988). Detection of DNA fingerprints of cultivated rice by hybridization with a human minisatellite probe. *Proceedings of the National Academy of Sciences, USA*, **85**, 6831–6835.

Daugherty, C. H., Cree, A., Hay, J. M. & Thompson, A. M. B. (1990). Neglected taxonomy and continuing extinctions of tuatara (*Sphenodon*). *Nature*, **347**, 177–179.

Davies, N. B., Hatchwell, B. J., Robson, T. & Burke, T. (1992). Paternity and parental effort in dunnocks *Prunella modularis*: how good are male chick-feeding rules? *Animal Behaviour*, **43**, 729–745.

Fisher, R. A. (1930). *The Genetical Theory of Natural Selection*. Clarendon Press, Oxford, UK.

Gardes, M., White, T. J., Fortin, J. A., Bruns, T. D. & Taylor, J. W. (1991). Identification of indigenous and introduced symbiotic fungi in ectomycorrhizae by amplification of nuclear and mitochondrial ribosomal DNA. *Canadian Journal of Botany*, **69**, 180–190.

Gibbs, H. L., Weatherhead, P. J., Boag, P. T., White, B. N., Tabak, L. M. & Hoysak, D. J. (1990). Realized reproductive success of polygynous red-winged blackbirds revealed by DNA markers. *Science*, **250**, 1394–1397.

Gilbert, D. A., Lehman, N., O'Brien, S. J. & Wayne, R. K. (1990). Genetic fingerprinting reflects population differentiation in the California Channel Island fox. *Nature*, **344**, 764–767.

Giovannoni, S. J., Britschgi, T. B., Moyer, C. L. & Field, K. G. (1990). Genetic diversity in Sargasso Sea bacterioplankton. *Nature*, **345**, 60–63.

Goff, L. J. & Coleman, A. W. (1988). The use of plastid DNA restriction endonuclease patterns in delineating red algal species and populations. *Journal of Phycology*, **24**, 357–368.

Goff, W., Barbet, A., Stiller, D., Palmer, G., Knowles, D., Kocan, K., Gorham, J. & McGuire, T. (1988). Detection of *Anaplasma marginale*-infected tick vectors by using a cloned DNA probe. *Proceedings of the National Academy of Sciences, USA*, **85**, 919–923.

Gowaty, P. A. & Droge, D. L. (1991). Sex ratio conflict and the evolution of sex-biased provisioning in birds. *Acta XX Congressus Internationalis Ornithologici*, **II**, 932–945.

Greer, C. E., Lund, J. K. & Manos, M. M. (1991). PCR amplification of paraffin-embedded tissues: recommendations on fixatives for long term storage and prospective studies. *PCR Methods and Applications*, **1**, 46–50.

Griffiths, R. (1991). The isolation of conserved DNA sequences related to the human sex-determining region Y gene from the lesser black-backed gull (*Larus fuscus*). *Proceedings of the Royal Society of London*, B, **244**, 123–128.

Griffiths, R. & Holland, P. (1990). A novel avian W chromosome DNA repeat sequence in the lesser black-backed gull (*Larus fuscus*). *Chromosoma*, **99**, 243–250.

Gubbay, J., Collignon, J., Koopman, P., Capel, B., Economou, A., Munsterberg, A., Vivian, N., Goodfellow, P. & Lovell-Badge, R. (1990). A gene mapping to the sex-determining regions of the mouse Y chromosome is a member of a novel family of embryonically expressed genes. *Nature*, **346**, 245–250.

Hadrys, H., Ballick, M. & Schierwater, B. (1992). Applications of random amplified polymorphic DNA in molecular ecology. *Molecular Ecology*, **1**, 55–63.

Hagelberg, E., Sykes, B. & Hedges, R. (1989). Ancient bone DNA amplified. *Nature*, **342**, 485.

Hanotte, O., Burke, T., Armour, J. A. L. & Jeffreys, A. J. (1991a). Hypervariable minisatellite DNA sequences in the Indian peafowl *Pavo cristatus*. *Genomics*, **9**, 587–597.

Hanotte, O., Burke, T., Armour, J. A. L. & Jeffreys, A. J. (1991b). Cloning, characterization and evolution of Indian peafowl *Pavo cristatus* minisatellite loci. *DNA Fingerprinting: Approaches and Applications* (Ed. by T. Burke, G. Dolf, A. J. Jeffreys & R. Wolff), pp. 193–216. Birkhäuser, Basel, Switzerland.

Hanotte, O., Cairns, E., Robson, T., Double, M. & Burke, T. (1992). Cross-species hybridization of a single locus minisatellite probe in passerine birds. *Molecular Ecology*, **1**, 127–130.

Harnett, W., Chambers, A. E., Renz, A. & Parkhouse, R. M. E. (1989). An oligonucleotide specific for *Onchocerca volvulus*. *Molecular and Biochemical Parasitology*, **28**, 77–84.

Harrison, R. G. (1989). Animal mitochondrial DNA as a genetic marker in population and evolutionary biology. *Trends in Ecology and Evolution*, **4**, 6–11.

Hayashi, K. (1991). PCR-SSCP: A simple and sensitive method for detection of mutations in the genomic DNA. *PCR Methods and Applications*, **1**, 34–38.

Helm-Bychowski, K. M. & Wilson, A. C. (1986). Rates of nuclear DNA evolution in pheasant-like birds: evidence from restriction maps. *Proceedings of the National Academy of Sciences, USA*, **83**, 688–692.

Hewitt, G. M., Johnston, A. W. B. & Young, J. P. W. (Eds) (1991). *Molecular Techniques in Taxonomy*. Springer Verlag, Berlin, Germany.

Higuchi, R., von Beroldingen, C. H., Sensabaugh, G. F. & Erlich, H. A. (1988). DNA typing from single hairs. *Nature*, **332**, 543–546.

Hillis, D. M. & Dixon, M. T. (1991). Ribosomal DNA: molecular evolution and phylogenetic inference. *Quarterly Review of Biology*, **66**, 411–453.

Hillis, D. M. & Moritz, C. (Eds) (1990). *Molecular Systematics*. Sinauer, Sunderland, MA, USA.

Hoelzel, A. R. (Ed.) (1992). *Molecular Genetic Analysis of Populations: A Practical Approach*. IRL Press, Oxford, UK.

Innis, M. A., Gelfand, D. H., Sninsky, J. J. & White, T. J. (Eds) (1990). *PCR Protocols: A Guide to Methods and Applications*. Academic Press, New York, NY, USA.

Ito K. (1992). Nearly complete loss of nucleic acids by commercially available highly purified ethanol. *Biotechniques* **12**, 69–70.

Jeffreys, A. J., Wilson, V. & Thein, S. L. (1985a). Hypervariable 'minisatellite' regions in human DNA. *Nature*, **314**, 67–73.

Jeffreys, A. J., Wilson, V. & Thein, S. L. (1985b). Individual-specific 'fingerprints' of human DNA. *Nature*, **316**, 76–79.

Jones, C. S., Lessells, C. M. & Krebs, J. R. (1991). Helpers-at-the-nest in European bee-eaters (*Merops apiaster*): a genetic analysis. *DNA Fingerprinting: Approaches and Applications* (Ed. by T. Burke, G. Dolf, A. J. Jeffreys & R. Wolff), pp. 169–192. Birkhäuser, Basel, Switzerland.

Kocher, T. D., Thomas, W. K., Meyer, A., Edwards, S. V., Pääbo, S., Villablanca, F. X. & Wilson, A. C. (1989). Dynamics of mitochondrial evolution in animals: amplification and sequencing with conserved primers. *Proceedings of the National Academy of Sciences, USA*, **86**, 6196–6200.

Kreitman, M. (1983). Nucleotide polymorphism at the alcohol dehydrogenase locus of *Drosophila melanogaster*. *Nature*, **304**, 412–417.

Kreitman, M. (1991). Variation at the DNA level: something for everyone. *Molecular Techniques in Taxonomy* (Ed. by G. M. Hewitt, A. W. B. Johnston & J. P. W. Young), pp. 15–32. Springer Verlag, Berlin, Germany.

Kukla, B. A., Majiwa, P. A. O., Young, J. R., Moloo, S. K. & ole-Moiyoi, O. (1987). Uses of species-specific DNA probes for detection and identification of trypanosome infection in tsetse flies. *Parasitology*, **95**, 1–16.

Laerm, J., Avise, J. C., Patton, J. C. & Lansman, R. A. (1982). Genetic determination of the status of an endangered species of pocket gopher in Georgia. *Journal of Wildlife Management*, **46**, 513–518.

Learn, Jr. G. H. & Schaal, B. A. (1987). Population subdivision for ribosomal repeat variants in *Clematis fremontii*. *Evolution*, **41**, 433–438.

Lee, J. S. (1991). Alternative dideoxy sequencing of double-stranded DNA by cyclic reactions using Taq polymerase. *DNA and Cell Biology*, **10**, 67–73.

Lessa, E. P. (1992). Analysis of DNA sequence variation at the population level by PCR and denaturing gradient gel electrophoresis. *Methods in Enzymology* (in press).

Lucchini, G. M. & Altwegg, M. (1992). Ribosomal-RNA gene restriction patterns as taxonomic tools for the genus *Aeromonas*. *International Journal of Systematic Bacteriology*, **42**, 384–389.

McDonald, B. A. & Martinez, J. P. (1990). DNA restriction fragment length polymorphisms among *Mycosphaerella graminicola* isolates collected from a single wheat field. *Phytopathology*, **80**, 1368–1373.

Moritz, C., Dowling, T. E. & Brown, W. M. (1987). Evolution of animal mitochondrial DNA: relevance for population biology and systematics. *Annual Review of Ecology and Systematics*, **18**, 269–292.

Mullis, K. B. & Faloona, F. A. (1987). Specific synthesis of DNA in vitro via a polymerase catalysed chain reaction. *Methods in Enzymology*, **55**, 335–350.

Myers, R. M., Sheffield, V. C. & Cox, D. R. (1989). Mutation detection by PCR, GC-clamps and denaturing gradient gel electrophoresis. *PCR Technology: Principles and Applications for DNA Amplification* (Ed. by H. A. Erlich), pp. 71–88. Stockton Press, New York, NY, USA.

Nybom, H. & Schaal, B. A. (1990). DNA 'fingerprints' reveal genotypic distributions in natural populations of blackberries and raspberries (*Rubus*, Rosaceae) *American Journal of Botany*, **77**, 883–888.

O'Brien, S. J. & Mayr, E. (1991). Bureaucratic mischief: recognizing endangered species and subspecies. *Science*, **251**, 1187–1188.

Olson, R. R., Runstadler, J. A. & Kocher, T. D. (1991). Whose larvae? *Nature*, **351**, 357–358.

Packer, C., Gilbert, D. A., Pusey, A. E. & O'Brien, S. J. (1991). A molecular genetic analysis of kinship and cooperation in African lions. *Nature*, **352**, 562–565.

Page, R. D. M. (1990). Temporal congruence and cladistic analysis of biogeography and cospeciation. *Systematic Zoology*, **39**, 205–226.

Palmer, J. D. (1987). Chloroplast DNA evolution and biosystematic uses of chloroplast DNA variation. *American Naturalist*, **140**, S6–S29.

Pamilo, P. & Nei, M. (1988). Relationships between gene trees and species trees. *Molecular Biology and Evolution*, **5**, 568–583.

Parker, J. S., Birkhead, T. R., Joshua, S. K., Taylor, S. & Clark, M. S. (1991). Sex ratio in a population of guillemots *Uria aalge* determined by chromosome analysis. *Ibis*, **133**, 423–424.

Persing, D. H., Telford, III S. R., Rys, P. N., Dodge, D. E., White, T. J., Malawista, S. E. & Spielman, A. (1990). Detection of *Borrelia burgdorferi* DNA in museum specimens of *Ixodes dammini* ticks. *Science*, **249**, 1420–1423.

Quinn, T. W. & White, B. N. (1987). Identification of restriction-fragment length polymorphisms in genomic DNA of the lesser snow goose (*Anser caerulescens*). *Molecular Biology and Evolution*, **4**, 126–143.

Quinn, T. W., Cooke, F. & White, B. N. (1990). Molecular sexing of geese using a cloned Z chromosomal sequence with homology to the W chromosome. *Auk*, **107**, 199–202.

Quinn, T. W., Quinn, J. S., Cooke, F. & White, B. N. (1987). DNA marker analysis detects multiple maternity and paternity in single broods of the lesser snow goose (*Anser caerulescens*). *Nature*, **326**, 392–394.

Rabenold, P. P., Piper, W. H., Decker, M. D. & Minchella, D. J. (1991). Polymorphic minisatellite amplified on avian W chromosome. *Genome*, **34**, 489–493.

Rabenold, P. P., Rabenold, K. N., Piper, W. H., Haydock, J. & Zack, S. W. (1990). Shared paternity revealed by genetic analysis in cooperatively breeding tropical wrens. *Nature*, **348**, 538–540.

Rassmann, K., Schlötterer, C. & Tautz, D. (1991). Isolation of simple sequence loci for use in polymerase chain reaction-based DNA fingerprinting. *Electrophoresis*, **12**, 113–118.

Raymond, M., Callaghan, A., Fort, P. & Pasteur, N. (1991). Worldwide migration of amplified insecticide resistance genes in mosquitoes. *Nature*, **350**, 151–153.

Richman, A. D. & Price, T. (1992). Evolution of ecological differences in the Old World leaf warblers: roles of history and adaptation. *Nature*, **355**, 817–821.

Riesner, D., Steger, R., Zimmat, R., Owens, R. A., Wagenhofer, M., Hillen, W., Vollbach, S. & Henco, K. (1989). Temperature-gradient gel electrophoresis of nucleic acids: Analysis of conformational transitions, sequence variations and protein-nucleic acid interactions. *Electrophoresis*, **10**, 377–389.

Rogstad, S. H. Surveying plant genomes for VNTR loci. *Molecular Evolution: Producing the Biochemical Data* (Ed. by E. A. Zimmer, T. J. White, R. L. Cann, & A. C. Wilson). Academic Press, San Diego, CA, USA (in press).

Rosa, P. A., Hogan, D. & Schwan, T. G. (1991). Polymerase chain reaction analyses identify two distinct classes of *Borrelia burgdorferi*. *Journal of Clinical Microbiology*, **29**, 524–532.

Rowan, R. & Powers, D. (1991). A molecular genetic classification of zooxanthellae and the evolution of animal algal symbioses. *Science*, **251**, 1348–1351.

Saiki, R. K., Gelfand, D. H., Stoffel, S., Scharf, S. J., Higuchi, R., Horn, G. T., Mullis, K. B. & Erlich, H. A. (1988). Primer-directed enzymatic amplification of DNA with a thermostable DNA polymerase. *Science*, **239**, 487–491.

Schäfer, R., Zischler, H., Birsner, U., Becker, A. & Epplen, J. T. (1988). Optimized oligonucleotide probes for DNA fingerprinting. *Electrophoresis*, **9**, 369–374.

Schlötterer, C., Amos, B. & Tautz, D. (1991). Conservation of polymorphic simple sequence data in cetacean species. *Nature*, **354**, 63–65.

Seutin, G., White, B. N. & Boag, P. T. (1990). Preservation of avian blood and tissues for DNA analyses. *Canadian Journal of Zoology*, **69**, 82–90.

Sibley, C. J. & Ahlquist, J. E. (1990). *Phylogeny and Classification of Birds: A Study in Molecular Evolution*. Yale University Press, New Haven, CT, USA.

Sinclair, A. H., Berta, P., Palmer, M. S., Hawkins, J. R., Griffiths, B., Smith, M. J., Foster, J. W., Frischauf, A. M., Lovell-Badge, R., Goodfellow, P. N. (1990). A gene from the human sex-determining regions encodes a protein with homology to a conserved DNA-binding motif. *Nature*, **346**, 240–244.

Smith, L. J., Braylan, R. C., Nutkis, J. E., Edmundsen, K. B., Downing, J. R. & Wakeland, E. K. (1987). Extraction of cellular DNA from human cells and tissues fixed in ethanol. *Analytical Biochemistry*, **160**, 135–138.

Soltis, P. S., Soltis, D. E. & Doyle, J. J. (1992). *Plant Molecular Systematics*. Chapman & Hall, London, UK.

Taberlet, P. & Bouvet, J. (1991). A single plucked feather as a source of DNA for bird genetic studies. *Auk*, **108**, 959–960.

Taberlet, P., Gielly, L., Pautou, G. & Bouvet, J. (1991). Universal primers for amplification of three non-coding regions of chloroplast DNA. *Plant Molecular Biology*, **17**, 1105–1109.

Taggart, J. B. & Ferguson, A. (1990). Minisatellite DNA fingerprints of salmonid fishes. *Animal Genetics*, **21**, 377–389.

Tautz, D. (1989). Hypervariability of simple sequences as a general source for polymorphic DNA markers. *Nucleic Acids Research*, **17**, 6463–6471.

Templeton, A. R. (1992). Human origins and analysis of mitochondrial DNA sequences. *Science*, **255**, 737.

Thomas, R. H. & Hunt, J. A. (1991). The molecular evolution of the alcohol dehydrogenase locus and the phylogeny of Hawaiian *Drosophila*. *Molecular Biology and Evolution*, **8**, 687–702.

Thomas, R. H., Schaffner, W., Wilson, A. C. & Pääbo, S. V. (1989). DNA phylogeny of the extinct marsupial wolf. *Nature*, **340**, 465–467.

Thomas, W. K., Pääbo, S., Villablanca, F. X. & Wilson, A. C. (1990). Spatial and temporal continuity of kangaroo rat populations shown by sequencing mitochondrial DNA from museum specimens. *Journal of Molecular Evolution*, **31**, 101–112.

Trivers, R. L. & Willard, D. E. (1973). Natural selection of parental ability to vary the sex ratio of offspring. *Science*, **179**, 90–92.

Turner, B. J., Elder, J. F. Jr, Laughlin, T. F. & Davis, W. P. (1990). Genetic variation in clonal vertebrates detected by simple-sequence DNA fingerprinting. *Proceedings of the National Academy of Sciences, USA*, **87**, 5653–5657.

Vigilant, L., Stoneking, M., Harpending, H., Hawkes, K. & Wilson, A. C. (1991). African populations and the evolution of human mitochondrial DNA. *Science*, **253**, 1503–1507.

Ward, D. M., Weller, R. & Bateson, M. M. (1990). 16S rRNA sequences reveal numerous uncultured microorganism in a natural community. *Nature*, **345**, 63–65.

Wayne, R. K. & Jenks, S. M. (1991). Mitochondrial DNA analysis implying extensive hybridization of the endangered red wolf *Canis rufus*. *Nature*, **351**, 565–568.

Welsh, J., Pretzman, C., Postic, D., Saint Girons, I., Baranton, G. & McClelland, M. (1992). Genomic fingerprinting by arbitrarily primed polymerase chain reaction resolves *Borrelia burgdorferi* into three distinct phylogenetic groups. *International Journal of Systematic Bacteriology*, **42**, 370–377.

Whittemore, A. T. & Schaal, B. A. (1991). Interspecific gene flow in sympatric oaks. *Proceedings of the National Academy of Sciences, USA*, **88**, 2540–2544.

Williams, J. G. K., Kubelik, A. R., Livak, K. J., Rafalski, J. A. & Tingey, S. V. (1990).

DNA polymorphisms amplified by arbitrary primers are useful as genetic markers. *Nucleic Acids Research*, **18**, 6531–6535.

Williams, S. M. & Strobeck, C. (1986). Measuring the multiple insemination frequency of *Drosophila* in nature: use of a Y-linked molecular marker. *Evolution*, **40**, 440–442.

Winship, P. R. (1989). An improved method for directly sequencing PCR amplified material using dimethyl sulphoxide. *Nucleic Acids Research*, **17**, 1266.

Woese, C. (1987). Bacterial evolution. *Microbiological Reviews*, **51**, 221–271.

Wong, Z., Wilson, V., Patel, I., Povey, S., Jeffreys, A. J. (1987). Characterization of highly variable minisatellites cloned from human DNA. *Annals of Human Genetics*, **51**, 269–288.

10. ECOLOGICAL GENETICS OF PARASITISM

RICHARD ENNOS
Institute of Ecology and Resource Management, University of Edinburgh, Darwin Building, Mayfield Road, Edinburgh EH9 3JU, UK

INTRODUCTION

Ecological studies of parasitism are concerned with developing an understanding of the dynamic behaviour of parasite populations and the impact they have on their hosts. They deal with processes which occur over a relatively short time scale, of the order of a few host generations, and are therefore distinct from, but related to, evolutionary studies of parasitism. Another important aspect of ecological, as opposed to evolutionary, studies is that they incorporate spatial aspects of the interactions between parasites and their hosts. The aim of this chapter is to illustrate the contribution which genetic approaches can make to our understanding of the ecology of parasitism.

Research in parasite ecology has three main strands. The first is essentially descriptive, providing an accurate picture of the way in which parasites and hosts interact at the population level. The second is analytical and seeks to identify the various factors which influence the outcome of parasite–host interactions. The final, and perhaps most neglected line of research is that concerned with synthesizing the information from descriptive and analytical investigations so as to produce models capable of predicting the joint dynamics of parasite and host populations.

In this contribution I focus on the progress that has been made in descriptive and analytical studies of parasite ecology. The first section outlines the role which genetic studies can play in refining our description of the ecological interactions between parasite and host populations. The second section analyses the various forms of genetic variation which could influence the joint behaviour of parasite and host populations, and assesses the extent of such variation within and among natural and managed pathosystems. The synthesis of these ideas to produce models of parasite–host population behaviour that are both ecologically and genetically realistic remains a major challenge for the future.

GENETIC CONTRIBUTIONS TO DESCRIPTIVE ECOLOGY

Parasite taxonomy

Accurate description of parasite ecology is founded on a thorough understanding of the taxonomy of the groups involved. Problems can arise with the classification of parasites which express few reliable morphological characters for delineation of taxa. The situation is particularly acute in such groups as the protozoa where convergent evolution tends to minimize morphological differentiation among species with quite distinct ecological attributes, and in the parasitic fungi where high levels of phenotypic plasticity have evolved (Tait 1990).

The taxonomic solution to these problems has often been to create taxa with wide limits. From the ecological point of view such classification schemes often prove inadequate. Within broad taxa there may be a number of biological species possessing quite distinct ecological characteristics which may influence both their transmission behaviour and their impact on hosts. In these situations, genetic analysis in conjunction with ecological studies can be useful for drawing up appropriate classification schemes.

Work on the taxonomy of the root-infecting fungal pathogen *Armillaria* illustrates this point. *Armillaria mellea sensu lato* includes a wide range of forms with a broad range of pathogenic potential. Genetic studies of mating behaviour reveal that it comprises a number of reproductively isolated biological species (Korhonen 1978). Ecological investigations show that each biological species possesses distinct attributes. For instance, *A. mellea sensu stricto* is a primary pathogen of broadleaved trees, *A. ostoyae* a primary pathogen of conifers, and *A. bulbosa* is largely saprotrophic and can only invade weakened trees (Rishbeth 1982). As a result of the clarification of the taxonomy of this group by complementary genetic and ecological analysis, previously puzzling aspects of parasite behaviour can be reconciled. A similar combination of genetic and ecological approaches has been used to draw up ecologically appropriate classification schemes in a range of other pathogenic fungi (Brasier & Gibbs 1976, Brasier 1990, Chase & Ullrich 1990).

Although the most direct way to identify a biological species is by showing reproductive isolation among groups, this is not technically feasible in the majority of parasite taxa. Under these circumstances indirect genetic methods must be employed. These are based on the premise that genetic identity among individuals will be high within biological species sharing in the same gene pool, whereas significant genetic divergence will be found among biological species. A choice of genetic techniques is available for measuring genetic relationships among groups. The most sophisticated involves the DNA sequencing of loci present in all groups. The degree of genetic identity is then determined from the sequence similarity between groups. Genes coding for ribosomal subunits, particularly the 5S ribosomal RNA gene, have been widely used in this work and to clarify taxonomic relationships in such diverse parasite groups as the protozoa, the helminths and the fungi (Walker & Doolittle 1982, Förster *et al.* 1990, Tait 1990). This technique has the disadvantage that it provides information on only a small fraction of the total genome. Rates of divergence within the gene sequenced may not be representative of overall levels of genetic divergence among the groups. An additional drawback is that few individuals can be sampled because DNA sequencing remains a relatively time-consuming procedure.

An alternative to DNA sequencing for indirect identification of biological species is to analyse DNA restriction site variation within taxa, restriction fragment length polymorphism (RFLP). The technique is sufficiently simple that large numbers of individuals can be studied. Provided that appropriate gene probes are available, RFLP variation can be assessed at a range of loci within both the mitochondrial and nuclear genomes. This form of analysis has revealed genetic markers which can be used to distinguish species and subspecies within the human parasite genera *Leishmania* and *Trypanosoma* (Paindavoine *et al.* 1986, Beverley *et al.* 1987) and the plant parasite genera *Armillaria*, *Phytophthora*, *Rhizoctonia* and *Fusarium* (Förster *et al.* 1988, Smith & Anderson 1989, Manicom *et al.* 1990, Vilgalys & Gonzalez 1990).

A third important genetic technique for assessing taxonomic relationships among parasitic groups makes use of naturally occurring variation at loci coding for soluble enzymes (isozyme variation). Allele frequencies at large numbers of loci (20 or 30) can be scored relatively cheaply, and these data can be used to calculate genetic identity among groups (Nei 1973). The power of this technique, when used in conjunction with ecological studies, to clarify taxonomic relationships is exemplified by work on the fungal parasite *Atkinsonella hypoxylon*. This taxon is found on the grass genera *Danthonia* and *Stipa*. Analysis of isozyme variation among isolates from each host genus indicated substantial genetic differentiation between the groups, suggesting that isolates from the two host genera were likely to belong to different species (Leuchtmann & Clay 1990a). This conclusion was supported by artificial inoculation studies indicating complete host specificity of isolates from the two host genera (Leuchtmann & Clay 1990b).

Population biology of parasites

Establishing the identity of interacting species involved in parasite–host systems is a first step in understanding their behaviour. The next objective must be to describe as fully as possible the population biology of the organisms involved. Many aspects of parasite population biology have proved difficult to establish from simple field observations. However, insights into a number of important questions can be gained from analysis of the distribution of genetic marker variation (e.g. RFLP, isozyme variation) within and among populations. Questions which can be addressed include the origin of parasite populations, their mode of reproduction, patterns of distribution of parasite genotypes and the extent of parasite dispersal. Basic data of these kinds must be to hand when models describing parasite and host dynamics are being developed.

To derive maximum benefit from information on the population genetic structure of parasites, carefully planned hierarchical sampling schemes are desirable. These allow for analysis of the distribution of genetic variation at various levels (within family, within host, within population etc.). From quantitative measures of genetic population structure valuable inferences about parasite populations can be drawn. Further useful information can be derived from knowledge of the multilocus structure of populations so, wherever possible, data on genetic variation at a number of different loci should be obtained.

Genetic diversity

The primary data available from surveys of RFLP or isozyme genetic markers are estimates of total genetic diversity within populations. This can be measured quantitatively in terms of gene diversity (Nei 1973). RFLP and isozyme analyses detect different fractions of the genetic variation present at the DNA sequence level. Values of gene diversity obtained by either method are therefore only relative measures of total genetic variation present. However, valid comparisons of the amount of genetic variation within populations can be made if data have been collected by scoring the same type of genetic markers.

Before the publication of data on gene diversity in parasites the accepted wisdom was that they lived in small isolated populations vulnerable to loss of genetic variation through genetic drift (Price 1980). However, the results gathered over the last 10 years show that levels of (selectively neutral) genetic marker variation are often as high in parasitic species as in their free-living relatives (Thompson & Lymbery 1990, Ennos & Swales 1991a). The genetically effective population size of many parasite populations is large, and their evolutionary potential is unlikely to be restricted by lack of genetic variation.

There are certain situations, however, where levels of parasite gene diversity have turned out to be very low. Reductions in genetic diversity are expected to occur where populations have passed through a bottleneck, perhaps because they have been founded from a very small number of genotypes. The discovery of very low levels of gene diversity in Australian populations of the fungal pathogen *Phytophthora cinnamomi* suggests that it has only recently been introduced to the continent on a very limited number of occasions and has the status of an exotic pathogen (Old *et al.* 1984). This would account for the severity of the ecological damage caused by this pathogen in the Jarrah forests of Western Australia (Weste & Marks 1987).

Another set of parasite populations which often show strikingly low levels of gene diversity are those on cultivated hosts (Newton *et al.* 1985, Leung & Williams 1986). In the rice blast fungus a direct comparison of isolates on wild hosts and on cultivated rice illustrate that there has been a dramatic reduction in diversity associated with transfer to the crop population (Leung & Williams 1986). These findings suggest that the parasite populations on crops have been derived from a small sample of available genotypes, or that the populations are periodically subject to severe bottlenecks.

Reproduction

The mode of parasite reproduction plays a key role in determining the distribution of variation within and among individuals and has a major influence on the dynamics of genetic changes which may occur as a result of interaction with the host population. Where rates of outcrossing are high, genetic change at loci concerned with parasite virulence, for instance, can occur independently of changes at other genetic loci. Where sexual outcrossing is absent, changes in virulence will be coupled to changes at other loci throughout the genome.

The most direct method for obtaining a detailed description of the mating system of parasites is to analyse genetic marker variation in parents and the progeny which they produce in the field (Ennos & Swales 1987). Where such methods are not technically possible, indirect approaches based on analysis of single and multilocus genotype distributions at marker genes can be employed. For instance in diploid populations deviations from Hardy–Weinberg genotype frequencies provide information on the extent of non-random mating and/or asexual reproduction. The degree of non-random association between alleles at different marker loci (linkage disequilibrium) in both diploid and haploid parasites provides further clues as to the extent of sexual and asexual reproduction in the life cycle.

Within the parasitic protozoa these type of studies reveal that sexual outcrossing occurs within *Plasmodium falciparum* and *Trypanosoma brucei* (Tait 1990, Conway & McBride 1991). Populations of *T. cruzi* on the other hand consist of a mixture of asexually reproducing clones among which very little gene exchange takes place (Tibayrenc & Ayala 1988). In some parasites the predominant mode of reproduction may vary among populations. A study of the population genetic structure of the rust *Puccinia graminis* shows that in regions where the secondary host, barberry, is present, sexual reproduction and random association of alleles at different loci are found. On the great plains, however, from which barberry has been eliminated, asexual reproduction predominates with strong association between genetic markers (Burdon & Roelfs 1985). Similar difference in reproductive behaviour can be shown among populations of the potato blight fungus from different geographic areas (Tooley *et al.* 1985). Such major reproductive differences can have a very profound influence on the epidemiological behaviour of parasite populations (McDonald *et al.* 1989).

Spatial distribution

To understand the population ecology of parasites it is often important to establish the distribution of parasites within and among hosts. Genetic markers are an invaluable tool for such work. By using surface protein antigen markers, Conway *et al.* (1991) have shown that some 55% of malarial patients in their study population are infected with more than one genotype of *Plasmodium falciparum*. In a fungal pathogen, *Crumenulopsis sororia*, isozyme analysis has demonstrated that at least five different genotypes may occupy a single branch lesion (Ennos & Swales 1987). A contrasting situation is shown by the root-infecting forest pathogen *Heterobasidion annosum* where genetic analysis reveals the presence of single genotypes spreading over a distance of 30 m infecting up to 13 mature trees (Stenlid 1985).

Transmission and dispersal

As we shall see later, the dynamic behaviour of parasite populations and the degree to which local adaptation takes place is critically affected by the dispersal characteristics of the species. Dispersal parameters are technically difficult to measure directly, though there would appear to be scope for using genetically marked individuals to measure parasite dispersal in much the same way that pollen movement has been monitored in plant populations (Schaal 1980).

In the absence of direct measurements of parasite dispersal, analyses of the distribution of genetic variation within and among appropriate levels (demes within hosts, subpopulations, geographically isolated populations) can provide useful qualitative information. This method of indirect analysis is based on the fact that divergence at selectively neutral marker loci will only occur among groups if there is restricted gene flow among them.

Evidence from parasitic helminth populations suggests that isozyme variation is distributed predominantly within, rather than among populations occupying the same geographic area (Thompson & Lymbery 1990). Substantial differentiation implying restricted gene flow has only been detected between well-isolated island populations (Agatsuma & Habe 1986). Analogous studies of parasitic fungal species with airborne spores indicate very low levels of genetic differentiation among populations separated by hundreds of kilometres (Leuchtmann & Clay 1990a, Ennos & Swales 1991a). Comparable studies of the splash-dispersed fungal parasite *Rhyncosporium secalis* on the other hand indicate that significant genetic differentiation at selectively neutral marker loci is present among subplots within single fields, suggesting restricted dispersal of spores within the field (McDonald *et al.* 1989).

Apart from providing indications of the extent of passive parasite dispersal, analysis of population genetic structure can be used to elucidate patterns of transmission by vectors from reservoirs of infection. A good illustration of this application comes from studies of epidemics of sleeping sickness in Kenya caused by the protozoon parasite *Trypanosoma brucei*. Populations of this parasite from wildlife and from domestic cattle in the Lambwe Valley are distinguishable on the basis of isozyme phenotype. Changes in the virulence of the disease through the 1970s and 1980s can be traced to changes in the pattern of transmission over this period. During the 1970s human infections were shown, on the basis of isozyme phenotype, to have been derived by transmission from the wildlife reservoir. In the 1980s new parasite genotypes with higher virulence were transmitted from domestic cattle (Mihok *et al.* 1990). Such major changes in transmission characteristics of parasites can have major impacts on the epidemiology of disease, and the knowledge gained from genetic analysis may be useful in the design of effective disease control programmes.

GENETIC EFFECTS ON PARASITE–HOST DYNAMICS

The discussion so far has concentrated on the role of genetics in expanding our knowledge of the descriptive aspects of parasite ecology. We now wish to turn our attention to the analysis of population dynamics in parasite–host systems. Our objective is to establish the impact which genetic variation either within populations or between populations of parasites and hosts could have on their joint dynamic behaviour. The first step in dealing with this topic must be to identify the types of genetic variation which may influence parasite–host population dynamics.

For simplicity and generality we will consider a system in which a single parasite species infects a single host species. No assumptions are made as to the exact nature of interaction between parasite and host (e.g. presence/absence of immune system, fixed infection period, etc.). The parasite establishes infection at some host infection sites, grows and reproduces on the host, and parasite propagules are dispersed to new host infection sites. These may be present on the same host or on different hosts within the same population. The host suffers some loss of reproductive potential as a consequence of parasite infection.

In this highly simplified and generalized system we anticipate that parasite–host dynamics will be influenced by two parameters whose values are affected by the interaction between parasite and host. The first of these is the parasite transmission parameter (Fig. 10.1a). Consider a single parasite propagule that has been dispersed to a host infection site. The parasite transmission parameter is defined as the expected number of parasite propagules derived from this parent propagule which are successfully dispersed to fresh infection sites. The parasite transmission parameter is thus a measure of the absolute fitness of the parasite which acknowledges that to complete a full generation a parasite must not only produce propagules but must also successfully transmit them to new host infection sites.

The second parameter that we expect to affect parasite–host population dynamics is the host impact parameter, which quantifies the reduction in host reproduction attributable to parasites (Fig. 10.1b). It can be defined more formally as the expected reduction in the number of offspring contributed by a host to the next generation due to the presence of a certain density of parasite propagules in the community. Note that the two parameters are related to, but are much more generalized than, the parasite transmission rate β and parasite induced death rate α used by Anderson and May (1979) and May and Anderson (1979) in their much

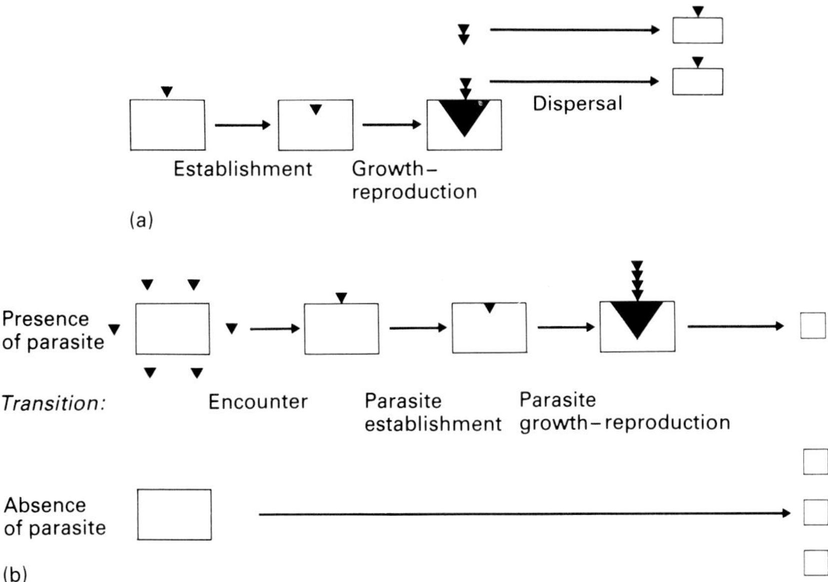

FIG. 10.1. (a) Processes involved in successful parasite (▼) transmission between host (□) infection sites. (b) Reproduction of host (□) in presence and absence of parasite (▼) indicating processes that influence the extent of host fitness reduction.

more specific and explicit treatment of the dynamics of parasite–host systems.

In the following section we look in some detail at the various processes which ultimately determine the values of the parasite transmission and host impact parameters in real systems. We review the evidence for the existence of genetic variation affecting these parameters in both managed and natural populations. It is these forms of genetic variation that must be studied if we wish to understand the importance of genetic factors in determining the population dynamics of parasite–host systems.

Parasite transmission parameter

Successful transmission of parasites from one generation to the next involves three sequential steps: establishment of infection, development and reproduction on the host, and dispersal of propagules to new infection sites (Fig. 10.1a). What is the evidence that genetic variation within and among parasite–host systems can influence these components of parasite transmission?

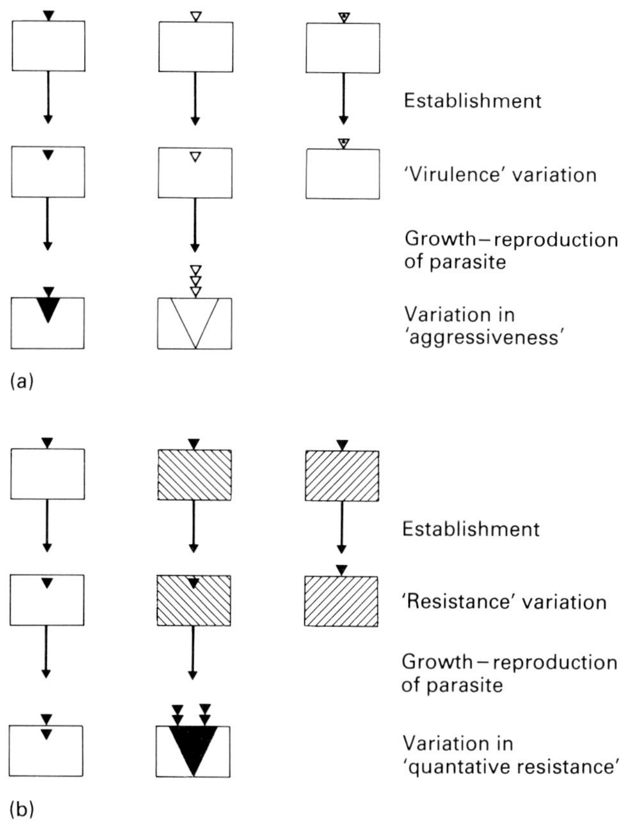

FIG. 10.2 (a) Innoculation of parasite genotypes (▼) on a single host genotype (□) to detect variation in 'virulence' and 'aggressiveness'. (b) Innoculation of single parasite genotype (▼) on host genotypes (□) to detect variation in 'resistance' and 'quantitative resistance'.

Parasite establishment

Genetic variation affecting parasite establishment can be detected by biological assays which take the form of artificial inoculation experiments. To reveal genetic variation in the parasite a sample of parasite genotypes from the relevant population is inoculated on to a standard set of host genotypes (Fig. 10.2a). Parasites that establish on the host are referred to as virulent on that particular host, whereas those that fail to establish are avirulent. Note that this is a qualitative distinction. To detect host genetic variation affecting establishment, a sample of host genotypes from the population is probed with a standard set of parasite genotypes (Fig. 10.2b). Where parasites establish the host is described as susceptible to that parasite genotype, and where establishment fails the host is described as resistant or immune. Once again the distinction is qualitative. Note that simple biological assays of this kind detect the presence of genetic variation in parasite and host but do not reveal its mode of inheritance.

Experimental procedures of this kind have been used to reveal virulence variation within parasite population and resistance variation within hosts. Although the work has concentrated on crop pathosystems (Day 1974, Burdon 1987 for reviews) these types of variability have also been found in systems with animal (Wassom *et al.* 1974, Wakelin 1978, 1985) and wild plant hosts (Wahl 1970, Dinoor 1977, Wahl *et al.* 1978, Kinloch 1982, Parker 1985, 1988, Harry & Clarke 1986, Burdon 1987, Crute 1990). The diversity of virulence and resistance phenotypes detected can often by very high. For instance in the groundsel–powdery mildew system, variation for 10 resistance factors was detected among 50 host lines tested, and 12 virulence phenotypes were found among a sample of 24 parasite lines (Clarke *et al.* 1990).

Where genetic analysis has been carried out, it has often been found that virulence and resistance variation can be accounted for by segregation at one, or a small number of genetic loci in the parasite and host respectively (Flor 1956, Day 1974, Barrett 1985 for reviews). Studies in wild pathosystems suggest that gene-for-gene systems, in which virulence alleles in the parasite are matched by resistance alleles in the host are not necessarily an artefact of crop breeding practices (Barrett 1985) but may be a general feature of parasite–host systems (Harry & Clarke 1987, Farrara *et al.* 1987, Parker 1988). A picture begins to emerge of parasite populations that are polymorphic for virulence alleles interacting with host populations that are polymorphic for complementary resistance alleles. How widespread and important is this variability likely to be in wild pathosystems?

One fact must be emphasized at this point. The identity of the standard host and parasite genotypes used in the bioassay for virulence and resistance dictate the variation detectable. The variation we should be measuring is that which affects the establishment of parasites in the community being studied. This can be referred to as the ecologically relevant variation. To detect this variation it is essential that the standard host and parasite genotypes used in the inoculation tests be derived from the same community. Variation detected using genotypes of host and parasite from other communities may be irrelevant (Dinoor & Eshed 1990). Recent work from wild pathosystems shows that if test genotypes from alien populations are used substantial virulence and resistance variation can be detected (Parker 1985, Dinoor & Eshed 1990). However, if test genotypes are restricted to those coming from the immediate locality, the degree of polymorphism detected for virulence and resistance may be rather low. Most pathogen genotypes are capable of establishing on most host genotypes (Parker 1985, Burdon *et al.* 1990, Clarke *et al.* 1990). These type of results highlight a common problem in ecological genetic studies whose importance has been overlooked. This is the problem of measuring phenotypic variation for ecologically relevant traits in environments other than those in which the genotypes naturally grow. Transfer of genotypes to novel environments (in this case novel biotic environments) can reveal phenotypic variation which would not be expressed if the plants were growing under natural conditions. We obtain an inflated estimate of the extent of genetic variation for ecologically relevant traits within the population (Mitchell-Olds 1986).

Another reason for suspecting that the importance of gene-for-gene systems may have been over-emphasized comes from a consideration of the biological basis for such interactions. In animals with immune systems, and in plants defending themselves against biotrophic parasites which operate by stealth, recognition of the parasite is a key process that is essential for the success of the defence reaction. It is relatively easy to imagine that simple changes at one or a few genetic loci in the parasite or host could render a parasite undetectable to the host, thus allowing establishment; or detectable, in which case the defence reaction would be triggered and the parasite would be eliminated. Single locus changes could therefore give qualitative differences in ability of parasites to establish (Keen 1982). There is a reasonable biological explanation for gene-for-gene interaction systems.

The situation is rather different for necrotrophic pathogens which advertise their presence to the host by the damage that they cause. Here the outcome of attempted infection will be determined by the ability of the parasite to tolerate the defence measures of the host. In this situation it is more difficult to imagine that genetic changes at single loci would lead to qualitative changes in parasite establishment, though quantitative changes in the probability of establishment could result. Thus gene-for-gene systems controlling virulence and resistance may not be so important in determining the outcome of necrotrophic parasite–host interactions. It is pertinent to note that studies on the genetics of parasite–host interactions have tended to concentrate on systems where gene-for-gene interactions are most likely to occur. A different picture of their importance might emerge if more studies of necrotrophic parasites were conducted (de Nooij & van Damme 1988a, 1988b).

A final point that needs to be made about the genetic control of parasite establishment is that although resistance/susceptibility may be clear-cut in controlled parasite inoculation trials, it may be much less so under field conditions. Even where gene-for-gene systems have been established, the environment may modify the expression of the resistance/susceptible reaction (Browder 1985). Hosts under stress may be unable to prevent parasite establishment, even though they possess the relevant genotype, because their defence reactions are compromised.

Parasite growth and reproduction

Following establishment, parasites must produce propagules for dispersal to ensure transmission to the next host infection site. Where parasites have overlapping generations, both the number of propagules produced and the timing of propagule production will influence the parasite transmission rate. Therefore if we wish to assess how genetic factors affect parasite transmission it is necessary to measure their influence on parasite life history (Antonovics & Alexander 1989).

Life-history attributes such as rate of growth, time to first reproduction, rate of reproduction in different age classes, etc., are quantitative characters whose values are determined by the genotype of the organism involved and the environment that it occupies. Parasites are special because they occupy an environment provided by their host. This environment, the host phenotype, is governed by the host genotype and the host environment. A parasite's life-history characteristics can therefore be influenced by its own genotype, the genotype of its host, and the environment of this host.

The importance of parasite genotype in determining its life-history characters can be found using the same artificial inoculation experiments that were described for investigating virulence variation (Fig. 10.2a). In this case, however, records must be kept of parasite growth and reproduction for those parasite genotypes which succeed in establishing on hosts. There is clear evidence from the plant pathology literature that parasite genotype can influence such life-history characters as growth rate, time to lesion production, lesion size, etc., when inoculations are made on single host cultivars (Caten 1974, Clifford & Clothier 1974, Hamid *et al.* 1982, Prakash & Heather 1986, Tooley *et al.* 1986). This has sometimes been referred to as variation in 'aggressiveness' among parasite genotypes. Similar techniques have been used to detect variation in life-history traits for the myxoma virus infecting rabbits (Fenner & Ratcliffe 1965). Where sexual crosses can be carried out, or where families of related isolates can be collected in parasite populations, biometrical genetic analysis can be used to estimate the genetic component of the variation in parasite life-history characters (Kolmer & Leonard 1986, Ennos & Swales

1991b). Despite the importance that this quantitative genetic variation affecting life-history traits is likely to have on the parasite transmission parameter, there have been few attempts to measure the levels or distribution of this variation in natural parasite populations. The work of de Nooij and van Damme (1988a) is a notable exception. They were able to show significant differences in rate of lesion development produced by isolates of the pathogen *Phomopsis subordinaria* collected from host plants growing only a few metres apart.

In the studies mentioned so far, life-history traits of parasites were measured *in vivo* on defined host genotypes. An alternative approach to measuring parasite variation affecting life history is to identify and measure *in vitro* parasite attributes which are likely to influence life history. Where possible the relationship between *in vitro* measurements and performance *in vivo* should be determined to confirm the ecological relevance of measurements made *in vitro*. Suitable parasite attributes which can be studied in plant parasites using such an approach are ability to tolerate and detoxify host defensive chemicals.

Substantial genetic variations for tolerance of host defensive monoterpene compounds has been found in two necrotrophic species of fungi that invade coniferous trees (Thibault-Balesdent & Delatour 1985, Ennos & Swales 1988). In the ascomycete *Crumenulopsis sororia* isolates from the same population may differ by as much as 50% in their monoterpene tolerance. Such large differences in response to host defensive compounds are likely to have significant effects on parasite life history. Extensive variation is also found within populations of the fungal parasite *Nectria haematococca* for ability to detoxify the host defensive compound pisatin. There is a good correlation between an isolate's ability to detoxify pisatin and its growth rate on peas (Van Etten *et al.* 1989). Further experiments of this type would give a clearer picture of how much quantitative genetic variation affecting parasite growth and reproduction is present within parasite populations.

As we have already argued, both host genotype and host environment will affect the life history characteristics of parasites. In agricultural pathosystems where host environment is relatively uniform, differences in host genotype may contribute significantly to variation in parasite life history. However in wild pathosystems, where environmentally induced host variability may be very large in comparison with genetically determined variation among hosts, host genotypes may have far less influence on parasite life history characteristics. It is no coincidence that crop pathologists concentrate their attention on the role of crop genotype in determining parasite growth and reproduction rates, whereas forest pathologists dealing with heterogeneous host environments emphasize the importance of environmentally induced host variation, particularly that associated with environmentally induced stress (Shoeneweiss 1975).

Recognition by crop pathologists that host genotype can influence the life-history characteristics of parasites has led to 'quantitative resistance' or 'field resistance' breeding programmes (Leonard & Mundt 1984, Parlevliet 1989). Here the objective is to select host genotypes on which parasite growth and reproductive rates following establishment are low. Artificial inoculation experiments such as those used to uncover qualitative resistance variation (i.e. ability/inability of parasites to establish) can also be used to study quantitative differences in the rate of parasite development and reproduction on those hosts which are susceptible (Fig. 10.2b). Host genetic variation with effects on parasite latent period, rate of lesion production, size of lesions and time course of propagule release have all been uncovered (Caten 1974, Clifford & Clothier 1974, Klittich & Bronson 1986, Prakash & Heather 1986, Parlevliet 1989). Genetic variation affecting parasite life history can also be demonstrated within populations of animal hosts. For instance artificial selection of laboratory mice for high and low levels of infection by the nematode *Nematospiroides dubius* resulted in labile and refractory lines which differed very significantly in their worm burdens (Brindley & Dobson 1981).

Fewer data are available on quantitative resistance in wild populations. However in their classic study of the myxoma virus–rabbit system, Fenner and Ratcliffe (1965) were able to show quantitative changes in the resistance of the rabbit population following exposure to the virus, implying that genetic variation affecting parasite development and reproduction had existed in the original rabbit population. Although many studies of genetic variation in natural plant pathosystems have been set up with the intention of looking at qualitative differences in host resistance to parasites, closer inspection of the results often reveals quantitative differences in parasite development on different susceptible host genotypes (Parker 1985, Clarke *et al.* 1990, Crute 1990). Artificial inoculation of a collection of *Plantago lanceolata* genotypes with a single isolate of the fungus *Phomopsis subordinaria* revealed a highly significant effect of host genotype on such pathogen life-history characters as lesion development rate and rate of progress of the pathogen through the host plant when measurements were made under controlled conditions (de Nooij & van Damme 1988b). However, the authors concluded that host genetic effects were only likely to account for a small fraction of the variation in pathogen behaviour seen under field conditions. Environmental variation was of overriding importance. Once again the problem of extrapolating from experiments conducted under environmental conditions which differ from those in the natural population becomes evident.

Before leaving this subject, one additional complication needs to be recognized. This is that in natural pathosystems parasites encounter a diversity of host phenotypes, the diversity being generated by both genetic and environmental variation. If we wish to understand the behaviour of parasites in terms of their growth and reproduction it will be necessary to measure how parasite genotypes perform not on one host phenotype but on the spectrum of host phenotypes likely to be encountered in the system. It is then possible to see whether parasites with high reproductive rates on one host phenotype maintain this on other host phenotypes. Alternatively there could be 'trade-offs' in performance on different host phenotypes. Analysis of genetic correlation for life-history characteristics across host phenotypes can usefully summarize information in this area (Via 1984). Very few data on the genetic correlations in performance of parasite genotypes over a range of host phenotypes have yet been collected (Ennos & Swales 1991b).

Parasite dispersal

Completion of the parasite transmission process requires effective dispersal between infection sites (Fig. 10.1a). The efficiency of this process will be dependent upon such characteristics as the timing of propagule production, the longevity of propagules, the dispersal range of propagules and the degree of selective transmission to appropriate infection sites. Genetic variation having significant effects on any of these attributes could alter the value of the parasite transmission parameter, with consequences for parasite–host population dynamics.

The timing of propagule production is important because for parasites with short-lived propagules, effective transmission can only be achieved where propagule release and availability of infection sites are coincident. As we have already seen, the timing of propagule production is one aspect of the life-history characteristics of the parasite and may be significantly affected by genetic variation in both parasite and host. A consideration of life history in parasites and its influence on transmission must therefore take into account not only effects on net reproductive rate but also on efficiency of transmission to host infection sites.

To our knowledge there has been very little work conducted on genetic variation for propagule longevity and dispersal characteristics in parasite populations. However we do know that in many parasite species distinctly different types of propagules are produced by asexual and sexual reproduction. Asexually dispersed propagules may be short lived and their dispersal characteristics are often quite different from those of their sexually produced counterparts. Thus differences in the balance of asexual and sexual propagule production among parasite genotypes could confer quite different propagule dispersal properties upon them. Substantial genetic variation affecting the rate of sexual reproduction has been detected among isolates of the southern leaf blight fungus *Cochliobolus heterostrophus* (Kolmer & Leonard 1985). In the field such variations could lead to differences in the efficiency of long-distance dispersal among genotypes of the fungus, thereby influencing the parasite transmission parameter. Further study of variation in the relative investment in sexual/asexual reproduction by parasite genotypes would be illuminating. This character could be regarded as another aspect of parasite life-history variation and may well be controlled not only by parasite genotype but also by host genotype. There is much anecdotal evidence that suggests that population of plant parasitic fungi on crop plants show very low levels of sexual reproduction compared with their counterparts on wild hosts. It is interesting to speculate that this may be due to selection of genotypes showing rapid short-distance propagule dispersal in the dense crop population where fresh host infection sites are available in very large numbers within short distances. In wild pathosystems, where host distribution is likely to be much more patchy and hosts are at much lower density, parasites investing more in sexual reproduction, producing propagules with superior long-distance dispersal characteristics, may be favoured. Comparison of the relative propensity for sexual reproduction between pathogen populations from wild and crop hosts would be illuminating.

Apart from the mere production and release of parasite propagules, effective transmission requires that they ultimately arrive at a very specific host infection site. Parasite characteristics that affect the probability of achieving such precise dispersal will, therefore, influence the value of the parasite transmission parameter. In passively dispersed propagules morphological features of the propagule (size, shape, adhesive properties, etc.) will undoubtedly influence their probability of arriving and lodging at a specific host infection site. Genetic variation for these morphological features of the propagule could therefore have an influence on the parasite transmission parameter. In parasites with animal hosts, parasites may induce changes in host behaviour which can alter the probability of parasite transmission (Dawkins 1990). Again, genetic variation in the parasite that affects host behaviour may be important. Finally in parasite–host systems where propagule vectors are involved, many features expressed directly by the parasite, or indirectly through its influence on the host, many alter the probability that propagules are acquired by vectors. Genetic variation in the parasite affecting attractiveness to vectors could significantly affect the parasite transmission parameter. The influence of variation in attractiveness to vectors on transmission of propagules has been demonstrated very conclusively in analogous studies of pollen transmission rates in pollinator–plant systems (Stanton *et al.* 1986).

Host impact parameter

We have argued in an earlier section that the dynamic behaviour of parasite–host systems is determined not only by the parasite transmission parameter, which we have analysed in some detail, but also by the host impact parameter, which measures the extent to which host reproduction is reduced by the presence of parasites in the community.

It is a curious fact that while many applied studies are motivated by the effect of parasites on their hosts, very few quantitative estimates of the impact of parasites on the lifetime reproductive success of their hosts have been attempted (Antonovics & Alexander 1989). Attention has been focused instead on the reproductive behaviour of parasites making the (not unreasonable) assumption that the larger the parasite population, the larger its impact on the host population. However, for understanding the joint behaviour of parasite and host populations this type of information alone is inadequate, and explicit measures of reduction in reproductive fitness caused by parasites are required.

Measuring host fitness in the field is an extremely difficult undertaking and there have been few attempts to quantify the effects of parasite infection on host reproductive success. Exceptions to this are the work of Clay (1984) and Parker (1986) for fungal infections of plants and Gill and Mock (1985) and Schaal (1990) for malarial infections of newts and lizards. For the purposes of this discussion we will assume that parasite infection causes deleterious effects on host reproduction and will attempt to identify the types of genetic variation that could affect the size of these deleterious effects.

In general terms the impact of parasites on host reproduction will depend on the frequency with which the host encounters parasites present in the community, the probability that such dispersed parasites will establish infection, and the extent to which host reproduction is reduced by successful infection. In the following sections we will discuss how genetic variation may affect each of these components of the host impact parameter.

Frequency of parasite encounters

We are concerned here with encounters where parasites succeed in reaching host infection sites. The frequency of such encounters experienced by a host will be determined by the number of infection sites which it possesses, the time period over which they are susceptible to infection and (in animals) by the behaviour of the host. Appropriate genetic variation affecting host morphology, host phenology and/or behaviour could therefore influence the frequency of parasite encounters and ultimately the host impact parameter.

The influence of genetically determined morphological variation on parasite encounter rates is suggested by a study of natural infection of white campion by an anther-smut fungus (Alexander 1989). Genotypes differ in the mean number of flowers per plant and, because infection takes place on flowers, genotypes therefore differ in the mean number of infection sites per plant. Among male plants a positive correlation between flower number per plant and mean infection frequency was found providing circumstantial evidence that genetic variation in host morphology, through its influence on the frequency of parasite encounters, can influence the host impact parameter.

Susceptible host infection sites are commonly present over only a fraction of the host life cycle. Genetic differences in host development and phenology may therefore influence the period of time over which they are susceptible to infection, and ultimately the reduction in fitness which they suffer. In oak, leaves are vulnerable to infection by oak mildew at the time of flushing but thereafter show reduced susceptibility. Lower infection of sessile than of English oak has been attributed to its earlier leaf flushing which occurs before the main period of spore production by the fungus (Anon 1956).

Behavioural variation with a genetic basis may also affect the probability of encounter with parasites and hence the host impact parameter. For instance where parasites have limited dispersal ranges, hosts that live in colonies are more likely to be exposed to infection than those that lead a solitary existence. If there is a genetic component to such variation in behaviour it will clearly influence the host impact parameter.

Parasite establishment

As already discussed (pp. 264–267), there is a substantial body of evidence for genetic variation in both parasite and host populations (virulence and resistance variation respectively) which controls the ability/inability of parasites to establish. So long as infection by parasites produces measurable reductions in the reproductive output of the host, this genetic variation will have significant effects on the host impact parameter.

Reproductive impact of infection

If there is quantitative variation in the reproductive impact caused by different parasite infections this too can affect the host impact parameter. As we have already seen (pp. 267–270), there may be considerable variation in the speed, extent and timing of growth and reproduction by parasites which can be affected by genetic variation in both parasite and host populations. It is not unreasonable to believe that the life-history characteristics displayed by parasites will be correlated with the impact they have on host reproductive success. Early and abundant parasite reproduction for instance would be expected to have a more serious impact on host reproduction than later and less extensive parasite reproduction. Therefore we would expect that the types of genetic variation affecting parasite life-history characters would also affect in a quantitative manner the host impact parameter. However, to confirm this it is clearly necessary to make explicit measurements of host reproductive success alongside measurements of parasite life-history characteristics.

The assumption mentioned above, that the 'aggressiveness' of parasites is positively correlated with the impact which they have on host reproductive success provides a link between the parasite transmission parameter, which we discussed earlier, and the host impact parameter. It is a link that leads to feedback in many models of parasite–host co-evolution, and underpins many of our theories of such co-evolution. Despite its importance, there have been very few experimental confirmations of this relationship. Analysis of artificial inoculation experiments in which simultaneous measurement of parasite life-history characteristics and reductions in host fitness were made could provide the data needed to make good this deficiency.

Conclusions

The aim of this section has been to highlight the types of genetic variation that could potentially influence the dynamic behaviour of parasite–host systems. The analysis has revealed the very wide range of forms that such variations could take. A consideration of the relevant literature suggests that our knowledge of this area is both unbalanced and very patchy.

Variation affecting parasite establishment has been investigated exhaustively. We have much less data on quantitative variation for parasite virulence and host resistance. Our knowledge of genetic variation affecting parasite dispersal and the impact of parasite infection on host reproduction is rudimentary. Unless our understanding of these areas is improved it is unlikely that we will achieve a balanced perspective on the genetics of parasite–host systems. Lack of knowledge also hinders the development of ecologically realistic models of parasite–host dynamics which take into account the effects of genetic variation on the behaviour of the interacting populations.

REFERENCES

Agatsuma, T. & Habe, S. (1986). Genetic variability and differentiation of natural populations in three Japanese lung flukes, *Paragonimus ohirai*, *Paragonimus iloktsuenensis* and *Paragonimus sadoensis*. (Digenea: Troglotematidae). *Journal of Parasitology*, **72**, 417–433.

Alexander, H. M. (1989). An experimental field study of anther-smut disease of *Silene alba* caused by *Ustilago violacea*: genotypic variation and disease incidence. *Evolution*, **43**, 835–847.

Anderson, R. M. & May, R. M. (1979). Population biology of infectious diseases: Part I. *Nature*, **280**, 361–367.

Anon (1956). Oak mildew. *Forestry Commission Leaflet* No. 38.

Antonovics, J. & Alexander, H. M. (1989). The concept of fitness in plant–fungal pathogen systems. *Plant Disease Epidemiology*, Vol. 2. *Genetics, Resistance and Management* (Ed. by K. J. Leonard & W. E. Fry), pp. 185–214. McGraw-Hill, New York, USA.

Barrett, J. (1985). The gene-for-gene hypothesis: parable or paradigm. *Ecology and Genetics of Host–Parasite Interactions* (Ed. by D. Rollinson & R. M. Anderson), pp. 215–225. Academic Press, London, UK.

Beverley, S. M., Ismach, R. B. & Pratt, D. M. (1987). Evolution of the genus *Leishmania* as revealed by comparison of nuclear DNA restricted fragment patterns. *Proceedings of the National Academy of Sciences, USA*, **84**, 484–488.

Brasier, C. M. (1990). China and the origins of Dutch elm disease: an appraisal. *Plant Pathology*, **39**, 5–16.

Brasier, C. M. & Gibbs, J. N. (1976). Inheritance of pathogenicity and cultural characters in *C. ulmi* I. Hybridisation of aggressive and non-aggressive strains. *Annals of Applied Biology*, **83**, 31–37.

Brindley, P. J. & Dobson, C. (1981). Genetic control of liability to infection with *Nematospiroides dubius* in mice: selection of refractory and labile populations of mice. *Parasitology*, **83**, 51–65.

Browder, L. E. (1985). Parasite : Host : Environment specificity in the cereal rusts. *Annual Review of Phytopathology*, **23**, 201–222.

Burdon, J. J. (1987). *Diseases and Plant Population Biology*. Cambridge University Press, Cambridge, UK.

Burdon, J. J. & Roelfs, A. P. (1985). The effect of sexual and asexual reproduction on the isozyme structure of populations of *Puccinia graminis*. *Phytopathology*, **75**, 1068–1073.

Burdon, J. J., Brown, A. H. D. & Jarosz, A. M. (1990). The spatial scale of genetic interactions in host–pathogen coevolved systems. *Pests, Pathogens and Plant Communities* (Ed. by J. J. Burdon & S. R. Leather), pp. 233–247. Blackwell Scientific Publications, Oxford, UK.

Caten, C. E. (1974). Intra-racial variation in *Phytophthora infestans* and adaptation to field resistance for potato blight. *Annals of Applied Biology*, **77**, 259–270.

Chase, T. E. & Ullrich, R. C. (1990). Genetic basis of biological species in *Heterobasidion annosum. Mycologia*, **82**, 67–72.

Clarke, D. D., Campbell, F. S. & Bevan, J. R. (1990). Genetic interactions between *Senecio vulgaris* and the powdery mildew fungus *Erisiphe fischeri. Pests, Pathogens and Plant Communities* (Ed. by J. J. Burdon & S. R. Leather), pp. 189–201. Blackwell Scientific Publications, Oxford, UK.

Clay, K. (1984). The effect of the fungus *Atkinsonella hypoxylon* (Clavicipitaceae) on the reproductive system and demography of the grass *Danthonia spicata. New Phytologist*, **98**, 165–175.

Clifford, B. C. & Clothier, R. B. (1974). Physiologic specialisation of *Puccinia hordei* on barley hosts with non-hypersensitive resistance. *Transactions of the British Mycological Society*, **63**, 421–430.

Conway, D. J. & McBride, J. S. (1991). Population genetics of *Plasmodium falciparum* within a malaria hyperendemic area. *Parasitology*, **103**, 7–16.

Conway, D. J., Greenwood, B. M. & McBride, J. S. (1991). The epidemiology of multiple-clone *Plasmodium falciparum* infections in Gambian patients. *Parasitology*, **103**, 1–6.

Crute, I. R. (1990). Resistance to *Bremia lactacae* (downy mildew) in British populations of *Lactuca serriola* (prickly lettuce). *Pests, Pathogens and Plant Communities* (Ed. by J. J. Burdon & S. R. Leather) pp. 203–217. Blackwell Scientific Publications, Oxford, UK.

Dawkins, R. (1990). Parasites, desiderata lists and the paradox of the organism. *Parasitology* **100**, 563–573.

Day, P. R. (1974). *Genetics of Host–Parasite Interaction*. W. H. Freeman, San Francisco, CA, USA.

de Nooij, M. P. & van Damme, J. M. M. (1988a). Variation in pathogenicity among and within populations of the fungus *Phomopsis subordinaria* infecting *Plantago lanceolata. Evolution*, **42**, 1166–1171.

de Nooij, M. P. & van Damme, J. M. M. (1988b). Variation in host susceptibility among and within populations of *Plantago lanceolata* L. infected by the fungus *Phomopsis subordinaria. Oecologia*, **75**, 535–538.

Dinoor, A. (1977). Oat crown rust resistance in Israel. *Annals of the New York Academy of Sciences*, **287**, 357–366.

Dinoor, A. & Eshed, N. (1990). Plant diseases in natural populations of wild barley (*Hordeum spontaneum*). *Pests, Pathogens and Plant Communities* (Ed. by J. J. Burdon & S. R. Leather), pp. 169–186. Blackwell Scientific Publications, Oxford, UK.

Ennos, R. A. & Swales, K. W. (1987). Estimation of the mating system in a fungal pathogen *Crumenulopsis sororia* (Karst.) Groves using isozyme markers. *Heredity*, **59**, 423–430.

Ennos, R. A. & Swales, K. W. (1988). Genetic variation in tolerance of host monoterpenes in a population of the ascomycete canker pathogen *Crumenulopsis sororia. Plant Pathology*, **37**, 407–416.

Ennos, R. A. & Swales, K. W. (1991a). Genetic variability and population structure in the canker pathogen *Crumenulopsis sororia. Mycological Research*, **95**, 521–525.

Ennos, R. A. & Swales, K. W. (1991b). Genetic variation in a fungal pathogen: response to host defensive chemicals. *Evolution*, **45**, 190–204.

Farrara, B. F., Ilott, T. W. & Michelmore, R. W. (1987). Genetic analysis of factors for resistance to downy mildew (*Bremia lactucae*) in species of lettuce (*Lactuca sativa* and

L. serriola). *Plant Pathology*, **36**, 499–514.

Fenner, F. & Ratcliffe, F. N. (1965). *Myxomatosis*. Cambridge University Press, Cambridge, UK.

Flor, H. H. (1956). The complementary genic systems in flax and flax rust. *Advances in Genetics*, **8**, 29–54.

Förster, H., Coffey, M. D., Elwood, H. & Sogen, M. L. (1990). Sequence analysis of the small subunit ribosomal RNAs of three zoosporic fungi and implications for fungal evolution. *Mycologia*, **82**, 306–312.

Förster, H., Kinschert, T. G., Leong, S. A. & Maxwell, D. P. (1988). Estimation of relatedness between *Phytophthora* species by analysis of mitochondrial DNA. *Mycologia*, **80**, 466–478.

Gill, D. E. & Mock, B. A. (1985). Ecological and evolutionary dynamics of parasites: the case of *Trypanosoma diemyctyli* in the red-spotted newt *Notophthalmus viridescens*. *Ecology and Genetics of Host–Parasite Interactions* (Ed. by D. Rollinson & R. M. Anderson), pp. 157–183. Academic Press, London, UK.

Hamid, A. H., Ayers, J. E., Schein, R. D. & Hill, R. R. (1982). Components of fitness attributes in *Cochliobolus carbonum* Race 3. *Phytopathology*, **72**, 1166–1169.

Harry, I. B. & Clarke, D. D. (1986). Race specific resistance in groundsel (*Senecio vulgaris*) to the powdery mildew *Erisiphe fischeri*. *New Phytologist*, **103**, 167–175.

Harry, I. B. & Clarke, D. D. (1987). The genetics of race-specific resistance in groundsel (*Senecio vulgaris* L.) to the powdery mildew *Erisiphe fischeri*. *New Phytologist*, **107**, 715–723.

Keen, N. T. (1982). Specific recognition in gene-for-gene host-parasite systems. *Advances in Plant Pathology*, **1**, 35–82.

Kinlock, B. B. (1982). Mechanisms and inheritance of rust resistance in conifers. *Resistance to Diseases and Pests in Forest Trees* (Ed. by H. M. Heybroek, B. R. Stephan & K. von Weissenberg), pp. 119–129. Pudoc, Wageningen, The Netherlands.

Klittich, C. J. R. & Bronson, C. R. (1986). Reduced fitness associated with TOXI of *Cochliobolus heterostrophus*. *Phytopathology*, **76**, 1294–1298.

Kolmer, J. A. & Leonard, K. J. (1985). Genetic variation and selection for fertility in the fungus *Cochliobolus heterostrophus*. *Heredity*, **55**, 335–339.

Kolmer, J. A. & Leonard, K. J. (1986). Genetic selection and adaptation of *Cochliobolus heterostrophus* to corn hosts with partial resistance. *Phytopathology*, **76**, 774–777.

Korhonen, K. (1978). Interfertility and clonal size in the *Armillaria mellea* complex. *Karstenia*, **18**, 31–42.

Leonard, K. J. & Mundt, C. C. (1984). Methods for estimating epidemiological effects of quantitative resistance to plant disease. *Theoretical and Applied Genetics*, **67**, 219–230.

Leuchtmann, A. & Clay, K. (1990a). Isozyme variation in the fungus *Atkinsonella hypoxylon* within and among populations of its host grasses. *Canadian Journal of Botany*, **67**, 2600–2607.

Leuchtmann, A. & Clay, K. (1990b). Experimental evidence for genetic variation in compatibility between the fungus *Atkinsonella hypoxylon* and its three host grasses. *Evolution*, **43**, 825–834.

Leung, H. & Williams, P. H. (1986). Enzyme polymorphism and genetic differentiation among geographic isolates of the rice blast fungus. *Phytopathology*, **76**, 778–783.

Manicom, B. Q., Bar-Joseph, M., Kotze, J. M. & Becker, M. M. (1990). A restriction fragment length polymorphism probe relating vegetative compatibility groups and pathogenicity in *Fusarium oxysporum* f. sp. *dianthi*. *Phytopathology*, **80**, 336–339.

May, R. M. & Anderson, R. M. (1979). Population biology of infectious diseases: Part II. *Nature*, **280**, 455–461.

McDonald, B. A., McDermott, J. M., Goodwin, S. B. & Allard, R. W. (1989). The population biology of host–pathogen interactions. *Annual Review of Phytopathology*, **27**, 77–94.

Mitchell-Olds, T. (1986). Quantitative genetics of survival and growth in *Impatiens capensis*. *Evolution*, **40**, 107–116.

Mihok, S., Otreno, L. H. & Darji, N. (1990). Population genetics of *Trypanosoma brucei* and the epidemiology of human sleeping sickness in the Lambwe Valley, Kenya. *Parasitology*, **100**, 219–233.

Nei, M. (1973). Analysis of gene diversity in subdivided populations. *Proceedings of the National Academy of Sciences, USA*, **70**, 3321–3323.

Newton, A. C., Caten, C. E. & Johnson, R. (1985). Variation for isozymes and double stranded RNA among isolates of *Puccinia striiformis* and two other cereal rusts. *Plant Pathology*, **34**, 235–247.

Old, K. M., Moran, G. F. & Bell, J. C. (1984). Isozyme variability among isolates of *Phytophthora cinnamomi* from Australia and Papua New Guinea. *Canadian Journal of Botany*, **62**, 2016–2022.

Paindavoine, P., Pays, E., Laurent, M., Geltmeyer, Y., le Ray, D., Mehlitz, D. & Steinert, M. (1986). The use of DNA hybridisation and numerical taxonomy in determining relationships between *Trypanosoma brucei* stocks and subspecies. *Parasitology*, **92**, 31–50.

Parker, M. A. (1985). Local population differentiation for compatibility in an annual legume and its host specific fungal pathogen. *Evolution*, **39**, 713–723.

Parker, M. A. (1986). Individual variation in pathogen attack and differential reproductive success in the annual legume *Amphicarpaea bracteata*. *Oecologia*, **69**, 253–259.

Parker, M. A. (1988). Polymorphism for disease resistance in the annual legume *Amphicarpaea bracteata*. *Heredity*, **60**, 27–31.

Parlevliet, J. E. (1989). Identification and evaluation of quantitative resistance. *Plant Disease Epidemiology*, Vol. 2. *Genetics, Resistance and Management* (Ed. by K. J. Leonard & W. E. Fry), pp. 215–248. McGraw-Hill, New York, USA.

Prakash, C. S. & Heather, W. A. (1986). Relationship between increased virulence and the aggressiveness traits of *Melampsora medusae*. *Phytopathology*, **76**, 266–269.

Price, P. W. (1980). *Evolutionary Biology of Parasites*. Princeton University Press, Princeton, NJ, USA.

Rishbeth, J. (1982). Species of Armillaria in southern England. *Plant Pathology*, **31**, 9–17.

Schaal, B. A. (1980). Measurement of gene flow in *Lupinus texensis*. *Nature*, **284**, 450–451.

Schaal, J. J. (1990). Virulence of lizard malaria: the evolutionary ecology of an ancient parasite–host association. *Parasitology*, **10**, S35–S52.

Schoeneweiss, D. F. (1975). Predisposition, stress and plant disease. *Annual Review of Phytopathology*, **13**, 193–211.

Smith, M. L. & Anderson, J. B. (1989). Restriction fragment length polymorphism in mitochondrial DNAs of Armillaria: identification of North American biological species. *Mycological Research*, **93**, 247–256.

Stanton, M. L., Snow, A. A. & Handel, S. N. (1986). Floral evolution: attractiveness to pollinators increases male fitness. *Science*, **232**, 1625–1627.

Stenlid, J. (1985). Population structure of *Heterobasidion annosum* as determined by somatic incompatibility, sexual incompatibility, and isoenzyme patterns. *Canadian Journal of Botany*, **63**, 2268–2273.

Tait, A. (1990). Genetic exchange and evolutionary relationships in protozoan and helminth parasites. *Parasitology*, **100**, S75–S87.

Thibault-Balesdent, M. & Delatour, C. (1985). Variabilité du comportement de *Heterobasidion annosum* (Fr) Bref. à trois monoterpenes. *European Journal of Forest Pathology*, **15**, 301–307.

Thompson, R. C. A. & Lymbery, A. J. (1990). Intraspecific variation in parasites — What is a strain? *Parasitology Today*, **6**, 345–348.

Tibayrenc, M. & Ayala, F. J. (1988). Isozyme variability in *Trypanosoma cruzi*, the agent of Chaga's disease: genetical, taxonomical and epidemiological significance. *Evolution*, **42**, 277–292.

Tooley, P. W., Fry, W. E. & Villarreal Gonzalez, M. J. (1985) Isozyme characterisation of sexual and asexual *Phytophthora infestans* populations. *Journal of Heredity*, **76**, 431–435.

Tooley, P. W., Sweigard, J. A. & Fry, W. E. (1986). Fitness and virulence of *Phytophthora infestans* isolates from sexual and asexual populations. *Phytopathology*, **76**, 1209–1212.

Van Etten, H. D., Matthews, D. E. & Matthews, P. S. (1989). Phytoalexin detoxification: importance for pathogenicity and practical implications. *Annual Review of Phytopathology*, **27**, 143–164.

Via, S. (1984). The quantitative genetics of polyphagy in an insect herbivore II. Genetic correlations in larval performance within and among host plants. *Evolution*, **38**, 896–905.

Vilgalys, R. & Gonzalez, D. (1990). Ribosomal DNA restriction fragment length polymorphisms in *Rhizoctonia solani*. *Phytopathology*, **80**, 151–158.

Wahl, I. (1970). Prevalence and geographic distribution of resistance to crown rust in *Avena sterilis*. *Phytopathology*, **60**, 746–749.

Wahl, I., Eshed, N., Segal, A. & Sobel, Z. (1978). Significance of wild relatives of small grains and other wild grasses in cereal powdery mildews. *The Powdery Mildews* (Ed. by D. M. Spencer), pp. 83–100. Academic Press, London.

Wakelin, D. (1978). Genetic control of susceptibility and resistance to parasitic infection. *Advances in Parasitology*, **16**, 219–308.

Wakelin, D. (1985). Genetics, immunity and parasite survival. *Ecology and Genetics of Host–Parasite Interactions* (Ed. by D. Rollinson & R. M. Anderson), pp. 39–54. Academic Press, London, UK.

Walker, W. F. & Doolittle, W. F. (1982). Redividing the basidiomycetes on the basis of 5SRNA sequences. *Nature*, **299**, 723–724.

Wassom, D. L., Dewitt, C. W. & Grundmann, A. W. (1974). Immunity to *Hymenolepis citelli* by *Peromyscus maniculatus*: genetic control and ecological implications. *Journal of Parasitology*, **60**, 47–52.

Weste, G. & Marks, G. C. (1987). The biology of *Phytophthora cinnamomi* in Australian forests. *Annual Review of Phytopathology*, **25**, 207–229.

11. GENES AND ECOLOGY: TWO ALTERNATIVE PERSPECTIVES USING *DROSOPHILA*

MARTIN KREITMAN*, BRYAN SHORROCKS† AND CALVIN DYTHAM†

**Committee on Evolutionary Biology, University of Chicago, 1025 East 57th Street, Chicago, IL 60637, USA and †Drosophila Population Biology Unit, Department of Pure and Applied Biology, University of Leeds, Leeds LS2 9JT, UK*

INTRODUCTION

It is now 26 years since G. E. Hutchinson wrote his book *The Ecological Theater and the Evolutionary Play*. This was one of the earliest attempts to place genes within an ecological framework. In this present chapter, biologists from two laboratories that have extensively used *Drosophila* as a model organism, to examine both genes (M.K.) and ecology (B.S. & C.D.), outline their respective approaches to the interface examined by Hutchinson and the subject of this symposium volume.

THE ECOLOGICAL THEATRE (B.S., C.D.)

Drosophila ecology

Most of the early work on *Drosophila* ecology involved the infamous milk-bottle and laboratory medium (Sang 1950, Chiang & Hodson 1950). We now have an extensive knowledge of the natural ecology of *Drosophila* flies (Shorrocks 1982, Lachaise & Tsacas 1983, Heed & Mangen 1986). While we (B.S. & C.D.) agree with Kareiva (1989) that ecology needs more bottle experiments, we feel that certain aspects of the bottle ecology of *Drosophila* have misled biologists. Below we highlight some aspects of fruitfly ecology that we feel have important implications for ecological and genetic diversity.

Survival and fecundity

In the laboratory, female *Drosophila* can survive for weeks laying eggs each day, except for the first one or two. The experiments of Birch *et al.*

(1963) using the Australian species, *D. serrata* Malloch, are representative of such laboratory studies and the survival rates found in the work are frequently quoted (e.g. Jaenike 1986). The average daily survival rate for Birch's five races of *D. serrata* at two different temperatures was 0.98. In contrast, Fig. 11.1 shows survival rates for five species, estimated from multiple capture–recapture experiments on wild populations, with values in the range 0.45–0.85, 0.7 being representative. With constant daily survival (ϕ) average expectation of life is $-1/\ln(\phi)$. For the values in Fig. 11.1, this implies a mean adult life expectancy of between 1.3 and 6.2 days, with a most representative value of 2.8 days. This is in stark contrast to the figure of 49.5 days, obtained by using the laboratory value of survival. One implication of this low survival is that realized fecundity is drastically lower in the field compared to the bottle. Figure 11.2 shows the $l_x m_x$ curves produced using Birch's fecundity schedule for *D. serrata* and a daily survival rate of 0.98 (laboratory) and 0.7 (field). Total productivity ($\Sigma l_x m_x$) is 461 using the laboratory survival rate and 14.6 using the field rate.

Small patches

Flies of the genus *Drosophila* are primarily consumers of the yeasts and bacteria associated with the fermentation and decay of plant material. This material is patchy and ephemeral, in that it supports only one or two generations of flies, and is spatially unpredictable. In terms of the numbers

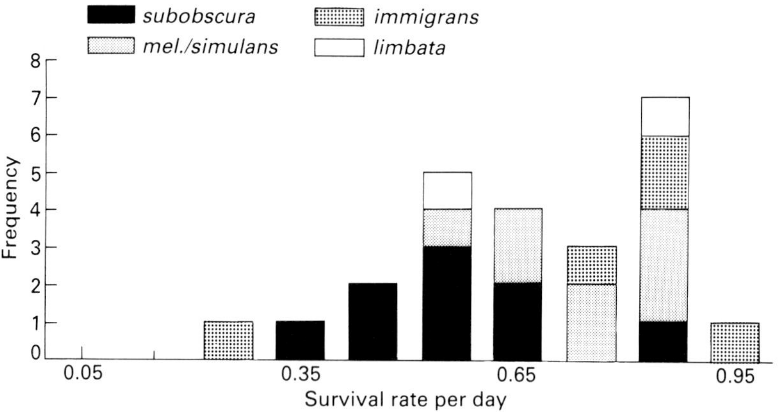

FIG. 11.1. Distribution of daily survival rates for *Drosophila* species under field conditions. (After Rosewell & Shorrocks 1987.)

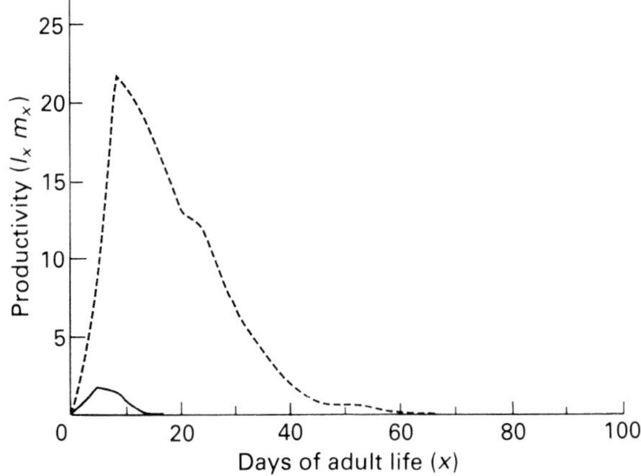

FIG. 11.2. Comparison of the effects of laboratory and field survival on realized fecundity. Data for fecundity are from Birch *et al.* (1963) for the Brisbane race of *D. serrata* at 25°C. Laboratory daily survival is taken as 0.98 while the field value is taken as 0.7. (After Rosewell & Shorrocks 1987.)

of flies emerging (Fig. 11.3), these patches are quite small compared to laboratory bottles. Surprisingly, given the large amount of information on *Drosophila* breeding sites (Shorrocks 1982), these data are not extensive, because most studies do not publish records for individual patches. The modal class is always less than 15, although species of fungi producing up to an average of 40 emerging adults are quite common.

Aggregation

Figure 11.4 shows the distribution of *D. subobscura* Colin eggs over single fruits of *Prunus cerasifera*. The eggs show an aggregated distribution over the patches (variance ≫ mean) with most patches containing few or even no eggs and only a few containing large numbers. This picture is typical for wild flies. Rosewell *et al.* (1990) tested 360 datasets representing distributions of Diptera, particularly drosophilids, on a total of 7638 resource patches. Excluding species with predaceous larvae, 314 of 337 datasets (93%) were significantly aggregated when tested by the variance to mean ratio.

Patches and competition

The general view of *Drosophila* ecology that emerges from the above studies is that of ephemeral flies, aggregating their eggs and larvae over

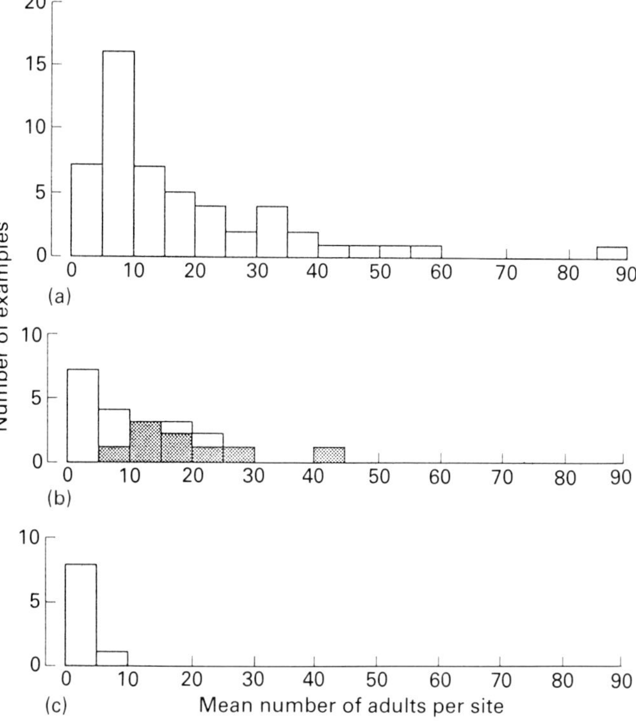

FIG. 11.3. Frequency histogram of mean numbers of drosophilid flies emerging from different breeding sites. (a) Fungi, (b) fruit, (c) flowers. (After Shorrocks & Rosewell 1986.)

small ephemeral patches. This view inspired the 'aggregation model' of competition (Shorrocks *et al.* 1979, 1984, Atkinson & Shorrocks 1981) that allows a competitively inferior species to survive in probability refuges. These are patches with no or a few superior competitors, that arise as a result of the aggregated distributions mentioned above. An independent model proposed by Hanski (1981, 1983) also incorporates spatial variance and similarly promotes coexistence. These probability refuges will persist because the patches are ephemeral and aggregation increases mean crowding (Lloyd 1967). Mean crowding (m^*) is the mean density experienced by randomly chosen individuals and is equal to $m + s^2/m - 1$, where m and s^2 are the mean and variance of the distribution over patches. With a random distribution $s^2 = m$ and $m^* = m$ but with an aggregated distribution $s^2 \gg m$ and $m^* \gg m$. Thus global population density is limited by strong intraspecific competition in patches with high

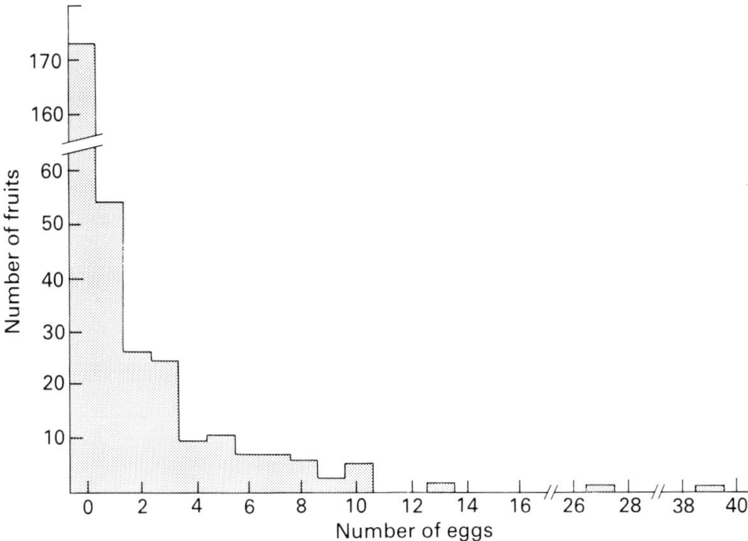

FIG. 11.4. Distribution of *Drosophila subobscura* eggs over patches (fruits) of *Prunus cerasifera*.

local density while low-density patches still exist. In fact, coexistence is promoted in this model because aggregation of the superior species increases its intraspecific competition and reduces interspecific competition. Ives and May (1985) and de Jong (1982) also point out that increased aggregation will usually reduce the equilibrium population and so lessen competition pressure but this is not necessarily true for all local competition models (Ives 1988, Rosewell 1990).

The model

In the model, the eggs of both species are independently distributed over the patches according to a negative binomial distribution, which has an exponent, k, inversely related to the degree of aggregation. The use of the negative binomial and the assumption of independence have been justified for drosophilids (Rosewell *et al.* 1990, Shorrocks *et al.* 1990). In the initial model (Atkinson & Shorrocks 1981) the parameter k was constant, rather than density dependent. This is not valid for real drosophilid populations but relaxing the assumption does not prevent coexistence (Rosewell *et al.* 1990).

Within a patch, competition is modelled by the equation of Hassell and Comins (1976):

$$N_i(t + 1) = \lambda_i N_i(t)[1 + a_i(N_i(t) + \alpha_{ij}N_j(t))]^{-b_i},\ i \neq j$$

where $N_i(t)$ and $N_j(t)$ are the numbers of each species in a breeding site at time t, λ_i is the net reproductive rate, α_{ij} is a competition coefficient and a_i and b_i are constants. The parameter a_i (equal to $(\lambda_i - 1)/N_i^*$, where N^* is the carrying capacity of a patch) is related to the population size per patch at which density dependence starts to act and b_i describes the type of competition. At $b = 1$, competition is contest with density dependence exactly compensating. With increasing values of b, competition becomes increasingly scramble with density dependence being over-compensating (Nicholson 1954, Hassell 1975). This type of difference equation has been shown to model insect competition in general (Stubbs 1977, Bellows 1981) and drosophilid competition in particular (Gilpin & Ayala 1973) very well. Figure 11.5 shows an example with *D. subobscura* on individual rowan (*Sorbus aucuparia* L.) berries (Shorrocks 1982). Values of b appear mainly to vary between 1 and 3 for drosophilids (Shorrocks & Rosewell 1987). The survivors of competition within each patch disperse, reproduce and die. However, there is no difference in dispersal ability between the two species; the inferior one is not a fugitive.

The conclusion that emerges from these simulations is summarized in Fig. 11.6 for $\lambda = 5$, $b = 1$ and $N^* = 10$, values that are quite representative of drosophilids (Shorrocks & Rosewell 1987). Also shown in Fig. 11.6 are the distributions of α and k collected by Shorrocks & Rosewell (1987).

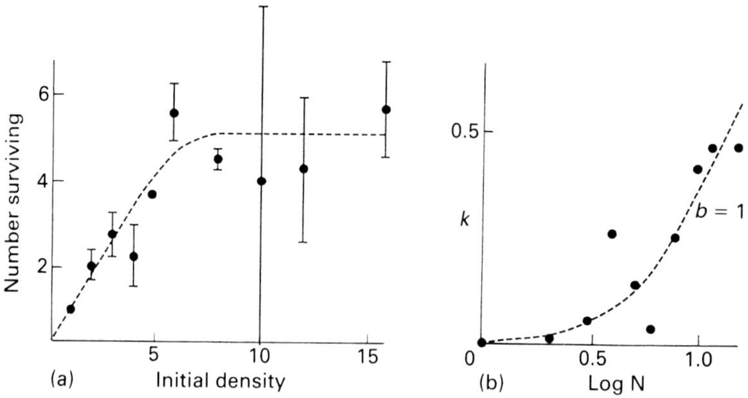

FIG. 11.5. Survival of *Drosophila subobscura* larvae on individual rowan berries. (a) number surviving versus initial numbers. (b) k value versus log initial numbers.

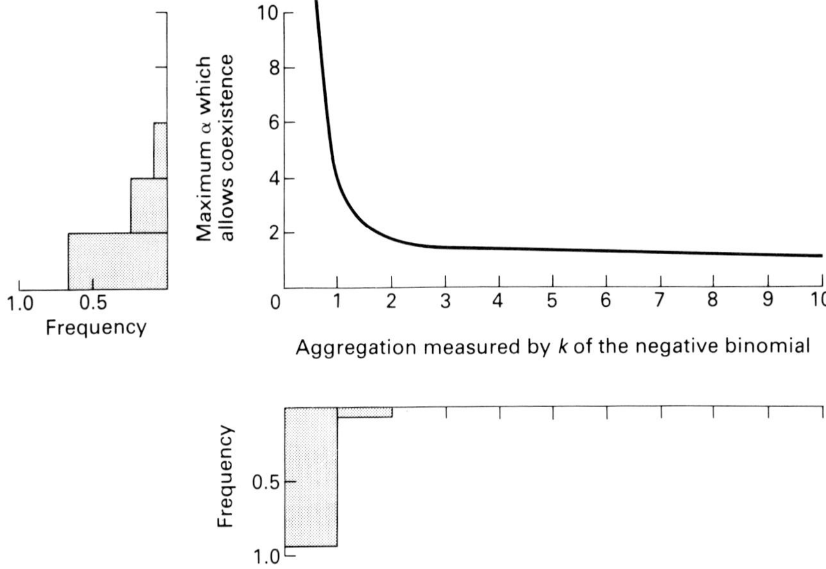

FIG. 11.6. Relationship between aggregation (k) and the maximum value for the competition coefficient (α) of the 'superior' species which allows coexistence. Also shown are the distribution of α and k values from *Drosophila* laboratory and field experiments.

Clearly, probability refuges can promote species diversity in drosophilids. But what about genetic diversity?

Patches and selection

Marginal overdominance

A number of models have been proposed (Levene 1953, Li 1955, Levins & MacArthur 1966, Maynard Smith 1966, 1970, Wallace 1968a, Bulmer 1972, Christianson 1974, 1975, Strobeck 1974, Yokoyama & Schaal 1985) in which environmental heterogeneity/patchiness promotes genetic diversity. However, these models effectively describe the situation in which genotypes have different fitness values in different environments.

These multiple-niche polymorphism models are the genetic equivalent of the traditional resource partitioning models in ecology. The aggregation model described in the last section does not involve traditional resource refuges and this section will examine a parallel model for 'competition' between genotypes.

Soft and hard selection

Before examining the effect of patches and aggregation on the maintenance of genetic diversity we should distinguish between two types of selection. In the multiple-niche polymorphism models above, selection was presented as hard-selection. With probability refuges, selection will be presented as soft-selection (Wallace 1968b, 1975, Christianson 1975).

Let us imagine that in a certain drosophilid there are two larval genotypes, 'slow' and 'fast'. These refer to the rate of feeding and therefore the rate of depletion of resources. Larvae that are slow can survive within a patch containing only slow genotypes. In a patch that contains fast genotypes, they may fail to obtain enough food before resources are depleted. This would be soft-selection, where a genotype's fitness is dependent upon which other genotypes are present. Alternatively with hard-selection, a genotype's fitness is not dependent upon the presence of other genotypes. For example, suppose the above drosophilid had two larval genotypes, 'warm' and 'cold', which referred to the ability of the larvae to withstand low temperature. The fitness of the more susceptible, warm genotype would be a function of temperature but not of how many cold genotypes were present in the patch. Notice that in both types of selection, genotypes fail to leave offspring. Soft does not, in this instance, imply a less severe type of selection. However, a consideration of a number of examples and some simple models leads to the conclusion (Wallace 1975, 1981) that soft-selection is both frequency- and density-dependent. Conversely, hard-selection is both frequency- and density-independent (see Clarke & Beaumont, Ch. 14, this volume). *Drosophila* frequently encounter a rather restricted set of genotypes within a patch. This is suggested by the work of Jaenike & Selander (1979) on the fungal-breeding *D. falleni*, where emerging flies appeared to be the progeny of a single female. It has also been demonstrated by Cooper (1990) for *D. melanogaster* on grapes, that fitness is a product of which genotypes (Adh^f/Adh^f, Adh^f/Adh^s or Adh^s/Adh^s) a larva encounters within a patch.

Despite the fact that many of the traditional models used by population geneticists do not involve 'density' or 'frequency' and are consequently depicting hard-selection, there are theoretical reasons for believing that soft-selection is the norm. Clarke (1973a, b) has presented a genetic model in which the competition between two phenotypes is represented by the equations:

$$dN_1/dt = N_1(w_1k_1/(k_1 + w_1N_1 + \alpha_1w_2N_2)-1)$$

$$dN_2/dt = N_2(w_2k_2/(k_2 + w_2N_2 + \alpha_2w_1N_1)-1)$$

where w and k are constants with effects similar to those of r and K in the more familiar Lotka–Volterra model of two-species competition. The relative competitive ability of the two phenotypes (M– and mm) are represented by α_1 and α_2, N is the number of fertile adults, fertility and fecundity of all genotypes are equal and young are produced in excess. Only if $\alpha_1 = \alpha_2 = 1$ and $k_1 = k_2$ will selection be frequency- and density-independent and therefore hard. In other words the conditions for hard-selection to operate exclusively are rather restrictive. Most individuals in populations experience soft-selection of the type incorporated into the probability refuge model below.

The model

The genetic model (Shorrocks 1990) is an extension of the ecological model described in the last section, with an additional third species. However, the three 'species' are treated as genotypes, AA (genotype 1), Aa (genotype 2) and aa (genotype 3) which can interbreed. Each genotype is independently distributed over the available patches according to a negative binomial distribution. As in the ecological model, survival in a patch is determined by the competition equations of Hassell and Comins (1976). Emerging adults disperse, interbreed at random with respect to this locus, reproduce and die. All three genotypes have identical parameters, $\lambda = 5$, $N^* = 10$, $b = 1$ (therefore $a = 0.04$), which are within the range shown by Shorrocks and Rosewell (1986) to be typical of many drosophilids in the field. Within a simulation, each genotype has the same value of the exponent k of the negative binomial. Between simulations this was varied so that the importance of the degree of aggregation over patches could be assessed. With three 'species' or genotypes there are six competition (fitness) values.

Shorrocks (1990) analysed two different situations, both with complete dominance. Figure 11.7 shows the results for selection acting only against genotype 3 (the homozygous recessive). The fitness values are $\alpha_{21} = \alpha_{12} = 1$, $\alpha_{13} = \alpha_{23} = 0$ and $\alpha_{31} = \alpha_{32} =$ variable. In other words, AA and Aa are identical in their effects upon themselves and each other ($\alpha = 1$), and upon aa (α variable). Genotype aa has no effect upon AA or Aa ($\alpha = 0$). Figure 11.8 shows the corresponding graph for selection acting equally against Aa and aa ($\alpha_{21} = \alpha_{31} =$ variable, $\alpha_{32} = \alpha_{23} = 1$ and $\alpha_{12} = \alpha_{13} = 0$). In both figures the degree of selection imposed, on either aa or Aa and aa, has been converted from α into the more usual selection coefficient (s) used by population geneticists. This was achieved by equating the change in the frequency of allele a (δq) that could be brought about by a particular value of both α and s in an undivided environment simulation.

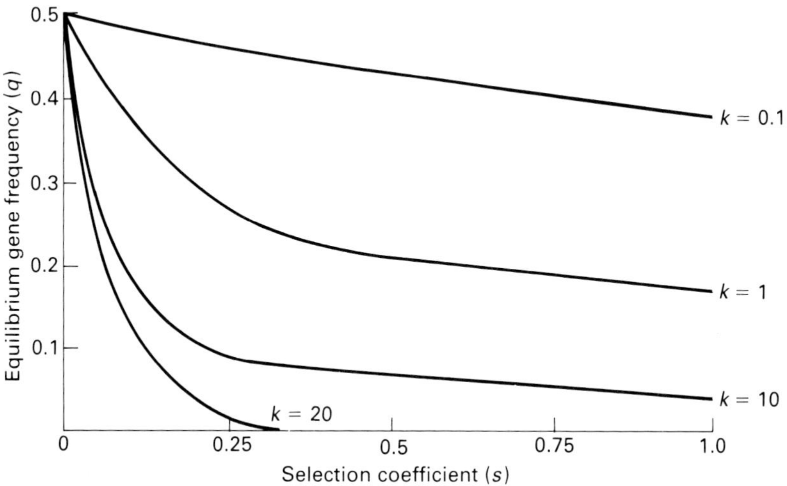

FIG. 11.7. The effect of aggregation upon selection. Each curve (different degrees of aggregation) represents the relationship between the intensity of selection against aa and the equilibrium frequency (q) of the allele a.

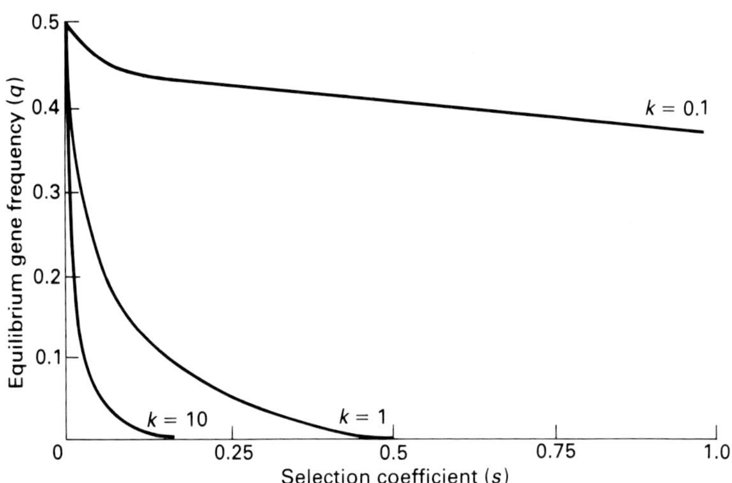

FIG. 11.8. The effect of aggregation upon selection. Each curve (different degrees of aggregation) represents the relationship between the intensity of selection against Aa and aa and the equilibrium frequency (q) of the allele a.

For different degrees of aggregation over patches (k of the negative binomial), both figures show the relationship between s and the equilibrium allele frequency (q). What is quite clear is that under both selection regimes, a degree of aggregation ($k < 1$) is sufficient to keep the 'inferior' allele in the population, despite very strong selection against it. With selection acting only on the recessive homozygote (aa), even a modest degree of aggregation ($k = 10$) is sufficient to maintain a polymorphic locus. In the latter case the 'inferior' allele has a refuge in both the heterozygotes and the low-density patches.

A cellular automaton

Cellular automata are a class of model that are increasingly being used by biologists to investigate spatial processes. A cellular automaton can be thought of as a stylized universe. Space is represented by a uniform grid, with each cell containing a few bits of data. Time advances in discrete steps and the laws of the universe are represented by simple rules which allows each cell to compute its new state from that of its immediate neighbors. In this section we describe a cellular automaton for drosophilids.

The model

The details of the model are shown in Fig. 11.9. Parameter values have been selected from the literature to simulate a drosophilid system on fungal patches. For most of the simulations detailed later the grid size was $9 \times 9 = 81$ cells. Each cell can be regarded as a fungal fruiting body, with a carrying capacity (*patch size*) = 50 (Fig. 11.3). However, with suitable modification of the *patch size* and *arrival rate* (see later), the cells could be regarded as clumps of fungi or even woods. In fact each cell only has the potential of containing a fungal body, so that the distribution of the breeding patches is not uniform. The fungus in each cell is ephemeral and lasts for one generation. Another fungus 'grows' in a cell with a certain *regeneration probability*. In most of the simulations this was 0.7. That is, on average, only 70% of the 81 cells actually contained fungi. Single genotype simulations, in which the observed variable was population size, showed that *regeneration probabilities* lower than about 0.5 produced a non-viable system. The same simulations showed that *arrival rates* less than 0.5 and $\lambda < 4$ also produced non-viable systems. However, above these values these parameters had little effect upon population size and the viability of the system.

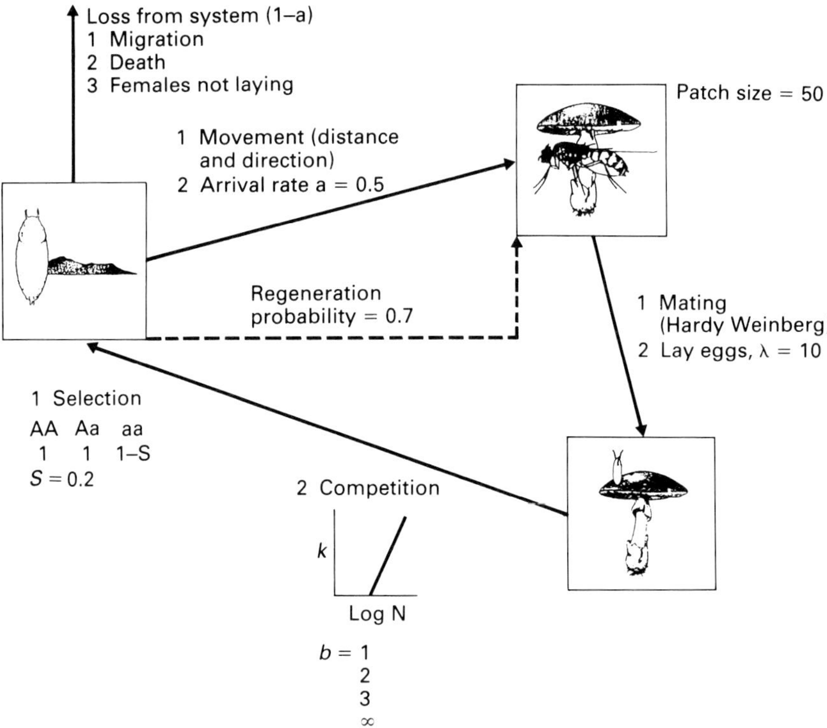

FIG. 11.9. A cellular automaton for fungal drosophilids. The flow diagram illustrates the main components of the system and the parameter values used in the simulations described in the text.

In the three genotype system (AA, Aa and aa), each simulation was initiated by placing two females (Aa) in each cell of the right to left diagonal of the 9 × 9 matrix. After the adults have emerged from a cell they move to another cell. The distance moved is one cell and the direction is random. Only a proportion of the flies survive to find fungi, mate and produce offspring (Figs 11.1 & 11.2). This is represented by the *arrival rate*, and was set at 0.5. Once all the flies have arrived at a fungus, they mate (Hardy–Weinberg) and the females lay eggs. This *clutch size* was set at 10, although because of the *arrival rate* of 0.5 it is equivalent to a value of 5 used in the models above. During the larval stage, the genotypes compete. This process has been separated into a traditional 'selection phase' in which the homozygous recessives (aa) are selected against (s = 0.2) in all patches (hard selection) or only in those patches in which AA and Aa are also present (soft selection). In other patches, s = 0.

In fact with soft selection the value of s increases progressively from 0 to 0.2 as the density of the 'superior' phenotype increases from 0 to 25. Thus the 'probability refuges' are all the low-density sites, not just the ones that are empty. All genotypes also experience an 'ecological phase' in which density dependence operates. In addition to the extremes of pure contest ($b = 1$) and pure scramble ($b = \infty$) competition, the model has also run at $b = 2$ and 3 which are more similar to real values (Shorrocks & Rosewell 1987). Thus the 'selection phase' regulates genotype frequency and the 'ecological phase' regulates numbers. With this version of the cellular automaton the distribution of the flies is effectively random over the patches.

The results of the simulations are shown in Fig. 11.10 which records the average time to elimination (generations) of the 'inferior' allele (a). Three observations can be made. First, the outcome is extremely variable. Second, there is only a small effect of 'hard' versus 'soft' selection. Third, there is a noticeable difference between contest competition ($b = 1$) and any degree of scramble competition ($b > 1$). Clearly the patch-work nature of the environment, in conjunction with the density dependence

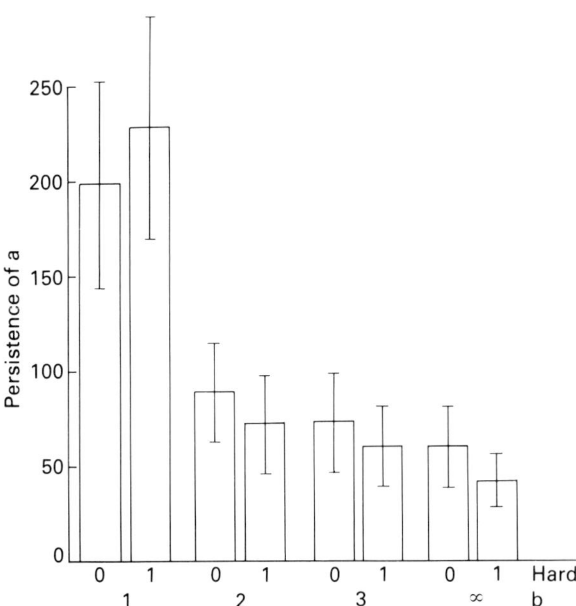

FIG. 11.10. Results of the 'random' cellular automaton. Results are shown as the time to extinction of the allele selected against (a). Error bars are one standard deviation.

within a patch is having an effect upon the course of selection. As yet we only have a transient polymorphism but ecology does affect genes.

Aggregation

Aggregation was introduced into the cellular automaton by changing the rules of dispersion, the rest of the model remained the same. Emerging flies still moved one cell but, for the dominant phenotype (AA and Aa), the direction was no longer random. Within each simulation, each fly 'examined' the eight adjacent cells, and moved to the cell already having the most flies, with a defined *attraction probability*. If this *attraction probability* was less than 1.0 and the fly did not move to the most crowded site, it then moved to one of the eight adjacent sites at random. The effect of this kind of conspecific attraction has also been examined by Ray and Gilpin (1991) in a metapopulation context. Preliminary evidence (Shorrocks 1991, Shorrocks & Davis unpublished) suggests that such attraction in real flies is a product of patch quality and visible fly presence. Figure 11.11 shows the results of these simulations, with 'soft' selection and $b = 2$. With sufficient aggregation of the 'superior' phenotype we now have a stable polymorphism.

Rosewell *et al.* (1990) have modified the non-cellular ecological aggregation model, outlined above, to allow aggregation to be density dependent. The cellular automaton detailed here, will automatically show such density dependence. It is interesting therefore to examine the nature of this

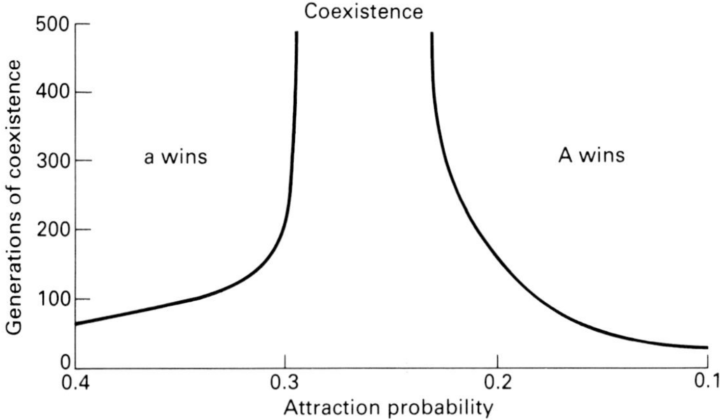

FIG. 11.11. Results of the 'aggregated' cellular automaton. The graph shows the relationship between time to extinction and the *attraction probability*. See text for further details.

relationship for the model to see if it resembles that found in nature. It does. For an *attraction probability* of 0.25 the Taylor power law relationship (Taylor 1961) is depicted in Fig. 11.12. For this graph, the intercept is 6.68 and the slope 1.56. This corresponds very closely to the values of 5.94 and 1.63 for British drosophilids breeding in fungi (Rosewell *et al.* 1990).

What kind of ecological theatre?

As indicated above, our general view of *Drosophila* ecology is that of ephemeral flies, aggregating their eggs and larvae over small ephemeral patches. This is a 'local' view of ecology but we believe that it has 'global' consequences. At the level of the local patch competition and selection can remove both species and genetic variation, yet on a larger scale variation is maintained because there is a 'spreading of risk' (den Boer 1968) so far as inferior species and genotypes are concerned. Each species/genotype alone achieves the same fitness in all patches but fitness does vary according to the other species/genotypes in that patch. Consequently, even in the absence of resource partitioning/multiple-niche polymorphism, aggregation of species/genotypes in these transient, patchy drosophilid environments can maintain high levels of species/genetic diversity or slow down the removal of 'inferior' species/alleles.

These ideas about patchy distributions of individuals, within populations, have clear parallels with ideas about metapopulation dynamics

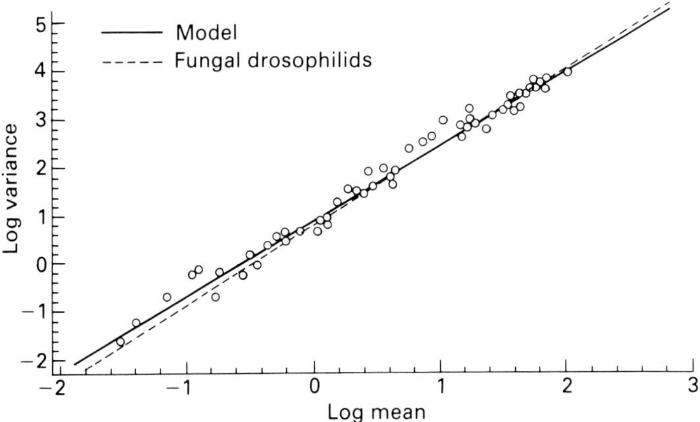

FIG. 11.12. Power law relationship for simulations run with an *attraction probability* of 0.25. The relationship for British fungal-breeding drosophilids (Rosewell *et al.* 1990) is also shown.

(Andrewartha & Birch 1954, Gilpin 1990, Hanski & Gilpin 1991). Populations are ensembles of interacting individuals, within patches; metapopulations are ensembles of interacting populations. They move the emphasis away from 'local' mechanisms that promote stability, such as resource partitioning and balancing selection, to metapopulation mechanisms that are a result of the probability of 'local' patch configurations and the migration that inevitably occurs between these 'local' patches.

THE EVOLUTIONARY PLAY (M.K.)

Why fly population geneticists ignore habitat patchiness

Although *Drosophila* ecology may be characterized by ephemeral patches and its population biology governed by density dependence, the ecology and population biology of flies are generally ignored by population geneticists who ask questions about the evolutionary mechanisms maintaining genetic variation or causing phylogenetic change. Although this time-honoured practice in *Drosophila* population genetics reflects a tactical necessity — Dobzhansky never did discover the breeding site for *D. pseudoobscura* — it is also a justifiable strategy. In the following sections I review some difficulties in identifying evolutionary forces from geographic dissection of genetic variation, which as a kind of gross habitat analysis illustrates the limitations of this approach. I then describe recent developments in the analysis of DNA polymorphism, which have the potential of distinguishing evolutionary forces without requiring assumptions about specific ecology and population biology. With this analysis it is possible to know that there is selection operating at a locus; the challenge for ecologists will be to identify the environmental factors and form of selection acting on this selected variation.

By and large, the attempt to distinguish natural selection from purely historical factors to account for the distribution of genetic variation in natural populations of *Drosophila* (and almost all other organisms) has been a disappointment. Consider — Lewontin and Hubby's classical 1966 paper introducing allozyme studies to *Drosophila* population genetics (Lewontin & Hubby 1966). Of 18 electrophoretic loci surveyed in five populations of *D. pseudoobscura*, eight were polymorphic and only two had allelic variants unique to one population. Thus, over half of the loci were polymorphic and 39% of them had shared polymorphic alleles in all populations. At face value the data suggest high levels of migration and/or uniform selection at many of the polymorphic loci but the authors were unable to distinguish between the alternatives. The geographical analysis of gene frequencies as an approach for detecting selection culminated in a statistical test of the population structure/migration hypothesis, based on testing for heterogeneity in gene frequencies (Lewontin & Krakauer 1973) but subsequent criticisms of the test have diminished its applicability (Nei & Maruyama 1975, Robertson 1975), and with it the appeal of this approach.

We now know that migration rates in many *Drosophila* species must be quite high, certainly greater than the critical one individual per generation needed to maintain genetic homogeneity in face of the local differentiation caused by genetic drift. Keith and associates studied allozyme variation at two loci, xanthine dehydrogenase and esterase-5 in two large collections (sample sizes of approximately 100 genes) of *D. pseudoobscura* separated by approximately 500 km (Keith 1983, Keith *et al.* 1985). A total of 41 electromorphs were identified for esterase-5 (33 in one population and 22 in the other) and 20 electromorphs were identified for xanthine dehydrogenase (12 in one population and 15 in the other). In both studies the electromorph frequencies were statistically indistinguishable.

An equally dramatic uniformity of genetic variation across populations spanning large geographic distances was demonstrated in *D. melanogaster* with restriction fragment length polymorphisms (RFLP). Using 10 four-base-recognizing restriction enzymes, Kreitman and Aguadé (1986) identified 50 different RFLP haplotypes in 87 *Adh* genes from two populations, Raleigh, North Carolina and Davis, California. Except for the allozyme polymorphism (Adh^f and Adh^s) only two of 29 restriction and insertion/deletion polymorphisms occurred at significantly different frequencies in the two samples. The haplotype frequencies were not significantly different. Figure 11.13 shows the distribution of the haplotypes in three population samples collected on the East Coast of the United States, where there is a well-established gene frequency cline for the Adh^f/Adh^s allozyme (Simmons *et al.* 1989). Again there is a striking co-occurrence of haplotypes among the populations, and with the exception of a couple of them (such as haplotype AC) there is an equally striking similarity of frequencies. Thus there can be little doubt but that there is substantial exchange of individuals across populations.

Although there are strong indications of homogenizing effects of migration in *Drosophila*, there are nevertheless a number of gene frequency clines for allozymes. Clines are, of course, of particular interest in highly vagile species because their persistence must require recurrent selection to counterbalance the homogenizing effect of migration. Figure 11.14 illustrates the *D. melanogaster* Adh^f/Adh^s allozyme cline along the East

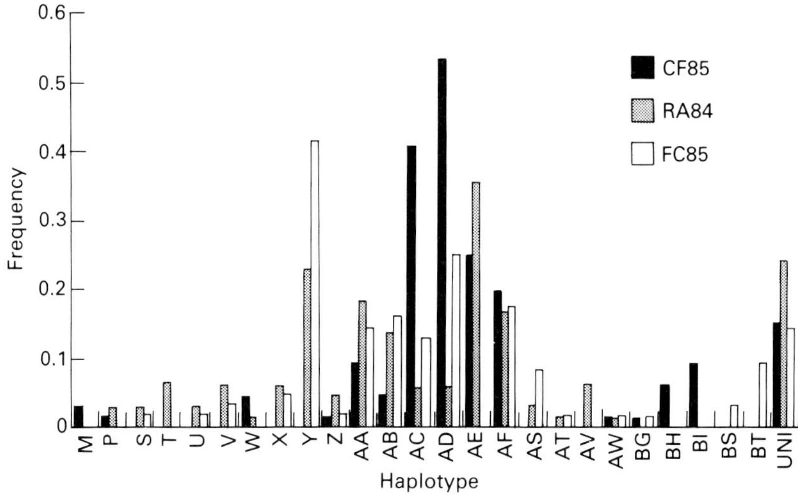

Fig. 11.13. Distribution of *Adh* 4-cutter RFLP haplotypes from three East Coast US populations of *D. melanogaster*. CF85: Cherryfield, Maine; RA84: Raleigh, North Carolina; FC85: Florida City, Florida. Uni: unique haplotypes. The frequency of each haplotype is the relative frequency within each of the two protein alleles, Adh^f or Adh^s.

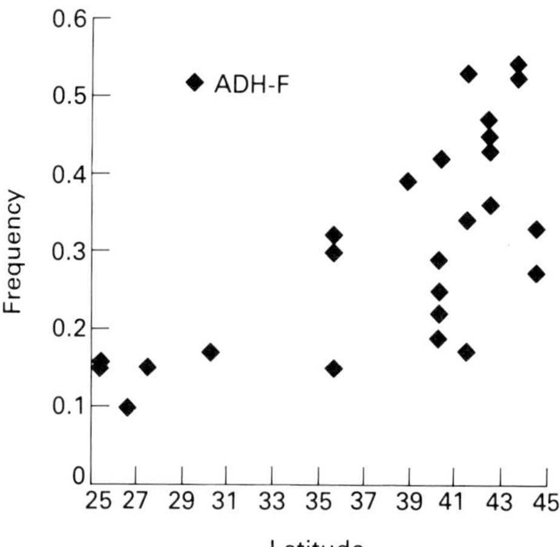

Fig. 11.14. *Adh* allozyme cline of *D. melanogaster* along the US East Coast. (After A. Berry & M. Kreitman, unpublished.)

Coast. Are these clines maintained by natural selection? Simmons and coworkers argued that the relative homogeneity of haplotypes within *Adh*^{s} allozymes and within *Adh*^{f} allozymes in the three populations strengthen the argument for natural selection. Oakeshott *et al.* (1982) reached a similar conclusion from an analysis showing the presence of the *Adh* allozyme cline on several continents. Yet, even with these strong indications of selection, it has not been possible to exclude specific historical scenarios for the presence of the cline. For example, if the southern United States was colonized by a population of flies homozygous for *Adh*^{s} and the north was similarly colonized by only *Adh*^{f}-bearing flies, subsequent mixing could produce a cline in which the within-allozyme haplotype frequencies are the same across populations. In summary, the presence of gene frequency clines in certain species of *Drosophila* indicate the presence of natural selection, but this hypothesis cannot be proven at a gross geographic scale of gene frequency analysis. Even in the face of high migration rates, it may be impossible to reject all historical models in favour of selection. From this point of view, the possibility of detecting microgeographic selection on genetic variation seems quite beyond our current capability.

The fact that many species of *Drosophila* are so highly polymorphic for allozymes and nucleotides suggests that the appropriate unit of evolution for understanding genetic variation may not be small numbers of flies occupying ephemeral habitats but relatively large, stable metapopulations. Table 11.1 contains a summary of polymorphism levels based on RFLP and DNA sequence analyses at several loci in four species of *Drosophila*, *D. melanogaster*, *D. simulans*, *D. ananassae* and *D. pseudoobscura*. Heterozygosity per nucleotide site, a standard measure of polymorphism, is lowest at four sites per thousand in two randomly chosen genes in

TABLE 11.1. Nucleotide heterozygosity in four species of *Drosophila*. (After Aquadro 1991.)

Locus	*D. melanogaster*	*D. simulans*	*D. ananassae*	*D. pseudoobscura*
per	0.001	0.007	–	–
forked	0.004	–	0.01	–
Om(1D)	–	–	0.009	–
vermilion	0.006	–	0.003	–
Adh	0.006	0.015	–	0.026
Amy	0.008	–	–	0.019
rosy	0.005	0.018	–	0.013
Average	0.004	0.014	0.010	0.022

D. melanogaster and highest in *D. pseudoobscura* at 22 per 1000. Under the assumption of selective neutrality for all changes at all sites, these estimates approximate $4N\mu$, where N is the evolutionary effective population size and μ is the neutral mutation rate per nucleotide site per generation. If we assume a mutation rate of $10^{-8}-10^{-9}$ then estimates of N are in the range 10^6-10^7 for these species. This calculation, which is likely to be conservative, and the fact that these high levels of polymorphism obtain in local populations, indicate that population sizes are very large. This pattern of polymorphism focuses attention on evolutionary processes affecting large numbers of flies, and possibly the whole species, rather than microgeographic heterogeneity affecting particular genotypes in particular places. It should not be surprising that many *Drosophila* population geneticists have ignored local habitat patchiness as a factor in the maintenance of polymorphism.

Recent developments for detecting selection at the molecular level

A new approach for detecting certain forms of natural selection has been developed recently based on DNA sequence comparison within and between species. This approach, described below, has the remarkable property of being relatively insensitive to the exact form of selection. So, for example, the approach should be able to identify overdominant selection whether it results from unconditional heterozygote advantage, or from marginal overdominance resulting from scramble selection. Although it will not distinguish between the two, it nevertheless allows us to ask the question, is natural selection acting to maintain a polymorphism in natural populations? Answering this question, in our view, is a necessary first step in a logical progression of investigation leading to an understanding of the actual ecological factors causing fitness differences between genotypes under selection.

The correlation between nucleotide polymorphism and divergence

The neutral theory of molecular evolution predicts a positive correlation between the level of nucleotide polymorphism at a locus and the rate of evolution (see Fig. 11.15). Mutations are assumed to be either selectively neutral or definitely deleterious. A locus in which mutations are largely neutral is expected to evolve faster than a locus with mostly deleterious mutations because more mutations are free to drift to fixation. Similarly, the largely neutral locus should have a correspondingly larger standing crop of polymorphism than the evolutionarily constrained locus. Thus, a

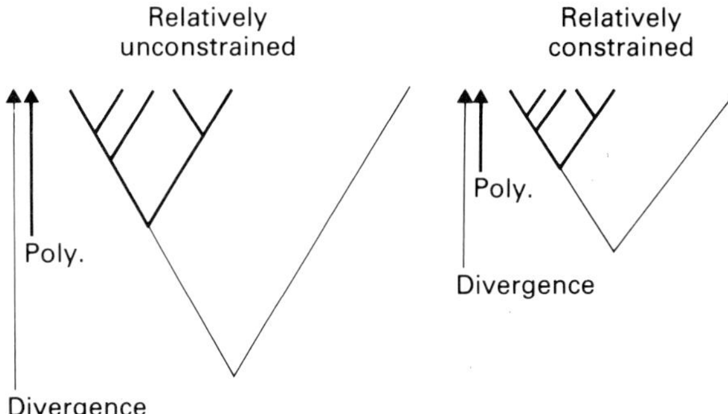

FIG. 11.15. Gene genealogies illustrating selectively neutral polymorphism within a species (heavy lines) and divergence between species in unconstrained versus constrained regions. Polymorphism and divergence are expected to be positively correlated.

simple test prediction of this neutral model is that the levels of polymorphism and sequence divergence at two or more loci (or regions) of a gene, should be positively correlated. Hudson *et al.* (1987) developed a conservative statistical test of this neutral hypothesis. This Hudson, Kreitman, Aguadé (HKA) test requires nucleotide polymorphism estimates from two (or more) regions or loci, and a between-species divergence estimate for the same regions. A significant test result indicates the presence of natural selection affecting levels of polymorphism in one or more region or other factors affecting rates of divergence, such as changing population size and slightly deleterious mutations (see Hudson *et al.* 1987).

What is the expected effect of natural selection on patterns of polymorphism and divergence? The simplest case is to consider one in which natural selection is acting at one site, possibly a balanced polymorphism for an amino acid replacement or a selectively favoured mutation in the process of sweeping to fixation, and ask what effect this selection will have on the level of polymorphism or rate of divergence at linked neutral sites. The rationale for considering this situation is that most nucleotide polymorphism and divergence occurs either in non-coding regions of genes, such as introns, or if it occurs in the coding regions of a gene, it is silent (synonymous change). Under the assumption that most of these mutations are selectively neutral, we are interested in knowing whether natural selection at another site affects the distribution of linked neutral mutations.

Two kinds of selection have been considered theoretically, balancing selection (Strobeck 1983, Hudson & Kaplan 1988, Kaplan *et al.* 1988) and directional selection (Maynard Smith & Haigh 1974, Kaplan *et al.* 1989). The two types of selection are illustrated in Figs 11.16 and 11.17. First, it should be apparent from these figures that natural selection affecting variation within a species is expected to have no effect on the number of accumulated differences between species. This is because the rate of neutral evolution is only dependent on the mutation rate to neutral alleles, and is unaffected by selection acting at linked sites. A significant departure from neutrality under the HKA test must indicate the presence of higher- or lower-than-expected levels of polymorphism in one (or more) loci rather than a departure in the amount of divergence. (With slightly deleterious mutations and changes in population size of sufficient magnitude, it is possible for rates of 'effectively' neutral evolution to vary. Whether or not such changes have occurred, or whether there are

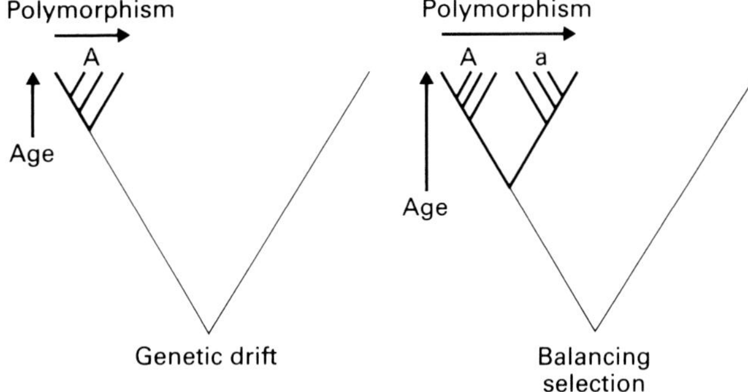

FIG. 11.16. Gene genealogies illustrating the effect of a balanced polymorphism (alleles A and a) on level of linked neutral polymorphism. See Fig. 11.18 for an example.

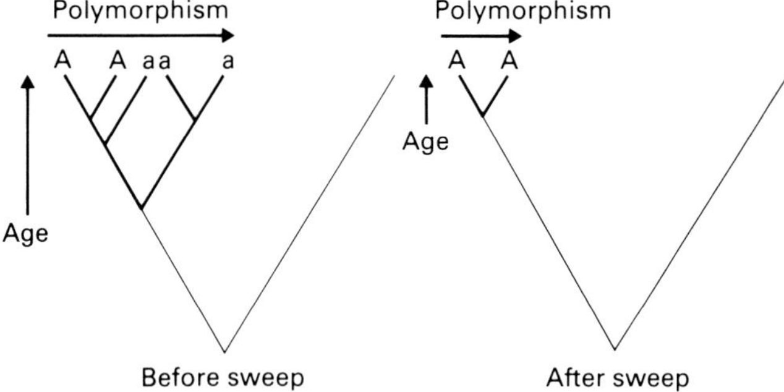

FIG. 11.17. Gene genealogies illustrating the effect of a selective substitution (allele A replaces a) on level of linked neutral polymorphism.

sufficient numbers of mutations of small absolute fitness effect is a problem well worth future investigation).

Higher-than-neutral levels of polymorphism are expected around a balanced polymorphism. The effect of a balanced polymorphism is to indefinitely maintain two (or possibly more) alleles in a population. The tightly linked region around the balanced polymorphism accumulates neutral mutations over time, and this accumulation of neutral differences between the two selected alleles is the source of 'excess' polymorphism. This excess neutral polymorphism is expected to be greatest around the site of selection and will rapidly decline to the neutral level as the recombinational distance increases.

Lower-than-neutral levels of polymorphism are expected around a site which has recently swept to fixation by natural selection. The effect of a selective sweep is to fix a single allele in the population or species. To the extent that recombination does not bring pre-existing neutral variation back on to the selected allele, the 'old' neutral variation will be swept away in the process of selection. This effect, as in the case of a balanced polymorphism, is expected to fall off with recombinational distance and also with the intensity of selection and the time since the selection event. Unlike balancing selection, this is an evolutionarily transient effect. However, the time to recovery can be very long.

Balancing selection and genetic drift at the Adh locus in D. melanogaster and D. simulans

Two examples comparing patterns of polymorphism and divergence of two loci, *Adh* and *Adh-dup* in *D. melanogaster* and *D. simulans* are shown in Figs 11.18 and 11.19. The *Adh-dup* locus is located immediately downstream from *Adh* and represents an ancient tandem duplication. The reading frame has been confirmed by cDNA analysis (Denker & Kreitman, unpublished) and the *Adh-dup* gene must encode a functional protein because the reading frame has been conserved between distantly related *Drosophila* species (Shaeffer & Aquadro 1987). The *Adh* locus of *D. melanogaster* shows a significant departure from neutrality when compared to either *Adh-dup* or to a 5′ flanking region (Kreitman & Hudson 1991). Figure 11.18 compares levels of polymorphism across *Adh* and *Adh-dup* to the levels predicted from a *D. melanogaster*–*D. simulans* between-species sequence comparison. Details of the procedure used in the figure for calculating the expected values from between-species sequence divergence are given in Kreitman and Hudson (1991). A higher-than-expected level of polymorphism is observed in *Adh* and it is centred

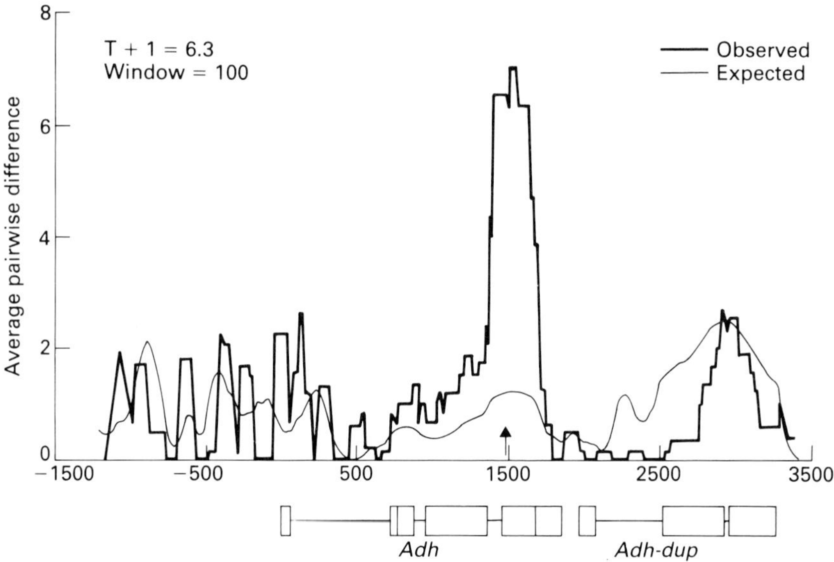

FIG. 11.18. Sliding window (100 bp width) for observed within-species silent polymorphism in *D. melanogaster* (sample size = 11) and for between-species silent divergence between *D. melanogaster* and *D. simulans* (expected). If every silent site was completely neutral the expected level should be a constant. The higher-than-expected silent polymorphism around position 1490, the site of the Adh^f/Adh^s protein polymorphism, may be a consequence of balancing selection. From Kreitman and Hudson (1991).

around the site of the Adh^f/Adh^s polymorphism (position 1490). Although the actual cause of the excess polymorphism in *Adh* may only partly have to do with the allozyme polymorphism (for explanation see Kreitman & Hudson 1991), the overall pattern is consistent with the presence of a balanced polymorphism for Adh^f/Adh^s.

Drosophila simulans does not have the allozyme polymorphism at position 1490, nor does it have any major protein polymorphism. Interestingly, the patterns of polymorphism and divergence are remarkably close, as shown in Fig. 11.19, and there is no indication of a departure from neutrality.

Adaptive evolution of Adh?

We have recently developed a statistical test to ask whether amino acid substitutions are accumulating between species at the rate expected if they are selectively neutral (McDonald & Kreitman 1991). Like the HKA

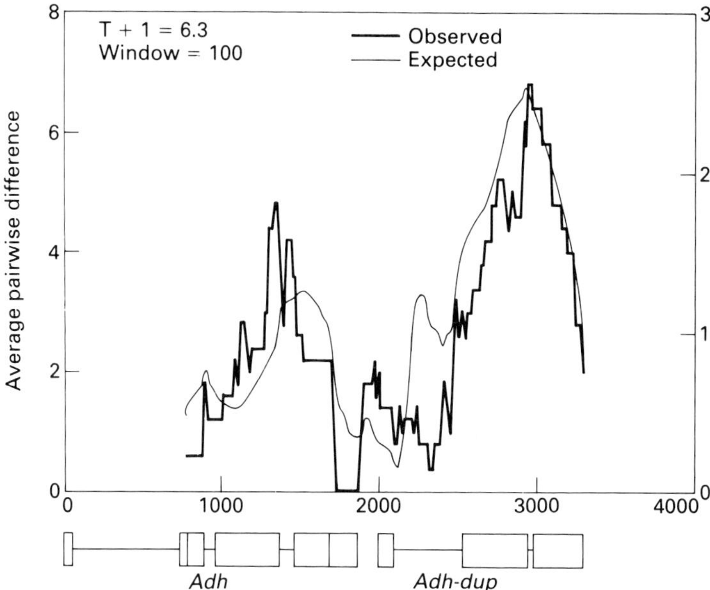

FIG. 11.19. Sliding window (100 bp width) for observed within-species silent polymorphism in *D. simulans* (sample size = 5) and for between-species silent divergence between *D. melanogaster* and *D. simulans* (expected). From Sumner (1991).

test, this new test compares nucleotide polymorphism and divergence in two regions, but in this case the two regions are amino acid replacement changes and synonymous changes in the coding regions of a gene. Under neutrality the expected ratio of replacement : synonymous polymorphisms within species should be the same as the expected ratio of fixed replacement : synonymous differences between species. As a selective alternative, if some amino acid replacement changes are selectively favoured, then the fixed amino acid replacements between species will consist of both neutral and selectively favoured mutations. Then the replacement : synonymous ratio should be higher for fixed differences between species than for within-species polymorphism.

The data consist of 12 *Adh* sequences of *D. melanogaster*, 6 of *D. simulans* and approximately 18 of *D. yakuba*. Forty-two synonymous changes and two amino acid replacement changes were polymorphisms within species. In contrast, there were 17 synonymous fixed differences between the species and 7 fixed amino acid differences. A *G* test of independence to test the null hypothesis that the proportion of replacement substitutions is independent of whether the substitutions are fixed or polymorphic was highly significant ($G = 7.43$, $p = 0.006$). The departure from neutrality is consistent with the selection model. We suggest that there has been selective pressure on the *Adh* enzyme since the divergence of these closely related species. But, we have no direct information on the environmental factors giving rise to the selection.

Enzyme evolution and enzyme performance

ADH enzyme function of three alleles of *D. melanogaster*, Adh^f, Adh^s and Adh^{71k} and the major allele of *D. simulans* has been studied in detail (Heinstra *et al.* 1988, and many other references). ADH-F and ADH-71k differ from ADH-S by a single substitution, a Thr for Lys substitution at position 192. ADH-71k differs from ADH-F by one additional substitution, a Ser for Pro substitution at position 214. A cladistic analysis using *D. yakuba* as outgroup shows that ADH-F is derived from ADH-S, and ADH-71k is derived from ADH-F. The *D. simulans* ADH differs from the *D. melanogaster* ADHs at two positions, Ala for Ser and Lys for Gln at 1 and 82, respectively. The Ala substitution at position 1 in *D. melanogaster* and the Lys substitution at position 82 in *D. simulans* are derived. The *in vitro* activities of fly extracts towards ethanol has the following rank order: ADH-71k > ADH-F > ADH-S > *simulans*-ADH. Heinstra has noted the ordering of activity mimicks the ordering of mutational changes from the common ancestor of the two species and may indicate natural selection for increased alcohol tolerance/utilization. *Drosophila melanogaster* is more tolerant of high concentrations of primary alcohol (David & van Herrewege 1983, many references in Chambers 1988) and uses ethanol more efficiently (Geer *et al.* 1985). *Drosophila melanogaster* adults are attracted to alcohols more readily than *D. simulans* (Hoffmann & Parsons 1984) and *D. melanogaster* females prefer ethanol-containing media for egg-laying (Hougouto *et al.* 1982).

The activity difference between ADH-F and ADH-S is largely due to protein quantity rather than catalytic properties but is not reflected in RNA level (Laurie & Stam 1988). The enzyme is inhibited by NADH, the reduced cofactor, and order of inhibition of the four alleles is ADH-F < ADH-71k < ADH-S < ADH-*simulans*. Product inhibition may be important at low concentrations of ethanol, where ADH-*simulans* will show a greater inhibition. Understanding the kinetics of catalysis, and the differences between the alleles, is complicated by the fact that ADH catalyzes not only the oxidation of alcohol to aldehyde, but also aldehyde to acetaldehyde. More than 90% of ethanol is degraded by this pathway (Geer *et al.* 1985, Heinstra *et al.* 1988).

An incredibly large number of cage experiments have been done with Adh^f and Adh^s alleles, varying an equally incredible number of environmental factors (most importantly alcohol and temperature) to decipher the cause of the protein polymorphism. The literature is reviewed by Van Delden (1982, 1984) and by Chambers (1988). Almost all conceivable results have been obtained with respect to the protein polymorphism. According to Chambers, 'For the present, it is probably fair to conclude that taken overall these experiments reveal the selection coefficients to be small and rather variable'.

Part of the explanation for the inconsistency of results with cages may be that there is considerable activity variation within alleles of *Adh* (Aquadro *et al.* 1986), some of which is now known to be caused by tightly linked *cis*-acting factors. There are also many *trans*-acting genetic factors affecting ADH activity (Laurie-Ahlberg *et al.* 1980). In an ongoing analysis of the Adh^f/Adh^s gene frequency cline along the East Coast of the United States we have recently discovered the cline may be caused by a distinct subset of Adh^f alleles (Berry & Kreitman, unpublished). The Adh^s allele can also show strong shifts in gene frequency in cage experiments when it is carried on a chromosome containing the cosmopolitan inversion In (2lt) (Van Delden 1984, Van Delden & Kamping 1989).

Another part of the explanation for the inconsistency of cage experiment results may have to do with the absolute selective difference between the two major alleles: it may, indeed, be small. How small can the selective difference between the alleles be before they are indistiguishable by selection? The answer is, $s < 1/(2N_e)$, a classic result from population genetics theory. Unfortunately, we do not know what N_e is for *D. melanogaster* but it has been indirectly estimated to be $N_e \approx 10^6$, based on calculations of $4N_e\mu$ from nucleotide polymorphism data (Kreitman 1983, 1991). The obvious implication is that selection coefficients may be very small, certainly orders of magnitude below the smallest detectable values in laboratory cage experiments. If this were so, then there would be no hope of using cage experiments to confirm observations in the wild. Unfortunately, we do not know even the order of magnitude of the selective difference between alleles.

Are we ready to place the evolutionary play into the ecological theatre?

Adh is certainly one of the best-studied protein polymorphisms in *Drosophila* and one of the best-studied polymorphisms in nature (Chambers 1988 review has 363 references!). Yet, even though the evidence for the polymorphism being subject to natural selection is overwhelming, we know almost nothing of the environmental factors affecting the gene frequencies. For example, essentially nothing is known about the environmental cause(s) of the latitudinal gene frequency clines (it does not correlate with temperature). With the exception of winery populations, almost no work has been done on the microgeographic distribution of the *Adh* genotypes. Maybe this would be a good place to start to look for habitat patchiness as a factor influencing polymorphism.

The same can be said of interspecific diversity and competition. Heinstra (1987) has made the very interesting observation that the evolution of *Adh* from the common ancestor of *D. melanogaster* and *D. simulans* has been towards increased activity in *D. melanogaster*, and this may reflect selective pressure for alcohol utilization and/or tolerance. That the amino acid differences between the species has been selected is supported by the recent findings of McDonald and Kreitman (1991). What habitat differences have driven the evolution of ADH? And do these differences contribute to the patterns of habitat segregation observed for the species? These are the kinds of questions we must answer before we can assess whether scramble competition in ephemeral patches is important for allowing coexistence of the species. They are also the kinds of questions we must answer if ever ecology and evolutionary genetics are to be unified.

ACKNOWLEDGEMENTS

B.S. and C.D. would like to thank Marc Bingley, David Coates and Andrew Davis for their helpful discussions. The ecological background was supported by NERC studentships to M. Bingley, W.D. Atkinson, M. Begon, R. Cooper, J. Kearney and J. Rosewell. The ecological work was also supported by NERC grants GR3/4736 and GR3/5464 to Bryan Shorrocks.

REFERENCES

Andrewartha, H. C. & Birch, L. C. (1954). *The Distribution and Abundance of Animals.* University of Chicago Press, Chicago, IL, USA.

Aquadro, C. F. (1991). Molecular population genetics of Drosophila. *Molecular Approaches to Fundamental and Applied Entomology* (Ed. by J. Oakeshott & M. Whitten), pp. 222–266. Springer Verlag, Berlin, Germany.

Aquadro, C. F., Deese, S. F., Bland, M. M., Langley, C. H. & Laurie-Ahlberg, C. C. (1986). Molecular population genetics of the alcohol dehydrogenase gene region of Drosophila melanogaster. *Genetics*, **114**, 1165–1190.

Atkinson, W. D. & Shorrocks, B. (1981). Competition on a divided and ephemeral resource: a simulation model. *Journal of Animal Ecology*, **50**, 461–471.

Bellows, T. S. (1981). The descriptive properties of some models for density dependence.

Journal of Animal Ecology, **50**, 139–156.

Birch, L. C., Dobzhansky, Th., Elliot, P. O. & Lewontin, R. C. (1963). Relative fitness of geographic races of *Drosophila serrata*. *Evolution*, **17**, 72–83.

Bulmer, M. G. (1972). Multiple niche polymorphism. *American Naturalist*, **106**, 254–257.

Chambers, G. K. (1988). The *Drosophila* alcohol dehydrogenase gene-enzyme system. *Advances in Genetics*, **25**, 39–107.

Chiang, H. C. & Hodson, A. C. (1950). An analytical study of population growth in *Drosophila melanogaster*. *Ecological Monographs*, **20**, 174–206.

Christianson, F. B. (1974). Sufficient conditions for protected polymorphism in a subdivided population. *American Naturalist*, **108**, 157–166.

Christianson, F. B. (1975). Hard and soft selection in a subdivided population. *American Naturalist*, **109**, 11–16.

Clarke, B. (1973a). The effect of mutation on population size. *Nature*, **242**, 196–197.

Clarke, B. (1973b). Mutation and population size. *Heredity*, **31**, 367–379.

Cooper, R. (1990). Competition and genetic variation in a patchy environment: a laboratory model. PhD Thesis, Leeds, UK.

David, J. R. & van Herrewege, J. (1983). Adaptation to alcoholic fermentation in *Drosophila* species: relationship between alcohol tolerance and larval habitat. *Comparative Biochemical Physiology*, **74A**, 283–288.

De Jong, G. (1982). The influence of dispersal pattern on the evolution of fecundity. *Netherlands Journal of Zoology*, **32**, 1–30.

den Boer, P. J. (1968). Spreading of risk and the stabilisation of animal numbers. *Acta Biotheoretica*, **18**, 165–194.

Geer, B. W., Langevin, M. L. & McKechnie, S. W. (1985). Dietary ethanol and lipid synthesis in Drosophila melanogaster. *Biochemical Genetics*, **23**, 607–622.

Gilpin, M. E. (1990). Extinction of finite metapopulations in correlated environments. *Living in a Patchy Environment* (Ed. by B. Shorrocks & I. Swingland), pp. 177–186. Oxford Science Publications, Oxford, UK.

Gilpin, M. E. & Ayala, F. J. (1973). Global models of growth and competition. *Proceedings of the National Academy of Sciences*, **70**, 3590–3593.

Hanski, I. (1981). Coexistence of competitors in patchy environments with and without predation. *Oikos*, **37**, 306–312.

Hanski, I. (1983). Coexistence of competitors in patchy environments. *Ecology*, **64**, 493–500.

Hanski, I. & Gilpin, M. E. (1991). Metapopulation dynamics: brief history and conceptual domain. *Biological Journal of the Linnean Society*, **42**, 3–16.

Hassell, M. P. (1975). Density dependence in single species populations. *Journal of Animal Ecology*, **42**, 693–726.

Hassell, M. P. & Comins, H. N. (1976). Discrete time models for two-species competition. *Theoretical Population Biology*, **9**, 202–221.

Heed, W. B. & Mangen, R. L. (1986). Community ecology of the Sonoran Desert *Drosophila*. *The Genetics and Biology of Drosophila* (Ed. by M. Ashburner, H. L. Carson & J. N. Thompson), Vol. 3e, pp. 311–345. Academic Press, London, UK.

Heinstra, P. W. H. (1987). Physiological significance of genetic variation in alcohol dehydrogenase of *Drosophila*. PhD Thesis, University of Utrecht, The Netherlands.

Heinstra, P. W. H., Thürig, G. E. W., Scharloo, W., Drenth, W. & Nolte, R. J. M. (1988). Kinetics and thermodynamics of ethanol oxidation catalyzed by genetic variants of the alcohol dehydrogenase from *Drosophila melanogaster* and *D. simulans*. *Biochimica et Biophysica Acta*, **967**, 224–233.

Hoffmann, A. A. & Parsons, P. A. (1984). Olfactory response and resource utilization in *Drosophila*: interspecific comparisons. *Biological Journal of the Linnean Society*, **22**, 43–53.

Hougouto, N., Lietaert, M. C., Libion-Mannaert, M., Feytmans, E. & Elens, A. (1982). Oviposition-site preference and Adh activity in *Drosophila melanogaster*. *Genetica*, **58**, 121–128.

Hudson, R. R. & Kaplan, N. R. (1988). The coalescent process in models with selection and recombination. *Genetics*, **120**, 831–840.

Hudson, R. R., Kreitman, M. & Aguadé, M. (1987). A test of neutral molecular evolution based on nucleotide data. *Genetics*, **116**, 153–159.

Hutchinson, G. E. (1965). *The Ecological Theater and the Evolutionary Play*. Yale University Press, New Haven, CT, USA.

Ives, A. R. (1988). Covariance, coexistence and the population dynamics of two competitors using a patchy resource. *Journal of Theoretical Biology*, **133**, 345–361.

Ives, A. R. & May, R. M. (1985). Competition within and between species in a patchy environment: relations between microscopic and macroscopic models. *Journal of Theoretical Biology*, **115**, 65–92.

Jaenike, J. (1986). Feeding behaviour and future fecundity in *Drosophila*. *American Naturalist*, **127**, 118–123.

Jaenike, J. & Selander, R. K. (1979). Ecological generalism in *Drosophila falleni*: genetic evidence. *Evolution*, **33**, 741–748.

Kaplan, N. R., Darden, T. & Hudson, R. R. (1988). The coalescent process in models with selection. *Genetics*, **120**, 819–829.

Kaplan, N. R., Hudson, R. R. & Langley, C. H. (1989). The 'hitchhiking effect' revisited. *Genetics*, **123**, 887–899.

Kareiva, P. (1989). Renewing the dialogue between theory and experiments in population ecology. *Perspectives in Ecological Theory* (Ed. by J. Roughgarden, R. M. May & S. A. Levin), pp. 68–88, Princeton University Press, Princeton, NJ, USA.

Keith, T. P. (1983). Frequency distribution of esterase-5 alleles in two populations of *Drosophila pseudoobscura*. *Genetics*, **105**, 135–155.

Keith, T. P., Brooks, L. D., Lewontin, R. C., Martinez-Cruzado, J. C. & Rigby, D. L. (1985). Nearly identical allelic distributions of xanthene dehydrogenase in two populations of *Drosophila pseudoobscura*. *Molecular Biology and Evolution*, **2**, 206–216.

Kreitman, M. (1983). Nucleotide polymorphism at the alcohol dehydrogenase locus of *Drosophila melanogaster*. *Nature*, **304**, 412–417.

Kreitman, M. (1991). Detecting selection at the level of DNA. *Evolution at the Molecular Level*. (Ed. by R. K. Selander, A. G. Clark & T. S. Whittam), Sinauer, Sunderland, MA, USA.

Kreitman, M. & Aguadé, M. (1986). Genetic uniformity in two populations of *Drosophila melanogaster* as revealed by filter hybridization of four-nucleotide-recognizing restriction enzyme digests. *Proceedings of the National Academy of Sciences, USA*, **83**, 3562–3566.

Kreitman, M. & Hudson, R. R. (1991). Inferring the evolutionary histories of the Adh and Adh-dup loci in *Drosophila melanogaster* from patterns of polymorphism and divergence. *Genetics*, **127**, 565–582.

Lachaise, D. & Tsacas, L. (1984). Breeding sites in tropical drosophilids. *The Genetics and Biology of Drosophila* (Ed. by M. Ashburner, H. L. Carson & J. N. Thompson), Vol. 3d, pp. 221–332, Academic Press, London, UK.

Laurie, C. C. & Stam, L. F. (1988). Quantitative analysis of RNA produced by Slow and Fast alleles of Adh in Drosophila melanogaster. *Proceedings of the National Academy of Sciences, USA*, **85**, 5161–5165.

Laurie-Ahlberg, C. C., Maroni, G., Bewley, G. C., Lucchesi, J. C. & Weir, B. S. (1980). Quantitative genetic variation of enzyme activities in natural populations of Drosophila melanogaster. *Proceedings of the National Academy of Sciences, USA*, **77**, 1073–1077.

Levene, H. (1953). Genetic equilibrium when more than one ecological niche is available. *American Naturalist*, **87**, 131–133.

Levins, R. & MacArthur, R. H. (1966). The maintenance of genetic polymorphism in a spatially heterogeneous environment: variation on a theme by Howard Levene. *American Naturalist*, **100**, 585–589.

Lewontin, R. C. & Hubby, J. L. (1966). A molecular approach to the study of genic heterozygosity in natural populations. II. Amount of variation and degree of heterozygosity in natural populations of *Drosophila pseudoobscura*. *Genetics*, **54**, 595–609.

Lewontin, R. C. & Krakauer, J. (1973). Distribution of gene frequency as a test of the theory of the selective neutrality of polymorphisms. *Genetics*, **74**, 175–195.

Li, C. C. (1955). The stability of an equilibrium and the average fitness of a population. *American Naturalist*, **89**, 281–296.

Lloyd, M. (1967). Mean crowding. *Journal of Animal Ecology*, 36, 1–30.

McDonald, J. H. & Kreitman, M. (1991). Adaptive protein evolution at the Adh locus in *Drosophila*. *Nature*, **351**, 652–654.

Maynard Smith, J. (1966). Sympatric speciation. *American Naturalist*, **100**, 637–650.

Maynard Smith, J. (1970). Genetic polymorphism in a varied environment. *American Naturalist*, **104**, 487–490.

Maynard Smith, J. & Haigh, J. (1974). The hitch-hiking effect of a favourable gene. *Genetical Research*, **23**, 23–35.

Nei, M. & Maruyama, T. (1975). Lewontin–Krakauer test for neutral genes. *Genetics*, **80**, 395.

Nicholson, A. J. (1954). An outline of the population dynamics of natural populations. *Australian Journal of Zoology*, **2**, 9–65.

Oakeshott, J. G., Gibson, J. B., Anderson, P. R., Knibb, W. R., Anderson, D. G. & Chambers, G. K. (1982). Alcohol dehydrogenase and glycerol-3-phosphate dehydrogenase clines in *Drosophila melanogaster* on different continents. *Evolution*, **36**, 86–96.

Ray, C. & Gilpin, M. (1991). The effect of conspecific attraction on metapopulation dynamics. *Biological Journal of the Linnean Society*, **42**, 123–134.

Robertson, A. (1975). Remarks on the Lewontin–Krakauer test. *Genetics*, **80**, 396.

Rosewell, J. (1990). The dynamics of a single-species population on a divided and ephemeral resource. *Living in a Patchy Environment* (Ed. by B. Shorrocks & I. Swingland), pp. 63–74. Oxford University Press, Oxford, UK.

Rosewell, J. & Shorrocks, B. (1987). The implication of survival rates in natural populations of *Drosophila*: capture–recapture experiments on domestic species. *Biological Journal of the Linnean Society*, **32**, 373–384.

Rosewell, J., Shorrocks, B. & Edwards, K. (1990). Competition on a divided and ephemeral resource: testing the assumptions. I. aggregation. *Journal of Animal Ecology*, **59**, 977–1001.

Sang, J. H. (1950). Population growth in *Drosophila* cultures. *Biological Review*, **25**, 188–217.

Shaeffer, S. W. & Aquadro, C. F. (1987). Nucleotide sequence of the Adh gene region of *Drosophila pseudoobscura*: evolutionary change and evidence for an ancient gene duplication. *Genetics*, **117**, 61–73.

Shorrocks, B. (1982). The breeding sites of temperate woodland *Drosophila*. *The Genetics and Biology of Drosophila*, Vol. 3b. (Ed. by M. Ashburner, H. L. Carson & J. N. Thompson Jr), pp. 385–428. Academic Press, London, UK.

Shorrocks, B. (1990). Competition and selection in a patchy and ephemeral habitat: the implications for insect life-cycles. *Insect Life Cycles* (Ed. by F. Gilbert), pp. 215–228, Springer Verlag, London, UK.

Shorrocks, B. (1991). Competition on a divided and ephemeral resource: a cage experiment.

Biological Journal of the Linnean Society, **43**, 211–220.

Shorrocks, B. & Rosewell, J. (1986). Guild size in drosophilids: a simulation model. *Journal of Animal Ecology*, **55**, 527–541.

Shorrocks, B. & Rosewell, J. (1987). Spatial patchiness and community structure: coexistence and guild size of drosophilids on ephemeral resources. *Organisation of Communities: Past and Present* (Ed. by J. H. R. Gee & P. S. Giller), pp. 29–51. Blackwell Scientific Publications, Oxford, UK.

Shorrocks, B., Atkinson, W. D. & Charlesworth, P. (1979). Competition on a divided and ephemeral resource. *Journal of Animal Ecology*, **48**, 899–908.

Shorrocks, B., Rosewell, J., Edwards, K. & Atkinson, W. D. (1984). Interspecific competition is not a major organizing force in many insect communities. *Nature*, **310**, 310–312.

Shorrocks, B., Rosewell, J. & Edwards, K. (1990). Competition on a divided and ephemeral resource: testing the assumptions. II. association. *Journal of Animal Ecology*, **59**, 1003–1017.

Simmons, G. M., Kreitman, M., Quattlebaum, W. F. & Miyashita, N. (1989). Molecular analysis of the alleles of alcohol dehydrogenase along a cline in *Drosophila melanogaster*. I. Maine, North Carolina, and Florida. *Evolution*, **43**, 393–409.

Strobeck, C. (1974). Selection in a fine-grained environment. *American Naturalist*, **109**, 419–425.

Strobeck, C. (1983). Expected linkage disequilibrium for a neutral locus linked to a chromosomal arrangement. *Genetics*, **103**, 545–555.

Stubbs, M. (1977). Density dependence in the life-cycles of animals and its importance in k-and r-strategies. *Journal of Animal Ecology*, **46**, 677–688.

Sumner, C. J. (1991). Nucleotide polymorphism in alcohol dehydrogenase duplicate locus of *Drosophila simulans*. Undergraduate thesis, Princeton University, NJ, USA.

Taylor, L. R. (1961). Aggregation, variance and the mean. *Nature, London*, **189**, 732–735.

Van Delden, W. (1982). The alcohol dehydrogenase polymorphism in *Drosophila melanogaster*. *Evolutionary Biology*, **15**, 187–222.

Van Delden, W. (1984). The alcohol dehydrogenase polymorphism in *Drosophila melanogaster*, facts and problems. *Population Biology and Evolution* (Ed. by K. Wührmann & V. Loeschcke). Springer Verlag, Berlin, Federal Republic of Germany.

Van Delden, W. & Kamping, A. (1989). The association between the polymorphisms at the Adh and αGpdh loci and the In(2L)t inversion in *Drosophila melanogaster* in relation to temperature. *Evolution*, **43**, 775–793.

Wallace, B. (1968a). Polymorphism, population size, and genetic load. *Population Biology and Evolution* (Ed. by R. C. Lewontin), pp. 87–108. Syracuse University Press, NY, USA.

Wallace, B. (1968b). *Topics in Population Genetics*. Norton, NY, USA.

Wallace, B. (1975). Hard and soft selection revisited. *Evolution*, **29**, 465–473.

Wallace, B. (1981). *Basic Population Genetics*. Columbia University Press, NY, USA.

Yokoyama, S. & Schaal, B. A. (1985). A note on multiple-niche polymorphism in plant populations. *American Naturalist*, **125**, 158–163.

PART 3
ECOLOGY IN GENETICS

12. GENETIC HETEROGENEITY AND ECOLOGY

JOHN A. ENDLER

Department of Biological Sciences, University of California, Santa Barbara, CA 93106, USA

SUMMARY

Genetic variation is widespread among many different species, so natural selection and genetic drift can alter the distribution of variants in time and space. Genetic variation in demographic parameters can have significant effects on population dynamics within species as well as affecting other species in the food web. In the longer term, genetic variation and evolution can also affect relationships in the food web. Natural selection of ecological traits may affect the form and dynamics of all ecological phenomena, and this will also affect genetic variation for these traits. Ecology and evolution are so closely interrelated that they should not be regarded as separate fields.

INTRODUCTION

Ecologists often treat all members of a single species as if they have identical biological properties (except age and sex). But in most species, individuals vary genetically, and the ecological consequences of individual variation are only just beginning to be appreciated (May 1986, Ohgushi 1987, 1988, Lomnicki 1988). Wherever there is genetic variation, natural selection and genetic drift can alter the distribution of variants in time, and local differences in the physical and biological environment can cause differentiation in space (Endler 1977, 1986, Ewens 1979). This chapter explores some of the ecological consequences of this genetic heterogeneity.

GENETIC VARIATION AND POPULATION DYNAMICS

Only a few models explicitly assume genetic variation in demographic parameters but they yield some fascinating yet largely ignored phenomena and insights (Endler 1990). In these models, population size and dynamics depend upon genotype or gene frequencies, and genotype and gene frequencies depend upon population size. The mutual dependence of genotype frequencies and total population size can make the dynamics very different from that expected if one considers either one independently. Excellent examples are given by Anderson and King (1970), King and Anderson (1971) and Roughgarden (1971). The following properties are characteristic of models including both ecology and genetics, where genotypes differ in demographic parameters such as age-specific survivorship, fecundity, *r* and *K* (from Anderson & King 1970, King & Anderson 1971, Roughgarden 1971, Charlesworth 1971, 1980, Clarke 1972, 1973, Lomnicki 1988).

1 The time course of total population size is not predictable from the average of the demographic parameters of all genotypes. The reason for this is that differences in genotypic parameters cause some genotypes to increase at the expense of others (natural selection). As a result, the genotypes contribute unequally and differently to population size as they change in frequency during the course of natural selection. This can result in, for example, a population growing for a while, remaining roughly constant, and then growing again, as the majority genotype changes from (say) one homozygote, to the heterozygote, to the other homozygote as allele frequencies change. An excellent example is given by Anderson and King (1970).

2 The mean number of progeny per individual will not be a good predictor of population dynamics in the absence of separate data for each genotype; the mean number of progeny per individual will change if natural selection results in turnover of genotypes varying in this parameter, or if they vary in the relationship between fecundity and population density. In addition, demographic differences may also result in gene frequencies and age class distributions oscillating until an equilibrium is reached. This can also result in oscillation of progeny per individual as frequencies or age classes oscillate.

3 Oscillation in *N* (total population size) and *p* (allele frequency), due to genotypic variation in demography, may be damped, exist as stable limit cycles, or unstable cycles, depending upon the magnitude of the *r*s (intrinsic rates of increase) of the genotypes. The average *r* over all genotypes may not be a good predictor of the presence or absence of oscillations because the genotypic composition of the population may change during the oscillations, changing the average *r*. Because oscillations in *N* may increase the probability of extinction, it is extremely dangerous from a conservation viewpoint to assume that, because an *r* calculated on all individuals predicts decaying or no oscillations, that oscillations will not necessarily occur.

4 Smooth changes in population size are not necessarily expected as long as natural selection proceeds. With density dependence, there can be temporary plateaux in N. These could be mistakenly interpreted as resulting from brief periods of environmental stability rather than temporary population stasis as one set of genotypes replaces another set. In some cases polymorphic populations may have larger population densities than monomorphic populations. If such a polymorphism is transient, then a population will start small, increase for a while, and then decline again, even if the environment remains constant. All these factors have important implications for monitoring endangered species and designing refuges with particular target population sizes.

5 Age structure and gene frequencies are intimately related; a change in one may lead to a change in the other. If the age structure of a local population has reached equilibrium and there is a change in gene frequency (for example, resulting from immigration, habitat change, or even mutation), there can be large changes in age structure and life-history schedules. This will then have profound effects on the population size and population dynamics, influencing the probability of extinction.

6 In the initial stage of growth of a population, it will probably consist mostly of high r genotypes. High K individuals will be at a relative disadvantage if there is a negative relationship between r and K properties among genotypes. If so, then high K individuals may initially decline in frequency during the growth phase of a population. Although high r genotypes may initially have an advantage, they will decline as the population approaches equilibrium, and this may be especially rapid in environments with low carrying capacity (K). This must be considered when reintroducing organisms into recovered habitats. If too few low r or high K genotypes are included in the reintroduction, then founder effects in K genotypes may result in a loss of genetic variation and a consequent inability to respond to further ecological and evolutionary change, even if initially large numbers of individuals were introduced — large numbers do little good if most of them (r genotypes) are removed by natural selection in a few generations. On the other hand, in heavily or frequently disturbed habitats, the population may never approach equilibrium and the genetic composition of the initial population may be a good predictor of its later composition. Such a population may also not change so much nor as irregularly as one living in a stable enough habitat so that it could approach equilibrium.

7 Using a similar argument, if the environment is seasonal, random, or harsh, making r aspects of fitness more important than K, then the predicted most common genotypes will follow the relative values of their

r rather than both r and K. If the environment is relatively aseasonal, constant, or non-harsh, the population may be near equilibrium so K genotypic properties will be better than r in predicting the most common genotypes, though both will be important. Again, these phenomena can have profound effects on population dynamics and the probability of local extinction.

In summary, population dynamics cannot be fully understood, or reliably predicted, unless the demographic parameters of all distinct genotypes are well known. This is especially true for rare, endangered and reintroduced species, which may experience large changes in allele frequencies as a result of genetic drift or founder events.

GENETIC VARIATION IN ECOLOGICALLY IMPORTANT BIOLOGICAL PROPERTIES

Stable environments are almost certainly the exception rather than the rule; climatic and other environmental parameters change over many different time scales and have done so for millions of years (Davis 1986). If the environment changes so rapidly that the genetic variation in a population does not allow a parallel response to natural selection, then the population, and perhaps even the species, may go extinct. Although genetic variation is widespread in animals and plants, we really do not know how much is needed to respond to major and rapid changes in the environment such as that experienced in the transitions between glacial and interglacial periods or human-induced disturbance, and ecological genetical studies of primary succession at high latitudes or altitudes are rare.

Although surveys of genetic variation cannot yet seriously address the response of species to radically changing environments, they do suggest that genetic variation itself can have direct ecological consequences. In a variety of animals and plants, there is a tendency for more heterozygous individuals to have faster growth rates, lower metabolic demands, faster developmental rates, shorter developmental times, greater developmental stability and greater disease resistance (Mitton & Grant 1984, Mitton *et al.* 1986, Allendorf & Leary 1986, Ledig 1986). Small populations are likely to become more homozygous, making deleterious recessive alleles homozygous, allowing them to be expressed, with consequences opposite to increased heterozygosity — this is collectively known as inbreeding depression (summaries in Ralls *et al.* 1986 and Ledig 1986). If population dynamics results in drastically reduced population size, this may result in periods of inbreeding depression, further affecting population dynamics, and possibly increasing the probability of extirpation of the population or extinction of the species. Crossing of individuals from different populations may in some cases have no effect, positive effects, and in other cases negative effects ('outbreeding depression'), depending upon the species, local differentiation, coadaptation and the distance of dispersal and gene flow (Endler 1977, Ledig 1986, Templeton 1986). These effects vary widely among species and populations within species, suggesting that the effects of genetic variation should not be ignored in ecological studies, and that we cannot generalize among populations or among species.

IMPLICATIONS OF GENETIC VARIATION IN SPACE

Not only is there extensive evidence for genetic variation of ecologically important traits within populations but there is also evidence for geographic variation in these traits. Guppies provide an excellent example. Guppies are small Poeciliid fishes and live in small northeastern South American streams with a variety of predators. The numbers and kinds of predators vary within and among streams (Haskins *et al.* 1961, Seghers 1973, Liley & Seghers 1975, Endler 1978, 1983, Fig. 12.1). Within streams, as elevation declines, the number and danger (to guppies) of predators increases, and this occurs in two different fish faunas in Trinidad and Venezuela (Endler 1983). The increase in number and danger of predator species, with decreasing elevation, results in a predation intensity gradient. In addition, the more dangerous predators tend to prefer larger guppies (and other fish), and the least dangerous predators (*R. hartii*, *A. pulchur*) prefer smaller guppies and juveniles. The net effect is that at lower elevations there is intense predation predominantly on larger size classes and at higher elevations there is low predation mostly on juveniles (Fig. 12.1).

Gradients in numerous ecologically relevant traits parallel the gradients in predation intensity and size-specific predation, and some of these are shown in Fig. 12.1. As predation intensity increases, colour patterns become less conspicuous (Haskins *et al.* 1961, Endler 1978, 1980, 1983), bodies become more fusiform (Endler 1980), body size declines (Haskins *et al.* 1961, Seghers 1973, Liley & Seghers 1975, Endler 1978, 1980, Reznick & Endler 1982), fecundity increases, interbrood interval increases, age at maturity decreases, reproductive allocation increases (Reznick 1982a, b, Reznick & Endler 1982, Reznick & Bryga 1987, Reznick *et al.* 1990); schooling of adults and juveniles increases (Seghers 1974, Magurran & Seghers 1990a); guppies become more wary of predators (Magurran & Seghers 1990b) and spend less courtship time in conspicuous visual displays (Magurran & Seghers 1990c). There is also geographical variation in mate

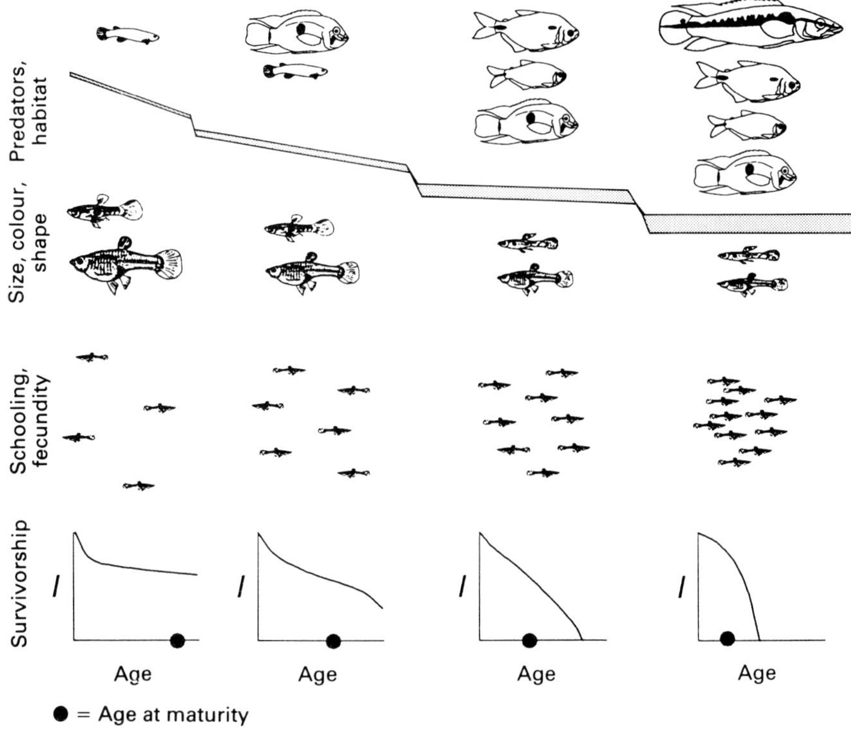

FIG. 12.1. Geographic variation in guppies (*Poecilia reticulata*). This figure is meant to show the qualitative but not the quantitative variation in guppies with predator community; differences are exaggerated for clarity. The upstream–downstream sequence (left–right) of diurnal visually hunting predators is (1) *Rivulus hartii*; (2) *Aequidens pulchur* + *R. hartii*; (3) *A. pulchur* + *Astyanax bimaculatus* + *Hemibrycon dentatum*; (4) *Crenicichla alta* + *A. pulchur* + *A. bimaculatus* + *H. dentatum*. Their risk to guppies is ranked as *R. hartii*, *A. pulchur*, *H. dentatum*, *A. bimaculatus* and *C. alta* the most dangerous (Haskins *et al.* 1961, Seghers 1973, Liley & Seghers 1975, Endler 1978). In some streams, community 2 is replaced with *H. dentatum* alone, *A. bimaculatus* alone, or both together. In addition, the crepuscular and nocturnal predators *Gymnotus carapo*, *Rhamdia quelen* and *Hoplias malabaricus* range through communities 3 and 4; they are about as dangerous to guppies as *H. dentatum*, *A. bimaculatus*, and *C. alta*, respectively. The distribution of all of these predators is limited by habitat preferences as well as waterfalls of various heights. See text for details of the correlated variation in guppies.

choice criteria, although it does not appear to parallel the variation in predation intensity (Houde 1988, Stoner & Breden 1988, Houde & Endler 1990). It is clear that many different ecologically important traits vary geographically in guppies, and the differences are heritable.

This pattern is likely to occur in many other species of animals and plants because the distribution of predators, parasitoids or herbivores of a given species never perfectly corresponds to the species of interest, and other ecological factors which may induce natural selection will also vary within the range of any species. Indeed, there is geographical and microgeographical variation in a variety of traits, including metal tolerance and nutrient requirements in plants (Bradshaw & Berry, Ch. 18, this volume), insect–plant interactions (Futuyma & May, Ch. 6, this volume, Edmunds & Alstad 1978, 1981, Alstad & Edmunds 1983a, b), food preferences (Partridge & Green 1985); timing of diapause in copepods (Hairston & Olds 1984) and insects (Denno & Dingle 1981, Dingle *et al.* 1982, Tauber & Tauber 1982, Palmer & Dingle 1989), migratory behaviour in birds (Berthold 1988) and insects (Andersen 1982, Palmer & Dingle 1989) and in which species is the best model in Mullerian and Batesian mimicry systems (Sheppard 1958, Endler 1982). Thus, we cannot extrapolate ecological parameters from one population to another.

IMPLICATIONS OF GENETIC VARIATION IN TIME

A distinction is often made between 'ecological time' and 'evolutionary time', presumably as a result of one or more of three implicit assumptions: (1) evolution is slow and gradual, and occurs at a sufficiently slow rate relative to ecological processes that evolutionary processes can be ignored during ecological studies; (2) natural selection (directional selection) is sufficiently weak that it results in slow evolution; (3) genetic drift predominates so evolution is slow. All three assumptions are likely to be wrong. Because ecologically relevant traits are unlikely to be selectively neutral, genetic drift in them should be uncommon, and will only occur in populations with small effective breeding populations. Natural selection can be quite strong in nature (Endler 1986). There are palaeontological objections to the assumption of constant gradual evolution; evolutionary rates are quite variable (Stanley 1981, Futuyma 1986). In addition, our field experimental work with guppies suggests that evolution can be quite rapid on very short time scales. Five field transfer experiments in which either guppies were moved from high to low predation streams, or dangerous (*Crenicichla alta*) predators were moved from high predation streams to low predation streams, resulted in large changes in colour patterns, body shape and size (Endler 1980 and unpublished) and life history patterns (Reznick & Endler 1982, Reznick & Bryga 1987, Reznick *et al.* 1990). These changes were large and involved most of the traits shown in Fig. 12.1, and in the same directions. Most of the change occurred within about two years of the transfers or of the order of 10 guppy generations, and divergence continued to develop over 11 years (Reznick *et al.* 1990 and unpublished). Experimental guppy populations in a greenhouse artificial stream evolved in the same directions within the same period of time (Endler 1980 and unpublished). The differences in both field and greenhouse populations were substantial (as in Fig. 12.1) even though they occurred in what is normally regarded as 'ecological time'. This suggests that the dichotomy between 'ecological time' and 'evolutionary time' is a false one, and might only apply to very long-lived species such as forest trees. But even in that case their generation time may be shorter than or similar to larger scale environmental changes such as glacial–interglacial transitions (Davis 1986, Anderson *et al.* 1988). We would probably make more progress if we considered the fact that natural selection and evolution can occur at all time scales. It is dangerous to assume that factors regulating population size should act at shorter time scales than factors affecting differences in demography among genotypes. In fact, put in these terms, the dichotomy between 'ecological time' and 'evolutionary time' makes no sense at all.

CONSEQUENCES OF EVOLUTIONARY CHANGE TO FOOD WEBS

Given that genetic variation for ecologically relevant traits is widespread, natural selection of these traits should also be widespread. If natural selection changes the distribution of these traits within and among populations (Endler 1986), then these changes can have far-reaching ecological consequences. As mentioned in the first section, changes in genotypic distributions can result in changes in population density, and these in turn can affect the probability of extirpation or extinction. This not only is important for the species of interest but also has strong implications for the local ecosystem because changes in the distribution of genetic variation for ecologically relevant characters will affect the connectedness, dynamics and stability of the entire food web. There are four main effects.

First, if natural selection results in a change in population density, this will affect parasite transmission rates, and hence parasite load, which can further affect the density of the species as well as that of the parasite. Changes in the density of a parasite with many (alternative) hosts at the same level in a food chain (alternate hosts), or at different levels of a food chain (primary and secondary hosts), will affect the densities of all the species, as well as the dynamics of the entire food web.

Second, foraging theory (Stephens & Krebs 1986) suggests that changes in density can affect the 'profitability' of a given species to predators, parasitoids (and if a plant, herbivores), causing them to use the species more intensely (higher density), or to choose other species (lower density). Such switching can affect the dynamics of all species in the food web.

Third, natural selection of ecologically relevant traits can alter the relationships among species at various places in a food web through evolutionary changes in competitive ability, character displacement, degree of mutualism, coevolution between predator and prey, host and parasite/parasitoid, herbivore and host plant. Some of these effects can follow directly from changes in density, such as the evolution of parasite virulence as a function of transmission rate (Ewald 1988). But many effects can arise simply as a result of changes in the evolutionary response of a species to all other species affecting in the food web. For example, if natural selection results in a prey species becoming better and better able to avoid or minimize predation, then it will become 'unprofitable'. As a result, its predators will switch to other species in the food web, reducing their density, and increasing the density of the original prey. If the predator switches to prey which it is less efficient at capturing, the predator's density may decline, resulting in its least favoured prey increasing in density. The multiple shifts in density could be felt throughout the food web in a very few generations, and could result in web instability. These phenomena are poorly studied.

Fourth, extinction associated with natural selection can have profound effects on food webs because extinction changes the form and connectedness of the web, which may further affect its stability and form. If densities decline as a result of natural selection through the direct or indirect effects described above, then extinction of the low-density species is more likely. Extinction might also occur through instability of the food web caused by changes in population density throughout the web and resulting changes in connectedness, as suggested above. Finally, extinction could also occur as a result of a new link in a food web causing a shift in natural selection that is so strong that there is not enough genetic variation to allow an evolutionary response. For example, suppose a predator switched to a prey species which formerly was a very minor part of the predator's diet, because the original prey evolved better defences against that predator. The formerly unimportant predator will then eat so many of the new prey species that one of four paths to extinction may be followed: (i) density becomes so low that random extinction occurs; (ii) density becomes so low that inbreeding occurs, resulting in inbreeding depression. Inbreeding depression may result in even greater reduction in density and genetic variation, preventing further response to selection for predator defence, increasing the probability of extinction; (iii) density or total population size becomes so low that genetic drift becomes significant, in some cases fixing deleterious genes, increasing the probability of extinction; (iv) the increased predation may induce such strong natural selection that there is not enough genetic variation for an evolutionary response to selection, and extinction may occur. Paths (i)–(iii) are related to the concept of minimum viable populations (Gilpin & Soulé 1986) and all of them have strong conservation as well as academic interest.

Speciation also affects the form of food webs, and can occur for a variety of ecological, geographical, and genetic reasons (Otte & Endler 1989). Although there is some controversy about exactly what a species is and which speciation mechanisms are most important (Otte & Endler 1989), it is generally agreed that when speciation occurs, the two new entities are evolutionarily independent. In other words, if two populations were diverging at a particular rate, and they speciate, then they will no longer exchange genes (or if so at a very low rate), and their rate of divergence can be very much faster (see also Endler 1977). This has at least two important consequences for food webs. First, if a food web extends over the area where the new species have formed, or nearby so that the new species invades the area of interest, a new species will be added to the web. The new species, because it is closely related to the old one (the sister species) will have very similar connections to other species in the web, and possibly antagonistic connections to the old species. This can strongly affect the dynamics and stability of the web. Second, whether or not the second species is within the area, both species involved in the speciation event will now diverge more rapidly, which may result in very rapid changes in connectedness in the local food web, altering its form and stability.

It is clear that the effects of natural selection on ecological properties which affect the position and connections of a given species in a food web can be profound. Changes in one or more species can result in instability of the food web, leading to a change in its form, and consequent further evolution of its components. This is a little-studied area and would yield some fascinating new insights into ecological as well as evolutionary processes.

CONSEQUENCES OF GENETIC VARIATION FOR LONG-TERM ECOLOGICAL CHANGES

The physical environment changes over various time scales, and so too does the biological environment of any one species (Davis 1986, Webb

1986, 1987, Anderson *et al.* 1988). Any large-scale change such as that resulting from climatic changes, advances and retreats of glaciers, large-scale primary or secondary succession, and even the large-scale effects of man's activity, induces changes in the direction and intensity of natural selection on all species in all food webs, either directly from the physical or biological environment, or indirectly through changes in other species in the food web. The amount of genetic variation will affect how well, and how rapidly, each species can respond to the changing environment, as well as their relative rates of extinction. Because these factors can affect food web dynamics and stability, it is possible that this will result in diversity gradients which correspond to rates of environmental change, such as during the transition from a glacial to an interglacial period, and the consequent poleward movement of food webs. The composition of the food webs is likely to change as their component species (i) differentially respond genetically, physiologically and behaviourally to the new selective regimes as a result of differing degrees of genetic variation, (ii) differentially disperse poleward, (iii) differentially go extinct locally, and (iv) respond to these changes in other species with which they interact. Even if the resulting changes in food web structure and dynamics do not produce a diversity gradient, they should result in varying combinations of species because there will be geographical variation in the form, connectedness and stability of the food web. For example, North American forest communities did not migrate as units during the ebb and flow of glacial and interglacial climatic conditions (Webb 1986, 1987). The effects of natural selection-induced changes in food web structure and stability may have contributed as much to this pattern as species-specific physiological requirements.

Large-scale changes in habitats and food web form will have additional effects which are mediated through genetic variation in ecological traits. One effect of evolving food webs is the creation of new ecological relationships, which may favour speciation, or the divergence of sibling species. Large-scale changes in habitats and in species distributions may result in hybrid zones between closely related species, semispecies, or populations on the verge of speciation. Hybrid zones can lead to speciation (Stebbins 1950, Endler 1977, Barton & Hewitt 1985) further affecting the form and dynamics of food webs. In addition, hybrid zones are a source of new genetic variants with entirely new ecological properties, so a hybrid zone may result in three rather than two new species (Stebbins 1950). Many plant species are of hybrid origin; some of the newer species have ecological properties different from either 'parental' species whilst others have intermediate properties. The appearance of two or three new species, especially if one of them has new properties, can strongly affect the dynamics and form of food webs. It can also affect their geographical distribution. For example, if the species involved in a hybrid zone are very important in the food web's dynamics (for example, a 'keystone species') then the entire food web may change geographically in concert with the hybrid zone.

GENETIC VARIATION AND THE GEOGRAPHIC SCALE OF ECOLOGICAL PROCESSES

The geographic scale of population dynamics as well as genetic differentiation of ecologically relevant traits is dependent upon dispersal and gene flow (Endler 1977, Gilpin & Hanski 1991). If the distance travelled between birth and first reproduction is large, then the geographical scale of dynamics and trait variation will be large, and in the extreme case, nearly uniform over the entire species range. If the dispersal and gene flow distance is small, then strong geographical variation can occur over short distances such as metres or kilometres (as in Fig. 12.1), and the dynamics and form of ecological processes can become quite complex. The critical parameter is the ratio of scales of dispersal to the scales of ecological or selective processes; if this is small then geographical variation will be large, but if the ratio is large, then there will be little variation. This has important implications to species living in increasingly fragmented habitats because as a habitat patch declines in size, and distances between patches increase, the effective ratio will increase. This leads to homogeneity within patches, increasing vulnerability to extinction.

Dispersal and gene flow distances must not be regarded as constant within a species just as ecological parameters must not be so regarded — they all can vary geographically. For example, not all individuals dispersing to their breeding areas will survive, and not all individuals surviving dispersal will breed. Such mortality during dispersal means that the distribution of distances travelled by breeding individuals can be considerably less than the distribution of dispersing adults. Because mortality is likely to vary geographically, the resulting gene flow distance will also vary geographically, being smaller in areas of higher mortality, and larger in areas of lower mortality. This has two consequences, (i) more rapid dispersal in invading species where they disperse in favourable areas compared with unfavourable areas, and (ii) effectively more isolation-by-distance between unfavourable and favourable areas, resulting in more rapid genetic adaptation to unfavourable areas than would be possible if gene flow scale were constant (Endler 1979). In addition, in species which can reproduce at any time during dispersal (e.g. non-territorial animals), then the effective gene flow distance may be reduced even further relative to the dispersal distances of adults. For example, fecundity schedules usually have a form of a rapid increase of fecundity with age immediately after maturity, then a gradual decline. The effect of this on species which disperse and can lay eggs anywhere during their dispersal, is that more eggs will be laid per individual per unit time at short distances compared with longer distances from their birthplaces; as individuals disperse away from their birthplaces they age and fecundity drops. This further reduces gene flow, allowing increased local genetic adaptation to local conditions (Endler 1979). The interaction between dispersal, gene flow, demography and geographic differentiation needs further study.

Dispersal and gene flow can also affect rates of extinction and speciation, and so can have indirect as well as direct effects on food webs. Larger dispersal distances mean that local catastrophes are more likely to result in extirpation of populations than in extinction of the species. Larger dispersal distances also mean that catastrophes are less likely to reduce drastically the levels of local genetic variation than if gene flow was more restricted. But speciation is more likely for smaller dispersal and gene flow distances because this will generate more geographical variation and genetic differentiation of all traits (Endler 1977). There is actually some direct evidence for this population genetics prediction in the fossil record of gastropods; species with planktotrophic larvae, which are more likely to disperse greater distances than species with non-planktotrophic larvae, have lower speciation rates and lower extinction rates than species with non-planktotrophic larvae (Jablonski & Lutz 1983, Jablonski 1987). Limited gene flow, resulting in the subdivision of a species into metapopulations, can also have significant, interesting and complex effects on the differential spread of species invading new areas, and the consequent geographical variation in food web form and stability (Gilpin & Hanski 1991). This is a fertile area for future theoretical and empirical research.

As for most other traits, there is genetic variation in the tendency to disperse (Andersen 1982, Berthold 1988, Palmer & Dingle 1989), and the literature on the evolution of dispersal is rapidly increasing (for example, Wiener & Feldman 1991). This obviously has profound implications for the level of gene flow and hence the amount of local differentiation of ecologically relevant traits because they will all change as dispersal distances evolve. As discussed in the previous sections, the resulting ebb and flow of species, as well as locally differentiated ecotypes and subspecies, can profoundly affect the local food web. The resulting changing geographical variation in food web dynamics could have interesting and important consequences for both general ecological and evolutionary processes.

GENERAL CONCLUSIONS

Genetic variation has many effects on a variety of ecological phenomena, yet this has not been well or systematically studied. Table 12.1 summarizes some possible avenues of research. There are basically eight questions. (1) What is the effect of genetic variation on population dynamics? (2) What is the effect of genetic variation in one species on the joint population dynamics of two species? (3) What is the effect of genetic covariation between two species on the joint dynamics of the species? (Genetic covariation between two species may or may not arise as a result of coevolution; it may also arise by responses to common environments or accidents). (4) What is the effect of covariance between genotype and environment (which can arise from natural selection or phenotypic plasticity) on population dynamics? (5) What is the effect of genotype–

TABLE 12.1. Some possible effects of genetic variation on ecological phenomena

Process	Abundance	Distribution
$V_G \rightarrow V_N$	Dynamics	Geographical range
$V_{G_1} \rightarrow COV_{N_1N_2}$	Predation Parasitism Herbivory	Joint distribution of two or more species
$COV_{G_1G_2} \rightarrow COV_{N_1N_2}$	Competition Mutualism	Joint distribution of two or more species
$COV_{GE} \rightarrow V_N$	Fluctuating numbers	Distribution with environment
$COV_{GE} \rightarrow COV_{NE}$	Habitat choice Differential survival	Distribution with environment
$V_G \rightarrow \Delta G$	Response to stress Invasion of new habitats	Ecotypes, geographic variation in food webs, range changes
$COV_{GE} \rightarrow \Delta G$	Response to stress Plasticity	Environmentally induced geographical variation
$COV_{GE} \rightarrow$ extinction	Lack of response to stress	Variation in food webs

V_G, genetic variation; V_{G_1}, genetic variation of species 1; V_N, population size variation; $COV_{N_1N_2}$, covariance between population sizes of species 1 and 2; $COV_{G_1G_2}$, genetic covariance between species 1 and 2; COV_{GE}, covariance between genotype and environment; COV_{NE}, covariance between population size and environment; ΔG genetic change (natural selection and evolution). Arrows indicate causal relationships.

environment covariance on a population's ability to 'track' the environment numerically? (6) What is the effect of genetic variation on a population's ability evolutionarily to 'track' the environment, and invade new habitats? (7) What is the effect of genotype–environment covariance on the ability to 'track'? (8) What is the effect of genotype–environment interactions on the probability of extinction? These questions will have answers which will reveal interesting facts and phenomena concerning both the distribution and abundance of species (Table 12.1).

Ecologists are close to a consensus about the major unsolved questions in ecology. Lubchenco *et al.* (1991) summarized these as 12 questions, and they are shown in Table 12.2. As this chapter has shown, genetic variation within and among species will have profound effects on all of the phenomena addressed by these questions; some examples are given in Table 12.2. These effects can be summarized by considering that genetic variation in ecologically relevant traits is likely to result in natural selection of those traits. Natural selection of those traits may result in a shift in the trait distributions, and this evolution of ecological parameters will affect the form and dynamics of all ecological phenomena. The changes in ecological phenomena will induce additional natural selection, leading to mutual interactions between ecological and evolutionary phenomena; the arrows in Table 12.1 should probably be double-headed. There is every reason to regard ecology and evolution as two aspects of the same subject.

TABLE 12.2. The major unsolved questions in ecology (Lubchenco *et al.* 1991) and examples of how genetic variation (and natural selection) may affect them

1 *What are the patterns of diversity in nature, and what are their critical ecological and evolutionary determinants?*
Patterns of diversity will be affected by genetic variation; sometimes this will be represented by sibling species and at other times by polymorphisms. In fact one could ask if it matters whether or not two ecologically different forms interbreed

2 *How do morphological, physiological and behavioural traits of organisms interact?*
Genetic variation in the traits will affect how they interact

3 *How plastic are the morphology, physiology and behaviour of organisms in the face of environmental stresses? What are organisms' proximal limitations?*
The degree of genetic variation determines the degree of evolutionary plasticity; this is Fisher's fundamental theorem of natural selection (Ewens 1979). The degree of genetic variation, in conjunction with the time-scale of fluctuations in the environment, determines whether or not a species should be evolutionarily plastic or henotypically plastic (Bradshaw 1965)

4 *What are the determinants and consequences of dispersal and dormancy?*
Genetic variation for dispersal tendency and dormancy will alter the consequences for the population and food web

Cont'd

TABLE 12.2. *Continued*

5 *What factors explain the life history adaptations of organisms? What are the population-level consequences of these adaptations?*
Genetic variation for life-history traits will have profound consequences

6 *What factors control the sizes of populations? How are changes in population size related to processes mediated at the level of the individual?*
Genetic variation in demographic parameters affects equilibrium population size as well as dynamics

7 *How does the internal structure of a population affect its response to various stresses?*
Genetic variation, in combination with metapopulation structure, can result in strong local adaptation as well as complex population dynamics

8 *How does fragmentation of the landscape affect the spread and persistence of populations?*
Varying degrees of genetic variation for ecologically relevant traits will affect how each species responds to fragmentation and consequent stress. Genetic variation for dispersal ability and the evolution of dispersal may or may not allow local adjustment to the new habitat geometry

9 *What factors govern the assembly of communities and ecosystems and the ways those systems respond to various stresses? What patterns emerge from cross-system comparisons?*
Genetic variation within species may affect their population dynamics and probability of extinction, with effects throughout the food web

10 *What are the feedbacks between the biotic and abiotic portions of ecosystems and landscapes? How do climatic, anthropogenic and biotic processes regulate biogeochemical processes?*
Genetic variation for traits involved in the feedback will affect the form and magnitude of the feedback as the interacting species evolve

11 *How do patterns and processes at one spatial or temporal scale affect those at other scales?*
Evolution of species interacting with the environment at small scales will affect the population dynamics and evolution of species at large scales, and vice versa

12 *What are the consequences of environmental variability, including natural and anthropogenic disturbances, for individuals, populations or communities?*
The amplitude and time scale of the environmental variability will allow evolutionary response to the induced varying natural selection provided that it is small relative to the degree of genetic variation. If environmental variability and change is large relative to the amount of genetic variation, then the species may go extinct

REFERENCES

Allendorf, F. W. & Leary, R. F. (1986). Heterozygosity and fitness in natural populations of animals. *Conservation Biology, The Science of Scarcity and Diversity* (Ed. by M. E. Soulé), pp. 57–76. Sinauer, Sunderland, MA, USA.

Alstad, D. N. & Edmunds, G. F. Jr. (1983a). Selection, outbreeding depression, and the sex ratio of scale insects. *Science*, **220**, 93–95.

Alstad, D. N. & Edmunds, G. F. Jr. (1983b). Adaptation, host specificity, and gene flow in the Black Pineleaf Scale. *Variable Plants and Herbivores* (Ed. by R. F. Denno & M. S. McClure), pp. 413–426. Academic Press, New York, NY, USA.

Andersen, N. M. (1982). *The Semiaquatic Bugs (Hemiptera, Gerromorpha): Phylogeny, Adaptations, Biogeography, and Classification*. Entomonograph Vol. 3. Scandinavian Science Press, Klampenborg.

Anderson, P. M., Barnosky, C. W., Bartlein, P. J., Behling, P. J., Brubaker, L., Cushing, E. J., Dodson, J., Dworetsky, B., Guetter, P. J., Harrison, S. P., Huntley, B., Kutzbach, J. E., Markgraf, V., Marvel, R., McGlone, M. S., Mix, A., Moar, N. T., Morley, J., Perrott, R. A., Peterson, G. M., Prell, W. L., Prentice, I. C., Ritchie, J. C., Roberts, N., Ruddiman, W. F., Salinger, M. J., Spaulding, W. G., Street-Perrott, F. A., Thompson, R. S., Wang, P. K., Webb, T. II, Winkler, M. G. & Wright, H. E. Jr. (1988). Climatic changes of the last 18 000 years: observations and model simulations. *Science*, **241**, 1043–1052.

Anderson, W. W. & King, C. E. (1970). Age-specific selection. *Proceedings of the National Academy of Sciences, USA*, **66**, 780–786.

Barton, N. H. & Hewitt, G. M. (1985). Analysis of hybrid zones. *Annual Review of Ecology and Systematics*, **16**, 113–148.

Berthold, P. (1988). Evolutionary aspects of migratory behavior in European warblers. *Journal of Evolutionary Biology*, **1**, 195–209.

Bradshaw, A. D. (1965). Evolutionary significance of phenotypic plasticity in plants. *Advances in Genetics*, **13**, 115–155.

Charlesworth, B. (1971). Selection in density-regulated populations. *Ecology*, **52**, 469–474.

Charlesworth, B. (1980). *Evolution in Age-Structured Populations*. Cambridge University Press, Cambridge, UK.

Clarke, B. C. (1972). Density-dependent natural selection. *American Naturalist*, **106**, 1–13.

Clarke, B. C. (1973). The effect of mutation on population size. *Nature*, **242**, 196–197.

Davis, M. B. (1986). Climatic instability, time lags, and community disequilibrium. *Community Ecology* (Ed. by J. Diamond & T. J. Case), pp. 269–284. Harper & Row, New York, NY, USA.

Denno, R. F. & Dingle, H. (Eds) (1981). *Insect Life History Patterns: Habitat and Geographic Variation*. Springer Verlag, New York, NY, USA.

Dingle, H., Blau, W. S., Kice Brown, C. & Hegmann, J. P. (1982). Population crosses and the genetic structure of milkweed bug life histories. *Evolution and Genetics of Life Histories* (Ed. by H. Dingle & J. P. Hegmann), pp. 209–229. Springer Verlag, New York, NY, USA.

Edmunds, G. R. Jr. & Alstad, D. N. (1978). Coevolution in insect herbivores and conifers. *Science*, **199**, 941–945.

Edmunds, G. R. Jr. & Alstad, D. N. (1981). Responses of black pineleaf scales to host plant variability. *Insect Life History Patterns, Habitat and Geographic Variation* (Ed. by R. F. Denno & H. Dingle), pp. 29–38. Springer Verlag, New York, NY, USA.

Endler, J. A. (1977). *Geographic Variation, Speciation, and Clines*. Monographs in Population Biology 10. Princeton University Press, Princeton, NJ, USA.

Endler, J. A. (1978). A predator's view of animal color patterns. *Evolutionary Biology*, **11**, 319–364.

Endler, J. A. (1979). Gene flow and life history patterns. *Genetics*, **93**, 263–284.

Endler, J. A. (1980). Natural selection on color patterns in *Poecilia reticulata*. *Evolution*, 34, 76–91.

Endler, J. A. (1982). Comment on John Turner's paper. *Biological Diversification in the Tropics* (Ed. by G. T. Prance), pp. 331–332. Columbia University Press, New York, NY, USA.

Endler, J. A. (1983). Natural and sexual selection on color patterns in Poeciliid fishes. *Environmental Biology of Fishes*, **9**, 173–190.

Endler, J. A. (1986). *Natural Selection in the Wild*. Monographs in Population Biology 21. Princeton University Press, Princeton, NJ, USA.

Endler, J. A. (1990). Ecology and natural selection. *Physiological Ecology, Japan*, **27** (special number), 17–30.

Ewald, P. W. (1988). The evolution of virulence. *Oxford Surveys in Evolutionary Biology*, **5**, 215–245.

Ewens, W. J. (1979). *Mathematical Population Genetics*. Springer Verlag, New York, NY, USA.

Futuyma, D. J. (1986). *Evolutionary Biology*. Sinauer, Sunderland, MA, USA.

Gilpin, M. & Hanski, I. (Eds) (1991). Metapopulation dynamics. *Biological Journal of the Linnean Society*, **42**, 1–323.

Gilpin, M. & Soulé, M. E. (1986). Minimum viable populations: processes of species extinction. *Conservation Biology, The Science of Scarcity and Diversity* (Ed. by M. E. Soulé), pp. 19–34. Sinauer, Sunderland, MA, USA.

Hairston, N. G. Jr. & Olds, E. J. (1984). Population differences in the timing of diapause: adaptation in a spatially heterogeneous environment. *Oecologia, Berlin*, **61**, 42–48.

Haskins, C. P., Haskins, E. F., McLaughlin, J. J. A. & Hewitt, R. E. (1961). Polymorphism and population structure in *Lebistes reticulatus*, a population study. *Vertebrate Speciation* (Ed. by W. F. Blair), pp. 320–395. University of Texas Press, Austin, TX, USA.

Houde, A. (1988). Genetic difference in female choice between two guppy populations. *Animal Behaviour*, **36**, 510–516.

Houde, A. E. & Endler, J. A. (1990). Correlated evolution of female mating preferences and male color patterns in the guppy, *Poecilia reticulata*. *Science*, **248**, 1405–1408.

Jablonski, D. (1987). Heritability at the species level: analysis of geographic ranges of Cretaceous mollusks. *Science*, **238**, 360–363.

Jablonski, D. & Lutz, R. A. (1983). Larval ecology of marine benthic invertebrates: paleobiological implications. *Biological Reviews of the Cambridge Philosophical Society*, **58**, 21–89.

King, C. E. & Anderson, W. W. (1971). Age-specific selection. II. The interaction between *r* and *K* during population growth. *American Naturalist*, **105**, 137–156.

Ledig, F. T. (1986). Heterozygosity, heterosis, and fitness in outbreeding plants. *Conservation Biology, The Science of Scarcity and Diversity* (Ed. by M. E. Soulé), pp. 77–104. Sinauer, Sunderland, MA, USA.

Liley, N. R. & Seghers, B. H. (1975). Factors affecting the morphology and behaviour of guppies in Trinidad. *Function and Evolution in Behaviour* (Ed. by G. P. Baerends, C. Beer & A. Manning), pp. 92–118. Clarendon Press, Oxford, UK.

Lomnicki, A. (1988). *Population Biology of Individuals*. Princeton University Press, Princeton, NJ, USA.

Lubchenco, J., Olson, A. M., Brubaker, L. B., Carpenter, S. R., Holland, M. M., Hubbell, S. P., Levin, S. A., MacMahon, J. A., Matson, P. A., Melillo, J. M., Mooney, H. A., Peterson, C. H., Pulliam, H. R., Real, L. A., Regal, P. J. & Risser, P. G. (1991). The sustainable biosphere initiative: an ecological research agenda. *Ecology*, **72**, 371–412.

Magurran, A. E. & Seghers, B. H. (1990a). Population differences in the schooling behaviour of newborn guppies, *Poecilia reticulata*. *Ethology*, **84**, 334–342.

Magurran, A. E. & Seghers, B. H. (1990b). Population differences in predator recognition and attack cone avoidance in the guppy, *Poecilia reticulata*. *Animal Behaviour*, **40**, 443–452.

Magurran, A. E. & Seghers, B. H. (1990c). Risk sensitive courtship in the guppy (*Poecilia reticulata*). *Behaviour*, **112**, 194–201.

May, R. M. (1986). The search for patterns in the balance of nature: advances and retreats. *Ecology*, **67**, 1115–1126.

Mitton, J. B. & Grant, M. C. (1984). Associations among protein heterozygosity, growth rate, and developmental homeostasis. *Annual Review of Ecology and Systematics*, **15**, 479–499.

Mitton, J. B., Carey, C. & Kocher, T. D. (1986). The relation of enzyme heterozygosity to standard and active oxygen consumption and body size of tiger salamanders, *Ambystoma tigrinum*. *Physiological Zoology*, **59**, 574–582.

Ohgushi, T. (1987). Factors affecting body size variation within a population of an herbivorous lady beetle, *Henosepilachna niponica* (Lewis). *Research in Population Ecology*, **29**, 147–154.

Ohgushi, T. (1988). Temporal and spatial relationships between an herbivorous lady beetle, *Henosepilachna niponica* and its predator, the earwig *Anechura harmandi*. *Research in Population Ecology*, **30**, 57–68.

Otte, D. & Endler, J. A. (1989). *Speciation and its Consequences*. Sinauer, Sunderland, MA, USA.

Palmer, J. O. & Dingle, H. (1989). Responses to selection on flight behavior in a migratory population of milkweed bug (*Oncopeltus fasciatus*). *Evolution*, **43**, 1805–1808.

Partridge, L. & Green, P. (1985). Intraspecific feeding specializations and population dynamics. *Behavioural Ecology, Ecological Consequences of Adaptive Behaviour* (Ed. by R. M. Sibly & R. H. Smith), pp. 207–226. Blackwell Scientific Publications, Oxford, UK.

Ralls, K., Harvey, P. H. & Lyles, A. M. (1986). Inbreeding in natural populations of birds and mammals. *Conservative Biology, The Science of Scarcity and Diversity*. (Ed. by M. E. Soulé), pp. 35–56. Sinauer, Sunderland, MA, USA.

Reznick, D. (1982a). The impact of predation of life history evolution in Trinidadian guppies: genetic basis of observed life history patterns. *Evolution*, **36**, 1236–1250.

Reznick, D. (1982b). Genetic determination of offspring size in the guppy (*Poecilia reticulata*). *American Naturalist*, **120**, 181–188.

Reznick, D. N. & Bryga, H. (1987). Life-history evolution in guppies (*Poecilia reticulata*) 1. Phenotypic and genetic changes in an introduction experiment. *Evolution*, **41**, 1370–1385.

Reznick, D. & Endler, J. A. (1982). The impact of predation on life history evolution in Trinidadian guppies (*Poecilia reticulata*). *Evolution*, **36**, 160–177.

Reznick, D. A., Bryga, H. & Endler, J. A. (1990). Experimentally induced life-history evolution in a natural population. *Nature*, **346**, 357–359.

Roughgarden, J. (1971). Density-dependent natural selection. *Ecology*, **52**, 453–468.

Seghers, B. H. (1973). An analysis of geographic variation in the antipredator adaptations of the guppy *Poecilia reticulata*. PhD Thesis, Zoology, University of British Columbia, Vancouver, Canada.

Seghers, B. H. (1974). Schooling behavior in the guppy *Poecilia reticulata*: an evolutionary response to predation. *Evolution*, **28**, 486–489.

Sheppard, P. M. (1958). *Natural Selection and Heredity*. Hutchinson University Library, London, UK.

Stanley, S. M. (1981). *The New Evolutionary Timetable*. Basic Books, New York, NY, USA.

Stebbins, G. L. (1950). *Variation and Evolution in Plants*. Columbia University Press, New York, USA.

Stephens, D. M. & Krebs, J. R. (1986). *Foraging Theory*. Princeton University Press, Princeton, NJ, USA.

Stoner, G. & Breden, F. (1988). Phenotypic differentiation in female preference related to geographic variation in male predation risk in the Trinidad guppy (*Poecilia reticulata*). *Behavioural Ecology and Sociobiology*, **22**, 285–291.

Tauber, C.A. & Tauber, M. J. (1982). Evolution of seasonal adaptations and life history traits in *Chrysopa*: response to diverse selective pressures. *Evolution and Genetics of Life Histories* (Ed. by H. Dingle & J. P. Hegmann), pp. 51–72. Springer Verlag, New York, NY, USA.

Templeton, A. R. (1986). Coadaptation and outbreeding depression. *Conservation Biology, The Science of Scarcity and Diversity* (Ed. by M. E. Soulé), pp. 105–116. Sinauer, Sunderland, MA, USA.

Webb, T. III. (1986). Is vegetation in equilibrium with climate? How to interpret late-Quaternary pollen data. *Vegetatio*, **67**, 75–91.

Webb, T. III. (1987). The appearance and disappearance of major vegetational assemblages: long-term vegetational dynamics in eastern North America. *Vegetatio*, **69**, 177–187.

Wiener, P. & Feldman, M. W. (1991). Evolution of dispersal in a model of mixed selfing and random mating. *Evolution*, **45**, 1717–1726.

13. DENSITY AND FREQUENCY DEPENDENCE IN ECOLOGY: MESSAGES FOR GENETICS?

MICHAEL BEGON

Department of Environmental and Evolutionary Biology, University of Liverpool, P.O. Box 147, Liverpool L69 3BX, UK

INTRODUCTION

This chapter and Chapter 14 by Clarke and Beaumont examine, together, for both genetics and ecology, the questions of density dependence (where vital rates — birth, death, growth, migration or, in the case of genetics, the intensity of selection — vary with population density) and frequency dependence (where these same rates vary with the frequency of a given type of individual in a population). We have tried to avoid going over old ground, but to concentrate instead on what we consider to be important recent advances and stimulating current controversies. We have also tried, in the spirit of this volume, to avoid examining either population ecology or population genetics in isolation, but to concentrate instead on interactions between the two. Hence, I, as a population ecologist, begin by answering two questions that I imagined my collaborators, Clarke and Beaumont, might want to ask, namely 'What's new in density and frequency dependence in ecology that we, as population geneticists, ought to know about?', 'And how might these things change our lives?'. Clarke and Beaumont then consider the validity and pertinence of these answers before asking, and answering, further questions of their own. Necessarily, the answers we provide, and indeed the questions we choose to ask, reflect our personal biases.

CHAOS

Perhaps the most visible revolution in ecologists' thinking on density dependence has been the recognition that density-dependent processes can give rise to chaotic population dynamics (May 1974, 1976, Godfray *et al.*, Ch. 3, this volume, and references therein). This revolution has had two main facets. The first has been the absorption of the underlying message: that simple and apparently regulatory biological processes can give rise to complex, apparently unstable and certainly unpredictable population dynamics. The second has been the search for deterministic chaos in real, even natural populations (Schaffer 1984, 1985, Schaffer & Kot 1986, Sugihara & May 1990) and even the more precise characterization of the chaos itself (Godfray & Blythe 1990).

The question naturally arises: can density- and frequency-dependent selection generate chaotic gene frequency dynamics in some related manner? If they can, then a number of gene frequency patterns that would seem superficially to suggest little influence from selection might need to be interpreted far more cautiously. Two immediately obvious examples are gene frequencies within a population taking an apparently random walk, and gene frequencies in separate but apparently ecologically equivalent populations being quite different (with, perhaps, fixation of different alleles). Both patterns are shown by the data in Table 13.1 (from Lewontin 1974), which were indeed interpreted as providing 'no convincing case for selection', on the basis that if sufficiently powerful selection were operating, a detectable trend of convergence ought to be observable.

In fact, the question of whether such chaotic dynamics are likely seems to have been answered, implicitly, in the affirmative in the early studies of density-dependent (which was also frequency-dependent) selection by Charlesworth (1971) and Clarke (1972). Both authors clearly recognized the interdependence of gene frequency and population size, and Charlesworth (1971) actually plotted the results of a computer simu-

TABLE 13.1. Frequency of a particular allele at the pt-8 locus in population cages of *Drosophila pseudoobscura* followed over time in a number of replicates at each of two temperatures. (After Lewontin, 1974.)

	25°C				18°C			
Months	Cage: I	II	III	IV	V	VI	VII	VIII
0	0.69	0.80	0.20	0.30	–	–	–	–
6	0.75	0.68	0.23	0.27	0.74	0.67	0.24	0.28
12	0.69	0.72	0.29	0.27	0.70	0.69	0.31	0.27
18	0.62	0.51	0.11	0.10	0.60	0.70	0.31	0.22
24	0.50	0.62	0.09	0.09	0.59	0.60	0.32	0.20
30	0.41	0.59	0.13	0.08	0.61	0.64	0.36	0.21
36	0.41	0.64	0.17	0.12	0.61	0.68	0.40	0.21
42	0.37	0.64	0.14	0.09	0.59	0.66	0.39	0.18
48	0.58	0.66	0.28	0.14	0.45	0.68	0.36	0.28
54	0.60	0.77	0.30	0.20	0.38	0.67	0.34	0.32

lation in which appropriately high values of *r* (intrinsic rates of increase) generated permanent two-point limit cycles in both population size and gene frequency (Fig. 13.1). In cases where the population dynamics are chaotic, it seems likely that the gene frequency dynamics will be so too. Consider the alternative: a population exhibiting chaotic population dynamics, with density- and frequency-dependent selection acting on many of its alleles, but in which the gene frequencies nonetheless contrive to remain constant or trace some simpler, non-chaotic pattern. This strains credulity too far. On the other hand, the amplitude of even chaotic fluctuations in gene frequency will be limited by the extent of the selective differentials. That is to say, the amount of change in gene frequency from generation to generation, largely determined by selective differentials, is likely to be very much less than the amount of change in total numbers, largely determined by reproductive rates. Chaos is likely, therefore, to be even more difficult to detect in genetics than in ecology. These points, and others, are taken up in more detail by Clarke and Beaumont.

SPATIAL HETEROGENEITIES

The role of spatial heterogeneity, and as part of this, the role of spatial density dependence, in density-dependent processes generally remains, despite considerable interest in recent years, an area of active controversy

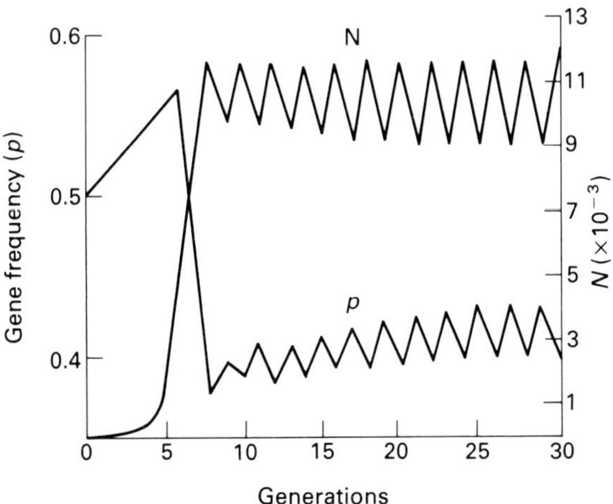

FIG. 13.1. Two-point limit cycle behaviour of both population size (N) and the gene frequency (p) of one of two possible alleles, in a simulation in which the fitnesses of genotypes are logistic functions of population size. (After Charlesworth 1971.)

(see, for example, Dempster 1983, Hassell 1985, 1987, Dempster & Pollard 1986, Mountford 1988, Murdoch & Stewart-Oaten 1989, Pacala *et al.* 1990, Stewart-Oaten & Murdoch 1990, Hassell *et al.* 1991, Pacala & Hassell 1991, Godfray & Pacala 1992). Nonetheless, a number of conclusions seem worth drawing.

The first is that it is important to distinguish between two rather separate questions. One is the question of what, if any, is the role of spatial heterogeneity in generating stable equilibria. A separate issue is then whether empiricists ought to structure their sampling programmes spatially as well as temporally, on the grounds that temporal runs of data alone, based on averages for each generation (or year), will not provide answers to the questions that are likely to be posed.

Starting with the question of whether spatial variation stabilizes dynamics, the answer seems to be that it does so in most, though not necessarily in all biologically reasonable circumstances (see, for example, Murdoch & Stewart-Oaten 1989, Pacala *et al.* 1990, Pacala & Hassell 1991, Godfray & Pacala 1992). It is important to realize, however, that spatial variation alone, whether density dependent or not, can play no part in stabilizing populations unless it translates into temporal density dependence (see Fig. 13.2 for an explanation). Although this has sometimes been treated as a contentious point (e.g. Stewart-Oaten & Murdoch 1990), there is no good evidence that anyone has seriously thought otherwise.

Furthermore, it has become clear recently that this stabilizing spatial variation can be density dependent, inversely density dependent or density independent (Fig. 13.3), so long as there is sufficient variation (Chesson & Murdoch 1986, Pacala *et al.* 1990, Hassell *et al.* 1991); and indeed that in practice, density-independent spatial variation is most likely to be important (Pacala & Hassell 1991).

Might it, though, be necessary to sample spatially in order to establish that a population is subject to regulatory phenomena, and if so, to establish what these are? May (1989) provides a clear view on this question. When the regulatory phenomena themselves are capable of producing oscillatory or chaotic dynamics (e.g. Hassell 1987), perhaps by overcompensating density dependence, then this 'density-dependent noise', combined with 'density-independent noise' (generated directly by environmental stochasticity) in a patchy world, is likely to make density dependence very difficult to detect in temporal runs of averages, whereas it may be readily apparent by sampling spatially on an appropriate scale. However, if the regulatory phenomena are contest-like, incapable of producing oscillatory dynamics (e.g. Mountford 1988), then spatial hetero-

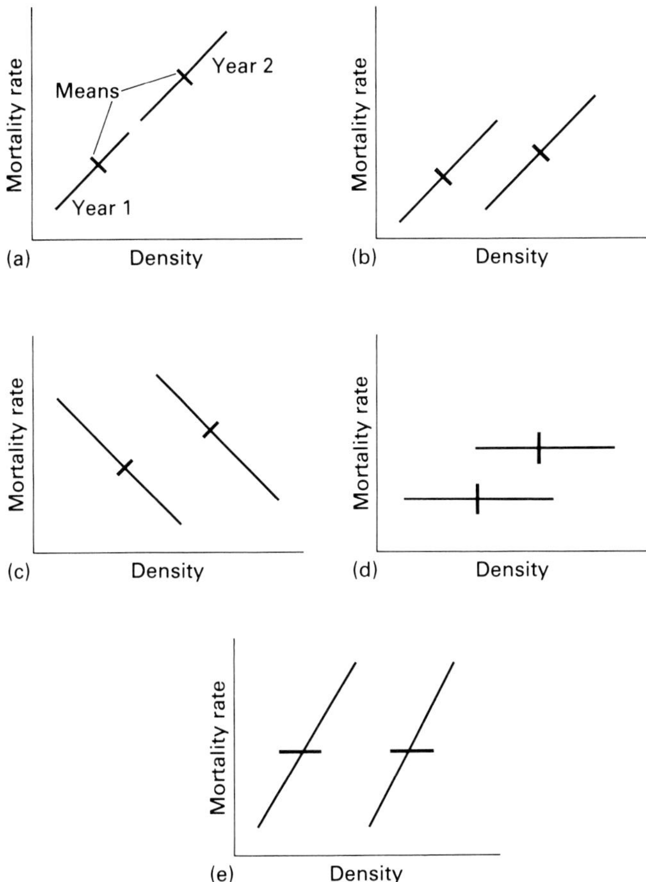

FIG. 13.2. Spatial heterogeneity in mortality rate within a year must translate into density dependence between years ((a)–(d) but not (e)) in order to have a stabilizing effect. This is so whether the spatial heterogeneity is density dependent ((a), (b), (e)), inversely density dependent (c) or density independent (d). In each case, lines represent the relationship within a year, with the temporal relationship given by the disposition of the two means.

geneity may actually enhance our ability to detect density dependence in temporal runs of averages.

The answer for empiricists is therefore clear: if the causes of population stability are being sought, then sampling programmes with a spatial structure are likely to be essential.

As far as population genetics is concerned, it is tempting to play safe and suggest simply that where there is interest in density- and/or frequency-dependent causes of polymorphisms or their stability, then the spatial

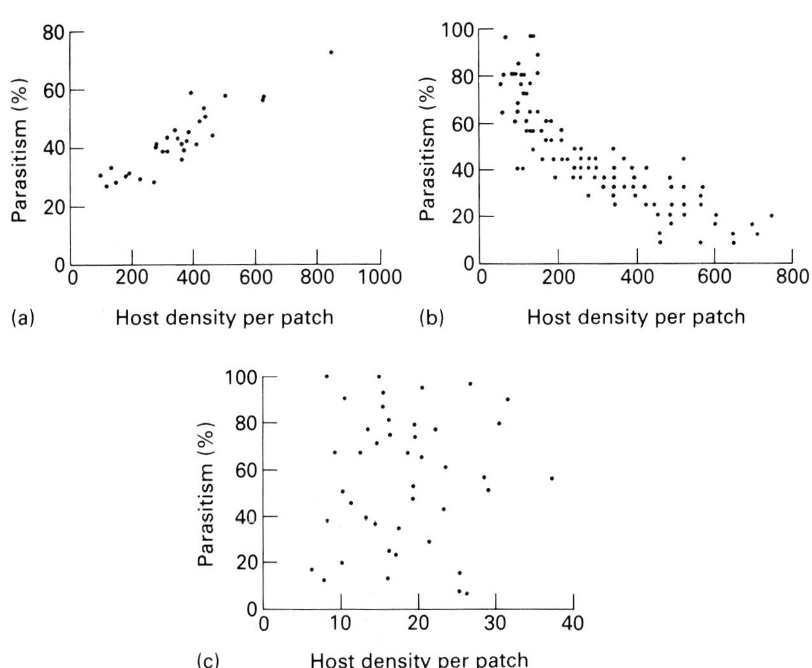

FIG. 13.3. Data sets indicating that density-dependent spatial variation (a), inversely density-dependent variation (b) and density-independent variation (c) can all stabilize, so long as there is sufficient variation (in this case, in percentage parasitism), which in these cases there is. (After Pacala & Hassell 1991.)

dimension cannot be ignored. However, the same proviso applies here as in the discussion of chaos, regarding the likely limits to the rate of change in gene frequency. Thus, if unstable dynamics in gene frequencies are correspondingly less likely, then spatial sampling may be correspondingly less necessary.

PROBABILITY REFUGES FOR COMPETITORS

Another manifestation of ecologists' recent interest in spatial heterogeneity has been the work of Shorrocks and co-workers on interspecific competition in a habitat comprising ephemeral patches (Atkinson & Shorrocks 1981, 1984, Shorrocks *et al.* 1984, 1990, Rosewell *et al.* 1990, Kreitman *et al.*, Ch. 11, this volume; see also Hanski 1981, 1983, Ives & May 1985). The essence of the work is that aggregation in the distribution of a superior competitor, in particular, gives rise to a 'probability refuge' for an inferior competitor, and thence to coexistence of competitors where, in a homogeneous environment, none would be possible. Competitors can coexist without niche differentiation. Shorrocks (1990) has himself made the point that the same processes that promote coexistence among competing species can maintain polymorphisms by promoting coexistence among competing morphs within a single species.

Frequency dependence provides a useful framework for combining ideas on conventional, niche-differentiated coexistence on the one hand, and probability refuge coexistence on the other. In both cases, the frequency of both competing species (or both competing morphs) increases at low frequency (see Fig. 13.4), and in both cases the essence of the coexistence is the balance between intra- and interspecific effects, arising either from niche differentiation or aggregation. On the other hand, this underlying unity should not be taken as equivalence (Chesson 1991, notwithstanding). Probability refuges provide a quite distinct (albeit frequency dependent) path to the coexistence of competitors.

It follows, though, that in terms of what is observed — species (or morphs) coexisting, and increasing when rare — the distinction between niche differentiation and probability refuges, and indeed between these and some combination of the two, disappears. This suggests a number of related observations in the present context. Firstly, it seems likely that

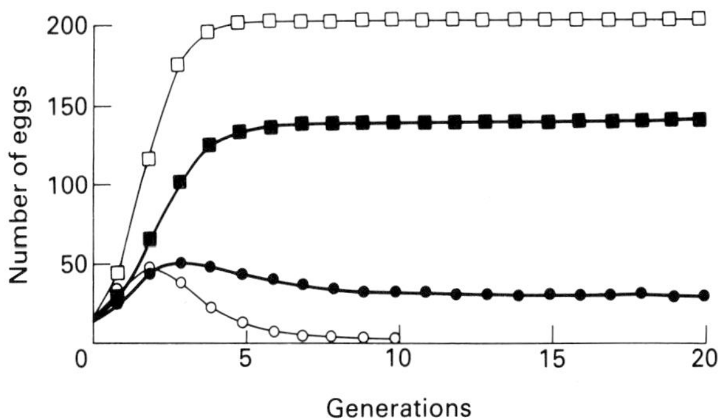

FIG. 13.4. Coexistence of competitors without niche differentiation (computer simulations). The niche of species 2 is included entirely within the niche of species 1 and, in competition, species 2 has no realized niche. In a homogeneous environment species 1 (□) excludes species 2 (○). But in a patchy environment, over which both species are distributed in an aggregated manner, there is coexistence. In addition, both species 1 (■) and species 2 (●) have densities lower than they would achieve in the absence of interspecific competition (200 in both cases). The aggregated distributions, not niche differentiation, have led to coexistence. (After Atkinson & Shorrocks 1981.)

many alleles that are deleterious can nonetheless persist in stable polymorphisms. (Here, an allele is defined as deleterious when there are no circumstances in which it contributes to the fittest genotype, either as a homozygote or a heterozygote.) Hence, the search by population geneticists — for example those interested in the visible polymorphisms of *Cepaea* (Jones *et al.* 1977, Clarke *et al.* 1978) — for the circumstances favouring each morph, and indeed for some balance in selective advantage between different morphs, may ultimately be unnecessary, given that the resource distributions of many, if not most, species are, to some extent at least, patchy and ephemeral.

Furthermore, two alleles may be close enough in selective value to be maintained in a stable polymorphism via the probability refuge route, without the variation qualifying as being 'selectively maintained.' Neither, though, would it be neutral, either by strict definition (equal selective value), or in the sense of being subject only to stochastic phenomena. Thus, probability refuges may impinge on the whole neutralist–selectionist controversy, blurring the distinction between neutral and selectively maintained variation by introducing a third type of variation which is neither neutral nor selectively maintained.

INDIVIDUAL DIFFERENCES AND EFFECTIVE POPULATION SIZE

The end result of spatial variation is often that individuals differ in the density dependence they experience. This, though, is an end result that can be arrived at by other means.

There has been a growing recognition among ecologists of what, to population geneticists, is axiomatic, namely that individuals differ. Insofar as they differ in ways that affect their competitive ability, this tends naturally to bring an asymmetry to the competitive process; and this asymmetric competition (Begon 1984) tends naturally, in turn, to exaggerate such initial differences as there were. This is especially apparent in plants (Fig. 13.5; see Weiner (1990) for a recent review) and perhaps in sessile animals, where the suppressed weaklings are most likely to survive to exhibit their competitive failure. It can also be observed in other animals (Fig. 13.6; Wall & Begon 1987), though the weaklings, being unitary rather than modular organisms, are much more likely to die before they can be captured in a snap-shot of a pattern of this type. To put it briefly: individual differences affect, and are affected by, the competitive process, and discussions of competition framed only in terms of averages will therefore necessarily ignore a great deal of potentially valuable information.

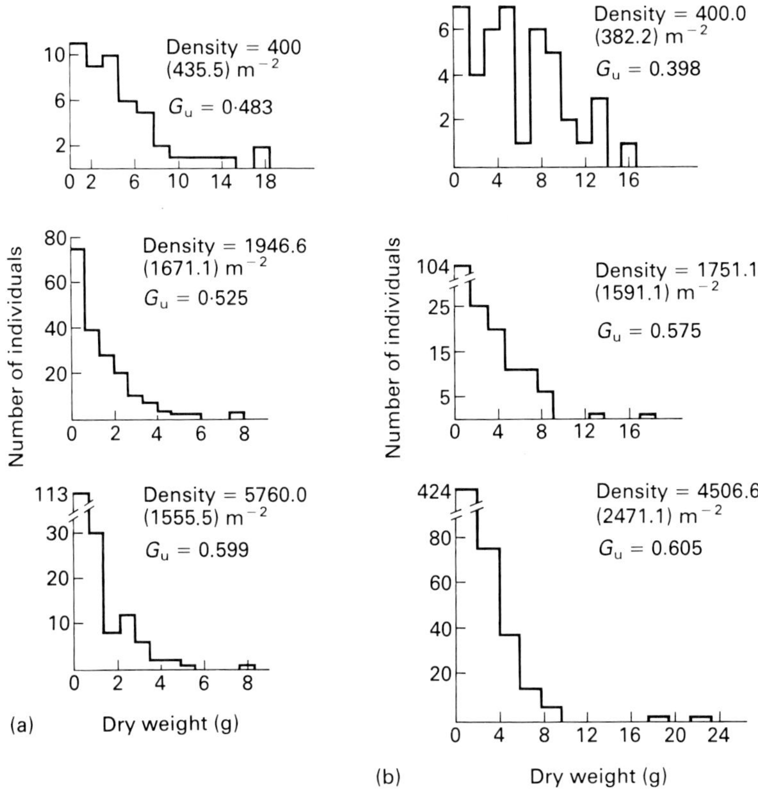

FIG. 13.5. Individuals differ, and differences increase with competition. Biomass distributions for experimental populations of (a) *Plantago major* and (b) *P. rugelii* grown at three densities, with the density of survivors in parentheses. G_u is an unbiased estimate of the Gini coefficient, a measure of the inequitability of the distribution of (in this case) biomass. (After Weiner & Thomas 1986; data from Hawthorn & Cavers 1982.)

One way of describing these patterns, which may be particularly appropriate in the present context, is to note that the variation within a population in the intensity of density dependence is, as a result of individual differences, often far greater than the variation in density. 'Density' and 'perceived density' are by no means necessarily the same thing. Similar comments can clearly be applied to density-dependent selection.

An alternative way of describing the outcome of these patterns is to say that the variance-to-mean ratio of family sizes in a population is typically much greater than unity (which is what it would be if the distribution was Poisson). This is important from the point of view of population genetics because of the effect of the ratio on the 'effective

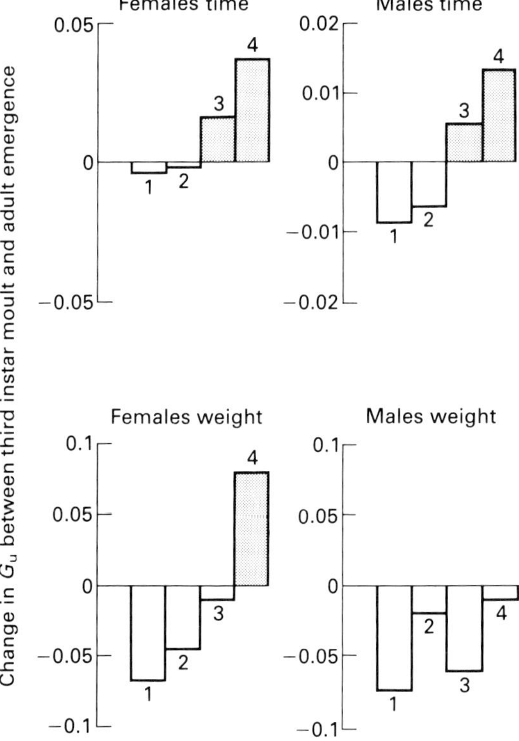

FIG. 13.6. Individuals differ, and differences increase with competition. The difference in phenotypic inequality (measured as a Gini coefficient, G_u, see Fig. 13.5) between moult to third instar and adult emergence at four densities (1 lowest, 4 highest) for male and female weight and developmental time in experimental populations of the grasshopper *Chorthippus brunneus*. Solid bars indicate an increase in inequality, open bars a decrease. (After Wall & Begon 1987.)

size' of a population (Crow 1954, Crow & Morton 1955, Wright 1969). The effective size of a population is the size of the 'genetically ideal' population with which an actual population can be equated genetically. Variance-to-mean ratios in excess of unity lead to effective population sizes lower than a census would suggest. In populations with low effective size, inbreeding may become relatively intense and/or genetic drift may become relatively important. That the effect can be significant is shown in Table 13.2, which contains estimates of the effective size of a natural population of *Drosophila subobscura* (Begon 1977). Inclusion of family size data took the estimate down almost an order of magnitude to a figure on the fringes of where drift and inbreeding have to be considered as potentially potent forces.

TABLE 13.2. Estimates of the effective size of a population of *Drosophila subobscura* in a woodland in northern England. An experimentally derived variance-to-mean ratio of family sizes of 14.78 reduces the size by an approximate order of magnitude compared to a 'default' assumption of a random distribution (ratio = 1). (After Begon 1977.)

	Variance-to-mean ratio		
	1	14.78	
Population		Variance number	Inbreeding number
April	923	120	1928
June	9392	1221	133
July	11 077	1440	550
August	12 158	1581	1373
September	15 787	2100	1522
Total (5 generations)	3507	456	445
Total (4 generations)	3217	364	382

It is, perhaps, particularly worth mentioning that the increasing number of ecologists studying life-history evolution through laboratory experiments are typically at pains to assert that their laboratory populations are 'outbreeding' (i.e. not subject to serious inbreeding). Clearly, it would be dangerous to place too much reliance on censuses alone in justifying this assertion.

Finally here, it should be noted that the extent of individual variation has been reported typically to increase with density (Weiner & Thomas 1986, Weiner 1990; see also Figs 13.5 and 13.6). This may seem to provide some reassurance in the context of conservation: small, threatened populations should be little affected, and their actual and effective population sizes should therefore be similar. However, in the data on individual differences that have been analysed (Weiner & Thomas 1986) density, population size and the intensity of competition have marched side by side. If, on the contrary, a small, threatened population nonetheless experiences intense competition, then the effects described here are likely to be of profound importance and reassurance is no longer appropriate.

MULTISPECIES SYSTEMS AND THE MANY PATHS TO FREQUENCY-DEPENDENT COEXISTENCE

Another growth point in population ecology in recent years has been the study of multi- (usually three) species systems, as opposed to those limited to single species or species pairs in isolation (see, for example, Hassell & Anderson 1989). One by-product of this has been that the range of frequency-dependent interactions receiving careful attention from ecologists has itself increased.

Discussions of frequency-dependent selection in the past have been dominated by two ecological processes. The first is conventional competition, i.e. competition for resources (see, for example, Antonovics & Kareiva 1988, Christiansen 1988); the second is predation (see, for example, Allen 1988), including attacks by pathogens (see, for example, Barrett 1988, Ennos, Ch. 10, this volume). This itself has reflected the preoccupations of population ecologists: most interest has been focused on conventional competition and predation, with rather less interest (though more, recently) in disease.

The range of demographically important interactions in nature, however, is likely to be much wider. Hochberg and Holt (1990), for example, have examined a model of an interaction in which two parasites subsist on a single host, and have shown that a parasite can play three roles: as a predator or true parasite of healthy hosts; as an intraguild predator of a competing parasite; and as a competitor with a second parasite species or strain.

Another interaction on which multispecies models have thrown light, and which is likely to be much more widespread in its occurrence, is 'apparent competition' for 'predator-free space'. This has been recognized for some time (by Charles Darwin, quoted in Hutchinson (1978), by Grinnell (1917), Lotka (1925) and Williamson (1957)) but very largely

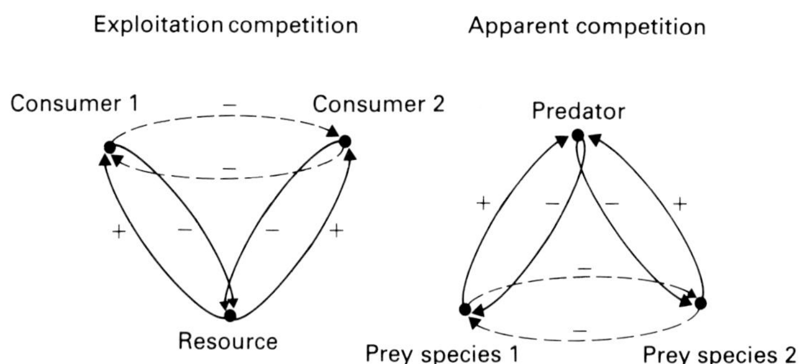

FIG. 13.7. In terms of the signs of their interactions, two prey species being attacked by a common predator ('apparent competition') are indistinguishable from two species consuming a common resource (exploitation competition). Solid lines are direct interactions, dotted lines indirect interactions. (After Holt 1984.)

neglected until quite recently (Holt 1977, 1984, Jeffries & Lawton 1984, 1985, Holt & Pickering 1985, Bowers & Begon 1991, Begon *et al.* 1992). The basis for it is quite simple, and is set out in Fig. 13.7. Essentially, two prey types (species or morphs) sharing a predator or pathogen have the same numerical response to one another as two consumer types sharing a resource: increases in one lead to decreases in the other.

Here, attention is focused on a model in which two hosts share a common, directly transmitted pathogen, and in which the hosts are also both subject to self-regulation (Begon *et al.* 1992). The model is as follows:

$$\frac{dH_1}{dt} = r_1 H_1 \left(1 - \frac{H_1}{K_1}\right) - \alpha_1 Y_1$$

$$\frac{dY_1}{dt} = \beta_{11} (H_1 - Y_1) Y_1 + \beta_{12} (H_1 - Y_1) Y_2 - \Gamma_1 Y_1$$

$$\frac{dH_2}{dt} = r_2 H_2 \left(1 - \frac{H_2}{K_2}\right) - \alpha_2 Y_2$$

$$\frac{dY_2}{dt} = \beta_{22} (H_2 - Y_2) Y_2 + \beta_{21} (H_2 - Y_2) Y_1 - \Gamma_2 Y_2$$

where H_i is the total size of the population of host species i, Y_i is the number of infected (and also infectious) individuals in this population and $(H_i - Y_i)$ is therefore the number of susceptible, uninfected individuals; r_i is the intrinsic rate of increase of species i; K_i is its carrying capacity, the density at which it would be regulated by intraspecific competition in the absence of disease, so that $(1 - H_i/K_i)$ is a measure of the intensity of intraspecific competition in species i; α_i is the rate of pathogen-induced mortality species i experiences from the single species of pathogen assumed here; Γ_i is the net rate of loss of infected individuals (including not only pathogen-induced mortality but also natural mortality and recovery back to the susceptible state); and β_{ij} is the transmission coefficient of the disease from host species j to host species i, such that $\beta_{ij} (H_i - Y_i) Y_j$ measures the rate of infection of hosts of species i as a consequence of their interaction with hosts of species j.

The details of the model, however, are not so important in the present context as a number of more general points. The first, simply, is that apparent competition can occur in the model, giving rise sometimes to the coexistence of both hosts with the pathogen (where there is sufficient differentiation of pathogen-free space), sometimes to the predictable elimination of one of the hosts, and sometimes to the elimination of one or other host, contingent on the initial densities in the system.

A more important point, though, is that this is not the only path to (frequency dependent) coexistence of both hosts with the pathogen. It can occur, too, for example, by what can be called 'resource mediation' (by analogy with predator-mediated coexistence in conventional competition). In other words, here, the free availability of resources can protect the hosts from competitive exclusion, even in the absence of a sufficient differentiation of pathogen-free space. Perhaps most important of all, however, coexistence can also occur by a combination of some differentiation of pathogen-free space and some resource mediation, where neither alone would have been sufficient to give rise to coexistence.

A final point is illustrated in Fig. 13.8: the complexity that arises in models of this type (that is, here, a model with four variables and the additional non-linearities arising from self-regulation). The figure plots curves bearing a superficial resemblance to the familiar zero isoclines of Lotka–Volterra competition. (In fact, here, the curves have $\mathrm{d}Y_1/\mathrm{d}t = \mathrm{d}Y_2/\mathrm{d}t = 0$ and either $\mathrm{d}H_1/\mathrm{d}t = 0$ or $\mathrm{d}H_2/\mathrm{d}t = 0$.) In this case there are 16

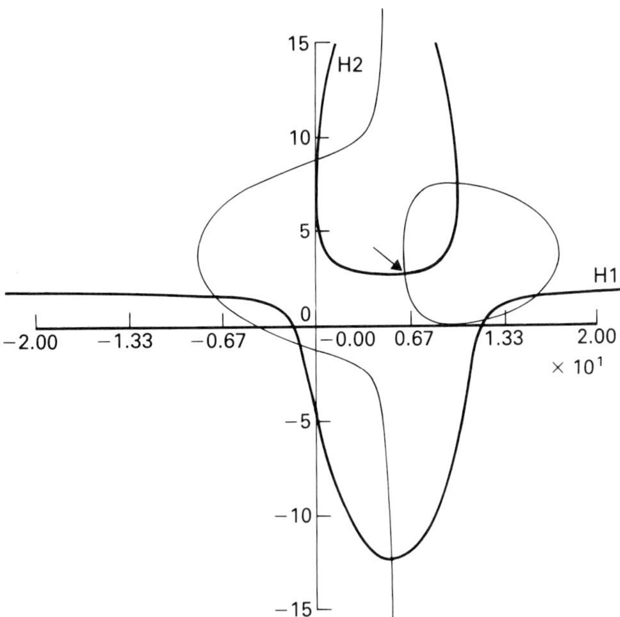

FIG. 13.8. A graph, from a host–host–pathogen model with host self-regulation, of (i) $\mathrm{d}Y_1/\mathrm{d}t = \mathrm{d}Y_2/\mathrm{d}t = \mathrm{d}H_1/\mathrm{d}t = 0$ (this includes the H_2 axis) and (ii) (in bold) $\mathrm{d}Y_1/\mathrm{d}t = \mathrm{d}Y_2/\mathrm{d}t = \mathrm{d}H_2/\mathrm{d}t = 0$ (this includes the H_1 axis). Equilibria occur at the intersections of the two graphs. Here, of 16 possible equilibria, the single stable, biologically relevant equilibrium, at which both hosts coexist with the pathogen, is indicated by the arrow.

equilibrium points, that is 16 points where the two sets of curves cross; but of these, only one is a biologically relevant, stable, coexistence equilibrium.

Of course, not all of this will come as news to all population geneticists. In particular, a role for apparent competition for pathogen-free space was clearly recognized by, for example, Antonovics & Kareiva (1988) in discussing the coexistence of different genotypes of *Anthoxanthum odoratum*. Nonetheless, the model nicely illustrates that there are many paths to coexistence, that there are frequency-dependent processes beyond the more conventional that can give rise to this coexistence, and that these frequency-dependent processes can intertwine quite subtly with other processes in exerting their effects. It seems clear that there may be lessons here for population geneticists seeking to understand the role of frequency-dependent selection in promoting the maintenance of polymorphisms.

ACKNOWLEDGEMENTS

I am most grateful to Bryan Clarke, Charles Godfray, Michael Hassell, Bryan Shorrocks and Dave Thompson for discussions and comments on a previous draft of this paper.

REFERENCES

Allen, J. A. (1988). Frequency-dependent selection by predators. *Philosophical Transactions of the Royal Society of London*, B, **319**, 485–503.

Antonovics, J. & Kareiva, P. (1988). Frequency-dependent selection and competition: empirical approaches. *Philosophical Transactions of the Royal Society of London*, B, **319**, 601–613.

Atkinson, W. D. & Shorrocks, B. (1981). Competition for a divided and ephemeral resource: a simulation model. *Journal of Animal Ecology*, **50**, 461–471.

Atkinson, W. D. & Shorrocks, B. (1984). Aggregation of larval Diptera over discrete and ephemeral breeding sites: the implications for coexistence. *American Naturalist*, **124**, 336–351.

Barrett, J. A. (1988). Frequency-dependent selection in plant–fungal interactions. *Philosophical Transactions of the Royal Society of London*, B, **319**, 473–483.

Begon, M. (1977). The effective size of a natural *Drosophila subobscura* population. *Heredity*, **38**, 13–18.

Begon, M. (1984). Density and individual fitness: asymmetric competition. *Evolutionary Ecology* (Ed. by B. Shorrocks), pp. 175–194. Blackwell Scientific Publications, Oxford, UK.

Begon, M., Bowers, R. G., Kadianakis, N. & Hodgkinson, D. E. (1992). Disease and community structure: the importance of host self-regulation in a host–host–pathogen model. *American Naturalist*, **139**, 1131–1150.

Bowers, R. G. & Begon, M. (1991). A host–host–pathogen model with free-living infective stages, applicable to microbial pest control. *Journal of Theoretical Biology*, **148**, 305–329.

Charlesworth, B. (1971). Selection in density-regulated populations. *Ecology*, **52**, 469–474.

Chesson, P. (1991). A need for niches? *Trends in Ecology and Evolution*, **6**, 26–28.

Chesson, P.L. & Murdoch, W. W. (1986). Aggregation of risk: relationships among host–parasitoid models. *American Naturalist*, **127**, 696–715.

Clarke, B. (1972). Density-dependent selection. *American Naturalist*, **106**, 1–13.

Clarke, B., Arthur, W., Horsley, D. T. & Parkin, D. T. (1978). Genetic variation and natural selection in pulmonate molluscs. *Pulmonates*, Vol. 2A, *Systematics, Evolution and Ecology* (Ed. by V. Fretter & J. Peake), pp. 219–270. Academic Press, London, UK.

Christiansen, F. B. (1988). Frequency dependence and competition. *Philosophical Transactions of the Royal Society of London*, B, **319**, 587–600.

Crow, J. F. (1954). Breeding structure of populations. II. Effective population number. *Statistics and Mathematics in Biology* (Ed. by O. Kempthorne, T. A. Bancroft, J. W. Gowen & J. L. Lush), pp. 543–556. Iowa State University Press, Ames, IA, USA.

Crow, J. F. & Morton, N. E. (1955). Measurement of gene frequency drift in small populations. *Evolution*, **9**, 202–214.

Dempster, J. P. (1983). The natural control of populations of butterflies and moths. *Biological Reviews*, **58**, 461–481.

Dempster, J. P. & Pollard, E. (1986). Spatial heterogeneity, stochasticity and the detection of density dependence in animal populations. *Oikos*, **46**, 413–416.

Godfray, H. C. J. & Blythe, S. P. (1990). Complex dynamics in multispecies communities. *Philosophical Transactions of the Royal Society of London*, B, **330**, 221–233.

Godfray, H. C. J. & Pacala, S. W. (1992). Aggregation and the population dynamics of parasitoids and predators. *American Naturalist*, **140**, 30–40.

Grinnell, J. (1917). The niche-relationships of the California thrasher. *Auk*, **34**, 427–433.

Hanski, I. (1981). Coexistence of competitors in patchy environments with and without predation. *Oikos* **37**, 306–312.

Hanski, I. (1983). Co-existence of competitors in patchy environments. *Ecology*, **64**, 492–500.

Hassell, M. P. (1985). Insect natural enemies as regulating factors. *Journal of Animal Ecology*, **54**, 323–334.

Hassell, M. P. (1987). Detecting regulation in patchily distributed animal populations. *Journal of Animal Ecology*, **56**, 705–713.

Hassell, M. P. & Anderson, R. M. (1989). Predator–prey and host–pathogen interactions. *Ecological Concepts* (Ed. by J. M. Cherret), pp. 147–196. Blackwell Scientific Publications, Oxford, UK.

Hassell, M. P., May, R. M., Pacala, S. W. & Chesson, P. L. (1991). The persistence of host–parasitoid associations in patchy environments. I. A general criterion. *American Naturalist*, **138**, 568–583.

Hawthorn, W. R. & Cavers, P. B. (1982). Dry weight and resource allocation patterns among individuals in populations of *Plantago major* and *P. rugelii*. *Canadian Journal of Botany*, **60**, 2424–2439.

Hochberg, M. E. & Holt, R. D. (1990). The coexistence of competing parasites. 1. The role of cross-species infection. *American Naturalist*, **136**, 517–541.

Holt, R. D. (1977). Predation, apparent competition and the structure of prey communities. *Theoretical Population Biology*, **12**, 197–229.

Holt, R. D. (1984). Spatial heterogeneity, indirect interactions, and the coexistence of prey species. *American Naturalist*, **124**, 377–406.

Holt, R. D. & Pickering, J. (1985). Infectious disease and species coexistence: a model in Lotka–Volterra form. *American Naturalist*, **126**, 196–211.

Hutchinson, G. E. (1978). *An Introduction to Population Ecology*. Yale University Press, New Haven, CT, USA.

Ives, A. R. & May, R. M. (1985). Competition within and between species in a patchy environment: relations between microscopic and macroscopic models. *Journal of Theoretical Biology*, **115**, 65–92.

Jeffries, M. J. & Lawton, J. H. (1984). Enemy-free space and the structure of ecological communities. *Biological Journal of the Linnean Society*, **23**, 269–286.

Jeffries, M. J. & Lawton, J. H. (1985). Predator–prey ratios in communities of freshwater invertebrates: the role of enemy free space. *Freshwater Biology*, **15**, 105–112.

Jones, J. S., Leith, B. H. & Rawlings, P. (1977). Polymorphism in *Cepaea*: a problem with too many solutions? *Annual Review of Ecology and Systematics*, **8**, 109–143.

Lewontin, R. C. (1974). *The Genetic Basic of Evolutionary Change*. Columbia University Press, New York, NY, USA.

Lotka, A. J. (1925). *Elements of Physical Biology*. Williams & Wilkins, Baltimore, USA.

May, R. M. (1974). Biological populations with nonoverlapping generations: stable points, stable cycles, and chaos. *Science*, **186**, 645–647.

May, R. M. (1976). Simple mathematical models with very complicated dynamics. *Nature*, **261**, 459–467.

May, R. M. (1989). Detecting density dependence in imaginary worlds. *Nature*, **338**, 16–17.

Mountford, M. D. (1988). Population regulation, density dependence, and heterogeneity. *Journal of Animal Ecology*, **57**, 845–858.

Murdoch, W. W. & Stewart-Oaten, A. (1989). Aggregation by parasitoids and predators: effects on equilibrium and stability. *American Naturalist*, **134**, 288–310.

Pacala, S. W. & Hassell, M. P. (1991). The persistence of host–parasitoid associations in patchy environments. II. Evaluation of field data. *American Naturalist*, **138**, 584–605.

Pacala, S. W., Hassell, M. P. & May, R. M. (1990). Host–parasitoid associations in patchy environments. *Nature*, **344**, 150–153.

Rosewell, J., Shorrocks, B. & Edwards, K. (1990). Competition on a divided and ephemeral resource: testing the assumptions. I. Aggregation. *Journal of Animal Ecology*, **59**, 977–1001.

Schaffer, W. M. (1984). Stretching and folding in lynx fur returns: evidence for a strange attractor in nature? *American Naturalist*, **124**, 798–820.

Schaffer, W. M. (1985). Order and chaos in ecological systems. *Ecology*, **66**, 93–106.

Schaffer, W. M. & Kot, M. (1986). Chaos in ecological systems: the coals that Newcastle forgot. *Trends in Ecology and Evolution*, **1**, 58–63.

Shorrocks, B. (1990). Competition and selection in a patchy and ephemeral habitat: the implications for insect life-cycles. *Evolution of Insect Life Cycles* (Ed. by F. Gilbert), pp. 215–228. Springer Verlag, London, UK.

Shorrocks, B., Rosewell, J. & Edwards, K. (1990). Competition on a divided and ephemeral resource: testing the assumptions. II. Association. *Journal of Animal Ecology*, **59**, 1003–1017.

Shorrocks, B., Rosewell, J., Edwards, K. & Atkinson, W. D. (1984). Interspecific competition is not a major organizing force in many insect communities. *Nature*, **310**, 310–312.

Sugihara, G. & May, R. M. (1990). Nonlinear forecasting as a way of distinguishing chaos from measurement error in time series. *Nature*, **344**, 734–741.

Stewart-Oaten, A. & Murdoch, W. W. (1990). Temporal consequences of spatial density dependence. *Journal of Animal Ecology*, **59**, 1027–1045.

Wall, R. & Begon, M. (1987). Individual variation and the effects of population density in the grasshopper *Chorthippus brunneus*. *Oikos*, **49**, 15–27.

Weiner, J. (1990). Asymmetric competition in plant populations. *Trends in Ecology and Evolution*, **5**, 360–364.

Weiner, J. & Thomas, S. C. (1986). Size variability and competition in plant monocultures. *Oikos*, **47**, 211–222.

Williamson, M. H. (1957). An elementary theory of interspecific competition. *Nature*, **180**, 422–425.

Wright, S. (1969). *Evolution and the Genetics of Populations*. Vol. II. *The Theory of Gene Frequencies*. University of Chicago Press, Chicago, IL, USA.

14. DENSITY AND FREQUENCY DEPENDENCE: A GENETICAL VIEW

BRYAN C. CLARKE AND M. A. BEAUMONT
Department of Genetics, Queens Medical Centre, Clifton Boulevard, University of Nottingham, Nottingham NG7 2UH, UK

SUMMARY

In this chapter we discuss the genetic effects of numerical chaos, and of 'probability refuges'. When selective values depend on density, the movement or stability of gene frequencies is remarkably little affected by numerical fluctuations, even when the numbers are chaotic and vary by many orders of magnitude. The main causes of this relative stability are (1) competition, which ties numerical fluctuations of competing genotypes (or species) together, so that their proportions change very much less than their absolute numbers, and (2) diploidy and recombination, which also buffer gene frequencies against changes in population size.

It is suggested that the relatively stable proportions of competing species in the face of large numerical fluctuations could be used to detect competition in nature. Natural selection usually favours genotypes that stabilize numbers, so we should not expect intra- or interspecific competition often to bring about chaotic behaviour in natural systems. The same may be true of interactions between parasites and hosts.

We argue here that probability refuges are unlikely to be important factors in maintaining genetic variation, and that more attention should be given to the mechanisms by which organisms 'choose' their habitats and the habitats of their offspring.

INTRODUCTION

We discuss in this chapter two issues raised by Dr Begon (Ch. 13, this volume), and allow them to lead us into answering the question posed at the beginning of his chapter; what is new in ecology, and how might it change the life of a population geneticist? In the process we hope to show that population genetics can also change the life of an ecologist. The two issues are (1) numerical chaos, and (2) probability refuges.

CHAOS

Most of theoretical population genetics is built on the myth that selective values are constant, and are not influenced by the frequencies of genotypes or the densities of populations. We know that it is indeed a myth. In truth, apart from cases of unconditional lethality, it is difficult to imagine how any selective agent can be entirely independent of the biotic environment. Nonetheless theorists continue to make models with constant selective values. How do they get away with it?

The answer seems to be that although selective values are very often affected by numbers, the resulting gene frequencies are generally insensitive to them. Gene frequencies can remain relatively constant, or proceed in an orderly manner to fixation or loss, while numbers fluctuate wildly. The sources of this orderliness are interesting, and can be shown by the following models.

We imagine two situations. In the first there are two competing genotypes of a haploid organism, a state of affairs that is formally equivalent to two competing species. The selective values are:

Genotype and phenotype	A	a
Frequency	$1 - q$	q
Selective value	$\dfrac{w_1}{1 + \left(\dfrac{N(w_1[1 - q] + \alpha w_2 q)}{k_1}\right)^{b_1}}$	$\dfrac{w_2}{1 + \left(\dfrac{N(w_2 q + \beta w_1[1 - q])}{k_2}\right)^{b_2}}$ (1)

where N is the population density, w_1 and w_2 represent density-independent rates of increase, k_1 and k_2 are measures of 'carrying capacity', and α and β are competition coefficients representing the effects of each genotype upon the other. The constants b_1 and b_2 measure the strength of feedback between density and selective value. When $b_1 = b_2 = 1$ the competition between genotypes is purely a contest. As b increases the competition moves from a contest to a scramble. This formulation is identical to the model of population growth proposed by Maynard Smith and Slatkin (1973; see also Bellows 1981), except that intergenotypic competition has been introduced.

In the second situation that we envisage, there is a diploid species with two alleles, one completely dominant to the other. Mating is random and the selective values of the two phenotypes are:

Phenotype	A–		a
Genotype	AA	Aa	aa
Frequency	$1 - q^2$		q^2

$$\text{Selective value} \quad \frac{w_1}{1 + \left(\dfrac{N(w_1[1 - q^2] + \alpha w_2 q^2)}{k_1}\right)^{b_1}} \qquad \frac{w_2}{1 + \left(\dfrac{N(w_2 q^2 + \beta w_1[1 - q^2])}{k_2}\right)^{b_2}} \tag{2}$$

When $b_1 = b_2 = 1$ this reduces exactly to the model of density-dependent selection proposed by Clarke (1972).

The first mechanism of buffering can be seen in the formulae for selective values. When $w_1 = w_2$ and $b_1 = b_2$ any equilibrium value of q becomes independent of N, even when the two phenotypes differ in their carrying capacities or competition coefficients. In this condition a balanced polymorphism is unaffected by fluctuations in density.

It is more interesting, however, to examine a case that *a priori* would be expected to produce the strongest fluctuations in q. This is illustrated in Fig. 14.1. Here it is assumed that the two phenotypes differ in their density-independent rates of increase ($w_2 > w_1$) and in their carrying capacities ($k_1 > k_2$). The differences are appreciable (20% in each case) and opposite in sense. We would therefore expect A– to be relatively favoured (or less disfavoured) at high densities and a to be relatively favoured (or less disfavoured) at low densities. We assume that $b_1 = b_2 = 5$, putting the population firmly into the region of chaotic numbers. Thus the model describes a situation in which the effects of numerical fluctuations on gene frequencies are expected to be maximal.

It can be seen (Fig. 14.1) that when the competition coefficients, α and β, are zero (i.e. when the two phenotypes occupy completely different 'niches' and do not interact at all), the chaotic densities are reflected in extreme fluctuations of gene frequencies, although the range of fluctuation is lower among the diploids. However, with increasing values of α and β the gene frequencies fluctuate less and less, in both haploids and diploids. At the higher values of the competition coefficients (α and $\beta > 0.4$) the fluctuations of q in diploids become small enough to be detectable only in large samples, despite the fact that the densities are varying by six or seven orders of magnitude. We note that competing genotypes of the same species are likely to have high values of α and β.

Evidently competition acts as a very effective buffer. In retrospect the reason is obvious. As competition increases, the numbers of the two phenotypes become more and more closely tied together because the numbers of one phenotype necessarily affect the numbers of the other, so

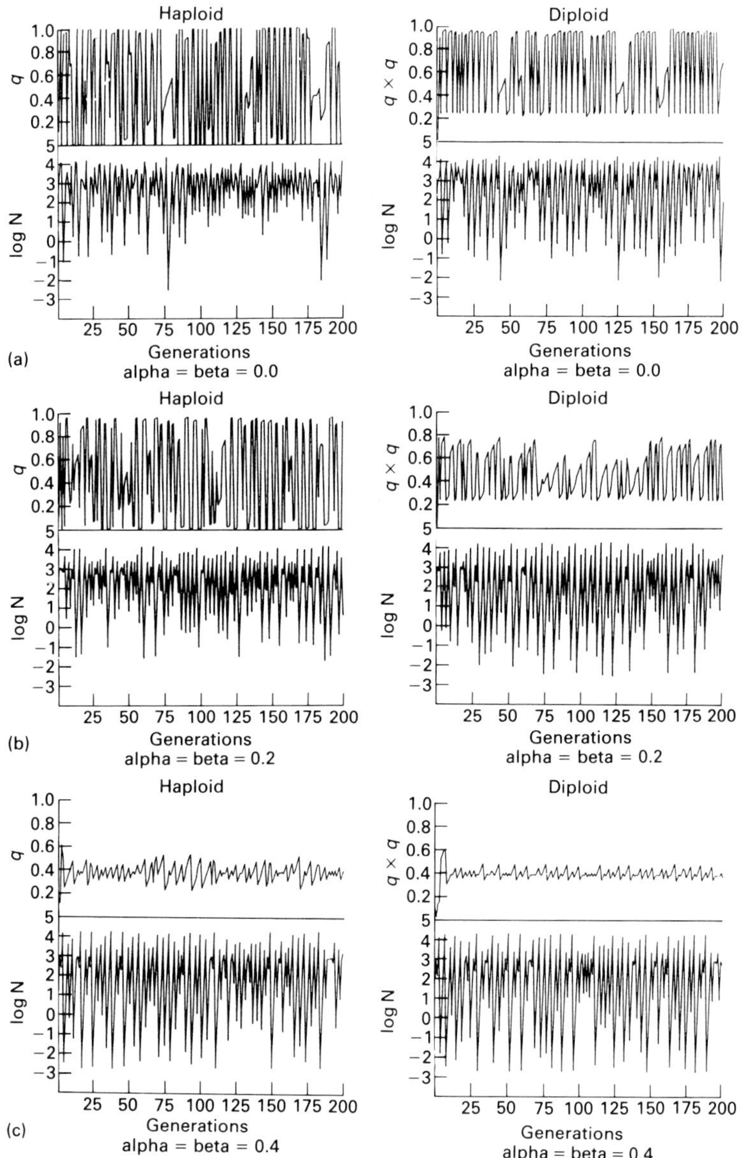

FIG. 14.1. Changes in genotype frequencies and population densities with progressively higher levels of competition. In each pair of diagrams, the left-hand one shows competition between two clones of a haploid, and the right-hand one shows competition between the dominant and recessive phenotypes (A−, and aa) of a diploid. The formulae for the selective values are given in the text.

In all cases, $w_1 = 100$, $w_2 = 120$, $k_1 = 24\,000$, $k_2 = 20\,000$, and $b_1 = b_2 = 5$. The starting value of N is 10 and of q is 0.1 (except in (f), where the starting value of q is 0.9). The values of α and β are assumed to be equal, and are 0 in (a), 0.2 in (b), 0.4 in (c), 0.6 in (d), 0.8 in (e) and 1.0 in (f). The upper half of each diagram shows q for haploids or q^2 for

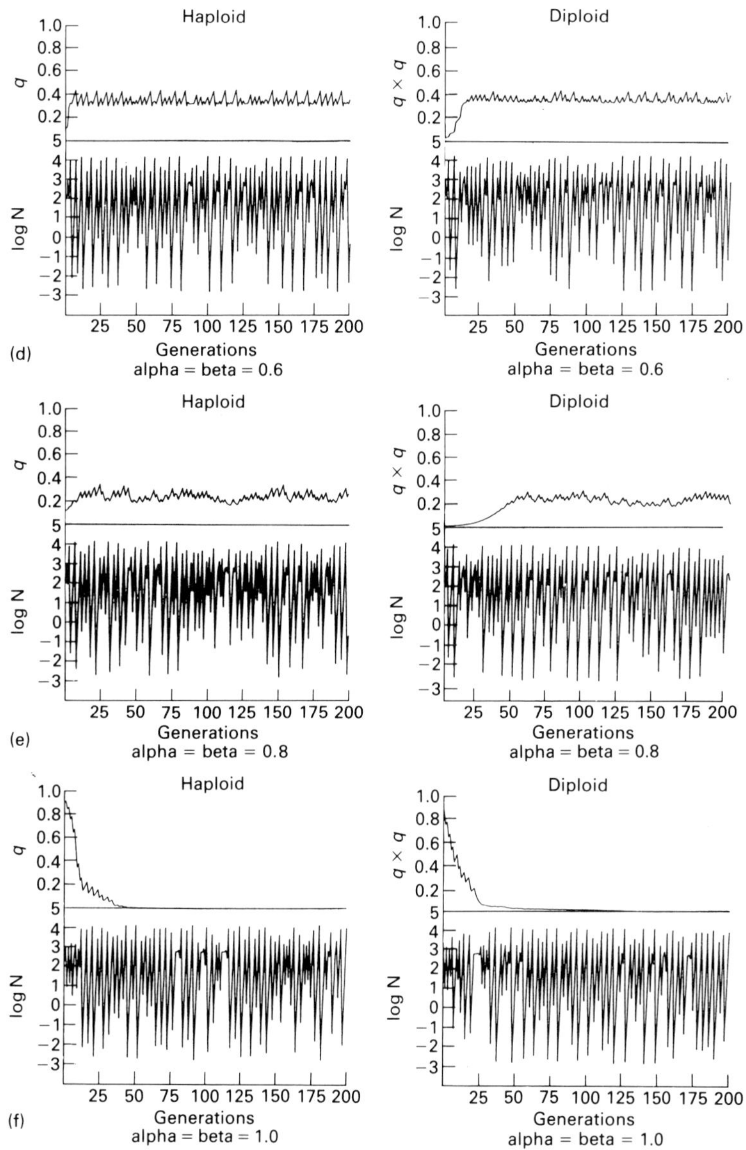

diploids, and the lower half shows the common logarithm of overall population density (N).

The fluctuations in genotype frequency become progressively smaller as the level of competition increases (note that when α and β reach 0.8 the polymorphism becomes less stable and there is a slight rise in the fluctuation). In general diploids show less variation in q^2 than haploids show in q. In the progression from $\alpha = \beta = 0$ to $\alpha = \beta = 0.4$ the stabilization of gene frequencies seems to be associated with a greater variation in N, and the variation in N is larger in diploids than in haploids. The diagrams for $\alpha = \beta = 1.0$ (f), show that the polymorphism has then become unstable, and allele A moves to fixation. Its advantage in k overcomes its disadvantage in w. Here the simulation was started at $q = 0.9$, to show more clearly the decline of a.

that they vary in unison. Consequently their relative proportions vary less and less. Since this effect is seen in haploids as well as diploids, it applies also to competing species. It leads us to suggest that relatively stable proportions of species, despite large movements of their absolute numbers, could be used as indicators of competition in natural ecosystems. Of course, it would be necessary to eliminate other factors, such as climatic variations, that could bring about concordance between species.

Figure 14.1 illustrates another aspect of buffering. The fluctuations in gene frequencies are consistently lower in diploids than they are in haploids (note that in the figure we plot q for haploids, but q^2 for diploids, thereby representing in each case the frequency of the equivalent genotype). The lower fluctuations in diploids come, at least in part, from the fact that selection on a recessive homozygote has a weaker effect on gene frequency than has selection on a hemizygote. There is another reason, not shown in the models, why haploids should be more prone to fluctuating gene frequencies. Many of them have only occasional bouts of recombination, and their populations are collections of clones that differ at large numbers of loci (for example, see Levin 1981 on *Escherichia coli*). Such clones are more likely than individual genotypes to suffer strong selective differentials, and the effects of differentials will show themselves at more loci. Diploids with recombination in every generation will be relatively immune. Thus, recombination itself acts as a buffer.

At this point we should emphasize that our model errs on the side of exaggerating the effects of density on gene frequencies, and that there must often be occasions when selection is effectively independent of density. If two genotypes differ in such a way that one is superior to the other with respect to both w and k, the effects of numerical fluctuations will be minimized. Furthermore, some mutants are unequivocally disadvantageous, in any known environment. They are often mutations that affect essential metabolic pathways, or essential structures. Their elimination comes into Wallace's (1975) category of 'hard selection'. It seems entirely likely that there are advantageous mutants in the same category.

We conclude that population geneticists, most of whom study diploids, have been able to get away with models assuming constant selective values because gene frequencies are buffered in various ways against the most drastic effects of density. The neglect of frequency- and density-dependent selection has not, perhaps, been disastrous to most studies of evolutionary change. It has, however, done serious damage to studies of evolutionary stability.

The supposition that selective values are constant leads inexorably to the view that the most important selective mechanism for the maintenance of polymorphism is heterozygous advantage. The fact that heterozygous advantage cannot comfortably explain the common occurrence of multiple alleles at unequal frequencies (Lewontin *et al.* 1978) has led many workers to abandon selection altogether as an explanation of polymorphism, and to appeal to selective neutrality and random genetic drift. Frequency- and density-dependent selection, however, are perfectly capable of supporting many alleles at a wide range of frequencies, and indeed there is much evidence that they play an important role. Predators and parasites seem to be major agents of frequency and density dependent selection, although competitors also have their part (Clarke 1979).

Shelton (1986) has shown that predators can exert frequency-dependent selection on quantitative (metrical) variation in the shapes of their prey, consequently maintaining variation at loci that influence morphological characters. Models of quantitative characters subject to a combination of frequency dependent and stabilizing selection produce patterns of genetic polymorphism that match those observed in nature, and do so more closely than models based on selective neutrality (Mani *et al.* 1990). The evidence that selection is important in maintaining molecular variation (see for example, Kreitman *et al.*, Ch. 11, this volume) forces us to take frequency and density dependence very seriously indeed.

It is worth remarking that the agents of frequency-dependent selection acting to maintain a balance of genotypes can also favour a balance of species. Furthermore they can bring about divergence between the species in relevant characters (such as colour or shape when predators are producing the selection, or biochemical characters when parasites are doing so; see Clarke 1962). Such divergence will strengthen the stability of the system, as defined by the lasting coexistence of the species, as well as raising the numbers of the prey. When competitors are the selective agents, selection will usually lead to a lowering of competition, and therefore to a greater likelihood of coexistence. It is important here to distinguish between the stability of the system in terms of coexistence, and its stability in terms of absolute numbers. Figure 14.1 illustrates that the maintenance of genotypic or specific variety is either independent of, or in some cases antagonistic to, numerical stability. Nonetheless, as Godfray *et al.* have suggested (Ch. 3, this volume), evolution can act to stabilize numbers, moving intraspecific competition away from a scramble and towards a contest (see also Wallace 1977, 1982, Lomnicki 1988).

This leads us to examine the evolutionary behaviour of the constant b in models (1) and (2). Ecological geneticists routinely consider the effects of inherited changes in the density-independent rate of increase (w), the carrying capacity (k) or the competition coefficients (α and β). However, we also need to understand the evolution of feedback between density and growth (i.e. the consequences, in this model, of natural selection acting on genotypes that differ only in b). Our simulations show that, other things being equal, a genotype having a lower value of b is almost invariably favoured. When the difference in b is large, the gene with the lower value spreads very rapidly to fixation, even when numbers are initially chaotic. In situations where polymorphism can otherwise be maintained (e.g. $\alpha = \beta = 0.5$, $w_1 = w_2 = 110$, $k_1 = k_2 = 22\,000$) but the difference in b is large (e.g. $b_1 = 5$, $b_2 = 2$), the gene with the lower value will still be fixed. When the difference in b is small (e.g. $b_1 = 5$, $b_2 = 4.9$) a balanced polymorphism may ensue but the equilibrium will be moved to favour the allele with the lower value of b. This strengthens the point made by Godfray *et al.* (Ch. 3, this volume) that selection will shift populations away from chaotic behaviour, and towards numerical stability. It is another reason why population geneticists have been able to ignore the more drastic effects of fluctuations in numbers. It is also a reason why ecologists should not expect chaotic behaviour to be a common property of natural competitive systems (despite, for example, the arguments of Schaffer & Kot 1985).

It is necessary to point out here that interactions between parasites and hosts involving complementary genotypes, such that each host genotype is vulnerable to one parasite genotype, can easily give rise to chaotic gene frequencies (see, for example, Seger 1988). In simple models the fluctuations can be extreme, because the mechanism of frequency dependence operates with a time delay. So far the theory does not tell us whether natural selection in parasite–host systems should act consistently in the long term to stabilize numbers and gene frequencies, although there is some empirical evidence that it does so (Fenner & Ratcliffe 1965, Holmes 1982, Levin *et al.* 1982). It seems that hosts and parasites usually evolve towards peaceful coexistence, although not necessarily to avirulence. Again there are reasons for expecting chaotic behaviour to be uncommon.

PROBABILITY REFUGES

After the finding by Atkinson and Shorrocks (1981) that the independent aggregation of two or more species on a divided and ephemeral resource can permit their coexistence under a wider range of conditions than would be the case if they were not aggregated, Shorrocks (1990) has extended the argument to genotypes. Begon (Ch. 13, this volume) has supported Shorrocks's view that the existence of probability refuges could maintain genetic variability.

While this may be correct, we doubt that it will prove to be important. In the probability refuge model, the likelihood that an inferior competitor will be able to coexist with a superior one depends not only on their relative competitive abilities but also on the extent to which their two patterns of aggregation are independent. The greater the positive correlation between the species in their patterns of aggregation, the smaller is the difference in competitive abilities that is compatible with coexistence.

Although Shorrocks *et al.* (1990) found evidence that different species of *Drosophila* show enough independence in their patterns of aggregation to allow coexistence at realistic levels of competition, the mechanism of aggregation is not known. When we come to consider competing genotypes, this mechanism becomes very important. We have to ask how likely it is that one genotype will aggregate with its fellows but do so independently of the other genotypes. At first sight it seems very unlikely. What cues might be used? If the cues reflect differences between the patches of resource, then it is admitted that the resource is not homogeneous, opening up the possibility that the heterogeneity is important to the survival of the different genotypes, and threatening the whole concept of probability refuges. If the cues for aggregation are given by the presence of other individuals, how do genotypes recognize their fellows? Postulating pheromones or other characteristics specific to each genotype complicates the hypothesis too much.

This argument about genotypes brings us back to competition between species. Suppose the species were detecting different environmental cues related to the probability of their survival. We would see aggregation, and we would see a degree of independence. How could we distinguish this state from the occurrence of probability refuges? Someone at the conference said, 'The mechanism of aggregation does not matter. If the aggregation is there, balance will ensue'. In a trivial sense this statement is true but in another it is profoundly wrong. The ecologist needs to know whether species are aggregating at random or choosing habitats particularly suitable for their own needs.

In this context we are reminded of two North American snails (*Mesodon normalis* and *Triodopsis albolabris*) that feed on the same species of fungus. When they are sympatric they feed on it at different times. When they are allopatric each species feeds on it throughout the night (Asami 1989). This is *prima facie* evidence that they are competing for a resource, but how do they avoid competition by feeding at different times? There must either be some temporal change in the fungus that is not detectable to the human eye, or some interaction between the snails so that each avoids the other. In either event they appear to be exploiting the habitat differentially in a way that favours their own survival, even though the habitat seems homogeneous.

There is an interesting way in which genotypic diversity might be promoted by a progress from refuges to specialization for particular components of the habitat. Let us suppose that the resource is heterogeneous in subtle ways, but that initially this heterogeneity has no relevance to the differential survival of the available genotypes. A mutant that favoured the choice of one type of habitat might still start to spread because the individuals carrying it would aggregate with a degree of independence from those not carrying it. Its advantage would decline as its frequency increased, until a point of balance was reached, and a polymorphism maintained. At this point selection would favour the accumulation of linked genes that adjusted the genotype to its chosen component of the habitat, and the polymorphism would be strengthened by the formation of a 'supergene'. Selection would then favour genes that helped other genotypes to escape competition by avoiding this component of the habitat. The divergence of adaptations would grow.

An alternative possibility does not even need a specific behavioural mutant. A tendency to favour familiar and distinguishable patches of resource would cause the population to break up into 'culturally inherited' subpopulations. If those in a patch were more likely to mate with each other, subpopulations on different groups of patches could specialize genetically and diverge from each other, perhaps even to the point of speciation (see Diehl & Bush 1989).

In our studies of the snail *Theba pisana* on Portugese sand dunes, we have found that some individuals rest on sea holly (*Eryngium maritimum*) and some on marram grass (*Ammophila arenaria*). Within a small area, we collected snails from each plant and marked them accordingly. In the evening the snails were taken to a different area, and placed on the border between a patch of sea holly and a patch of marram. Their positions on the following morning are shown in Table 14.1. It can be seen that the snails tended significantly to choose the habitat from which they came (Hamshere 1989). Evidently behaviour like this could initiate genetic differentiation between groups of animals that inhabit different

TABLE 14.1. *Theba pisana*: choice of habitat

	Collected on	
Went to	Marram	Sea holly
Marram	15	3
Sea holly	7	14

$\chi^2_{(1)} = 7.93$, $p < 0.01$.

host plants. On patches of resource that look the same but differ in subtle ways, distinguishable to the organism, such behaviour could produce aggregations that mimic probability refuges.

THE IMPORTANCE OF MECHANISMS

We believe that a useful contribution of population genetics to ecology is its emphasis on mechanisms. We hope to have shown how a concern with genetics leads to different ways of viewing ecological problems, sometimes beneficially. The importance of studying mechanisms, particularly genetic ones, can be illustrated by the following tale.

Once upon a time an ecologist found an array of divided resources. They all looked more or less identical but the distribution of species within them was aggregated, and the aggregations of different species were partially independent. After puzzling over these distributions for a while, the ecologist read some papers by Shorrocks, and concluded that there were probability refuges. There was no encouragement to study the matter further because 'the mechanism is unimportant. If the aggregation is there, balance will ensue'.

This tale is untrue. The habitats were patches of soil under electricity pylons, polluted with zinc from galvanized iron in the pylons. They were studied by Professor A. D. Bradshaw and his colleagues, who found that whether or not a particular patch was inhabited by a particular species of plant depended upon whether or not the surrounding populations of the species carried genes for zinc resistance (Al-Hiyaly *et al.* 1991).

The moral of our untrue tale, and its true counterpart, is obvious.

ACKNOWLEDGEMENTS

We thank Michael Begon for stimulating our interest in these matters, and for valuable discussions. We are grateful to the Science and Engineering Resource Council for financial support.

REFERENCES

Al-Hiyaly, S. A., McNeilly, T. & Bradshaw, A. D. (1992). The effects of zinc contamination from electricity pylons — genetic constraints on selection for zinc tolerance. *Heredity* (in press).

Asami, T. (1989). Temporal segregation of two sympatric species of land snails. *Venus, Japanese Journal of Malacology*, **47**, 278–297.

Atkinson, W. D. & Shorrocks, B. (1981). Competition on a divided and ephemeral resource: a simulation model. *Journal of Animal Ecology*, **50**, 461–471.

Bellows, T. S. (1981). The descriptive properties of some models for density dependence. *Journal of Animal Ecology*, **50**, 139–156.

Clarke, B. (1962). Balanced polymorphism and the diversity of sympatric species. *Taxonomy and Geography* (Ed. by D. Nichols), pp. 47–70. Systematics Association, Oxford, UK.

Clarke, B. (1972). Density-dependent selection. *American Naturalist*, **106**, 1–13.

Clarke, B. (1979). The evolution of genetic diversity. *Proceedings of the Royal Society of London*, B, **205**, 453–474.

Diehl, S. R. & Bush, G. L. (1989). The role of the habitat preference in adaptation and speciation. *Speciation and its Consequences* (Ed. by D. Otte & J. Endler), pp. 345–365. Sinauer, Sunderland, MA, USA.

Fenner, F. & Ratcliffe, F. N. (1965). *Myxomatosis*. Cambridge University Press, Cambridge, UK.

Hamshere, M. (1989). Visible, molecular and behavioural polymorphisms of the land snail *Theba pisana*: a study of population structure in central Portugal. Unpublished BSc Thesis, University of Nottingham, UK.

Holmes, J. C. (1982). Impact of infectious disease agents on the population growth and geographical distribution of animals. *Population Biology of Infectious Diseases* (Ed. by R. M. Anderson & R. M. May), pp. 37–51. Springer Verlag, Berlin, Germany.

Levin, B. R. (1981). Periodic selection, infectious gene exchange and the genetic structure of *Escherichia coli* populations. *Genetics*, **99**, 1–23.

Levin, B. R., Allison, A. C., Bremermann, H. J., Cavalli-Sforza, L. L., Clarke, B., Frentzel-Beyme, R., Hamilton, W. D., Levin, S. A., May, R. M. & Thieme, H. R. (1982). Evolution of parasites and hosts. *Population Biology of Infectious Diseases* (Ed. by R. M. Anderson & R. M. May), pp. 212–243. Springer Verlag, Berlin, Germany.

Lewontin, R. C., Ginzburg, L. R. & Tuljapurkar, S. D. (1978). Heterosis as an explanation for large amounts of genetic diversity. *Genetics*, **88**, 149–170.

Lomnicki, A. (1988). *Population Ecology of Individuals*. Princeton University Press, Princeton, NJ, USA.

Mani, G. S., Clarke, B. & Shelton, P. R. (1990). A model of quantitative traits under frequency-dependent balancing selection. *Proceedings of the Royal Society of London*, B, **240**, 15–28.

Maynard Smith, J. & Slatkin, M. (1973). The stability of predator–prey systems. *Ecology*, **54**, 384–391.

Schaffer, W. M. & Kot, M. (1985). Do strange attractors govern ecological systems? *Bioscience*, **35**, 342–350.

Seger, J. (1988). Dynamics of some simple host–parasite models with more than two genotypes in each species. *Philosophical Transactions of the Royal Society of London*, B, **319**, 541–555.

Shelton, P. R. (1986). Some studies of frequency-dependent selection on metrical characters. PhD Thesis, University of Nottingham, UK.

Shorrocks, B. (1990). Competition and selection in a patchy and ephemeral habitat: the implications for insect life-cycles. *Insect Life Cycles* (Ed. by F. Gilbert), pp. 215–228. Springer Verlag, London, UK.

Shorrocks, B., Rosewell, J. & Edwards, K. (1990). Competition on a divided and ephemeral resource: testing the assumptions. II. Association. *Journal of Animal Ecology*, **59**, 1003–1017.

Wallace, B. (1975). Hard and soft selection revisited. *Evolution*, **29**, 465–473.

Wallace, B. (1977). Automatic culling and population fitness. *Evolutionary Biology*, **10**, 265–276.

Wallace, B. (1982). Phenotypic variation with respect to fitness: the basis for rank-order selection. *Biological Journal of the Linnean Society*, **17**, 269–274.

15. FUNCTIONAL BIOLOGY OF ADAPTATION

MARTIN E. FEDER* AND WARD B. WATT†

**Department of Organismal Biology and Anatomy and Committee on Evolutionary Biology, University of Chicago, 1025 East 57th Street, Chicago, IL 60637, USA, and †Department of Biological Sciences, Stanford University, Stanford, CA 94305 and Rocky Mountain Biological Laboratory, P.O. Box 519, Crested Butte, CO 81224, USA*

INTRODUCTION

Although both genetical and ecological research can proceed without considering adaptation, understanding the adaptive process and its outcome can inform both genetical and ecological work. For ecologists, that organisms should work sufficiently well (or at least not poorly) is a cornerstone of the analysis of pattern and process. For geneticists, that selection constrains genetic variation is often a starting point for diverse viewpoints or forms of analysis. A challenge for both genetics and ecology is to take best advantage of the insights provided by adaptational analysis while avoiding its pitfalls. Our objectives are: (1) to consider why the nature of adaptation necessitates an interdisciplinary approach to its analysis; (2) to explore the characteristics of ideal study systems and approaches for such work; (3) to suggest advantageous modes of investigation for the future.

WHY GO TO THE TROUBLE?

We believe, as did Darwin (1859), that the adaptive process and its outcomes are primarily, though not solely, responsible for our planet's present biota. As Bartholomew has written (1987), '. . .every organism alive today is a link in a chain of parent–offspring relationships that extends back unbroken to the beginning of life on earth. Every organism is a part of an enormously long success story — each of its direct ancestors has been sufficiently well adapted to its physical and biological environments to allow it to mature and reproduce successfully. Viewed thus, adaptation is not a trivial facet of natural history but a biological attribute so central as to be inseparable from life itself.' Viewed in another way, the multidimensional niche concept (Hutchinson 1957, 1978), a landmark in ecological thought, is 'a fitness measure on an environment space' (Levins 1968) and hence an intrinsically evolutionary idea. Indeed, the process and outcome of adaptation is responsible for the positive fitness values that may occur along specific niche axes; adaptation is as much a part of ecology in particular as of evolutionary biology in general.

The process of adaptation by natural selection involves the recursive interaction of four different elements or foci of biological study: variation in allele frequencies → variation in morphological or physiological design → variation in ecological performance → variation in demographic output, hence in fitness → changed distribution of genetic variants in the

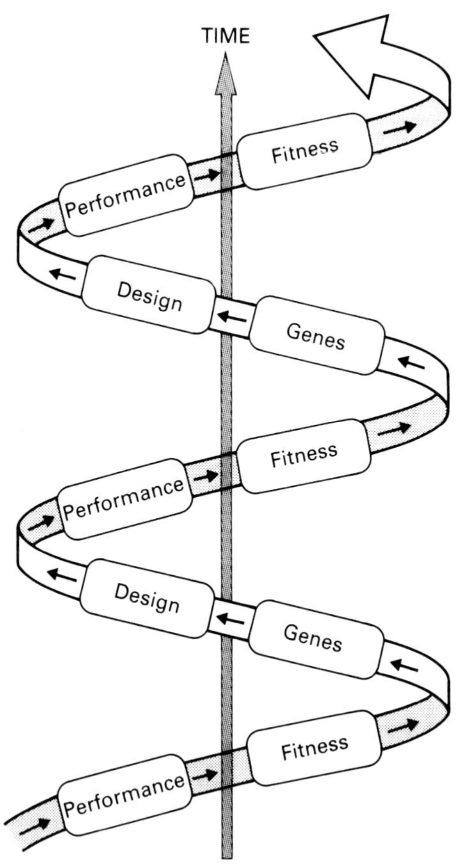

FIG. 15.1. The 'single helix', a visual model of the recursive process of adaptation, incorporating the relations among variation in genes, design, performance and fitness through time as the central axis.

new generation, etc. (Fig. 15.1). (We use 'performance' to denote anything an organism does (after Arnold 1983), e.g. growth, reproduction, photosynthesis, predator defence or oxidative phosphorylation. We use 'design' to refer to the organization of biological structure at any level from the gene product to the entire organism (after Lauder 1982).) We particularly stress the recursiveness of this interaction (cf. Schmalhausen 1960, Watt 1990). For a change in any one element to effect selection, it must affect each other element in turn, hence its own future value. The great challenge to adaptational analysis is to establish unequivocally how each element in the evolutionary recursion affects and is affected by the others. Because each element may vary without change in its predecessors and each may change without affecting its successors, patterns of cause and effect need not be simple or straightforward.

Despite this, students of adaptation have tended to focus on one or another pairwise interaction of elements within the recursive sequence: geneticists on *genes → design*, functional biologists (*sensu lato*, including ecologists, comparative physiologists, biomechanics) on *design → performance*, and population geneticists on *fitness → genes*. The causes of such specialization have received extensive analysis elsewhere and are not at issue here. Its consequences, on the other hand, have immense implications for adaptational analysis. Progress in understanding some of these interactions has been so rapid that biologists are hard pressed to keep abreast of developments (or even jargon) in their own specialties, let alone those of others. The remaining link *performance → fitness*, has received very little attention. To observe performances or fitnesses of organisms in nature may be very difficult for some taxa; the measurements may be time-consuming, tedious and readily go awry. A common response to such problems is that investigators restrict their work to their own close interests, avoiding analysis of performance → fitness in the wild. This omission, while perhaps understandable, leads to many flaws in adaptational analyses, as detailed elsewhere (e.g. Gould & Lewontin 1979). Also as a result, rigorous analyses of performance → fitness are so few that generalizations may be premature (Feder 1987, Bennett & Huey 1990).

The most basic relationships among genes, design, performance and fitness have long ago passed from scientific debate to become textbook knowledge. Biologists typically derive common expectations about how any pairwise interaction should work from this general knowledge. By contrast, the subtleties of these basic relationships, the constraints upon them and exceptions to them, the procedures by which exceptions are evaluated, and the standards of analysis may not be general knowledge, nor may the most recent insights or revisions of the general expectations.

They may be common knowledge within the specialized subdiscipline that concerns them but obscure to outsiders. One example concerns the regulation of intermediary metabolism. Unknown to many former students in biochemistry courses or even to present 'comprehensive' textbooks, quantitative theory about the organization of metabolic pathways has undergone major development in the past two decades (e.g. Easterby 1973, Kacser & Burns 1979, Heinrich & Rapoport 1983, Westerhoff & van Dam 1987, Savageau & Sorribas 1989). Whereas this theory is essential to evolutionary evaluation of the consequences of variation in metabolic design for performance and fitness (Watt 1985, 1986), few comparative biochemists, physiological ecologists and population geneticists have been familiar with it until recently. Such specialized knowledge from disciplines external to one's own can revolutionize the interpretation of any particular study, extending its generality and avoiding errors.

Pough (1989) reviewed successful attempts to relate genes to design, design to performance or performance to fitness. Our intent here is to advocate studies that examine the entire adaptive recursion. To do so, we emphasize instances in which the links between elements in the adaptive recursion are not straightforward, components of the recursion that are not well-studied, and ways in which non-adaptive considerations can influence the outcome of the recursion. We ask to what extent, in the light of these examples, the usual expectations of biologists about genes → design → performance → fitness are realized. Our goal is to rationalize the importance of broad interest and communication across the boundaries of the several specialized subdisciplines involved.

Genes to design

Genetic variation need not lead to changes in adaptive design. Neutral genetic variants may have no detectable effect at any given level of the phenotype. For example, so-called 'silent' nucleotide substitutions, e.g. in the third positions of codons, do not change the amino acid specified by that codon; 'pseudogenes', or unexpressed and often defective copies of functional genes, likewise have no phenotypic consequences above the level of genomic integrity itself, if indeed they have significance there. Neutral variants of genes, whose products differ in peptide sequence but not detectably in function, also occur (e.g. Dykhuisen & Hartl 1983). Indeed, a major school of population genetics rests on the premise that much genetic variation is selectively neutral (Kimura & Ohta 1971).

Of course, genes *do* encode much of design, and genetic variation clearly underlies much variation in design and resulting performance.

Moreover, selection on genetic variation in one trait can cause other traits to change in unanticipated ways along with the first trait. Such effects are often termed 'genetic correlations' (cf. Sulzbach & Lynch 1984, Endler 1986, Arnold 1987), and may arise from diverse causes. These include linkage disequilibrium among genes for the traits in question, multiple effects of single genes (pleiotropy), or even simply by interactions among the various developmental pathways that the 'correlated' genes subserve.

Conversely, mechanisms that buffer development against environmental perturbation may also buffer phenotypes against the effects of some genetic variation, and indeed decrease pleiotropic expression of genes. One such mechanism, often discussed in evolutionary genetics, is canalization (e.g. Rendel 1967, Waddington 1953). An exemplary study, one of the most thorough dissections ever made of a naturally occurring polygenic system, is that of Milkman (1960a, b, 1961, 1965, 1967) on the '*crossveinless* complex' of *Drosophila melanogaster*. Briefly, the structural integrity of the posterior crossvein in this fly's wing is essential for flight. Waddington (1953) showed that high-temperature shock at particular times of pupal development not only could damage this crossvein, but also could expose small, polygenically determined heritable defects in the crossvein. These polygenic variants are distributed throughout the genome but have no visible phenotypic effect unless heat shock or a single dose of *cv-c* depletes the canalization of 'crossvein-making ability' (cma), a trait that shows characteristic parallel distributions in males and females (Milkman 1960a, b, 1961). In 1967, Milkman associated 'Protein A', whose electrophoretic mobility changed with heat shock, with cma. This protein and its role in the crossvein–canalization system now invite further investigation with modern molecular biological techniques to understand the mechanistic basis of both polygenic control of the phenotype and of phenotypic buffering against genetic or environmental disruption.

Although genes control much of design, they are not omnipotent. An organism's phenotype is not rigidly determined by its genome at the start of development; as many studies show, organisms have an enormous capacity to modify design and thereby exhibit a range of phenotypes for any particular genotype. Of this capacity, behaviour can be the most rapidly acting component. Although the harsh cold environment of montane North America might predispose the geneticist to believe that the thermal sensitivities of genetic variants should rigidly restrict the distribution of ectothermic insects, a modest behavioural change in a butterfly's orientation to the sun can transform a cold mountain top to a warm grassland (Watt 1968). Through diverse processes collectively termed acclimation, short-term (days or weeks) exposure to a non-lethal stress can induce a dramatic alteration of the phenotype to a form that putatively or actually functions better in the face of that stress. Exposure to cold, for example, which reduces the catalytic activity of enzymes, might induce increased concentrations of enzymes and their positive modulators (e.g. Crawford & Powers 1989). Comparable examples of acclimation are available for most environmental stresses and physiological systems (Prosser 1986), and may also result from stresses of an organism's own making (e.g. responses to training in animals and human athletes). Alternatively, circadian, circannual and other rhythms may act to deploy organismal responses to stress before the advent of that stress. Environmental signals early in development may cue the expression of very different phenotypes later in development, each of which may demonstrably be suited to the particular environment in which the developing organism finds itself (e.g. Hoffmann 1978, Shapiro 1976; see also Stearns 1989 for a general discussion). Each of these responses, from behaviour to 'polyphenism', has a genetic basis and may itself be the result of selection. In general, however, they permit broad-ranging variation in design within the lifetime of an organism. Accordingly, the 'one genotype—one phenotype' premise, if extrapolated through the entire adaptive recursion, can yield quite unrealistic expectations.

Design to performance

Studies of design → performance provide a basic set of expectations that inform both ecology and genetics. The theory of enzyme kinetics, as a specific example, provides an analytical framework for evaluating whether allozymic variants are selectively neutral (Powers 1987); biomechanics and functional morphology suggest how genetic variation in structure and biological materials ought to affect the roles that organisms play in natural ecosystems (Gans 1986). Thus the ongoing explosive expansion in our understanding of how organisms work, particularly (but not exclusively) at the molecular level, ought to potentiate parallel growth in genetical and ecological aspects of adaptations (Feder & Block 1991, Watt 1991).

Textbooks are replete with examples of design → performance relationships at every level of biological organization, in every taxon and for every function. Biologists may thus understandably assume that a particular variation in design inexorably affects performance, or that variation in performance ineluctably reflects the limitations or potentiation of design. Often their assumption is warranted; in others, as several examples demonstrate, it is not.

Design ≠ performance. A classic adaptive story concerns scales in reptiles, which for years have been touted as the basis for the integumental impermeability that enabled the reptiles to exploit terrestrial environments fully. Discovery of a population of scaleless snakes and subsequent physiological measurements show that snakes lacking scales have water loss rates no different from those of snakes with scales (Licht & Bennett 1972, Bennett & Licht 1975).

Performance ≠ design. As do many groups of animals, lizards vary in foraging mode (Huey & Bennett 1986). Some sit and wait for prey to approach, and thereupon capture prey in a burst of rapid but non-sustainable movement; some forage widely and seek out prey. Closely related and syntopic species of lacertid lizards from the Kalahari desert exemplify both the sit-and-wait approach and the widely foraging style, as confirmed by measurements of movement and feeding performance in the field. Laboratory measurements of performance (the speed–stamina relationship, maximum sustainable speed, maximum burst speed and aerobic and anaerobic metabolic capacity) correspond to the field measurements of performance. Huey and Bennett (1986) hypothesized that variation in the design of muscle should underlie these differences in performance: muscles from the widely foraging species ought to have greater fatigue resistance, slower contractile velocities, greater activity of aerobic enzymes, and lesser myosin ATPase activity than in the sit-and-wait species. Measurements reveal, however, no difference between these muscle properties of the lizard species despite vast differences in capacity for performance and actual performance in the field.

Performance and design correlated without a known causal relationship. In tiger salamanders (*Ambystoma tigrinum*), the aerobic metabolic scope for activity (the difference between the minimum and maximum rate of oxygen consumption) is related to heterozygosity at the alcohol dehydrogenase (ADH) locus (Mitton *et al*. 1986). Insofar as the ADH-catalysed reaction plays no known role in aerobic metabolism during activity in amphibians, the implications of the correlation for locomotor performance are obscure.

These cautionary tales are intended to emphasize that the connection between design and performance can be tenuous indeed. Individuals, populations and species can vary in design but not in performance, can vary in performance but not in design, or can vary independently in both performance and design. Not every design → performance relationship will be as problematic as in these examples (indeed, most may not be) but adaptational biologists obviously need to take care of their analyses.

Performance to fitness

Ewens and Feldman (1976) wrote wryly that to develop a general evolutionary theory of the phenotype would require '...more ecology than population geneticists have been willing to use'. Population genetics needs functional biology, in all its aspects from comparative metabolism to 'environmental biogeography', to solve the evolutionary problems of the transformation of ecological performance, through its demographic consequences, into fitness measures. Studies of the *esterase-5* locus of *Drosophila pseudoobscura* exemplify the futility of proceeding without such information. Yamazaki (1971) found no fitness differences among polymorphic alleles at this locus in a massive laboratory population study. However, soon thereafter Marincovic and Ayala (1975) found significant fitness differences, also in the laboratory, at the same locus. Without knowledge of the metabolic function of this enzyme in the fly, or of ecological pressures which might impinge on that function in the wild, no evolutionary interpretation of either study is possible: failure to find fitness differences could have been due to absence of an ecologically relevant opportunity for selection, while fitness differences found could have been due to variants at closely linked loci in linkage disequilibrium with the *esterase-5* alleles. Each study, carefully executed (and expensive of time and resources) as it was, requires additional work to elaborate its evolutionary implications.

By contrast, Powers and colleagues more successfully studied a two-allele polymorphism at a lactate dehydrogenase (LDH) locus in the estuarine fish *Fundulus*. Their work began with prior knowledge both of the enzyme's metabolic role and of the fish's geographic distribution and environment. Functional differences among the three genotypes are essentially nil at 25°C (a typical temperature of routine enzyme assays, largely a matter of convenience for the enzymologist), but are large at 10°C and 40°C, both of which temperatures are ecologically important to *Fundulus* in parts of its American Atlantic Coast range. Without designing their biochemical–functional evaluation to include these temperatures, Powers *et al.* might have missed the whole basis of the polymorphism; instead, they produced a superb case study of the interaction of biochemical-level genetic variation with strong selection in nature (Powers 1987).

A key feature of the success of Powers *et al.* was prediction, from differences among genotypes in metabolic context, of performance differences that plausibly affect fitness. Understanding this transformation in general, by abstraction from specific cases in which performance → fitness is demonstrated directly, is central to understanding the evolutionary recursion and the predictability of microevolution, including adjustment of ecological relationships. Yet neither the transformation of design into performance, nor that of performance into fitness, is likely to be linear or otherwise simple. Threshold effects, interaction of one aspect of phenotypic performance with others, etc., may complicate analysis. These facts, and perceived difficulties with field measurement of performance and fitness components, may discourage such measurements. However, if one examines systems in the wild whose basic biology is accessible, perhaps already partially known, often new routes, direct or indirect, to the study of performance → fitness become apparent.

Examples of both the non-linearity of the transformation and its accessibility are evident in *Colias* butterflies. These insects must fly to express any component of adult fitness, and must behaviourally achieve a high and narrow T_b to fly (Watt 1968, Kingsolver & Watt 1984, Watt 1990). A key parameter in behavioural thermoregulation in *Colias* is their absorptivity for sunlight (Watt 1968). Fitness, however, is by no means linearly proportional to this phenotypic character. Because *Colias* fly only when T_b exceeds a particular threshold, a 17% reduction in absorptivity can result in as much as a *fourfold* decrease in the opportunity of females to fly and to lay eggs under low-temperature habitat conditions (Watt 1990).

On the other hand, elaborate as such biological interactions may be, *Colias* also show that one aspect of an organism's adaptive biology can potentiate the study of another, which might seem utterly inaccessible to the evolutionist *a priori*. From *in vitro* study of kinetics and thermal stability differences among the 10 common polymorphic genotypes for phosphoglucose isomerase (PGI), Watt (1983, Watt *et al.* 1983) predicted which genotypes should have the greatest capacity for flight and hence the greatest mating success. Testing these predictions might have been intractable if not for investigations of parental investment strategy in butterflies (a typical focus of evolutionary ecology), which showed that sperm precedence in *Colias* is absolute: although both sexes mate multiply, the male most recently mating a given female fathers all her eggs until he in turn is superseded by another male (Boggs & Watt 1981, Carter & Watt 1988). Absolute sperm precedence means that the eggs laid at any one time by a female, whether she has mated multiply or not, all have one and the same father. Thus by sampling wild males and females, and genotyping enough progeny from each wild female to determine their father's genotype, PGI genotype frequencies among males mating females were compared with those among males merely flying with the females. The results thoroughly confirm the predicted consequences of PGI variation for this crucial fitness component (Watt *et al.* 1985, 1986, Watt 1991), showing the advantage of well-characterized study systems.

A final example may alternately, depending on one's ratio of pessimism to optimism, demonstrate the troublesome complexity of performance → fitness transformations or illuminate a different aspect of transformation complexity that is nonetheless analysable from the proper viewpoint. In an important series of studies, Snyder and colleagues (Snyder 1981, Chappell & Snyder 1984, Snyder *et al.* 1988) studied an α-haemoglobin polymorphism in the deer mouse, *Peromyscus maniculatus*, of western North America, and clearly established relationships among genes, design and performance. Allele frequency varies predictably with elevation, and major allelic variants correspond to gradients in oxygen partial pressure along an altitudinal transect. Allele frequency variation, however, is *statistically* detectable only across broad geographic ranges. These workers suggested that in any local region, mice may traverse a broad altitudinal range in even a single night, adjusting blood oxygen carriage with acute regulatory mechanisms and/or embodying 'gene flow' among demes, thus blurring the differential effects of the haemoglobin alleles at specific locations or elevation. Acute regulation of blood oxygen carriage might well suffice for limited challenges to gas exchange, with genetic alterations reserved for major challenges to oxygen transport (cf. Savageau 1976, Watt 1986).

Even when variation in performance affects survivorship l_x or fecundity m_x, the translation of these effects into net fitness for subsequent population genetic analysis can be nontrivial. A common procedure, for example, is first to calculate the net reproductive rate, R_{ij} for each genotype (made up of alleles $1 \ldots i \ldots j \ldots k$) at a gene locus from the life-time sums or integrals (depending on population age structure and life cycle strategy) of that genotype's survivorship l_x and fecundity m_x. Next, dividing each R_{ij} value by an arbitrary standard value produces the relative fitness (W_{ij}) of the population geneticist. Often, for algebraic simplicity, this standard is the R_{ij} of the most fit genotype, so that the maximum relative fitness is 1.0 and the relative fitness of other genotypes is <1.0. However, if some common genotypes have an R_{ij} greater than 1.0 (so that the absolute frequency of such genotypes will increase with time), this standardization of relative fitness will nonetheless yield a *mean* population fitness (as defined below) of <1.0, erroneously suggesting that the entire population should decrease with time. Such suggestions can obviously be very misleading for the overall interpretation of natural variation (cf. Wallace 1981).

At a different level, many functional biologists are concerned not with allelic or individual variation among members of a population but with traits common to many if not all members of a population, species or higher taxon. They may wish to quantitate the benefit due to such a trait or the penalty of its absence for the entire group under study, i.e. the population, species or higher taxon counterpart of allelic fitness. A first challenge to this kind of analysis is that a consensus measure of this counterpart of fitness is lacking. Reproductive rate, group size, geographic range and persistence in evolutionary time, among others, are possible metrics, but these may yield different (even contradictory) measures of group 'fitness'. A second challenge is that within-group variation may be insufficient for analysis. If all reptiles have scales, for example, the assessment of the benefit of scales for reptiles becomes problematic (see earlier). Faced with this problem, some biologists turn to 'natural experiments' (e.g. naturally occurring scaleless snakes (Licht & Bennett 1972, Bennett & Licht 1975) or lungless salamanders (e.g. Feder 1976)), some to experimental manipulation of traits (e.g. Feder 1988), but most to comparison among groups possessing or lacking the trait under study. A third challenge is that each population, species or higher taxon being compared to others will have its own evolutionary history, and so factors other than the trait under study can affect the comparison (Huey 1987, Feder 1988). Techniques are available to minimize the impact of these confounding variables (e.g. Huey 1987) but cannot eliminate them entirely.

Fitness to genes

The genetical 'response to selection' (Lande & Arnold 1983) is a well-studied central theme of mathematical population genetics (e.g. Hartl & Clark 1989) and does not require extensive review here. Indeed, population geneticists have developed a large body of theory than can predict the impact of selection upon the distribution of genotypes in the subsequent generation for each of a diverse set of assumptions and boundary conditions (Hartl & Clark 1989). For example, according to the comprehensive but simple 'gametic excess equation' (e.g. Hartl & Clark 1989) if varying genotypes ij have frequencies p_{ij} in the population and expected fitnesses (averaging over the rest of the segregating genome) W_{ij}, the mean fitness of the population with respect to this locus is:

$$\overline{W} = \Sigma\, p_{ij}\, W_{ij} \qquad (1)$$

The change in frequency of the ith allele for a single generation, as a function of all genotypic fitnesses, is then:

$$\Delta p_i = p_i[(\Sigma p_j W_{ij}) - \overline{W}]/\overline{W}$$

where the bracketed expression in the numerator is the 'gametic excess' of the ith allele. This particular formula accommodates all manner of diverse selective regimes, arbitrary numbers of segregating alleles/genotypes and the like.

Importantly, many different agents may obscure or frustrate a straightforward response to selection as described by the above equation. First, genetic drift can influence allele frequencies even in the face of selection; its power to do so varies inversely with the effective population size N_e. In general, selection does not exert thorough control over allele frequency change in a gene pool unless the selection coefficients (i.e., differences among the W_{ij} relative to the standard genotype), are larger than $1/2N_e$, and drift dominates allele frequencics if the selection coefficients are less than $1/4N_e$ (e.g. Hartl & Clark 1989). Next, if alleles at two or more linked genes experience linkage disequilibrium among the frequencies of the various possible gamete types, then selection on some of the linked loci in disequilibrium may oppose or delay the effects of selection on other linked loci. Chromosomal inversions in *Drosophila*, for example, represent huge blocks of genetic material apparently held in linkage disequilibrium by selection combined with a lack of recombination, itself brought about by the inversions (cf. Dobzhansky 1970, Lewontin 1974). Lastly, catastrophes can overwhelm the effects of usual intensities of selection, and these need not be events on the scale of asteroid collisions! For example, Ehrlich *et al.* (1972) report the outright extinction of a montane Colorado population of the lycaenid butterfly *Glaucopsyche lygdamus* by unusual snowfall. The snowfall eliminated any adaptations that had arisen in this population, regardless of their refinement or usual impact on fitness. Thus, even dramatic cause-and-effect relationships between design, performance and fitness may fail to bring about persistent genetic change. Alternatively, traits previously lacking any selective advantage (e.g. cold tolerance in an equable climate) may suddenly become the basis of major evolutionary change (e.g. Jablonski 1986).

Other than drift and the response to selection, both new genetic variation and 'extra-Mendelian' genetic mechanisms can also affect genetic variation in the next generation. Mutation is the indispensable source of new variants; however, its rate is so small, roughly 10^{-8} per base pair per generation, that it does not affect allele frequencies significantly other than to bring new alleles into being. By contrast, gene conversion, post-meiotic segregation, and intragenic recombination all can arise from local chromosomal damage and its repair in association with the molecular processes of recombination. These phenomena can not only change frequencies of existing alleles at rates as high as 10^{-3} to 10^{-4} per base pair per generation but in some situations can generate new alleles at similar rates, i.e. at least four orders of magnitude greater than classical mutation (reviewed by Leslie & Watt 1986). Thus the genetic transmission machinery itself can alter the allelic contribution of one generation to the next.

The adaptive recursion reconsidered

The links between the elements of the adaptive recursion, genes, design, performance and fitness, are sometimes straightforward but sometimes are not. All of the elements, as well as the transformations among them, are affected by agents outside the adaptive recursion and are subject to constraint. Each element may vary without affecting the others. When present, the effects may vary depending upon the environment and population structure in which they occur. What appears at first glance a straightforward chain of cause and effect (Fig. 15.1) may actually be quite elaborate (Fig. 15.2). We regard this elaboration not as a cause for despair or frustration but as a worthy challenge to the combined ingenuity of geneticists, functional biologists and evolutionists alike. Indeed, how much of the evolution of genes and organisms has been a result of adaptation, and how much is due to other evolutionary and non-evolutionary processes, are open questions.

THE HOLY GRAIL OF EXPERIMENTAL EVOLUTIONARY BIOLOGY

Even if an individual biologist or collaborative group can master all recent developments in each of the necessary disciplines and is willing to undertake meaningful measurements of fitness in the field, substantial barriers to examining the whole of the adaptive recursion may remain. These impediments are rooted in limitations not of biologists but of species. The same attributes that make a species especially tractable for study of genetics may frustrate analysis of its functional biology. *Drosophila*, for example, excel as subjects of genetical study, but have a long-neglected functional biology in the wild that is only recently (and reluctantly) yielding to the ingenuity of investigators (e.g. Courtney *et al.* 1990, Shorrocks 1977). Alternatively, Galapagos finches (Grant 1986), red deer (Clutton-Brock *et al.* 1982) and ground squirrels (Sherman 1981) have

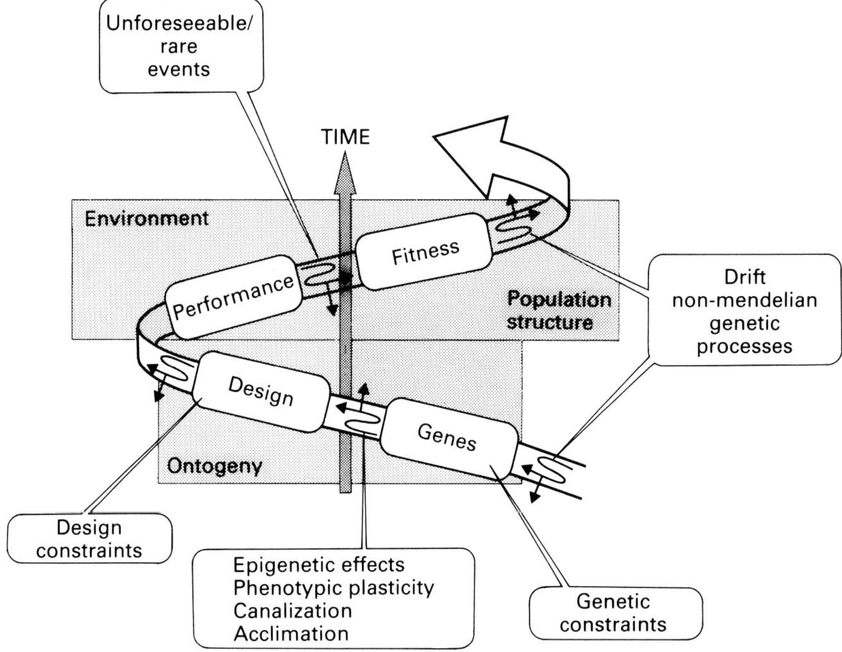

FIG. 15.2. A more realistic version of the 'single helix' depicted in simplified form in Fig. 15.1. The connections between elements are not always straightforward but are sometimes quite elaborate and limited in effect by various constraints. Sometimes change in one element may have no discernable effect on the others. In addition, many agents outside the adaptive recursion may affect the relationships among genes, design, performance and/or fitness. The transformation of variation in performance to variation in fitness occurs against a background of environment and population structure; i.e. a change in performance can have very different consequences for fitness depending upon the environment and population in which it occurs. Similarly, genes → design occurs against a background of developmental processes. Indeed, 'environment' and 'ontogeny' can interact, producing a series of phenotypes for a single genotype. A final point is that through behaviour, animals can mitigate environmental stresses and remove themselves from otherwise intense selection. In the light of these interactions, a challenge for adaptational biologists, geneticists and ecologists is to ascertain how much of evolution has been the result of adaptation.

furnished important insights to field workers but the genetic bases of the traits under study are often obscure. Both the genetic basis of traits in garter snakes and the relationship of these traits with fitness have been elucidated (e.g. Arnold & Bennett 1988, Garland & Bennett 1990, Jayne & Bennett 1990); the mechanistic basis for these relationships, however, is speculative because snakes are often unobservable in the field.

August Krogh, the father of comparative physiology, articulated the principle that 'for every biological question is an organism best suited to its solution'. Such an organism, the squid giant axon or *Caenorhabditis elegans* of experimental evolutionary ecology, has been a Holy Grail for those who wish to examine the entire adaptive recursion (Fig. 15.3). Pursuit of this grail has not been much more successful than in Arthurian times. Instead, experimental evolutionary ecologists have had to settle for a 'holey' grail, in which at least one (and typically more) components of the evolutionary recursion are unexamined. We suggest that the identification of suitable subject species may engender considerable progress in the field, and consider the characteristics of such species.

Substantial literature and knowledge and natural history and systematics. Unambiguous analyses of genes, design, performance and fitness require that these components be examined in the context of environments actually or potentially experienced by a subject species or population. To this

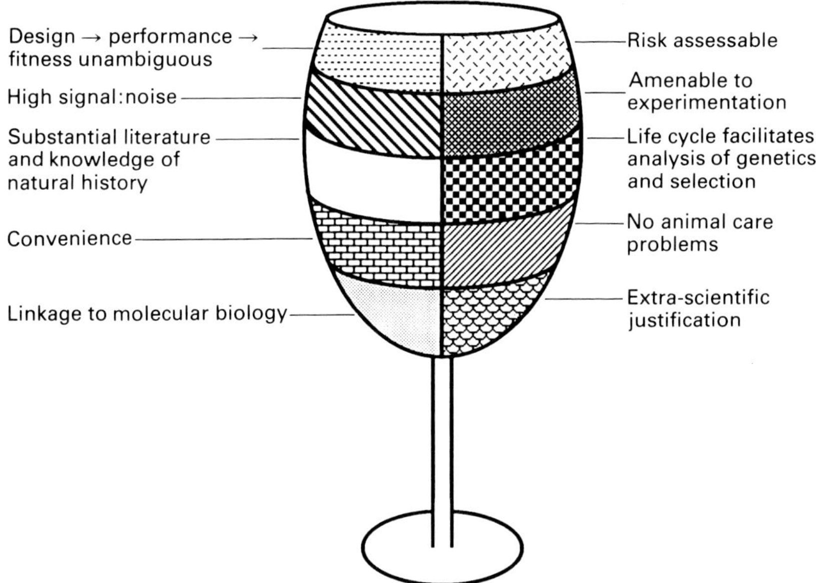

Fig. 15.3. The holy grail of experimental evolutionary biology. Each component of the grail is a characteristic of a species that either permits or facilitates the comprehensive experimental investigation of the role of selection and other evolutionary processes. Frequently, however, evolutionary studies investigate a 'holey' grail, a species in which one or more of the grail's components is absent.

end, knowledge of the actual challenges to an organism's exploitation of environments and the opportunities an organism may face are invaluable to the examination of adaptation (Greene 1986). Obviously, choosing a species for study whose natural history is patently unobservable can frustrate analysis, and choosing a species whose natural history lends itself to characterization can facilitate study. Best of all would be a species whose natural history is already understood in detail. We discussed earlier how this kind of knowledge (e.g., sperm precedence in *Colias*) can facilitate testing the predicted consequences of genetic variation. Ideally, also, the species might be one of several close relatives whose phylogenetic interrelationships are unambiguous and in which the trait under study has arisen independently. The study of independent trait origins in closely related species could be an excellent test of the generality of conclusions based on study of a single species (Huey 1987, Harvey & Pagel 1991), if such situations could be identified.

The entire study system should be amenable to experimentation. Genetic variation and its effects on organismal design can often be altered experimentally in the analysis of the evolutionary recursion, whether by new mutation, choice of alternative polymorphs for study, or even surgical manipulation (Sinervo 1990). By contrast, save for those 'natural experiments' in which an investigator takes advantage of pre-existing environmental variation (e.g., plants growing on heavy metal-laden soil), experimental manipulation of the organisms' environment is often thought to be beyond the grasp of scientists, who must content themselves with the particular circumstances offered by their subject species. Some species (and their habitats) are amenable to such manipulations, however. Perhaps the greatest successes with experimental manipulations of environmental variables have concerned the biotic environment: e.g. enclosures manipulating competitor density (e.g. Pacala *et al.* 1983, Pacala & Roughgarden 1984, Roughgarden *et al.* 1984), removal or addition of key predators or competitors (Paine 1966, Hairston 1980), food/water supplementation (e.g. Licht 1974) and wholesale removal of species (e.g., Wilson & Simberloff 1969). Abiotic variables (e.g. temperature, light, water potential) can also be controlled in the field, as in common garden or reciprocal transplantation experiments (e.g. Palumbi 1984; Trexler & Travis 1990), by study of 'natural experiments', and by direct manipulation (e.g. exclusion of mechanical forces, rainfall, sunlight, etc.). Purely descriptive studies of adaptation can be misleading or prone to erroneous conclusions (Gould & Lewontin 1979, Endler 1986), and experimentation is an underused but very powerful way to avoid such errors. The capacity for experimentation, moreover, enables investigators to benefit from tools such as the use of particular experimental designs, positive and negative controls, and the ability to repeat experiments and examine results statistically. Not every species is amenable to field experimental study, and we recommend that the potential of species for experimental manipulation of their environments be considered when choosing subjects for analysis.

Life cycle should facilitate analysis of genetics and selection. That so many model organisms for the study of genetics and selection in the laboratory are small, short-lived with brief generation times, and easily cultured is no accident. If students of adaptation wish to understand the genetic basis of traits of interest, know in detail how variation in gene products affects design, performance and fitness, and ascertain unambiguously that expected results of selection actually do obtain, the ability to breed multiple generations of a subject species can be a tremendous advantage. Not only should the ideal subject species have a life cycle that will facilitate the examination of multiple generations, it should be amenable to the tracking of individuals with known pedigrees in the field.

Design → performance → fitness should be unambiguous. First, each of these elements should be amenable to analysis; i.e. observable and in a well-developed analytical framework. In Powers's (1987) analysis of variation in *Fundulus*, for example, the structural differences in the LDH variants are known to the level of amino acid sequence, the particular variant residues with implications for enzyme function have been identified, and a well-developed body of theory and technique of enzyme kinetics is available to characterize the functional differences. Similar depth of analysis is available for characterizing the rate and force with which muscle contracts. Study systems that are now poorly known and therefore require extensive background development are less preferable than well-characterized ones.

Second, the links between the elements must be unambiguous and demonstrable. The mechanistic underpinnings of performance are well-known in many cases, having long been a central focus of functional biology (e.g. physiology, morphology, biomechanics), and our knowledge of these continues to grow as analytical technology improves. The design → performance gradient (Arnold 1983) seems, at first glance, not particularly problematic; by contrast, major challenges lie in the elucidation of the performance → fitness gradient, as noted earlier. Further, the choice of an appropriate performance for analysis is critical. The performance should be unambiguously relatable to a component of fitness. As Huey and

Stevenson (1979) and Bartholomew (1987), among others, have emphasized, such performance must be 'ecologically relevant' (i.e. demonstrably of consequence in the field); speculation on fitness consequences of performance based on laboratory measurements may be useful but is not sufficient (see earlier). Often, whole-organism performance will be the kind of performance most readily related to fitness and least likely to suffer from ecological irrelevance (Huey & Stevenson 1979). Frustratingly, the standard laboratory assays of performance that have been used to study design → performance, which often rely on stereotypic performance, steady-state phenomena, or turnkey instrumentation that is not easily modified, may often be unable to accommodate suitable whole-organism performance (but see Burggren 1987 and below).

Too often, a performance whose underlying design is well characterized does not yet meet rigorous standards of ecological relevance and relationship to fitness, and a performance that satisfies the latter criteria may lack a satisfactory mechanistic explanation or not be amenable to measurement. The challenge is to find a species in which both design → performance and performance → fitness can be analysed.

Notable successes in identifying strong and straightforward causal relationships among design, performance and fitness (reviewed by Watt 1985, Powers 1987) examine traits that are biochemical variants of single gene products, whole-organism performances whose rate or duration are amenable to measurement in the field (e.g. flight in insects, growth in molluscs), and fitness components that are simple, unambiguous functions of performance and readily observable in non-cryptic organisms (e.g. mating success in butterflies that mate only after a highly visible flight, survivorship of mollusc larvae in osmotically stressful environments). Often, studies that examine other kinds of traits can contribute valuable information on particular aspects of design → performance → fitness, but cannot address the adaptive recursion in its entirety. For example, Arnold, Bennett and colleagues have found heritable differences in design of garter snakes (*Thamnophis*) that seem causally related to variation in performance, which is in turn linked to differential survivorship of snakes (e.g. Arnold & Bennett 1988, Garland & Bennett 1990, Jayne & Bennett 1990). How the performance variation may lead to differential fitness is the subject of well-reasoned speculation but is still uncertain because snakes are difficult to observe in the field during most of their lives.

Falsifying candidate causal relationships among design, performance and fitness can be relatively easy; this requires only experimentally demonstrable lack of relationship between any two components in the evolutionary recursion. In toads, for example, Walton (1988) found no correlation between aerobic capacity (design) and prey capture (performance), and Wells and Taigen (1984) found no correlation between aerobic capacity and male mating success (fitness). Perhaps, as some have argued (Gould & Lewontin 1979), the armchair biologist can always invent a plausible adaptive scenario, realistic or not, for any combination of design and performance — but when experiments can be done crisply in the field, 'hyperadaptationist' scenarios have little refuge from hard data.

Alternative forms of selection (e.g. species selection) and sources of evolution other than selection should be assessable. Genetic drift, straying meteorites or other rare events, and the bad luck for a population or species to have been at the wrong place at the wrong time, all may contribute to the assortment of traits and species in a given environment. Although such occurrences can be rare, they can nonetheless have a greater impact on evolution in a few generations than can numerous generations of micro-evolutionary change (Jablonski 1986). Rare events, however, require either prolonged observation or numerous repeated trials to record their occurrences, assess their probability over time, and document their impact. Species that occur in multiple independent populations under identical conditions (in a series of separate but similar ponds, host plants, quadrats, caves, islands, mountain tops, etc.), or those with short generation times lend themselves to this kind of analysis; other forms do not.

Convenience. Analysing adaptation is difficult enough without the myriad of practical details that plague investigators: obtaining funding, generating enough publications sufficiently rapidly to be tenured, travelling to remote sites where the otherwise perfect study organism lives, obtaining permission to work with live animals, and so on. In this spirit, we offer a modest checklist of other attributes of the ideal organism. It should live in a habitat so pleasant that field studies might otherwise be regarded as a vacation but not so distant, exotic, or developed that field study presents a logistical or financial difficulty. It should readily adapt to laboratory culture, presenting animal care difficulties no greater than those of *Drosophila melanogaster*. To minimize animal care problems, it should not be a vertebrate or, better still, it should be an organism whose elimination society would favour (e.g. the cockroach). One should be able to construct a compelling case as to why knowledge of adaptation in the organism has substantial societal value (e.g. the species could be a pest or medically relevant). Some traits that would intrigue molecular biologists, especially the well-funded variety, would be nice. That the organism should lend a hand (or fin, tarsus, tendril or hypha) in analysing data or writing manuscripts is probably too much to hope for, however.

MAKING RIGOROUS ADAPTIVE STUDIES MORE FEASIBLE

The successful cases already mentioned demonstrate that the rigorous study of adaptation in organisms is far from hopeless but can be challenging. Even though the most rapid progress might have to await ideal study organisms, progress could still be more rapid than it now is. Accordingly, we consider ways to make the most of existing knowledge, techniques and study species to maximize future research success in this important area of biology.

Quite possibly, the search for the holy grail of an 'ideal' study species will yield but a few species whose biology is amenable to examination of the entire adaptive recursion, and even these species may well be uncharacteristic of biological species in general. This potential outcome raises valid concerns about the generality of conclusions that the study of these 'ideal' species may yield. Indeed, some (e.g. G.G. Simpson, quoted in Lauder 1982; Bartholomew 1986, 1987) have argued that every species has such an idiosyncratic evolutionary history that few generalities can be derived, that every taxon may represent a highly individualistic solution to the problems posed by its environment, and that any case study of adaptation may have limited applicability to other taxa. For example, the possibility exists that the haploidy of prokaryotes may lead to rather different options for their metabolic evolution than those available to diploid eukaryotes, in which heterozygosity at individual gene loci, and therefore modes of selection other than directional selection, are routinely possible (e.g. Hartl *et al.* 1985, Watt 1991). The mechanisms of internal energy processing and allocation may be very different in mobile consumers, e.g. most Metazoa, and in sessile consumers, e.g. many Fungi, yielding different evolutionary expectations (Perkins & Turner 1988). If we are to derive generalities about adaptation from the study of biological diversity, we must eschew an exclusive focus on a few ideal species. On the other hand, the need for a reasonable diversity of test systems must be balanced by the need to avoid dilution of effort among too many diverse taxa, so that few are understood in enough detail.

A particularly important development for the generality–individuality problem discussed above and the overall investigation of adaptation has been the application of modern systematic and comparative techniques (e.g. Huey 1987, Maddison 1990, Harvey & Pagel 1991, Martins & Garland 1991). These techniques explicitly recognize differing evolutionary histories as a potentially confounding variable (see earlier), and directly incorporate phylogeny into analyses as one of several candidate independent variables. In so doing, these techniques can recast comparative studies as a series of independent evolutionary trials from common starting points, i.e. replicated natural experiments. With a phylogeny in hand, an evolutionary biologist can ask the following questions for example. Of the various character states of a trait, which is primitive and which are derived? How many times has a particular trait evolved in a given taxon or clade? How often has a particular character state evolved in association with a particular environmental variable (e.g. invasion of a new habitat) or *not* in association with any environmental variable in particular, and how often has a particular trait coevolved with another trait or only in the absence of another trait (suggesting a correlated response to selection or constraint)? With the answers to such questions, an adaptational biologist can grapple with issues such as the repeatability, variability and taxon-specificity of evolutionary outcomes; the magnitudes of the gradients among genes, design, performance and fitness; and other general issues (e.g. see Feder 1987).

Another important strategy for understanding the evolutionary recursion is to exploit systems whose study has already begun. This may involve the continued study of particular populations by different workers with different viewpoints. More often, one research group's approach will show how an organismal system can be approached in new ways, with new power, thus opening that system up to the use of others at other times and places.

For example, Twitty's early work on the development of the western 'newt' *Taricha* was followed by his own later extensive study of the population structure and homing behaviour of *Taricha* (Twitty 1966). This body of combined laboratory and field knowledge of *Taricha* now makes the animal practical as a test system for pursuing other aspects of amphibian adaptation. Though work has begun on the population genetics of *Taricha* (Hedgecock 1976, 1978), many genetical and functional aspects of the animal's evolution are still enigmatic and ripe for new study. In another example of the power of new analysis of an already well-studied system, Gottlieb and colleagues have for some time (Gottlieb & Weeden 1979, Gottlieb & Higgins 1984, Tait *et al.* 1988) pursued diverse biochemical- and molecular-population genetic studies of the plant genus *Clarkia*, whose systematics and local biogeography Lewis (1953, Lewis & Lewis 1955) had previously elaborated. Their work already includes collaboration with metabolic specialists and the explicit use of laboratory mutagenesis to manipulate otherwise natural *Clarkia* stocks (Jones *et al.* 1986, Kruckeberg *et al.* 1989, Neuhaus *et al.* 1989). Again, functional study of the photosynthetic performance of *Clarkia* under natural conditions (in the manner of Berry & Bjorkman 1980, Mooney & Gulmon 1979 or Woolhouse 1981) could further increase the productivity of *Clarkia* as a system for adaptive studies.

New technology is a powerful ally in such work, particularly in enabling investigators to reach scientific goals that previously were inaccessible. In addition to the aforementioned advances, compact, flexible data loggers and miniaturized sensors have led to a genuine revolution in biophysical ecology during the last two decades. DNA 'fingerprinting' and other molecular genetic tools are now available to trace parentage in the wild, making possible whole classes of sociobiological or sexual selection studies that previously were impossible. Special photographic methods and light-amplification devices may allow field study of behaviour in nocturnal animals. If technological innovation is coupled with the energy and ingenuity of field biologists, whether by extensive collaboration or by multidisciplinary education of individuals, questions whose answering was once not feasible may become routine (Burggren 1987).

The study of species of economic importance also represents an important opportunity. In addition to direct financial support, engagement with 'applied issues' may both benefit from and contribute to an understanding of the evolutionary recursion. Pest species often are pests *because of* their short generation time, effective adaptation to a crop-resource niche and the like, and thus may offer themselves as highly practical subjects for mechanistic study of their functional biology. Study of near relatives of endangered species may shed light on what adaptive strategies predispose toward fragility of population distribution or demographic persistence. Study of adaptive mechanisms in crop species or their near relatives may not only contribute directly to practical agricultural success but also illuminate questions of the origins by artificial selection of crop species. Never has the urgency or diversity of needs for the effective application of basically evolutionary approaches been greater in human affairs. However, with the advent of a functional evolutionary biology such as we advocate, never has the opportunity been greater for evolutionary studies to realize their immense, if long latent, applications potential.

CONCLUSION

Our goal has been to rationalize a broadly interdisciplinary approach to the analysis of adaptation. While we have emphasized *how* best to perform adaptive studies, we have but briefly considered a more basic issue: *whether* to do so. Has adaptational analysis fallen out of fashion, due to the immense challenge of deploying a sufficiently interdisciplinary approach to its understanding, over-reaction to justifiable criticism of adaptational biology (Gould & Lewontin 1979), diminishing returns in some of its aspects (Ross 1981, Feder 1987), or simple senescence? We are optimistic that it has not. Adaptational biology may have its problems (and what discipline does not?), but it is central to current thinking in genetics, ecology and evolutionary biology. Adaptational biology has yet to reap the benefits of the revolutions in molecular biology (Prosser 1986, Feder & Block 1991), comparative biology and systematics (Huey 1987). Adaptational biology has the potential to become 'the experimental arm of evolutionary biology' (Watt 1991). These potential rewards should be more than sufficient incentive for biological scientists to surmount the challenges of interdisciplinary adaptational studies.

ACKNOWLEDGEMENTS

This essay is dedicated with respect and affection to George A. Bartholomew and the late G. Evelyn Hutchinson, in recognition of their many and complementary contributions to the growth and conceptualizing of our science.

We thank D. Clemens, D. Crawford, R. Huey and D. Zuccarello for thoughtful discussion of our manuscript; L.P. Wimsey for general editorial comments; and the National Science Foundation (BSR 87–05268 to WBW; DCB87–18264 to MEF) and National Institutes of Health (GM 26758 to WBW) for research support.

REFERENCES

Arnold, S. J. (1983). Morphology, performance and fitness. *American Zoologist*, **23**, 347–361.

Arnold, S. J. (1987). Genetic correlation and the evolution of physiology. *New Directions in Ecological Physiology* (Ed. by M. E. Feder, A. F. Bennett, W. W. Burggren & R. B. Huey), pp. 189–215. Cambridge University Press, Cambridge, UK.

Arnold, S. J. & Bennett, A. F. (1988). Behavioural variation in natural populations. V. Morphological correlates of locomotion in the garter snake (*Thamnophis radix*). Biological Journal of the Linnean Society, **34**, 175–190.

Bartholomew, G. A. (1986). The role of natural history in contemporary biology. *BioScience*, **36**, 324–329.

Bartholomew, G. A. (1987). Interspecific comparison as a tool for physiological ecologists. *New Directions in Ecological Physiology* (Ed. by M. E. Feder, A. F. Bennett, W. W. Burggren & R. B. Huey), pp. 11–37. Cambridge University Press, Cambridge, UK.

Bennett, A. F. & Huey, R. B. (1990). Studying the evolution of physiological performance. *Oxford Surveys in Evolution* 7 (Ed. by D. Futuyma & J. Antonovics), pp. 251–284.

Oxford University Press, Oxford, UK.

Bennett, A. F. & Licht, P. (1975). Evaporative water loss in scaleless snakes. *Comparative Biochemistry and Physiology*, **52A**, 213–215.

Berry, J. & Bjorkman, O. (1980). Photosynthetic response and adaptation to temperature in higher plants. *Annual Review of Plant Physiology*, **31**, 491–543.

Boggs, C. L. & Watt, W. B. (1981). Population structure of pierid butterflies. IV. Genetic and physiological investment in offspring by male *Colias*. *Oecologia*, **50**, 320–324.

Burggren, W. W. (1987). Invasive and noninvasive methodologies in ecological physiology: a plea for integration. *New Directions in Ecological Physiology* (Ed. by M. E. Feder, A. F. Bennett, W. W. Burggren & R. B. Huey), pp. 251–274. Cambridge University Press, Cambridge, UK.

Carter, P. A. & Watt, W. B. (1988). Adaptation at specific loci. V. Metabolically adjacent enzyme loci may have very distinct experiences of selective pressures. *Genetics*, **119**, 913–924.

Chappell, M. A. & Snyder, L. R. G. (1984). Biochemical and physiological correlates of alpha-chain hemoglobin polymorphisms. *Proceedings of the National Academy of Sciences, USA*, **81**, 5484–5488.

Clutton-Brock, T. H., Guinness, F. E. & Albon, S. D. (1982). *Red Deer: The Behavior and Ecology of Two Sexes*. University of Chicago Press, Chicago, IL, USA.

Crawford, D. L. & Powers, D. A. (1989). Molecular basis of evolutionary adaptation at the lactate dehydrogenase-B locus in the fish *Fundulus heteroclitus*. *Proceedings of the National Academy of Sciences, USA*, **86**, 9365–9369.

Courtney, S. P., Kibota, T. T. & Singleton, T. A. (1990). Ecology of mushroom-feeding Drosophilidae. *Advances in Ecological Research*, **20**, 225–274.

Darwin, C. R. (1859). *The Origin of Species*. Modern Library, Random House, NY, USA.

Dobzhansky, Th. (1970). *The Genetics of the Evolutionary Process*. Columbia University Press, New York, NY, USA.

Dykhuisen, D. E. & Hartl, D. L. (1983). Functional effects of PGI allozymes in *E. coli*. *Genetics*, **105**, 1–18.

Easterby, J. S. (1973). Coupled enzyme assays: a general expression for the transient. *Biochimica et Biophysica Acta*, **293**, 552–558.

Ehrlich, P. R., Breedlove, D. E., Brussard, P. F. & Sharp, M. A. (1972). Weather and the 'regulation' of subalpine populations. *Ecology*, **53**, 243–247.

Endler, J. A. (1986). *Natural Selection in the Wild*. Princeton University Press, Princeton, NJ, USA.

Ewens, W. J. & Feldman, M. W. (1976). The theoretical assessment of selective neutrality. *Population Genetics and Ecology* (Ed. by S. Karlin & E. Nevo), pp. 303–337. Academic Press, New York, NY, USA.

Feder, M. E. (1976). Lunglessness, body size, and metabolic rate in salamanders. *Physiological Zoology*, **49**, 398–406.

Feder, M. E. (1987). The analysis of physiological diversity: the prospects for pattern documentation and general questions in ecological physiology. *New Directions in Ecological Physiology* (Ed. by M. E. Feder, A. F. Bennett, W. W. Burggren & R. B. Huey), pp. 38–75. Cambridge University Press, Cambridge, UK.

Feder, M. E. (1988). Exercising with and without lungs. II. Experimental elimination of pulmonary and buccopharyngeal gas exchange in individual salamanders (*Ambystoma tigrinum*). *Journal of Experimental Biology*, **138**, 487–497.

Feder, M. E. & Block, B. A. (1991). On the future of physiological ecology. *Functional Ecology*, **5**, 136–144.

Gans, C. (1986). Functional morphology of predator–prey relationships. *Predator–Prey Relationships: Perspectives and Approaches from the Study of Lower Vertebrates*

(Ed. by M. E. Feder & G. V. Lauder), pp. 6–23. University of Chicago Press, Chicago, IL, USA.

Garland, T. & Bennett, A. F. (1990). Quantitative genetics of maximal oxygen consumption in a garter snake. *American Journal of Physiology*, **259**, R986–R992.

Gottlieb, L. D. & Higgins, R. C. (1984). Phosphoglucose isomerase expression in species of *Clarkia* with and without a duplication of the coding gene. *Genetics*, **107**, 131–140.

Gottlieb, L. D. & Weeden, N. F. (1979). Gene duplication and phylogeny in *Clarkia*. *Evolution*, **33**, 1024–1039.

Gould, S. J. & Lewontin, R. C. (1979). The spandrels of San Marco and the Panglossian paradigm: a critique of the adaptationist program. *Proceedings of the Royal Society of London*, B, **205**, 581–598.

Grant, P. (1986). *Ecology and Evolution of Darwin's Finches*. Princeton University Press, Princeton, NJ, USA.

Greene, H. W. (1986). Natural history and evolutionary biology. *Predator–Prey Relationships: Perspectives and Approaches from the Study of Lower Vertebrates* (Ed. by M. E. Feder & G. V. Lauder), pp. 99–108. University of Chicago Press, Chicago, IL, USA.

Hairston, N. G. (1980). Evolution under interspecific competition: field experiments in terrestrial salamanders. *Evolution*, **34**, 409–420.

Hartl, D. L. & Clark, A. G. (1989). *Principles of Population Genetics* (2nd edn). Sinauer, Sunderland, MA, USA.

Hartl, D. L., Dykhuisen, D. E. & Dean, A. M. (1985). Limits of adaptation: the evolution of selective neutrality. *Genetics*, **111**, 655–674.

Harvey, P. H. & Pagel, M. D. (1991). *The Comparative Method in Evolutionary Biology*. Oxford University Press, Oxford, UK.

Hedgecock, D. (1976). Genetic variation in two widespread species of salamanders, *Taricha granulosa* and *Taricha torosa*. *Biochemical Genetics*, **14**, 561–576.

Hedgecock, D. (1978). Population subdivision and genetic divergence in the red-bellied newt, *Taricha rivularis*. *Evolution*, **32**, 271–286.

Heinrich, R. & Rapoport, S. M. (1983). The utility of mathematical models for the understanding of metabolic systems. *Transactions of the Biochemical Society*, **11**, 31–35.

Hoffmann, R. J. (1978). Environmental uncertainty and evolution of physiological adaptation in *Colias* butterflies. *American Naturalist*, **112**, 999–1015.

Huey, R. B. (1987). Phylogeny, history, and the comparative method. *New Directions in Ecological Physiology* (Ed. by M. E. Feder, A. F. Bennett, W. W. Burggren & R. B. Huey), pp. 76–101. Cambridge University Press, Cambridge, UK.

Huey, R. B. & Bennett, A. F. (1986). A comparative approach to field and laboratory studies in evolutionary biology. *Predator–Prey Relationships: Perspectives and Approaches from the Study of Lower Vertebrates* (Ed. by M. E. Feder & G. V. Lauder), pp. 82–98. University of Chicago Press, Chicago, IL, USA.

Huey, R. B. & Stevenson, R. D. (1979). Integrating thermal physiology and ecology of ectotherms: a discussion of approaches. *American Zoologist*, **19**, 357–366.

Hutchinson, G. E. (1957). Concluding remarks. *Cold Spring Harbor Symposia on Quantitative Biology*, **22**, 415–427.

Hutchinson, G. E. (1978). *An Introduction to Population Ecology*. Yale University Press, New Haven, CT, USA.

Jablonski, D. (1986). Background and mass extinctions: the alternation of evolutionary regimes. *Science*, **231**, 129–133.

Jayne, B. C. & Bennett, A. F. (1990). Selection on locomotor performance capacity in a natural population of garter snakes. *Evolution*, **44**, 1204–1229.

Jones, T. W. A., Gottlieb, L. D. & Pichersky, E. (1986). Reduced enzyme activity and starch level in an induced mutant of chloroplast phosphoglucose isomerase. *Plant Physiology*,

81, 367–371.

Kacser, H. & Burns, J. M. (1979). Molecular democracy: who shares the controls? *Transactions of the Biochemical Society*, **7**, 1149–1160.

Kimura, M. & Ohta, T. (1971). *Theoretical Population Genetics*. Princeton University Press, Princeton, NJ, USA.

Kingsolver, J. G. & Watt, W. B. (1984). Mechanistic constraints and optimality models: thermoregulatory strategies in *Colias* butterflies. *Ecology*, **65**, 1835–1839.

Kruckeberg, A. L., Neuhaus, H. E., Feil, R., Gottlieb, L. D. & Stitt, M. (1989). Decreased-activity mutants of phosphoglucose isomerase in the cytosol and chloroplast of *Clarkia xantiana*. *Biochemical Journal*, **261**, 457–467.

Lande, R. & Arnold, S. J. (1983). The measurement of selection on correlated characters. *Evolution*, **37**, 1210–1226.

Lauder, G. V. (1982). Historical biology and the problem of design. *Journal of Theoretical Biology*, **97**, 57–67.

Leslie, J. F. & Watt, W. B. (1986). Some evolutionary consequences of the molecular recombination process. *Trends in Genetics* **2**, 288–291.

Levins, R. (1968). *Evolution in Changing Environments*. Princeton University Press, Princeton, NJ, USA.

Lewis, H. (1953). The mechanism of evolution in the genus *Clarkia*. *Evolution*, **7**, 1–20.

Lewis, H. & Lewis, M. E. (1955). The genus *Clarkia*. *University of California Publications in Botany*, **20**, 241–392.

Lewontin, R. C. (1974). *The Genetic Basis of Evolutionary Change*. Columbia University Press, NY, USA.

Licht, P. (1974). Responses of *Anolis* lizards to food supplementation in nature. *Copeia*, **1974**, 215–221.

Licht, P. & Bennett, A. F. (1972). A scaleless snake: tests of the role of reptilian scales in water loss and heat transfer. *Copeia*, **1972**, 702–707.

Maddison, W. P. (1990). A method for testing the correlated evolution of two binary characters: are gains and losses concentrated on certain branches of a phylogenetic tree. *Evolution*, **44**, 539–557.

Marincovic, D. & Ayala, F. J. (1975). Fitness of allozyme variants in *Drosophila pseudoobscura*. II. Selection at the *est-5*, *odh*, and *mdh-2* loci. *Genetical Research*, **24**, 137–149.

Martins, E. P. & Garland, T. (1991). Phylogenetic analyses of the correlated evolution of continuous characters: a simulation study. *Evolution*, **45**, 534–557.

Milkman, R. D. (1960a). The genetic basis of natural variation. I. Crossveins in *Drosophila melanogaster*. *Genetics*, **45**, 35–48.

Milkman, R. D. (1960b). The genetic basis of natural variation. II. Analysis of a polygenic system in *Drosophila melanogaster*. *Genetics*, **45**, 379–391.

Milkman, R. D. (1961). The genetic basis of natural variation. III. Developmental lability and evolutionary potential. *Genetics*, **46**, 25–38.

Milkman, R. D. (1965). The genetic basis of natural variation. VII. The individuality of polygenic combinations in *Drosophila*. *Genetics*, **52**, 789–799.

Milkman, R. D. (1967). Kinetic analysis of temperature adaptation in *Drosophila* pupae. *Molecular Mechanisms of Temperature Adaptation* (Ed. by C. L. Prosser), pp. 147–162. American Association for the Advancement of Science, Washington, DC, USA.

Mitton, J. B., Carey, C. & Kocher, T. D. (1986). The relation of enzyme heterozygosity to standard and active oxygen consumption and growth rate of tiger salamanders, *Ambystoma tigrinum*. *Physiological Zoology*, **59**, 574–582.

Mooney, H. A. & Gulmon, S. (1979). Environmental and evolutionary constraints on the photosynthetic characteristics of higher plants. *Topics in Plant Population Biology* (Ed. by O. T. Solbring *et al.*), pp. 316–337. Columbia University Press, NY, USA.

Neuhaus, H. E., Kruckeberg, A. L., Feil, R. & Stitt, M. (1989). Reduced-activity mutants of phosphoglucose isomerase in the cytosol and chloroplast of *Clarkia xantiana*. *Planta*, **178**, 110–122.

Pacala, S. & Roughgarden, J. (1984). Control of arthropod abundance by *Anolis* lizards on St. Eustatius (Neth. Antilles). *Oecologia*, **64**, 160–162.

Pacala, S., Rummel, J. & Roughgarden, J. (1983). A technique for enclosing *Anolis* lizard populations under field conditions. *Journal of Herpetology*, **17**, 94–97.

Paine, R. (1966). Food web complexity and species diversity. *American Naturalist*, **100**, 65–75.

Palumbi, S. R. (1984). Tactics of acclimation: morphological changes of sponges in an unpredictable environment. *Science*, **225**, 1478–1480.

Perkins, D. D. & Turner, B. C. (1988). *Neurospora* from natural populations: toward the population biology of a haploid eukaryote. *Experimental Mycology*, **12**, 91–131.

Pough, F. H. (1989). Organismal performance and Darwinian fitness: approaches and interpretations. *Physiological Zoology*, **62**, 199–236.

Powers, D. A. (1987). A multidisciplinary approach to the study of genetic variation within species. *New Directions in Ecological Physiology* (Ed. by M. E. Feder, A. F. Bennett, W. W. Burggren & R. B. Huey), pp. 102–134. Cambridge University Press, Cambridge, UK.

Prosser, C. L. (1986). *Adaptational Biology: Molecules to Organisms*. John Wiley & Sons, New York, NY, USA.

Rendel, J. M. (1967). *Canalization and Gene Control*. Logos Press, London, UK.

Ross, D. M. (1981). Illusion and reality in comparative physiology. *Canadian Journal of Zoology*, **59**, 2151–2158.

Roughgarden, J., Pacala, S. & Rummel, J. (1984). Strong present-day competition between the *Anolis* lizard populations of St. Maarten (Neth. Antilles). *Evolutionary Ecology* (Ed. by B. Shorrocks), pp. 203–219. Blackwell, Oxford, UK.

Savageau, M. A. (1976). *Biochemical Systems Analysis*. Addison Wesley, Reading, MA, USA.

Savageau, M. A. & Sorribas, A. (1989). Constraints among molecular and systemic properties — implications for physiological genetics. *Journal of Theoretical Biology*, **141**, 93–115.

Schmalhausen, I. I. (1960). Cybernetics and evolution. *Evolution*, **14**, 509–524.

Shapiro, A. M. (1976). Seasonal polyphenism. *Evolutionary Biology*, **9**, 259–333.

Sherman, P. W. (1981). Reproductive competition and infanticide in Belding's ground squirrels and other animals. *Natural Selection and Social Behavior: Recent Research and New Theory* (Ed. by R. D. Alexander & D. W. Tinkle), pp. 311–331. Chiron Press, New York, NY, USA.

Shorrocks, B. (1977). An ecological classification of European *Drosophila* species. *Oecologia*, **26**, 335–345.

Sinervo, B. (1990). The evolution of maternal investment in lizards: an experimental and comparative analysis of egg size and its effects on offspring performance. *Evolution*, **44**, 279–294.

Snyder, L. R. G. (1981). Deer mouse hemoglobins: is there genetic adaptation to high altitude? *BioScience*, **31**, 299–304.

Snyder, L. R. G., Hayes, J. P. & Chappel, M. A. (1988). Alpha-chain hemoglobin polymorphisms are correlated with altitude in the deer mouse, *Peromyscus maniculatus*. *Evolution*, **42**, 689–697.

Stearns, S. C. (1989). The evolutionary significance of phenotypic plasticity. *BioScience*, **39**, 436–445.

Sulzbach, D. S. & Lynch, C. B. (1984). Quantitative genetic analysis of temperature regulation in *Mus musculus*. III. Diallel analysis of correlation between traits. *Evolution*, **38**, 541–552.

Tait, R. C., Froman, B. E., Laudencia-Chingcuanco, D. L. & Gottlieb, L. D. (1988). Plant phosphoglucose isomerase genes lack introns and are expressed in *Escherichia coli*. *Plant Molecular Biology*, **11**, 381–388.

Trexler, J. C. & Travis, J. (1990). Phenotypic plasticity in the sailfin molly, *Poecilia latipinna* (Pisces: Poeciliidae). I. Field experiments. *Evolution*, **44**, 143–156.

Twitty, V. C. (1966). *Of Scientists and Salamanders*. W. H. Freeman, San Francisco, CA, USA.

Waddington, C. H. (1953). Genetic assimilation of an acquired character. *Evolution*, **7**, 118–126.

Wallace, B. (1981). *Basic Population Genetics*. Columbia University Press, New York, NY, USA.

Walton, B. M. (1988). Relationships among metabolic, locomotory, and field measures of organismal performance in Fowler's toad *(Bufo woodhousei fowleri)*. *Physiological Zoology*, **61**, 107–118.

Watt, W. B. (1968). Adaptive significance of pigment polymorphisms in *Colias* butterflies. I. Variation of melanin pigment in relation to thermoregulation. *Evolution*, **22**, 437–458.

Watt, W. B. (1983). Adaptation at specific loci. II. Demographic and biochemical elements in the maintenance of the *Colias* PGI polymorphism. *Genetics*, **103**, 691–724.

Watt, W. B. (1985). Bioenergetics and evolutionary genetics: opportunities for new synthesis. *American Naturalist*, **125**, 118–143.

Watt, W. B. (1986). Power and efficiency as indexes of fitness in metabolic organization. *American Naturalist*, **127**, 629–653.

Watt, W. B. (1990). The evolution of animal coloration — adaptive aspects from bioenergetics to demography. *Adaptive Coloration in Invertebrates* (Ed. by M. Wicksten), pp. 1–15. Texas A&M University Press, College Station, TX, USA.

Watt, W. B. (1991). Biochemistry, physiological ecology, and evolutionary genetics — the mechanistic tools of evolutionary biology. *Functional Ecology*, **5**, 145–154.

Watt, W. B., Cassin, R. C. & Swan, M. S. (1983). Adaptation at specific loci. III. Field behavior and survivorship differences among *Colias* PGI genotypes are predictable from *in vitro* biochemistry. *Genetics*, **103**, 725–739.

Watt, W. B., Carter, P. A. & Blower, S. M. (1985). Adaptation at specific loci. IV. Differential mating success among glycolytic allozyme genotypes of *Colias* butterflies. *Genetics*, **109**, 157–175.

Watt, W. B., Carter, P. A. & Donohue, K. (1986). Females' choice of 'good genotypes' as mates is promoted by an insect mating system. *Science*, **233**, 1187–1190.

Wells, K. D. & Taigen, T. L. (1984). Reproductive behavior and aerobic capacities of male American toads *(Bufo americanus)*: is behavior constrained by physiology. *Herpetologica*, **40**, 292–298.

Westerhoff, H. V. & van Dam, K. (1987). *Thermodynamics and Control of Biological Free-energy Transduction*. Elsevier, Amsterdam, The Netherlands.

Wilson, E. O. & Simberloff, D. S. (1969). Experimental zoogeography of islands: defaunation and monitoring techniques. *Ecology*, **50**, 267–278.

Woolhouse, H. W. (1981). Aspects of the carbon and energy requirements of photosynthesis considered in relation to environmental constraints. *Physiological Ecology: An Evolutionary Approach to Resource Use* (Ed. by C. R. Townsend & P. Calow), pp. 51–85. Sinauer, Sunderland, MA, USA.

Yamazaki, T. (1971). Measurement of fitness at the esterase-5 locus in *Drosophila pseudoobscura*. *Genetics*, **67**, 579–603.

16. LIFE HISTORY AND MECHANICAL CONSTRAINTS ON REPRODUCTION IN GENES, CELLS AND WATERFLEAS

J.S. JONES*, D. EBERT[†] AND S.C. STEARNS[‡]

*Department of Genetics and Biometry, University College London, 4 Stephenson Way, London NW1 2HE, UK; [†]Department of Zoology, South Parks Road, Oxford OX1 3PS, UK and [‡]Zoology Institute, University of Basle, Rheinsprung 9, CH-4051 Basle, Switzerland

INTRODUCTION

No organism can do everything. Every creature is restricted by constraints of various kinds. Many of these arise from the facts of history and the nature of evolution, both of which can proceed only from where they left off. This systems view of constraint — that living things have so many functional interconnections that it becomes difficult for evolution to reverse itself — is implicit in much of the literature. Natural selection has, it is supposed, produced the best available balance between components of life history such as age at maturation and number of offspring.

Physical and chemical laws also impose mechanical limits on how an animal, a cell or a genome operates. Molecular biology sees the structure of genes as being as much a chemical consequence of the nature of the genetic material as an evolved trade-off among its functions. Both views of constraint are needed to understand how any living system operates but neither is in itself enough to explain its limitations.

Here we illustrate the dual nature of constraint on patterns of reproduction and survival in relation to size, the causes of being small and fast as opposed to large and slow. Limits to growth and reproduction arise both from evolutionary history and from the mechanics of replication, from Darwin's organ-grinder and Mendel's monkey. The balance between them has some surprising effects on life history. Nearly all living systems — genes, cells and organisms — grow discontinuously as one generation succeeds another. This leads to a mechanical constraint as dividing systems have a size threshold below which the next stage of development cannot be initiated. There may also be natural selection on growth through variations in size at the beginning of each growth cycle, and through variation in growth rates. This produces a trade-off between size, age at maturation and rate of multiplication. Reproductive constraints on size may be similar at the organismal, the cellular and the DNA level. Research on tractable systems showing mechanical constraint may give an insight into the behaviour of systems less open to experiment.

DAPHNIA MOULTING: A MECHANICAL CONSTRAINT ON LIFE HISTORY

The life history of *Daphnia* (Fig. 16.1) has several elements: discontinuous growth (an unavoidable consequence of a rigid exoskeleton); genetic or environmental variation in size at birth; a threshold size for initiation of maturation and ovarian development; and variation in growth rates. Consider a series of freshly hatched first instar *Daphnia*, each slightly larger than the last (Fig. 16.1). The first just crosses the size threshold in its third moult. After two more moults it matures, having had five juvenile instars. The next four, each slightly larger at birth, also cross the threshold in their third moult. They define an *instar group*, within which all individuals have had five instars. Within this instar group and when growth rates are constant, the pattern is simple; size at maturity increases with size at birth. In contrast, the size at birth of the sixth individual in Fig. 16.1 is so

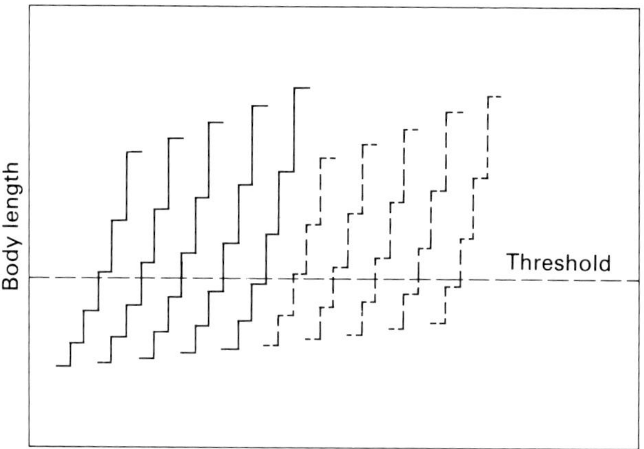

FIG. 16.1. The threshold model. Simulated growth steps for 10 female *Daphnia* from the first instar to the instar of first reproduction. Each step represents one instar, and the next instar length is 30% greater than the one preceding it. In the instar reached after passing the threshold egg production is initiated and takes two instars. The five animals smallest at birth (solid lines) took six instars to reach the reproductive stage, while the five larger newborns (dashed lines) took five instars to do so.

great that the threshold is crossed in the second moult and it matures after four moults. This means that the sixth individual is larger at birth than the fifth but smaller at maturity. Discontinuous growth coupled with a size threshold can reverse the ranks of sizes at birth and sizes at maturity but only does so between instar groups, not within them (Ebert 1991).

This can have unexpected effects on life history. Figure 16.2a shows the relation between size at birth and size at maturity for two groups of

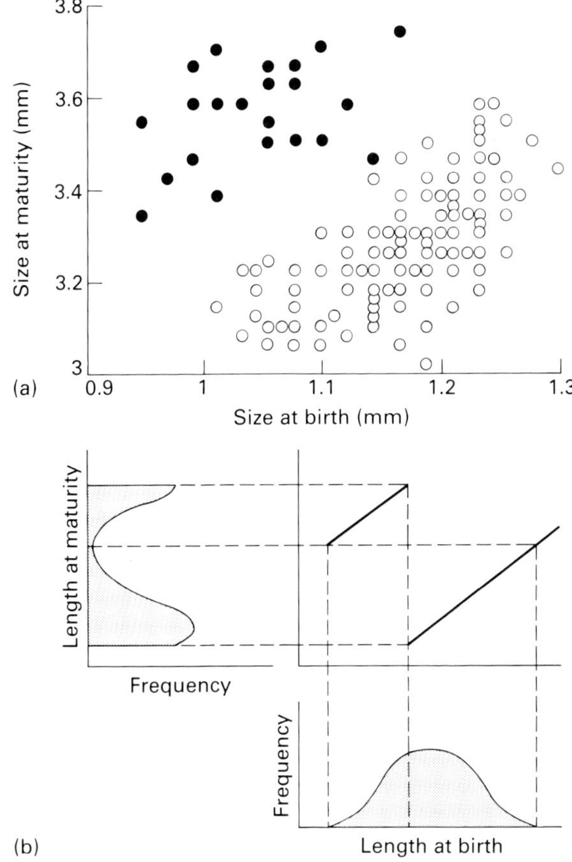

Fig. 16.2. Transformation of a distribution of size at birth into a distribution of size at maturity. (a) Relationship between length at birth and length at maturity. Newborns too small to reach the threshold size in the same instar as their larger sibs grow through one instar more and become larger at maturity. (b) A distribution of sizes at birth is transformed into a distribution of sizes at maturity.

Daphnia females with different numbers of instars at maturity. Figure 16.2b shows a typical unimodal distribution of sizes at birth. Individuals in the right-hand portion of the distribution are large enough at birth to cross the threshold in their second moult and mature in the fifth instar. Within this instar group, size at maturity increases with size at birth in a straightforward fashion. Those in the left-hand portion of the distribution are smaller at birth, require one more instar to mature, and are larger at maturity than those in the other instar group. They form a second mode in the distribution, which is unimodal at birth but bimodal at maturity. There may hence be very different distributions for size at maturity from particular ranges of size at birth.

This can have important selective effects. For example, there is selection for large size at birth under conditions of limited food (Tessier *et al.* 1983). Mean size at maturity would then decrease rather than increase. How selection on size at maturity might be transformed into selection on size at birth depends on several factors (Fig. 16.3). Figure 16.3a shows the relationship of size at birth to size at maturity for two instar groups (6 instars and 5 instars). The points are laboratory data from *D. magna*, and the lines are the best fit to these points. They represent the situation depicted schematically in Fig. 16.2a. Figure 16.3b shows five hypothetical ranges of size at birth, with the hatched portions indicating individuals that are killed and the white portions those selected. The influence on size at birth of selection for large or small adult size is not simple.

In distribution 1, all individuals are large enough at birth to need only five juvenile instars. If there is directional selection on size at maturity so that all individuals larger than 3.3 mm at maturity are killed, there is also directional selection for the individuals that were smaller at birth. Distribution 2, however, has a range that overlaps the five and six instar groups. Individuals requiring five instars to mature are smaller than those needing six instars to do so, so that directional selection downwards on size at maturity is transformed into directional selection upwards on size at birth. Distribution 4 is just as broad as distribution 3 but is shifted with respect to the threshold sizes at birth that separate the instar classes. It results in a transfer of directional selection on size at maturity into disruptive selection on size at birth. Distribution 5, broadest of all, results in a transformation of size at maturity into a more complex kind of disruptive selection. It emphasizes the unexpected consequences of small changes in the initial conditions of growth.

This has implications for phenotypic covariance. Within an instar group, for a fixed growth rate, size at maturity increases with size at birth. Under the same conditions age at maturity also increases with size at birth (Ebert 1991) and the phenotypic correlation between age and size at

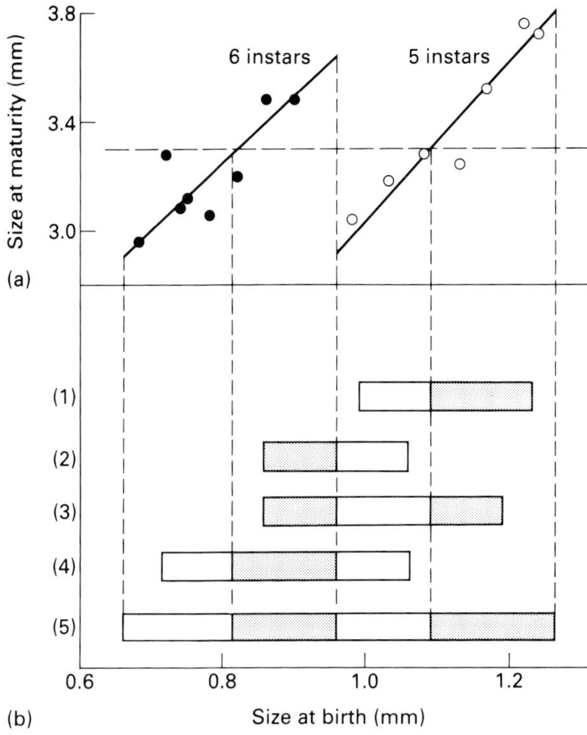

FIG. 16.3. (a) Plot of size at maturity on size at birth in 15 *Daphnia* females. The horizontal dashed line marks a hypothetical mortality threshold, above which all females suffer from high mortality. (b) Five examples of different ranges of offspring size distribution. If heritability of offspring size and mortality above the dashed line were both 100%, all clones producing offspring of the size shaded would be eliminated in one generation. For the ranges of offspring size in both (1) and (2) selection on offspring size would be directional, in (3) stabilizing and in (4) and (5) disruptive. Lower mortality or heritability would both slow the elimination of offspring size classes.

maturity is positive. If size at birth is fixed and growth rates vary (for example, because of variation in juvenile food supply), then the correlation becomes negative. In nature there will be diversity in size at birth and in juvenile growth rate. Depending on which combination applies the phenotypic correlation of age and size at maturity could vary from strongly positive to strongly negative. A small change in the initial conditions of size and growth rate can have large effects on the phenotypes of the adult population, and hence on subsequent generations. In particular, it may alter their demography because of the effects of adult size on fecundity, leading, for example, to a loss of synchrony and the rapid appearance of a wide range of age and size classes.

In *Daphnia* an ancient constraint on growth, the exoskeleton, combined with a size threshold for maturation leads to complex and surprising relationships between size, selection and phenotypic covariances. The *Daphnia* size-dependent maturation threshold ensures, at the cost of additional instars, that individuals do not mature at too small a size. There is variation in instar numbers in spiders (Deevey 1949), decapods (Hartnoll 1985), Lepidoptera (Clare & Singh 1991) and locusts (Uvarov 1966) and other groups. However, in Diptera, Hymenoptera and Coleoptera the number of pre-adult instars is fixed. If this were true in *Daphnia*, adults would be small when growth is poor (as in fruitflies and bumblebees; Plowright & Jay 1968, Gebhardt & Stearns 1988). If, as in *Daphnia*, juvenile growth is about equal in each juvenile instar, a fixed number of instars leads to a positive correlation between size at birth (or egg size) and size at maturity. It also predicts age at maturity, which is then likely to be a continuous rather than a discontinuous function of growth, as is the case when instar number varies (see Fig. 16.1). This may help to ensure synchrony of mating partners, or the ratio of adults to juveniles in social organisms. When a fixed number of juvenile instars leads to costs in terms of small adult size these may be convertible into a cost in age at maturity. The tobacco horn worm *Manduca sexta* always pupates in the fifth instar. If growth is poor, maturation can be delayed until this instar reaches a critical weight (Nijhout & Williams 1974).

MECHANICAL CONSTRAINTS AND CELL DIVISION

This mechanism of growth, with its need to attain a threshold before reproduction, has consequences for the ecology, demography and evolution of *Daphnia*. It amplifies small differences in growth rate to produce large differences in life history. There may be analogies here with the life histories of cells and genes. The rate of cell division is itself subject to mechanical constraint. For example, rapidly growing *E. coli* cells can divide every 20 minutes or so, twice as fast as the maximum rate of DNA replication. The cost of replicating the DNA is deferred by initiating a subsequent cycle of DNA replication before the end of the preceding cell division. Individual *E. coli* cells may contain one, two, three or more replication forks; and as cell size depends on DNA content they differ in size at cellular maturity (Lewin 1990). This mechanism means that any slight genetic or environmental difference in growth rate early in the history of an *E. coli* population is rapidly amplified as particular cells attain (or fail to attain) the critical ratio between DNA content and cell mass needed for the subsequent division; a pattern comparable to that in

Daphnia and one which may have similar demographic effects on subsequent generations. In particular it may lead to the rapid loss of synchrony in cell cultures.

In eukaryotes, too, a cell must attain a critical point in the cell cycle before it is primed for division (Alberts *et al.* 1989). There is a series of controls which trigger the onset of mitosis in developing tissues (O'Farrell *et al.* 1989). Any slight variation, genetic or environmental, which affects the time when it reaches the trigger point and the decision whether to divide or to continue to grow can have large effects on later cell generations. In cells — as in *Daphnia* — limitation of growth leads to an arrest at some point in the division cycle (Pardee 1989). Any such mechanism which involves discontinuous growth and a size threshold will ensure that a newly founded population — of bacteria, yeast or *Daphnia* — rapidly develops a wide range of age and size classes, thus reducing intraspecific competition. It will also affect patterns of tissue differentiation in multicellular organisms.

Tissue growth is limited by the need to replicate DNA and assemble each new cell. The strength of this constraint is manifest in the early embryo (Alberts *et al.* 1989, Hartwell & Weinert 1989). DNA replication takes place very rapidly after fertilization but this can be achieved only by the mother's provisioning the unfertilized egg with the precursors needed for cell division. Although the cells divide rapidly, they do not grow: thousands of cells may arise by cleavage of the egg within a few hours with no increase in overall mass as succeeding cells become smaller and smaller. Once the developing embryo begins to grow the rate of cell division decreases greatly; there is a trade-off between size at cellular maturity and rate of growth. The existence of cell cycle mutations which change the relationship between cell size and cell maturity (Murray & Kirschner 1989) may provide an experimental system for exploring the effects of growth thresholds on the life histories of cells.

DNA REPLICATION AS A MECHANICAL CONSTRAINT

DNA replication is a physically and chemically complicated business which takes time and energy, so that the rate of reproduction can be constrained by the nature of the genetic material. The *E. coli* genome has about two million base pairs (bp). At optimal temperatures replication proceeds at about 50 000 bp per minute, so that it cannot take less than 40 minutes to produce the new copy of the DNA required by a daughter cell (Lewin 1990, Watson *et al.* 1987). Any increase in genome size has a physical cost in terms of reproductive rate. The insertion of a plasmid slows the replication process (Zund & Lebek 1980).

E. coli, unlike most eukaryotes, has little repetitive DNA or untranscribed sequences within functional genes. The traditional view that bacteria are primitive has been abandoned: modern bacteria are a diverse and highly adapted group. Their lack of introns and repeated sequences may be a size trade-off arising from the strong selection for life history components, in particular for rapid reproduction in creatures who repeatedly show exponential growth in numbers. The need to copy the functional minimum of DNA may hence limit the age at which reproduction takes place. Any excess genetic material slows this process and selection has eliminated it. The same process may explain why most eukaryotic mitochondria are free of intervening sequences. Mitochondria can divide rapidly. They compete for membership in the fraction passed on at cell division. All their genes are functional, and indeed some seem to have been shipped off to the nucleus during their evolution. To be speedy, the mitochondrial genome is forced to be small; and how quickly it can replicate is constrained by how small it can get.

The same life history trade-offs apply in viruses, whose economical genome is the epitome of the sacrifice of size for speed of reproduction. Viral genes may even overlap, with the same DNA sequence coding for different products when read from different starting points (Lewin 1990). 'Incomplete' viruses of plants have a shorter genome than do their complete relatives and reproduce at their expense by taking advantage of some of their DNA sequence. This provides an escape from the constraints imposed by the mechanics of replication but imposes an evolved constraint of its own, a dependence on the presence of complete viruses. Mobile DNA elements have to face the same mechanical compromises. In *Drosophila*, shorter transposable elements (such as P elements) multiply more frequently than do longer ones (Charlesworth & Langley 1989). 'Incomplete' P elements have deleted part of their sequence. They increase their reproductive rate by taking advantage of the replication machinery of complete elements to escape from the mechanical constraint on speed and size at maturity. Their number is limited by the number of complete elements available; and the number of complete elements is itself restricted by their cost to the host.

DISCUSSION

The 10^8 range in body size in the living world is accompanied by a 10^6 difference in the length of DNA. In many creatures, the vast majority of the genome seems to be without function and must exert a cost in replication. There are some correlations between the amount of DNA and life history parameters at both cellular and organismal levels, suggesting that the mechanics of replication may act as a constraint (Cavalier-Smith 1985). In protozoa, genome size is negatively correlated with intrinsic rate of natural increase (Shuter *et al.* 1983). Eukaryotic cells with excess chromosomes (such as B chromosomes and perhaps trisomic cells in humans) appear to divide more slowly. Cancer cells treated with methotrexate may produce multiple copies of detoxifying genes; and this slows their division. Metastasizing cells in a tissue may have aberrant amounts of DNA when compared to normal cells (Weatherall 1991). They frequently lose any of the synchrony present in the parental tissue (Pardee 1989), perhaps because of the effects of DNA content on changing growth rate and, as in *Daphnia*, amplifying small initial differences in rate of growth because of the presence of a threshold size for division.

At the organismal level, too, the amount of DNA is correlated with life history parameters such as age at maturation. In copepods, species with larger genomes grow more slowly (McLaren *et al.* 1989). In Amphibia, developmental time may increase with DNA content. This is well seen in plethodontid salamanders, in which those with high C-value have a torpid life-style, with a low rate of limb differentiation and long lives (Sessions & Larson 1987). Although there is no general fit between DNA content and life history parameters in plants, those species whose growth involves increase in cell size rather than in cell number do have larger genomes (Grime *et al.* 1985). Other associations between genome size and life history are reviewed by Cavalier-Smith (1985). Although genome size tends to be correlated with slow growth or cell division, this is not always so: in cyprinid fishes, for example, in which there is variation in DNA content among individuals and among species there is no apparent fit of genome size with variation in life history (Gold *et al.* 1990).

Of course, not all cases of delayed maturity are related to such mechanical constraints. Maturity may be delayed for adaptive reasons of life history: a delay increases size and hence fecundity, or improves physiological condition so that offspring mortality is reduced to an extent which compensates for a longer juvenile period (Stearns & Crandall 1981). However, there are real mechanical constraints on age at maturity: these range from the basic need to carry out a set number of DNA replications and cell divisions to the equivalent need to pass through a series of instars before maturity. There is enough phenotypic plasticity in rate of growth and age at maturity to ensure that when growth rates are reduced and maturity delayed there may — as in *Daphnia* — be either larger or smaller size at maturity, and hence changes in the demography of the populations of cells or organisms being studied. However, the commonest pattern is that reduced growth rates result in delayed maturity at a smaller size (Stearns & Koella 1986).

Why, then, are some genomes congested with DNA that has no apparent function and seems to slow replication? It is possible that such DNA has some as yet unknown role but most favour the idea that such sequences are 'selfish'; that they multiply without reference to the effects on the fitness of their carriers. For example, the numbers of copies of mobile elements such as *Drosophila* P elements is limited by their deleterious effects on their carriers (Charlesworth & Langley 1989). Although the target of selection is not known, reduced growth rate imposed by the need to replicate excess DNA may be a good candidate.

It may be that delayed maturity usually evolves for some adaptive reasons, and that only then can excess DNA accumulate. Studies of cell size (a good measure of DNA content) in some fossils do suggest that species early in an evolving lineage have relatively small genomes, and that large quantities of DNA accumulate in derived taxa (Conway Morris & Harper 1988). In a slowly growing species, selection pressures to keep the cell cycle short and the genome small are considerably reduced. This could allow DNA content to increase to an extent determined by the delay in maturity. It may then be difficult to get rid of this excess DNA should demographic pressures be reversed. In creatures with short life cycles, selection is stronger on age at maturity than it is on other fitness components (such as fecundity). However, in those with long slow life cycles selection on fecundity becomes much more important than that on age at maturity (Stearns 1992). Only in species that already mate at a relatively early age is selection likely to be able to lead to the ejection of excess DNA and to even earlier maturity. A slow life cycle may be an evolutionary impasse whose limits are defined by the invasion of redundant DNA.

These speculations — and they are little more than that — about the interaction between life-history theory and molecular biology suggest some avenues which might be explored. Do taxa which appear to have gained large amounts of repeated sequence DNA recently have a later age at maturity than their relatives? Are evolutionary reversals of size and life history accompanied by decrease in DNA content? This seems to be true for bacteria and mitochondria but is it the case for, say, dwarf mammals on islands and hymenopteran parasitoids of insect eggs which have been selected for small size and speedy lives? An apparent contradiction to this view is that the tiny plethodontid salamander *Thorius* (which matures relatively young) has a very large genome but in this species cells divide slowly but differentiate rather rapidly (Roth *et al.* 1988). Might there be differences in DNA content or cell size among *Drosophila* lines selected for high or low rates of maturation; or an association between the response to selection for early maturation and DNA content? It may be possible to use lines differing in DNA content to test whether redundant DNA does have a direct effect on body size and on age at maturity.

Whatever the merit of these ideas it is clear that demographic adjustments of the timing of age at maturity operate under constraints set by the mechanics of molecular biology and cell division as much as by the machinations of natural selection.

REFERENCES

Alberts, B., Bray, D., Lewis, J., Raff, M., Roberts, K. & Watson, J. D. (1989). *Molecular Biology of the Cell.* Garland, New York, NY, USA.

Cavalier-Smith, T. (1985). *The Evolution of Genome Size.* John Wiley & Sons, New York, NY, USA.

Clare, G. K. & Singh, P. (1991). Variation in the number of larval instars of the brownheaded leafroller *Ctenopseustis obliquana* (Lepidoptera: Tortricidae). *New Zealand Journal of Zoology*, **17**, 141–146.

Conway Morris, S. & Harper, E. (1988). Genome size in Conodonts (Chordata): inferred variations during 270 million years. *Science*, **241**, 1230–1232.

Charlesworth, B. & Langley, C. H. (1989). The population genetics of transposable elements. *Annual Review of Genetics*, **23**, 251–287.

Deevey, G. B. (1949). The developmental history of *Latrodectus mactans* (Fabr) at different rates of feeding. *American Midland Naturalist*, **42**, 189–219.

Ebert, D. (1991). The effect of size at birth, maturation threshold and genetic differences on the life history of *Daphnia magna*. *Oecologia*, **86**, 243–250.

Gebhart, M. D. & Stearns, S. C. (1988). Reaction norms for developmental time and weight at eclosion in *Drosophila mercatorum*. *Journal of Evolutionary Biology*, **1**, 335–354.

Gold, J. R., Ragland, C. J. & Schliesing, L. J. (1990). Genome size variation and evolution in North American cyprinid fishes. *Génétique, Sélection, Évolution*, **22**, 11–29.

Grime, J. P., Shacklock, J. M. L. & Band, S. R. (1985). Nuclear DNA contents, shoot phenology and species coexistence in a limestone grassland community. *New Phytologist*, **100**, 435–445.

Hartnell, L. H. & Weinert, T. A. (1989). Checkpoints: controls that ensure the order of cell cycle events. *Science*, **246**, 629–634.

Hartnoll, R. G. (1985). Growth, sexual maturity and reproductive output. *Factors in Adult Growth* (Ed. by A. M. Wenner), pp. 101–128. Balkema, Rotterdam, The Netherlands.

Lewin, B. (1990). *Genes* (4th edn). Oxford University Press, Oxford, UK.

McLaren, I. A., Sevigny, J.-M. & Frost, B. W. (1989). Evolutionary and ecological significance of genome sizes in the copepod genus *Pseudocalanus*. *Canadian Journal of Zoology*, **67**, 565–569.

Murray, A. W. & Kirschner, M. W. (1989). Dominoes and clocks: the union of two views on the cell cycle. *Science*, **246**, 614–621.

Nijhout, H. F. & Williams, C. M. (1974). Control of moulting and metamorphosis in the tobacco hornworm, *Manduca sexta* (L): growth of the last instar larva and the decision to pupate. *Journal of Experimental Biology*, **61**, 481–491.

O'Farrell, P. H., Edgar, B. A., Lakich, D. & Lehner, C. F. (1989). Directing cell division during development. *Science*, **246**, 635–640.

Pardee, A. B. (1989). G1 events and the regulation of cell proliferation. *Science*, **246**, 603–640.

Plowright, R. C. & Jay, S. C. (1968). Caste differentiation in bumblebees (*Bombus* Latr.: Hymenoptera). I. The determination of female size. *Insectes Sociaux*, **15**, 171–192.

Roth, G., Rottluff, B. & Linke, R. (1988). Miniaturization, genome size and origin of functional constraints in the visual system of salamanders. *Naturwissenschaften* **75**, 297–304.

Sessions, S. K. & Larson, A. (1987). Developmental correlates of genome size in plethodontid salamanders and their implication for genome evolution. *Evolution*, **41**, 1239–1251.

Shuter, B. J., Thomas, J. E., Taylor, W. D. & Zimmerman, A. M. (1983). Phenotypic correlations of DNA content in unicellular eukaryotes and other cells. *American Naturalist*, **122**, 26–44.

Stearns, S. C. (1992). *The Evolution of Life Histories*. Oxford University Press, Oxford.

Stearns, S. C. & Crandall, R. C. (1981). Quantitative predictions of delayed maturity. *Evolution*, **35**, 455–463.

Stearns, S. C. & Koella, J. C. (1986). The evolution of phenotypic plasticity in life-history traits: predictions of reaction norms for age and size at maturity. *Evolution*, **40**, 893–913.

Tessier, A. J., Henry, L. L., Goulden, C. E. & Durand, M. W. (1983). Starvation in *Daphnia*: energy reserves and reproductive allocation. *Limnology and Oceanography*, **28**, 667–676.

Uvarov, B. (1966). *Grasshoppers and Locusts*. Cambridge University Press, Cambridge, UK.

Watson, J. D., Hopkins, N. H., Roberts, J. W., Steitz, J. A. J. & Weiner, A. M. (1987). *Molecular Biology of the Gene* (4th edn). Benjamin/Cummings, Menlo Park, CA, USA.

Weatherall, D. J. (1991). *The New Genetics and Clinical Practice* (3rd edn). Oxford University Press, Oxford, UK.

Zund, P. & Lebek, G. (1980). Generation time-prolonging R plasmids: correlation between increases in the generation time of *Escherischia coli* caused by R plasmids and their molecular size. *Plasmid*, **3**, 65–69.

17. CONSERVATION BIOLOGY: THE ECOLOGY AND GENETICS OF ENDANGERED SPECIES

ANDREW P. DOBSON*, GEORGINA M. MACE†, JOYCE POOLE‡ AND ROBERT A. BRETT‡

**Department of Ecology and Evolutionary Biology, University of Princeton, Princeton, NJ 08544–1003, USA; †Institute of Zoology, Regents Park, London NW1 4RY, UK and ‡Kenya Wildlife Service, P.O. Box 40241, Nairobi, Kenya*

INTRODUCTION

Population genetics and population dynamics are both crucial in the conservation and management of endangered species of animals and plants. However, a considerable change in emphasis occurs as we move from captive populations in zoos, through managed populations in nature reserves to whole communities of free-living organisms. Genetic considerations tend to guide the management of captive populations, while demographic, and often purely taxonomic, considerations tend to dominate studies of free-living populations and communities. To a large extent this continuum reflects the different types of information collected in studies designed to address different types of question.

This chapter attempts to partly redress the balance. First we review captive breeding in zoos where genetic conservation tactics are mainly concerned with maintaining a maximum level of genetic diversity. We then move on to discuss problems in free-living populations where both genetic and ecological considerations have been shown to be important. We conclude by discussing the relative time scales at which genetic, ecological and economic events affect endangered species, and the efficiency with which they can be managed. Throughout the chapter we emphasize areas where interactions between ecologists and geneticists will be important in improving the effectiveness of attempts to conserve endangered species. We centre our discussion around populations of large mammals but many of our conclusions will be relevant to other kinds of organisms.

CAPTIVE POPULATIONS

In captive populations the primary management and research objectives are education and propagation, possibly for eventual reintroduction. Close genetic management is possible because individuals are usually both identifiable and under close management. Moreover, in many cases family relationships or sometimes extended pedigrees are available, and the capture site of wild caught individuals that founded the captive populations may be known. Increasingly, this kind of information is being recorded in zoo record systems, and for many endangered species studbooks and other databases that facilitate population management are maintained with detailed pedigree and other life history information on individuals (Olney 1980, Flesness & Mace 1988). Perhaps because of the availability of this kind of information, and the close control over the formation of breeding pairs that the captive environment presents, zoo breeding plans have tended to concentrate heavily on genetic management, especially based upon detailed pedigree analysis.

Captive populations: detailed records available

A variety of pedigree analysis methods have been applied but all involve tracing living individuals back to wild caught founders and calculating inbreeding coefficients. Generally the overall aims of genetic management are to maximize founder number, to equalize founder representation and to minimize inbreeding levels (Foose & Ballou 1988).

Founder animals are the source of all genetic variability in the population and the preservation of variation is generally the aim of captive management programmes. However, often little is known about the origins or relationships of founder animals and actual genetic information (e.g. from molecular studies) is rarely available. Genetic management, therefore, tends to be based around a simple though unrealistic assumption that all founders are genetically unique. Maximizing founder number and equalizing founder representation should maximize the probability of preserving genetic variation. Since inbreeding depression has now been demonstrated in a variety of both captive and wild populations (Ralls *et al.* 1979, Ballou & Ralls 1982, Ralls *et al.* 1988) minimizing inbreeding levels is another common aim. In a population with a completely known pedigree it should therefore be possible to design an ideal breeding plan. However, in reality there are a number of serious complications:

1 *Data are rarely complete.* Frequently there are unknown parents, unknown founder origins or parts of the pedigree where almost nothing

was recorded. When missing data are a relatively small fraction of the total it may be reasonable to fill in gaps with assumed events according to some 'worst case scenario' (Carroll & Mace 1988, Ballou in press). This is frequently done in captive management plans but it may influence the results of analyses quite markedly, especially where a significant portion of the pedigree is unknown. Under these circumstances it may be preferable to base management decisions on population-level analyses (see later). In the future we hope that molecular genetic data will contribute this kind of historical information, though there are methodological as well as technical difficulties (Lynch 1990).

2 *Pedigrees are bottlenecked and complex*. Often the pedigrees of captive populations are extended over many generations with cross-generation mating, periodic bottlenecks and extensive inbreeding. Under these circumstances, analytical methods for calculating relationship coefficients are inaccurate. For example, in the pedigrees in Fig. 17.1, all the living individuals have the same level of relationship to founder animals, and all founders have four living descendants. However, the probability that founder genes are preserved will vary. With inbreeding and family size variation, equalizing founder representation will tend to lead to multiple copies of the same founder genes, rather than maximizing genetic variation in the living population. To take this into account, pedigree simulation methods, known as 'gene dropping' are used to establish target representation levels for each founder based upon the probability that a founder allele is expected to be preserved in the living population (see MacLuer *et al.* 1986, Lacy 1989).

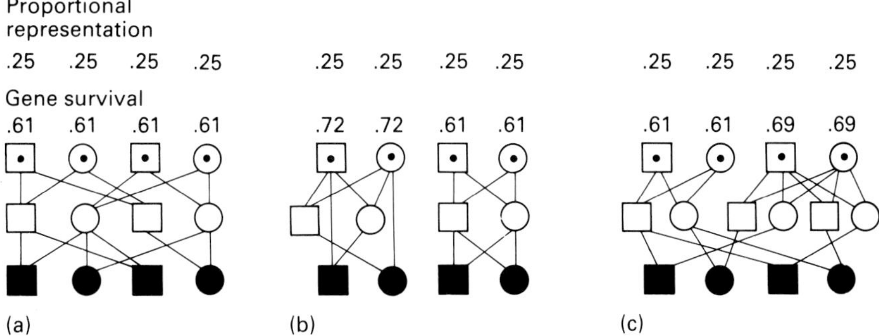

FIG. 17.1. Three simple pedigrees (a, b, c) in which two founder males (⊡) and two founder females (⊙) leave two surviving male (■) and female (●) offspring. Although the proportional genetic representation in the surviving population is the same for each founder, the probability that any one founder gene survives (gene survival) varies with the amount and nature of inbreeding and backcrossing (pedigree b) and on family size (pedigree c). See MacLuer *et al.* (1986) for more information.

3 *Inbreeding depression versus optimal outbreeding*. Evidence for inbreeding depression is now widespread from studies of captive, laboratory and wild populations (Ralls *et al.* 1979, Ralls & Ballou 1983, Ralls *et al.* 1986). However, several authors have suggested that minimization of inbreeding may not necessarily be best. Most natural populations are subdivided and outcrosses could potentially lead to the loss of locally adapted genotypes or to reduced fertility due to the breakdown of intrinsic genetic coadaptation (see Templeton 1986). These processes are often called 'outcrossing depression', though actual examples are rare. The most commonly cited case of outbreeding depression through loss of a locally adapted genotype concerns the unsuccessful translocation of ibex subspecies from Austria and Sinai to the Tatra mountains in Czechoslovakia, where the native subspecies had gone extinct. The introduced population rutted early and young were born in the coldest part of the year and died, leading to the extinction of the population (Greig 1979, Templeton 1986).

Intrinsic coadaptation refers to the way in which genetic or karyotypic characters are expected to evolve in response to others in the population, so that outcrosses could lead to the breakdown of these coadapted complexes. This process has been extensively studied in *Drosophila* (Templeton 1986) and plants (Ledig 1986) but is rarely documented in vertebrates. One clear-cut case is seen in captive populations of the douroucouli (*Aotus trivirgatus*) where chromosome studies have revealed polymorphisms in chromosome number both within and between different wild populations (de Boer 1982). Fertility is likely to be reduced from crossing some chromosome races because of difficulties at meiosis.

The degree of inbreeding depression or 'outcrossing depression' that a population will suffer will partly be a function of its recent history. Templeton *et al.* (1986) suggest a method to determine the impact of each in a captive pedigree as a prelude to devising a detailed management plan. In a recent study that adopted this method on 40 pedigrees of captive mammals, nine showed statistically significant inbreeding depression, but none showed significant outbreeding depression (Ralls *et al.* 1988). Inbreeding depression is probably a more significant factor in genetic management than outcrossing depression.

4 *Dealing with real animals*. Genetic management plans have to consider practical limitations imposed by economics, legislation, the logistics of zoo management, and most significantly by the behaviour of the species and individual animals involved in the programme. Behavioural considerations are extremely important, not only because failure to recognize them can lead to reduced viability and fertility, but also because inappro-

priate genetic management can have negative consequences. For example, polygynous species are subject to both natural and sexual selection but genetic management schemes based around the preservation of heterozygosity *per se* may tend to select against sexually selected characters perhaps to the detriment of population survival (Arnold in press). Polygynous species generally present more difficulties, especially in restricted populations where single males have dominated breeding over many breeding seasons.

Table 17.1 shows estimates of variance in life-time reproductive success for a selection of species maintained in captivity for which long-term data are available. The standardized variance ($\sigma^2/\bar{x}^2$), denoted by I, is used to reflect the potential for selection among individuals (Arnold & Wade 1984a, b). The estimates were based on individuals whose whole life-time was recorded, except for the Asian lion (*Panthera leo persica*) where all individuals that had a breeding lifespan over at least 5 years were included. Compared with similar data on wild African lions (*Panthera leo*) (Packer *et al.* 1988) variances for both males and females are significantly higher in captive than in wild animals (males: wild I = 1.18, captive I = 4.27, $F_{36,90} = 3.82$, $p < 0.001$; females: wild $I = 0.41$, captive $I = 4.40$, $F_{59,53}$ =

TABLE 17.1. Estimated life-time reproductive success for seven captive species. For each sex the sample size (N), mean (x), variance (σ^2) and standardized variance ($I = \sigma^2/\bar{x}^2$) are shown. Data analysed are from published data in international studbooks (see Olney & Ellis 1990 for details)

Species	Sex	N	$\bar{x}^2$	$\bar{\sigma}^2$	I	I_m/I_f
Red crowned-crane	m	30	3.10	9.10	0.95	1.44
	f	42	2.70	4.80	0.66	
Pink pigeon	m	72	2.38	31.24	5.50	1.18
	f	91	1.11	5.74	4.66	
Asian lion	m	37	2.70	31.10	4.27	0.97
	f	60	2.78	34.00	4.40	
Grevy's zebra	m	75	3.60	34.00	2.63	3.70
	f	209	1.30	1.20	0.71	
Przewalski horse	m	408	1.40	23.44	11.96	3.16
	f	382	1.62	9.92	3.78	
Scimitar-horned oryx	m	103	2.18	127.90	26.90	6.18
	f	65	1.55	10.44	4.35	
Golden-headed lion tamarin	m	94	1.15	7.27	5.49	1.18
	f	91	1.11	5.74	4.66	

10.86, $p < 0.001$). Comparable species were not otherwise available for direct comparison, but Fig. 17.2 shows standardized variances for a range of wild species compiled by Clutton-Brock (1988a) compared with the captive species in Table 17.1. For both sexes, higher variances are common in captive species. The reasons for this probably lie in low adult mortality in captive species and the tendency for some individuals to continue to dominate breeding over long time periods. High juvenile mortality may be a confounding factor in the estimation of I in both captive and wild species (Clutton-Brock 1988b) but would not be sufficient to explain the differences in Fig. 17.2. Whereas the variation observed in the free-living populations reflects differences in the breeding systems of the species, the

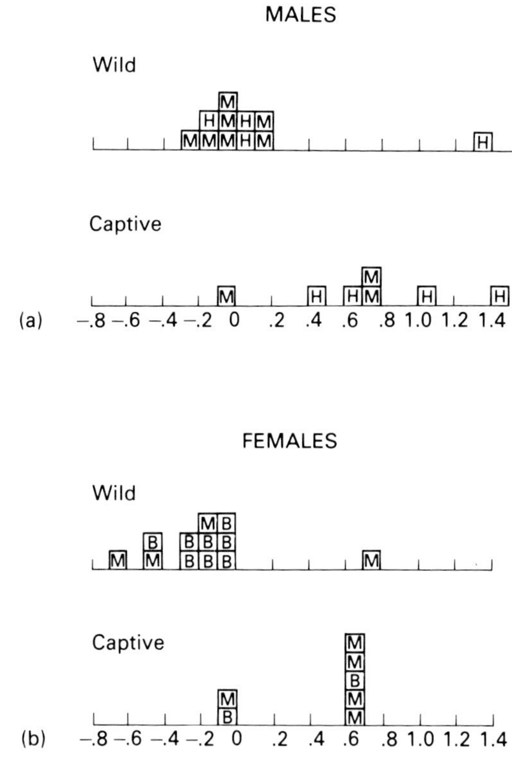

FIG. 17.2. Frequency distributions of log (standardized variance in reproductive success) for free-living species (wild) and seven captive species. The wild data are those compiled by Clutton-Brock (1988a). (a) Males: M, monogamous; H, harem. (b) Females: M, mammal; B, bird.

data from captive populations are due to differences in management practice that do not necessarily reflect the natural breeding system, and will result in strong selection pressures for certain traits that may well not be adaptive in more natural circumstances.

5 *Planning for the future*. Pedigree analyses are by definition retrospective but for conservation-sensitive species the analyses should be able to provide statistics useful for future planning. Although gene drop methods can provide some of this kind of information (MacLuer *et al.* 1986) and new methods are now being developed to identify genetically important individuals in a population (Ballou in press), many genetic plans are still based around quite general models predicting loss of genetic variability (heterozygosity) over specified time periods with given effective population sizes (Soulé *et al.* 1986). These methods are dominated by the effects of genetic drift and do not incorporate the effects of selection or population subdivision, both of which are likely to be significant.

Captive populations: individuals and breeding not completely known

In the case of many group-living species in captivity, and many wild populations, detailed studies can only provide a limited amount of information and this is never likely to be as complete as the full pedigrees discussed earlier (p. 406). Although genetic management will have similar aims in these populations, it has to be based upon population rather than individual data. The key statistic used in the genetic management of this type of population is effective population size, N_e, an estimate of the number of unique genetic individuals in the population contributing to subsequent generations. This can be estimated from breeding data on the mean and variance in family size for males and females (Lande & Barrowclough 1987, Harris & Allendorf 1989).

In theory, N_e may be greater than N (the census size) in a closely managed population but this is only achieved in very closely controlled circumstances, e.g. with laboratory animals (Falconer 1981). Estimates of N_e/N in natural and captive populations, based on demographic data are generally in the range 0.2–0.6 (Mace 1986, Carroll & Mace 1988). Nunney (1991) has shown that a good approximation of N_e is found simply from 0.5 N_b, where N_b is the number of breeding individuals. However, some recent studies based on genetic data suggest that these are overestimates (e.g. Tomlinson *et al.* 1991) and in a recent study of large *Drosophila* populations N_e/N ratios were rarely more than 0.2 and usually less than 0.1 (Briscoe *et al.* in press). These differences are important because species conservation plans are usually based on assumptions about N_e/N

ratios (Soulé *et al.* 1986, Lande & Barrowclough 1987, Mace & Lande 1991).

THE POPULATION BIOLOGY OF INTENSIVELY MANAGED SPECIES

Genetic management has tended to dominate techniques for population management in captivity. However, this bias may not be appropriate in more natural environments (or in captivity). Demographic extinction factors are more difficult to quantify but simulation studies suggest their impact may be more significant in the short term. Here we present an example that uses data from some small populations of rhinos in Kenyan game sanctuaries.

Black rhino populations in Kenya

Black rhinos (*Diceros bicornis*) are now threatened across their entire range (IUCN 1990); in East Africa no single population numbers more than 60 animals (Brett 1990). Some of these populations are in closely protected sanctuaries or reserves where detailed population monitoring is now under way. Their continued survival is critical for the species and population simulation studies are being undertaken to aid effective population management. Preliminary analyses presented here allow an insight into the significance of demographic and genetic factors in extinction rates, and the ecological and behavioural factors that will need to be taken into consideration in management strategies.

We have used the GAPPS animal population modelling software which is a discrete time, stochastic computer program that follows the history of each individual from birth to death (Harris *et al.* 1986). Input is in the form of a series of data files containing identities and parentage of each individual, age and sex-specific rates of survival and reproduction as well as rates of immigration of different age and sex classes. Data from rhino sanctuaries were used as input, and the populations were modelled for 200 years with no immigration or with one immigrant every 10 years up to year 50. The immigrant was set to be aged between 8 and 14 years, and to have an equal probability of being male or female. GAPPS also allows inbreeding depression to be modelled by adjusting the age-specific probability of survival or reproduction (P) to be reduced according to the function:

$$P \times \mathrm{e}^{-(bF)}$$

where F is the animal's inbreeding coefficient, and e is the base of natural logarithms. b is the slope of the line relating some fitness character to the level of inbreeding. In a set of 40 populations studied by Ralls *et al.* (1988), b was found to vary between −0.68 and 15.16 with a mean of 2.33 and a median of 1.57 with juvenile survival as the dependent variable. In this study, female breeding rates were set as a function of b, and b was set to 2.0, close to the median value for large mammals found by Ralls *et al.* (1988). The populations were modelled with and without inbreeding depression. Rates of breeding and survival were also adjusted by a function to incorporate density dependence. The carrying capacity of each reserve was estimated independently (Brett 1990) and at each breeding and survival event probabilities were adjusted by a modified Michaelis–Menton equation to:

$$\text{Min} + (\text{Max} - \text{Min}) \times (1 - [V^x/(0.05P_{95}{}^x + V_x)])$$

where Min and Max are the minimum and maximum probabilities allowed, V is an independent variable set to N (population size)/K (carrying capacity), P is the value of V at which the function takes a value 95% of the distance between Min and Max, and x is an exponent controlling the shape of the function (see Harris *et al.* 1986).

The results from two populations are presented here. The sanctuary population at Lewa Downs consists of 3 males and 10 females, 1 and 5 of which are adults respectively. The sanctuary is estimated to have a carrying capacity of 20. Nakuru National Park contains 11 males and 7 females, 8 and 5 of which are adults respectively, and has a carrying capacity of 71. Each population was modelled under three management options:

1 With no inbreeding depression and no immigration.
2 With inbreeding depression affecting female fertility and no immigration.
3 With inbreeding depression and immigration.

Population survival, population size and structure, average neonatal inbreeding coefficients and heterozygosity were recorded over 200 years; each simulation was repeated 200 times. The results are summarized in Figs 17.3 and 17.4.

Population survival for both populations was lowest in option 2, with 26% survival at Lewa Downs and 78% at Nakuru. The comparison between options 1 and 2 give insight into the relative significance of demographic and genetic extinction factors over the 200-year period. The extinction rates for the two options are initially similar when demographic extinction factors dominate. After about 100 years at Lewa Downs and 60 years at Nakuru the extinction curves diverge and inbreeding depression starts to have a significant impact (Fig. 17.3). Two general conclusions may be drawn. In the short term, i.e. the next few decades, demographic extinction factors are more significant and it is only after this time that genetic considerations become important. Secondly, demographic extinction is considerably more of a threat to the smaller population at Lewa Downs than at Nakuru.

Even low levels of immigration by unrelated individuals have quite a major effect on population size and persistence. Once immigration was

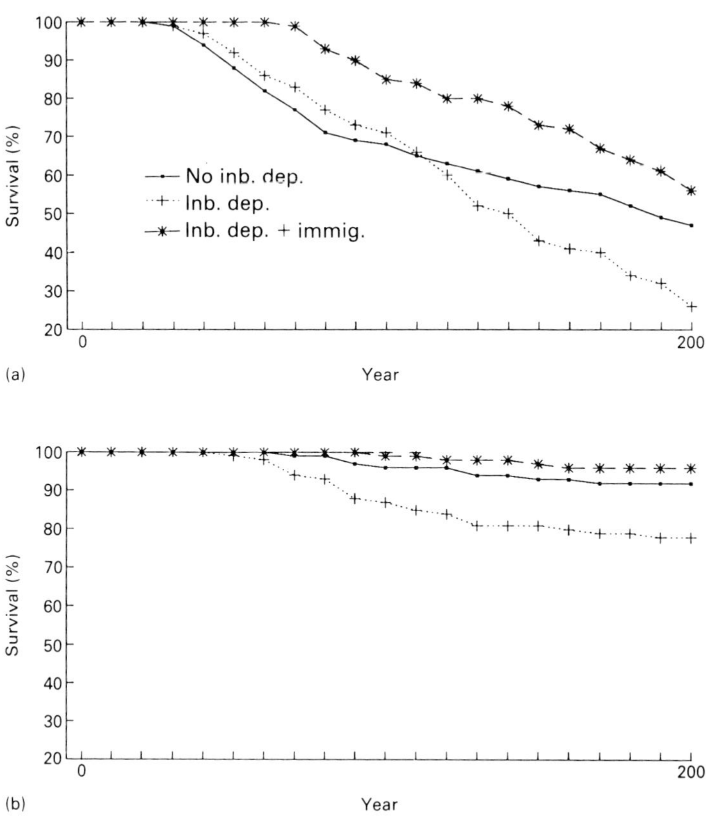

Fig. 17.3. The effect of inbreeding depression (Inb. dep.) and immigration (immig.) on the survival of populations of rhinoceros at Lewa Downs (a) and Nakuru National Parks (b). In both cases the probabilities of the present population surviving over the next 200 years are considered assuming no inbreeding depression, when extinction would be due entirely to stochastic events; inbreeding depression which lowers the survival of offspring as heterozygosity decreases; and immigration of new individuals into the population for the first 50 years of the project.

stopped, these benefits deteriorated quite rapidly due to inbreeding depression. At both Lewa Downs and Nakuru this option led to the highest persistence rate at 200 years (Fig. 17.3). However, 100 years after immigration has ceased the population sizes were again low and similar to those achieved with no immigration (Fig. 17.4). It was only under option 1, with no inbreeding depression, that population size was maintained close to carrying capacity after about 150 years. Two general conclusions can be drawn from this analysis. In small populations demographic forces are likely to dominate rates of extinction but even low levels of immigration can have a significant beneficial influence, especially by reducing the demographic extinction factors and delaying the effects of inbreeding depression. These benefits deteriorate rapidly once immigration is halted.

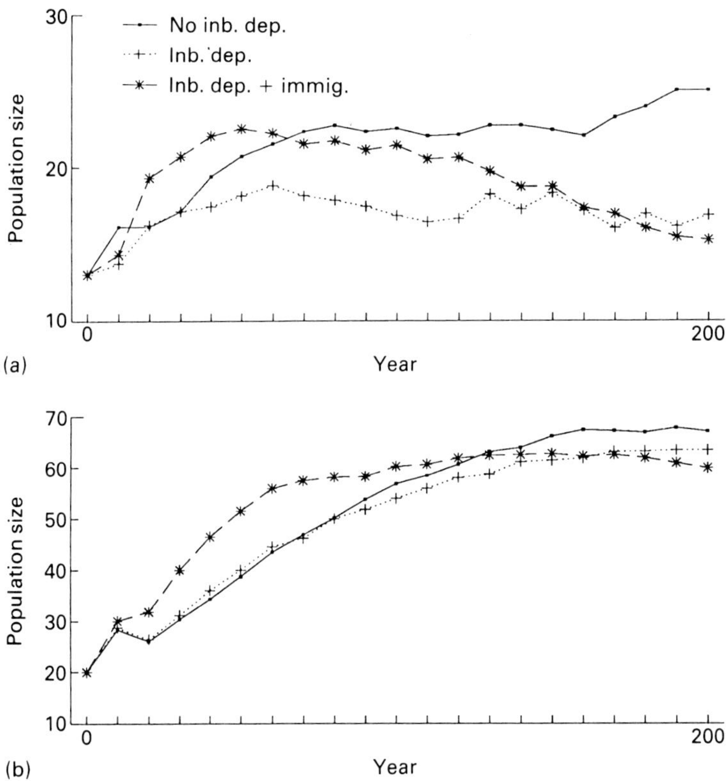

FIG. 17.4. The effect of inbreeding depression (lnb. dep) and immigration (immig.) on the size of populations of rhinoceros at Lewa Downs (a) and Nakuru National Parks (b). In both cases the average size of the population over the next 200 years is illustrated under the same set of assumptions as were used in the simulations of Fig. 17.3.

In very small populations, such as that at Lewa Downs, the effect is particularly marked. However, in all small populations genetic factors will eventually become significant.

These models are relatively simple and the results should not be taken too literally. In several ways the population survival rates are likely to be overestimates. The model does not incorporate the effects of extrinsic extinction factors such as disease, food supply failure or loss of more habitat, all of which are likely to influence all populations throughout time. Secondly, the simulation assumes that mating pairs are selected at random, thus ignoring the influence of male dominance and territoriality characteristic of the species; in natural populations this will generally lead to higher levels of relatedness and hence more pronounced inbreeding depression. The model does not allow any adaptation to inbreeding depression in the population; this might be expected over the course of several generations of inbreeding (Templeton & Read 1983), and would tend to slow down the delcterious genetic effects that dominate the dynamics towards the end of the 200-year period.

A general conclusion is that most of these small populations in Kenya are non-viable without intensive management, involving continuous monitoring of population size and structure and periodic introduction of unrelated individuals. Applying these recommendations presents a series of practical difficulties resulting from the ecology and behaviour of the species (Brett 1990). In many areas the vegetation is extremely dense and monitoring individuals is difficult and dangerous. Immobilization of individuals for monitoring or transfer is difficult and costly with high risks to both rhinos and biologists. Considerable aggression from resident animals may pose problems for immigrants, especially for older animals. Finally, habitat differences in browse, disease, temperature, disturbance, etc., may pose adaptational problems for new immigrants. All these factors will have to be quantified and costed in the future as the biological factors clearly indicate that unless some kind of intensive management is undertaken these small populations are not viable.

THE DEMOGRAPHY OF FREE-LIVING ENDANGERED SPECIES

The diversity of problems facing population biologists interested in conserving endangered species is nowhere more acutely apparent than when we consider the primates. Current estimates suggest that more than 50% of the 230 extant primate species may become extinct sometime in the next 20–50 years (Mittermeier *et al.* 1986). The world population size of many primate species is smaller than that of most towns or villages (Jolly 1985). Although nearly all species have now been studied in the wild, the average duration of a primate field study is less than 3 years; this is considerably less than the life expectancy of most primate species and close to the average interbirth interval of most (Dobson & Lyles 1989). The demographic data available for most primate populations is scant at best and there are almost no studies of the genetics of wild primate populations. Nevertheless, the recent rapid developments in DNA fingerprinting technology should allow the reconstruction of pedigrees from long-term studies of primates and other species in the wild.

Merenlender and Dobson have begun such a study at Ranomafana National Park in Madagascar, and we hope to compare the demography *and* genetics of two closely related lemur species with different social systems. One particular irony of the study is that the techniques for genetic analysis develop at a much faster rate than the data accumulates. When the study was initiated we concentrated on determining if Jeffrey's probe could be used to construct pedigrees for captive populations of lemurs (Jeffreys *et al.* 1985). As the field study developed we realized that serious ambiguities could result in our assessment of paternity if we relied on these techniques (Lynch 1990), and we have subsequently developed single-locus probes with which to undertake these studies. The advent of the polymerase chain reaction (PCR) means that we could do many more things with the limited amount of tissue collected in the field. It is a full-time job keeping up with the genetic techniques and there is a constant temptation to adopt new techniques before we have used those available to address our initial questions.

The extensive marking and monitoring of animals required by the study has already revealed something that would have taken considerably longer in a more conventional primate field study: *Lemur rubriventer*, previously supposed to be monogamous, frequently change mates between breeding seasons; in contrast, *L. fulvus rufus* have very stable group structure. The full implications of these differences between social systems for the genetic structure of the population will become apparent as the study progresses.

SELECTION IN EXPLOITED POPULATIONS OF ENDANGERED SPECIES

Many endangered populations have become reduced in numbers through human exploitation. Economic analyses indicate that it is often in the interest of those exploiting a population to use it to the brink of extinction

(Clark 1976, Walters 1986). Intense selection may ultimately lead to genetic changes in the population that allow it to better withstand the impact of humans. However, the time scale at which the population responds to selection may be considerably longer than either the time scale determining changes in numbers or the time scale at which economic markets create opportunities for exploitation. An analysis of a hypothetical gene for tusklessness in elephant populations can illustrate these problems.

Elephants, ivory and poaching

The African elephant, *Loxodonta edentata*, was recently declared endangered on a global scale and placed on Appendix 1 of Convention on Trade in Endangered Species (CITES), resulting in a complete ban on trade in elephant products by all the countries that are signatories to CITES. The ban was initiated following a series of analyses which suggested that elephants would be driven to extinction in many parts of Africa if poaching continued at the rates prevalent in the early 1980s. Levels of trade in ivory had been increasing rapidly following increases in the price of ivory over the last 30 years (Fig. 17.5). The huge volume of ivory moved through the markets was observed to consist of tusks from increasing numbers of smaller individuals, suggesting that the demand for ivory had led to a switch from the older males to immature males and females (Poole & Thomsen 1989). By the mid-1980s the volume of ivory entering the trade was diminishing rapidly suggesting that stocks were rapidly being overexploited. Field surveys recorded widespread decreases in the size of Africa's elephant populations (Douglas-Hamilton 1987).

The demography of African elephants has been examined using a number of mathematical models (Caughley *et al.* 1990, Basson *et al.* 1991, Milner-Guillard & Mace 1991, Dobson & Poole in preparation). A variety of sources suggest that both age at first reproduction and interbirth interval are dependent upon available resources (Fig. 17.6; Laws 1969, Eltringham 1982). These density dependent relationships can be readily included into age-structured (Leslie matrix) models and stock recruitment relationships derived for elephant populations under different exploitation assumptions. The simplest (and least accurate) way to do this is to assume random harvesting (Fig. 17.7). Such models suggest that elephant populations may be driven to extinction by harvest levels in excess of 6% per annum. Furthermore, the time taken to drive populations to extinction decreases rapidly as annual exploitation rates exceed 10% per annum. Estimates of average exploitation rates for the late 1970s and early 1980s suggest that poaching levels may have been as high as 15–20% per

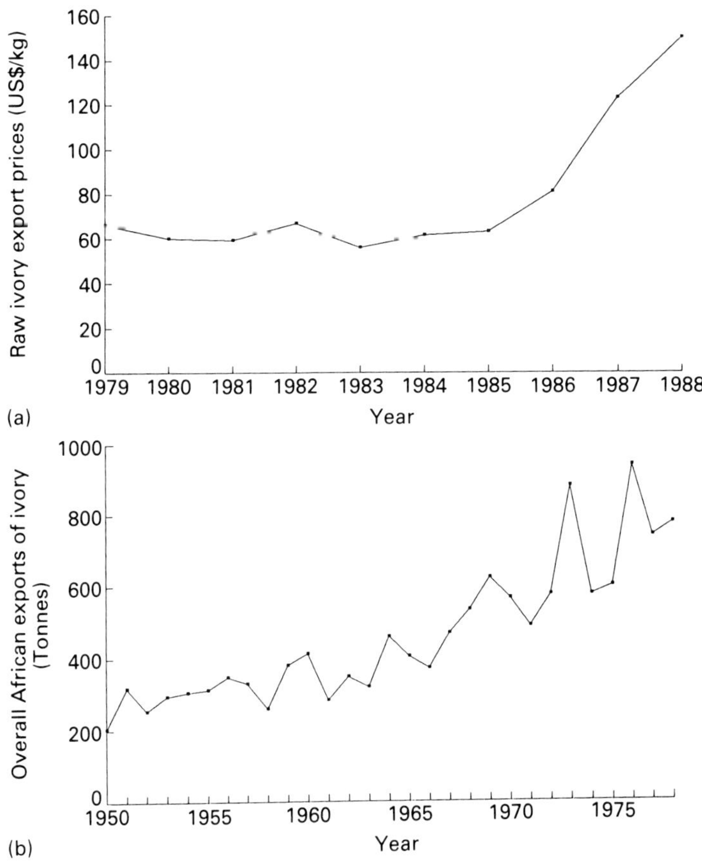

FIG. 17.5. (a) The raw ivory export prices for the years 1979–1988. (b) The amount of ivory exported from Africa in the years 1950–1978. (After Barbier *et al.* 1990.)

annum (Milner-Guillard & Mace 1991); had this continued it would have driven elephants to extinction by the beginning of the next century.

The models of elephant demography can be modified to consider rates of gene frequency change under exploitation. There is empirical evidence to suggest that tusklessness has increased in frequency in heavily poached populations (Fig. 17.8; Douglas-Hamilton personal communication, Hall-Martin 1980). Tusks have also completely disappeared in female Indian elephants (Sukumar 1990). In this example we consider a simple one locus, two allele model for tusklessness. We assume that tusked is the dominant trait and that tusklessness is only expressed in homozygous

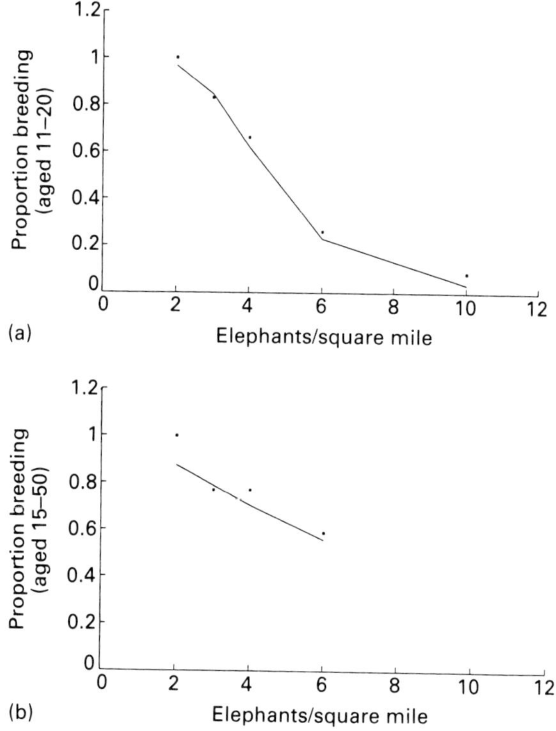

FIG. 17.6. The observed relationship between age at (a) first reproduction and (b) interbirth interval for African elephants (data from Laws 1969). Fecundity is expressed as the proportion of female elephants breeding in any time interval.

recessive individuals. Because male elephants use their tusks in fights to control access to females, we assume that the fitness of a tuskless individual is a function of their frequency in the population. When tusked individuals are common, tuskless individuals are unable to win fights and fail to obtain matings, as the frequency of tusked individuals is reduced by poaching, the relative ability of tuskless individuals to obtain matings increases (Fig. 17.9). In the absence of poaching, tuskless individuals only appear in the population when two heterozygous individuals mate and produce an offspring. The model is obviously a caricature of reality. However, in the absence of any real information on the genetic mechanisms determining these traits in elephants, it acts as a phenomenological example which serves to illustrate the rate at which gene frequencies respond to selection in populations with this type of age structure.

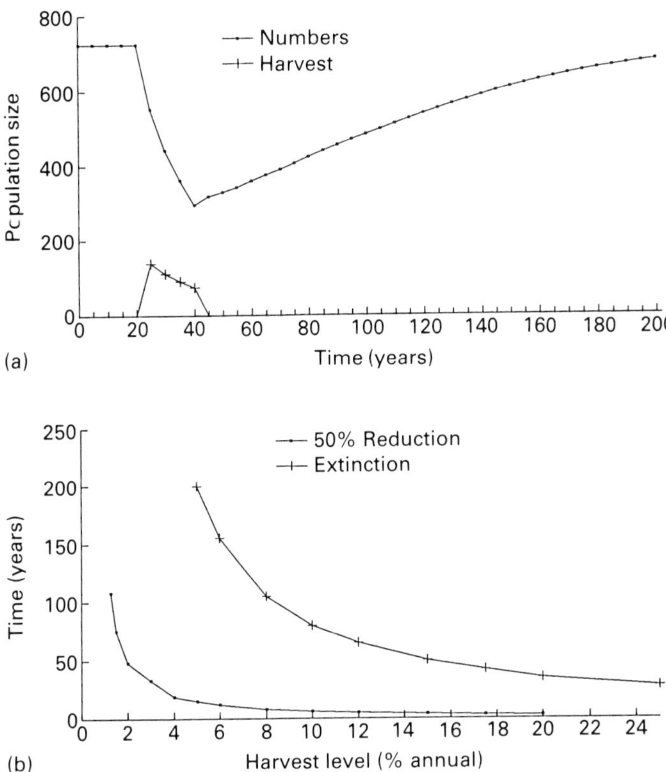

FIG. 17.7. (a) The effect of randomly harvesting 5% of the elephants in a population over a 20-year time interval. The upper line shows total population size, the lower shows resultant ivory yield. (b) The time taken to reduce an elephant population by 50% and to drive it to extinction at a range of different harvesting levels. (After Dobson & Poole in preparation.)

The initial conditions for the simulations were determined by running the model in the absence of poaching until all age classes and gene frequencies arrived at stable numbers and frequencies, these were then used as the initial conditions for the exploited population. In the absence of any selection for tusks, random harvesting of the population at an annual level of 5% is sufficient to drive the population almost to extinction (Fig. 17.7). In contrast, when only tusked individuals are removed from a population containing genes for tusklessness, the population initially declines to a low level where it remains stable for around 200 years (Fig. 17.10). During this time the relative frequencies of tusked and tuskless genes changes. Eventually, the mating success of the tuskless individuals

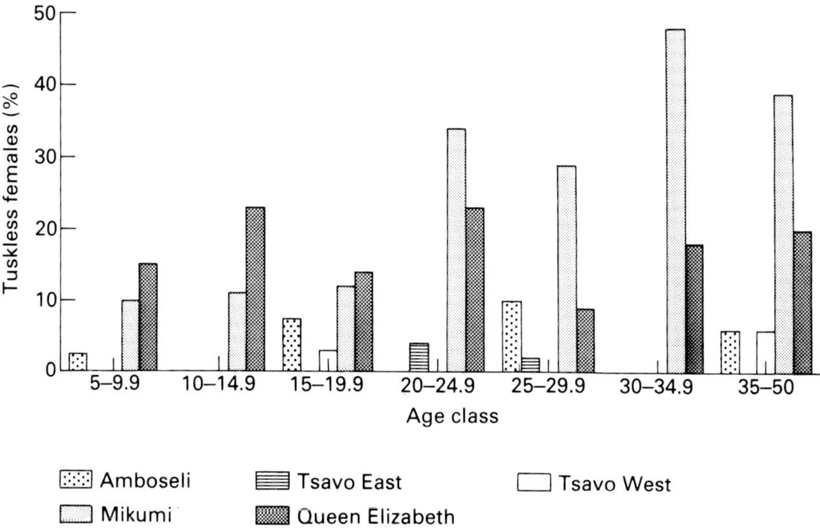

FIG. 17.8. The numbers of tuskless individuals observed in four populations of elephants surveyed by Poole (unpublished). The Amboseli population is relatively unpoached, the populations in Tsavo, Mikumi and Queen Elizabeth Parks have been subjected to increasing levels of poaching.

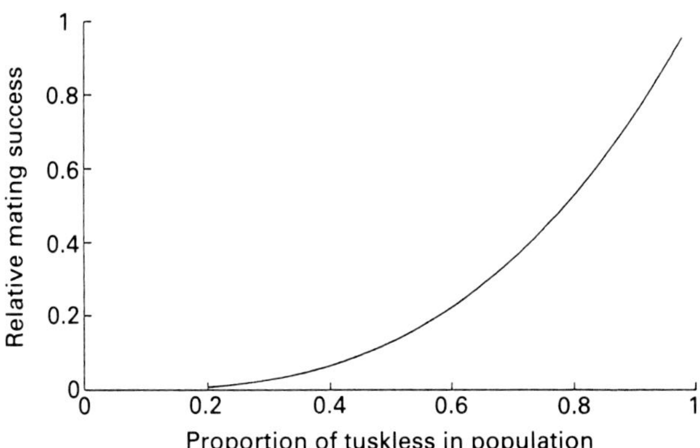

FIG. 17.9. Hypothetical relationship between the relative number of matings obtained by tuskless individuals as a function of their frequency in the population. The graph assumes that tusked males have an average relative mating success of unity.

approaches parity with the tusked individuals, and the tuskless population increases to the carrying capacity of the previously predominantly tusked population. The most important point to emerge is that even in the face of strong selection, the rates of gene frequency change are slow when

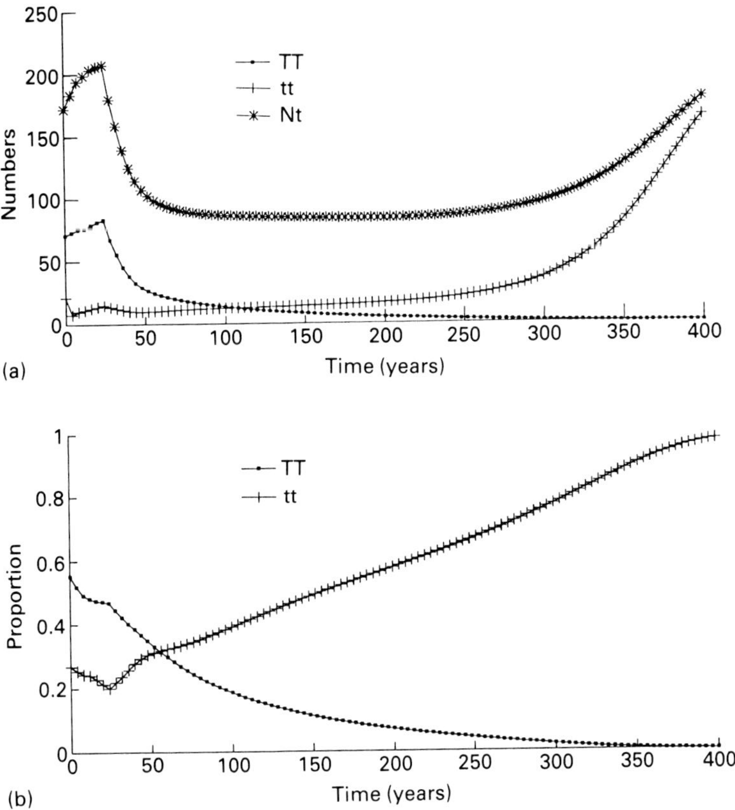

FIG. 17.10. The effect of a 5% harvest rate on the total population size of a hypothetical elephant population. (a) The total numbers of individuals (Nt) and the numbers homozygous for tusked (TT) or tuskless (tt). (b) The frequency of the tusked and tuskless alleles.

compared with the changes in population density. The age structure of the elephant population gives the species considerable resilience to selection operating over quite long time intervals.

It is also possible to examine what happens if we stop harvesting the population once it has reached either a low density or after the tusked trait is almost completely removed from the population (Fig. 17.11). In both cases the frequency of tusked individuals increases and ultimately their frequency and numbers return to a stable polymorphic frequency. However, this adjustment takes over two to four centuries, a period of time considerably longer than the time scale at which the elephants respond to exploitation.

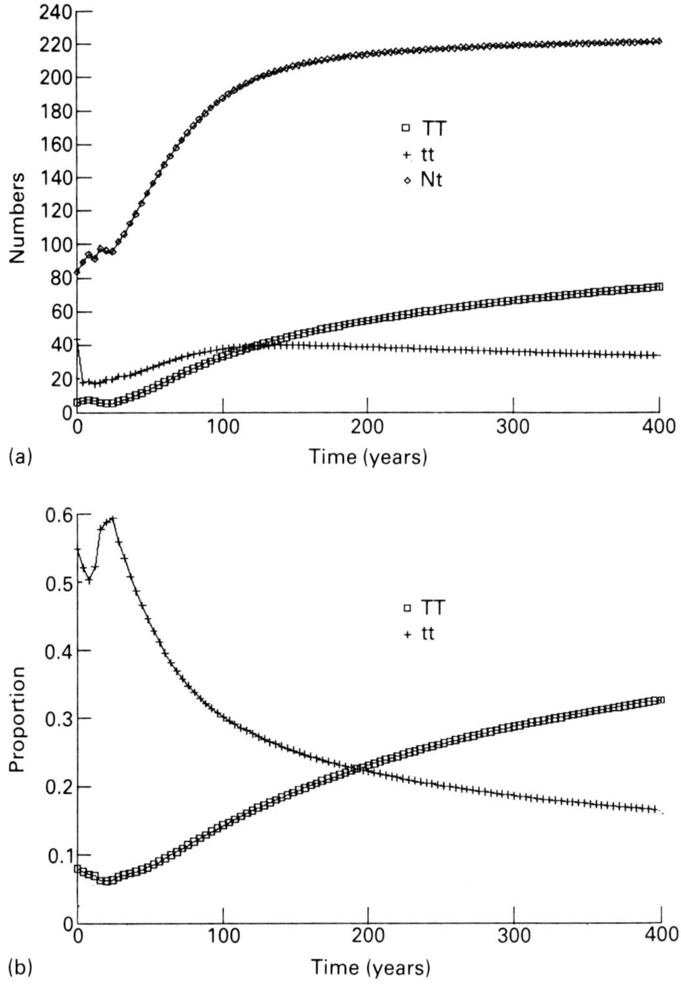

FIG. 17.11. Recovery of a previously harvested population from it's minimum density. (a) The total numbers of individuals (Nt) and the numbers homozygous for tusked (TT) and tuskless (tt) conditions. (b) The frequency of the tusked and tuskless alleles.

The effect of elephant social systems on demography

The models can be further modified to examine the effect of elephant social systems on demography (Dobson & Poole in preparation). Inclusion of different features of elephant social systems (mate choice, allomothering) into population models always produce an Allee effect, a deterministic threshold below which the populations collapse to extinction. These thresholds, or breakpoints, were originally postulated to occur for parasitic helminths (May 1977). They have also been examined in models for primates where the magnitude of the breakpoint is dependent on the social system of the species. In general, monogamous, more solitary species tend to have higher thresholds than group-living promiscuous species (Dobson & Lyles 1989). The magnitude of these thresholds will also be important in determining the size and composition of populations that are reintroduced to the wild. Furthermore, in declining populations, the social structure of the population may be such that the population may be in danger of deterministic collapse at population sizes higher than those where inbreeding has a significant effect on viability.

An important additional exercise is to examine the impact deterministic Allee effects have on rare alleles in more complex genetic models. Unpublished work by Gupta *et al.* (personal communication) on selection in parasite models suggest these 'Allee-type' effects lead to enhanced rates of loss of heterozygosity at densities where drift may not be leading to significant losses. Inclusion of these effects into estimates of N_e might perhaps explain some of the anomalies between observed and estimated values of N_e/N discussed earlier (Dobson in preparation).

ECONOMICS, GENES, ECOLOGY AND CONSERVATION

All of the analyses discussed in this chapter suggest that the conservation and management of endangered species present a number of problems that require further interactions between ecologists and geneticists. In each of the four areas described earlier, more basic scientific information is required about the interactions between changes in population size and changes in levels of genetic heterozygosity. In particular, we need to know more about how human modification and reduction of natural habitats is likely to affect the persistence of increasingly fragmented populations and rates of gene flow between these populations. Consideration of human activities is crucial as most of the economic processes that encroach on natural populations and communities operate on a much faster time scale than the demographic and genetic events that determine the ability of any individual population to respond and adapt to changes in its natural environment.

Although captive breeding programmes have been developed for many endangered species, it is essential that some vestige of a truly natural habitat be available for the reintroduction to the wild that is the ultimate aim of these programmes. Although captive populations of some animals have been successfully reintroduced into the wild (Stanley-Price 1986), the costs of maintaining species in captivity are significant and there is a definite limit on space in zoos and conservation centres (Conway 1986). The costs of captive propagation are dependent upon the social system of the species; solitary, territorial species usually cost more than more gregarious species (Table 17.2). Plans for captive propagation and release will ultimately only be successful if they proceed in conjunction with projects that maintain the integrity of the species' natural habitat in the wild. Reintroduction will only be successful if the habitat is maintained so that the reintroduced individuals can use resources in a way that is

TABLE 17.2. Comparative annual upkeep of 11 species maintained at an effective population size (N_e) sufficient to sustain 90% of founder heterozygosity over 200 years. (After Conway 1986.)

Species	Generation time (years)	N_e	Annual upkeep (US$ × 10^4)
Siberian tiger *Panthera tigris altaica*	7	136	57.7
Indian rhinoceros *Rhinoceros unicornis*	18	53	44.4
Nyala *Tragelaphus angasi*	8	115	15.3
Striped grass mouse *Lemniscomys striatus*	0.75	1275	13.1
Brush-tailed betong *Bettongia penicillata*	6	159	9.0
Mauritius pink pigeon *Besoenas mayeri*	10	95	8.7
Arabian oryx *Oryx leucoryx*	10	95	7.8
African black-necked cobra *Naja nigricollis pallida*	10	95	6.3
Bullfrog *Rana catesbeiana*	7	136	4.0
White-naped crane *Grus vipio*	26	37	3.1
Caribbean flamingo *Phoenicopterus r. ruber*	26	37	1.1

beneficial to themselves and not excessively detrimental to the structure of the community (Lyles & May 1988).

The importance of social systems in determining both demographic and genetic effects is still an area that requires intensive collaborative studies if realistic species survival plans are to be assembled for endangered species. A better understanding is required of the role of social systems in determining both the size of populations where inbreeding effects become important and the interaction of this with deterministic and stochastic mechanisms which may cause populations to collapse to extinction.

All of the work we have discussed here requires more interactions between ecologists and geneticists. It seems unlikely that these collaborations will come to fruition unless more imaginative funding is available for interdisciplinary projects from research foundations. The predetermined scepticism of geneticists towards ecology, and vice versa, will have to be discounted by 'research boards' reviewing grants for interdisciplinary projects. Most major breakthroughs in science have come from hybrid projects that seek to cross-fertilize ideas from different disciplines. The conservation of the world's natural plant and animal resources requires fertile interactions not only between ecologists and geneticists, but also with economists, and even sociologists and politicians. If the ecologists and geneticists continue to have difficulties in communicating, there is little hope for the discussions between all of these groups that are required to provide viable means of managing natural populations of endangered species.

ACKNOWLEDGEMENTS

A.P.D. was supported by Princeton University and Wildlife Conservation International, G.M.M. was supported by the Pew Scholars Program in Conservation and the Environment. J.B. and R.A.B. were supported by Kenya Wildlife Service and R.A.B. also by the Zoological Society of London.

REFERENCES

Arnold, S. J. Monitoring qualitative genetic variation and evolution in captive populations. *Population Management for Survival and Recovery* (Ed. by J. Ballou, T. Foose & M. Gilpin). Chicago University Press, Chicago, IL, USA (in press).

Arnold, S. J. & Wade, M. (1984a). On the measurement of natural and sexual selection: theory. *Evolution*, **38**, 709–719.

Arnold, S. J. & Wade, M. (1984b). On the measurement of natural and sexual selection: applications. *Evolution*, **38**, 720–734.

Ballou J. D. Diagnostic methods for identification of genetically important individuals and groups. *Population Management for Survival and Recovery* (Ed. by J. Ballou, T. Foose & M. Gilpin). Chicago University Press, Chicago, IL, USA (in press).

Ballou, J. D. & Ralls, K. (1982). Inbreeding and juvenile mortality in small populations of ungulates: a detailed analysis. *Biological Conservation*, **24**, 239–272.

Barbier, E. B., Burgess, J. C., Swanson, T. M. & Pearce, D. W. (1990). *Elephants, Economics and Ivory*. Earthscan, London, UK.

Basson, M., Beddington, J. R. & May, R. M. (1991). An assessment of the maximum sustainable yield of ivory from African elephant populations. *Mathematical Biosciences* (in press).

Brett, R. A. (1990). The black rhino sanctuaries of Kenya. *Pachyderm*, **13**, 31–34.

Briscoe, D. A., Malpica, J. M., Robertson, A., Smith, G. J., Frankham, R., Banks, R. G. & Barker, J. S. F. Rapid loss of genetic variation in large captive populations of *Drosophila* flies. *Conservation Biology* (in press).

Carroll, J. B. & Mace, G. M. (1988). Population management of the Rodrigues fruit bat (*Pteropus rodricensis*) in captivity. *International Zoo Yearbook*, **27**, 70–78.

Caughley, G., Dublin, H. & Parker, I. (1990). Projected decline of the African elephant. *Biological Conservation*, **54**, 157–164.

Clark, C. W. (1976). *Mathematical Bioeconomics: The Optimal Management of Renewable Resources*. Wiley, New York, NY, USA.

Clutton-Brock, T. H. (1988a). Reproductive success. *Reproductive Success* (Ed. by T. H. Clutton-Brock), pp. 472–485. Chicago University Press, Chicago, IL, USA.

Clutton-Brock, T. H. (Ed.) (1988b). *Reproductive Success*. Chicago University Press, Chicago, IL, USA.

Conway, W. G. (1986). The practical difficulties and financial implications of endangered species breeding programs. *International Zoo Yearbook*, **24/25**, 210–219.

de Boer, L. E. M. (1982). Karyological problems in breeding owl monkeys. *International Zoo Yearbook*, **22**, 119–124.

Dobson, A. P. & Lyles, A. M. (1989). The population dynamics and conservation of primate populations. *Conservation Biology*, **3**, 362–380.

Douglas-Hamilton, I. (1987). African elephant population trends and their causes. *Oryx*, **21**, 11–34.

Eltringham, S. K. (1982). *Elephants*. Blandford Press, Poole, Dorset, UK.

Falconer, D. S. (1981). *Introduction to Quantitative Genetics* (2nd edn). Longman, New York, NY, USA.

Foose, T. J. & Ballou, J. D. (1988). Management of small populations. *International Zoo Yearbook*, **27**, 26–41.

Flesness, N. R. & Mace, G. M. (1988). Population databases and zoological conservation. *International Zoo Yearbook*, **27**, 42–49.

Greig, J. C. (1979). Principles of genetic conservation in relation to wildlife management in Southern Africa. *South African Journal of Wildlife Research*, **9**, 57–78.

Hall-Martin, A. (1980). Elephant survivors. *Oryx*, **15**, 355–362.

Harris, R. B. & Allendorf, F. W. (1989). Genetically effective population sizes of large mammals: an assessment of estimators. *Conservation Biology*, **3**, 181–191.

Harris, R. B., Metzgar, L. H. & Bevins, C. D. (1986). *GAPPS – Generalized Animal Population Projection System*. Montana Cooperative Wildlife Research Unit, Montana, Missoula, USA.

IUCN (1990). *1990 IUCN Red List of Threatened Animals*. IUCN, Gland, Switzerland.

Jeffreys, A. J., Wilson, V. & Thein, S. L. (1985). Hypervariable minisatellite regions in human DNA. *Nature*, **316**, 76–80.

Jolly, A. (1985). *The Evolution of Primate Behaviour* (2nd edn). Macmillan, New York, NY, USA.

Lacy, R. C. (1989). Analysis of founder representation in pedigrees: founder equivalents and founder genome equivalents. *Zoo Biology*, **8**, 111–123.

Lande, R. & Barrowclough, G. F. (1987). Effective population size, genetic variation and their use in population management. *Viable Populations for Conservation* (Ed. by M. E. Soulé), pp. 87–124. Cambridge University Press, Cambridge, UK.

Laws, R. M. (1969). Aspects of reproduction in the African elephant, *Loxodonta africana*. *Journal of Reproduction and Fertility* (Supplement 6), 193–217.

Ledig, F. T. (1986). Heterozygosity, heterosis and fitness in outbreeding plants. *Conservation Biology: The Science of Scarcity and Diversity* (Ed. by M. E. Soulé), pp. 77–104. Sinauer, Sunderland, MA, USA.

Lyles, A. M. & May, R. M. (1988). Problems in leaving the ark. *Nature*, **326**, 245–246.

Lynch, M. (1990). The similarity index and DNA fingerprinting. *Molecular Biology and Evolution*, **7**, 478–484.

Mace, G. M. (1986). Genetic management of small populations. *International Zoo Yearbook*, **24/25**, 167–174.

Mace, G. M. & Lande, R. (1991). Assessing extinction threats: towards a re-evaluation of IUCN threatened species categories. *Conservation Biology*, **5**, 148–137.

MacLuer, J. W., VandeBerg, J. L., Read, B. & Ryder, O. A. (1986). Pedigree analysis by computer simulation. *Zoo Biology*, **5**, 147–160.

May, R. M. (1977). Togetherness among schistosomes: its effects on the dynamics of the infection. *Mathematical Biosciences*, **35**, 301–343.

Milner-Guillard, E. J. & Mace, R. (1991). The impact of the ivory trade on the african elephant (*Loxodonta africana*) population as assessed by data from the trade. *Biological Conservation* **55**, 215–229.

Mittermeier, R. A., Oates, J. F., Eudey, A. E. & Thornback, J. (1986). Primate conservation. *Comparative Primate Biology*, Vol. 2 (Ed. by G. Mitchell & J. Erwin), pp. 3–72. Alan R. Liss, New York, NY, USA.

Nunney, L. (1991). The influence of age structure and fecundity on effective population size. *Proceedings of the Royal Society, London*, B, **246**, 71–76.

Olney, P. J. (1980). Report on the international symposium on the use and practice of wild animal studbooks. *International Zoo Yearbook*, **20**, 485–490.

Olney, P. J. & Ellis, P. (1990). *International Zoo Yearbook* Vol. 30. Zoological Society of London, London.

Packer, C., Herbst, L., Pusey, A. E., Bygott, J. D., Hanby, J. P., Cairns, S. J. & Mulaer, M. B. (1988). Reproductive success of lions. *Reproductive Success* (Ed. by T. H. Clutton-Brock), pp. 363–383. University of Chicago Press, Chicago, IL, USA.

Poole, J. H. & Thomsen, J. B. (1989). Elephants are not beetles: implications of the ivory trade for the survival of the African elephant. *Oryx*, **23**, 188–198.

Ralls, K. & Ballou, J. (1983). Extinction: Lessons from zoos. *Genetics and Conservation: a Reference for Managing Wild Animal and Plant Populations* (Ed. by C. Schonewald-Cox, S. M. Chambers, B. MacBryde and L. Thomas). Benjamin Cummings, Menlo Park, CA, USA.

Ralls, K., Ballou, J. D. & Templeton, A. (1988). Estimates of lethal equivalents and the cost of inbreeding in mammals. *Conservation Biology*, **2**, 185–193.

Ralls, K., Brugger, K. & Ballou, J. (1979). Inbreeding and juvenile mortality in small populations of ungulates. *Science*, **206**, 1101–1103.

Ralls, K., Harvey, P. H. & Lyles, A. M. (1986). Inbreeding in natural populations of birds and mammals. *Conservation Biology: The Science of Scarcity and Diversity* (Ed. by M. E. Soulé), pp. 35–56. Sinauer, Sunderland, MA, USA.

Soulé, M. E., Gilpin, M., Conway, W. & Foose, T. (1986). The millenium ark: how long the voyage, how many staterooms, how many passengers? *Zoo Biology*, **5**, 101–113.

Stanley-Price, M. R. (1989). *Animal Reintroductions: The Arabian Oryx in Oman*. Cambridge

University Press, Cambridge, UK.

Sukumar, R. J. (1990). *The Asian Elephant: Ecology and Management*. Cambridge University Press, Cambridge, UK.

Templeton, A. R. (1986). Coadaptation and outbreeding depression. *Conservation Biology: The Science of Scarcity and Diversity* (Ed. by M. E. Soulé), pp. 105–116. Sinauer, Sunderland, MA, USA.

Templeton, A. R. & Read, B. (1983). The elimination of inbreeding depression in a captive herd of Speke's gazelle. *Genetics and Conservation: A Reference for Managing Wild Animal and Plant Populations* (Ed. by C. M. Schonewald-Cox, S. M. Chambers, F. MacBryde & L. Thomas), pp. 241–261. Benjamin/Cummings, Menlo Park, CA, USA.

Templeton, A. R., Hemmer, H., Mace, G., Shields, W. M. & Woodruff, D. S. (1986). Coadapted gene complexes and population boundaries. *Zoo Biology*, **5**, 115–126.

Tomlinson, C., Mace, G. M., Black, J. M., & Hewston, N. (1991). Improving the management of a highly inbred species: the case of the white-winged wood duck (*Cairina scutulata*) in captivity. *Wildfowl*, **42**, 123–133.

Walters, C. (1989). *Adaptive Management of Renewable Resources*. Macmillan, New York, NY, USA.

18. GENES IN THE REAL WORLD

R. J. BERRY* AND A. D. BRADSHAW[†]
*Department of Biology, University College London, London WC1E 6BT, UK and [†]Department of Environmental and Evolutionary Biology, University of Liverpool, P.O. Box 147, Liverpool L69 3BX, UK

INTRODUCTION

Ecology and genetics have always been uneasy bedfellows, despite their intrinsic complementarity; genetics is about what exists, ecology is about how it exists. Darwin was uncomfortably aware of the need for a physical basis to variation, and the discoveries of genetics in the years following 1900 provided this (Fisher 1954). But the biometrical–Mendelist disputes of the 1900s, the geneticist–palaeontological debates of the 1920s and 1930s, and the neutralist controversies of the 1970s and 1980s have repeatedly forced the disciplines apart (Provine 1971, Mayr & Provine 1980). The chapters in this volume have explored the current situation, in particular the contribution that genetics can (and should) make to ecology and vice versa. In this concluding chapter, we seek lessons from the past and pointers for the future. Our conviction is that any understanding of the 'real world' will be incomplete and potentially distorted unless it is based on all relevant factors, and not merely those tractable to particular viewpoints.

LEARNING FROM MISTAKES

Ecology lacks an agreed theoretical core and is therefore easily destabilized and subject to intellectual fashion. At times it's development has been driven by deterministic models, ecosystem studies, energetics, physiological understanding and others (Berry 1989a); ecologists tend to carry personal prejudices from their own experiences, with the additional complication that 'very general events are only seen by ecologists with rather blurred vision. The very sharp-sighted always find discrepancies and are able to say that there is no generality, only a spectrum of special cases' (MacArthur 1968).

It would be presumptuous (and reminiscent of past mistakes) to claim we have identified *the* key to ecology but we are impressed by the number of times that deterministic models tested (or often not) under simplified conditions, have confused their users.

For example, the distribution of the melanic form (*edda*) of the autumnal rustic moth (*Paradiarsia (Amathes) glareosa*) in Shetland can be 'explained' by a model of a cline devised by J.B.S. Haldane (1948) (Kettlewell & Berry 1961, Slatkin 1973). This use of a model was heavily criticized by E.B. Ford (1964) on the grounds that it involved over-simplification of both theory and fact; Ford believed 'no valid conclusions can be drawn from Haldane's model of a cline'. However, Wallace (1968), in evaluating the significance of ecological genetics models quotes Ford's comment and then goes on, 'without some sort of theoretical model, one has no basis for assuming that a second analysis of the same material would agree with the first. Nor would one know on what basis to compare the observations in Shetland with those made in other localities, nor the *edda* cline with clines of other sorts. Actually, without a model, it is *unimportant* what happened to *edda* on Shetland where Kettlewell made his studies; this fine work takes on meaning only in relation to other studies and from the generalizations which emerge from them. It has no meaning standing in splendid isolation'. This is true when the context and reason for studying melanic moths in Shetland is considered, but Ford was almost certainly correct in his rejection of the model's validity, albeit for the wrong reasons. Further field studies showed that the moth exists in a mosaic of different populations in Shetland, and it was certainly inappropriate to apply to it a model involving general gene flow (Berry & Johnston 1980).

In higher plants, where the organisms sit still (apart from vegetative spread) and only gametes and seeds move, there is perhaps more regularity which is capable of being modelled (e.g. Jain & Bradshaw 1966). Nevertheless, discrepancies between models and actuality appear here also (May *et al.* 1975), almost certainly because of a failure to appreciate the effects of density and population compactness in reducing gene flow (Gleaves 1973).

P. glareosa in Shetland is divided in a way unsuspected from normal perceptions of a strongly flying insect. The opposite situation occurs in mammals, where many species are divided into defended territories, but where models showing the genetic consequences of population subdivision have been equally misleading. Such models have been derived from both behavioural and genetical studies, and at one time achieved considerable acceptance. Klein (1975) reviewed more than 40 published studies of house mice (*Mus domesticus*) and concluded, 'These studies reveal that the mouse population is divided into small subpopulations or *demes* (breeding units, family units, tribes, colonies)...occupying no larger than a few square meters.... An average deme consists of 7–12 adult mice'.

De Fries & McClearn (1972) judged likewise, 'It is quite conceivable that the effective population size in natural populations is less than four.... With such a small effective population size, random drift would be an important factor in determining allelic frequencies in local populations'.

However, these deductions are too restrictive. Although mice certainly live in defended territories, a degree of population churning takes place, particularly as animals die and are replaced, and many mouse populations can be treated as random mating ones, with relatively large effective breeding groups (Berry 1986). Identical considerations apply to plants: the leptokurtic distribution of pollen means that populations can behave either as isolates, particularly when natural selection is acting against the influx of unwanted genes (Jain & Bradshaw 1966), or connected to each other when genes are being favoured by selection. The isolation can operate over distances of a few metres, as with population differentiation at mine boundaries (Antonovics & Bradshaw 1970); the connection can extend over distances of many kilometres, as with the spread of tolerance genes away from an area of metal contamination (Bradshaw 1971).

There are many comparable examples in the key ecological topics reviewed in Cherrett (1989). The problem is not the use of models, but over-reliance on deductions from them. It is often difficult to test ecological ideas adequately in the field, and both ecologists and geneticists retain misapprehensions about the applicability of ideas in both their own and the others' discipline. This is particularly true when applying genetical ideas (founded on a firm physical base) to field situations. A good example of this is the notion of 'genetic load': no one doubts that mutations repeatedly occurring in all organisms and that most of these reduce fitness to some extent. But there is no good evidence for genetic load detriment in natural populations (Brues 1969, Berry 1982). Likewise many workers warn of the dangers of genetic drift in producing non-adaptive change. However, there are very few examples of genetical changes produced by drift outside the laboratory (with the exception of the special case of founder effects) (Berry 1992). As A.J. Cain (1977) has written, 'the golden rule is always to ask questions of the animals, not of the pundits'. Our only addition to this is a preparedness to quiz plants as well as animals.

Another category of a persisting mistake is the temptation to regard natural selection (or adaptation) as a perfecting agent. It is not: it is a wholly pragmatic response; Darwin (1859) himself recognized this (Chapter VI of the *Origin of Species*). Integration at the individual, population and ecosystem level which so impressed such pre-Darwinian observers as John Ray and William Paley ought to be seen as adjustment to effective functioning, not as the outworking of an inexorable coevolutionary principle. For example, succession has occupied an inordinate amount of ecologists' time, yet it is no more than the response of communities to invadability produced by change in the communities themselves. The interesting biological question is why some species fail to survive, not what are the general principles of succession. Indeed, succession can be more sensibly interpreted simply as a general case of island biogeography, than as an example of a wholly illusory balance or equilibrium in nature (Elton 1949, Connell 1979, Hengeveld 1989).

LEARNING FROM HISTORY

Many evolutionary debates are recurrences of earlier ones. For example, the neutralism debate of the 1970s had close parallels to the controversy sparked by the saltationist ideas of Hugo De Vries almost a century ago; Hoyle's doubts about evolutionary probability were dealt with by Darwin in the *Origin* (Fisher 1954, Huxley 1983); palaeontological 'punctuations' are little more than examples of changes in evolutionary rates, discussed by Simpson (1944) and Mayr (1954) — and by Darwin in the *Origin*; and so on. Unfortunately, ecologists are as reticent to learn from history as are evolutionary biologists.

Numerous ecologists have urged their colleagues to think evolutionarily (e.g. Orians 1962, Harper 1967) but there is still a tendency to regard 'evolutionary ecology' as a distinct branch of ecology, somehow separate from 'pure' ecology. In fact ecology, like evolutionary biology, is a synthesis of disciplines. The genius of Darwin and Wallace was to bring together the concepts of a 'struggle for existence' (as basic an ecological idea as any) and variation (to whose understanding, genetics can particularly contribute). The tragedy is, in Harper's (1967) words, 'ecology has abandoned evolution to genetics'. Our contention is that ecology will only mature when it brings together all relevant disciplines — extinction with colonization, life history variation with life tables, population numbers with population 'quality' (Birch 1960), energetics with ecosystem integrity, individual performance with genotype potential (Lomnicki 1988), and so on.

It is here we can learn from the travails of evolutionary biology. Evolutionary mechanisms have almost always been challenged when viewed from a specialist viewpoint (by geneticists and embryologists in the first decades of the century; palaeontologists and biogeographers in the 1920s; theoreticians in the 1950s; biochemists in the 1960s; systematists in the 1970s), and the challenge has faded when the insights of the disciplines concerned have been integrated (or usually, re-integrated) into the corpus of overall biological knowledge.

The most informative episode in the history of evolutionary biology was the establishment of the 'neo-Darwinian synthesis'. The key factor was a re-interpretation of the nature of inherited variation by the geneticists themselves (Yule 1907, Fisher 1922, 1928), with the end result that Darwin's original synthesizing glue adhered again 'not by one side being proved right and the others wrong, but by an exchange of the most viable components of the previously competing research traditions' (Mayr 1980). The significant movers in the synthesis were scientists like R.A. Fisher who transferred ideas from one discipline to another, iconoclasts like Cyril Darlington and G.G. Simpson who broke the boundaries of traditional subject areas, and individuals like Julian Huxley who moved between research groups. And as an indication of the importance of mutual comprehension in this process it is worth quoting Fisher (1932) when presenting his ideas to a general audience of biologists, 'As I am a mathematician by trade perhaps I should explain that I shall use no mathematics, partly because I recognize that the first duty of a mathematician, rather like that of a lion tamer, is to keep his mathematics in their place, but chiefly because I think that mathematics, though well fitted to elucidate points of special intricacy, are after all only a special means of carrying out reasoning processes common to all scientific work...'.

Our contention is that ecology needs its own 'synthesis'. We are encouraged in this belief by McIntosh's (1985) conclusion in his masterly history of ecology, that key experiments or breakthroughs are rarely identifiable, and 'many of the key figures of ecology are recognised primarily for bringing together and ordering disparate aspects of the works of others'.

An example of the sort of problem to be overcome in forging an ecological synthesis is that ecologists have traditionally assumed that phenotypes remain constant in the time span they are concerned with, while geneticists have tended to assume that fitnesses are virtually constant (Clarke & Beaumont, Ch. 14, this volume). True, genetical (evolutionary) models have become more realistic, and now treat fitness as capable of varying in time and space (shown so clearly by Allard *et al.* 1966, as well as with allele frequency and population density, q.v. Endler, Ch. 12, this volume). Such models are both ecological and genetical and therefore intrinsically better than ones concerned exclusively with genetical or ecological variables. However, their analysis has tended to depend on an assumption that population density changes more rapidly than allele frequency, and hence that, densities are at equilibrium values for the contemporary values of the allele frequencies (Slatkin & Maynard Smith 1979). In other words, they are based on equilibria which probably do not exist (or only transitorily).

This is bad enough, but the search for order through coevolutionary models may be misplaced (Berry 1985). Time after time, coevolutionary relationships disappear on close examination. Host–parasite interaction is a classical case. There is no doubt that hosts and parasites adjust to each other in a rapid and precise manner but this is probably no more than hosts and parasites responding independently to separate selection pressures. May and Anderson (1983) have reviewed the evidence for the myth of a perfect parasite, harmless to its host. They argue that the relationship between parasite and the host follows no fixed path but depends on the cost to the host of evolving resistance. They quote data on the myxoma virus, which has apparently stabilized at an intermediate level of virulence in both Britain and Australia after beginning at a very high level.

The notion that parasitism evolves towards some ideal state of harmonious benevolence has received even shorter shrift from Rothschild and Clay (1952). After an extensive survey, they conclude, 'Parasitism can develop gradually or suddenly. It can be the outcome of complicated interactions or the result of isolated accidents which occurred a million years ago or only this morning.... There is only one vital factor in the genesis of a parasitic relationship, and that is opportunity'.

Mimicry is another classical example of ecological–genetical interaction where similar considerations apply (Berry 1981, Endler 1981). The clear lesson from the history of biological science as a whole and from consideration of particular cases of interdisciplinary interaction, is that assimilation and possibly reinterpretation of all relevant data are a better guide than dependence on increasingly complex models. As so often, we can do no better than follow Darwin (1876):

> I have no great quickness of apprehension or wit which is so remarkable in some clever men, for example, Huxley. I am therefore a poor critic; a paper when first read generally excites my admiration, and it is only after considerable reflection that I perceive the weak points.... On the positive side of the balance, I think I am superior to the common run of men in noticing things which easily escape attention, and in observing them carefully. My industry has been as great as it could have been in the observation and collection of facts.

VARIATION

There are undoubtedly lessons that we can learn from the past, but there is a major perceptual block that has to be overcome before genetics and ecology can properly integrate and ecology develop a general theory. Although they would doubtless recoil from the accusation, most ecologists tend to be practising typologists, neglecting variation except when it is convenient to do otherwise. All the plants and animals in a population are treated as effectively identical, or at best differentiated only by sex or age. There are, of course, many distinguished exceptions to this generalization (most notably the exploitation of polymorphism by Ford, Cain, Allard, Sheppard, Clarke and their colleagues, and the studies of quantitative variation carried out by Mather and Jinks, Robertson, Falconer and Hill) but the bulk of ecological studies wilfully ignores both individual and intraspecific variation, and consequently misses important interactions, both biotic and abiotic (although see Endler 1986, Lomnicki 1988).

The danger of this tunnel vision can be illustrated by examples from house mouse studies, trivial in themselves but indicative of processes that can be missed. Virtually all wild caught mice are superficially alike but almost all populations are polymorphic for two alleles at a locus controlling the β-chain of haemoglobin. On the small Welsh island of Skokholm, the frequency of heterozygotes increases during the summer breeding season and decreases during the winter survival phase (Berry *et al.* 1987); Petras & Topping (1983) calculated that the overall fitnesses of the two homozygotes were 0.49 and 0.24, compared with unity for the heterozygote (they quote similar fitnesses for experimental colonies they maintained in Ontario). Berry *et al.* (1979) found significant changes in allozyme frequencies during life in mice living in tussock grass on South Georgia, indicating differential death of particular genotypes. Such selective loss is relatively common (Bumpus 1899, Berry & Crothers 1968, Berry *et al.* 1978); the surprising fact in the South Georgia mice was that the change in frequencies was in opposite directions in the two sexes, indicating precise, rapid adaptation.

Another unexpected selective adjustment in house mice occurred in a population on the Isle of May, Firth of Forth, where the introduction of animals from Orkney into an existing population was followed by allele frequencies changing rapidly, and then stabilizing — but at levels different from those in both parental groups and in the population whence the introduced animals came (Berry *et al.* 1992). This stabilization indicates that there are factors affecting allele frequencies which are not merely historical. The factors are unknown but clearly important.

A different sort of example concerns laboratory investigations of aggression in house mice. This differs greatly between strains but one strain (C3H) always performs badly in fights with other strains. The reason for this is known (although the discovery was made much later than the original studies of fighting behaviour: Rodgers 1970); it is that C3H has defective vision, through homozygosity for an allele producing 'rodless retina'.

All these variations in mice do not change the appearance of the animals. A field ecologist would not distinguish between mice carrying the different alleles described, which affect a range of characteristics. But the fitness and viability of the animals concerned is greatly affected by the genes they carry, and the properties of the populations of which they are members will depend on the frequencies of the alleles therein. Measures of such population parameters as birth and death rates, longevity, turnover, etc., will vary according to hidden genetic factors as well as the extrinsic factors (food, climate, density, etc.) normally considered by ecologists. Life tables will reflect the genotypes present in particular populations, rather than strict species characteristics. Not surprisingly, 'replicate' experiments may produce very different outcomes unless genetic variation is controlled. For example, Southwick (1955) set up six apparent replicates of house mouse populations, beginning each with four pairs of assumedly identical mice. After 2 years, the numbers in each population had more or less stabilized but they varied from 25 to 140 in different cages. In each cage, the number of fights increased with population size, and numbers increased until aggression reached about one fight per mouse per hour, at which point reproduction ceased. Presumably the populations were initially heterogeneous for factors affecting aggressiveness.

House mice are among the more variable mammals on standard measures of heterozygosity, polymorphism, etc., but there is no reason to believe that they are exceptional in that their genes affect life history traits more than those of other mammals. The position is that *Mus domesticus* is one of the better known genetical species, and that similar genetical interactions with fitness traits must occur in other species; the inference is that as ecologists we neglect genetical variation to the detriment of our science.

We must however be careful not to be mesmerized by the subtleties of the variation which floats as polymorphism. The variation which becomes fixed in particular populations in response to individual selection pressures is almost certainly of greater importance. This is more obvious in plants than in animals, where populations of a single species occupying different habitats may be completely distinct in relation to certain genes or gene complexes (Clausen & Hiesey 1958). Transplant experiments, such as those originally pioneered by Clausen *et al.* (1948), show that such differences in genetic make-up are not trivial but critical to the survival of the species in particular habitats.

It was commonly inferred from earlier work, for example that of Turesson (1925), that the main interest of such genetic differentiation lay in the way it showed that the characteristics of a species could be influenced by the environment. Now we can appreciate its 'permissive' nature. Without such evolutionary differentiation many species would be excluded from many environments and have a much reduced distribution (Bradshaw 1991).

At the same time such evolutionary differentiation throws grave doubts on the wisdom of assuming that the characteristics of a species are revealed by a single population. As further work is carried out in plant populations, such as recent work on pasture grasses in British Columbia, it becomes increasingly clear that 'ecological theories based upon the performance of . . . species attributes must take into account experimental conditions, the variability of species and the dynamic nature of those species' (Mehrhoff & Turkington 1990).

A legitimate claim is that T.H. Huxley was a major despoiler of biology through his introduction of teaching through 'types' (earthworm, dogfish, frog and rabbit), distracting attention from the enormous variety of nature. In contrast, Carl Pantin (1968) argued that variation is such a major element in all biological situations that it is scientifically culpable to eschew it. He believed that 'physics and chemistry have been able to become exact and mature just because so much of the wealth of natural phenomena is excluded from their study'. He called physics and chemistry 'restricted', in distinction to biology (and geology) which is 'unrestricted'. He wrote, 'Men of science devoted to these fields must be prepared to follow the analysis of their problems into every other kind of science'. And as far as ecology is concerned, this means that we are brought back to the point we made earlier, that ecology should be treated as a synthesizing discipline, joining with genetics, microbiology, physiology, chemistry and other sciences; a pure ecologist is likely to be a poor ecologist.

ECOLOGICAL AND EVOLUTIONARY CONSTRAINTS

There is a paradox to variation which may go some way to excusing its neglect by ecologists: although electrophoretic studies have shown it to be almost omnipresent and although conventional wisdom is that adaptation is not limited by lack of variation (at least in the longer term), the fact is that populations continually fail and become extinct through the absence of appropriate variation (Bradshaw 1991). The conventional explanation is that relevant variations will sooner or later appear and be available for selection. For example, more than 200 species of trunk-sitting Lepidoptera in Britain have acquired melanic forms in polluted areas (Kettlewell 1973), and in some cases the spread of the new form has been traced from a single locality (e.g. Steward 1977). Notwithstanding, melanics may take some time to arise. *Mesoligia (Procus) literosa* was extinct in the Sheffield area for many years, and only reappeared (and spread) about 1940, albeit in a melanic rather than the non-cryptic typical form (Kettlewell 1973).

However, there are unexplained anomalies in the occurrence of variation: for example, insecticide resistance is common in many insects but has never appeared in tsetse flies, despite exposure over years to a range of poisons. More striking is the extremely common phenomenon of unexplained limits to species ranges. Some limits can be accounted for by a physical barrier or replacement by a similar form but it is not obvious why other species have not extended their range (Fig. 18.1). The common finding of 'selection limits' in plant and animal breeding can explain a temporary restriction to spread into a harsh environment but not why such a restriction may persist over periods long enough for new variation to be produced by recombination or mutation.

It is commonly taken for granted that species must have limits to their capabilities, and that it is not surprising that one species can occupy a habitat while another does not. Yet, as in the case of metal-contaminated habitats, often no reason can be seen for this, and it has to be inferred that it is an absence of the appropriate variability (providing tolerance) which is a real constraint to adaptive evolution. For copper tolerance there is good evidence that this is the case (Bradshaw 1984). The part played by the presence or absence of genetic variability in determining evolutionary pathways and the resulting situations which are analysed by ecologists has hardly been examined (Bradshaw 1991). Genes have repeatedly turned out to be the ultimate constraint.

GENE ACTION AND INTERACTION

Explanations based on mechanisms are both more convincing and more satisfactory than those based on correlation. Continental drift was posited by biogeographers many years before the discovery of tectonic plates and their movement made it widely accepted. Few people believed that bird predation could explain the distribution of *Biston betularia* melanics until

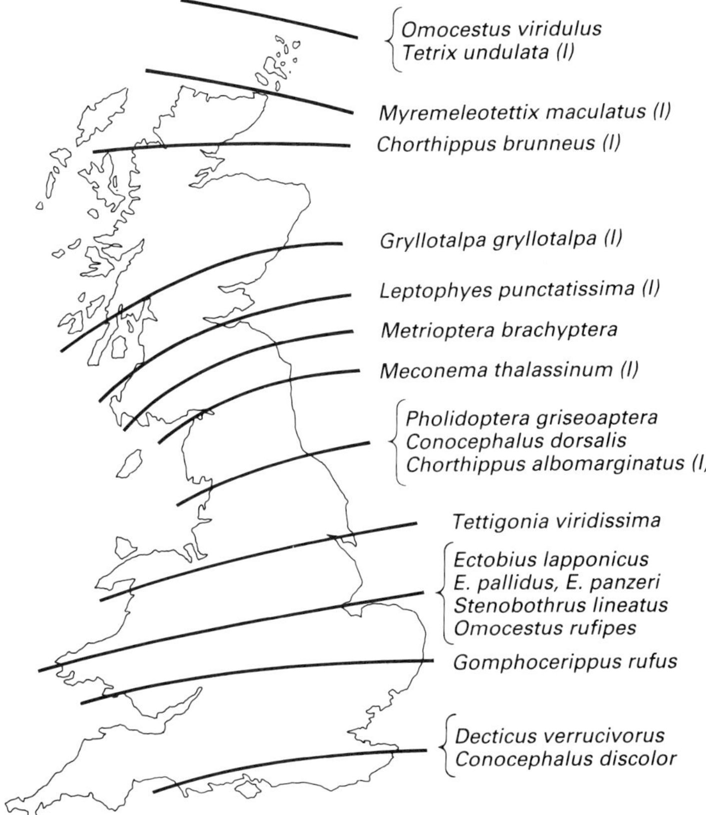

Fig. 18.1. Approximate northern limits of some British grasshopper species. 'I' indicates species recorded in Ireland. Note that such species are the most northerly and presumably hardier ones, which entered Britain from Continental Europe first, and presumably colonized Ireland before the land-bridge between Britain and Ireland was broken (from Berry 1977, after Ragge 1963).

Kettlewell and Tinbergen filmed it happening (Berry 1990). One of the catalysts for the neo-Darwinian synthesis was the disentangling of the effects of single allele substitutions from general genetic determinants; one of the failures of electrophoretic examination of population samples has been the inability to link biological properties to individual loci (although correlative and biochemical properties have been identified: Bryant 1974, Harris 1974, Clarke 1979). With new tools for dissecting the genome it should be possible to associate gene action with biological properties.

Two research directions need emphasis:

Genetic architecture produced by the linkage of genes on chromosomes and the need to maintain biochemically complementary mechanisms means that developmentally essential gene combinations will be protected. This is important for considerations about genetic conservation because it will retard gene erosion (Berry 1971) but it has been largely neglected (e.g. Lande 1988; although see Templeton 1986); virtually all discussions have been conducted on the straighforward probabilistic axioms of 'bean-bag genetics' (Haldane 1964). The most likely reason for this has been the lack of strong evidence for gene associations in wild populations, apart from a limited number of special cases of linkage disequilibria (such as the mammalian histocompatibility complex, incompatibility controls in flowering plants, mimicry patterns in butterflies, colour and shell banding in *Cepaea*) (e.g. Barton & Charlesworth 1984). However, failure to find evidence does not mean that genetic architecture is unimportant. Recent interest has concentrated on testing Mayr's (1954) hypothesis of 'genetic revolutions', which is only a particular case of genetic architecture; memories of the early work of Mather (1943, 1974), Clausen & Hiesey (1958), Thoday (1961), and others have been displaced by later observations (or the lack of them) on allozyme associations. We must not forget that species are determined by gene associations rather than genes per se, and that theoretical considerations indicate that complex traits are likely to be controlled by many loci, with selection favouring the formation of 'balanced' chromosomes with positive and negative alleles intermingled. Experimental results (mainly from selection experiments in *Drosophila*) confirm this expectation (Bodmer & Parsons 1962). For example, about one in six of the 1300 identified gene loci in house mice can be regarded as affecting behaviour, and they are distributed over 19 out of the 20 chromosomes in the species (Berry 1989b).

Stress. The second neglected topic in evolutionary ecology is stress, possibly because of disputes over its correct use (Calow & Berry 1989). A useful working definition for ecologists is that stress 'is any environmental influence that impairs the structure and functioning of organisms such that their neo-Darwinian fitness is reduced' (Calow 1989). This incorporates survival probability, developmental rate and fecundity, and hence links responses at the level of individuals to parameters that influence the density of their populations and their future contribution to the gene pool.

The advantage of this definition is that it invites tests in a variety of situations (e.g. Parsons 1989). A particular topic of interest for conservation biology is the link between genetic variation and life history traits (Allendorf & Leary 1986). The most intensive investigations on this have been carried out by Koehn, Bayne and their collaborators on the physiological responses of marine molluscs with different genotypes to varying temperature and food stresses. They have shown that the association found for various traits between heterozygosity and growth (or productivity) is between particular phenotypes, rather than heterozygosity per se, with homozygous individuals liable to suffer more than more heterozygous ones from a negative energy balance in environments that deviate from the optimum for the phenotype concerned (Koehn & Bayne 1989, Koehn 1991).

Again we must not be seduced by polymorphisms. There is very good evidence that genes and gene systems with major effects have the major part to play in providing adaptation to stress. These can become fixed in different populations and species to provide radically different responses. In both plants and animals the adaptation can be either facultative or constitutive. The facultative responses may have great elegance, tailored by selection to the nature of the environmental stresses involved (Bradshaw & Hardwick 1989). Indeed the variety of responses, such as that of plants to light quality and quantity, show the remarkable diversity of genes which must be available. Response to stress is not just an incidental outcome of other adaptation but a character which can be finely tuned in its own right.

The importance of an adequate concept of stress is that it provides a framework for recognizing the dynamic complex of interactions between phenotype and environment (Parker & Maynard Smith 1990). Survival is a property of these interactions, not of either phenotype or environment alone (Fig. 18.2); the same genotype will respond differently to a range of conditions through life, and different genotypes will respond differently to a particular environmental stress (Berry *et al.* 1973). For example, Sikes (1968) found a high incidence of arterial disease in African elephants living at high densities or in disturbed habitats but virtually none in low-density populations in their natural habitat. Clearly harsh environmental pressures cause problems for living organisms but to evaluate these problems we need to study organism–environment interactions (or levels of stress) and not merely extrapolate from a knowledge of either genetics or environment.

SCIENTIFIC NATURAL HISTORY

Although Haeckel (deriver of the name 'ecology') regarded the subject as simply a branch of physiology, ecology in Britain from Darwin through

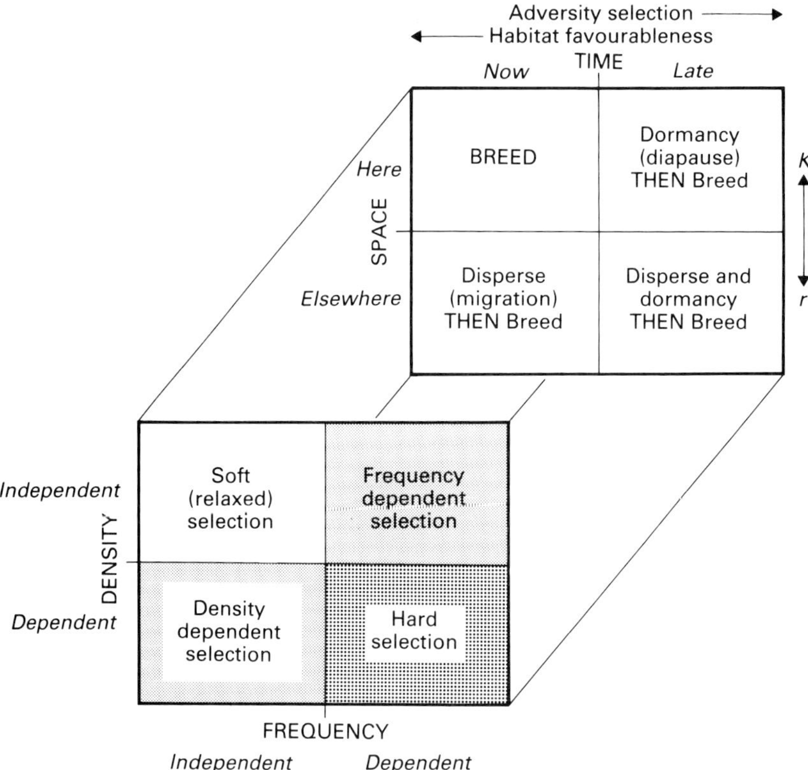

FIG. 18.2. Wallace's (1975) classification of selection and Southwood's (1977, 1988) habitat templet complement each other, putting the adaptive adjustability of genetical constitution alongside environmental heterogeneity and introducing the variable stresses experienced by organisms. The links between the two models are not causal: although allele frequencies are commonly regarded as changing with time and density with space, frequency may change in space (clinally) and density with time (through recruitment and/or mortality), i.e. selection modes interact with each other and with the environment. From Berry (1992).

William Smith, Tansley, Elton, Ford, Tinbergen and Sheppard (and Ray, Gosse and many others before them) has been based on scientific natural history — subjecting the whole range of natural phenomena to analysis and experiment. It has often lapsed into uncritical nature study (Tansley 1951, bemoaned the fact that 'ecology has a great attraction for weaker students.... A good many papers published during the first years of the century were rather trivial and some of them decidedly slovenly') or blinkered reductionism. [We should distinguish between operational reductionism necessary in all science, and ontological reduction which assumes that any science can be accounted for wholly by the properties of its components, and ignores emergent properties and variation (Ayala 1974).] Ecological problems have to take into account all relevant data, recognizing that nature is cruel and that in the real world, genes are subject to a range of pressures. Organisms are not simply vehicles for gene expression but are the outcome of complex interactions and opportunities in time and space. Ecology and genetics are complements, not alternatives. Only when we accept the need for an ecological synthesis will our subject come of age.

Charles Darwin is buried in Westminster Abbey. The organist at the time, F.W. Bridge, composed an anthem for the occasion, with words taken from the book of Proverbs (3 : 13, 15–17) 'Happy is the man that findeth wisdom and getteth understanding'. Whether or not Darwin died happy, we do not know. But we have no doubts at all that a proper understanding of genes in the real world depends on a wisdom based on studying genes and ecology together, and not merely accumulating data about either on their own. After all, organisms live in the real world.

REFERENCES

Allard, R. W., Harding, J. & Wehrhahn, C. (1966). The estimation and use of selective values in predicting population change. *Heredity*, **21**, 547–564.

Allendorf, F. W. & Leary, R. F. (1986). Heterozygosity and fitness in natural populations of animals. *Conservation Biology* (Ed. by M. E. Soulé), pp. 57–76. Sinauer, Sunderland, MA, USA.

Antonovics, J. & Bradshaw, A. D. (1970). Evolution in closely adjacent plant populations. VIII. Clinical patterns at a mine boundary. *Heredity*, **25**, 349–362.

Ayala, F. J. (1974). Introduction. *Studies in the Philosophy of Biology* (Ed. by F. J. Ayala & T. Dobzhansky), pp. vii–xvi. Macmillan, London, UK.

Barton, N. H. & Charlesworth, B. (1984). Genetic revolutions, founder effects and speciation. *Annual Review of Evolution and Systematics*, **15**, 133–164.

Berry, R. J. (1971). Conservation aspects of the genetical constitution of populations. *The Scientific Management of Animal and Plant Communities for Conservation* (Ed. by E. Duffey & A. S. Watt), pp. 177–206. Blackwell Scientific Publications, Oxford, UK.

Berry, R. J. (1977). *Inheritance and Natural History*. Collins New Naturalist, London, UK.

Berry, R. J. (1981). Mimicry 1981. *Biological Journal of the Linnean Society*, **16**, 1–3.

Berry, R. J. (1982). Atom bombs and genetic damage. *British Medical Journal*, **284**, 366–367.

Berry, R. J. (1985). The processes of pattern: genetical possibilities and constraints in coevolution. *Oikos*, **44**, 222–228.

Berry, R. J. (1986). Genetical processes in wild mouse populations. Past myth and present knowledge. *Current Topics in Microbiology and Immunology*, **127**, 86–94.

Berry, R. J. (1989a). Ecology: where genes and geography meet. *Journal of Animal Ecology*, **58**, 733–759.

Berry, R. J. (1989b). Genes, behaviour and fitness in mice: concepts and confusions. *House Mouse Aggression: a Model for Understanding the Evolution of Social Behaviour* (Ed.

by P. T. Brain, D. Mainardi & S. Parmigiani), pp. 23–48. Harwood Academic, Chur, Switzerland.

Berry, R. J. (1990). Industrial melanism and peppered moths (*Biston betularia* (L)). *Biological Journal of the Linnean Society*, **39**, 301–322.

Berry, R. J. (1992). The role of ecological genetics in biological conservation. *Conservation of Biodiversity for Sustainable Development* (Ed. by O. T. Sandlund, K. Hindar & A. H. D. Brown), pp. 107–123. Scandinavian University Press, Oslo, Norway.

Berry, R. J. & Crothers, J. H. (1968). Stabilizing selection in the Dog whelk (*Nucella lapillus*). *Journal of Zoology, London*, **155**, 5–17.

Berry, R. J. & Johnston, L. (1980). *The Natural History of Shetland*. Collins New Naturalist, London, UK.

Berry, R. J., Bonner, W. N. & Peters, J. (1979). Natural selection in mice from South Georgia (South Atlantic Ocean). *Journal of Zoology, London*, **189**, 385–398.

Berry, R. J., Jakobson, M. E. & Peters, J. (1987). Inherited differences within an island population of the House mouse (*Mus domesticus*). *Journal of Zoology, London*, **211**, 605–618.

Berry, R. J., Jakobson, M. E. & Triggs, G. S. (1973). Survival in wild-living mice. *Mammal Review*, **3**, 46–57.

Berry, R. J., Peters, J. & Van Aarde, R. J. (1978). Sub-antarctic House mice: colonization, survival and selection. *Journal of Zoology, London*, **184**, 127–141.

Berry, R. J., Triggs, G. S., King, P., Nash, H. R. & Noble, H. R. (1991). Hybridisation and gene flow in House mice introduced into an existing population. *Journal of Zoology, London*, **225**, 615–632.

Birch, L. C. (1960). The genetic factor in population ecology. *American Naturalist*, **94**, 5–24.

Bodmer, W. F. & Parsons, P. A. (1962). Linkage and recombination in evolution. *Advances in Genetics*, **11**, 1–100.

Bradshaw, A. D. (1971). Plant evolution in extreme environments. *Ecological Genetics and Evolution* (Ed. by R. Creed), pp. 20–50. Blackwell Scientific Publications, Oxford, UK.

Bradshaw, A. D. (1984). The importance of evolutionary ideas in ecology — and vice versa. *Evolutionary Ecology* (Ed. by B. Shorrocks), pp. 1–25. Blackwell Scientific Publications, Oxford, UK.

Bradshaw, A. D. (1991). Genostasis and the limits to evolution. *Proceedings of the Royal Society, London*, B, **333**, 289–305.

Bradshaw, A. D. & Hardwick, K. (1989). Evolution and stress — genotypic and phenotypic components. *Biological Journal of the Linnean Society*, **37**, 137–155.

Brues, A. M. (1969). Genetic load and its varieties. *Science*, **164**, 1130–1136.

Bryant, E. H. (1974). On the adaptive significance of enzyme polymorphisms in relation to environmental variability. *American Naturalist*, **108**, 1–19.

Bumpus, H. C. (1899). The elimination of the unfit as illustrated by the introduced sparrow, *Passer domesticus*. *Biological Lectures, Marine Biological Laboratory, Wood's Hole (1898)*, 209–226.

Cain, A. J. (1977). The efficacy of natural selection in wild populations. *Academy of Natural Sciences* (Special Publication No. 12), 111–133.

Calow, P. (1989). Proximate and ultimate responses to stress in biological systems. *Biological Journal of the Linnean Society*, **37**, 173–181.

Calow, P. & Berry, R. J. (Eds) (1989). *Evolution, Ecology and Environmental Stress*. Academic Press, London, UK.

Cherrett, J. M. (1989). Key concepts, the results of a survey of our members' opinions.

Ecological Concepts (Ed. by J. M. Cherrett), pp. 1–16. Blackwell Scientific Publications, Oxford, UK.

Clarke, B. C. (1979). The evolution of genetic diversity. *Proceedings of the Royal Society of London*, B, **205**, 453–474.

Clausen, J. & Hiesey, W. M. (1958). Experimental studies on the nature of species. IV. Genetic structure of ecological races. *Carnegie Institute of Washington*, No. 615, 312 pp.

Clausen, J., Keck, D. D. & Hiesey W. M. (1948). Experimental studies on the nature of species. III. Environmental responses of climatic races of *Achillea*. *Carnegie Institute of Washington*, No. 581, 129 pp.

Connell, J. H. (1979). Tropical rain forests and coral reefs as open non-equilibrium systems. *Population Dynamics* (Ed. by R. M. Anderson, L. R. Taylor & B. D. Turner), pp. 141–163. Blackwell Scientific Publications, Oxford, UK.

Darwin, C. (1859). *On the Origin of Species by Means of Natural Selection*. John Murray, London, UK.

Darwin, C. (1876). *Autobiography*, Oxford Paperback Edition (Ed. by G. R. De Beer, 1983). Oxford University Press, Oxford, UK.

De Fries, J. C. & McClearn, G. E. (1972). Behavioral genetics and the fine structure of mouse populations: a study in microevolution. *Evolutionary Biology*, **5**, 279–291.

Elton, C. S. (1949). Population interspersion: an essay on animal community patterns. *Journal of Ecology*, **37**, 1–23.

Endler, J. A. (1981). An overview of the relationships between mimicry and crypsis. *Biological Journal of the Linnean Society*, **16**, 25–31.

Endler, J. A. (1986). *Natural Selection in the Wild*. Princeton University Press, Princeton, NJ, USA.

Fisher, R. A. (1922). On the dominance ratio. *Proceedings of the Royal Society of Edinburgh*, **42**, 321–341.

Fisher, R. A. (1928). The possible modification of the response of the wild type to recurrent mutations. *American Naturalist*, **62**, 115–126.

Fisher, R. A. (1932). The evolutionary modification of genetic phenomena. *Proceedings of the VIth International Congress of Genetics*, **1**, 165–172.

Fisher, R. A. (1954). Retrospect of the criticisms of the theory of natural selection. *Evolution as a Process* (Ed. by J. Huxley, A. C. Hardy & E. B. Ford), pp. 84–98. Allen & Unwin, London, UK.

Ford, E. B. (1964). *Ecological Genetics*. Methuen, London, UK.

Gleaves, T. (1973). Gene flow mediated by wind-borne pollen. *Heredity*, **31**, 355–366.

Haldane, J. B. S. (1948). The theory of a cline. *Journal of Genetics*, **48**, 277–284.

Haldane, J. B. S. (1964). A defense of beanbag genetics. *Perspectives in Biology and Medicine*, **7**, 343–360.

Harper, J. L. (1967). A Darwinian approach to plant ecology. *Journal of Ecology*, **55**, 247–270.

Harris, H. (1974). Common and rare alleles. *Science Progress, Oxford*, **16**, 495–514.

Hengeveld, R. (1989). *Dynamics of Biological Invasions*. Chapman & Hall, London, UK.

Huxley, A. (1983). Anniversary address. *Proceedings of the Royal Society of London*, B, **217**, 117–128.

Jain, S. K. & Bradshaw, A. D. (1966). Evolutionary divergence in adjacent plant populations. I. The evidence and its theoretical analysis. *Heredity*, **21**, 407–441.

Kettlewell, H. B. D. (1973). *The Evolution of Melanism*. Clarendon Press, Oxford, UK.

Kettlewell, H. B. D. & Berry, R. J. (1961). The study of a cline. *Heredity*, **16**, 403–414.

Klein, J. (1975). *The Biology of the Mouse Histocompatibility Complex*. Springer Verlag, Berlin, Federal Republic of Germany.

Koehn, R. K. (1991). The cost of enzyme synthesis in the genetics of energy balance and physiological performance. *Biological Journal of the Linnean Society*, **44**, 231–247.

Koehn, R. K. & Bayne, B. L. (1989). Towards a physiological and genetical understanding of the energetics of the stress response. *Biological Journal of the Linnean Society*, **37**, 157–171.

Lande, R. (1988). Genetics and demography in biological conservation. *Science*, **241**, 1455–1459.

Lomnicki, A. (1988). *Population Ecology of Individuals*. Princeton University Press, Princeton, NJ, USA.

MacArthur, R. H. (1968). The theory of the niche. *Population Biology and Evolution* (Ed. by R. C. Lewontin), pp. 159–176. Syracuse University Press, New York, NY, USA.

Mather, K. (1943). Polygenic inheritance and natural selection. *Biological Reviews*, **18**, 32–64.

Mather, K. (1974). *Genetical Structure of Populations*. Chapman & Hall, London, UK.

May, R. M. & Anderson, R. M. (1983). Epidemiology and genetics in the coevolution of parasites and hosts. *Proceedings of the Royal Society of London*, B, **219**, 281–313.

May, R. M., Endler, J. A. & McMurtrie, R. E. (1975). Gene frequency clines in the presence of selection opposed by gene flow. *American Naturalist*, **109**, 659–676.

Mayr, E. (1954). Change of genetic environment and evolution. *Evolution as a Process* (Ed. by J. S. Huxley, A. C. Hardy & E. B. Ford), pp. 157–180. Allen & Unwin, London, UK.

Mayr, E. (1980). Some thoughts on the history of the evolutionary synthesis. *The Evolutionary Synthesis* (Ed. by E. Mayr & W. B. Provine), pp. 1–48. Harvard University Press, Cambridge, MA, USA.

Mayr, E. & Provine, W. B. (1980). *The Evolutionary Synthesis*. Harvard University Press, Cambridge, MA, USA.

McIntosh, R. P. (1985). *The Background of Ecology*. Cambridge University Press, Cambridge, UK.

Mehrhoff, L. A. & Turkington, R. (1990). Microevolution and site-specific outcomes of competition among pasture plants. *Journal of Ecology*, **78**, 745–756.

Orians, G. H. (1962). Natural selection and ecological theory. *American Naturalist*, **96**, 257–263.

Pantin, C. F. A. (1968). *Relations between the Sciences*. Cambridge University Press, Cambridge, UK.

Parker, G. A. & Maynard Smith, J. (1990). Optimality theory in evolutionary biology. *Nature, London*, **348**, 27–33.

Parsons, P. A. (1989). Environmental stresses and conservation of natural populations. *Annual Review of Ecology and Systematics*, **20**, 29–49.

Petras, M. L. & Topping, J. C. (1983). The maintenance of polymorphisms at two loci in house mouse (*Mus musculus*) populations. *Canadian Journal of Genetics and Cytology*, **25**, 190–201.

Provine, W. B. (1971). *The Origins of Theoretical Population Genetics*. Chicago University Press, Chicago, IL, USA.

Ragge, D. R. (1963). First record of the grasshopper *Stenobothrus stigmaticus* (Rambur) (Acrididae) in the British Isles, with other new distribution records and notes on the origin of the British Orthoptera. *Entomologist*, **96**, 211–217.

Rodgers, D. A. (1970). Mechanism-specific behavior: an experimental alternative. *Contributions to Behavior–Genetic Analysis. The Mouse as a Prototype* (Ed. by G. Lindzey & D. D. Thiessen), pp. 207–218. Appleton-Century-Crofts, New York, NY, USA.

Rothschild, M. & Clay, T. (1952). *Fleas, Flukes and Cuckoos*. Collins New Naturalist, London, UK.

Sikes, S. K. (1968). Observations on the ecology of arterial disease in the African elephant (*Loxodonta africana*) in Kenya and Uganda. *Symposia of the Zoological Society of London*, **21**, 251–269.

Simpson, G. G. (1944). *Tempo and Mode in Evolution*. Columbia University Press, New York, NY, USA (revised as *Major Features of Evolution*, 1953).

Slatkin, M. (1973). Gene flow and selection in a cline. *Genetics*, **75**, 733–756.

Slatkin, M. & Maynard Smith, J. (1979). Models of coevolution. *Quarterly Review of Biology*, **54**, 233–263.

Southwick, C. H. (1955). Regulatory mechanisms of house mouse populations: social behaviour affecting litter survival. *Ecology*, **36**, 627–634.

Southwood, T. R. E. (1977). Habitat, the templet for ecological strategies. *Journal of Animal Ecology*, **46**, 337–365.

Southwood, T. R. E. (1988). Tactics, strategies and templets. *Oikos*, **52**, 3–18.

Steward, R. C. (1977). Industrial and non-industrial melanism in the peppered moth *Biston betularia* (L). *Ecological Entomology*, **2**, 231–243.

Tansley, A. G. (1951). *What is Ecology*? Council for the Promotion of Field Studies, London (reprinted in *Biological Journal of the Linnean Society*, **32**, 5–16, 1987).

Templeton, A. R. (1986). Coadaptation and outbreeding depression. *Conservation Biology* (Ed. by M. E. Soulé), pp. 105–116. Sinauer, Sunderland, MA, USA.

Thoday, J. M. (1961). The location of polygenes. *Nature, London*, **191**, 368–370.

Turesson, G. (1925). The plant species in relation to habitat and climate. *Hereditas*, **6**, 147–234.

Wallace, B. (1968). *Topics in Population Genetics*. Norton, New York, NY, USA.

Wallace, B. (1975). Hard and soft selection revisited. *Evolution*, **29**, 465–473.

Yule, G. U. (1907). On the theory of inheritance on the basis of Mendel's Laws — a preliminary note. *Report of the Third International Conference on Genetics*, pp. 140–142. Spottiswoode, London, UK.

PART 4
TECHNIQUES AND PROTOCOLS

1. USE OF PCR TECHNIQUES IN *DROSOPHILA* POPULATION BIOLOGY

LYNNE O'BRIEN, DAVID COATES, JANE ARNOLD AND BRYAN SHORROCKS

Drosophila Population Biology Unit, Department of Pure and Applied Biology, University of Leeds, Leeds LS2 9JT, UK

POLYMERASE CHAIN REACTION (PCR)

PCR is a technique for amplifying short specific regions of DNA. It therefore allows rapid identification of individuals in a population which carry specific DNA markers, and so complements a mark/release/recapture approach where phenotypic traits are not readily scorable. In principle it can differentiate not only between individuals having or not having a specific DNA sequence but also between allelic variants which differ at the DNA level, or between individuals with tandem duplications as opposed to individuals with single copy genes.

An advantage that PCR has over other techniques is that the amount and purity of the DNA is not critical. This allows large numbers of samples to be prepared and screened relatively quickly. It is possible to go from the intact sample to a final result within the space of a single day.

PCR is based on the fact that if DNA is denatured by heating and short DNA sequences, known as primers, are annealed to it, then these primers can act as starting blocks for the synthesis of a new strand of DNA by DNA polymerase. In PCR reactions the DNA polymerase most commonly used is a thermostable enzyme obtained from *Thermophilus aquaticus* known as Taq. This enzyme is able to withstand the high temperatures required for the DNA denaturation stage without losing its activity. Primers are prepared that hybridize to either end of a particular gene or region of DNA of interest and that are complementary to opposite strands of the DNA. In the presence of Taq polymerase and various other components it is possible to initiate DNA synthesis across the region of interest between the two primers.

PCR is carried out by incubating the samples at three temperatures. First of all the DNA is denatured by heating the sample to 92–95°C. Then the primers are annealed to the target DNA at 40–60°C. The temperature used depends on the sequence of the primers and target DNA. Finally the sample is incubated at 72°C to allow the polymerase to extend the annealed primers to give two new strands of DNA. If this amplification process is repeated 20–30 times, the amount of DNA doubles every cycle, increasing to a level where it is clearly visible on a stained agarose gel. Temperature cycling machines make this process quite straightforward.

Reaction components

1	10 × PCR buffer	0.1% gelatine
	500 mM KCl	1% Triton X-100
	100 mM Tris pH 9	

2 $MgCl_2$. The Mg^{2+} concentration needs to be determined for each set of primers. This reaction component greatly affects the specificity of the PCR and therefore the optimum Mg^{2+} concentration should be titrated. A final concentration of 0.5–2.5 mM should give the best results, the optimum is normally around 1.5 mM.

3 dNTPs. These are the building blocks for the synthesis of the new strands of DNA. They are stored as 100 mM stocks of dATP, dCTP, dGTP and dTTP at −20°C. The working stock is 2 mM for each dNTP and the final concentration of dNTPs in the reaction is 0.2 mM.

4 Taq polymerase. This is stored at −20°C, and about 2 units (U) are required per reaction.

5 Primers. These are stored dry at −70°C and are used at a final concentration of 100 pmol.

6 DNA. Great care must be taken to ensure that there is no cross-contamination of any of the solutions with the DNA preps. Owing to the high sensitivity of the PCR this would lead to a large potential number of false positives. Single fly DNA is prepared using the method described in Ashburner (1989).

Standard reaction protocol

The reaction is set up with a final volume of 50 μl overlaid with 50 μl of mineral oil to prevent evaporation.

Input	Final concentration
5 μl 10 × PCR buffer	1 × PCR buffer
5 μl 10 mM $MgCl_2$	1 mM $MgCl_2$
5 μl 2 mM dNTPs	0.2 mM dNTPs
1 μl primer 1 (100 pmol)	
1 μl primer 2 (100 pmol)	

4 μl Taq polymerase (2 U)
2 μl DNA (200 ng)
plus deionized water to 50 μl

Standard reaction conditions

1 95°C–5 min
2 95°C–1 min
3 55°C–1 min 30 s   Stages 2–4 are repeated 20–30 times.
4 72°C–2 min
5 72°C–5 min

Refrigerate overnight if necessary.

Materials

PCR machine. We are using the PREM III thermal cycler from Luminar Technology. This machine costs about £4000, including the extra heating block.

Taq polymerase. Purchased from Northumbria Biologicals Ltd, Cramlington, Northumberland NE23 9BL, UK. The cost is £320 for 1000 U: this is sufficient for 500 reactions using the protocol described above.

dNTPs. Purchased from Boehringer Mannheim. Each dNTP costs about £10 for 10 mg.

Primers. These can be obtained from commercial sources, or made by your local molecular biology friend with access to an Oligonucleotide Synthesizer. For hints on the design of primers, see Erlich (1989) and Innis *et al.* (1990).

Most other reagents were purchased from Sigma, Poole, Dorset

REFERENCES

Ashburner, M. (1989). *Drosophila. A Laboratory Manual.* Cold Spring Harbor Laboratory Press, New York, NY, USA.

Erlich, H. A. (Ed.) (1989). *PCR Technology. Principles and Applications for DNA Amplification.* Stockton Press, New York, NY, USA.

Innis, M. A., Gelfand, D. H., Sninsky, J. J. & White, T. J. (Eds) (1990). *PCR Protocols. A Guide to Methods and Applications.* Academic Press, London, UK.

2. POLYMERASE CHAIN REACTION

INGER ARNAU AND STEVEN COOPER
School of Biological Sciences, University of East Anglia
Norwich NR4 7TJ, UK

PRINCIPLE

The polymerase chain reaction (PCR) is an *in vitro* method for amplification of a specific DNA sequence, using two oligonucleotide primers that flank the region of interest in the target DNA.

1 Initial denaturation
94–97° C for 1–5 min

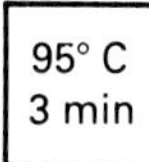

Separating the strands

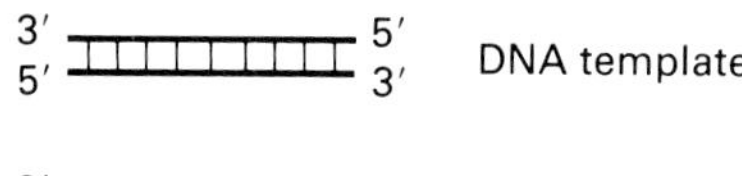

2 Annealing
40–70° C for 30 s – 5 min

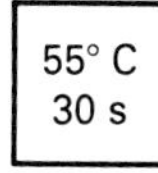

Annealing of primer to DNA — template

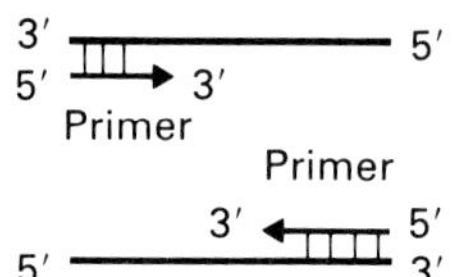

3 Extension
70–75° C for 30 s – 2 min

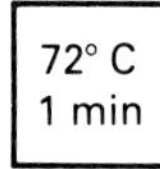

Amplification of target DNA

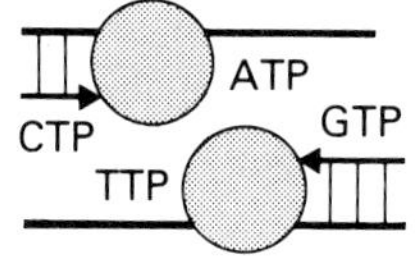

Taq. polymerase

☐ = standard

4 Denaturation
90–95° C for 20 s – 1 min

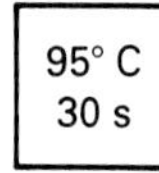

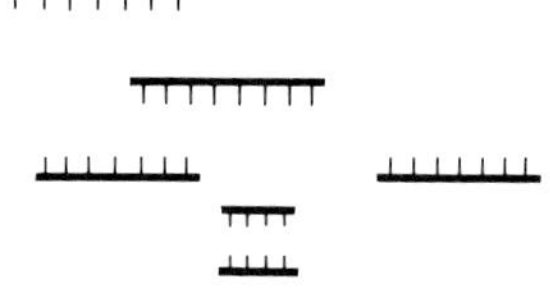

5 Repeat cycles 2–4: 25–40 times

6 Final extension
71 – 72° C for 5–10 min

72° C
5 min

To make sure that the amplified DNA are double-stranded

PCR product

PROCEDURES TO MINIMIZE CONTAMINATIONS

1 If it is possible, reactions should be set up in a separate room or a DNA-free area. Care must be taken to ensure that amplified DNA is not brought into this area.
2 Have a set of pipettes for use with PCR reagents only and a separate pipette for adding DNA to the PCR.
3 Use a new bottle of H_2O every time or day.
4 Autoclave the equipment needed such as Eppendorf tubes, tips, etc.
5 Do not reuse the tips.
6 Change gloves frequently.
7 Uncap and close tubes carefully to prevent aerosols.
8 Add the DNA as the last component, and cap the tube before proceeding to the next.

STANDARD PROTOCOL

The standard PCR is typically done in a 50 or 100 µl volume.
Store all components at −20°C and keep them on ice, while performing the reactions.

For a 50 µl reaction volume

5 µl 10 × Taq polymerase buffer
5 µl 1 mg/ml Bovine Serum Albumin (optional)
5 µl 2 mM dNTP
0.2 µl = 1 U Taq polymerase (5 U/µl)

1 µl primer x_1 (0.2–20 µM, depending on size and specificity)
1 µl primer x_2 (0.2–20 µM, depending on size and specificity)
x µl DNA template (conc. 10–100 ng, depending on copy number of gene)

Adjust the volume up to 50 μl with H_2O.
Add a few drops of mineral oil to seal the reaction and to prevent condensation.
Spin tubes briefly before running the PCR programme.
Include positive + negative control(s) in the experiment.

Positive control(s). To check if all the solutions in the PCR are OK. Use primers from a conserved region, which always amplified a certain sequence.

Negative control(s). Samples with no DNA. To check if the primer solutions are contaminated with DNA, which can give false positive results.

ANALYSIS OF THE AMPLIFIED PCR PRODUCTS

By electrophoresis on agarose gel.

OPTIMIZATION AND FUNCTION OF PCR CONDITIONS

It can be highly advantageous to optimize the PCR for a given application. Even if the standard protocol seems to work, a small change in the protocol can lead to a higher yield of the amplification product and minimize artefacts and non-specific background.

The recipe of the Taq polymerase buffer below (Table 1) is more or less standard but there are many variations, depending on the supplier.

The annealing temperature and incubation time plus number of cycles are other parameters which can be adjusted to optimize the PCR reaction.

TABLE 1. Taq polymerase buffer ×1

Components	Changing range	Standard conditions	Function
KCl	Max. 50 mM	50 mM	Facilitate primer annealing
Tris-HCl pH 9.0	10–20 mM	10 mM	Stabilize the DNA
$MgCl_2$	1.4–2.5 mM	1.5 mM	(1)
Gelatine	0.01% (w/v)		Stabilize the enzyme
Triton X–100	0.1%		

(1) $MgCl_2$ affects primer annealing, strand dissociation temperature of both template and PCR product, product specificity, formation of primer–dimer artefacts and enzyme plus fidelity. So the $MgCl_2$ concentration in the buffer is extremely important because it affects the whole PCR. If the Mg^{2+} concentration increases, then the specificity of the primer annealing decreases.

For more detailed discussions of these parameters see the references listed.

REFERENCES

Erlich, H. A. (Ed.) (1989). *PCR Technology. Principles and Applications for DNA Amplification*. Macmillan, London, UK.

Innis, M. A., Gelfand, D. H., Sninsky, J. J. & White, T. J. (Eds) (1990). *PCR Protocols: A Guide to Methods and Applications*. Academic Press, London, UK.

3. THE DETECTION OF ORGANISMS AT FAMILY, GENUS AND SPECIES LEVEL USING THE POLYMERASE CHAIN REACTION TO AMPLIFY SPECIFIC TARGET DNA SEQUENCES

RAYMOND A. McKEE , CHRISTOPHER M. GOODING, STEPHEN D. GARRETT AND HILARY A. POWELL

AFRC Institute of Food Research, Norwich Research Park, Colney, Norwich NR4 7UA, UK

The polymerase chain reaction (described in detail elsewhere in this volume; for example, Arnau & Cooper, Techniques and Protocols section 2, p. 456) is an *in vitro* enzymatic method for the specific amplification of a target DNA sequence. The DNA sequence of, at least, the ends of the target must be known so that oligonucleotide primers may be constructed to prime DNA synthesis of the desired region.

Various procedures have been published detailing the detection of bacteria using the polymerase chain reaction. To illustrate the use of the technique we have selected three applications: (1) detection of the presence of the family bacteriaceae, (2) detection of members of the genus *Listeria*, and (3) detection of the species *Listeria monocytogenes*.

PROTOCOLS

Polymerase chain reaction (PCR)

Any standard protocol may be used, see for example that described by Arnau and Cooper (p. 456).

Reaction volumes are typically 50 or 100 μl
Taq is used at 0.5 U/reaction.
Primers are constructed on an Applied Biosystems Ltd, Warrington, UK, DNA synthesizer Model 381A
Primers are used at 20 pmol final concentration
Target DNA is *not* generally isolated, cells are added to the reaction with or without a boiling (5 min) step
Positive and negative controls are always included

Detecting at the level of family

The following primers are based on regions of the 16S ribosomal RNA (rRNA) and are essentially conserved throughout bacteria (Lane *et al.* 1985, Border *et al.* 1990). They amplify a product of 408 bp derived from the 16S rRNA genes present on the bacterial chromosome.

Primer 1: 5′ cagcagccgcggtaatac 3′
c t

Primer 2: 5′ ccgtcaattcatttaagttt 3′
c g

Reaction conditions

95°C 4.0 min 50°C 2.0 min 72°C 1.0 min	1 cycle	95°C 1.0 min 50°C 2.0 min 72°C 1.0 min	29 cycles

Detecting at genus level

Using primer 1 above and primer 3 detailed below, which is based on *Listeria* sp. 16S rRNA sequence data, species of the genus *Listeria* can be detected using PCR; a product of 938 bp is produced (Stackenbrandt & Curiale 1988, Border *et al.* 1990).

Primer 3: 5′ ctccataaaggtgaccct 3′

Reaction conditions

95°C 4.0 min 50°C 2.0 min 72°C 1.0 min	1 cycle	95°C 1.0 min 50°C 2.0 min 72°C 1.0 min	29 cycles

Detection at species level

The detection of particular species usually requires the cloning and sequencing of unique genes or fragments specific to that organism. Fragments (primers 4 and 5 below) of the listeriolysin gene from *Listeria monocytogenes* have been used as probes for *L. monocytogenes*; those shown yield a product of 702 bp. (Mengaud *et al.* 1988)

Primer 4: 5′ cctaagacgccaatcgaa 3′

Primer 5: 5′ aagcgcttgcaactgctc 3′

Reaction conditions

95°C 4.0 min 50°C 2.0 min 72°C 1.0 min	1 cycle	95°C 1.0 min 50°C 2.0 min 72°C 1.0 min	29 cycles

DNA sequences from other *L. monocytogenes* genes have been used in a similar fashion. The primers detailed below are taken from the sequence of another Listeria gene, DTH, encoding a delayed hypersensitivity factor, and giving a product of 326 bp. (Wernars *et al.* 1991.)

Primer 6: 5′ ccgggagctgctaaagcggt 3′
Primer 7: 5′ gccaaaccaccgaaaagacc 3′

Reaction conditions
94°C 3.0 min

94°C 1.0 min 54°C 2.0 min 72°C 3.0 min	30 cycles

VALUE AND LIMITATIONS OF THE TECHNIQUE

The polymerase chain reaction has been used to amplify target sequences from a wide variety of organism and tissue types. The value of the technique is that one does not necessarily need to isolate and purify the DNA to be used as substrate. Once the specific target DNA sequences have been identified and sequenced, the sequence can be amplified (under the right conditions) from a background of a large amount of competing material.

One limitation of the methodology is that DNA sequence is required in order that synthetic oligonucleotide primers may be synthesized. Another potential serious limitation relates to cross-contamination of different samples, or contamination of an unamplified sample with previously amplified DNA. This can be avoided to a large extent by taking a few simple precautions:

1 Physically isolate the PCR preparation and products.
2 Autoclave all solutions.
3 Aliquot reagents.
4 Use disposable gloves.
5 Avoid splashes.
6 Use positive displacement pipettes.
7 Where possible prepare pre-mixed reagents.
8 Add the DNA/sample last.
9 Always include positive and negative controls.
10 Treat gel apparatus, combs and surfaces (where possible) with 1.0 M HCl.

REFERENCES

Border, P. M., Howard, J. J., Plastow, G. S. & Siggens, K. W. (1990). Detection of *Listeria* species and *Listeria monocytogenes* using polymerase chain reaction. *Letters in Applied Microbiology*, **11**(3), 158–162.

Lane, D. J., Pace, B., Olsen, G. J., Stahl, D. A., Sogin, M. L. & Pace, N. R. (1985). Rapid determination of 16S ribosomal RNA sequences for phylogenetic analysis. *Proceedings of the National Academy of Sciences, USA*, **82**, 6955–6959.

Mengaud, J., Vicente, M. F., Chenevert, J., Pereira, J. M., Goeffroy, C., Gicquel-Sanzey, B., Baquero, F., Perez-Diaz, J. C. & Cossart, P. (1988). Expression in *Escherichia coli* and sequence analysis of the listeriolysin O determinant of *Listeria monocytogenes*. *Infection and Immunity*, **56**, 766–772.

Stackenbrandt, E. & Curiale, R. M. (1988). Detection of *Listeria*. European Patent Application 88308820.5.

Wernars, K., Heuvelman, C. J., Chakraborty, T. & Notermans, S. H. W. (1991). Use of the polymerase chain reaction for direct detection of *Listeria monocytogenes* in soft cheeses. *Journal of Applied Bacteriology*, **70**, 121–126.

4. SELECTION OF DNA SEQUENCES FOR USE AS PROBES

RAYMOND A. McKEE, CHRISTOPHER M. GOODING, STEPHEN D. GARRETT, HILARY A. POWELL, BARBARA M. LUND AND MARGARET R. KNOX

AFRC Institute of Food Research, Norwich Research Park, Colney, Norwich NR4 7UA, UK

PRINCIPLE

The use of nucleic acid probes for the detection of genes within particular organisms and for the positive identification of the organism itself is based on the unique ability of a molecule of DNA or RNA to hybridize specifically with a complementary sequence.

There are a number of choices as to which nucleic acid sequence should be used as the target. Genomic DNA sequences from known cloned genes such as those encoding toxins have been used and offer high specificity.

Ribosomal RNA (rRNA), which can be present at 1000–10 000 copies per cell, is another potential target. One of the drawbacks to this approach is the high degree of conservation of primary sequence in rRNA from different species, particularly those closely related.

We have used an approach developed by Welcher *et al.* (1986) which allows the selective enrichment of DNA sequences specific to a particular organism, for example microbial pathogens. This is effected by the removal of those cross-hybridizing sequences which are present in other species, and with which one does not want the particular probe to react.

SUBTRACTION PROTOCOL

The protocol given is that used to obtain specific probes for *Listeria monocytogenes*, and it has given useful results in our hands (see also Welcher *et al.* 1986). The method could benefit from a number of minor modifications, for example the use of PCR technology to generate larger amounts of DNA on both sides of the subtraction.

1 *Listeria monocytogenes* (ATCC 19111) DNA was terminally digested with *Sau*3A and ^{32}P-labelled with dCTP using the random primer method.

2 *Alu*I-digested *Listeria innocua* DNA was denatured and biotin-labelled with biotin (bio-11-dUTP) using an adaptation of the primer method used in (1) above.

3 6.0 μl 5.0 M NaCl, 4 μl 0.5 M sodium phosphate pH 6.8, were added to 10 μg *Listeria innocua* DNA (labelled with bio-11 dUTP) and 3 μg *Listeria monocytogenes* DNA (labelled with [^{32}P]-dCTP), in 30 μl of sterile distilled water (SDW).

4 The DNA in the solution was then heat denatured at 100°C for 4 minutes, quickly chilled on ice, spun down and then overlaid with paraffin oil. The tube was placed in a heating block at 55°C and hybridization was allowed to continue for 15 hours.

5 On completion of the hybridization reaction the paraffin oil was removed and the volume adjusted to 90 μl with a freshly prepared solution of 20 mM $NaHCO_3$, 1.0 M NaCl (pH 7.7).

6 60 μl of 5.0 M NaCl was then added, followed by 150 μl of a 1 mg/ml solution of Avidin-DN in 0.05 M $NaHCO_3$ pH 8.2, 0.1% thimerosal (Vector Labs, Peterborough, UK). The tube was gently mixed and placed at 55°C before application to the copper chelate column, prepared as in (7) below.

7 A siliconized 1.0 ml disposable syringe was plugged with sterile polypropylene wool and packed with 0.4 ml iminodiacetic acid agarose. The column was washed with 10 volumes SDW, and 0.2 ml of a 5.0 mg/ml $CuSO_4$ solution was passed through the column, turning the column light blue.

8 The column was washed 10 times with SDW, followed by 10 volumes of 20 mM $NaHCO_3$, 1.0 M NaCl (pH 7.7). 300 μl of the bicarbonate solution was also added to the hybridization mix (see 7 above), and the sample was gently mixed and carefully added to the top of the column.

9 Fractions were collected and the column was washed with the bicarbonate solution until the radioactivity of the eluate was reduced to background levels. The bound, biotinylated DNA was eluted by washing the column in 50 mM EDTA, 1.0 M NaCl, 0.1% SDS. As the copper ion is stripped off, the column turns from blue to white. The trapped DNA was usually found in the first couple of drops of eluate. The distribution of the labelled *Listeria monocytogenes* DNA could be assessed by Cerenkov counting, and an estimate made as to the percentage of homologous *Listeria monocytogenes* DNA removed.

10 The unbound *Listeria monocytogenes* DNA samples were pooled in siliconized tubes, isopropanol precipitated and resuspended in 25 μl SDW.

11 The complete hybridization and column procedure was then repeated a further three times until a solution suitable for probing the library was obtained. At each subtraction step a small sample of the probe was removed and used to probe slot-blots containing DNA from a range of bacterial species.

Following the subtraction process the radiolabelled probe DNA, enriched for sequences specific for *Listeria monocytogenes*, was used to screen a pre-prepared genomic library of the *L. monocytogenes* strain used in the subtraction.

Of 7500 individual library colonies screened, approximately 120 were selected as probes possibly specific for *L. monocytogenes*. On further characterization under stringent hybridization conditions several isolates have been found to be specific for *Listeria monocytogenes* and not to cross-react with any of the other *Listeria* species or non-*Listeria* species so far tested. To date the DNA sequences of the subtraction isolated probes show no homologies to any known DNA sequences.

APPLICATIONS

The method of subtractive hybridization has proved to be a useful generic technique in the isolation of DNA sequences specific to *Listeria monocytogenes*. The procedure as described by Welcher *et al.* (1986) and modified in our hands is fairly tedious. A potential alternative application for the isolation of specific DNA probes for eukaryotes is described by Anamthawat-Jonsson *et al.* (1990).

REFERENCES

Anamthawat-Jonsson, K., Schwarzacher, T., Leitch, A. R., Bennett, M. D., & Heslop-Harrison, J. S. (1990). Discrimination between closely related *Triticeae* species using genomic DNA as a probe. *Theoretical and Applied Genetics*, **79**, 721–728.

Welcher, A. A., Torres, A. R. & Ward, D. C. (1986). Selective enrichment of specific DNA, cDNA and RNA sequences using biotinylated probes, avidin and copper-chelate agarose. *Nucleic Acids Research*, **14** (24), 10027–10044.

5. RAPDs: RANDOM AMPLIFIED POLYMORPHIC DNAs

DIANE HOWLAND AND JOSE ARNAU
School of Biological Sciences, University of East Anglia, Norwich, NR4 7TJ, UK

PRINCIPLE

This is an adaptation of the PCR, named AP-PCR (for Arbitrarily Primed PCR) (Welsh & McClelland 1990). Its use permits the detection of polymorphisms (as different PCR products) between different strains, isolates, subspecies, etc. Since this technique uses arbitrary primers to amplify random segments of genomic DNA, revealing polymorphisms, those markers are called RAPDs (Williams *et al.* 1990). It is equivalent to the RFLP (Restriction Fragment Length Polymorphisms) techniques, but considerably less time-consuming, and does not require the use of complicated protocols.

The rationale for the AP-PCR is as follows. At low temperature, a given primer is likely to find many sequences in the template DNA (i.e. DNA from the organism being studied), to which it can anneal with a variety of mismatches, provided the right temperature and salt concentration are used.

If the frequency of these sequences in the template DNA is relatively high, there will be a chance that pairs of sequences lie close to one another, and arranged in opposite orientation, such that the 3′ ends of the primer will point to each other. Given these facts, the PCR will amplify a set of fragments, which can vary in size when different individuals, isolates, subspecies, etc., are analysed (Williams *et al.* 1990).

The arbitrary primers may then reveal polymorphisms which function as genetic markers in the construction of genetic maps. The segregation of the PCR fragments can be readily studied in genetic crosses.

No previous genetic or molecular knowledge of the organism is required using this technique. The RAPDs (also named RAPiDs) are therefore suitable for genetic mapping, taxonomic and population studies. These PCR fragments can also be cloned and used, for example, to initiate a chromosome walk.

We are using this technique to produce markers useful in the establishment of a genetic map in the plant pathogenic fungus *Cladosporium fulvum*, as well as for the detection of polymorphisms between isolates of birch tree (*Betula*) populations in East Anglia.

PCR PROTOCOL FOR RAPDs

PCR mixture

25–100 ng genomic DNA (template). (DNA purification in CsCl–EtBr gradients is recommended to prevent variable results, due to different salt concentration.)
200 μM dNTPs (dATP, dTTP, dGTP, dCTP)
200 nM primer (10-mer)
Taq polymerase buffer (containing $MgCl_2$ to give a final concentration in the PCR mixture ranging from 1.0 to 5.0 mM). Different primers show different optimum [$MgCl_2$]
1 U Taq polymerase
H_2O up to 50 μl

Spin down briefly, add 50 μl mineral oil to seal the PCR mix, and perform PCR cycles as follows:

1 min at 94°C (denaturing step)
1 min at 35°C (primer annealing)
2 min at 72°C (extension of the annealed primer)

Repeat this cycle 35–45 times. After PCR, 10–25 μl of the reaction are sufficient to run a 1% agarose TBE gel (containing 0.5 μg/μl EtBr).

As in any other application of the PCR technique, it is important to run controls in which either the primer or the template DNA is omitted. It is also important to use sterile H_2O, Eppendorf tubes and pipette tips, and to wear gloves while preparing the reaction mixture to prevent contamination of samples with foreign DNA.

RAPDs versus RFLPs

Advantages of RAPD–PCR technique over RFLP methods

1 Universal set of primers which can be used on a wide variety of species with different genome sizes.
2 Large number of primers available.
3 Small amount of template DNA required.
4 No Southern blotting or radioactive probes.
5 Quick and simple protocol.

Disadvantages

1 Reaction conditions are very sensitive:
(a) Mg^{2+} concentration can vary from 1 to 5 mM. Optimum may differ for each primer and each species being studied.
(b) Taq polymerase. Some brands are not suitable for RAPDs. We recommend Amplitaq (Perkin-Elmer-Cetus, Connecticut, USA).

2 Reproducibility of bands. Larger bands may not always be produced. Standardization of reaction conditions, especially DNA concentration, is important.

3 No indication of which part of the genome is amplified.

4 Initial cost of primers and Amplitaq.

REFERENCES

Welsh, J. & McClelland, M. (1990). Fingerprinting genomes using PCR with arbitrary primers. *Nucleic Acids Research*, **18**, 7213–7218.

Williams, J. G. K., Kubelik, A. R., Livak, K. J., Rafalski, J. A. & Tingey, S. V. (1990). DNA polymorphisms amplified by arbitrary primers are useful as genetic markers. *Nucleic Acids Research*, **18**, 6531–6535.

6. DNA FINGERPRINTING

ROYSTON E. CARTER

Eleanor Roosevelt Institute for Cancer Research, 1899 Gaylord Street, Denver, CO 80206, USA

Laboratory protocols used at Nottingham for producing DNA fingerprints from birds, mammals and invertebrates are described.

DNA EXTRACTION

High-quality, high-molecular-weight genomic DNA is essential for successful DNA fingerprint analysis, and time spent on this aspect of the protocol is never wasted. One of the most common causes of failure to produce good fingerprints is poorly prepared, semidegraded or only partially digested DNA. DNA is conveniently prepared from avian erythrocytes or for mammalian studies from isolated leucocytes; alternatively, for all species homogenized tissues (e.g. liver) may be used.

1 Avian whole blood (15 μl) is suspended in 600 μl of isotonic buffer (1 × SET: 0.15 M NaCl, 1 mM EDTA, 50 mM Tris, pH 8.0). The cells are lysed by the addition of 7.5 μl of 25% w/v sodium dodecyl sulphate solution. Lysis causes the release of nucleases, which are inactivated by incubating with 15 μl of proteinase K solution (10 mg ml^{-1}) overnight at 55°C.
2 Proteins contaminating the DNA are denatured and removed during a series of extractions with immiscible organic solvents.
3 To the DNA solution is added 500 μl of buffered phenol (pH 8.0), the phases are mixed for 15–30 minutes then separated by centrifugation. Proteins partition to the lower organic phase or precipitate at the solvent interface. The aqueous phase is recovered and additionally extracted either with repeated phenol or phenol/chloroform/isoamyl alcohol (24:23:1 v/v) until no further precipitation occurs at the interface. The final traces of phenol are removed by a brief chloroform/isoamyl alcohol (23:1 v/v) extraction. The DNA is then recovered by the addition of 2 × volumes of cold (−20°C) absolute ethanol, for 30 minutes at −20°C which causes the precipitation of the DNA. This is collected by centrifugation. Traces of ethanol are removed by drying *in vacuo* and the DNA is dissolved in TE buffer (10 mM Tris, 1 mM EDTA, pH 8.0) at 55°C overnight.

DNA RESTRICTION

The genomic DNA isolated is a suitable substrate for digestion with a variety of restriction enzymes. Ideally a restriction enzyme is chosen which cuts frequently in most genomic DNA but not within tandemly repeated minisatellite sequences. A variety of such 'four base pair' restriction enzymes exist, e.g. *Hae*III, *Alu*I and *Hinf*I, although their suitability varies with different species.
1 An aliquot (10 μl) containing excess (>10 μg) genomic DNA is digested to completion with 10 U of the chosen 'four base pair' restriction enzyme according to the manufacturers instructions, usually overnight and in the presence of 4 mM Spermidine HCl.
2 The extent of the digestion is monitored by a 'minigel assay'. A small aliquot is electrophoresed through an 0.8% agarose minigel, stained with ethidium bromide and the resulting smear is examined, for both even staining and the presence of characteristic (species/enzyme specific) satellite bands. All samples are also quantitatively assayed fluorometrically, and are adjusted to 0.15 μg μl^{-1} with 2 × bromophenol blue (BPB). (10 × BPB: 20% w/v Ficoll® 400, 0.2 M EDTA, 0.25% w/v BPB, 0.25% Xylene cyanol FF.)

ELECTROPHORESIS

DNA fragments are separated by electrophoresis according to size by molecular sieving through an agarose gel under the influence of an applied electrical field.

1 A 0.7–1.0% w/v agarose gel is prepared by dissolving by microwave the appropriate mass of LE agarose into 375 ml 1 × TAE buffer (1 × TAE: 0.04 M Tris acetate, 1 mM EDTA, pH 8.0). The agarose solution is cooled to 55°C and poured into a gel mould to set. The gel is placed into an electrophoresis tank containing 2.5 l 1 × TAE electrophoresis buffer. The samples and appropriate molecular weight markers (e.g. bacteriophage λ DNA digested with the restriction enzyme *Hind*III) are heated to 65°C for 10 minutes then rapidly quenched on ice to dissociate fragments which have joined by their restriction generated cohesive termini. They are micropipetted into the preformed sample wells of the gel. The samples are allowed to equilibrate with the electrophoresis buffer for 10 minutes before starting electrophoresis. Electrophoresis is necessarily long and slow (40–72 hours at 40 V depending on the species and chosen enzyme), in order to minimize 'band smiling'.

BLOTTING

For ease of handling the DNA fragments are transferred from the gel to a solid support matrix by capillary blotting, thus maintaining their relative positions.

Two routine methods of preparing blots are used depending upon the membrane chosen: Southern transfer (Sambrook *et al.* 1989) must be used for nitrocellulose and can be used for all nylon varieties. Alternatively, some nylon membranes are amenable to 'alkali transfer' (Sambrook *et al.* 1989).

Southern transfer

Large DNA fragments (>10 kb) retained within the gel are further fragmented *in situ* by brief acid hydrolysis by soaking the gel in 0.2 M HCl for 10 minutes. The double-stranded DNA is then separated by alkali in 1.5 M NaCl, 0.5 M NaOH for 35 minutes, followed by a gel neutralization in 3 M NaCl, 0.5 M Tris pH 8.0 for 45 minutes. The DNA fragments are then transferred to the membrane by blotting. The gel is placed on a wick in contact with a reservoir of the high ionic strength buffer 20 × SSC (20 × SSC: 3 M NaCl, 0.3 M sodium citrate), a membrane is then placed on to the gel surface. DNA fragments are eluted from the gel and deposited on to the membrane surface, as the 20 × SSC is absorbed into paper towels above the filter membrane.

Alkali transfer

Acid hydrolysis and denaturation are performed as above, but the neutralization step is omitted and transfer is in either 0.4 M NaOH or 0.25 M NaOH, 1.5 M NaCl. DNA is then fixed to the membrane by drying *in vacuo* for 2 hours at 80°C, or by brief exposure to UV.

PRE-HYBRIDIZATION, HYBRIDIZATION AND WASHING

A probe capable of recognizing and binding to minisatellite DNA is prepared and used to wash the filter, so that it may bind to homologous sequences immobilized on the membrane surface. The required match between a probe and target can be regulated by controlling temperature and/or the ionic strength (stringency) during the hybridizing step or may occur during the post-hybridization washing.

Pre-hybridization

Non-specific hybridization of the labelled probe to positively charged sites on the membrane surface is prevented by a pre-hybridization step. The membrane is washed with proteinaceous 'blocking' agents at the desired stringency, e.g. 1% BLOTTO, 1 × SSC, 1.0% SDS at 65°C for several hours (typically 8–10). This is done either in bottles or cake boxes depending upon the number of filters to be processed (Carter *et al.* 1989).

Hybridization

In our procedures stringency is regulated during hybridization. Usually a moderate stringency (1 × SSC at 65°C) is used – it is easier to prevent hybrids forming than to dissociate them during the washing stage.

Post-hybridization washing

Non-bound probe is removed from the membranes by washing them at 65°C in several changes of wash solution (1 × SSC, 0.1% SDS).

PREPARATION OF A HYBRIDIZATION PROBE

A hybridization probe is a piece of nucleic acid which can be hybridized to specific target sequences, and which is 'labelled' to allow their detection. A probe may be DNA or RNA, and can be labelled either radioactively or chromogenically. For genetic fingerprint analyses a high-activity label is necessary and for this reason we routinely use $[^{32}P]$-RNA probes.

The minisatellite region from the multilocus fingerprint probes 33.6 and 33.15 (Jeffreys *et al.* 1985) were subcloned into a transcription vector (Carter *et al.* 1989). Radiolabelled $[\alpha^{32}P]$-CTP is incorporated into multiple RNA copies using a commercial kit transcribing from a T_7 RNA polymerase promoter (Little & Jackson 1987).

Plasmid (1 μg) containing the minisatellite region that has previously been linearized distal to the polymerase promoter is labelled in a reaction containing unlabelled UTP, GTP and ATP, transcription buffer, DTT, T_7 RNA polymerase and $[\alpha^{32}P]$-CTP. The probe is separated from unincorporated nucleotides by spun column chromatography (Sambrook *et al.* 1989), and is added (120 000 counts ml^{-1}) after pre-hybridization is complete.

AUTORADIOGRAPHY

Labelled probe hybridized to target sequences on the membrane may be detected by autoradiography. Beta-radiation emitted from $[^{32}P]$-labelled nucleotides incorporated in the probe will expose X-ray film. Intensifying screens are used for initial exposures to amplify the image exposures without amplification offer improved resolution but require much longer exposures even when probes of high specific activity are used.

After washing is complete the filters (while still damp) are wrapped in Saran wrap and exposed to pre-flashed X-ray film for 4 hours at −80°C in a cassette with two tungsten intensifying screens. This autoradiograph is developed photographically and used to gauge additional exposures with screens, if necessary, or exposures without screens (3−10 days at room temperature).

The Jeffreys' probes 33.6 and 33.15 and pSPT derivatives are the subject of patent No. GBA 2166445 and worldwide patents (pending) for commercial diagnostic use. All enquiries regarding the probes should be directed to ICI Diagnostics, Gadbrook Park, Northwich, Cheshire, UK.

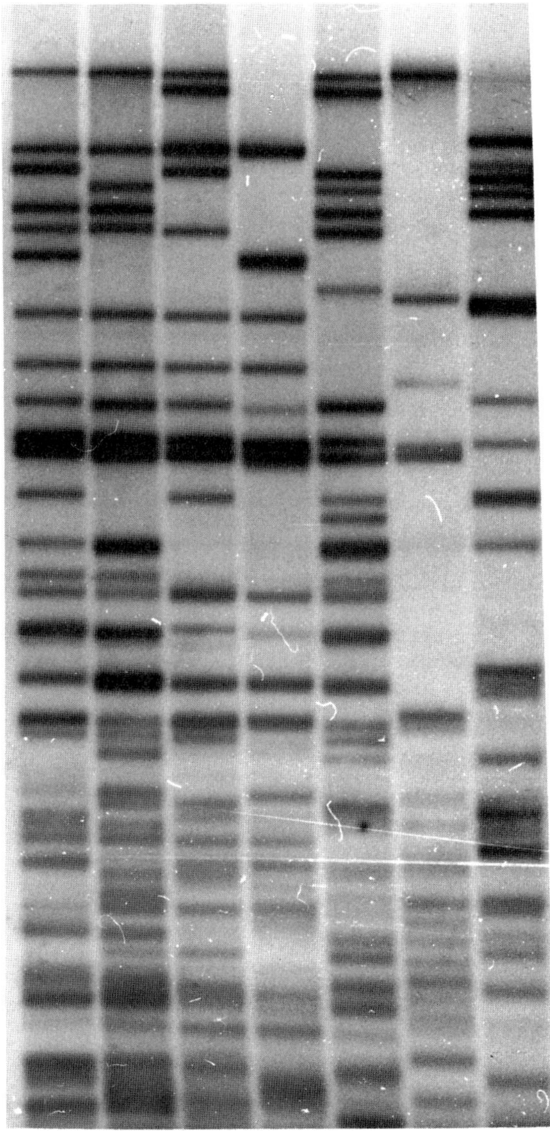

FIG. 1. Genetic fingerprints of seven House Sparrows (*Passer domesticus*) revealed by RNA probe pSPT 19.6. *Hae*III (3 μg) restricted DNA from three sibs (1–3), their parents (4 and 5) and two unrelated adults (6 and 7) (reading from left to right).

REFERENCES

Carter, R. E., Wetton, J. H. & Parkin, D. T. (1989). Improved genetic fingerprinting using RNA probes. *Nucleic Acids Research*, **17**, 5867.

Jeffreys, A. J., Wilson, V. & Thein, S. L. (1985). Hypervariable 'minisatellite' regions in human DNA. *Nature*, **314**, 67–73.

Little, P. F. R. & Jackson, I. J. (1987). Application of plasmids containing promoters specific for phage-encoded RNA polymerases. *DNA Cloning*, Vol. III (Ed. by D. M. Glover). IRL Press, Oxford, UK.

Sambrook, J., Fritsch, E. F. & Maniatis, T. (1989). *Molecular Cloning – A Laboratory Manual* (2nd edn). Cold Spring Harbor Laboratory Press, New York, NY, USA.

7. DNA FINGERPRINTING USING MULTILOCUS AND SINGLE LOCUS PROBES

ROYSTON E. CARTER* AND DAVID T. PARKIN†
**Eleanor Roosevelt Institute for Cancer Research, 1899 Gaylord Street, Denver, CO 80206, USA and †Department of Genetics, Queens Medical Centre, Clifton Boulevard, University of Nottingham, Nottingham NG7 2UH, UK*

A *m*ulti*l*ocus DNA fingerprint is the familiar 'bar code' pattern produced by hybridizing a minisatellite DNA *p*robe (MLP) to the restriction fragments of an individual separated according to size by agarose gel electrophoresis and then immobilized as single-stranded DNA on to a nitrocellulose or nylon membrane (Fig. 2).

The structure of the minisatellite DNA is represented in Fig. 3. A short 'core sequence' of about 9–15 bp of DNA together with additional flanking DNA (total length up to about 70 bp) represents a single minisatellite unit. Variable numbers of units are arranged in tandem and the polymorphic variation in repeat number may be very great (one to several thousand). It is this size variation that determines the mobility of the DNA fragments during electrophoresis.

Several families of minisatellite DNA exist; most contain the 'core like' sequence but have different additional flanking DNA within the repeat units.

Under appropriate detection (low stringency) conditions, minisatellite probes simultaneously detect alleles from many loci by hybridizing to the

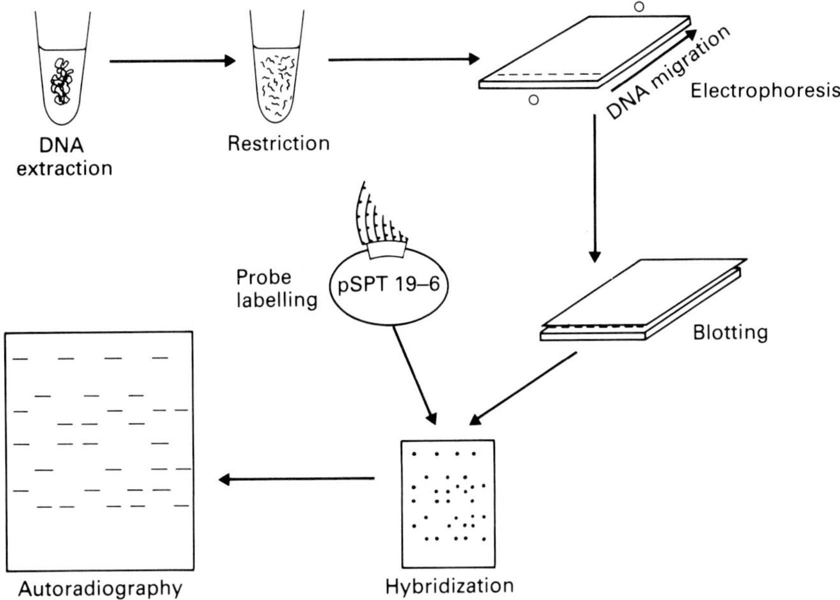

FIG. 2. Outline of the DNA fingerprinting technique.

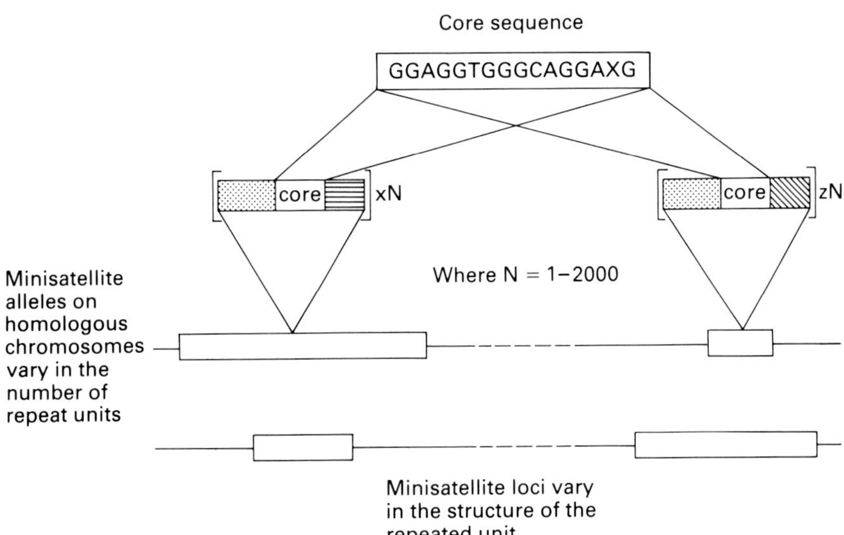

FIG. 3. Minisatellite structure.

'core region'. The fingerprint revealed is unique to an individual (or to a given pair of monozygotic twins) but is governed by very simple genetic principles. Approximately half of the bands in an individual come from each parent (one allele from each parent from each of the loci). Consequently related individuals (sibs) will share bands with each other which they have inherited from their parents. However, because of the large number of bands involved each sib will inherit a different combination of parental bands and will therefore possess its own individual specific pattern.

If a probe is prepared from an individual cloned locus and hybridized at high stringency, it will detect the alleles from that and only that locus. In an individual, such a *s*ingle *l*ocus *p*robe (SLP) will usually detect two bands (heterozygote) or one band (homozygote). Very high levels of heterozygosity (>80%) are normal for minisatellite loci. This means that most individuals will be heterozygous for different alleles. Consequently, the exclusion of paternity/maternity can easily be determined. Probing with several single locus probes either serially or in parallel can provide high levels of statistical certainty.

PROS AND CONS

It must at the outset be stressed that multilocus and single locus fingerprinting are *both* powerful analytical techniques of considerable importance to some types of population analysis, and that their use is not mutually exclusive but rather complementary. The choice of system depends upon the nature of the available samples and the questions to be answered.

Multilocus probes work well. Informative DNA fingerprints can be obtained from most species (plant, invertebrate or vertebrate) with readily available probes, e.g. Jeffreys 33.6 and 33.15, M13, 3′ HVR. Individual identification and familial delineation are relatively straightforward. However, multilocus fingerprints are complex. Very large numbers of bands need to be resolved and accurately scored. This is a technically difficult and time-consuming operation.

Single locus probes offer major advantages over MLPs. They are significantly more sensitive and are technically easier to use (the gel quality need not be so high). The interpretation of SLP profiles is easy and the ability to obtain allele frequency estimates allows important population genetic questions to be addressed. The data obtained are also amenable to database formation. These allow comparisons between experiments to be made, e.g. the assignment of paternity from a large pool of males.

The major drawback of SLPs is their unavailability. Although hybridization occurs to closely related species, at present the SLPs isolated have proved to be species specific. Consequently, for investigations of a new species probes must be isolated from complex genomic libraries. This is a very long and laborious exercise in molecular biology, not to be taken lightly. Realistically, at least a year would be required for success.

8. FINGERPRINTING FUNGI

PAUL NICHOLSON, JAMES BROWN AND MARK ATKINSON

Cambridge Laboratory, John Innes Centre, Colney Lane, Norwich NR4 7UH, UK

DNA fingerprinting is a very powerful technique with the potential to identify individuals and to estimate relatedness amongst individuals within populations. In the past, identification of fungal isolates has generally relied upon phenotypic markers which, because they are dependent upon gene expression, may be affected by cultural and other environmental factors. A further complication for the study of biotrophic fungi is the difficulty of isolating them from the host.

In our laboratory two general approaches have been used with cereal pathogens depending on whether the organism of interest can be cultured axenically:

1 For biotrophic fungi — axenic culture not possible; species-specific probe E9

2 For necrotrophic fungi — axenic culture possible; general fingerprinting probe M13

BIOTROPHIC FUNGI

This approach requires that DNA is isolated from fungal material which should, ideally, be free from contamination with host material. The DNA is then cut with restriction enzymes and cloned into plasmids. These plasmids are used to transform bacteria in which the plasmids replicate. Individual bacterial colonies are then screened to identify those containing DNA fragments of the fungus (clones) which do not cross-react with

DNA from the host. Using 'dot-blot' procedures a large number of clones may be screened at one time.

Clones that do not cross-react with host DNA are then hybridized to labelled DNA from the fungus. The extent of the signal obtained gives an indication of the number of copies, in the fungal genome, of sequences similar to those in the clone.

Clones of high copy number must then be analysed in detail by hybridization to 'Southern' membranes. DNA of the fungus is cut with restriction enzymes and size fractionated by electrophoresis through agarose gel. Following treatment to denature the DNA it is transferred by capillary action (Southern blotting), to either nylon or nitrocellulose membranes. The plasmid fraction is isolated from clones of interest and labelled (generally by incorporation of [^{32}P]-nucleotides) before hybridization to the membranes. Those clones that exhibit highly polymorphic restriction fragment length profiles characteristic of fingerprinting probes are selected and analysed further to establish the extent of their potential for particular purposes.

One such probe isolated from the biotrophic fungus *Erysiphe graminis* f. sp. *hordei*, which causes powdery mildew of barley, is E9. E9 hybridizes only to mildew DNA, not that of barley. This has been successfully used to investigate populations of this fungus in the UK and to follow the spread of clonally derived isolates over wide areas.

NECROTROPHIC FUNGI

A different system has been used for analysing necrotrophic fungi such as *Pseudocercosporella herpotrichoides* which can be cultured axenically.

The bacteriophage M13 has been found to contain regions of tandemly repeated DNA sequences with characteristics similar to the minisatellite sequences identified in human DNA and which form the basis of most forensic genetic fingerprinting. The sequences in M13 have been found to hybridize to almost all species tested to date, ranging from animals and plants to protists and bacteria. Use of this off-the-shelf 'general' probe, of course, means that the complex procedure for isolating species-specific probes is not required and so greatly simplifies matters, which is especially useful for newcomers to the field. For many purposes the human-derived probes 33.15 and 33.6 may be equally useful. Other general probes now in use are short oligonucleotides produced synthetically and which consist of repeats of 3–5 nucleotides in a total probe of 15–20 nucleotides. Each probe/'target organism' combination must be tested empirically to determine which probe is most suitable for each organism and requirement.

Different types of probe may require different labelling procedures, for instance, E9, 33.15, 33.6 and other double-stranded DNA probes are best labelled by 'oligo-labelling'. The oligonucleotide probes must be 'end-labelled' and a specific labelling procedure is used with M13 the DNA of which is generally single stranded. A protocol for the labelling of M13 as used in our laboratory is given below.

A final note for the near future is the non-radioactive labelling of fingerprinting probes using biotin, digoxigenin-11-dUTP and other labels which will permit fingerprinting to be carried out without the restrictions associated with radioactivity.

PROTOCOL FOR PROBING WITH WHOLE M13 (AFTER WELLS 1988)

Pre-hybridization

Buffer: for 50 ml (2–6 filters)

Water	30 ml
5 × HSB*	10 ml
(*3 M NaCl, 0.1 M Pipes, 0.05 M Na_2EDTA)	
Denhardt's III	5 ml
2.5% skimmed milk stock	5 ml (0.5 g in 20 ml)

(Warm in 65°C waterbath to clear cloudiness)

1 Soak filters with 2 × SSC.

2 Place filters in a sandwich box and cover each with pre-hybridization buffer before laying the next on top.

3 Place in shaking waterbath at 65°C for 5–6 hours (or overnight).

4 Cover with two sheets of Saran wrap (Dow Chemical Co.) at right angles.

Labelling

For 2–6 filters

1 To an Eppendorf tube add:
  (a) 100 ng of single-stranded M13 (0.4 μl),
  (b) 4 ng of 17-mer primer (4 μl),
  (c) 4 μl of 10 × common restriction enzyme buffer,
  (d) 14 μl sterile distilled water.

2 Incubate at 55°C for 1 hour.

3 Spin briefly in microfuge.

4 Add:
(a) 10 μl AGT mixture (deoxynucleoside 5′-triphosphates of adenine, guanine and thymine) (Wells 1988),
(b) 4 μl Klenow fragment,
(c) 4 μl BSA (bovine serum albumin),
(d) 1 μl [^{32}P]-dCTP (deoxcytidine 5′-triphosphate).
5 Incubate at 37°C for 15 minutes.
6 Stop by adding 140 μl 3 × SSC.

Hybridization

Buffer: for 20 ml (2–6 filters)

Water	12 ml
5 × HSB	4 ml
Denhardt's III	2 ml
2.5% skimmed milk stock	2 ml

(Warm in 65°C waterbath to clear cloudiness)

1 Add labelled probe to hybridization buffer, add labelled λ/*Hin*dIII digest.
2 Cover filters with two layers of Saran wrap.
3 Place in 65°C shaking waterbath overnight.

Washing membranes

1 Rinse a small volume of 2 × SSC, 1% SDS (65°C).
2 Wash at least twice for 15 minutes in 500 ml 2 × SSC, 1% SDS (65°C).
3 Blot dry between filter paper and rapidly seal in Saran wrap.
4 Expose to X-ray film at −70°C.

REFERENCE

Wells, R. A. (1988). DNA fingerprinting. *Genome Analysis: A Practical Approach* (Ed. by K. E. Davies), pp. 153–169. IRL Press, Oxford, UK.

9. ANALYSIS OF GENETIC VARIATION IN POPULATIONS: SOUTHERN BLOTTING AND RESTRICTION FRAGMENT LENGTH POLYMORPHISM (RFLP) ANALYSIS

STUART NOBLE, RICHARD OLIVER AND TONY DAVY

School of Biological Sciences, University of East Anglia, Norwich, NR4 7TJ, UK

PRINCIPLE

DNA from individual plants or animals in a given population is cut into fragments of different sizes using restriction enzymes which cut DNA at particular 4 or 6 base pair recognition sites in the genome. DNA fragments are separated by agarose gel electrophoresis and transferred to a nitrocellulose or nylon filter by capillary or vacuum action (Southern blotting). The filter is then incubated in a hybridization solution containing a radioactive or chemically labelled DNA fragment. This probe DNA will bind to any DNA fragments on the filter which are identical or very similar in sequence to itself. The position of those fragments which hybridize to the probe is revealed by exposing the filter to X-ray film (in the case of radioactive probes) or by adding suitable activators which result in a colour reaction (in the case of chemically labelled probes). This produces a particular banding pattern for each DNA sample. Genetic variation between individuals or populations in a particular gene of interest may be detected as differences in the sizes of DNA fragments which hybridize to the DNA probe for that gene.

PROTOCOL/TECHNIQUES

Isolation of DNA

Many different protocols have been developed. The simpler methods often involve only grinding of sample in extraction buffer, phenol extraction to remove proteins followed by precipitation of DNA with alcohol. In more difficult cases more complicated procedures such as isolation of nuclei may be required.

Restriction digestion of DNA

Simple reaction: DNA + enzyme + buffer (usually provided with enzyme when purchased). Usually 3-hour incubation at 37°C but occasionally overnight reaction required.

Agarose gel electrophoresis

Different sized DNA fragments migrate at different rates through the gel when current is applied. Gels usually run overnight at low voltage (20–30 V) to achieve good resolution of fragments.

Southern blotting

DNA fragments in the gel are denatured by washing the gel in 0.5 M NaOH, 1.5 M NaCl (2 × 30 minutes), followed by neutralization in 0.5 M Tris, 3 M NaCl (2 × 30 minutes). The DNA fragments in the gel are then transferred to a nitrocellulose or nylon filter by capillary action. The gel is placed upside down on a solid support which is covered by wicks cut from Whatman 3MM paper and soaked in transfer buffer (3 M NaCl, 0.3 M sodium citrate). The nitrocellulose or nylon filter is placed on the gel and then covered with several sheets of dry 3MM paper and tissues cut to the same size as the gel. A weight (about 500 g) is then applied to the top of the tissues. The transfer buffer moves up the wicks, through first the gel and then the filter and into the tissues. The denatured DNA fragments are transferred from the gel to the filter during this process. Blotting is usually done overnight. Alternatively, a vacuum pump can be used to transfer the DNA to the filter; in this case transfer takes about one hour. Following blotting the DNA is fixed to the filter by baking it at 65°C overnight or 80°C for 2 hours under vacuum.

DNA hybridization to detect RFLPs

Following a short period of pre-hybridization to prevent background problems caused by non-specific binding of probe DNA, the filter is incubated usually at 65°C overnight in a small volume of hybridization solution containing radioactively or chemically labelled probe. In most cases probe labelling is a relatively simple reaction taking between about 15 or 20 minutes and a few hours depending on which type of reaction is being used. Several types of DNA-labelling kits are commercially available or the users can make up their own buffers, etc., and simply add bought-in enzyme. During incubation the probe DNA will bind to DNA on the filter which is identical or similar in sequence to itself. Hybridization conditions can be varied to alter the efficiency of probe binding.

Post-hybridization washes and autoradiography/colour visualization

After hybridization the filter is washed in a series of salt solutions to remove unbound probe and probe which is non-specifically bound to target DNA. The filter is dried and exposed to X-ray film to detect radioactive probes; in the case of non-radioactive probes appropriate developers/colour activators are added to visualize hybridizing fragments.

APPLICATIONS

Southern blotting and DNA hybridization form the basis of a number of different types of molecular investigations that have been carried out in the areas of population/evolutionary biology and ecology. These techniques have provided new information on the nature and levels of genetic variation present in a number of naturally occurring plant populations (for example, Learn & Schaal 1987, Schaal *et al.* 1987, Davy *et al.* 1990, Noble 1990). They are fundamental to the many studies involving DNA fingerprinting in animal populations (see other contributions in this volume). They also provide an initial means of assessing whether interesting types of variation are present for a particular gene when one is considering whether to carry out a detailed PCR-based study of large numbers of individuals from different populations.

REFERENCES

Detailed protocols for DNA isolation, Southern blotting and DNA hybridization:

Ausubel, F. M. ***et al.*** **(Eds) (1987).** *Current Protocols in Molecular Biology*. Wiley Interscience, New York, NY, USA.

Maniatis, T. ***et al.*** **(Eds) (1989).** *Molecular Cloning*. Cold Spring Harbor Laboratory Press, New York, NY, USA.

Other references:

Davy, A. J., Noble, S. M. & Oliver, R. P. (1990). Genetic variation and adaptation to flooding in plants. *Aquatic Botany*, **38**, 91–108.

Learn, G. L. & Schaal, B. A. (1987). Population subdivision for rDNA repeat variants in *Clematis fremontii*. *Evolution*, **41**, 433–437.

Noble, S. M. (1990). Molecular variation between populations of annual haplophytes. PhD Thesis, University of East Anglia, UK.

Schaal, B. A., Wesley, J. L. & Nieto-Sotelo, J. (1987). Ribosomal DNA variation in the native plant *Phlox divaricata*. *Molecular Biology and Evolution*, **4**, 611–621.

10. THE USE OF REPETITIVE DNA PROBES IN THE ANALYSIS OF NATURAL POPULATIONS OF INSECTS AND PARASITES

PAUL K. FLOOK, MICHAEL D. WILSON AND RORY J. POST
Department of Biological Sciences, University of Salford, Salford M5 4WT, UK

PRINCIPLE

Many sibling species of insects and parasites are morphologically indistinguishable and reliable methods of identification are essential. In many instances species-specific repetitive DNA sequences have been isolated and may be used to assign species membership using the method of dot blotting DNA.

1 DNA is isolated from single specimens.
2 Denatured DNA is immobilized on nitrocellulose or nylon membrane in small dots.
3 Membranes are incubated with radiolabelled DNA sequences.
4 DNA hybridization is detected by autoradiography.

Using appropriate interspersed repetitive DNA probes and the method of Southern blotting, intraspecific polymorphisms can be detected in a similar way.

STANDARD PROTOCOL

DNA isolation

(NB. Material preserved in alcohol should be rehydrated in Tris-EDTA buffer for about 5 minutes before DNA extraction.)

1 Homogenize specimen (something the size of *Drosophila* works very well with this method) in 1.5 ml Eppendorf tube in 100 μl of 0.1 M NaCl, 0.2 M sucrose, 0.1 M Tris-HCl, 0.05 M EDTA pH 8, 0.5% SDS.
2 Incubate at 65°C for 30 minutes.
3 Add 15 μl of pre-chilled 8 M K acetate. Mix well by tapping tube.
4 Leave on ice for 45 minutes.

5 Centrifuge for 5 minutes at 15 000 rev min^{-1}.
6 Add supernatant to 2× volume of ethanol in a 0.5 ml Eppendorf tube, mix well and leave to stand at room temperature for 5 minutes (if the DNA is to be digested with restriction enzymes for Southern blotting two further ethanol precipitations should be included at this stage).
7 Spin down in microfuge for 10 minutes at room temperature.
8 Discard supernatant and resuspend pellet in 15 μl 0.1 × SSC + RNAase (50 μg/ml) to redissolve DNA. Allow 1 hour on ice to redissolve.

Dot blot procedure (Sim *et al.* 1979)

1 Samples diluted in 300 μl 6 × SSC and denatured in a boiling waterbath for 10 minutes.
2 A nitrocellulose membrane is set up in dot blot manifold (e.g. BRL Hybri-Dot) and vacuum applied.
3 DNA samples are transferred to wells. After a few minutes the wells are rinsed with 6 × SSC.
4 Filter is baked at 80°C for 2 hours and may be stored at room temperature for several weeks before hybridization.

Hybridization and autoradiography

1 Incubate filter overnight at 42°C in 10 ml 5 × SSC, 5 × Denhardt's solution, 5 mM phosphate buffer, 50 μg ml^{-1} denatured herring sperm DNA, 50% deionized formamide (this can be performed in a sealed plastic bag or lunch box in a waterbath or in a hybridization oven).
2 Appropriate DNA sequence(s) is labelled with [α^{32}P]-dCTP using a random primed DNA-labelling kit (e.g. Boerhinger Mannheim, Germany). The probe is denatured by boiling for 10 minutes.
3 Pre-hybridization solution is replaced with 5 ml of 5 × SSC, 5 × Denhardt's solution, 2 mM phosphate buffer, 50 μg ml^{-1} denatured herring sperm DNA, 50% deionized formamide + labelled probe (10^8 cpm ml^{-1}) and the filter incubated overnight at 42°C.
4 Filters are removed from hybridization mixtures and washed in 0.1 × SSC, 0.1% SDS at 42°C for 30 minutes.
5 Membranes are blotted dry with filter paper and placed on to a piece of card wrapped in cling film. Filters and card are then wrapped in a second piece of cling film.
6 DNA hybridization is then detected by autoradiography by exposing Fuji RX film to the filter at −80°C.

GENERAL CONSIDERATIONS

1 Repetitive DNA sequences are often repeated in a single genome many thousands of times and only very small amounts of DNA are necessary for detection (<100 ng).

2 For some species there exist DNA probes which hybridize to only one species e.g. *Onchocerca armillata* (Murray *et al.* 1990) and *Anopheles gambiae* (Gale & Crampton 1987). Alternatively, in more complex taxonomic situations, there may exist a number of probes which when used in combination show distinct patterns of hybridization to different species e.g. *Simulium damnosum* s.l. (Post & Crampton 1988). Besides species-specific probes genus specific probes may also be found (Post *et al.* 1991).

3 Nylon membranes (e.g. Amersham Hybond-N) may be used in place of nitrocellulose without any increase in background hybridization and with the added advantage of increased strength.

4 Non-radioactive DNA-labelling techniques (e.g. Enhanced chemiluminescence, Digoxigenin) are becoming increasingly popular and have the added advantage of making the method applicable in the field.

5 The stringency of the post-hybridization washing may be altered to increase the sensitivity of the probe. Often washing at higher temperatures, e.g. 65°C will improve the ability of a probe to differentiate species.

6 Nuclear DNA probes can also detect variation at both inter- and intrapopulation levels using Southern blotting (e.g. Hall 1990).

REFERENCES

Gale, K. R. & Crampton, J. M. (1987). DNA probes for species identification in the *Anopheles gambiae* complex. *Medical and Veterinary Entomology*, **1**, 127–136.

Hall, H. G. (1990). Parental analysis of introgressive hybridization between African and European Honeybees using Nuclear DNA RFLPs. *Genetics*, **125**, 611–621.

Murray, K. A., Post, R. J., Crampton, J. M., McCall, P. J. & Kouyate, B. (1990). Cloning and characterization of a species-specific DNA sequence for *Onchocerca armillata*, *Molecular Biology and Parasitology*, **30**, 209–216.

Post, R. J. & Crampton, J. M. (1988). The taxonomic use of variation in repetitive DNA sequences in the *Simulium damnosum* complex. *Biosystematics of Haematophagous Insects* (Ed. by M. W. Service), pp. 245–256. The Systematics Association Special Volume. Oxford University Press, Oxford, UK.

Post, R. J., Murray, K. A., Flook, P. K. & Millest, A. L. (1991). Molecular taxonomy in the control of West African Onchocerciasis. *Molecular Techniques in Taxonomy* (Ed. by G. M. Hewitt), pp. 271–281. NATO ASI Series Vol. H57, Springer Verlag, Berlin.

Sim, G. K., Kafatos, F. C., Jones, C. W., Koehler, M. D., Efstratiadis, A. & Maniatis, T. (1979). Use of a cDNA library for studies on evolution and developmental expression of the chorion multigene families. *Cell*, **18**, 1303–1316.

11. C-BANDING AND THE CHARACTERIZATION OF HETEROCHROMATIC REGIONS

JOSE M. RUBIO AND COLIN FERRIS

School of Biological Sciences, University of East Anglia, Norwich NR4 7TJ, UK

INTRODUCTION

C-banding of chromosomes was first described as a result of the pretreatment of preparation for *in situ* hybridization (Pardue & Gall 1970). Arrighi and Hsu (1974) modified the *in situ* hybridization pretreatment steps by staining with Giemsa producing a pattern of transverse bands over the centromeres which corresponds to the satellite DNA regions. The bands were termed C-bands because of the correlation with the centromeric heterochromatin, although the same technique gave a pattern of pericentric bands in other species.

C-banding procedures do in fact extract DNA from non-C-banded regions of the chromosomes (the lightly staining regions) and C-banding can be produced by mild deoxyribonuclease digestion (Alfi *et al.* 1973). However, there is no firm correlation between the degree of condensation of blocks of DNA and their ability to C-band. There is also no correlation between the type of sequence and C-banding. C-banding does stain predominantly satellite DNA-rich regions but not exclusively so. The classical example of satellite DNA-rich C-bands are those in the mouse, where the C-bands correlate both in size and in quantity with the amount of satellite DNA. In other instances, however, C-bands do not contain appreciable amounts of satellite DNA, the best known example being the sex chromosomes of the Chinese hamster (*Clicetulus gliseus*; Arrighi *et al.* 1974). In some species, C-bands may contain more than one satellite sequence, possibly interspersed with a chromatic DNA, as in man and primates (Gosden *et al.* 1975).

In view of the diversity in both the type of DNA sequences present in C-bands and in the base composition of these sequences, it seems likely that C-banding results from a specific DNA–protein interaction rather than as a function of the DNA itself as was initially postulated. However, as yet no differences in the DNA–protein composition of the chromosomes have been identified that could explain the differential C-band staining, and the nature of the interaction between DNA and protein and its correlation between C-banding remain to be characterized.

METHODOLOGY

The procedure described below was developed by Sumner (1972) and modified by Bella *et al.* (1986).

1 Squash tissue in 45% acetic acid, remove cover-slip and air dry. Use as soon as possible.

2 Incubate the slide in 0.2 M HCl for 1 hour at room temperature. This step is not essential.

3 Rinse the slide in distilled water.

4 Place in freshly prepared barium hydroxide octahydrate solution (5%) at 60°C for between 5 and 30 minutes. This step depends upon the tissue used. We use 5 minutes for embryo and 30 minutes for testis material.

5 Rinse thoroughly in several changes of distilled water.

6 Incubate in 2 × SSC (0.3 M NaCl, 0.03 M Trisodium citrate, pH 7.0) at 60°C for 30 minutes.

7 Rinse briefly in distilled water.

8 Stain in 2% Giemsa in phosphate buffer for 1–2 minutes. It is possible before this step to stain with a solution of 0.001% acridine orange which improves the resolution of the bands, for observation under ultraviolet radiation.

9 Rinse in distilled water, dry thoroughly and mount.

VALUE AND LIMITATIONS OF C-BANDING

C-bands are constant within any one species. In two subspecies of *Chorthippus parallelus, C. p. parallelus* and *C. p. erythropus*, which meet and form a hybrid zone at the Pyrenees (Butlin & Hewitt 1985a, b), it is possible to distinguish the karyotypes of both subspecies by the localization of heterochromatin in the sex chromosomes with the C-banding technique. In *C. p. parallelus* (Fig. 4a) the sex chromosome shows a centromeric and a distal band while *C. p. erythropus* (Fig. 4b) shows a centromeric and an interstitial band but not the distal one (Gosalvez *et al.* 1988).

The size of the C-bands or heterochromatic regions can be polymorphic within a species. An example of such polymorphism is the Y chromosome in man, in which the long arm has a prominent C-band that varies greatly in size (Geraedts *et al.* 1975). Also, in *C. parallelus* it is possible to find a polymorphic pattern of C-banding within the smallest autosomal chromosomes. Some of them are shown in Fig. 4a.

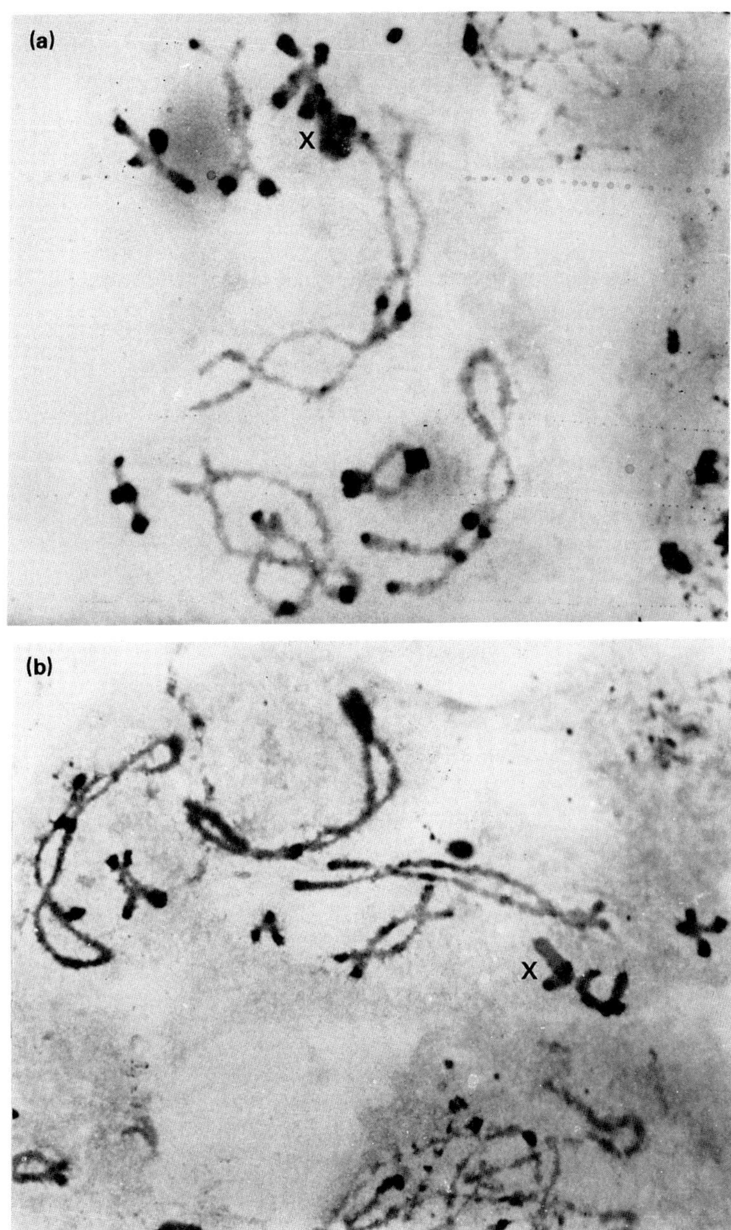

Fig. 4. C-banding in *Chorthippus parallelus*. (a) *C. p. parallelus*. (b) *C. p. erythropus*. Notice sex chromosomes and polymorphic pattern.

Although this technique is useful in some organisms, it is not always possible to find a clear pattern of C-banding within species with small chromosomes or within some species where no C-bands can be obtained.

MATERIALS REQUIRED

Apparatus: microscope, slides, cover-slips, waterbath.
Chemicals: acetic acid, hydrochloric acid, barium hydroxide octahydrate, sodium chloride, trisodium citrate, Giemsa or acridine orange.

REFERENCES

Alfi, O. S., Donnell, G. N. & Derencsenyi, A. (1973). C-banding of human chromosomes produced by DNase. *Lancet*, **ii**, 505.

Arrighi, F. E. & Hsu, T. C. (1974). Staining constitutive heterochromatin and Giemsa crossbands of mammalian chromosomes. *Human Chromosome Methodology* (Ed. by J. J. Yunis), ch. 4. Academic Press, New York, NY, USA.

Arrighi, F. E., Hsu, T. C., Pathak, S. & Sawada, H. (1974). Sex chromosomes of Chinese hamster. Constitutive heterochromatin deficient in repetitive DNA sequences. *Cytogenetics and Cell Genetics*, **13**, 268–274.

Bella, J. L., Garcia de la Vega, C., Lopez-Fernandez, C. & Gosalvez, J. (1986). Changes in acridine orange banding and its use in the characterization of heterochromatic regions. *Heredity*, **57**, 79–83.

Butlin, R. K. & Hewitt, G. M. (1985a). A hybrid zone between *Chorthippus parallelus parallelus* and *Chorthippus parallelus erythropus* (Orthoptera: Acrididae): morphological and electrophoretic characters. *Biological Journal of the Linnean Society*, **26**, 269–285.

Butlin, R. K. & Hewitt, G. M. (1985b). A hybrid zone between *Chorthippus parallelus parallelus* and *Chorthippus parallelus erythropus* (Orthoptera: Acrididae): behavioural characters. *Biological Journal of the Linnean Society*, **26**, 287–299.

Geraedts, J. P. M., Pearson, P. L., Van Der Ploeg, M. & Vossepoel, A. M. (1975). Polymorphism for human chromosome I and chromosome Y: Feulgen and UV DNA measurements. *Experimental Cell Research*, **95**, 9–14.

Gosalvez, J., Lopez-Fernandez, C., Bella, J. L., Butlin, R. & Hewitt, G. M. (1988). A hybrid zone between *Chorthippus parallelus parallelus* and *Chorthippus parallelus erythropus* (Orthoptera): chromosomal differentiation. *Genome*, **30**, 656–663.

Gosden, J. R., Mitchell, A. R., Buckland, R. A., Clayton, R. P. & Evans, H. J. (1975). Location of four human satellite DNAs on human chromosomes. *Experimental Cell Research*, **92**, 148–158.

Pardue, M. L. & Gall, J. C. (1970). Chromosomal localization of mouse satellite DNA. *Science*, **168**, 1356–1358.

Sumner, A. T. (1972). A sample technique for demonstrating centromeric heterochromatin. *Experimental Cell Research*, **75**, 304–306.

12. SILVER STAINING

COLIN FERRIS AND JOSE M. RUBIO
School of Biological Sciences, University of East Anglia, Norwich NR4 7TJ, UK

PRINCIPLES

The genes encoding ribosomal DNA (rDNA) are arranged in tandem arrays of multiple copies. Such regions of rDNA are primarily represented by the genes for 18 + 28S rRNA. The frequency of such regions of rDNA is related to the number of nucleoli in the cell, and such regions were termed nucleolar organizing regions (NORs).

While in some species NORs can be recognized on mitotic chromosomes as secondary constrictions and satellites, in many species this is not possible. NORs were conventionally visualized in animals and plants using N-banding techniques (Funaki *et al.* 1975) and by *in situ* hybridization (Hsu 1973). However, these conventional techniques had their limitations. *In situ* hybridization is both expensive and time consuming and N-banding sometimes fails to identify terminal and centromeric NORs. As a consequence, Goodpasture and Bloom (1975) developed a more reliable, cheaper method of visualizing NORs using silver staining.

The silver staining technique outlined here stains the products of the NOR rather than the NOR itself; thus a large silver spot is produced adjacent to the NOR site on the chromosome. The technique was modified for grasshoppers by Rufas *et al.* (1983) and is further modified for *Chorthippus* species by Bella *et al.* (1990).

PROTOCOL

1 Testis follicles are fixed in 3:1 absolute alcohol and acetic acid. Tap out and squash follicles in 45% acetic acid.

2 Remove cover-slips by freezing in liquid nitrogen and snapping off with a razor blade. Allow to air dry for 2 weeks.

3 Place 3 drops of stain on to a slide and place a cover-slip on top. Stain mixture: 0.2 ml formic acid solution (100 ml dH_2O + 2 drops of acid), and 0.2 g silver nitrate in a foil-wrapped tube. Keep away from light and use immediately. This is enough for 3 slides.

4 Incubate slides in a moist chamber at 60°C for about 2 minutes or until a golden glow is produced around the edges of the cover-slip.

5 Wash cover-slip off immediately with cold running water for several minutes.

6 Stain slides in 2% Giemsa for 1 minute.

7 Rinse in cold water and air dry.

MATERIALS REQUIRED

Apparatus: microscope, slides, cover-slips, small glass tubes, oven and moist chamber.

Chemicals: acetic acid, liquid nitrogen, formic acid, silver nitrate, Giemsa.

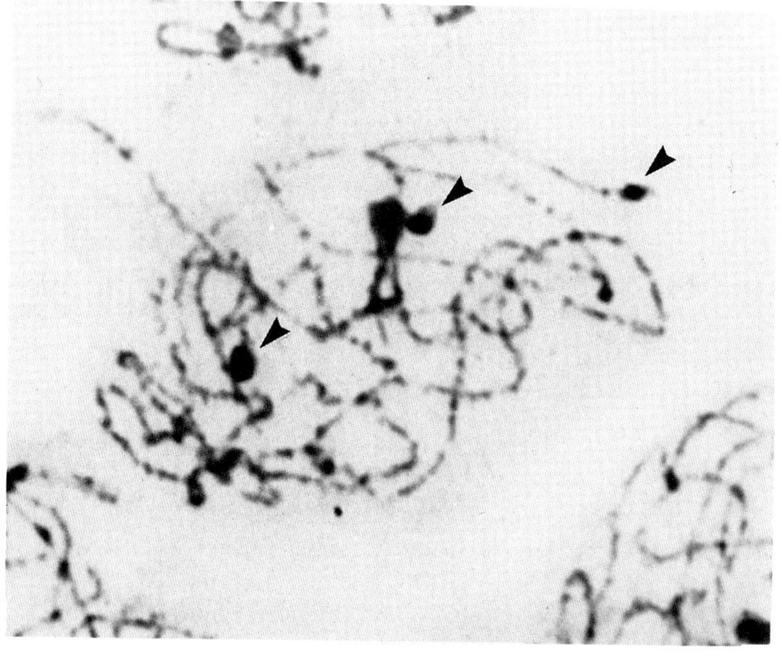

FIG. 5. Silver staining pattern of *Chorthippus parallelus parallelus* showing three nucleolar organizers (NORs). One can be seen to be associated with the heterochromatic X chromosome, while the terminal location of the NOR on the L3 autosome can be seen. *C. p. erythropus* lacks the X chromosome NOR.

COMMENTS ON THE TECHNIQUE

This technique is more easily applied to some groups of organisms than others due to the availability of meiotic prophase cells for staining. Thus in mammals, for example, it is necessary to culture cell lines whilst in plants and invertebrates such as the grasshopper used above, meiotic cells are more easily obtained.

The staining itself will only reliably distinguish NORs and cannot be used to detect small regions of rDNA activity. Such secondary rDNA sites require analysis by *in situ* hybridization.

Where natural variation in the numbers and/or positions of NORs occurs in a species, this technique can be used for genetic analysis. In the cotton rat *Sigmodon arizonae*, the 11 pairs of chromosomes of the karyotype can all be identified using their patterns of silver staining. Furthermore, variation in the staining patterns has been found between individuals (Zimmerman & Sirohnen 1973).

In the meadow grasshopper *Chorthippus parallelus* a hybrid zone is formed along the Pyrenees where the subspecies *C. p. parallelus* and *C. p. erythropus* meet. Silver staining has revealed a difference between the two subspecies with *C. p. parallelus* containing a NOR on the X chromosome (Fig. 5) which is absent from *C. p. erythropus* and can thus be used as a genetic marker for the X chromosome in studies of this hybrid zone (Hewitt *et al.* 1988).

REFERENCES

Bella, J. L., Hewitt, G. M. & Gosalvez, J. (1990). Meiotic imbalance in laboratory-produced hybrid males of *Chorthippus parallelus parallelus* and *Chorthippus parallelus erythropus*. *Genetical Research*, **56**, 43–48.

Funaki, K., Matsui, S. & Sasaki, M. (1975). Location of nucleolar organizers in animal and plant chromosomes by means of an improved N-banding technique. *Chromosoma*, **49**, 357–370.

Goodpasture, C. & Bloom, S. E. (1975). Visualization of Nucleolar Organizing Regions in mammalian chromosomes using silver staining. *Chromosoma*, **53**, 37–50.

Hewitt, G. M., Gosalvez, J., Lopez-Fernandez, C., Ritchie, M. G., Nichols, W. & Butlin, R. K. (1988). Differences in the nucleolar organisers on sex chromosomes and Haldane's Rule in a hybrid zone. *Kew Chromosome Conference III* (Ed. by P. E. Brandham), pp. 109–119. HMSO, London, UK.

Hsu, T. C. (1973). Longitudinal differentiation of chromosomes. *Annual Review of Genetics*, **7**, 153–175.

Rufas, J. S., Gosalvez, J., Lopez-Fernandez, C. & Cardoso, H. (1983). Complete dependence between Ag-NORs and C-positive heterochromatin revealed by simultaneous Ag-NOR C-banding method. *Cell Biology International Reports*, **7**, 275–281.

Zimmerman, E. G. & Sirohnen, D. A. (1973). Chromosomal banding pattern and idiogram of the cotton rat *Sigmodon arizonae* (Rodentia, Muridae). *Chromosoma*, **41**, 85–91.

13. USE OF A CELLULOSE ACETATE SYSTEM FOR ALLOZYME ELECTROPHORESIS

IAN R. WYNNE, HUGH D. LOXDALE AND CLIFF P. BROOKES
Entomology and Nematology Department, AFRC Institute of Arable Crops Research, Rothamsted Experimental Station, Harpenden, Hertfordshire AL5 2JQ, UK

INTRODUCTION

Since the early 1970s, allozyme electrophoresis has been extensively used in studies of the taxonomy, systematics and population genetics of a wide range of animal and plant species (Ayala 1976, Oxford & Rollinson 1983, Loxdale & den Hollander 1989). Most of these studies have used starch, polyacrylamide, and to a lesser extent agarose, as supporting media for electrophoretic separation of proteins.

Hitherto, our studies at Rothamsted, which have been mainly on aphids, have used PAGE (polyacrylamide gel electrophoresis) (Loxdale & Brookes 1989). However, recently we have been introduced to a cellulose acetate system which has many advantages, particularly with respect to studies concerning small invertebrates such as *Drosophila*, mites (Easteal & Boussy 1987), thrips (Lewis *et al.* 1991) and aphids and their wasp parasitoids (Loxdale & Brookes, unpublished data). Presently, we are also using this system to study the population genetics of moths. Because of the advantages and flexibility of the cellulose acetate system, we believe it will prove a very useful technique for population biologists and ecologists and hence describe it here.

MATERIALS AND METHODS

Electrophoresis equipment

Although there are a number of companies producing cellulose acetate (CA) electrophoresis systems, we found the system supplied by Helena Laboratories (PO Box 752, Beaumont, TX 77704, USA) to be convenient and relatively cheap. It consists of an electrophoresis chamber (UK Cat. No. 1283) and an applicator kit (UK Cat. No. 4093), which consists of two sample plates with 12 wells each, an applicator with 12 microtips and a plate-aligning base. Although we use the CA plates produced by Helena (Titan III, UK Cat. No. 3033), those supplied by Gelman Sciences (Optiphor-10 triacetate, UK Cat. No. 51240) are also suitable for use with this system (Thompson *et al.* 1989).

Sample preparation

All insects are homogenized in a solution as described by Loxdale *et al.* (1983) (see Wynne & Brookes, Techniques and Protocols, section 14, this volume for details). Aphids, parasitoid wasps, thrips and mites are homogenized in 5–10 μl of solution using either the end of a heat-sealed Pasteur pipette or the multiple homogenizer described by Brookes and Loxdale (1985). Moths are homogenized in greater volumes (e.g. 1.5 ml for *Autographa gamma*) in a larger version of the multiple homogenizer and preserved, in small aliquots, in the manner described by Wynne and Brookes (Techniques and Protocols, section 14, this volume).

Sample loading and electrophoretic conditions

The CA plates are carefully immersed vertically in the running buffer and left to soak for at least a few minutes. This may be done in a purpose-built device supplied by Helena (UK Cat. No. 5093) but a 500 ml beaker will suffice. Once soaked, the CA plates are blotted firmly (using Whatman No. 1 filter paper) before being placed on the aligning base. The sample is then loaded using the applicator. For enzymes with high activity (e.g. PGI in moths) only one application (0.25 μl) is required, but others may need up to five applications to achieve reasonable staining.

Electrophoresis is performed at constant voltage (200 V) for 20–40 minutes. Refrigeration is not usually necessary though ice may be used to cool the apparatus. The current drawn during the run is dependent on the running buffer (3 mA/plate for 25 mM Tris-glycine, pH 8.5 and 15 mA/plate for 50 mM Tris-citrate, pH 7.8).

Enzyme staining recipes

Richardson *et al.* (1986) give a wide range of staining recipes suitable for use with the Helena system. A selection of recipes for enzymes that we have found to be polymorphic in insects (particularly moths) is presented here. The recipe for PEP is modified from Baker (1974). Stains should be prepared in the order described in the recipes.

Aconitate hydratase (ACON; EC 4.2.1.3): 0.2 ml aconitate (50 mg/ml, pH 8.0), 2 ml stain buffer, 0.1 ml each of NADP, 0.2 M $MgCl_2$, PMS and MTT. 1 U isocitrate dehydrogenase.

Glutamate-oxaloacetate transaminase (GOT; EC 2.6.1.1): 5 mg Fast Garnet GBC salt, 2 ml stain buffer, 0.2 ml α-ketoglutarate (50 mg/ml, pH 8.0), 0.2 ml L-aspartate (50 mg/ml, pH 8.0). Adjust pH with 4 M NaOH.

Hydroxybutyrate dehydrogenase (HBDH; EC 1.1.1.30): 20 mg β-hydroxybutyrate, 2 ml stain buffer, 0.1 ml each of NAD, PMS and MTT.

Mannose-phosphate isomerase (MPI; EC 5.3.1.8): 8 mg mannose 6-phosphate, 2 ml stain buffer, 0.1 ml each of NADP, 0.2 M $MgCl_2$, PMS and MTT. 2 U glucose-phosphate isomerase, 2 U glucose-6-phosphate dehydrogenase.

Peptidase (PEP; EC 3.4.11) (PEP-D): 10 mg phenylalanine-proline, 5 mg peroxidase, 2 mg snake venom (from *Bothrops atrox*), 2 ml PEP buffer pH 7.6 (18.9 ml 0.2 M KH_2PO_4; 127 ml 0.2 M Na_2HPO_4. 12 H_2O diluted to 400 ml — to this add 14 ml 0.1 M $MnCl_2$, then filter), 0.1 ml 3-amino-9-ethylcarbazole in *N,N*-dimethylformamide (40 mg/ml).

6-Phosphogluconate dehydrogenase (6PGD; EC 1.1.1.44): 5 mg 6PGA, 2 ml stain buffer, 0.1 ml each of NADP, 0.2 M $MgCl_2$, PMS and MTT.

Phosphoglucose isomerase (PGI; EC 5.3.1.9): 5 mg fructose 6-phosphate, 2 ml stain buffer, 0.1 ml each of NADP, 1 M $MgCl_2$, PMS and MTT. 2 U glucose-6-phosphate dehydrogenase.

Phosphoglucomutase (PGM; EC 2.7.5.1): 5 mg glucose 1-phosphate (containing at least 1% glucose 1,6-diphosphate), 2 ml stain buffer, 0.1 ml each of NADP, 1 M $MgCl_2$, PMS and MTT. 2 U glucose-6-phosphate dehydrogenase.

The stain buffer in all recipes except PEP is 0.1 M Tris-HCl, pH 8.0 (100 mM Tris adjusted to pH 8.0 with 4 M HCl). The concentrations of the stock solutions are as follows: NADP, NAD = 20 mg/ml; 1 M $MgCl_2$ = 95 mg/ml; 0.2 M = 19 mg/ml; PMS = 2 mg/ml; MTT = 6 mg/ml.

Running buffers

Richardson *et al.* (1986) provide a comprehensive list of buffers suitable for allozyme electrophoresis. However, we have found that for insects, a few continuous buffer systems will suffice for most enzymes used regularly. For GOT, MPI, PEP, PGI and PGM, 25 mM Tris-glycine pH 8.5 (25 mM

Tris, 192 mM glycine) provides good resolution and staining whilst 50 mM Tris-citrate pH 7.8 (50 mM Tris, 12.5 mM citric acid) is good for ACON, HBDH and 6PGD. However, the suitability of a running buffer does vary between taxa and often a modification (of pH or ionic strength) is needed.

Staining

After electrophoresis, CA plates are stained using the agar overlay technique described by Easteal and Boussy (1987). To 2–3 ml of staining mixture, an equal volume of molten agar (360 mg/25 ml maintained molten at 60°C) is added and mixed before being poured on to the CA plate. Once the agar has hardened (usually within 2 min), the plates are placed in the dark at room temperature (though PEP may stain better if incubated at 37°C) until the protein bands become visible (Fig. 6). After staining, the CA plates may be fixed using 7% (v/v) acetic acid.

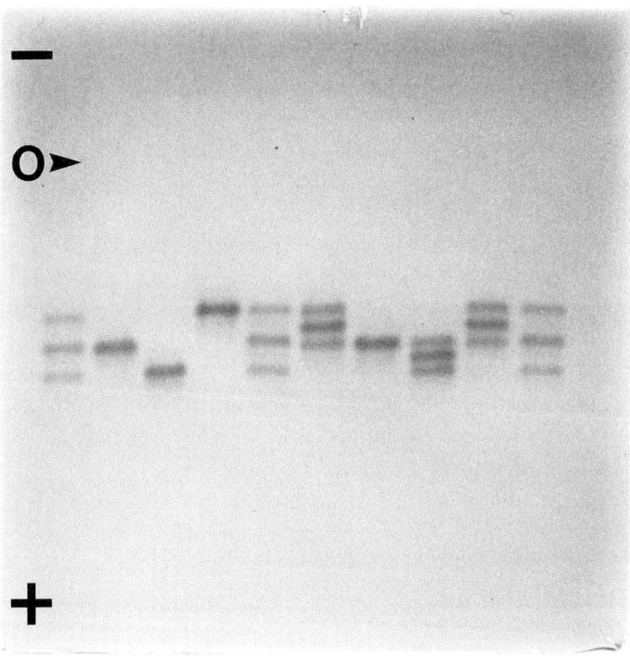

FIG. 6. Photograph of a cellulose acetate plate stained for PGI in 10 individuals of the November moth, *Epirrita dilutata* (Lepidoptera: Geometridae). Three alleles, fast (F), medium (M) and slow (S), are displayed in six genotypes. Reading from left to right, homozygotes: F/F (track 3), M/M (2 and 7) and S/S (4). Heterozygotes: S/M (6 and 9), S/F (1, 5 and 10) and M/F (8). O = position of origin.

DISCUSSION

Enzyme electrophoresis using the Helena cellulose acetate system is quick, simple and has many advantages over starch and PAGE systems. For example, the run time is very short (20–40 minutes) compared with ≥ 2 hours for PAGE (as used by Loxdale *et al.* 1983). A cooling system is not essential (Thompson *et al.* 1989 performed CA electrophoresis at temperatures of up to 34°C) and more electrophoretic runs per day are possible. Also, the volume of staining mixture used (approx. 4 ml per plate) is much less than that required for similar sized PAGE gels (i.e. 25 ml per gel), reducing the cost of stains containing expensive ingredients. The volume of electrode buffer needed for the electrophoresis chambers is also reduced (c. 100 ml per trough).

A problem with many PAGE systems is that for small invertebrates, it is only possible to stain for one or two enzymes per individual (due to the small volume of homogenate available for testing). In contrast, the more sensitive CA system requires smaller volumes of homogenate, enabling the running of a range of enzymes per individual (five in some aphid spp.). This means that more information is gained, making studies of linkage disequilibria easier.

Although, compared to starch or polyacrylamide gels, the CA plates are expensive, they are easy to use, non-toxic (unlike acrylamide) and have a long shelf life. Since the CA plates draw little current it is possible to run four or more chambers from one power pack or even to run one chamber using a 12 V car battery as a power supply. Thus, unlike starch or polyacrylamide the CA system can be used in the field away from a mains electricity supply (Thompson *et al.* 1989).

The use of the applicator with the CA system means that loading is simple, accurate and quick and, as the samples can be applied to any region of the CA plate, cathodal and anodal isozymes may be detected on the same plate and multiple origins are possible.

A potential problem with CA systems is the phenomenon of evaporative drift whereby, unlike starch or polyacrylamide, molecular migration through the matrix is not at a constant rate (see Richardson *et al.* 1986 for details). This problem may, however, be overcome by use of a standard sample.

Overall, we have found this system to be ‘user friendly’, quick, cheap and particularly suitable for allozyme studies involving the screening of a large number of specimens and loci.

ACKNOWLEDGEMENTS

Our thanks are extended to Dr Roy Wiles, Buckingham University for introducing us to the Helena cellulose acetate system. This work was supported by the AFRC/NERC/ESRC under the Joint Agriculture and Environment Programme.

REFERENCES

Ayala, F. J. (1976). *Molecular Evolution*. Sinauer, Sunderland, MA, USA.

Baker, J. P. (1974). A new method for staining for peptidase on polyacrylamide gels. *Biochemical Genetics*, **12**, 199–201.

Brookes, C. P. & Loxdale, H. D. (1985). A device for simultaneously homogenizing numbers of individual small insects for electrophoresis. *Bulletin of Entomological Research*, **75**, 377–378.

Easteal, S. & Boussy, I. A. (1987). A sensitive and efficient isoenzyme technique for small arthropods and other invertebrates. *Bulletin of Entomological Research*, **77**, 407–415.

Lewis, T., Loxdale, H. D. & Brookes, C. P. (1991). Prospects for studying the persistence and dispersal of pear thrips populations using genetic markers (allozymes). *Proceedings of the 1990 Conference on Thysanoptera*. Bulletin 698, pp. 1–7. Agricultural Experimental Station, University of Vermont, USA.

Loxdale, H. D. & Brookes, C. P. (1989). Use of genetic markers (allozymes) to study the structure, overwintering and dynamics of pest aphid populations. *Electrophoretic Studies on Agricultural Pests* (Ed. by H. D. Loxdale & J. Den Hollander), pp. 231–270. The Systematics Association Special Volume No. 39. Clarendon Press, Oxford, UK.

Loxdale, H. D. & den Hollander, J. (1989). *Electrophoretic Studies on Agricultural Pests*. The Systematics Association Special Volume No. 39. Clarendon Press, Oxford, UK.

Loxdale, H. D., Castañera, P. & Brookes, C. P. (1983). Electrophoretic study of enzymes from cereal aphid populations. I. Electrophoretic techniques and staining systems for characterising isoenzymes from six species of cereal aphids (Hemiptera: Aphididae). *Bulletin of Entomological Research*, **73**, 645–657.

Oxford, G. S. & Rollinson, D. (1983). *Protein Polymorphism: Adaptive and Taxonomic Significance*. The Systematics Association Special Volume No. 24. Academic Press, London, UK.

Richardson, B. J., Baverstock, P. R. & Adams, M. (1986). *Allozyme Electrophoresis*. Academic Press, Sydney, Australia.

Thompson, M. C., Davies, J. B. & Wilson, M. D. (1989). A portable allozyme electrophoresis kit used to identify members of the *Simulium damnosum* Theobald complex (Diptera: Simuliidae) in the field. *Bulletin of Entomological Research*, **79**, 685–691.

14. A DEVICE FOR PRODUCING MULTIPLE DEEP-FROZEN SAMPLES FOR ALLOZYME ELECTROPHORESIS

IAN R. WYNNE AND CLIFF P. BROOKES
Entomology and Nematology Department, AFRC Institute of Arable Crops Research, Rothamsted Experimental Station, Harpenden, Hertfordshire AL5 2JQ, UK

A device is described for producing multiple aliquots of cryogenically preserved homogenates suitable for allozyme electrophoresis. Richardson *et al.* (1986) describe many of the routine methods for preparation and long-term storage of homogenized samples for electrophoresis. One method involves dripping homogenates from a Pasteur pipette into liquid nitrogen to produce a series of snap-frozen droplets. We have found this method to be particularly useful but have modified it using a device which allows simultaneous processing of a number of different samples (e.g. individual insects).

The device consists of a funnel unit and a collar. The funnel unit carries a series of seven funnels made from medical plastic specimen tubes with a hole drilled in the bottom (5 mm diameter) and four or more small drainage holes (<2 mm diameter) drilled in the sides (Fig. 7d). Each of these sits on a 1.8 ml Nunc cryotube (labelled and lid removed) (Fig. 7d). The tubes are held together in three perspex rings (3 mm thick) connected by brass studding (Fig. 7c). The whole construction fits neatly into a 1 l dewar flask (Phillip Harris Scientific Supplies, Cat. No. D36436) filled with liquid nitrogen (not shown). If alternative materials are used in the construction of the funnel unit, their low temperature tolerance must be determined. The collar (Fig. 7a) fits over the neck of the flask and holds seven 'drippers' (Fig. 7b). These consist of 2 μl disposable micropipettes ('Microcaps' – Drummond Scientific Company, Broomfield, PA, USA) held in cut-down C200 Gilson disposable pipette tips by rubber bungs.

The size of micropipette used depends on the viscosity of the homogenate and determines the volume of the snap-frozen droplet. Using the homogenizing solution described by Loxdale *et al.* (1983) (15% (w/v) sucrose, 50 mM Tris-HCl, pH 7.1 in 0.5% (v/v) Triton X-100) we found

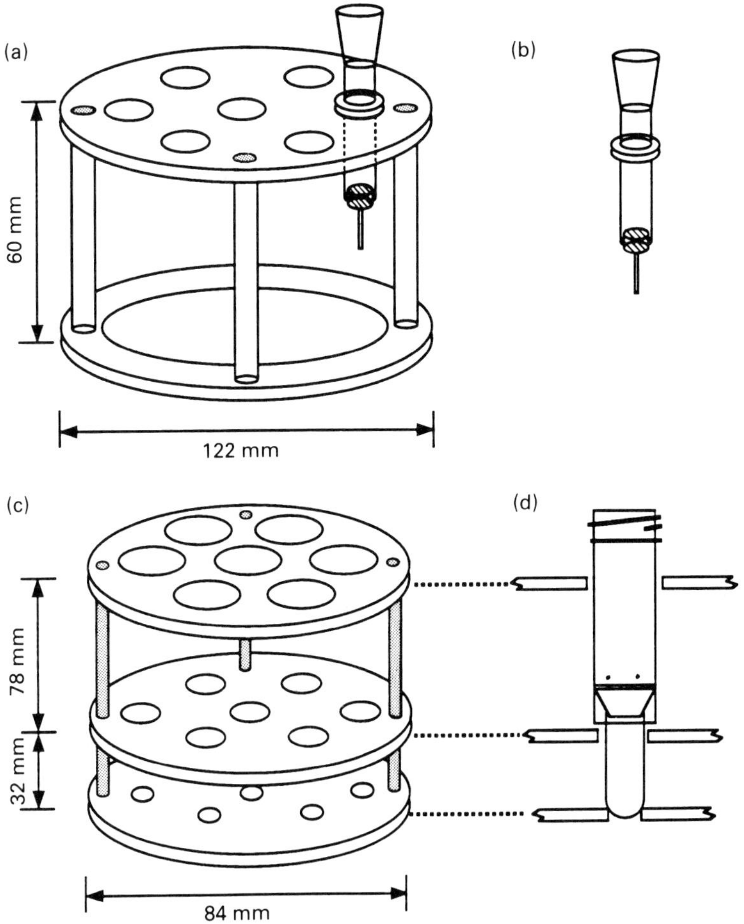

FIG. 7. Diagrams showing construction of device. (a) Collar with one 'dripper'. (b) Dripper. (c) Funnel rack shown without funnels. (d) Funnel with cryotube. Note: diagrams are not to scale and measurements are intended as a rough guide only.

that 2 μl pipettes were the most satisfactory and produced a droplet with an average volume of 6 μl. The interval between drips is also important as if this falls below 6 seconds the droplets tend to aggregate. This is because the drops float on the surface of the liquid nitrogen for several seconds before sinking.

Crude homogenates which have been centrifuged at 14 000 rev min^{-1} for a few minutes, to remove most of the debris, are loaded into the drippers using disposable Pasteur pipettes. Once all seven are loaded they may be left for 10–15 minutes until empty. To retrieve the frozen samples, the collar is removed and the funnel unit lifted out gently (allowing the liquid nitrogen to drain). The cryotubes can then be capped and transferred to permanent low-temperature storage. Eye and hand protection must be worn when handling liquid nitrogen, and great care taken when submerging the funnel unit.

An advantage of storing samples as small aliquots is that there is no need to thaw the whole sample each time an aliquot is required. Since all the aliquots are stored in one tube the method saves space (an important consideration in population studies where large numbers of individuals are involved). As many aliquots are produced from one homogenate , it also offers a simple way of producing a genotype library. We have found this technique particularly convenient in conjunction with our studies on moth population genetics using the Helena cellulose acetate electrophoresis system (see Wynne *et al.*, Techniques and Protocols, section 13, this volume).

ACKNOWLEDGEMENTS

Our thanks to Mr Ian Lowles, Imperial College, Silwood Park, for drawing Fig. 7 and Hugh Loxdale for commenting on the manuscript. This work was supported by the AFRC/NERC/ESRC under the Joint Agriculture and Environment Programme.

REFERENCES

Loxdale, H. D., Castañera, P. & Brookes, C. P. (1983). Electrophoretic study of enzymes from aphid populations. I. Electrophoretic techniques and staining systems for characterising isozymes from six species of cereal aphids (Hemiptera: Aphididae). *Bulletin of Entomological Research*, **73**, 645–657.

Richardson, B. J., Baverstock, P. R. & Adams, M. (1986). *Allozyme Electrophoresis*. Academic Press, Sydney, Australia.

AUTHOR INDEX

Figures in *italics* refer to pages where full references appear.

SUBJECT INDEX